Dictionary of Chinese Biography

BERKSHIRE

Dictionary of Chinese Biography

宝库山中华传记字典

Kerry Brown

China Studies Centre at the University of Sydney

Editor in Chief

VOLUME 2

BERKSHIRE PUBLISHING GROUP
Great Barrington, Massachusetts

Berkshire Publishing Group
122 Castle Street
Great Barrington, Massachusetts 01230-1506 USA
Email: info@berkshirepublishing.com
Tel: +1 413 528 0206
Fax: +1 413 541 0076

Digital editions. All volumes of the *Berkshire Dictionary of Chinese Biography* are available online through Oxford Reference Library, Oxford University Press, at www.oxfordreference.com.

Library of Congress Cataloging-in-Publication Data

Names: Brown, Kerry, 1967-
Title: Berkshire dictionary of Chinese biography/Kerry Brown, Lau China Institute, King's College, London.
Description: Paperback edition. | Great Barrington, Massachusetts : Berkshire Publishing Group, 2015. | Includes bibliographical references and index.
Identifiers: LCCN 2015015350 | ISBN 9781614720010 (v. 1 : pbk. : color) | ISBN 9781614728757 (v. 2 : pbk. : color) | ISBN 9781614728764 (v. 3 : pbk. : color) | ISBN 9781614728771 (v. 4 : pbk. : color) | ISBN 9781614720058 (set : pbk. : color) | ISBN 9781614720065 (v. 1 : pbk. : b&w) | ISBN 9781614720072 (v. 2 : pbk. : b&w) | ISBN 9781614720089 (v. 3 : pbk. : b&w) | ISBN 9781614720096 (v. 4 : pbk. : b&w) | ISBN 9781614720102 (set : pbk. : b&w)
Subjects: LCSH: China—Biography—Dictionaries.
Classification: LCC DS734 .B47 2015 | DDC 951.003—dc23 LC record available at http://lccn.loc.gov/2015015350

Kazakhstan
Mongolia
Urumqi
Kyrgyzstan
Tajikistan
Xinjiang
新疆维吾尔自治区
Afghanistan
Gansu
甘肃
宁夏回族自治区
Ningxia
Pakistan
Xining
Qinghai
青海
Lanzhou
Xizang
(Tibet)
西藏自治区
Lhasa
Chengdu
Nepal
Sichuan
四川
Bhutan
India
Bangladesh
Kunming
Yunnan
雲南
Myanmar
(Burma)
Vietnam
Laos
Thailand

21st Century
CHINA
中华
Russia
Kuril Islands
N
Hailar
Heilongjiang
黑龙江
Harbin
Changchun
Jilin
吉林
Nei Monggol
(Inner Mongolia)
内蒙古自治区
Liaoning
辽宁
North Korea
South Korea
Japan
Hohhot
Beijing
Beijing
Tianjin
Tianjin
Dalian
Hebei
河北
Shanxi
山西
Jinan
Shandong
山东
YELLOW SEA
Xi'an
Zhengzhou
Jiangsu
江苏
Shaanxi
陕西
Henan
河南
Hefei
Nanjing
Shanghai
Anhui
安徽
Hubei
湖北
Hangzhou
Chongqing
Zhejiang
浙江
EAST CHINA SEA
Changsha
Nanchang
Guizhou
貴州
Guiyang
Hunan
湖南
Jiangxi
江西
Fuzhou
Fujian
福建
Taipei
Taiwan
台湾
Guangxi
广西壮族自治区
Nanning
Guangdong
广东
Guangzhou
Macao
Hong Kong
SOUTH CHINA SEA
Haikou
Hainan
海南
Philippines
0
300
600 Miles
0
300
600 Kilometers

Table of Contents

Volume 4 will continue with figures from the post-1979 era of the People's Republic of China.

Editors and Staff

List of Entries: Volume 2

Song Dynasty–Jurchen Jin Dynasty–Yuan Dynasty–Ming Dynasty

Sòng 宋 Dynasty (960–1279 CE)

Jurchen Jin 女真金 Dynasty (1115–1234 CE)

Yuán 元 Dynasty (1279–1368 CE)

Full List of Entries in Volumes 1–3

VOLUME 1: Xia and Shang Dynasties–Zhou Dynasty–Spring and Autumn Period–Warring States Period–Qin Dynasty–Southern and Northern Dynasties–Sui Dynasty–Tang Dynasty

VOLUME 2: Song Dynasty–Jurchen Jin Dynasty–Yuan Dynasty–Ming Dynasty

VOLUME 3: Qing Dynasty–Republic of China–People's Republic of China (until 1979)

Volume 4 will continue with figures from the post-1979 era of the People's Republic of China, Taiwan, and Hong Kong.

Sòng Dynasty

宋朝

960 – 1279 CE

Detail of the famous scroll *Along the River During Qingming Festival* 清明上河图 by Zhang Zeduan (1085–1145). It portrays a bustling city scene during the Qingming Festival (or Tomb Sweeping Day) in Kaifeng, the capital of the Northern Song dynasty.

The Song dynasty defined a new and enduring phase in China's premodern civilization, with a shift of the economic center to the south and the development of a market economy, the flourishing of urban culture, and a revival of classical heritage. The dynasty is divided into two periods: the Northern Song 北宋 (960–1127 CE), with its capital in Kāifēng 开封, and the Southern Song 南宋 (1127–1279), which coexisted with the Jurchen Jin (Nǚzhēn Jīn 金女真; 1125–1234) dynasty in the north. (The Jurchen Jin dynasty is covered in the next section.) The Song dynasty produced many leading intellectuals. Marked by the rise of the scholar-official class, the full implementation of a national official examination system, rapid urbanization, the spread of print technology, and a revival of Confucian thought known as Neo-Confucianism (*lǐxué* 理学), this era forms a pivotal "middle period" that set the mold for cultural developments in the subsequent Yuán 元, Míng 明, and Qīng 清 dynasties.

List of Entries

Bì Shēng
毕升

c. 990–c. 1051—Inventor of movable type printing

Summary

Bi Sheng is considered the inventor of movable type printing, one of China's "four great inventions." He lived during the Song dynasty, a time of great technological and social change. Virtually nothing is known about his life, or even what he printed from his movable type, although it is thought that he was a commoner. His techniques followed upon centuries of print- and papermaking innovations in China, and were in turn improved upon by innovators in Korea, Holland, and, most famously, by the German printer Johannes Gutenberg. Bi Sheng's invention was not fully utilized in China for several hundred years after his death.

Bi Sheng holds credit for one of China's "four great inventions," movable type printing, but very little is known about him. (The other inventions are paper, gunpowder, and the compass.) He pioneered the technological innovation that revolutionized human communication when it was perfected by Johannes Gutenberg in Europe four centuries later. Bi Sheng's innovation, in contrast, did not leave his own country for eight hundred years.

The legendary figure Bi Sheng appeared sometime between 1040 and 1050 CE, during the Sòng 宋 dynasty (960–1279 CE), a time of rapid innovation that many historians say bordered on the revolutionary. In addition to printing, great strides were made in the fields of agriculture and iron-working. China experienced its first real population explosion during this time, and the eating of rice and the drinking of tea both became prevalent.

The only evidence that exists about the inventor appears in a passage of the book *Writings Beside the Dream Creek* (*Mèngxī Bǐtán* 梦溪笔谈), written in Bi's time by the renowned man of letters and science Shěn Kuò 沈括 (1031–1095 CE), who wrote, "During the Qingli reign period (1041–1048 CE), Bi Sheng, a cotton-robed man, made movable type." There is no further record, not even in Shen Kuo's book, of who Bi Sheng was, what his occupation was, where he lived, what he printed from his movable type, and for what purpose he invented the movable type.

Bi is thought to have lived somewhere in or near Hangzhou, modern-day Zhejiang Province, the commercial capital of the Southern Song dynasty. Inferences of his life can be drawn only from the passage in Shen Kuo's book. As Shen Kuo wrote, Bi was a "cotton-robe" man—a commoner who did not wear the silk robes that symbolized officialdom. The use of silk in everyday dress was strictly regulated by law; there were also laws against "foreign" styles of dress and clothes of certain colors, as well as the use of gold thread and embellished silk.

Bi's invention was one of the first movable type sets in the world, but even that is uncertain: there is evidence that the Minoan civilization of Crete created a clay disk around 1700 BCE that was punched mechanically with spiraling arrays of 241 symbols that constituted 45 syllabic signs: a rudimentary and unwieldy form of movable type.

Bi Sheng's moveable type was later improved upon by King Taejong of Korea, around 1400, and, on the other side of the world, by Dutch printer Laurens Janszoon around 1430. Johannes Gutenberg perfected the movable type printing technology in Germany in 1455 with his first printing of bibles. The course of the technological improvements around the world before and after is both complicated and fuzzy. As author Jared Diamond writes, "A more accurate rendering of [Gutenberg's] achievements would be something like the following legalistic sentence: 'Gutenberg played a major practical and symbolic role in independently reinventing, in a greatly improved form and within a more receptive society, a printing technique previously developed in Minoan Crete around 1700 BC, if not long before that'" (Diamond 1999). Bi Sheng's role in the long history of printmaking is even more difficult to pinpoint.

Whatever the later significance of Bi Sheng's innovation, Shen Kuo described his process in detail in his book:

> He took sticky clay and cut in it characters as thin as the edge of a coin. Each character formed, as it was, a single type. He baked them in the fire to make them hard. . . . When he wished to print, he took an iron frame and set it on [an] iron plate. In this he placed the types, set close together. When the frame was full, the whole set made one solid block of type. . . . For each character there were several types, and for certain common characters there were twenty

> or more types each, in order to be prepared for the repetition of characters on the same page. (Tsien 1985).

It is not known how many characters Bi Sheng was able to make because of insufficient historical records; nor is it clear how much time Bi spent in making his type. According to Shen Kuo's description, however, Bi managed to build a set that had enough characters to print an ordinary book, because he needed to make new characters only when rare characters were needed. Shen Kuo further stated that "for printing hundreds or thousands of copies, it was marvelously quick."

Paper and Other Printing Techniques

Bi Sheng's invention of movable type was made possible by the earlier invention of one of China's other four great inventions—paper—followed by numerous other technological innovations. The invention of paper has long been attributed to a court official named Cài Lún 蔡伦 (c. 50–121 CE) of the Hàn 汉 dynasty (206 BCE–220 CE), who in 105 CE presented the Han emperor with a new writing material: a composite paper perhaps made from plant fibers (such as hemp and bark), textile fibers (such as silk), and perhaps other ingredients as well, although the exact formula was lost. Han records mention that the emperor was pleased when Cai Lun gave him the gift, and understandably so: transporting even a small number of bamboo record books required the use of a cart; storing them was unwieldy at best. With the rise of the first Chinese empire (the short-lived Qín 秦 dynasty [221–206 BCE], which gave way to the Han), came an expansion in imperial bureaucracy, and an increasingly urgent need for new writing materials and methods of keeping records. The earliest Chinese records from the sixteenth to eleventh centuries BCE were etched on tortoise shells and animal bones; these cumbersome materials were gradually replaced with wooden tablets and strips of bamboo. The imperial bureaucracy generated huge quantities of records on these new, unrefined materials.

Early papermakers macerated old rope ends, rags, and fishing nets in water to free the component vegetable fibers, then sifted the solution through a screen to form a thin sheet of matted fibers. The wet sheets were left to dry on the screen or placed on another drying surface. Once dry, the fibers in paper form chemical bonds and create a strong but light writing surface.

Paper was in common use in China by the third century CE, though it would be several more centuries before the technology made its way to the Arab world, and not until the twelfth century would knowledge of papermaking spread to Europe. By the twelfth century, Europeans learned to make paper from the Arabs, who had captured several

Cai Lun's Invention of Paper

In *The 100: A Ranking of the Most Influential Persons in History,* author Michael H. Hart placed the supposed inventor of paper, the Han-dynasty eunuch Cai Lun, as the seventh most influential figure in human history, beating both Johannes Gutenberg and Christopher Columbus, and coming in just behind Confucius and St. Paul. (Bi Sheng does not make Hart's list; the Chinese figures in the top 100, besides Cai Lun, are all philosophers or rulers.) Hart bases his ranking of Cai Lun above Gutenberg on three factors:

(1) paper's cost-effectiveness and its versatility as a material for applications other than writing;
(2) the possibility that Gutenberg would never have invented (or, more accurately, "perfected") the movable-type printing press had paper not been invented; and
(3) the assumption that if only one of the two had been invented, more books would have been block-printed on paper (a technique known in China as early as the seventh century) than produced by using movable type on parchment.

Hart credits paper, and by extension Cai Lun, as a key factor that allowed Chinese civilization to surpass the West: paper enabled a more rapid dissemination of knowledge and information than did parchment. But, Hart acknowledges, the West would soon narrow the gap when Gutenberg made possible the mass production of books.

Chinese papermakers in a battle near Samarqand (in present-day Uzbekistan) in 751 CE.

By the fourth century CE paper had replaced wood and bamboo strips as the writing material of choice; by the sixth century, Chinese papermakers had learned how to extract vegetable fiber from the bark of the mulberry tree, one of the best sources of paper fiber. Today mulberry bark is still favored by fine papermakers in China, Korea, and Japan because of its strength and beauty.

Having created an inexpensive, light medium on which to write, the Chinese next searched for a way to mass-produce written text and visuals, primarily for religious reasons. In the eighth century, devout Buddhists sought to spread their religion by making thousands of copies of the Buddha's word and image. One early technique used a stamp with an image carved in relief on its surface; once inked with a combination of black soot and oil, the stamp could be pressed onto a sheet of paper, sparing the patron the cost of reproducing the image by hand. This technique was suitable for relatively small images, but larger, more complex images and texts were much more difficult to reproduce.

Government artisans also frequently made rubbings from stone stele. Although this technique was not as fast as stamping, rubbings could be taken from large surfaces with complex engravings. To make a rubbing, the artisan needed to place a moist sheet of fine paper onto the surface of the text- or image-bearing stone stele or tablet. Once the paper adhered to the surface of the stele, the artisan carefully pressed some of the moist paper into the crevices of the stele or tablet with a pad. Then the artisan would take another pad, this time inked with water and black soot, and press the ink onto the surface paper. When the paper was dry, the artisan would peel the inked sheet off the stone, revealing a copy of the engraving in white on a black background. The rubbing technique is still valued today for its precision and aesthetic quality, and is still used to duplicate images of fine calligraphy for Chinese art collectors.

By the eighth century, all the prerequisites for printing were in place. Artisans knew how to take prints from both relief and engraved images with stamps and rubbings. Stamps could replicate small images quickly, and rubbings could reproduce large, detailed images, albeit slowly. But neither method could satisfy the increasing demand in Chinese society for more books: Buddhists, Daoists (Taoists), and Confucians all sought to produce more copies of their canonical texts for an increasingly literate public. At some point in the eighth century, an artisan thought of combining the advantages of stamps and rubbings by making woodblock prints.

Woodblock Printing

Xylography, or woodblock printing, is both a simple and sophisticated technique for printing, unrivaled until the advent of mechanical printing presses such as Gutenberg's. Three skilled artisans are needed to prepare a page of text for xylographic printing. First, using black ink, a calligrapher writes the text to be printed on a thin sheet of paper. Next, a woodcarver takes the sheet of paper and turns it over, pasting the right side of the sheet onto a foot-long block of fruitwood; once the sheet has dried onto the block, the carver can see the characters in reverse through the back of the paper. The carver then carefully cuts into the wood and removes the background, leaving the calligraphic characters raised in relief. When the remaining paper is rubbed off, the block is ready for printing. Finally, a printmaker inks the cut woodblock with an ink pad, carefully inking only the raised characters, and then lays a thin sheet of paper on top. The printmaker presses the sheet of paper onto the characters to take an impression. A skilled printmaker can make two or three impressions a minute this way. This technique was used to make the world's earliest extant printed book, the Buddhist *Diamond Sutra,* which is dated 868 CE.

Movable Type Around the World

Bi Sheng's invention did not catch on immediately. It was not until two hundred years after his invention of movable type sometime in the mid-eleventh century that the first books were printed from such type in China; another four hundred years after that, movable type was being used sporadically in some places in China; and it was not until the latter part of the nineteenth century that the Western movable type press was "re-imported" back into China and began to replace all other kinds of printing in the country.

In contrast, the similar but more refined technology invented by Gutenberg in 1455 rapidly diffused throughout the commercial centers of Europe within fifty years. By 1470, printing offices had been set up in at least fourteen cities in Germany and other European countries. From 1470 to 1480, the number grew to more than one hundred, and by 1500 there were more than eleven hundred shops in two hundred cities throughout Europe.

No records indicate that Bi Sheng ever printed a book, which is where Gutenberg found his fame (but not his fortune: he died in poverty). When Bi Sheng died, the type came into the possession of Shen Kuo's cousins, who stored the engraved characters simply as antique toys. They were never used for printing again.

This dramatically different diffusion pattern of a considerably similar invention has remained a puzzle. Scholars have attempted to offer some insight by looking at various factors that might have shaped the different diffusion paths of the invention. At the individual level, the motivations of Bi and Gutenberg for creating their inventions were quite different. Bi, though not a wealthy man, apparently considered his invention to be a hobby and was under no economic pressure to put his invention to commercial use. What might have motivated him was a desire to demonstrate what he could do with his gadget. In contrast, Gutenberg was a professional craftsman (he was a goldsmith and a blacksmith, in addition to being a publisher), driven by economic concerns from the very

A movable type printing set; each character has its individual block.

outset of his experiment. He had to turn his printing press into a profit-making operation quickly so that he could make money to repay his debts, to retain the tools and equipment he had tried to perfect for several years, and to make a good living (He 1994).

The Importance of Books in Chinese Culture

Chinese innovations from the third to eleventh centuries CE included not only the invention of paper, but the development of stamps, rubbings, and woodblock printing, as we have seen. The mass production of text and images made possible by these inventions resulted in the widespread dissemination of religious texts, the introduction of civil service examinations for government officials, the creation of storybooks for a mass audience, and an increase in public debate. Movable type, however, was not an especially important factor in the development of books in China.

Scholars have identified two major technical difficulties in the Chinese version of movable type that hindered its diffusion: 1) the water-based ink used in China did not adhere as well to paper as did the oil-based ink used in Europe; and 2) the numerous Chinese characters caused a tremendous problem for typesetting compared with the small number of letters used in European alphabets.

In addition to the personal and technical factors limiting the broad and rapid diffusion of Bi Sheng's movable type, his invention may have been deterred by several profound challenges in the Chinese social and cultural context: a unified ideology that stifled the pursuit of change and innovations; the emphasis on literary achievements rather than commercialism; a penchant for elegant calligraphy that could not be well replicated in printed material; and a series of destabilizing wars (He 1994).

Whether or not Bi Sheng's movable type played a part in their printing, books had tremendous influence on the development of Chinese society. Easy access to books allowed writers and scholars to compare ideas and to generate new ones with greater facility. When writing new books, Chinese writers could draw upon a wider variety of books and challenge old ideas. In his memoirs, Shen Kuo made over 250 citations of a wide variety of works that were available to him, sometimes using those works to support his conclusions, at other times challenging his sources. When he finished his memoirs in the 1080s, they were printed and sold to his peers and other aspiring members of Song society. This highlights another important aspect of print culture: not only could people now read and question older ideas, their own ideas could be easily published and disseminated, adding to the scope and intensity of public debate and discussion. Bi Sheng's legacy rests in his contribution to the long continuum of the printed word in China.

Zhou HE
The City University of Hong Kong

Paul FORAGE
Indian River State College

Further Reading

Cao Jiongzhen. (1986). *A comparative study of Chinese and Korean movable type*. Taipei, Taiwan: Xuehai Publishing Company.

Chappell, Warren. (1970). *The invention of printing in China and its spread westward*. New York: The Ronald Press Company.

Deng Yinke. (2005). *Ancient Chinese inventions*. (Wang Pingxing, Trans.). Beijing: China Intercontinental Press.

Diamond, Jared. (1999). Invention is the mother of necessity. *The New York Times Magazine*. Retrieved December 3, 2013, from http://partners.nytimes.com/library/magazine/millennium/m1/diamond.html

Ebrey, Patricia, & Schirokauer, Conrad. (Advisors.) (2008). The Song dynasty in China. *Asian Topics on Asia for Educators*. Retrieved December 3, 2013, from http://afe.easia.columbia.edu/song/

Hart, Michael H. (1978). *The 100: A ranking of the most influential persons in history*. New York: Kensington Publishing Group.

He Zhou. (1994). Diffusion of movable time in China and Europe: Why were there two fates? *Gazette*, 54, 153–173.

Tsien Tsuen-hsuin. (1985). Paper and printing. In Joseph Needham (Ed.), *Science and civilisation in China: Vol. 5. Chemistry and chemical technology* (p. 485). Cambridge, UK: Cambridge University Press.

Temple, R. (1986). *The genius of China: 3,000 years of science, discovery, and invention*. New York: Simon & Schuster.

Chéng Hào
程颢

1032–1085 CE—Neo-Confucianist thinker

Alternate names: Míngdào 明道; courtesy name: Bàichún 伯淳

Summary

Cheng Hao was a Confucian thinker during the Song dynasty. He strove to restore and reconstruct classical Confucianism. Although his theses were inherited from the Confucian classics, including the *Analects, Mencius, the Classic of Changes,* and the *Doctrine of the Mean,* his interpretations offer learners new insight and perspective in understanding Confucianism. He and his younger brother, Cheng Yi, are commonly referred to as the "Two Chengs" for their parallel efforts in laying the groundwork of Neo-Confucianism.

Cheng Hao, also widely known as Míngdào 明道, was a scholar during the Sòng 宋 dynasty (960–1279). He used Bàichún 伯淳 as a courtesy name and took restoring the tradition of *Confucius 孔子 (551–479 BCE) and *Mencius 孟子 (c. 372–c. 289 BCE) as his life career. His scholarship is crystallized in the "study of *Dao*" (*dàoxué* 道学), which eventually became the major concern of various schools of Neo-Confucianism. His younger brother, Chéng Yí 程颐 (1033–1107), is likewise regarded as an important figure of Neo-Confucianism. Although they diverged on some points in their philosophical thought, the Cheng brothers are often mentioned together as the Two Chengs (Èr Chéng 二程) for their parallel effort in the groundwork of Neo-Confucianism.

The Cheng brothers were the sons of a local official in Henan Province. A precocious child, Cheng Hao exhibited much talent at an early age. At age fifteen, he studied under a teacher, Zhōu Dūnyí 周敦颐 (1017–1073), who drew much from Daoism (Taoism) in his interpretation of Confucianism, and whose thinking is considered a precursor of Neo-Confucianism. Cheng was inspired by this study and resolved to dedicate his

*People marked with an asterisk have entries in this dictionary.

life to the search of *Dao*. His brother Cheng Yi was also a student of Zhou. In his brother's words, Hao's path to *Dao* was "browsing through various schools of thought, looking deeply into Taoism and Buddhism for many decades, coming back to the Six Classics and finally attaining it" (Cheng and Cheng 1981, 638).

In 1057, Cheng Hao was awarded the degree of *jìnshì* 进士 (presented scholar), and thereafter served in various government posts until he had the opportunity of meeting the emperor, Shénzōng 神宗, in person. His political career took a downturn, however, when he adamantly opposed the view of the leader of the reformation campaign, *Wáng Ānshí 王安石 (1021–1086), who then won the trust of the emperor. Cheng Hao was demoted and eventually dismissed. This career decline, nevertheless, opened up an opportunity for his deeper pursuit of *Dao*. He returned to Luoyang in 1072. There, together with his brother Cheng Yi, he set up a school where he taught for the rest of his life.

Cheng Hao inherited and developed the thought of classical Confucianism rather than drawing on preceding Neo-Confucian thinkers such as Zhou Dunyi, Shào Yōng 邵雍 (1011–1017), or Zhang Zai (1020–1077). The main corpus of Cheng Hao's work comprises conversations recorded by his disciples collected in *Literary Remains of the Two Chengs* (*Ér Chéng yíshū* 二程遗书). He also wrote short essays, poems, and letters. Two of his best known essays are "Letters on Stabilizing Nature" 定性书 and "On Understanding *Ren*" 识仁篇.

Heaven and Principle

For Cheng Hao, Heaven (*tiān* 天) is a transcendent entity. It has multiple names: the Way (*dào* 道), the Changes (*yì* 易), or the Spirit (*shén* 神). Each name signifies a specific aspect of the Heaven. The notion of Changes is to illustrate the ceaselessly producing nature of Heaven, the function of which is called the Spirit, as a description of its unpredictable creativity that renders the existence of innumerable things. Whereas the Spirit represents the function (*yòng* 用), the Changes and the Way refer to the substance. The Way denotes the Principle (*lǐ* 理) it contains, which is also called the Heavenly Principle (*tiānlǐ* 天理).

The Principle is one, which includes many. Within this Principle, hundreds of principles are implicitly there to be employed where particular issues arise. These can be considered different forms of the Principle, which is everlasting and without change, no matter what situation comes up. The Principle is the law of creation, equivalent to creativity. It is not only a static law providing governance and guidance to innumerable things; rather, the law has creative/productive power that makes their existence possible. Therefore the Principle can be viewed as the *principle* of production and the Way as the *way* of production. The Principle refers to both the law, based on which things are formed, and the creating activity, by which things come into existence. The literal meaning of the Changes is precisely a description of the activity of "production and reproduction" (*shēng shēng* 生生). This meaning has a long tradition, which can be traced back to the "Great Appendix" in the *Classic of Changes* (*I Ching* or *Yìjīng* 易经): "Production and reproduction is what meant by the Changes." Cheng Hao remarked on this text: "It is production which Heaven regards as its Way" (Cheng and Cheng 1981, 1.29). The Spirit shows the unlimited and unfathomable function of the activity of creation. Everything that shares the Principle thus has the potential of "production and reproduction." In sum, no matter which name it bears, Heaven is the transcendent Being that is completely embodied in its activity, and the activity is the manifestation of the Being. Therefore as Being (the creativity itself), it can be understood through activity (act of creation) and vice versa.

Heaven and Innumerable Things

Heaven no doubt belongs to the realm of "above-form" (*xíng ér shàng* 形而上), which is contrary to "below-form" (*xíng ér xià* 形而下) (realm of phenomenon) where instruments (*qì* 器) (innumerable things) emerge. Nevertheless, these two realms are in no way separate. It is because the Heaven or the Way is nothing but its manifestation through the instruments. Also, when the instruments are fully actualized, they embody the Way. Cheng Hao claimed, "Outside the Way there are no things and outside things there is no Way, so that between heaven and earth there is no direction to go which is not the Way" (Cheng and Cheng 1981, 1.73). He also said that "the Way is the instruments and the instruments are the Way" (Cheng and Cheng 1981, 1.4).

The Way and Vital Energy

The relationship between the Way and vital energy (*qì* 气) is analogous to the relationship between the Way and the instruments. Vital energy, which is divided into *yīn* 阴 and *yáng* 阳, belongs to the realm of below-form. All phenomena are formed by the operation of yin and yang, hence the former can be understood in terms of the latter. To quote an example from Cheng Hao, "The coldness of winter and the heat of summer are respectively yin and yang. That by which they [yin and yang] are moved and transformed is Spirit" (Cheng and Cheng 1981, 1.121). It is noteworthy that Cheng Hao distinguished with clarity yin and yang from their operations. Apparently he thought that only the above-form could be the explanatory and operational ground for the below-form. Yet he emphasized that "outside vital energy there is no Spirit and outside Spirit there is no vital energy" (Cheng and Cheng 1981, 1.121). Spirit is present in the vital energy, no matter if it is clear or turbid. This means that the Way may manifest itself in any form. Cheng Hao thought the Way should not be confined to a certain form; therefore he objected to the view that the source of the innumerable things is located only in the "clear, void, one and great," which are commonly considered as positive. The Way, for him, "becomes one substance with things without exception" (Cheng and Cheng 1981, 1.21).

Philosophy of Human Nature

Cheng Hao did not endorse what was advocated by Mencius, specifically that "human nature is good." He did focus, however, on the origin of human nature (*rénxìng* 人性). Mencius claimed that the greater body, by which humanity is capable of discerning good and evil, is decreed by Heaven (*Mencius* 6A.1). The greater body refers to the heart-mind, the actualization of human nature. Following this line of thinking, the passage that "by fully exhausting one's heart-mind one can apprehend one's own nature, by fully apprehending one's own nature one will apprehend Heaven" (*Mencius* 7A.1) is deemed intelligible. Even though the capacity of discerning good and evil is decreed by Heaven, it is by no means that goodness is decided by it. Therefore, Confucian ethics is not a kind of metaphysical ethics.

Cheng Hao held that the origin of human nature is Heaven, and both human nature and Heaven share the common quality of creativity. We have mentioned that everything shares the Principle of creation, including humanity. Therefore a human is endowed with the power of production and reproduction as to his/her nature. Although things and humans share a common nature, that is, the creativity by which they come into existence, they individually have different characteristics. Hence, on the one hand, all innumerable things are the same, and on the other, they differ.

Apart from attributing human nature to a specific content, Cheng Hao also gave his own interpretation of "good." He said, "it is production which Heaven regards as its Way, and what succeeds this productive Principle is goodness. Goodness has the implication 'Originating' (*yuán* 元). 'The Originating is at the head of goodness'" (Cheng and Cheng 1981, 1.29). This means that the productive power is the origin of goodness. Human nature, which possesses this productive power, also possesses the origin of goodness. Therefore the attribute "good" in the assertion "human nature is good" has a totally different meaning from that appearing in a moral judgment. The former indicates an inborn capacity of human beings, which is considered as the ground of making moral judgment. The actualization of human nature means the succession of the original good, which is also considered good. This is how Cheng Hao interpreted the passage in the "Great Appendix": "That which succeeds is goodness; that in which it is completed is the nature" (Cheng and Cheng 1981).

Cheng Hao quoted the saying of Gàozǐ 告子 (Mencius's contemporary), that "inborn is what is meant by the nature"; nevertheless, he and Gaozi did not hold the same view. It is true that both agreed on the view that every being possesses the inborn qualities of life to come into existence. For Gaozi, however, these qualities are composed of natural dispositions, desires, and abilities that make one species different from another, whereas for Cheng Hao the inborn quality refers to the productive power that is commonly shared by all kinds of things. Cheng Hao maintained that because the innumerable things share the same productive power, all things are the same. Based on this reason, he further claimed that humans and things can become one.

As was already mentioned, the innumerable things and humans obtain the ceaselessly productive power from Heaven as their nature. Since they completely possess this productive power once they are formed, in order to become one with Heaven they are complete within themselves without the need of attaining anything outside. Cheng Hao interpreted Mencius saying that "the innumerable things are all complete in myself" (*Mencius* 7A.4), as mentioned earlier, and he added that "this is so not only of human but of all things" (Cheng and Cheng 1981, 1.34). Having said that, in the phenomenal world (i.e., the world that is perceived by the sense), things differ from each other in kind, and also from humans. Cheng Hao explained this differentiation in terms of the vital energy with which things are endowed when they become an individual being. The vital energy obtained by things is impure or obscure. Although like humans, the innumerable things obtain the Way of Principle when they come into existence. They only possess it ontologically, meaning that the Way (of production) exists within things themselves merely as potential. (Ontology is a branch of metaphysics concerned with the nature of being.) Only humans are endowed with the vital energy that allows them to actualize their own nature as well as to extend it to actualize others' natures. Therefore, only humans can nurture their nature and cultivate the nature of things, and because of this capacity, they can form a trinity with Heaven and Earth as well.

The innumerable things receive the Principle from Heaven, but the Principle endowed only manifests as the structure of their existence. In the case of humans, the Principle endowed constitutes the human nature of ceaseless productive power. Since the Principle is one and the same, we as humans can get in touch with the Principle by watching the manifestation of productive power in living things, for instance, the activity of grass growing. Cheng Hao exclaimed, "It is most excellent to look into the vital impulses of the innumerable things" (Cheng and Cheng 1981, 1.120). It is because of the vital impulses that he can take a glimpse of the Changes.

Heart-Mind and the Theory of Cultivation

A human endowed with the Principle thus can extend his or her nature to the nature of things. Adopting Mencius's conception of heart-mind (*xīn* 心), Cheng Hao also took the heart-mind as the faculty of extension. Mencius said, "By fully exhausting one's heart-mind one can apprehend one's own nature, by fully apprehending one's own nature one will apprehend Heaven" (*Mencius* 7A.1). According to Mencius, through "extending from whom he/she (a person with *ren*) loves to whom he/she doesn't" (*Mencius* 7B.1) one will exhaust one's heart-mind, and then apprehend Heaven. Cheng Hao made a further claim that "the heart-mind alone is Heaven" (Cheng and Cheng 1981, 1.15). What he emphasized is that the heart-mind and the Heaven are originally one, given that they both have creativity (the ceaselessly productive power) as their virtue. Therefore one only needs to actualize or restore this virtue, which is inherent in one's own heart-mind.

The virtue of creativity inherent in the heart-mind is called *rén* 仁, sometimes translated as "benevolence" because one of its meanings is the capacity of loving people without discrimination. *Ren* presents the transference of feeling (*gǎntōng* 感通) with other people, which makes this universal love possible. Whereas love is empirical, the capacity of transference is transcendent because it is not conditioned by empirical factors. By activating *ren*, one will regard other's interest as one's own and will "help others to stand while wishing to stand oneself and help others to arrive while wishing to arrive oneself" (*Analects* 6.30). The creativity of *ren* presents in the ceaseless extension of care and love. Ultimately, one who fully activates *ren* will treat oneself and the innumerable things as one substance, "so that nothing is not Oneself" (Cheng and Cheng 1981, 1.15). Cheng Hao liked to take "the numbness in the hands and feet" as a metaphor to illustrate the unconnected condition of one and the others. He said the sage, who achieves *ren* to perfection, would regard Heaven and Earth as one body, and the innumerable things as four limbs and other organs—such a person would love the innumerable things as his/her own limbs. When the limbs are "unfeeling," then we would describe this situation as paralysis. By the same token, if one does not feel the suffering of others, then we would say that his or her heart-mind is paralytic, and the *ren* within it is not activated.

As mentioned, the heart-mind possesses the virtue of Heaven, that is, creativity as its own virtue. Therefore all one needs for actualizing the virtue of Heaven is to actualize one's heart-mind. Once the heart-mind is actualized then one can actualize the nature of others as well as that of innumerable things. When the nature of others and things are actualized, then one can assist Heaven in transforming and nurturing things. On the contrary, if the heart-mind has not been fully actualized, then one cannot apprehend the nature of things and that of Heaven. Cheng Hao said, "Exhausting the Principle, actualizing the nature and reaching the decree [of Heaven], these three events can altogether be completed at one time. Definitely there is no priority. Exhausting the Principle should not be regarded as a cognitive act. If the Principle is really exhausted, then the nature and the decree are also completed" (Cheng and Cheng 1981, 1.15). If exhausting the Principle is not a cognitive act, then the accomplishment of knowledge, even about the principles of innumerable things, is irrelevant to the apprehension of the Principle. Once the heart-mind is actualized, the Principle is exhausted; this idea is well developed from *Mencius* 7A.1.

Cheng Hao maintained that one can actualize one's heart-mind merely through sincerity (*chéng* 诚). He said, "By perfect sincerity one can take part in (*zàn* 赞) the cultivation of Heaven and Earth" (Cheng and Cheng 1981, 1.133). According to him, this is possible because perfect sincerity is the cultivation of Heaven and Earth, which is manifesting ceaseless creativity. This view can be traced back to Mencius, that sincerity is the way of Heaven and that aiming at sincerity is the way of man (*Mencius* 4A.12). Also in the *Doctrine of the Mean* (*Zhōngyōng* 中庸), it is claimed that "the Way of Heaven and Earth can be perfectly expressed in a single clause: 'It is without any doubleness (*bú èr* 不二), therefore its production of things is unfathomable'" (Ch. 26). "Double" or "two" (*èr* 二) symbolizes the dichotomy of true and false, real and illusory, and so forth. Only if the dualistic way of thinking is abolished can the ultimate truth that constitutes the ground for all existence be revealed. Hence the Way of production is, unequivocally, sincerity. In the *Doctrine of the Mean* it is held that through perfect sincerity one can actualize the nature of oneself, that of other people, and things. It is clear that Cheng Hao combined these two sources and concluded that by actualizing the heart-mind through sincerity one can realize the virtue of Heaven.

In sum, the ceaseless creative power, *ren*, and sincerity are but one virtue in the human's heart-mind as well as in Heaven. Therefore, through the actualization of this virtue, human and Heaven are united. For practice in daily lives, once one understands Heaven and the Principle, one merely needs to preserve *ren* by sincerity and composure (*jìng* 敬). Cheng Hao maintained that there is no need to be on one's guard or to conduct deep inquiries. He argued, "If the mind relaxes we must be on guard; but if not, what is there to guard against? Inquiry is necessary only because there are principles which have not yet been grasped; if they have been constantly preserved they will be clear of themselves, and what need is there to inquire?" (Cheng and Cheng 1981, 1.16–1.17) Precisely, for Cheng Hao, it is because the human and the Principle are originally one and both have *ren* as their content, therefore understanding the Principle means understanding human nature, which can be actualized by the heart-mind through sincerity.

The Highest Achievement of Cultivation

In Confucianism the ultimate goal of cultivation for an individual is to become a sage, a person who has achieved the highest state in the moral realm. To achieve the highest moral accomplishment, the sage cultivates his or her heart-mind so as to unlimitedly extend the circle of care and concern, and eventually treat others and things equally as treating oneself. For Cheng Hao, apart from devoting themselves to the moral pursuit, sages also aim at uniting with Heaven. As mentioned earlier, humans and Heaven are originally one because both share the common nature and virtue of the power of production. If human and Heaven are but one, however, there is no need to speak of the union of Heaven and human. By the same token, it is odd to speak of forming a trinity with Heaven and Earth or uniting with others and things. When Cheng Hao claimed that "outside the Way there are no things and outside the things there is no Way," and "the Way is instruments and instruments are the Way," what kind of expressions were they? Obviously they are neither empirical statements of fact nor a metaphysical belief. The former demands one way or another for verification or confirmation. The latter is commonly regarded as something speculative without a convincing ground. Rather, the expressions in question can be considered as a description of a vision that can only be achieved by a sage. A sage can achieve this kind of vision since as a sage he or she completely embodies the Way. Therefore, sages can apprehend the Way by apprehending the heart-mind; furthermore they will find that the Way manifests itself in their heart-mind and in any form of instruments without confinement. It seems that this explanation commits the fallacy of begging the question: the metaphysical claim is accounted for in terms of a sage and a sage is characterized in terms of the content in the metaphysical claim. If this is the case, then the metaphysical claim and the description about the sage are mutually dependent. This problem is analogous to that arising from the conceptual relationship between virtuous acts and virtuous persons. If a virtuous person is characterized in terms of virtuous acts—that is, a virtuous person is someone who always chooses virtuous acts for their own sake, and a virtuous act is what a virtuous person would do—then the conceptions of virtuous acts and virtuous persons will be mutually dependent. The British moral philosopher Bernard Williams comments on this relationship of dependence that "there is no problem just in this, but there will be a problem if it leads to vacuity" (Williams 1985, 16). Under what conditions will it constitute a problem? Williams proceeds, "This will be so, if we cannot distinguish one virtue from another, and/or the V [virtuous] agent is left with no determinate content to his thoughts" (Williams 1985, 16). In the present case, being a sage can be identified without depending on the metaphysical claim. Because after some practice one can completely apprehend one's heart-mind and thus knows vividly whether one treats others as oneself. This merely depends on personal reflection, which usually applies to inner experience. Thus from the perspective of a sage, when he or she sees that him- or herself and others are one, then he or she would also find that the Way and the instruments are one. Cheng Hao called the theses of this oneness apprehended by a sage "one-rootedness" (*yīběn* 一本).

A problem remains that if Heaven and human are originally one, then why is cultivation needed anyway? According to Cheng Hao, a human is endowed with vital energy that might hinder the actualization of his/her nature; therefore, a human needs to make an effort in order to resume the unity with Heaven. Through activating *ren*, sincerity, and the productive power, one is taking the path toward the aim.

The Duality of Good and Bad

In his book *Two Chinese Philosophers* (1992), Angus Graham discusses the issue of "monism or dualism" in Cheng Hao's thought. He singles out the contrariness of good and evil in one chapter and argues that Cheng Hao admits the bad, like the good, is a necessary part of the Way. Graham points out that Neo-Confucians in general and Cheng Hao in particular, make no distinction between descriptive and normative principles (Graham 1992, 127): since bad is a necessary part in the world of existence, it is equally so in the moral world. Graham thinks that it is a conceptual contradiction to prescribe that the human ought to do good and at the same time to regard bad as a necessary component of the natural harmony. He guesses that the solution for a modern European is to distinguish between the two senses of the principle.

In fact, Cheng Hao has distinguished between these two senses. As mentioned earlier, the Way decrees the human with the Principle as his or her nature. In the ontological sense of the principle—that is, the Principle (it is not proper to regard it as descriptive since the truth it refers to is not an empirical fact)—it possesses the power of production, which is the origin of good (that which succeeds is goodness); therefore human nature is good. Nevertheless, when an individual comes to existence, he or she is also endowed with vital energy, which might lead to the bad. Even though the bad is not originated from the Principle, the process of coming into existence is also under the governance of the Principle. This is what is meant by Cheng Hao's saying "there are good and bad events, all are heavenly Principle" (Cheng and Cheng 1981, 1.17). As far as the normative sense of Principle is concerned, however, one ought to exhaust one's heart-mind and thus actualize one's nature. This is the way of observing the Principle. But since one is endowed with vital energy, which might hinder one from actualizing one's own nature, therefore one needs to cultivate one's heart-mind to resume the Principle. It is in this sense that he speaks of good or bad acts in a normative sense.

In Cheng Hao's thought, however, it is admitted that the Principle has to manifest itself through vital energy, where the bad originates. It does not mean that the human is "born with good and bad as two contrasting things present in his/her nature from the very beginning" (Cheng and Cheng 1981, 1.11). Therefore, underlying the dualistic view of good and bad, for Cheng Hao, it is the original goodness that is the ultimate ground for the contrasting attributes. He uses a water parable to illustrate this: water is originally clean, and it becomes muddy only if it is polluted. The cleanliness and the muddiness are not two contrasting attributes in the nature of water. The water inevitably becomes muddy once it starts to flow; in this sense the nature of water also includes the possibility of being polluted. It does not follow from this, however, that it could not be purified to obtain clean water again. For the present issue, we have seen that the two principles—namely, the ontological principle and the normative principle—are one. The former accounts for the origin of good and bad, while the latter governs the good and the bad. Yet the fact that the principles are but one would not render Cheng Hao's ethics a metaphysical one. This is so because the recognition of the latter does not depend on that of the former; rather, it is through the heart-mind that both principles are apprehended. Therefore, contrary to Graham's view, firstly, the two principles have not been mixed up; secondly, there is no contradiction between these two principles.

The Significance of Cheng Hao's Thought

Cheng Hao was the first one to focus on the heart-mind and *ren* among the Neo-Confucians in the Song dynasty. He was also the first one who emphasized the unity of heart-mind, human nature, and Heaven, which is based on the one-rootedness doctrine.

Although his theses are inherited from the Confucian classics, including the *Analects*, *Mencius*, the *Classic of Changes*, and the *Doctrine of the Mean*, his interpretation and elaboration offer learners a new insight and perspective in understanding Confucianism. For example, the notion of Heaven has existed very early in the history of Chinese thoughts and in pre-Qin Confucianism, but Cheng Hao claimed that he picked up the notion of Principle by himself and developed it to refer to the ontological Being as well as activity. His thesis is so influential that the thoughts of various schools of Neo-Confucianism are commonly called "the study of Principle" (*lǐxué* 理学). Therefore, his contribution to Confucianism is regarded as going beyond restoration, serving as a revitalization and reconstruction of Confucianism.

Cheng Hao and his brother Cheng Yi shared the same interest in traditional Confucianism in theory and moral cultivation in practice. There is a wide range of disagreements between the views of the two brothers, however. Cheng Hao gave a significant role to the heart-mind in ontology and in moral philosophy. His thought was further developed by Lù Xiàngshān 陆象山 (1139–1193) and *Wáng Yángmíng 王阳明 (1472–1529), and has evolved into the tradition of the study of mind (*xīnxué* 心学). This tradition has become the rival school of the study of Principle (in a narrow sense), which was founded by Cheng Yi.

Wai-ying WONG
Lingnan University, Hong Kong

Further Reading

Cheng Hao 程颢, & Cheng Yi 程颐. (1981). *Er Cheng ji* 二程集 [Complete works of the Cheng brothers]. Beijing: Zhonghua Shuju.

Confucius. (2003). Analects: *With selections from traditional commentaries*. (Edward Slingerland, Trans.). Indianapolis: Hackett Publishing Company.

Graham, Angus C. (1992). *Two Chinese philosophers: The metaphysics of the brothers Ch'êng*. La Salle, IL: Open Court Publishing Company.

Guo Xiaodong 郭晓东. (2006). *Shi ren yu ding xing* 识仁与定性 [Understanding *ren* and stabilizing the nature]. Shanghai: Fudan University Press.

Huang Siu-chi. (1999). *Essentials of Neo-Confucianism: Eight major philosophers of the Song and Ming periods*. London: Greenwood Press.

Huang Yong. (2007). The Cheng brothers' onto-theological articulation of Confucian values. *Asian Philosophy, 17*(3), 187–211.

Mencius. (1979). *Mencius*. (D. C. Lau, Trans.). Hong Kong: The Chinese University Press.

Mou Tsung-san 牟宗三. (1968). *Xin ti yu xing ti* 心体与性体 [The substance of *xin* and the substance of *xing*], Vol. II. Taipei, Taiwan: Zhengzhong Shuju.

Muller, Charles A. (2011). *The Doctrine of the Mean (Zhongyong)* 中庸 (Rev. ed.). Retrieved September 11, 2013, from http://www.acmuller.net/con-dao/docofmean.html

Williams, Bernard. (1985). *Ethics and the limits of philosophy*. London: Fontana Press.

Wong, Wai-ying. (2009). The morally bad in the philosophy of Cheng brothers. *Journal of Chinese Philosophy, 36*(1), 141–156.

Wong, Wai-ying. (2010). The thesis of "single-rootedness" in the thought of Cheng Hao. In John Makeham (Ed.), *Dao companions to Chinese philosophy series: Neo-Confucianism* (pp. 89–104). London: Springer.

Huáng Tíngjiān
黄庭坚

1045–1105—Poet, calligrapher, art critic, official, and scholar

Alternate names: style name: Lǔzhí 鲁直; most common sobriquets: Shāngǔ lǎorén 山谷老人, Fúwēng 涪翁

Summary

Huang Tingjian was one of the Song dynasty's most notable scholars; his artistic achievements are still studied by scholars and artists. He escaped his humble origins to become an influential figure in reinterpreting antique ideals to create new literary and visual aesthetics. The main events in Huang's life affected his literary writings, as well as the aesthetics of his calligraphy. While he was proficient and excelled in several literary genres such as poetry and prose, he also studied the major calligraphy models of antiquity, ultimately reaching his own idiosyncratic style—one that would have been considered flawed in an earlier era. A later scholar would write that there was "not one idle idea" in Huang's calligraphy.

Even during his lifetime, Huang Tingjian was much admired in particular for his highly innovative style in calligraphy, but also for his originality in poetic writing, in which he successfully sought to create new expressions based on existing poetry. In addition to his duties as an official, Huang wrote extensively on calligraphy and was also a respected painting critic; among other genres, his writings on calligraphy and painting have been preserved as colophons (there is no systematic treatise on the arts by Huang), which form an important part of the *Complete Volumes of Huang Tingjian's Works* (*Huáng Tíngjiān quánjí* 黄庭坚全集). Some of these, such as the famous *Colophon to Su Shi's Poems Written at Huangzhou on the Cold Food Festival* (*Bá Dōngpō hánshí shītiē juàn* 跋东坡寒食诗帖卷; dated 1100, today in the National Palace Museum in Taiwan), have been preserved in his original handwriting, which makes them particularly valuable items for the study of texts that survive as original calligraphy as well as the role that they play in Sòng 宋 dynasty (960–1279) material culture.

Huang was one of the so-called four great masters of calligraphy of the Northern Song dynasty (960–1127 CE), which was a group of literati including the eminent artist, scholar, and friend *Sū Shì 苏轼 (1037–1101), the calligrapher Mǐ Fú 米芾 (1051–1107), and the scholar and writer Cài Xiāng 蔡襄 (1012–1067). While these scholars are most noted for their achievements in literature and the arts, they also successfully applied their talents in several other cultural spheres such as politics and governing, which is why the twentieth century sinologist James T. C. Liu described them as "somewhat like Renaissance men in Europe" (Franke 1976).

In the arts, Huang was particularly talented as a writer and calligrapher. For certain calligraphic styles such as cursive script (*cǎoshū* 草书), contemporary scholars such as the respected calligraphy expert Fù Shēn 傅申 from National Taiwan University even refer to Huang Tingjian as the most outstanding and influential in this style (Fu 1991). An example of the cursive script style is Huang's noted *Sayings of a Chan Buddhist Monk* (*Zhū shàng zuò* 诸上座, dated 1100) in the Palace Museum, Beijing.

In other styles such as running script (*xíngshū* 行书), Huang also had his own very distinctive approach, which involved highly individual large-character cursive script works. Three of the most famous examples in large running script calligraphy are his scroll *Dedicated to My Nephew Zhang Datong* (*Zèng shēng Zhāng Dàtóng juàn* 赠甥张大同卷, dated 1100; Princeton University Art Museum), *Passing the Shrine of the God Calming the Waves* (*Jīng Fúbō shéncí shī juàn* 经伏波神祠诗卷, dated 1101; Eisei Bunko Museum, Tokyo), and *Poem of the Pine Wind Pavilion* (*Sōng fēng gé shī* 松风阁诗, dated 1102; National Palace Museum, Taipei).

As a major cultural figure of the Song dynasty, Huang Tingjian was and still is influential in calligraphy and poetry, as well as a respected painting critic (Fu 1976). While these two media form part of a much wider corpus of Chinese material culture, they were also subject to a notable, and then-unique, trend in the Song dynasty, which was the reflection and hence acceptance of artists' idiosyncrasies within their works of art. Before the Song dynasty, such characteristics would have been criticized as "flaws." There were many important stages in Huang Tingjian's life that were crucial in the formation of his individual style and work, including historical context.

The Social and Cultural Context

The Song dynasty that Huang Tingjian was born into was a period of radical

*People marked with an asterisk have entries in this dictionary.

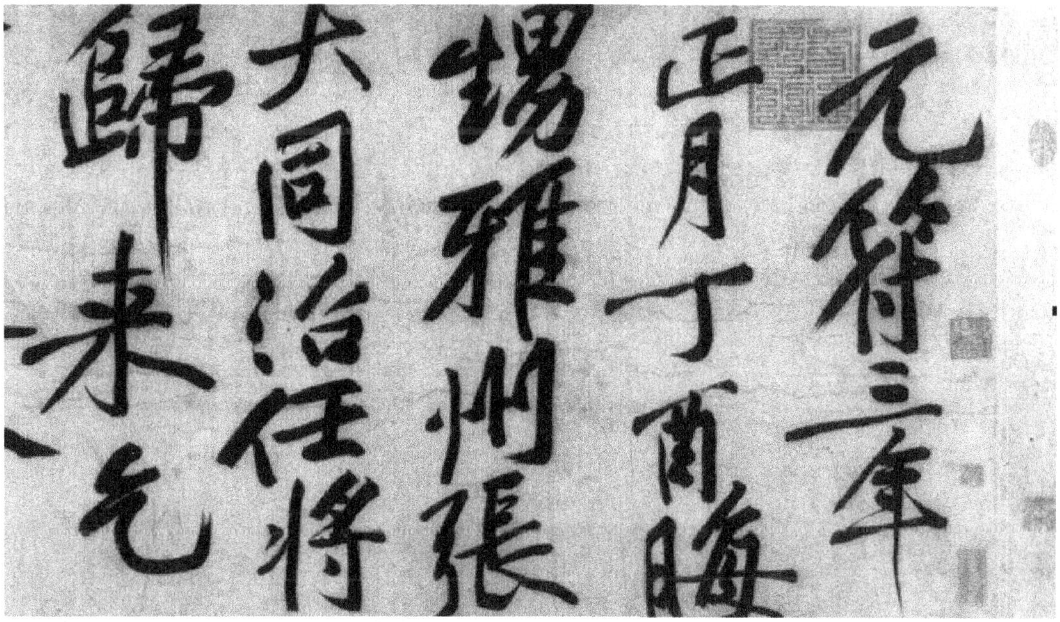

Initial section of *Dedicated to My Nephew Zhang Datong* (1100 CE) by Huang Tingjian. Handscroll, ink on paper. Princeton University Art Museum, Princeton, New Jersey.

changes in several areas. After several decades of political unrest, the first emperor Sòng Tàizǔ 宋太祖 (r. 960–976 CE) managed to stabilize the empire, along with the establishment of a civil order within China. Military officers were replaced with civil servants, and the standing army was diminished—hence the shift from *wǔ* 武 ("the martial") to *wén* 文 ("the civil"), which was a major reason the arts flourished during this period. Too much promotion of learning and refinement could, however, also prove disastrous, such as was the case with Northern Song Emperor Huīzōng 徽宗 (r. 1100–1126), who devoted himself to the arts and neglected politics.

Despite the fact that the Song dynasty has been described as one of the politically weakest (but also safest) dynasties in Chinese history, it nevertheless produced some of the greatest and most influential thinkers. This has led distinguished scholars, such as the historian and sinologist Naitô Torajirô 内藤虎二郎 (1866–1934), to redefine the beginning of "modern times" in Chinese history by claiming that China's modern period began with the Song dynasty. Naitô's theory involves the return to antiquity (*fùgǔ* 复古), i.e., a return to antique ideals, as an important notion.

The return to antique ideals also plays an important part in the arts. For example, the development of the so-called ancient style prose movement (*gǔwén yùndòng* 古文运动) was an important reform movement in Chinese literature, which had its origins in the Táng 唐 dynasty (618–907 CE). Its style involved a language that was seen as reflecting the simplicity and naturalness of the *dào* 道 ("The Way"). Historical issues and the studies of the Chinese classics were particularly appreciated, and the movement formed the foundation for learning based on the classics during the following centuries. In this context, the Neo-Confucian statesman and scholar *Ōuyáng Xiū 欧阳修 (1007–1072) was particularly important because he managed to pave the way for a new generation of scholars who were proficient in the ancient prose style. Ouyang had overhauled the structure of the state exams (*jìnshì* 进士) in 1057, which is when Huang's friend and mentor Su Shi passed his degree; both Huang and Su belonged to a new generation of highly talented scholars, Huang passing his degree in 1067.

The Life and Work of Huang Tingjian

The main events in Huang's life affected his literary writings, as well as the aesthetics of his calligraphy. While he was proficient and excelled in several literary genres such as poetry and prose, he also carefully and diligently studied the major calligraphy models of antiquity, ultimately reaching his own, very distinctive, style. Despite working as an official to support his family, Huang was very prolific in the arts, something that was marked by hardship due to several political banishments to remote and inhospitable places, particularly in his later years. Even more interesting is that many of his most excellent works were produced in exactly these circumstances.

Major Stages in Huang's Life

Huang Tingjian was born on 29 July 1045 in Hongzhou, Fenning County (now Xiushui, Jiangxi Province) into a once-wealthy family, which was already relatively poor by the time he was born. Huang's father, Huáng Shù 黄庶 (d. 1058), was a minor official and had high hopes for his children—there were five sons and four daughters—yet Huang Tingjian would be the only one to fulfill these hopes. Legend has it that his literary talent was such that he could recite the Five Classics (Wǔjīng 五经, a compendium of Confucian classics) by the time he was five years old, which certainly would have helped his official career and his wish to make enough money to help his family out financially after his father died in 1058. The family tradition of service in officialdom had become established as early as the tenth century through his grandfather, Huáng Zhōnglǐ 黄中理 (life dates unknown). Huang's father remained a minor official but provided the impetus for Huang's admiration and study of the famous Tang poets *Dù Fǔ 杜甫 (712–770) and *Hán Yù 韩愈 (768–824). When his father passed away, Huang's uncle Lǐ Cháng 李常 (1027–1090), who was an influential official and friend of the eminent Su Shi, took care of him.

Through Li Chang, an important statesman and scholar with a library of more than nine thousand volumes, the doors to a literary career were opened to Huang Tingjian. In addition to being very well-read, and excelling at calligraphy and poetry, Li was also a good teacher, and through this laid the foundation for Huang's own excellent scholarship. While in his early years, the core of Huang's scholarship consisted mainly of Confucian literature, it was Li's traditional Confucian views of the Chinese classics that led him to value the "way of the ancients" (*gǔrén fǎ* 古人法).

In 1067, after passing his state examinations, Huang Tingjian married the daughter of Sūn Jué 孙觉 (1028–1090), a scholar to whom he was introduced by his uncle Li Chang. They moved to Ruzhou (now Linru, Henan Province), where Huang started his career as a police prefect under the renowned statesman Fù Bì 富弼 (1004–1083). His work there made him understand the burden of the common people, who suffered famines and heavy taxation, and his sympathy for the poor and the wish to break out of officialdom became a crucial aspect of Huang's life. Despite him having to continue working until old age, it was these qualities that he admired in the famous recluse and poet Táo Yuānmíng 陶淵明 (365–427 CE), who had left government service and devoted himself to the arts.

Sun Jue, his father-in-law, was regarded as a fair official by the people, a fact that Huang wished to emulate in his own district; Sun also furthered his literary interests and taught him how to appreciate good literature, which enabled Huang to eventually find his own style. Huang's strain, however, intensified with the death of his first wife in 1070, and instead of granting his wish to be dismissed from court, he was promoted to a post in the capital by his eventual political enemy and reformer *Wáng Ānshí 王安石 (1021–86) of the progressive party, who admired the young official's writing skills. He started his career there as a higher official in 1072, and was supported by influential court officials such as Wén Yànbó 文彥博 (1006–1097). Equally important for his career was his marriage in 1073 to the daughter of the influential Xiè Jīngchū 谢景初 (1019–1084), who was the nephew of the renowned poet Méi Yáochén 梅尧臣 (1002–1062), and who counted the prominent statesmen Ouyang Xiu and Wang Anshi among his relatives. Unfortunately, his second wife also suffered an untimely death and died in 1079.

Huang's time at the capital from 1072 until 1079, however, still proved fruitful in several ways; during these years, he composed more than 293 pages of poetry, as opposed to only 273 pages from 1051 to 1071. In 1076, his daughter, Mù 睦, was born. In 1080, the breakthrough to a great literary career finally took place through an exchange of letters with the noted Su Shi, who admired the poems Huang had sent him; a close friendship ensued, and Huang became one of Su's four major students.

From 1080 to 1085, he first served as a magistrate in Jizhou (now Taihe, Jiangxi Province); on his way to his new post in 1080, he passed the Buddhist Shāngǔ 山谷 monastery, which provided the inspiration for his sobriquet, "Old Man from Shangu" (*Shāngǔ lǎorén* 山谷老人). At the end of 1083 he was sent away from Taihe to serve as a garrison overseer in Deping (now Deping Xian, Shandong Province), which may have been a demotion due to his criticism of the government's high taxation of poor people at his previous post. It was also around 1083 that his son, Xiāng 相, was born, probably to a concubine. On his way to Dezhou, Huang passed Sizhou (now Sixian, Anhui Province), where he visited the Sengjia Pagoda, which was built for the important Tang monk Sēng Jiā 僧加 (628–710). As Huang Tingjian had already become interested in Buddhism by then, he took the occasion to write the *Vow from the Sutra of Accumulated Treasures* (*Fǎ yuàn wén juàn* 法愿文卷, c. mid-1080s (attributed), Lin Boshou 林柏寿 Collection, Taipei), meaning that he renounced wine, meat, and women. After this experience, Huang would be attracted to Buddhism in the form of Chan meditational Buddhism. It was also in Deping that Huang Tingjian first encountered the official Zhào Tǐngzhī 赵挺之 (c. 1040–c.1107), who was a reformist and would later become one of his fiercest enemies at court.

Huang Tingjian's official career was at its peak from 1085 to 1091 at the capital Kaifeng, where he held several prestigious posts. By 1086, the noted official *Sīmǎ Guāng's 司馬光 (1019–1086) appreciation of Huang's scholarly talent resulted in further appointments to literary projects such as Sima Guang's *A Comprehensive Mirror to Aid Government* (*Zīzhì tōngjiàn* 资治通鉴), which covered the history of China from 403 BCE to 959 CE and was the first major work in its genre and thus enormously influential. In 1087, Huang was given the post of Secretary of the Imperial Office.

Huang Tingjian belonged to the conservative *Yuányòu* 元祐 party (named after the era from 1086–1093), and while prestigious, his positions at court would also lay the foundation for the later accusations by the reformists, who used his writings as the basis for those accusations. While in office, Huang was protected by his influential mentor Su Shi, who had gained substantial political influence. In 1089, he was promoted for the last time when he was appointed Subeditor of the Library of the Academy of Scholarly Worthies (Jíxián jiàolǐ 集贤校理).

His career was ended by the death of his mother in July 1091, when he returned to Jiangxi. Having previously requested to be relieved of his duties due to health reasons, he retired from court without regret. Huang had taken care of his ill mother for years before her death and spent the years from 1091 to 1093 mourning her death, which is seen as a time of "exemplary filial piety," yet also important as he found solace in Chan Buddhism (Zen in Japanese). The Chan monk Huìtáng Zǔxīn 晦堂祖心 (1025–1100) was his spiritual guide, and Huang had his moment of enlightenment (*lǐngjiě* 领解)—also referred to as "satori experience"—at the Huánglóngshān 黄龙山 monastery west of his native Fenning. This was also important regarding his calligraphy, as he claimed to have "become one with running script" during this time, this type of script being the one that allowed for the greatest amount of personal freedom when writing (Bieg 1975).

Again citing health reasons, he declined an assignment to a new post in the capital in 1093, which may also have shown foresight on his part, because the period of "post-reform" (1093–1125) soon followed. In Huang's case, there were two major phases: one from 1093 to 1101, and from 1102 until his death in 1105. Emperor Zhézōng 哲宗 (r. 1086–1101), under the guidance of the reformists, changed the political course in accordance with the aims of Wang Anshi (by then related to Huang) and his followers.

In early 1094, Huang had two official posts before being appointed intendant of Mingdao Monastery in Bozhou, yet this brief period of quiet would only last until the official Cài Biàn 蔡卞 (1054–1112), who was Wang Anshi's son-in-law and follower, renewed the political hunt against the conservatives. Cai Bian and Chancellor Zhāng Dūn 张惇 (1035–1105) were the main accusers against the conservatives, attacking them for wrongdoing in comparing the notes in the so-called *True Records* (*Shílù* 实录) of the court with Wang Anshi's own diary of the *Yuanyou* period; the aim was to "rectify" official records in favor of the reformists. A series of interrogations followed, directed at members of the *Yuanyou* fraction; Huang was ordered to the capital Kaifeng in 1094 to explain his entries in the records, but stuck to his views, which rejected the reformists' plans. His uprightness and fearlessness resulted in repeated banishment, yet impressed many of his contemporaries as well as later generations.

Despite the many years of banishment from 1094 onwards, the best of Huang Tingjian's works were written during 1095 to 1100, including poetry, prose, and several works on the classics (see details in the sections below on poetry and calligraphy); also, most of his extant works in calligraphy are dateable to the period after 1095. In his remote Qianzhou (Sichuan Province) exile in 1095, he lived in the Mowei Hall of the Kaiyuan temple, hence the sobriquet

"Old Man from Mowei" (Mówéi lǎorén 摩围老人); "Old Man from Fu [-river]" (Fúwēng 涪翁) was another name he took on during this period.

In 1098, further edicts against the conservatives were proclaimed, and he was ordered away to Rongzhou (today Xuzhou, also Sichuan). This trip proved the most productive in perfecting his calligraphy, with which he had not yet been satisfied in Qianzhou; he attributed this improvement to the careful observation of the rhythmic movements of experienced boatmen pulling oars and hawsers. This he meant as an analogy to the calligrapher's brush carefully and precisely "entering" a character (i.e., touching the paper), and upon finishing it swiftly "emerging" from a character (i.e., lifting the brush).

It was in the calm and quiet times he passed at Rongzhou that Huang again found solace in Chan Buddhism and appreciated the Daoist (Taoist) writings of the philosopher *Zhuāngzí 庄子 (c. 369–c. 268 BCE; works compiled c. 130 BCE). His friendship with the bamboo painter Huáng Bīnlǎo 黄斌老 (life dates uncertain), as well as the knowledge of living in the same place where the famous Tang poet Du Fu once dwelled, further inspired his poetry.

After a brief period of calm between the parties upon the ascension of artist-emperor Huizong in 1100, Huang and the reformists increasingly became the subject of new attacks, which intensified with the appointment of Cài Jīng 蔡京 (1046–1126) as vice chancellor in 1102. In November 1100, news of his brother Shūdá's 叔達 death reached him. From April 1101 until 1102, Huang and his family stayed in Jingzhou (now Jiangling, Hubei Province). As he was in bad health, he declined two invitations to serve in the capital, and was finally allowed to retire to Taiping (now Dangtu, Anhui Province). In May 1102, however, further repressions against the old party resulted in Huang being stripped of his official title, and he was forced to move again soon thereafter, this time to Ezhou (modern day Wuhan), where he arrived in September 1102. It was on this trip that he wrote the famous *Poem of the Pine Wind Pavilion,* which is to this day one of his most celebrated calligraphies. As Huang and his political allies were listed on a stele, which vice chancellor Cai Jing had erected in the capital, he was forced to move again the following year. It is interesting to note that even during the constant moving from 1100 to 1102, Huang wrote more than 200 poems: his artistic output was hardly affected by the constant political turmoil.

In early 1103, Huang was banished again, this time to Yizhou (now Yishan, Guangxi Province). As mentioned at the beginning of this section, it was the official Zhao Tingzhi who was directly responsible for this last demotion, and he now wrongly accused Huang of "joy about the malfortune of the state" (Liu et al. 2001). Huang left at the end of 1103 and arrived at Yizhou in March 1104. On

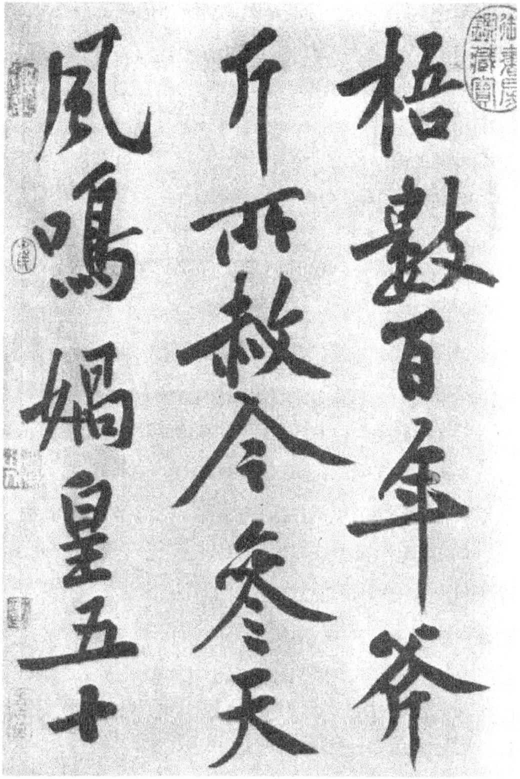

Detail of ***Poem of the Pine Wind Pavilion*** **(1102 CE) by Huang Tingjian. Handscroll, ink on paper.** National Palace Museum, Taipei.

his way he visited the Wuxi valley (now Lingling, Hunan Province), where he composed *Epilogue to the Moya Stele* (*Shū Móyá bēi hòu* 书磨崖碑后), one of his most famous poems. It refers to the restitution of the great Tang dynasty, which has been interpreted as an expression of Huang's disappointment with officialdom.

For the last year of his life, Huang Tingjian remained in Yizhou, accompanied by family and one of his students. Both Huang and Su Shi were mentioned as traitors of the state in June 1104, which was of little concern to him. He accepted his fate and never once complained about either his health or the harsh living circumstances. He died in November 1105, unaware of the amnesty granted to him by the imperial court.

Huang's Poetry and Calligraphy

Every piece of writing that Huang ever produced was once calligraphy itself—a seemingly obvious point, yet important to bear in mind when facing the fact that of more than three thousand pieces of *printed* literature in many genres contained in the *Complete Volumes of Huang Tingjian's Works,* only about forty remain as calligraphic works in museums and collections around the world. Huang managed to create not only original poetry known for qualities such as observation and phrasing, but became equally famous for turning elements of antiquity into his highly individual and celebrated calligraphic style.

Huang Tingjian's Poetry

Huang Tingjian's ideas on poetic writing can only be gathered through prefaces, colophons, letters, commentaries, and the poems themselves, which is also the case regarding his views on calligraphy. He considered the study of ancient models important, but also stressed the importance of going beyond this and finding one's own style in whatever genre. At the same time, Huang also helped establish hitherto less accepted genres such as *cí* 词 poetry (which may be described as "song lyrics," as opposed to classical *shī* 诗 poetry) within elite literati culture by writing about them as a literary genre that was primary to an author's work.

While neither doing the complexity of Huang Tingjian's concern with technical aspects of poetry or the sheer number of poems extant by him any justice, the following terms are crucial to an understanding of his views: "turning iron into gold" (*diǎn tiě chéng jīn* 点铁成金), "turning the old into the new" (*yǐ gǔ wéi xīn* 以古为新), "turning the vulgar into the refined" (*yǐ sú wéi yǎ* 以俗为雅), and "snatching the embryo and changing the bone" (*duó tāi huàn gǔ* 夺胎换骨). These terms coined by Huang can all be viewed as methods of creative imitation on behalf of the poet, and the use of earlier matter to create the new—in this case, literature—is at the heart of Huang's interests when writing. It is important to note that while these terms have their origins in his literary activities, they are evidence of a feature successfully implemented in both his poetry *and* calligraphy. Even though Huang was preceded by literary geniuses such as Ouyang Xiu and Su Shi, he successfully turned "the old into the new" and created what the contemporary sinologist Stephen Owen refers to as "a playfully urbane delight in language and poetic tradition" (Owen 1996). Unfortunately, translations of Huang's poetry hardly manage to convey this literary sophistication of the original, yet their contents do give an idea of his thinking. Compare the initial two lines from a poem where Huang describes the ceaseless alternation of things:

> 虚飄飄,　虚飄飄,　花飛不到地,
> 虹起漫成橋.
>
> 入夢雲千疊, 遊空[條]萬條.
>
> [Flickering and floating] lightly through emptiness, the flowers never touch the ground;
>
> a rainbow appears and forms a bridge [with its colors].
>
> [I enter] a dream through a thousand layers of clouds,
>
> roaming through emptiness and a myriad of silk ribbons. . . . (Liu et al. 2001)

Huang Tingjian's Calligraphy

Huang's highly individual and celebrated large running script style, visible in works such as *Passing the Shrine of the God Calming the Waves*, share several distinctive features: the use of the hidden-tip brush (i.e., the brush tip does not go outside the line), elongated and slanting diagonal strokes, a tendency for vertical columns to slant to the right, avoidance of parallels, and shifting vertical axes of individual characters within columns. All this adds up to what the calligraphy expert Fu Shen perfectly describes as "neighbors coming into each others' yards" (Fu 1976), meaning that individual characters do not reign exclusively over their territory, as one would expect from standard calligraphy in regular script, where each character is surrounded by imaginary squares. Despite this, Huang's overall compositions remain balanced and coherent.

Huang Tingjian's large running script as described here was influenced by the Daoist medical scholar and calligrapher *Táo Hóngjǐng's 陶宏景 (c. 456–c. 536) style, whose large stone inscriptions such as the *Epitaph for Burying a Crane* (*Yìhè míng* 瘗鹤铭; c. 512–514 CE) he greatly admired. The strength and boldness of his characters in turn derive from Huang's study of the eminent Tang general and calligrapher Yán Zhēnqīng 颜真卿 (709–85), who was famous for his masculine, bold, and forceful style in regular script calligraphy (*kǎishū* 楷书). Yan's style was the one that Huang Tingjian studied the most of all models, and he saw him as equal even to *Wáng Xīzhī 王羲之 (c. 303–361 CE), the fourth century sage of calligraphy. While these two calligraphers were, in the Song dynasty, normally regarded as alternatives, Huang looked upon them as individuals who had "transcended the ordinary" (*chāosú* 超俗). In addition, qualities such as the moral rectitude (*rénpǐn* 人品) of Yan Zhenqing also played an important role—the values of a person being an equally important characteristic for Huang to incorporate into his calligraphy.

In cursive-script works such as *Sayings of a Chan Buddhist Monk*, Huang was influenced by ancient calligraphy masters such as Zhāng Xù 张旭 (c. 710–750) and the monk Huáisù 怀素 (725–785), who served as prototypes to develop his own style in this script. In this style as well, Huang once again stressed the importance of being able to adapt fundamental tenets of "classical" calligraphy into one's own style, thus confirming the weight of the spirit of antiquity and the importance of turning the old into the new.

Public Reaction and Influence after Death

Huang's artistic oeuvre was already highly appreciated by his contemporaries, the most influential being the famous literatus Su Shi, who said the following about Huang's writing:

> 魯直以平等觀作欹側字，袖真實相出游戲法，以磊落人書細碎事，可謂三反.
>
> Luzhi [i.e., Huang Tingjian] uses a balanced and impartial view to create slanting yet balanced characters, truthfulness to create playfulness, and [his] upright character to write about the apparently unimportant; this may be called the "three contradictions." (Kong 1986)

The "balanced and impartial view" derives from the Buddhist notion of non-attachment, and illustrates the importance of this characteristic for Huang to

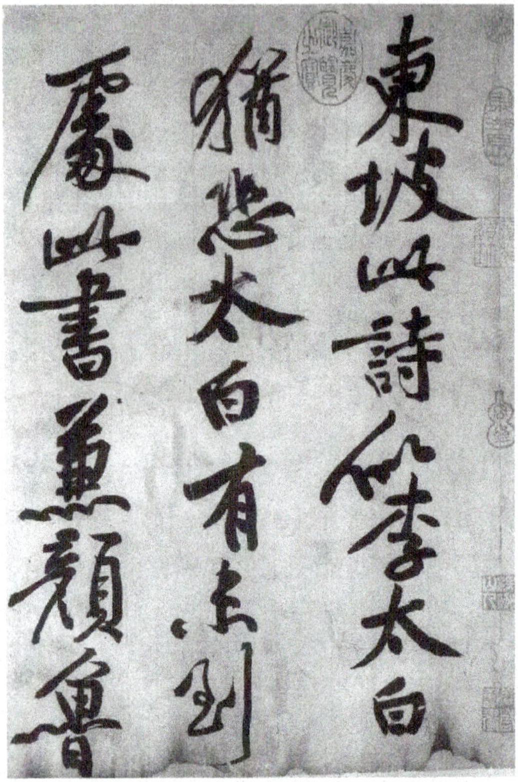

Detail from *Colophon to Su Shi's Poems Written at Huangzhou on the Cold Food Festival* (1100 CE) by Huang Tingjian. Handscroll, ink on paper. Collection of Wang Shijie 王世杰, Taipei, Taiwan.

reach his high standard. Notwithstanding his political affiliation to the conservatives, the quality of his literary and artistic works has been attested to in writings and the arts by countless individuals throughout the dynasties right down to the present.

In addition to Su Shi's patronage and appreciation of Huang's work during the Northern Song (960–1126), the reformer and later political enemy Wang Anshi appreciated his literary talent, and the artistically gifted Northern Song emperor Huizong studied Huang's style. In the Southern Song (1127–1279) his literary style was much imitated by poets who are collectively described as the Jiangxi School (*Jiāngxī shīpài* 江西诗派). The Song scholar and poetry critic Yán Yǔ 严羽 (c. 1200) vehemently condemned the literary style of the Jiangxi school, yet ironically, in his advocacy of Tang poets like Du Fu, as well as other points, shares many of Huang's own tenets.

Huang Tingjian's calligraphy and literary works also became much appreciated by Japanese monks during the Kamakura (1185–1333) and the Muromachi (1334–1564) periods, which may have its origins in the fact that Huang's satori, or enlightenment, at the Huanglongshan monastery had become known as an exemplary event. During the Míng 明 dynasty (1368–1644), history repeated itself as the eminent calligrapher and painter Wén Zhēngmíng 文徵明 (1470–1559) became strongly influenced by Huang's calligraphy and studied it to create his own distinctive style. The late Ming and early Qing dynasty scholar and official Sūn Chéngzé 孙承泽 (1592–1676) equally attests to the beauty of Huang Tingjian's calligraphy, referring to it as writing of "heavenly authenticity and unique in style" (Cai 1984). During the Qīng 清 dynasty (1644–1911/1912), the wealthy salt merchant and art connoisseur Ān Qí 安岐 (1683–1744)—like many emperors and collectors also once in possession of works by Huang—writes about a poem by Huang:

> The calligraphy of this poem is exquisite and delicate, [its] divine atmosphere brilliant; [. . .] the brush appears to naturally follow its inclination, [and the calligraphy] is difficult not to appear pleasing; there is not one idle idea. (An 1920)

Through the creation of a new aesthetic in both calligraphy and poetry, Huang's oeuvre has managed to survive for nearly a millennium and has itself become part of the corpus of antique ideals to be studied by subsequent scholars to this day. The novelties that were introduced by Huang and his circle—some of which would have been dismissed as "flaws" by the standards of the preceding Tang dynasty—had been the result of deliberate artistic choices that would henceforward extend the notion of aesthetics for subsequent generations of scholars and artists.

Patrick DE VRIES
University of Zurich

Further Reading

An Qi 安岐. (1920). *Mo yuan hui guan* 墨缘汇观 [*Collected notes on calligraphy I happened to see*]. Albany: State University of New York Press.

Bieg, Lutz. (1975). *Huang T'ing-chien (1045–1105): Leben und Dichtung* [*Huang Tingjian (1045–1105): Life and poetry*]. Darmstadt, Germany: Blaeschke Verlag.

Cai Chongming 蔡崇名. (1984). *Song sijia shufa xilun* 宋四家書法析論 [*An analysis of the calligraphy of the four great masters of the Song*]. Taipei, Taiwan: Huazheng shuju.

Egan, Ronald. (2006). *The problem of beauty: Aesthetic thought and pursuits in northern Song China*. Cambridge, MA, and London: Harvard University Press.

Franke, Herbert (Ed.). (1976). *Sung biographies*. Taipei, Taiwan: Southern Materials Center, Inc.

Fu Shen. (1976). *Huang T'ing-chien's calligraphy and his scroll for Chang Ta-t'ung: A masterpiece written in exile*. Princeton, NJ: Princeton University.

Fu Shen. (1991). Huang T'ing-chien's cursive script and its influence. In Alfreda Murck & Wen Fong (Eds.), *Words and images: Chinese poetry, calligraphy, and painting*. Princeton, NJ: Princeton University Press.

Hisayuki Miyakawa. (1969). The Naito hypothesis. In James T. C. Liu & Peter J. Golas (Eds.), *Changes in Sung China: Innovation or renovation?* (pp. 4–78). Lexington, MA: D. C. Heath and Co.

Idema, Wilt, & Haft, Lloyd. (1997). *A guide to Chinese literature*. Ann Arbor: University of Michigan Center for Chinese Studies.

Kong Fanli 孔凡礼. (1986). *Su Shi wenji* 苏轼文集 [*Collection of Su Shi's works, 6 volumes*]. Beijing: Zhonghua shuju.

Li Jie 李傑. (1978). *Song shi* 宋史 [*The History of the Song*]. Taipei, Taiwan: Jiushi chubanshe.

Liu Lin 李傑, et al. (Eds.). (2001). *Huang Tingjian quanji* 黄庭坚全集 [*The complete volumes of Huang*

Tingjian's works]. Chengdu, China: Daxue Chubanshe.

Owen, Stephen. (1996). *An anthology of Chinese literature: Beginnings to 1911.* New York & London: W. W. Norton & Co.

Rickett, Adele Austin. (1978). Method and intuition: The poetic theories of Huang Tingjian. In Adele Austin Rickett. (Ed.), *Chinese approaches to literature from Confucius to Liang Ch'i-ch'ao* (pp. 97–119). Princeton, NJ: Princeton University Press.

Wilkinson, Endymion. (2000). *Chinese history: A manual (revised and enlarged).* Cambridge, MA, and London: Harvard University Press.

Zhang Bingquan 张秉权. (1978). *Huang Shangu de jiaoyou yu zuopin* 黄山谷的交游与作品 [*Huang Shangu's circle of friends and his work*]. Xianggang, China: Zhongwen Daxue Chubanshe.

Lǐ Qīngzhào
李清照

1084–1151—Poet, calligrapher, and artist; China's foremost female literary figure

Alternate name: style name: Yì'ān Jūshì 易安居士

Statue of Li Qingzhao in Jinan Province.

Summary

Li Qingzhao is considered by many to be China's foremost female literary figure, embodying the height of cultural expression during the Song dynasty—the three perfections of poetry, calligraphy, and painting. Born and raised in a household where cultural and literary activities were encouraged, Li's talents developed under the watchful eye of many of the eras most famous scholars, writers, and artists. While her poetry reflects the social context of the eleventh century, it is also characterized by a universal humanity that makes it appealing to readers of any time period. Her tranquil life of scholarly pursuits was upended in 1127, when armies of the northern Jurchen Jin invaded Song territories, quickly overrunning them.

Painter, calligrapher, prose writer, poet famed in her own lifetime, antiquarian, book and art collector, and even inventor of a new card game—such are the accomplishments of Li Qingzhao, China's foremost historical female literary figure. She lived and created during the Sòng 宋 dynasty (960–1279) when much was changing and much was being violently destroyed. This change and violence would touch her life and compel her to clarify the core themes of her literary work—the ephemeral and poignant quality of beauty, the unpredictable demands of reality, the urgency of art which lifts life beyond the mundane and into the realm of ideals. The fall of a petal, the stirring of a breeze, the patter of raindrops, the undulation of a song—such images she holds up in her poems as mirrors into which we may gaze, not for narcissistic satisfaction, but to gauge the verity and purpose of our own lives. Her poems, however, are not essays expounding trite, predictable "lessons." Rather, she embodies that rarest of poetic expression—transcendence, in that her work is not dated or parochial. Her canvas is vaster than the space and time allotted to one particular life; her concern is humanity itself in that she truly understands those universal qualities that bind us all. This does not mean, however, that she harkens back to a Golden Age to which we must return. She is thoroughly grounded in the here-and-now, and she expresses great joy in the present moment lived thoroughly—no matter if it evokes a tear, a sigh, a smile, or laughter. Thus, she also becomes a profound commentator on beauty, which she knows is mesmerizing because it is fragile and fleeting—and this beauty she understands to be life itself. There is deep sadness in this knowledge, but she overcomes this desolation with her poems, which become, not monuments, but receptacles that hold some of the fugitive shimmer of life.

Historical Context

The time of the Song dynasty may best be described as one of immense innovation, during which social and cultural values were redefined to afford centrality to the individual. It was, therefore, a time in which Neo-Confucianism grew into prominence with its emphasis on the individual whose social obligation was to nurture innate moral principles by way of education. This philosophical outlook encouraged a heightened esthetical sensibility that sought to blend personal emotion and intellect with the world outside, especially the natural world. In this way, the arts became a crucial endeavor in the Song period, in that they allowed the individual not only the ability to be reflective but also to be educated, that is, refined. And the highest expression of refinement was delicacy; thus each word, each note of music, each hue spread by the paintbrush, each piece of ceramic had to express a soft tranquility; an intimate, private stillness that was serene and restrained and yet deeply, quietly passionate.

It is in this context that Li Qingzhao, China's greatest female poet, emerges, for not only was she the product of her time, but she was engaged in creating the very cultural identity of the Song era. Her poetry, her calligraphy, her painting, her commentary on antiquities and old books that she and her husband collected were seen, in her own lifetime, as encapsulating all that was highest and best in the arts of that age. She embodied all that was deemed to be the height of cultural expression—the three perfections of poetry, calligraphy and painting. The elegance of her expression, the fluidity with which she captured the ephemeral nature of beauty, made of her poems intense, concentrated "landscapes" of an inner world, a world steeped in private emotions that would then open out into the vastness of universal ideas. This quality of passionate privacy and forceful universality underlies and informs Li Qingzhao's art, so that her work becomes effortless because it moves by way of simplicity into profundity.

Despite her importance in Chinese literary history, facts about her life are meager at best, and rest on the reliability of her own comments, which are found in her colophons (inscriptions at the end of manuscripts) and descriptions appended to her catalogs of antiquities. It is from such scant evidence that the contours of her life may be traced. In effect, her life story is her own "self-portrait"—for it is what she wished to leave behind to posterity as a remembrance of her. It is of necessity, as it were, that the artist must vanish behind the work; for it is the work alone that can be immortal, and not its all-too-human creator.

Her reputation as a great poet rests on very few poems: just sixty extant poems in all. These, however, are enough; their like cannot be found in the work of her near contemporaries, such as the female poets, Zhū Shūzhēn 朱淑真 or Lady Huāruǐ 花蕊. This is why the Song dynasty scholar *Zhū Xī 朱熹 (1130–1200) considered Li Qingzhao to have drunk deeply at the well of great literary tradition. It is also why she fashioned her own niche in the tremendous ferment of the Song period.

*People marked with an asterisk have entries in this dictionary.

Life and Career

Although it is difficult to be precise, literary evidence suggests that Li Qingzhao was born sometime in 1084 in the city of Jinan, in Shandong Province, and spent her early years in that city. Her father, Lǐ Géfei 李格非 (d. 1106), authored a treatise, entitled *A Chronicle of the Famous Gardens of Luoyang* (*Luòyáng míngyuán jì* 洛阳名园记), which he wrote sometime after 1094 when he is known to have purchased a garden in Luoyang. He was among the "latter four disciples" of the poet-scholar *Sū Shì 苏轼 (1037–1101) and he therefore moved in the highest literary circles of the Song period. He carried the style name of Wenshu.

Li Qingzhao's mother also came from a learned family; her father was named Wáng Guì 王桂 (1019–1085) and her grandfather, named Wang Zhun, was a *zhuàngyuán* 状元 (somebody who achieves the highest score in the civil service examinations). It is said that she was a poet in her own right who had been taught by Wang Zhun; however, none of her poems have survived. Recently, some scholars have suggested that Li Gefei was married for the second time to a granddaughter of the poet and essayist Wáng Gǒngchén 王拱辰 (1012–1085).

The household into which Li Qingzhao was born and raised was one in which books, painting, and music were readily present and greatly valued. At literary gatherings, poets and thinkers shared their ideas and discussed the craft and discipline of writing. Her father did not exclude Li Qingzhao, but encouraged her to actively participate in these discussions. It is likely that in such get-togethers, she began to write verses and recite them before prominent writers of her day. It is also likely that her talent flourished under the guidance of both her father and Su Shi, as it is known that she gained a reputation for the quality of her verse while she was still in her teenage years. Her reputation as a great poet was assured when she wrote two *shi* poems in which she outdid the famed poet Zhāng Lĕi 张耒 (1054–1114), who was also known as Wenqian, or Master Wangqiu. She mastered both the earlier *shi* form and the more current *ci* form of poetry, and her verses enjoyed wide circulation in the capital, which was the hub of Song literary activity.

By the time of Li Qingzhao, the complex *shi* genre of poetry was a distinguished literary tradition, stretching back two millennia up until the Tang dynasty. The *shi* form, in its earliest form was tetrasyllabic and consisted of hymns (*sòng* 颂), airs (*fēng* 风), and odes (*yǎ* 雅). Later, the genre became more regulated regarding tone, which led to a twofold division into "old-form *shi*" (*gǔtǐ shī* 古体诗, *gǔshī* 古诗), which included the various sub-styles that did not follow particular tonal guidelines and were largely pentatonic, and the "new-form *shi*" (*jìntǐ shī* 近体诗), which adhered to the strictures of tonality, and gave rises to verses (*lǜshī* 律诗) and quatrains (*juéjù* 绝句), each line of which had a specific syllabic count—either pentasyllabic or heptasyllabic. The *ci* form as poetry came into prominence during the Song era and is a lyrical genre, divided by way of length—the short lyic (*xiǎolìng* 小令) and the long lyric (*màncí* 慢词). The genius of Li Qingzhao consists in the fact that she made important poetic contributions within the intricate parameters of such genres.

In 1101, at the age of seventeen or eighteen, she was married to Zhào Míngchéng 赵明诚 (1081–1129), who was a friend of her father. Perhaps the two became familiar with each other through the many literary gatherings that were a regular event in her paternal home. Zhao was born in Zhucheng, in the province of Shandong. He was the son of Zhào Tǐngzhī 赵挺之 (1040–1107), the prime minister and censor under Emperor Huizong (1082–1135; r. 1100–1126). Zhao Mingcheng grew up in the capital city of Bianjing, where he entered the academy to study the classics.

Zhao Mingcheng was still a student when the marriage took place, but it was a much-celebrated event in the Song intellectual community, for both the Li and Zhao families were prominent. The couple took up residence in Zhucheng. The marriage was a very happy one, for not only were they deeply in love, but theirs was also a true marriage of minds.

Husband and Wife at Work

Li Qingzhao matched her husband's deep love of the past and she was his able partner in his eventual scholarly work as antiquarian and epigrapher. The study of ancient ritual practices was being actively encouraged by the royal court. It was thus with official sanction that Zhao focused his attention on *jīnshí xué* 金石学, or epigraphy: the discovery, cataloging, and description of inscriptions found on metal and stone. This antiquarian work involved extensive research so that the historical contexts of these various ancient inscriptions might be validated and therefore established. In effect, Zhao was carefully providing artifacts with provenance, and establishing some very important methodologies for historiography. He stipulated that classical historical texts were often written much later than the events they described, and therefore the assertions found in them had to be verified before they could be accepted. He also demonstrated that epigraphical records should take precedence over classical texts since they were contemporary witnesses. Eventually he would write a thirty-volume catalog of the various inscriptions he had discovered, copied, and explained. After his death, Li Qingzhao would edit, collate, and publish these volumes, to which she would append her famous "Postscript," which described her life.

Zhao's work has proved to be of immense value not only for the light it sheds on things antiquarian, but because of the history and insights it provides for important buildings and temples, information which might otherwise have been lost.

This work of her husband's was also of immense interest to Li Qingzhao, for it appealed to her sensibility which saw in things a lineage, a process, a significance; and she became an eager partner as together they sought out old books, paintings, rubbings of inscriptions, ceramics, and sculpture. She relates that in their early years, while Zhao was still a student and with little money in his pocket, he would pawn a few pieces of clothing and with the proceedings purchase a stone rubbing or two. These he would bring back home and, together with Li Qingzhao, spend many happy hours over some wine or tea examining and studying the inscription. They valued the same things and derived immense pleasure in cultural and literary pursuits.

In 1103, Zhao graduated and took a post with the government in the city of Kaifeng. The new post saw an improvement in the couple's monetary situation, and they were now able to work carefully in expanding their collections to include paintings and antique bronzes and ceramics. Several rooms in their house were devoted to housing their ever-growing acquisitions. They expressed their joy in the objects they obtained by inventing a game in which each would question the other about the new purchase. The winner would get a cup of tea or wine. Li Qingzhao later recalled that by the end of the game both would be laughing so much that the cup would overturn in the lap of the winner, who got not a sip. Both of them greatly admired the paintings of Xu Xi, who lived in the Five Dynasties and Ten Kingdoms 五代十国 (907–960 CE) era, and they held in highest regard the poems of Táo Yuānmíng 陶渊明 (365–427 CE) who flourished during the Six Dynasties period (220–589 CE). This admiration was so great that they named the room in which they played their sport of knowledge, "Returning home" ("Guiqu lai xi ci"), which was the title of a celebrated poem by Tao Yuanming. Later, in 1114, when Li Qingzhao's portrait was painted, Zhao would inscribe it with a colophon that was the first line from this poem.

Zhao's work as a government official often took him away to various cities and towns, and these separations filled Li Qingzhao with feelings of extreme loneliness and longing. It appears that Zhao was similarly afflicted, for his preference was to spend time with his antiques and his wife rather than tend to government business. The couple would never have children, whose presence might have blunted these feelings. But these separations gave Li Qingzhao occasion to write poems that became profound meditations on separation, on the ephemeral nature of joy, and on the true quality of love which unites distant lovers.

A famous episode is associated with this early period of their marriage. During one of her husband's official absences from home, Li Qingzhao wrote a poem on a silken handkerchief and sent it to him. This is the famous poem, "Sorrow of Separation," which was composed to be sung to the tune, "A Sprig of Plum Blossom" ("Yī jiǎn méi" 一剪梅), The story goes that when Zhao received the poem, he was much taken by its delicacy and excellence, and he sought to excel it by writing verses of his own in the same meter and tune. After either fifteen or fifty attempts (records differ), he showed his efforts to a friend, and he included Li Qingzhao's original among them. After much consideration, the friend said that the best of the lot was a couplet that ended Li Qingzhao's poem:

This sorrow cannot be held back	此情无计可消除
as soon as it fades from the brow	才下眉头
it eats away at the heart	却上心头

This couplet was so often repeated that it would soon take on aphoristic status. Before long, her poems gained a larger readership and greater admiration, for they perfectly embodied musicality and *wǎnyuē* 婉約 or "delicate restraint."

Political Turmoil

These happy, carefree years were not entirely trouble-free, however. The court was a place of factionalism, where rivalries were bitterly fought by supporters of Minister of Revenue Cài Jīng 蔡京 and those who opposed him. Li Qingzhao's father, Li Gefei, supported Cai Jing, while Zhao Mingcheng's father (Zhao Tingzhi) opposed him. Eventually, Zhao Tingzhi's faction won, and Emperor Huizong impeached Cai Jing in 1102 and banished all his supporters. During this time, Zhao Mingcheng himself was briefly arrested and later released for lack of evidence. Li Qingzhao wrote many letters and poems to Zhao Tingzhi, who now held the post of deputy prime minister, on behalf of her father. She did not succeed in having her father's banishment rescinded. Family members of the two rival factions were also forbidden to marry; this decree made her own marriage to Zhao Mingcheng technically illegal. With all the rival factions gone from the capital, Zhao Tingzhi eventually became prime minister.

The couple supported each other through this turmoil and continued their antiquarian and epigraphical work while Zhao Mingcheng looked after his governmental responsibilities. In 1105, the emperor lifted her father's banishment, which allowed Li Gefei to return to his home in Jinan, although he would never regain his position at court. The old bitterness between the two families was eventually forgotten and life returned to its previous peaceful and happy mode. This, however, was short-lived. Much of court life depended on the whims of the emperor, and those who had the royal ear acquired power, which meant that things could always drastically change. In 1107, Zhao Tingzhi grew out of favor and was then banished from the capital. He was a broken man and he would die the same year.

The privilege that Li Qingzhao and her husband enjoyed because of his father suddenly vanished. Added to this was the fact that the entire Zhao family was held in contempt at the court. This made life difficult, and the couple decided to leave the capital and head south, where Zhao Mingcheng took work as a judicial officer, first in the city of Laizhou, and then in Qingzhou. They eventually settled in Itu, in Shandong Province, where they bought a house large enough to hold their books and antiquities. Here, the couple spent the next ten years, continuing to collect, discuss, and write. Despite the political climate, Li Qingzhao's poems were still eagerly read and highly praised. She also wrote prose works on literary, political, and historical subjects. Zhao Mingching worked on completing his massive and monumental work on epigraphy.

Move to the South

With the Zhao family still out of favor at court, Zhao Mingcheng was sent alone in 1126 as governor of Qinan city, also in Shandong Province. This was shattering for Li Qingzhao, because they had to be separated and live apart. Then, in 1127, Zhao Mingcheng's mother died in

Nanjing. This would prove to be a fateful year for the couple and for the Song era, for it was also when the Jingkang Incident took place. Armies of the northern Jurchen Jin (Nǚzhēn Jīn 金女真) invaded Song territories and quickly overran and destroyed the capital city of Kaifeng. They captured Emperor Qīnzōng 钦宗, along with his father, the retired emperor Huizong, stripped them of their royal rank, and then exiled them to Manchuria to live as commoners under humiliating circumstances. Most of the rest of the imperial family, as well as prominent courtiers, managed to flee south to Zhejiang Province and established themselves in Hangzhou, where the ninth son of the old emperor Huizong, Gāozōng 高宗 (1107–1187), became the first emperor of the newly established Southern Song dynasty (1127–1279).

Months of bloodshed and cruelty followed as the Jurchen spread through the north. In the spring of 1128, they struck Shandong Province. Refugees streamed to the south looking for safety. Among them was Li Qingzhao, who was alone, since her husband was still in Qinan. She had to abandon their house in Itu and flee with whatever she could easily carry. When the Jurchen attacked Itu, their house was burned down, where books alone filled a dozen rooms. She fled to Gianxian, in Jiangxi Province, with nothing but a few belongings, along with her poems and her husband's work on epigraphy. She eagerly waited for Zhao Mingcheng to join her, but he was again ordered to proceed as judicial officer to Jiaxing in Zhejiang Province. Li Qingzhao traveled on to Gaixia in Anhui Province, where she stayed.

Tragedy struck in 1128 when Zhao Mingcheng became sick at Nanjing (either of malaria or dysentery). Gravely weakened, he sent for Li Qingzhao. She found him at an inn; his last words to her were to ask for a brush because he wanted to write her a poem. He died in her arms at the age of forty-eight. She was only forty-five.

Devastated, she fell ill and remained sick for many months. When she recovered, she was a different woman; the poems she wrote were darker and quieter. Perhaps it was writing that gave her comfort and courage to continue with her life. She moved to Hangzhou, the Southern Song capital. She still had Zhao Mingcheng's work, and this she set about organizing and editing, and eventually publishing with a "Postscript" that described how her happiness was gone forever.

The Jurchen threat was still omnipresent, however, and this meant that she had to flee their raids again. As if this hardship were not enough, there was a rumor that she had sent a jade flask to a Jurchen general. The rumor came to Emperor Gaozong's attention, and it was officially seen as an act of treason, since the Zhao family was still not rehabilitated and actions by its family members, even those through marriage, were suspect. To avoid problems, she left

Hangzhou. This was a timely decision, for the Jurchen attacked Hangzhou soon thereafter and captured the city. She had no time to secure her remaining books, and they were all destroyed when the city was put to the torch.

She eventually made her way to her brother's home in Jinhua, in Zhejiang Province, where she took up residence and found a measure of peace after so much chaos and misfortune. She continued to write exquisite poems, transforming her sorrow into a grand, universal theme of the indomitable human spirit that must endure and overcome the calamity and heartbreak that life always brings. She also continued to study and write about antiques. She retained a zest for life, and even invented a new card game called *dama* ("driving horses"). The poems from this period reflect that life is bittersweet, and the burden she was destined to carry must be borne with courage—sorrow must not be allowed to stifle life. In 1141, Li Qingzhao died in her brother's home at the age of fifty-seven.

Li Qingzhao's Legacy

During her lifetime, Li Qingzhao published seven volumes of *shī* 诗 poetry and six volumes of *cì* 词 poetry. Time has thoroughly winnowed this output, however, so that we only have about eighteen of her *shi* verses and about seventy-eight of her *ci* poems (most scholars suggest that of these, only fifty are truly from her pen). She also wrote many works of prose, but only three have come down through the ages: a "Postscript" ("Hòuxù" 后序) to her husband's study of ancient inscriptions found on metal and stone; the *Lan ci,* which is a discourse on the *ci*-form; and a single letter to the scholar Qí Chónglǐ 綦崇礼 (1083–1142). Brief as these remnants are, they are enough to validate her position as the foremost female poet in Chinese literature.

Nirmal DASS
Wilfrid Laurier University

Further Reading

Chao Ho, Lucy. (1968). *More gracile than yellow flowers. The life and works of Li Ch'ing-chao*. Hong Kong: Mayfair Press.

Cryer, James. (Trans.). (1984). *Plum Blossom: Poems of Li Ch'ing-chao*. Durham, NC: Carolina Wren Press.

Hu, P'in-ch'ing. (1966). *Li Ch'ing-chao*. New York: Twayne Publishers.

Parnam, Clifford L. (2009). *Music from a jade flute: The* ci *poems of Li Qingzhao*. Ormond, Victoria, Australia: Hybrid Publishers.

Rexroth, Kenneth, & Chung, Ling. (Trans.). (1979). *Li Ch'ing-chao. Complete poems*. New York: New Directions.

Ting, Ch'uan-ching, & Chu Djang. (Trans.). (1989). *A compilation of anecdotes of sung personalities*. New York: St. John's University Press.

Wang Jiaosheng. (Trans.). (1989). *The complete ci-poems of Li Qingzhao: A new English translation*. Philadelphia: University of Pennsylvania.

Wei Djao. (2010). *A blossom like no other: Li Qingzhao*. Toronto: Ginger Post.

Ōuyáng Xiū
欧阳修

1007–1072—Neo-Confucian statesman and scholar

Summary

Ouyang Xiu was the leading intellectual and literary figure during the middle years of the Northern Song dynasty. His main contribution to prose writing was his revival of ancient-style prose. He was a vigorous advocate for ancient-style prose as a remedy to the obscurity of the "parallel prose" style that in his youth had dominated the civil service examination system, a method of recruiting civil service officials based on merit rather than family or political connections. He made important contributions to poetry and invented new genres for writing on aesthetics, connoisseurship, and daily life. He stands in Chinese literary and intellectual history as an innovator as well as an important transitional figure to future literary movements.

Ouyang Xiu was arguably the leading intellectual and literary figure of the middle years of the Northern Sòng 宋 dynasty (960–1127). He was a major participant in the political reform movements of the day and a leader in the intellectual revival of the Confucian classics that would become known as Neo-Confucianism. He initiated important changes in prose writing, expanded the range of topics and modes of expression in different poetic genres, and invented new genres that allowed for increasingly informal writing in the areas of aesthetics, connoisseurship, and daily life. He lived during the middle of the Song dynasty, a period generally recognized for its civil accomplishments. Marked by the rise of the scholar-official class, the full implementation of a national official examination system, rapid urbanization, the spread of print technology, and a revival of Confucian thought, this era forms a pivotal "middle period" that set the mold for cultural developments in the subsequent Yuán 元 (1279–1368), Míng 明 (1368–1644), and Qīng 清 (1644–1911/1912) dynasties. Ouyang Xiu's innovations in political, intellectual, and literary spheres set a standard for the aspirations and ethos of the scholar-official elite (literati) that greatly influenced important figures of the next generation like *Wáng Ānshí 王安石 (1021–1086) and *Sū Shì 苏轼 (1037–1101, also known as Sū Dōngpō 苏东坡).

Ouyang Xiu's Life and Times

Ouyang Xiu's life is representative of a group of up-and-coming literati families from southern China who rose from relative obscurity to the center of power and influence by means of the official civil service examination system (*kējǔ* 科举 or *kējǔ kǎoshì* 科举考试), a method of recruiting civil service officials based on merit rather than family or political connections. Although from a family based in Lúlíng 庐陵 (in the modern-day eastern province of Jiangxi), Ouyang Xiu was born in Miánzhōu 绵州, located in the modern-day western province of Sichuan. At the young age of four, his father died and he and his mother consequently moved to Suízhōu 随州 (modern-day Hubei Province) to live with an uncle. Suizhou was a remote and rustic central province, and Ouyang Xiu educated himself largely without the benefit of teachers or tutors. Ouyang Xiu sat for the provincial official examinations twice in Suizhou and failed both times, once for violating the required rhyme conventions that were part of the strict euphonic rules of the "current style" of prose at the time. After submitting his writings to the scholar-official Xū Yǎn 胥偃, however, he received the older scholar's patronage and traveled with him to the capital Kāifēng 开封, where he won first place in the departmental exams and fourteenth in the palace examination. Every three years, scholars who had passed the first-stage prefectural examinations came from all over the empire to the capital in order to take the departmental examinations held by the Ministry of Rites. Those who passed this second stage then gathered at the imperial palace for a last day of testing, known as the palace examination, under the personal supervision of the emperor to determine the candidates' final rankings. Ouyang Xiu's father and uncles were the first men in the family known to have obtained official status through the examinations. Thus, within two generations the Ouyang family changed its social status from commoner to scholar-official, illustrating the potential of the examination system to facilitate social mobility.

In his subsequent official career, Ouyang Xiu experienced both great success and significant setbacks that included two periods of exile. In the first phase of his official career in the 1030s, he served first in the western capital of the Northern Song, Luòyáng 洛阳, and then later in the central administration in the capital at Kaifeng. During his days in Luoyang, serving on the staff of the

*People marked with an asterisk have entries in this dictionary.

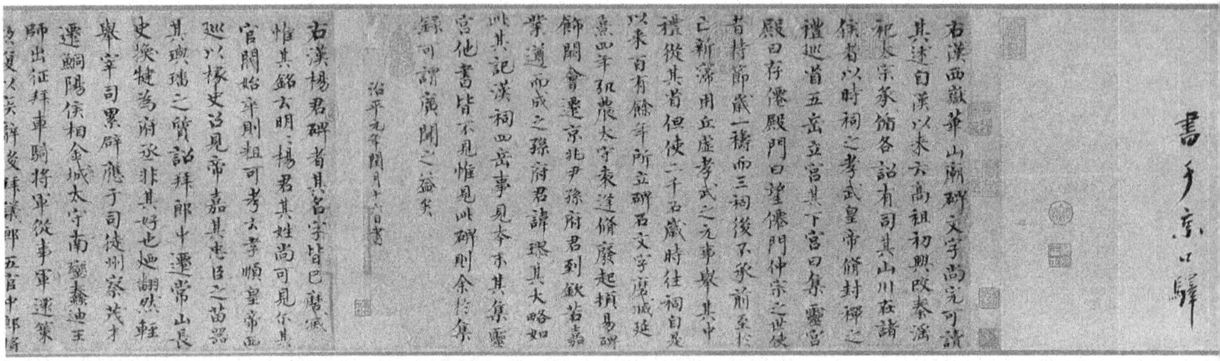

This and next page: One part of Ouyang Xiu's *Colophon to Catalogue of Antiquities*. The scroll is a collection of rubbings and colophons from earlier times, and Ouyang's comments upon these earlier writings. (A colophon is commentary written onto additional sheets of silk or paper that follows the image or text itself.) The scroll itself is read from right to left (starting with the four large characters on the right page). National Palace Museum, Taipei, Taiwan.

prefectural judge, Qián Wéiyǎn 钱惟演, he met a member of a group of young officials that included Méi Yáochén 梅尧臣 (1002–1060) who shared his views on the importance of ancient-style prose (i.e., the classical style by which non-fiction matters were recorded and relayed through the bureaucratic hierarchy), and developing a "simple" and "bland" style of poetry that was more accessible and allowed for a broader range of mundane topics. In Kaifeng, Ouyang Xiu served as a collator of texts in the Imperial Library where he began working on a massive annotated catalogue of the works in the library. It was at this time that Ouyang Xiu encountered the leading political reformer of the day, Fàn Zhòngyān 范仲淹 (989–1052). As the prefect of Kaifeng, Fan Zhongyan put forth a bold set of proposals to reform the bureaucracy and the criteria for advancement and demotion of officials. When entrenched forces in the bureaucracy denounced Fan Zhongyan, who was demoted accordingly, Ouyang Xiu wrote a scathing and sarcastic letter in his defense to Fan's principal critic. Although this resulted in Ouyang Xiu's exile to the small county of Yílíng 夷陵 (modern-day Yíchāng 宜昌 in Hubei Province) from 1036 to 1038, it also won him praise as a principled official among the literati.

The second phase of Ouyang Xiu's official career began with his return to the capital after Emperor Rénzōng 仁宗 (r. 1022–1063) reconsidered his position on Fan Zhongyan's ideas for the bureaucracy, promoted him to Assistant Chief Minister, and implemented Fan's proposed reforms. These reforms have come to be known as the "Qingli reforms" (*Qìnglì xīnzhèng* 庆历新政) named for the Qingli reign period (r. 1041–1048) during which they were implemented. Fan Zhongyan's Ten-Point

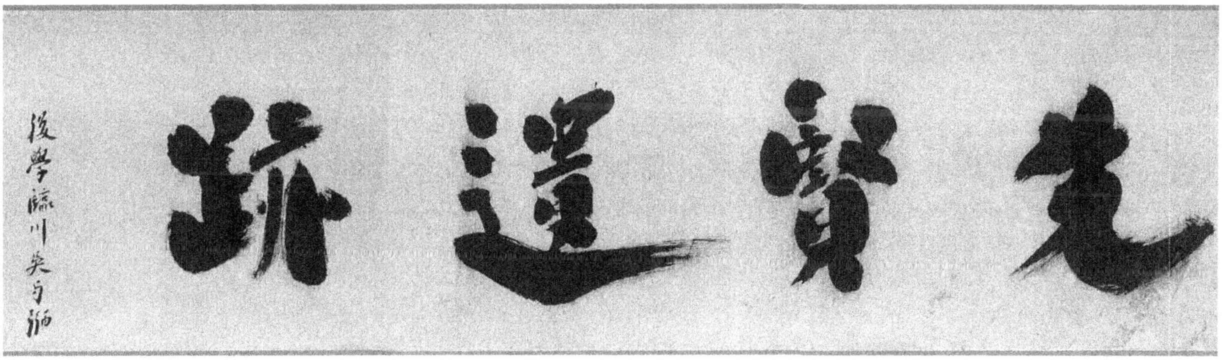

Memorial advocated administrative reforms, including a reduction in the number of privilege appointments (*yìn* 荫) through which officials above a certain rank were allowed to ensure appointments for their sons. The proposals also sought to change examination system standards by encouraging new interpretations of the Confucian classics that allowed greater application of the classics to practical matters, as well as the use of ancient-style prose in lieu of the rule-bound parallel prose or "current prose" (prose that was written strictly in strings of couplets, consisting of metrically and grammatically parallel lines) that had dominated the examinations up to that point (Liu 1967, 43–45).

Ouyang Xiu was the strongest advocate of ancient-style prose in his time. Ancient-style prose was based on the language of literary models dating from early China, and was characterized by a straightforward, non-parallel style that stressed the conveyance of meaning and philosophical argumentation. Support of this style was tied to an intellectual reengagement with the contemporary moral meanings of the classics. Despite this support among the literati, opponents accused the Qingli reformers of factionalism, and in 1045, the reforms were largely rescinded, and their proponents demoted or exiled. Ouyang Xiu entered his second period of exile to Chúzhōu 滁州 (in modern-day Anhui Province). This period of exile saw an upsurge in Ouyang Xiu's literary production, especially in prose works and *shī* 诗 poetry (classical poetry style characterized by fixed-length lines and rhyme placement on the final syllable of every couplet). During this time, he developed the literary persona of the "Old Tippler" through which he conveyed an attitude of resilience and even joy under conditions of adversity. Contemporary Japanese scholar Yoshikawa Kojiro argued that the "emancipation from the preoccupation with sorrow" that Ouyang Xiu's literary works epitomized helped distinguish Song dynasty literature as a whole in comparison to the earlier Chinese literary tradition (Kojiro 1967, 64).

During his late career, Ouyang Xiu was able to implement his ancient-style prose ideals in two important ways. In 1054, following two provincial appointments, the first in Yángzhōu 扬州 (1048–1049) and the second in Yīngzhōu 应州 (1049–1054), Ouyang Xiu was called back to the capital. There, along with the high official Sòng Qí 宋祁 (998–1061), he co-wrote the *New History of the Tang* (*Xīn Tángshū* 新唐书) completely in ancient-style prose. At the end of his life, Ouyang single-handedly completed a second important historical work: the *History of the Five Dynasties* (*Wǔdài shǐjì* 五代史记), also written entirely in ancient-style prose, thereby setting a new precedent for historical studies. Even more importantly, in 1057 Ouyang Xiu served as the administrator of the advanced (or presented) scholar (*jìnshì* 进士) examinations and, in a surprise decision, changed the standards from the traditionally required parallel prose to ancient-style prose. This controversial decision set a new standard for the official examination system during the Song dynasty. Two of the next generation's most important intellectual and literary figures, the neo-Confucian thinker Chéng Yí 程颐 (1033–1107) and Su Shi, came to the capital at this time to take the official examination. Su Shi passed the exam and became closely associated with the literary ideals promoted by Ouyang Xiu. As historian Peter Bol has pointed out, however, the style of both Cheng Yi and Su Shi showed that their pursuit of the way of ancients had largely shifted from institutional reform to a more personal and internal search (Bol 1992, 177). In the last years of his life, rather than return to his family's native home in Luling, Ouyang Xiu chose to retire to the place of his most fondly remembered provincial appointment, Yingzhou, with its beautiful West Lake. Some critics during the Southern Song dynasty (1127–1279) considered this decision controversial, but Ouyang's choice of Yingzhou as his place of retirement reflected the cosmopolitan life of a Northern Song scholar-official, which was a position that required frequent travel from post to post, and often resulted in less attachment to one's native province. In Yingzhou, Ouyang Xiu edited a compilation of his earlier writings, titled the *Collected Works of the Retired Scholar* (*Jūshì jí* 居士集), to which Su Shi wrote a preface in 1091.

The following will briefly introduce Ouyang Xiu's most important contributions to three areas of literary endeavor: ancient-style prose and official histories, poetry (*shi* and song lyrics), and informal genres on aesthetics and connoisseurship.

Ancient-style Prose and Official Histories

Ouyang Xiu's main contribution to prose writing was his revival of ancient-style prose and his vigorous advocacy for ancient-style prose as a remedy to the obscurity of the parallel prose that dominated the examination system in his youth. Ouyang Xiu recounted his early fascination with the prose works of the Táng 唐 dynasty (618–907) writer *Hán Yù 韩愈 (768–824) in an essay composed in the 1060s, in which he narrated his youthful "rediscovery" of an incomplete collection of the works of prose master Han Yu found in a basket of old books tucked away in a hole in the wall of his friend's home. In his own era, Han Yu had opposed the florid parallel prose common to the time, and advocated the idea that a return to ancient-style prose could be used to reengage the Confucian classics in a moral and didactic style of prose writing. Han Yu's prose works were life-changing to Ouyang Xiu, and served as a model of morally and politically engaged writing inspired by the Confucian classics. At the same time, as the modern scholar Yu-shih Chen has shown, the aspects of "loftiness" (gāo 高) and "extraordinariness" (*qí* 奇) to which Han Yu aspired ran contrary to Ouyang Xiu's aims. Ouyang sought instead to promote the principal of "universality" (*cháng* 常) and subject matter that was "immediate and tangible" (*shí* 实) (Chen 1988, 115–119). Ouyang implemented these principals in his substantial body of prose works in a variety of styles, including accounts of events, prefaces, letters, prose-style farewells, and even grave inscriptions.

As noted above, Ouyang Xiu applied his ancient-style prose principals to the writing of history. In a recent set of translations from Ouyang Xiu's *History of the Five Dynasties*, Richard Davis notes that Ouyang Xiu's adherence to the idea of "common sense" or "ordinary reason" led him to avoid or reduce emphasizing auguries and omens in his account of the Five Dynasties period (also known as the Five Dynasties and Ten Kingdoms 五代十国 [907–960 CE] period) and instead to focus on "historical reasoning grounded in human experience and tangible evidence" (Davis 2004, lii). Although auspicious omens or inauspicious auguries were often utilized in premodern Chinese historical writing as a way to legitimize or delegitimize different emperors or regimes, Ouyang Xiu rejected this practice, and "reasserted the centrality of personal merit to political development" in his account of the rulers of that period (Davis 2004, liii). A rather strict application of Confucian ethics is also apparent in Ouyang Xiu's historical writings. Ouyang Xiu was especially concerned with the Confucian principal of loyalty in his account of the Five Dynasties, which was a period of short-lived kingdoms during which frequent changing of allegiance was common practice among the political elite. Ouyang Xiu invented two new categories of biography in his *History of the Five Dynasties:* chapters on "martyrs to virtue" to praise those who maintained service to a single dynasty, and "martyrs in service" to praise those who died serving a second ruler. While Ouyang Xiu's historiographical works did not receive the same high critical praise that his other prose works garnered during later generations, they nonetheless exemplified the principals of "universal" and "tangible" prose, and reflected Ouyang's belief that writing should engage Confucian values.

Poetry: *Shi* and Song Lyrics

Although best known for his innovations in prose, Ouyang Xiu was also an important poet. In his *shi* poetry, he praised the "simple" or "bland" style epitomized by the works of his friend Mei Yaochen, and saw this style as an alternative to the *Xīkūn* 西昆 style that by conventional account dominated poetic practice and examination culture in his day. The *Xikun* style was based on the poems produced by a circle of seventeen literati led by Yáng Yì 杨亿 (974–1020), and compiled into the anthology, *Exchange Poems of Xikun* (*Xīkūn chóuchàng jí* 西昆酬唱集). *Xikun* style poetry was a florid, allusive, and heavily decorative style of poetry that took the later Tang poet, Lǐ Shāngyǐn 李商隐 (c. 813–858) as its ultimate model. By contrast, as Stanford University professor Ronald Egan has noted, many of Ouyang Xiu's *shi* are plain enough in diction and sufficiently unburdened by allusion to allow modern readers to browse them without heavy annotation. Egan outlines two major types of poetic treatment in Ouyang Xiu's *shi*. First, he composed poems that express "serene or even joyful sentiments," often set in bucolic settings. Second, he wrote long narrative or descriptive poems on "strange or fantastic subjects" (Egan 1984, 84–85). While the first category of poems fits well with Yoshikawa Kojiro's characterization of Song poetry as an "emancipation from sorrow," the second group, in Canadian scholar Colin Hawes view, complicates Kojiro's characterization of Song poetry as simply "joyful" or straightforward and accessible "realism." Hawes has shown that even in Ouyang Xiu's poems that contain detailed descriptions of objects or scenes from everyday life, he utilized the techniques of "caricature and structural ingenuity." He states that, "their realism is tinged with exaggeration, caricature and humor; their mundane situations are juxtaposed with imaginative leaps into distant visions of purity and freedom; trivial objects are often treated in an incongruously profound manner; and if there are moral judgments at all, they frequently appear in strangely unsuitable contexts" (Hawes 1999, 101). Hence, following Hawes, perhaps it is more appropriate to say that Ouyang Xiu's *shi* poems imbued "simple" or "bland" objects and scenes with a new level of imagination and intellectual rigor than had been typical of the Chinese poetic tradition heretofore.

Ouyang Xiu was also an avid writer of popular song lyrics, a genre of poetry set to music and generally performed by courtesans in a banquet setting during the Northern Song dynasty. In many ways, Ouyang's song lyrics followed closely literary conventions established for the genre by the tenth century court anthology *Among the Flowers* (*Huājiān jí* 花间集). Songs about love and romance predominated, especially those about nostalgia for past loves. As Egan points out, in many cases it is difficult to distinguish the song lyrics of Ouyang Xiu from those written by his senior contemporary, Yàn Shū 晏殊 (991–1055). Still, Egan identifies several salient distinguishing characteristics of Ouyang's song lyrics. First, Ouyang's song lyrics contain strong narrative elements and a penchant for dramatization. Along with this, they frequently display a personal tone and autobiographical persona. This was not typical of song lyrics that tended to highlight somewhat stereotyped female personas of the abandoned women or the love-sick singing girl.

Finally, although Ouyang Xiu wrote song lyrics exclusively in the shorter *xiǎolíng* 小令 form and never utilized the longer *màncí* 慢词, he did achieve a kind of narrative expansiveness in several sets of song lyric cycles that he composed. The most extended instance of this is the cycle of ten songs he wrote about the scenic West Lake in Yingzhou during his retirement there (Egan 1984, 140–180). Throughout the sequence, the poet observes the crowds of ordinary sightseers who gather at West Lake in Yingzhou and then, in a surprise twist at the end of the piece, reveals himself to the crowd to be the former magistrate of

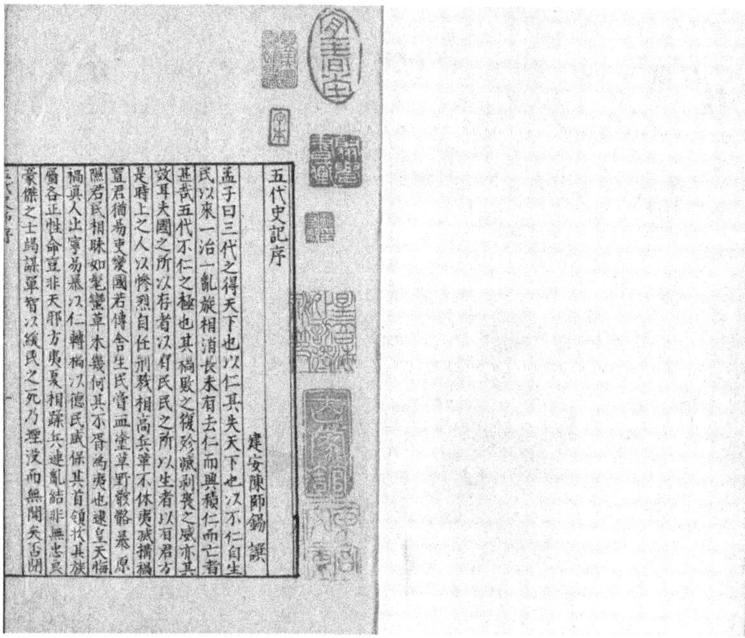

五代史記序

建安陳師錫 撰

孟子曰三代之得天下也以仁其失天下也以不仁自生
民以來一治一亂旋相消長未有去仁而興積仁而亡者
甚哉五代不仁之極也其禍敗之復殄滅剝喪之威亦其
效耳夫國之所以存者以有民民之所以生者以有君方
是時上之人以慘烈自任刑戮相高兵革不休夷滅構禍
置君猶易吏變國若傳舍生民膏血塗草野骸骼暴原
隰君民相眎如髦蠻草木幾何其不胥爲夷也逮皇天悔
禍眞人出寧易暴以仁轉禍以德民咸保其首領收其族
屬各正性命豈非天耶方更夏相蹂兵連亂結非無忠臣
豪傑之士竭謀單智以綏民之死乃埋沒而無聞矣否則

A page from the *History of the Five Dynasties* by Ouyang Xiu. National Archives.

town. For the first time in the genre's history, Ouyang Xiu utilized the song lyric cycle to explore the complex issue of literati identity in relation to a life of constant travel and settlement in the local place of his former service.

Remarks on Poetry and Botanical Treatises

Beyond his important contributions to established literary genres, Ouyang Xiu must also be credited with the creation of new genres that broadened the scope of intellectual activity and prose style considered proper for Song dynasty literati. He created two new genres that allowed for new explorations of aesthetics and connoisseurship that became mainstream media in late imperial China. The most important of these was his remarks on poetry (*shīhuà* 诗话), entitled *Six One's Remarks on Poetry* (*Liùyī shīhuà* 六一诗话), based on one of his pennames. The genre allowed for the collection of casual conversation or comments—suggested in the term *huà* 话 (speech)—on the topic of poetry and poetic craft. While such comments could be found in more general miscellanies, the *shihua* separated literati conversations about poetry into discrete works. After Ouyang Xiu's groundbreaking work, the genre quickly flourished with a few dozen *shihua* produced by the end of the Northern Song, and some 140 such works by the end of the Southern Song (Egan 2010, 460). Egan hypothesizes that the appeal of the genre lay in how it allowed literati to explore and argue issues of poetic craft to a broad audience in an impromptu fashion that did not necessarily require authors of *shihua* to situate their views in canonical or established systems of values (Egan 2010, 461). There is much to be explored in the rich terrain of Song dynasty *shihua* and miscellanies.

Another new genre invented by Ouyang Xiu was the botanical treatise (*huāpǔ* 花谱), which he introduced via his work, *Tree Peonies of Luoyang* (*Luòyáng mǔdān jì* 洛阳牡丹记) written in the 1030s during Ouyang Xiu's early official career in Luoyang. Ouyang's work categorizes twenty-four varieties of peony grown and cultivated in the city of Luoyang, including explanations of their names and a history of peony lore. His botanical treatise is fascinating in its level of detail and seemingly professional knowledge of the plant, the methods of its cultivation (including human manipulation of nature through grafting and other techniques), and even the market value of peonies. It was truly unprecedented for a scholar-official to show this level of interest in what was considered a craftsman's trade, but Ouyang Xiu seems to have shared the peony-craze that was current among the general populace of the city and wished to show his first-hand observations of this aspect of popular culture. This is apparent in the third and final chapter of his treatise that contained a description of local practices and lore concerning the plant (Egan 2006, 114–121). In addition to being an empirical catalogue of an important local flower, Ouyang Xiu's treatise also stands as an early study of urban popular culture by a member of the newly risen Song dynasty literati elite.

In summation, Ouyang Xiu was a pivotal figure of the mid-Song dynasty. In the rise of his family from commoner to scholar-official status through the examination system, he is representative of the aspirations and ideals of his age. His rigorous advocacy for a politically engaged Ancient-style prose aroused opposition in his lifetime, but inspired the next generation of scholar-officials, like Wang Anshi and Su Shi, to view the revival of the classics as a method of rediscovering the "way" to order the state and society. He is also a transitional figure, in that his early invention and adoption of genres related to poetic aesthetics and popular culture heralded the even greater flourishing of such works in the dynamic print culture of the Southern Song and later dynasties.

Benjamin RIDGWAY
University of Illinois, Urbana-Champaign

Further Reading

Bol, Peter K. (1992). *"This culture of ours." Intellectual Transitions in T'ang and Sung China*. Stanford, CA: Stanford University Press.

Chen, Yu-shih. (1988). *Images and ideas in Chinese classical prose, studies of Four Masters*. Stanford, CA: Stanford University Press.

Davis, Richard (Trans.). (2004). *Historical record of the Five Dynasties*. New York: Columbia University Press.

Egan, Ronald. (2010). The Northern Song (1020–1126). In Kang-I Sun Chang, & Stephen Owen (Eds.), *The Cambridge history of Chinese literature, Vol. 1: To 1375* (pp. 381–464). Cambridge, UK: Cambridge University Press.

Egan, Ronald. (2006). *The problem of beauty. Aesthetic thought and pursuits in Northern Song Dynasty China*. Cambridge, MA. Harvard University Press.

Egan, Ronald. (1984). *The literary works of Ou-yang Xiu*. Cambridge, UK: Cambridge University Press.

Hawes, Colin. (2005). *The social circulation of poetry in the Mid-Northern Song. Emotional energy and literati self-cultivation*. Albany: State University of New York Press.

Hawes, Colin. (1999). Mundane transcendence: Dealing with the everyday in Ouyang Xiu's poetry. *CLEAR, 21*, 99–129.

Liu, James T. C. (1967). *Ou-yang Hsiu, an eleventh-century Neo-Confucianist*. Stanford, CA: Stanford University Press.

Mote, Frederick. (1999). *Imperial China, 900–1800*. Cambridge, MA: Harvard University Press.

Strassberg, Richard E. (Trans.). (1994). *Inscribed landscapes. Travel writing from imperial China*. Berkeley: University of California Press.

Yoshikawa, Kojiro. (1967). *An introduction to Sung poetry* (Burton Watson, Trans.). Cambridge, MA: Harvard University Press.

Sīmǎ Guāng
司马光

1019–1086—Statesman and historian; rival of Wang Anshi

Alternate name: style name: Jūnshí 君实; posthumous title: Duke of Wēn 温国公

Summary

Sima Guang was one of China's leading political figures and the author of *Comprehensive Mirror for Aid in Government (Zizhi tongjian)*, a historical account of over a thousand years (403 BCE–959 CE) of China's early imperial past. Produced in the context of fierce disputes at the eleventh-century imperial court, *Zizhi tongjian*'s didactic message of how to maintain imperial power and ensure dynastic longevity helped to shape a belief in China's unbroken political tradition and contributed to the formation of a Chinese self-identity. He is often associated with his opposition to the reform proposals of his rival Wang Anshi.

Sima Guang lived almost a millennium ago, yet his name still resonates today for two reasons. First, he is seen as one of Chinese history's leading political figures. Much of his reputation has centered on one aspect of his career: the fierce factional dispute with his contemporary and rival *Wáng Ānshí 王安石 (1021–1086) between the late 1060s and the deaths of both men in 1086. When we hear about Sima Guang, it is often as a foil to Wang Anshi. He emerges from the comparison as a conservative statesman with a regressive influence on his times. But exclusive focus on one political rivalry, however explosive, mutes the range and richness of Sima Guang's thinking. We rarely hear of his early political experiences, though most of the policies that defined his opposition to Wang Anshi had already taken shape in the context of other debates. We should not underplay the importance of the political opposition between the two men, but neither should we let it obscure the ideological consistency of Sima Guang's overall career.

*People marked with an asterisk have entries in this dictionary.

Second, Sima Guang is known as author of *Comprehensive Mirror for Aid in Government* (*Zīzhì tōngjiàn* 资治通鉴), a keystone chronological account of over a thousand years of China's early imperial past. This work helped to shape later belief in China's integral, unbroken political tradition and, as a corollary, contributed to the formation of a Chinese self-identity. Against this politicized use of Sima Guang's work stand claims for its objectivity, which have dominated its reception from at least the fifteenth century. Yet Sima Guang's representation of China's past, though well-researched and written, was inevitably colored by the political and social environment of the eleventh century, and by his personal commitments. Once we restore *Zizhi tongjian* to the context of its composition and set it among the broader political activities of its author, it assumes a more complex function than much later scholarship suggests. Its force as a statement of political ideology, and not as a dispassionate account of the past, begins to emerge.

Early Life

Sima Guang was born on 17 November 1019 at the prefect's residence in Guangshan, modern Henan Province. He was named after his birthplace. He was the younger son of Sīmǎ Chí 司马池 (c. 980–1041), then prefect of the district, and Madame Niè 聶 (d. 1039); his brother, Sīmǎ Dàn 司马旦 (1006–1087), was older by thirteen years.

The Simas traced their ancestry back to Sīmǎ Fú 司马孚 (180–272 CE), an imperial prince and senior minister of Western Jìn 西晋 (265–316 CE). Geographically, that rooted them in Wen County, in modern Henan Province; Sima Guang received the posthumous title of Duke of Wēn 温国公. During Northern Wèi 北魏 (386–534 CE), the family moved northwest to Sushui village in Xia County, modern Shaanxi Province, when one of its members was buried there. That is where its family tomb remained during Sima Guang's lifetime, and where he was also buried. A collection of Sima Guang's jottings was later given the title *Records of Things Heard by [the Man from] Sushui* (*Sùshuǐ jì wén* 涑水记闻), reflecting a near-contemporary sense of his geographical identity.

By the Táng 唐 dynasty (618–907 CE) this branch of the Simas had fallen to the status of commoners. None of its members took office during the political fragmentation and social turmoil of the following Five Dynasties period 五代 (907–960 CE). It was Sima Guang's grandfather Sīmǎ Xuàn 司马炫 (fl. late tenth century), who obtained a prestigious *jìnshì* 进士 (presented scholar) degree by passing the metropolitan level of the newly revived civil service examinations. He eventually served as a county magistrate. Sima Guang's father, Sima Chi, also obtained office and reached the rank of prefect, which he held in six different regions. By the time of Sima Guang's birth, the family had begun to establish itself in political circles.

Sima Guang's formal academic education began at the age of five under the tutelage of his father and elder brother. It centered on the rote learning and recitation of texts, not on a close understanding of their meaning. Sima Guang later claimed to have dedicated particular effort to these studies for fear of academic inferiority to his contemporaries. It was not until the age of twelve, he suggested, that he moved beyond recitation and started to contemplate the significance of the texts under study. Sima Guang's contemporary and biographer, *Sū Shì 苏轼 (1037–1101), tells us that already by the age of fourteen, Sima Guang had developed an impressive erudition and was skilled at composition. Recitation later formed an important part of his approach to education: "Books have to be recited completely from memory," he insisted. "Whether on horseback or unable to sleep in the middle of the night, your gains will be manifold if you recite texts and contemplate their significance" (Zhu 1929, 7A.2b). It even echoed in examination reforms that he advocated in 1086, at the end of his career.

In 1033 Sima Guang received his first official appointments through the hereditary privilege (*yìn* 荫) system to which his father's high rank entitled him. Five years later, at the relatively young age of nineteen, he earned an official post in his own right when he ranked top among the *jinshi* examination candidates of 1038. He transferred to the Ministry of Rites 礼部 as a result—an early introduction to the theme of ritual, which he revisited in later writings—and then to a post as an administrative assistant in a region close his native Xiazhou and also close to his father's posting at the time.

This early period was important to Sima Guang's later career in forging relations of friendship and political patronage. Two men connected to his father had a particular impact. The first was Páng Jí 庞籍 (988–1063), with whom Sima Chi had served in the late 1020s. Pang held the young Sima Guang in high esteem and seems to have treated him as a son both during childhood and in later life. There was also a long political collaboration between the two: Pang recommended Sima Guang to a position in an imperial academy, they headed the Ritual Academy together in the early 1050s, and Pang appointed Sima Guang as his aide when he became a regional prefect in 1054 and 1055.

The second association was with Zhāng Cún 张存 (984–1071). Zhang and Sima Chi had known each other ever since they had both obtained their *jinshi* degrees in 1005. Zhang gained high office as Minister of Rites. Sima Guang's relationship with him was mainly a personal one, though: in 1038 he married Zhang's fifteen-year old daughter. Although we hear little of Madame Zhang in Sima

Guang's story, their marriage lasted until her death on 2 March 1082.

The Political Context

Sima Guang was born into a Sòng 宋 state that had held nominal power for nearly sixty years. Its actual political control was fragile, though, and attempts to subjugate rival states continued after its foundation in 960 CE. This process of military and political annexation was paralleled by the growing consolidation of barbarian polities to the north of Song territory. Song's main threats were the Khitan (Qìdān 契丹) state of Liáo 辽 (916–1125) to the northeast, and the Tangut state of Xià 夏 (1032–1227) to the northwest.

In 979 Song suffered a heavy defeat to Liao. Despite this, a rhetoric of Chinese superiority endured: Song officials continued to represent their barbarian neighbors as culturally and morally inferior. But a new dynamic of relative barbarian military strength and Song weakness demanded a nuanced foreign policy, based on diplomatic treaties that implied at least equality between Song and its rivals. Further defeats by Liao after 979 CE forced Song into the Treaty of Chanyuan in 1004. It agreed to pay an annual subsidy in silks and silver. Song foreign policy for the remainder of the eleventh century was colored by the treaty.

Foreign relations influenced domestic agendas. The maintenance of a large standing army increased government expenditure: by 1064, according to a contemporary estimate, 60–70 percent of government revenue went to supporting active and retired troops. An expanding civilian bureaucracy also consumed a large proportion of fiscal revenue. One way to meet the cost of this expenditure was to develop interregional and international trade, which promised to open up new sources of tax revenue for the government. As a result, the state became more closely involved than before in a range of economic activities. Social problems resulted, though, and government revenues were insecure as a result.

A foreign threat, together with the development of forms of civilian governance at home, prompted intellectual introspection. There was a revival in canonical Confucian thought. Debates erupted over an appropriate framework for official culture, or *wén* 文. Some scholars, including the prominent statesman and intellectual *Ōuyáng Xiū 欧阳修 (1007–1072), championed a culture based on antiquity. They sought to establish canonical Confucian moral values that excluded foreign influences such as Buddhism. Others argued for a catholic, all-embracing definition of culture that could accommodate ideological developments since antiquity and could even incorporate external influences. Early Song rulers and ministers at first pursued syncretism as a basis for domestic unity. By the late 1030s and early 1040s and the time of

Sima Guang's emergence into public office, those in favor of the model of antiquity had started to gain ascendance.

The past loomed large over the eleventh century. If they were to ensure their own survival, Song emperors needed to learn the lessons of political fragmentation and regional militarization of late Tang and the Five Dynasties. There was therefore a tendency toward the centralization of political power in the hands of the ruler and, as a corollary, a reduction in the influence of senior ministers in the routine administration of government. There was also a proliferation of civilian over military forms of governance—the context for debates on official culture. The foreign military threat had a role to play here, too: Song emperors worried that it would enable local military commanders to increase their power and undermine the central court, as had happened from the mid-eighth century CE on. Successive generations of Song scholars and statesmen therefore concerned themselves with ways of making their state strong and efficient, better able to hold its own in an insecure political environment and to avoid the mistakes of the past. That, too, was Sima Guang's aim from early in his political career.

The Local Official

In 1039 Sima Chi was posted to the eastern coastal region of Hangzhou. Sima Guang requested a transfer to nearby Suzhou to be close to his father. Before he could take up his post, his mother died. Mourning freed him from official duties, and he joined his father in Hangzhou. While there, in 1040, he produced his first major political statement, opposing increases to government-managed civilian security forces in the region. This early rejection of popular conscription and militarization prefigured arguments that he produced throughout the rest of his career.

Sima Chi died in 1041, aged sixty-two. Sima Guang returned to his native Sushui to bury both of his parents at the family tomb and to observe a three-year period of mourning. In 1044 he resumed official duties as an administrative assistant in regional government. Again he used his time in local politics to produce essays on political themes that would take center stage in his later ideology: on checks and balances in government and on the need for talented and virtuous men in the official bureaucracy. These were theoretical in tone, unlike the practical policy statement of 1040, and the statements of a man trying to establish his public ideological identity.

Pang Ji played a central role in Sima Guang's career at this time. The two were in contact over official business in the winter of 1046 and 1047, after Sima Guang had returned the previous year to the capital at Kaifeng. In 1049 Pang Ji recommended Sima Guang for appointment as an imperial academician, with greater access to court politics and to the emperor. Sima Guang transferred through a series of posts in various capital agencies as a result of this powerful patronage, including a move in 1052 to the Historiography Bureau.

In 1054 the professional relationship between the two men grew closer. Pang Ji appointed Sima Guang as a teaching aide when he became administrator of the northeastern region of Yunzhou. Later that year Sima Guang received a commission from the court to report on Pang Ji's work. In 1055, Sima Guang followed Pang Ji again to take up a post the northern borderland region of Bingzhou. While in Bingzhou, in 1057, Pang sent Sima Guang to resolve a local border dispute with Xia. Sima Guang submitted a plan to take advantage of perceived Xia military weakness by driving out Xia farmers from the area. Pang Ji adopted it despite contrary reports of a large enemy military presence. Song armies were ambushed as they moved into the disputed area; over a quarter of their troops perished. Pang Ji was demoted after an official investigation.

Though Sima Guang claimed personal responsibility for the defeat, he ultimately went unpunished. He left Bingzhou and transferred through a series of capital postings. By 1060 he had become supervisor of the Ministry of Revenue. It is tempting to trace his later economic concerns to this experience: he himself pointed up his post at the Ministry of Revenue in a long and involved discussion of state finances produced in the seventh lunar month of 1062.

Throughout the 1050s, Sima Guang issued statements on themes that would continue to concern him throughout his career. In late 1050 he worked on revisions to imperial sacrificial music, a topic that resulted in ongoing discussions with a colleague until the last years of his life. In 1051, from a post in the Ritual Academy, he issued essays on ritual protocols that included the granting of posthumous titles and funerary practices for the dead; this theme assumed a practical urgency in discussions surrounding Emperor Yingzong's succession during the mid-1060s. Also in 1051 Sima Guang turned to the theme of the employment of officials: he focused on the themes of talent (*cái* 才) and favoritism, central to his later discourse in court debate and in *Zizhi tongjian*. In 1057 he produced essays on the proper relationship between achievements and titles, and on knowing people—both extensions of the issue of official employment. And in 1058 he wrote on a related topic and one of the most pressing problems at court, which would engulf his own career over the following decade: factionalism.

Sima Guang's broader intellectual, as well as political, identity also took shape during the 1050s. In 1050 he requested the publication and dissemination of political and moral writings by *Xúnzǐ 荀子 (c. 312–c. 230 BCE) and *Yáng Xióng 杨雄 (53 BCE–18 CE), both of whom had "expanded orthodox methods" (Sima 1929a, 16.5a). Sima Guang later reversed his positive appraisal of

Xunzi, but Yang Xiong's thinking drew support throughout his career. In 1057 Sima Guang also produced a commentary on a version of the *Classic of Filial Piety* (*Xiàojīng* 孝经). Here was yet another concept with which he engaged early in his career and then revisited later on, both explicitly in debates about the Song line of imperial succession during the early 1060s, and in more general terms as a principle for the foundations of government.

Despite the dramatic upward trajectory of his career and his prolific intellectual output in the capital, Sima Guang made three requests in 1059 for a transfer to a provincial posting near to his native Xiazhou; he offered as a reason his long absence from his home region. Contrary to characterizations of him as preoccupied with central government, in the first two decades of his career Sima Guang was sensible to local concerns: he occupied several local posts and, even when in the capital, pursued local postings. And it was while in local government that he produced many of his most important political statements of the period.

The Remonstrator

In the seventh lunar month of 1061 Sima Guang took up two posts that with hindsight assume particular significance. The first was that of imperial diarist. He received the appointment together with his future political rival, Wang Anshi. Its main task was to record the emperor's daily actions. Wang Anshi refused the commission; Sima Guang accepted after five refusals. The appointment hints at two aspects of Sima Guang's ideology at this stage of his career. First, in the fourth of his petitions declining the post, he drew a marked comparison between Wang Anshi and himself, with a focus on their respective literary abilities; a debate over the role of literary talent in government would become one of their ideological battlegrounds. Second, we have here a picture of Sima Guang as a developing historian: the Imperial Diary was classified in Song as a genre of historiography.

Sima Guang also took a post as joint head of the Remonstrance Bureau 谏院, an agency that offered critical comment on central government policy. He held the post for five years, an unusually long tenure. Even after a professional transfer to the prestigious Hanlin Academy in 1067, Sima Guang continued to address many of the themes that preoccupied him in the Remonstrance Bureau. They recurred, too, in his responses to Wang Anshi's policies, after the latter received control of government on 10 September 1068. A basic continuity therefore makes itself felt in Sima Guang's statements from the early and the late 1060s. After Wang Anshi came to power, though, Sima Guang gave his policies a new focus.

The Need for Remonstrance

The most basic issue that Sima Guang addressed as head of the Remonstrance

Bureau was the need for remonstrance itself. Early in 1064 he produced a statement on the importance of the Remonstrance Bureau's functions. Its officials were to concern themselves solely with matters of magnitude and urgency, not with the trivialities of daily administration. They were also to work in the state's interest, not their own: loyalty and frankness were key character traits. Later in the same year, on 13 September, Sima Guang issued a further statement in which he criticized contemporary failures to heed remonstrance. The result was a loss of popular faith in government.

Similar memorials flowed throughout the decade. All urged the court to enable open expression. By 1067 this was more vital than ever, Sima Guang argued: senior ministers' power had been restricted at the beginning of the dynasty, but since the reign of Emperor Rénzōng 仁宗 (r. 1022–1063) it had grown to excess; there was a danger was that it would encroach upon the ruler's authority. Sima Guang restated the same charge in a statement to the throne on 30 August 1069, this time with Wang Anshi's suppression of criticism against his policies as a particular target.

Imperial Responsibilities

Two of the early notices that Sima Guang submitted to the throne from the Remonstrance Bureau addressed the theme of emperorship. For Sima Guang, an emperor needed three fundamental qualities if he were to achieve success: humanity (*rén* 仁), clarity (*míng* 明), and decisiveness (*wǔ* 武). He also had three central duties: the employment of officials, the administration of rewards, and the application of punishments. This was the major business of state, which would create an efficient official bureaucracy and would serve the interests of the common people. Conversely, Sima Guang urged against the emperor's involvement in matters of routine governance. Such a division of political responsibility ran against the grain of early Song politics, in which emperors had devolved power upon themselves at the expense of their chief ministers. Sima Guang therefore met with opposition from his contemporaries and even, in 1069, from the emperor himself. Yet he repeated the same formulation, both with identical rhetoric and in different guises, to each emperor under whom he served.

Also early in his tenure at the Remonstrance Bureau, on 3 September 1061, Sima Guang presented to the throne a five-part guide to imperial success. After a sweeping review of the rises and falls of past dynasties, he concluded that the conduct of the emperor determined political longevity. Continuity and the transmission of tradition were essential here: emperors who kept their polities in good repair could preserve the legacy of their forebears and, in their turn, transmit it to their descendants. The five guidelines for imperial longevity had a more practical focus than the imperial character traits and duties that Sima

Guang had identified earlier: timely preparation for foreign invasion and domestic disasters, careful selection of military and civil officials, military training for troops, management of grain storage, and efficient local administration. Common to all was the maintenance of proper hierarchical relations between the constituent parts of the polity, and the need to ensure that everyone (including the emperor himself) fulfilled their allotted roles. Political and social harmony, which clear hierarchies ensured by removing competition, was essential if Song were to survive.

Employing Officials

Court officials were the emperor's main source of information about events in the empire, and it was therefore essential for imperial control to have a close familiarity with members of bureaucracy, their individual talents, and their personal sentiments. On 4 January 1064, on 8 October 1067, and again in the sixth lunar month of 1069, Sima Guang cast the employment of suitable men to appropriate offices as the root of order and disorder throughout the empire.

This came with a qualification. Sima Guang pointed up Emperor Shenzong's inappropriate involvement in the business of employment and demotion: he acted against senior ministers' advice, and he exposed himself to the machinations of those with private, factional interests as well as to recriminations from others who bore the brunt of imperial decisions. Sima Guang therefore insisted on a division between senior ministers' recommendations of individuals for employment, and the emperor's power to follow those recommendations. When appointed joint head of the Recruitment Section on 7 February 1063, and then head of the Recruitment Bureau and Personnel Evaluation Section in the late 1060s, Sima Guang supplemented his theoretical statements on this issue with practical influence over policy for employing officials.

The civil service examinations were the main tool in the eleventh century for selecting candidates for office. Throughout the 1060s, Sima Guang produced discussions on the selection of *jinshi* degree holders. In particular, he criticized the content of the present examinations and argued against the inclusion of questions on poetry and rhapsodies. He demanded that these literary elements give way to a focus on prose compositions, policy analysis, and classical texts. This emphasis on employing men with talent in practical governance later folded into an attack on Wang Anshi, whom Sima Guang criticized for promoting men of literary ability over those with moral integrity and talent. There was also a personal aspect to his criticisms: in 1067 he declared his own inability to produce compositions in parallel prose, a generic form associated with literary ornament and elaboration; in a letter to Wang Anshi on 10 April 1070, he again cast himself as the antithesis of a literary man, coarse in his rhetoric but in tune with reality.

Ritual

Ritual took several forms for Sima Guang. First, it comprised the performative rituals of state, ancestral sacrifices, and funerals. For these, Sima Guang favored a definition of ritual (as part of a broader cultural sphere of *wen*) based on the prescriptions of antiquity, and in particular on canonical expectations of filial piety. In statements of the early 1060s he excluded from imperial ritual certain prevalent Buddhist and Daoist (Taoist) practices that, he claimed, fostered a conduct which was far removed from filial piety and so jeopardized the framework of traditional imperial authority. Second, ritual found expression in the social and political divisions of authority between superior and inferior, and especially between ruler and minister. Third, it was the observation of practices appropriate to the various roles that contributed to the larger social and political structure. We will hear more about the latter two types of ritual in what follows: for Sima Guang their collapse could endanger the state and, as he would show repeatedly in *Zizhi tongjian*, had actually done so in the past.

Filial ritual came to the fore of discussions at court after the death of Emperor Renzong on 30 April 1063, and with the succession of his adopted heir, Emperor Yīngzōng 英宗. Over the next three years, a tense debate erupted over the ritual status due to Emperor Yingzong's biological father. Sima Guang opposed senior statesmen of the time; he even differed with the emperor himself. Yingzong's legitimacy derived from status as Renzong's adopted son, Sima Guang argued, and any ambiguity in this status would weaken Yingzong's authority. Sima Guang therefore proposed that Yingzong's biological father should be referred to as an imperial uncle; the title of "imperial father" should be reserved for Renzong alone. These arguments fell on deaf ears. Yingzong ultimately accorded his biological father, not Renzong, the ritual title of imperial parent. Despite his defeat, Sima Guang had established a reputation for himself as a check against senior officials' monopolization of political authority, a role that he played in his opposition to Wang Anshi later in the decade.

Conscription and Military Service

Sima Guang's other political statements as a remonstrator during the 1060s revisited themes that he had already addressed earlier in his career. After the episode in Bingzhou in 1057, his foreign policy advocated a tolerant approach to dealing with barbarians and rejected the belligerent stance that he had once proposed to Pang Ji. The corollary to this was Sima Guang's opposition to a general increase in the militarization of Song society. He had already written on this theme in Hangzhou in 1040. On 1 January 1065 he issued the first in a series of statements that demanded an end to policies for the conscription of civilian militia. Sima Guang offered two arguments to support his case. First, such a policy would precipitate military defeat because Song civilian conscripts were unprepared for conflict. Second, the conscription of local civilian militia would subvert the divide between military and civilian life that underpinned the machinery of the state. These arguments established a recognizable pattern and rhetoric for Sima Guang's statements, made between 1070 and 1073, against Wang Anshi's implementation of compulsory military service through local security groups.

Economic Policy

In seventh lunar month of 1062 Sima Guang submitted to the throne an extensive discussion of the Song state's economic resources. Again, he raised familiar arguments. He prioritized the selection of talented men to administer finances, and advocated employing them for long periods of time. He argued for setting aside part of any annual surplus in preparation for unexpected expenditure in future. With echoes of representations of his own frugality, he urged the reduction of institutional waste and official opulence.

Sima Guang opposed the interference of the state in the economic affairs of society. He proposed instead a laissez-faire economic policy, allowing the common people to enrich themselves without government deterrents or controls. For Sima Guang, government taxation should serve only to satisfy the minimal requirements for maintaining public order and no more. When Wang Anshi came to power, all this took on a sharp focus with Sima Guang's opposition to the so-called Green Shoots policy (*qīngmiáo fǎ* 青苗法) of state farming loans, as well as to the Hired Service system (*miǎnyì qián* 免役钱), a tax that enabled local administrators to hire personnel for services once covered by corvée labor. The effect of such policies, Sima Guang argued, was social hardship, poverty, and an increase in levels of crime. Families would be discouraged from working to support themselves, since they would anticipate the loss of their wealth to the government. Wang's policies also undermined the existing social distinctions between rich and poor, which Sima Guang saw as economically beneficial to society.

In a long statement of 24 August 1069, he opposed a further instrument of government intervention in regional economies—the use of commissioners, a practice that Wang Anshi had introduced in the fourth lunar month of that year. Commissioners rushed into local areas to solve their financial and other problems with little sense of local economic and social conditions, Sima Guang claimed. They disrupted local affairs by interfering with local officials' jobs and creating personal and professional jealousies, but they brought little practical benefit. Hierarchies were again the issue here: the hierarchical divide between the demands of central government and the needs of local society. What was necessary for economic and social stability were competent men to observe those hierarchies, men like Sima Guang himself, in fact.

Historian of the Empire

On 1 November 1070, after numerous requests to be released from court duties, Sima Guang resigned from his post as an imperial academician. He left Kaifeng to become administrator of Yongxing Military Circuit, on the northwestern border with Xia. (A circuit was a historical administrative division similar to a prefecture.) While there, he made a number of statements on military affairs. The theme had preoccupied him during the 1060s, but now his opposition was underpinned by a close sense on the detrimental effects on local society. He also issued several strong statements against Wang Anshi's policies, especially the Green Shoots loans and the Hired Service taxes.

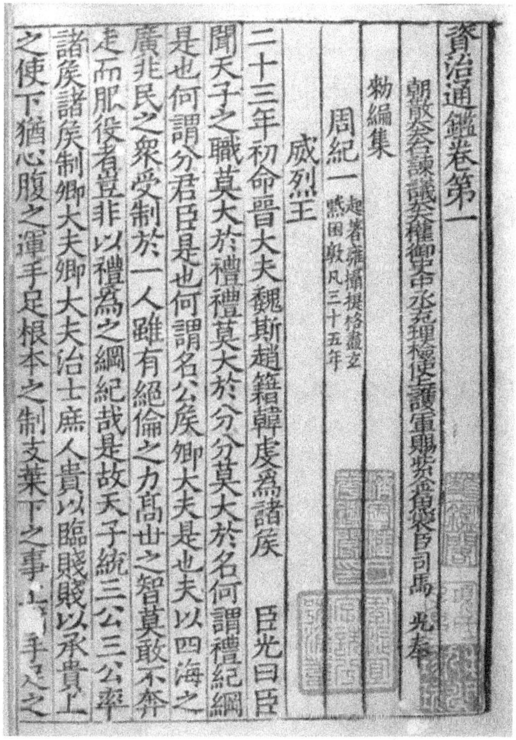
資治通鑑卷第一
朝散大夫右諫議大夫權御史中丞充理檢使上護軍賜紫金魚袋臣司馬光奉
勑編集
周紀一 起著雍攝提格盡玄黓困敦凡三十五年
威烈王
二十三年初命晉大夫魏斯趙籍韓虔爲諸侯 臣光曰臣
聞天子之職莫大於禮禮莫大於分分莫大於名何謂禮紀綱
是也何謂分君臣是也何謂名公侯卿大夫是也夫以四海之
廣兆民之衆受制於一人雖有絕倫之力高世之智莫敢不奔
走而服役者豈非以禮爲之綱紀哉是故天子統三公三公率
諸侯諸侯制卿大夫卿大夫治士庶人貴以臨賤賤以承貴上
之使下猶心腹之運手足根本之制支葉下之事上猶手足之

A page from Sima Guang's *Comprehensive Mirror for Aid in Government (Zizhi tongjian).*

Sima Guang did not remain long in Yongxing. On 20 May 1071 he took up a sinecure in Song's second city, Luoyang. This in effect marked a withdrawal from the forefront of political life for the next fourteen years; only occasional statements made their way from Luoyang to the court at Kaifeng. Though Sima Guang was a prominent figure in local society and maintained close social contacts with a community of retired statesmen, his writings at the time are shot through with the rhetoric of solitude and eremitism—rhetoric that had served historically as an expression of political discontent.

Sima Guang instead channeled his political energies in a different direction. He concerned himself with scholarly explications of a range of ritual matters, which favored inner moral self-cultivation over the conventional trappings of power and social success. He also produced a ten-chapter table of Song's official bureaucracy, a three-chapter tabulated genealogy of the imperial house, a series of essays expressing ideological opposition to the classical thinker *Mencius 孟子 (c. 372–c. 289 BCE), a commentary on Yang Xiong's *Canon of Supreme Mystery* (*Tàixuánjīng* 太玄经), and in 1085 a further commentary on the *Classic of Filial Piety*. Above all, though, he worked on the composition of *Zizhi tongjian*. On 1 January 1085, he finally submitted to the throne that 294-chapter work. A thirty-chapter source-critical *Consideration of Variants* (*Kǎoyì* 考异) and a thirty-chapter *General Outline* (*Mùlù* 目录) accompanied the main text.

Development of the Text

By the time he left for Luoyang, Sima Guang had already laid the foundations for *Zizhi tongjian*'s composition. The project had first taken shape in discussions of the late 1050s and early 1060s between Sima Guang and scholar-official Liú Shù 刘恕, who later assisted with *Zizhi tongjian*'s composition. It bore its first fruit in 1064: Sima Guang presented to the throne *A Chart of Historical Years* (*Lìnián tú* 历年图). This was a chronological table in five chapters that, like the later *Zizhi tongjian*, covered events from 403 BCE to 959 CE.

In 1066, while the Normans were conquering England on the other side of the world, Sima Guang presented to the throne *Comprehensive Notes* (*Tōng zhì* 通志). This chronicle covered the period between 403 and 207 BCE; it later formed *Zizhi tongjian*'s first eight chapters. On 14 May of the same year, Emperor Yingzong issued his order for Sima Guang to compile "the traces of the business of rulers and ministers of past ages" (Li 1979–1995, 208.5050). A year later, at an imperial lecture on 18 November 1067, Sima Guang read an extract from his new work. The recently enthroned Emperor Shenzong accorded it an imperial preface and its present title. The emperor also granted Sima Guang the use of books from his former residence and allowed him access to the resources of the imperial library collections, he offered financial support for necessary equipment, and he consented to a request for assistants. The court reading of 1067 was the first in a series that took place during the late 1060s and early 1070s. Each produced discussions of contemporary political issues at court, and it is useful to see *Zizhi tongjian* in this context—as a form of political memorial to the throne. The next seventeen years were punctuated by a steady stream of readings from *Zizhi tongjian*'s early drafts at imperial seminars. As work on each chronological section of *Zizhi tongjian*'s account was finished, final versions were sent to the emperor.

The Function of Historiography

Emperor Shenzong's choice of title for Sima Guang's work was heavy with significance. Among its several implications, it suggested that Sima Guang's work served as a "mirror" (*jiàn* 鉴). It used the past to reflect for the ruler on present political problems; it would thereby "aid government" (*zīzhì* 资治) and ensure the proper fulfillment of imperial functions. That is why it appeared in imperial seminars and in court debate. *Zizhi tongjian*'s didactic function was the product of a basic tenet of Chinese traditional historiography: works of history should inculcate moral and political lessons, and those lessons should emerge from the ways in which an author selected and organized his sources.

Sima Guang's thematic focus was expressly political; he was assiduous in meeting Emperor Yingzong's demand that he assemble "the traces of the business of rulers and ministers of past ages" (Li 1979–1995, 208.5050). He traced the fluctuating fortunes of the imperial institution. He was preoccupied with the major political figures of the past, individuals who had been responsible for making government function and who had exposed themselves to the processes of political unity and disunity and of dynastic rise and fall.

For Sima Guang, the political past taught a double-edged lesson. His ambivalent political vision was signaled by his choice of the starting date of 403 BCE for *Zizhi tongjian:* images of the political fragmentation and collapse of the great hereditary ruling house of the classical era, the house of Zhōu 周 (1045–256 BCE), greeted his readers, not descriptions of a strong and unified state. The same ambivalence received explicit expression in a phrase that appeared in statements on early drafts of *Zizhi tongjian* that Sima Guang produced during the 1060s. It culminated in the memorial that accompanied *Zizhi tongjian*'s presentation to the throne in 1084: "The good should be taken as models, the bad as warnings" (Sima Guang 1956, 9607; see also Sima Guang 1929a, 51.10b, 65.6b; Sima Guang 1929b, 16.86b; Li Tao 1979–1995, 208.5050).

Here was a familiar rhetoric of paired oppositions: Sima Guang echoed the celebrated antithetical coupling of "praise and blame" that had established itself in canonical texts as an ideal for representing the past; it was a common formulation at the time of *Zizhi tongjian*'s composition, too. In his rendering, as in the canonical precedent, Sima Guang accentuated the positive by placing it first. But while *Zizhi tongjian* offered examples of how rulers got things right in the past, it also supplied rich evidence of how far wrong individual emperors could go. Sima Guang not only represented the strength of dynastic control but also its frailty: the imperial institution was seen to be in constant, fraught danger.

The good and the bad of the past might reflect larger moral and political processes, but they were also shaped in their specific representation by historians' personal values. Here was another well-established tenet for historiography by Sima Guang's time. At least since Mencius in the fourth and third centuries

BCE, the function of historiography was not just to narrate what had happened but also to suggest what it meant. An omission might therefore resonate with ideological import; the phrasing of the text bristled with implication.

With these expectations hanging over him, Sima Guang was at pains to detail the meticulous process by which he had selected his sources for *Zizhi tongjian*. He did this through a text-critical commentary—the *Consideration of Variants*—which accompanied his main text. *Zizhi tongjian*'s ideological authority was at stake. Sima Guang's version of the past established itself as having been founded on the most rigorous standards of documentation: he had taken into account all available evidence. His *Consideration of Variants* therefore strengthened the claims of *Zizhi tongjian*'s main text by implying a process of careful objective judgment. But it also revealed the inherent subjectivity of the text's composition. As *Zizhi tongjian*'s historian and editor, Sima Guang first decided what material should inform his emperor in making political judgments, and then determined with what ideological slant that material should appear. The *Consideration of Variants* commentary showed the reasons why certain sources had been selected for inclusion, and what changes had been made to them. Sima Guang associated himself through citation with certain traditions of historical writing and, as a corollary, rejected rival traditions. He also claimed unique personal insights into the events that he recounted through personal interjections into his account in the explicit voice of historian. In the terminology of today, he placed his own spin on the past, and that was acknowledged in the eleventh century as the fulfillment of a canonical mode of historical writing.

Dynastic Rise and Fall

Zizhi tongjian's didactic message—its representation of the ways to maintain imperial power and to ensure dynastic longevity—resonated closely with the political agenda that Sima Guang set out in his memorials and statements of the 1050s and 1060s, the period of the work's conception and early development. At its heart was the need for clearly defined hierarchies in political and social rituals and relationships. That was what occupied the opening statement that Sima Guang made in the text in his own voice as *Zizhi tongjian*'s historian. He put it like this: "I, your minister, have heard that none of the duties of the Son of Heaven is greater than ritual; that in ritual nothing is greater than the division of roles; and that in divisions nothing is greater than titles" (Sima Guang 1956, 1.2). That, too, was the dominant theme that underpinned *Zizhi tongjian*'s account of the past. It made itself felt in a range of different contexts: the importance of strong titular and functional distinctions between the roles of rulers and ministers, and between different institutions within imperial government; the need for clearly defined relationships between civil and military governance; the necessity of divides between Chinese and barbarians in foreign policy; the importance of preserving distinctions between the secular and the religious; and so on. Those rulers who in the past had managed to secure such ritual hierarchies emerged from *Zizhi tongjian* as effective administrators and were usually seen to have achieved political stability and longevity; those who had neglected the importance of these fundamental political and social divisions had faced personal demise, had damaged the common weal, and had jeopardized the security of the polities over which they ruled. In short, here was the pivot on which turned the dynamic of dynastic rise and fall, and the thematic basis of *Zizhi tongjian*'s composition. We are on familiar ground here: these were ideological commitments that have emerged already in our analysis of Sima Guang's early career and of his role as remonstrator.

The Senior Statesman

Shortly after *Zizhi tongjian*'s submission to the throne, Sima Guang at last received the imperial patronage that he had long sought. After a serious illness, Emperor Shenzong died on 1 April 1085. His heir, the nine-year old Emperor Zhézōng 哲宗 (r. 1086–1101), acceded to the throne under the regency of Emperor Yingzong's widow, Empress Dowager Gāo 高 (1032–1093). On 18 April Sima Guang received a communication from the Empress Dowager urging him to return to the capital to offer advice to the throne. We hear that Sima Guang received a rapturous welcome on his return to Kaifeng, in which commoners and officials alike beseeched him to remain and serve as chief minister of state. On 21 June the Empress Dowager appointed him as Vice Director of the Chancellery, second only to the chief minister.

As soon as he had attained a position of substantial power, Sima Guang pressed for a repeal of Wang Anshi's policies. On the day after his appointment as Vice Director of the Chancellery, he requested wholesale changes that moved beyond the piecemeal alterations made since Zhezong's accession. He argued that the only justification for Wang Anshi's policies had been Emperor Shenzong's desire to expand Song borders. Without such a desire for military conquest, he reasoned, there was little reason to retain Wang Anshi's political program. So soon after Shenzong's death this was daring stuff; political opponents objected that Sima Guang had failed to respect Shenzong's legacy. But it was consistent with Sima Guang's broader conception of the structures of imperial power: by attributing blame to Shenzong, he revisited the idea that the emperor must take ultimate responsibility for the common weal.

By the end of 1085, despite the continued presence in government of political opponents, Sima Guang had abolished most of Wang Anshi's policies. Four major areas remained unaddressed, though. These formed the focus of Sima Guang's subsequent policies. They all revisited themes familiar from earlier in Sima Guang's political career: Hired Service taxes, the Green Shoots policy, ongoing military tensions with Xia, and the appointment of commander-officials. In the first lunar month of 1086 he claimed that "while these four scourges have yet to be eliminated, I shall not shut my eyes—even in death!" (Su Shi 1986, 16.490).

On 10 February 1086 Sima Guang requested the total abolition of Hired Service taxes and the restoration of an earlier system of corvée (i.e., conscripted) labor. He argued that Hired Service taxes harmed the livelihoods of both rich and poor, turned land-holding freemen into vagrants by causing farmers to lose their jobs, and bred negligence and corruption among local officials.

Sima Guang initially took a softer stance on Wang Anshi's Green Shoots policy. He proposed retaining the policy with the simple emendation that farmers be allowed to draw loans on a voluntary basis, rather than take the compulsory government loans that Wang Anshi had implemented. He was soon persuaded to abandon this moderate stance by colleagues such as Su Shi, who argued that even the availability of government loans would encourage farmers to spend beyond their means. On 16 September 1086, he therefore repealed the Green Shoots policy altogether and restored an earlier system of communal granaries.

Sima Guang attributed ongoing military tensions with Xia to Song belligerence and to the legacy of Wang Anshi's political program. On 19 February 1086 he submitted statements on Xia in which he advocated diplomacy over belligerence, requested an imperial pardon for Xia territorial encroachment in the past, and urged that cross-border trade between the two states be permitted. In the third lunar month of 1086 he submitted a further request to receive and console Xia immigrants to Song. In the seventh lunar month he proposed returning territory to Xia. These proposals initially met with opposition at court. When former chief minister Wén Yànbó 文彦博 (1006–1097) lent his support, though, they were finally implemented.

The one policy that Sima Guang ultimately failed to revoke was the appointment of commander-officials. These were men charged with providing training to local military units at a time when Emperor Shenzong had intended to launch a military campaign against Xia. Sima Guang claimed that they brought no benefit but, in stripping military control from regional administrators, they disrupted the institutional structures of local military. Despite falling short of a total repeal of Wang Anshi's policy, Sima Guang managed to modify it by returning military authority to local civil government.

These political measures were not entirely beneficial to the Song state. After the abolition of Wang Anshi's policies, for example, government revenue shrank dramatically. Within several years, the surplus accumulated during the late 1060s and 1070s had almost vanished. The government was forced to borrow from the imperial treasury to cover deficits in its spending.

Many of the other statements that Sima Guang made in 1085 and 1086 also revisited themes that he had first developed during the 1060s and before. There are few new insights into his ideology to be gained from these later policies. Their interest instead lies in their consistency: they consolidate and confirm the vision that Sima Guang had developed over two decades earlier. Though there were familiar refrains from his political statements of the 1060s, we should also note that Sima Guang avoided ideological rigidity in his statements of 1085 and 1086. Rather than the backward-looking outlook commonly ascribed to him, he showed willingness at this time to respond to present exigencies.

Early in 1086 Sima Guang suffered an illness that, despite periods of remission, afflicted him for the remaining nine months of his life. It was not the first time that he had suffered from poor health: while in Luoyang in the autumn of 1082 he had suffered a suspected stroke. Now, though, illness interfered with official duties. A pustule on his left foot left him unable to walk and prevented him from meeting the full ritual demands of court. It was a cause for personal concern. He submitted several memorials claiming that it was inappropriate for a senior official to recuperate at home and not to attend to his court duties; a concern with the division of titles and functions sounded again. He therefore tendered his resignation from his official posts. It was not accepted. Instead, the opposite happened: on 18 March 1086, he was appointed to an advanced post as a Vice Director of the Secretariat, giving him overall control of governance and a secure platform from which to revoke Wang Anshi's policies. He died still in office, in the Chancellery building, on 11 October 1086.

Mark STRANGE
The Australian National University

Further Reading

Bol, Peter. (1992). *"This culture of ours": Intellectual transitions in T'ang and Sung China*. Stanford, CA: Stanford University Press.

Bol, Peter. (1993). Government, society, and state: On the political visions of Ssu-ma Kuang and Wang An-shih. In Robert P. Hymes and Conrad Schirokauer (Eds.), *Ordering the world: Approaches to state and society in Sung Dynasty China* (pp.128–192). Berkeley, CA: University of California Press.

Cao Jiaqi 曹家琪. (1978). *Zizhi tongjian* bianxiu kao 资治通鉴" 编修考. [A study of the compilation of *Zizhi tong jian*] *Wenshi* 文史, *5*, 63–89.

Gu Donggao 顾栋高. (2006) *Sima Taishi Wenguo Wenzheng gong nianpu* 司马太师温国文正公年谱 in

Sima Guang nianpu 司马光年谱 [Chronological biography of Sima Guang]. Beijing: Zhonghua shuju. (Original work published 1737/1738)

Hartwell, Robert M. (1971). Historical analogism, public policy, and social science in eleventh- and twelfth-century China. *The American Historical Review*, *76*(3), 690–727.

Huang Yizhou 黄以周, et al. (2004). *Xu Zizhi tongjian changbian shibu* 续资治通鉴长编拾补 [Supplement to the Long draft of the Continuation of *Zizhi tongjian:* lost fragments]. Beijing: Zhonghua shuju. (Original work published 1883)

Xingzheng yuan wenhua jianshe weiyuan hui 行政院文化建设委员会 (Eds.) (1986). *Jinian Sima Guang Wang Anshi shishi jiubai zhounian xueshu yantao hui lunwen ji* 纪念司马光王安石逝世九百周年学术研讨会论文集 [Conference proceedings for the commemoration of the 900th anniversary of the deaths of Sima Guang and Wang Anshi]. Taipei, Taiwan: Guojia wenyi jijinhui, Guoli zhengzhi daxue.

Ji Xiaobin. (2005). *Politics and conservatism in Northern Song China: The career and thought of Sima Guang (A.D. 1019–1086)*. Hong Kong: The Chinese University Press.

Li Tao 李焘. (1979–1995). *Xu Zizhi tongjian changbian* 续资治通鉴长编 [Long draft of the Continuation of *Zizhi tongjian*] Beijing: Zhonghua shuju. (Original work submitted 1163–1183)

Liu Xizhong 刘羲仲. (1922). *Tongjian wenyi* 通鉴问疑 [Questions on *Tongjian*]. Shanghai: Bogu zhai. (Original work written late-eleventh century)

Pulleyblank, Edwin. (1961). Chinese historical criticism: Liu Chih-chi and Ssu-ma Kuang. In W. G. Beasley & E. G. Pulleyblank (Eds.), *Historians of China and Japan* (pp.135–166). London: Oxford University Press.

Sariti, Anthony William. (1972). Monarchy, bureaucracy, and absolutism in the thought of Ssu-ma Kuang. *The Journal of Asian Studies*, *32*(1), 53–76.

Sima Guang 司马光. (1929a). *Wenguo Wenzheng gong wenji* 温国文正公文集 [Collected works of Duke Wenzheng of Wen] (Sibu congkan 四部丛刊, Ed.). Shanghai: Shangwu yinshu guan. (Original work submitted 1133)

Sima Guang 司马光. (1929b). *Sima Wen gong Jigu lu* 司马温公稽古录 [Duke Sima of Wen's Records of studying the past] (Sibu congkan 四部丛刊, Ed.) Shanghai: Shangwu yinshu guan. (Original work submitted 1086)

Sima Guang 司马光. (1956). *Zizhi tongjian* 资治通鉴 [Comprehensive mirror for aid in government]. Beijing: Zhonghua shuju. (Original work submitted 1084)

Sima Guang 司马光. (1986). *Chuan jia ji* 传家集 [Collected works transmitted through the family] (Yingyin Wenyuan ge Siku quanshu 景印文渊阁四库全书 Ed.). Taipei, Taiwan: Taiwan shangwu yinshu guan. (Original work published c.1180)

Sima Guang 司马光. (1993). *Zengguang Sima Wen gong quanji* 增广司马温公全集 [*Zōkō Shiba On kō zenshū.* Duke Sima of Wen's complete works: expanded edition]. Tokyo: Kyūko shoin. (Original work published mid-twelfth century)

Sima Guang 司马光. (1994). *Sima Guang riji jiao zhu* 司马光日记校注 [Sima Guang's diary: critical and annotated edition]. Beijing: Zhongguo shehui kexue chubanshe. (Original work written c. 1068–1070)

Sima Guang 司马光 (1997). *Sushui jiwen* 涑水记闻 [Records of things heard by [the man from] Sushui]. Beijing: Zhonghua shuju. (Original work submitted 1136)

Strange, Mark. (2007). A reading of Hou Jing's rebellion in *Zizhi tongjian*: The construction of Sima Guang's imperial vision. In Daria Berg (Ed.), *Reading China: Fiction, history and the dynamics of discourse. Essays in honour of Professor Glen Dudbridge* (pp. 200–237). Leiden, The Netherlands: Brill.

Strange, Mark. (2008) *The construction of* Zi zhi tong jian*'s imperial vision: Sima Guang on the Southern and Northern Dynasties.* (Unpublished doctoral dissertation). University of Oxford, Oxford, UK.

Su Shi 苏轼. (1986). *Su Shi wenji* 苏轼文集 [Collected works of Su Shi]. Beijing: Zhonghua shuju. (Original work written eleventh century, published early sixteenth century)

Tuotuo 脱脱 [Toghto] et al. (1977). *Songshi* 宋史 [History of Song]. Beijing: Zhonghua shuju. (Original work submitted 1345)

Twitchett, Denis, & Smith, Paul Jakov. (Eds.). (2009). *The Cambridge history of China: Vol. 5, part 1. The Sung dynasty and its precursors, 907–1279.* Cambridge, UK: Cambridge University Press.

Yang Mingzhu 杨明珠. (Ed.). (2004). *Sima Guang ying ci beizhi: tulu yu jiaoshi* 司马光茔祠碑志: 图录与校释 [Epitaphs and inscriptions from Sima Guang's tomb and shrines: a catalogue, with critical annotations]. Beijing: Wenwu chubanshe.

Zhu Xi 朱熹. (1929). *Sanchao mingchen yanxing lu* 三朝名臣言行录 [Record of the utterances and actions of famous officials of three reigns] (Sibu congkan 四部丛刊, Ed.). Shanghai: Shangwu yinshu guan. (Original work submitted in 1172)

Sū Shì

苏轼

1037–1101—Poet, writer, humorist, alchemist, philosopher, and scholar-official

Alternate name: Sū Dōngpō 苏东坡 ("East Slope")

Summary

Su Shi was a Song dynasty poet and intellectual. Like many of his contemporaries he was a true polymath, excelling in poetry, painting, calligraphy, and philosophy. He served as an official in different positions and locations, but was exiled three times for his outspoken opposition to the reform policies of Wang Anshi. His poetry is beloved and remembered for its perceived spontaneity, showing the temporality and imperfection of the author's existence, with a timeless and universal appeal. Readers also relate to Su Shi's humor and stamina in the face of adversity.

Often known by his style name Dongpo, Su Shi was considered by many to be the preeminent figure of his age. Any biographical account cannot but begin with a list of his achievements: a major premodern Chinese poet; a prose master and eclectic thinker who was deeply and equally versed in Confucianism, Buddhism, and Daoism (Taoism); a calligrapher; painter; high-ranking official influential in national politics; a humorist; alchemist; and, finally, a gastronome who, according to legend, created the meat dish called Dongpo pork that still bears his name in the twenty-first century. Perhaps even more important than his reputation as an overachiever is the fact that Su Shi is also arguably the most beloved poet of generations of Chinese readers. What endears him to readers is a perceived spontaneity in his writing—evident as well in his visual artistic creations—that intimates the temporality and imperfection of the author's existence, while simultaneously rendering it timeless and universal. Readers can also relate to the humor and stamina that Su Shi demonstrated in the face of adversity. In response to his opposition to the "New

Policy" reforms of *Wáng Ānshí 王安石 (1021–1086), chancellor to Emperor Shénzōng 神宗 (r. 1067–1085), he was exiled on three occasions—the last time to Hainan, at the time an outermost frontier of Chinese cultural influence. He adapted and survived, but died shortly after his final return to the country's central region.

The Topography of Culture in the Early Song Dynasty

His dazzling variety of accomplishments qualified Su Shi as a leading *literatus*, or *wénrén* 文人, with the combined identity of poet-scholar-bureaucrat. The formation of the elite class of *literati* can be attributed to the social and institutional forces that defined the intellectual transition that occurred from the ninth to the eleventh century—or from the Late Tang to the Early Song.

The Sòng 宋 dynasty (960–1279 CE) emerged from the political disintegration and cultural destruction of the interregnum period that followed the fall of the Táng 唐 (618–907 CE). To avoid the armed rebellions and coups-d'état that had defined the Five Dynasties and Ten Kingdoms (907–960 CE) era of the north, the Song dynasty's founding emperors sought to curb the "power of the sword" while increasing that of "the brush." A series of changes was undertaken to optimize the civil service examination system, which began in 605 CE and was used to select government officials. These changes included dramatically increasing the numbers of degrees awarded, creating a three-tier examination system (comprising prefectural, departmental, and palace examinations), and articulating procedures to ensure the anonymity of the written examinations—and therefore the impartiality of those responsible for grading them. As a result, the state-education and examination systems were extended to attract increasing numbers of students from a broader spectrum of social strata to compete for seats in an ever-expanding civil government. Candidates who successfully passed the metropolitan examination given at the capital Kaifeng were called *jìnshì* 进士, "advanced" or "selected" scholars. Poetry, Confucian classics, and policy essays were routinely tested in the examinations, and constituted the core curricula of a general education. Furthermore, the purpose of education became, at that point, intrinsically tied to bureaucratic duties.

The most successful *jinshi* degree holders, Su Shi among them, entered Chóngwén Academy 崇文院, an institution set up by the second Song emperor, *Tàizōng 太宗 (939–997; r. 976–997), to collect books and talents. Chongwen consisted of three separate academies and an imperial library, located close to the imperial palace. Academicians served as literary attendants to the throne and carried

*People marked with an asterisk have entries in this dictionary.

out light administrative duties. Many would eventually enter the bureaucracy's top echelons. Calligraphy was deemed a necessary skill for executing imperial obligations. Often painting and connoisseurship were practiced to complement the academician's elegant lifestyle. These academicians were the earliest and archetypical "literati."

Scholarly talents could not be decoupled from the availability of books. During the interregnum period, northern China was devastated by internecine warfare and nomadic invasions resulting in the heavy loss of books and the disruption of knowledge transmission. Many scholars fled to the south, which enjoyed relative peace and prosperity during the ongoing struggles for power among regional kingdoms. Books were avidly collected and preserved by royal families eager to prove their cultural and political legitimacy. Block-printing technology, begun in the mid-Tang era, was improved and books became more accessible. The concentration of culture in the south was partly reflected in regional poetic styles. While in the north a colloquial style that focused on the quotidian prevailed, southern poetry tended to emphasize elegance and refinement. A touch of the northern easiness and southern elegance, combined with the erudition befitting a unified empire, would come to define the outlook expressed in Song poetry.

After the Song-era reunification of China, books collected in the south furnished the newly founded imperial library, providing resources for the editing and printing of imperial encyclopedias. The percentage of "degree-holders" from the south increased, partly due to the importance of poetry as a subject in the metropolitan test, to such an extent that, in 1064, the formidable *Sīmǎ Guāng 司马光 (1019–1086), himself a native of the north, petitioned to limit the number of southern *jinshi*. The topography of culture in the early Song helped to explain how the Su family—relatively obscure local gentry in southwestern Sichuan—could have produced three of the most brilliant talents of the period.

Su Shi's Early Life

Su Shi was born on 8 January 1037, during the reign of Rénzōng 仁宗 (1010–1063; r. 1022–1063), the fourth Song emperor. His family lived in Meishan County, Sichuan. Genealogical records have shown that Su's clan was related to the Tang magistrate Sū Wèidào 苏味道 (648–705), a talented (albeit notorious) character. Perhaps due to the chaos of the late Tang to the Song that severed the region from national politics, the Su clan harbored no grand ambitions. His father Sū Xún 苏洵 (1005–1066) began his serious studies only at the age of twenty-seven *sui* (a traditional Chinese way of recording age, counting the number of calendar years somebody had been alive, usually one or two years more than their actual age). Su Shi was his fifth child. Xun, Shi, and the equally precocious sixth child, Sū Zhé 苏辙 (1039–1112), would be later known as "the Three Sus from Meishan," all ranked among the eight greatest "ancient prose" (*gǔwén* 古文) masters of the Tang and the Song.

Su Shi's talent and career had been, in one way or another, shaped by his regional background. After the fall of the Tang dynasty, the Sichuan area was ruled by two successive Shu regimes until the Song conquest in 965. Decades after that conquest, the coercion policy of the central and local governments continued to result in cycles of rebellion and repression. Though the gentry continued to educate their youth, the purpose of that education became less focused on career success and more on maintaining a clan's prestige. Before Su Xun's uncle Sū Huàn 苏涣 (1001–1062) successfully passed the metropolitan exam in the year 1024, few students in this area had ever attempted the civil service examinations.

The separatist character of their region must have contributed to the three Sus' decision to employ the archaic essay style, so different from the highly ornamented and mannerist style popular among metropolitan students. By chance, when Su Xun brought his two sons to the capital for the *jinshi* exam in the year 1057, the statesman and scholar *Ōuyáng Xiū 欧阳修 (1007–1072) was then chief examiner. Unsatisfied with the popular contemporary style, Ouyang was determined to promote "ancient prose" that emphasized clarity and argumentation. This examination became a watershed in Song literary history. The two sons rode on a tide to success. Su Shi ranked second in the departmental examination; his younger brother, Zhe, trailed not far behind. The Sus won not only national acclaim but also the patronage of Ouyang Xiu, the most renowned *literatus* and statesman of the period.

The sudden death of their mother halted the Sus' career progress. After the required period of ritual mourning, in early 1061 they continued to succeed in the Decree Examination (*zhìkē* 制科), the highest level exams in the Song examination system; these special-purpose examinations were organized by imperial decree either in the case of a specific promotion or to identify particularly talented men. Throughout the three-hundred-year Song era, only thirty-five candidates passed this exam. Su Shi ranked third (i.e., the highest de facto) rank—the first three ranked candidates were given "first-class" status—and Su Zhe ranked fourth.

Their examination triumph did not immediately translate into political fortune; under the Song bureaucratic system that valued seniority above all else, they were required to begin as low-ranking officials in local governments. They had grabbed the attention of officials who had grand expectations for their futures, however. Su Shi began his bureaucratic career as an administrative assistant in Fengxiang (in modern-day Shaanxi Province) for three years. This was the standard term for a provincial tenure, after which an official was called back to the capital to report on his work and to be assigned another post. In 1063, when Emperor Renzong died without leaving an heir, his nephew Yīngzōng 英宗 (1032–1067; r. 1063–1067) succeeded him. Su finished his term and returned to the capital, where he was promoted to the post of Academician in the Academy of History, a coveted sinecure.

Once again, death visited the Su family. Su Shi's wife, Wáng Fú 王弗 (1039–1065), whom he had married in 1054, died, leaving behind a son, Sū Mài 苏迈 (1058-1112). The following year, his father Su Xun also passed away. Shi and Zhe escorted the two coffins back to Sichuan for interment. After the mourning period, he married Wang Fu's cousin, Wáng Rùnzhī 王闰之 (1048–1093), and returned once again to the capital during the second month of 1069.

That same month, Wang Anshi was promoted to the post of chancellor by the new emperor, Shénzōng 神宗 (1048–1085; r. 1067–1085). Aware of the deep social, economic, and military crises underlying an apparent prosperity, Wang managed to persuade the ambitious young emperor to push forward a series of socioeconomic reforms, known as the "New Policy" (*xīnfǎ* 新法). These methods soon encountered vehement resistance from more conservative-leaning officials. Their struggle foreshadowed a vicious cycle of reforms and restorations that would contribute to the steady decline of the Song vis-à-vis its nomadic neighbors. This powerful political whirlpool would also consume the political futures of Su Shi and his allies.

The Reformist Years

The theatrical antagonism between Su Shi and Wang Anshi would perhaps not have been inevitable had Wang been more moderate in the pace of his reform and more tolerant of different opinions. Wang wanted to radically modernize Song systems of agriculture, transportation, finance, and the military service. To a certain extent, he introduced a business model into the operation of the state. Leaving any issue of the practicality of these means aside, he was confident in his own integrity to a fault. His rejection of even well-intended and reasonable criticism alienated many, resulting in his speedy promotion of opportunists.

One of his major confrontations with Su Shi concerned education and examination policies. Since the seventh century CE, literary talent had been a major, if not the sole, concern of the *jìnshì* examination. Yet Wang Anshi, a poet himself, regarded literature as unrelated to practical matters and proposed to replace the literary composition section of the test with a section comprising commentary on the classics. Su Shi, in his later court indictment on Wang's reform, opposed this on the grounds that neither poetry nor the classics were of any pragmatic value for governance. He claimed that to write poetry well, however, an examinee must be familiar with the classics and history, and should apply their moral and historical lessons to actual governance. In contrast, classicists were opinionated and often versed only in one classic and little else, let alone history or literature. Emperor Shenzong was said to be an avid reader of Su Shi's prose and was not unsympathetic to his arguments, but Wang had a tighter grip on imperial aspirations. After repeated conflicts, Su Shi withdrew from this losing battle and petitioned for a provincial post. At the end of the year 1071, he became Censorial Vice Governor of Hangzhou (in modern Zhejiang Province).

In the picturesque city of Hangzhou, Su Shi enjoyed his association with poets, singing girls, and Buddhist monks. He began to compose lyric or *ci* poetry—sung according to one of a number of set patterns—called *cípái* 词牌—each associated with a specific title that dictated a particular tonal and rhythmic pattern. Several *ci* might share the same title, which may or may not have anything to do with the actual subject of the poems. Hangzhou was then the epicenter of Chán 禅 Buddhism (Zen in Japanese). At the time, Song Buddhism was divided into Chan, *vinaya* (律, or "discipline"), and "teaching" (*jiào* 教) lineages, although, in practice, the actual boundaries between these categories were not absolute. Su Shi's parents had been devout lay Buddhists, but their beliefs were apparently little affected by the novel Chan style. Perhaps because of their influence, the younger Su Shi showed little sympathy to Chan. He revered instead the *vinaya* lineage, regarding it the proper duty of a monk to abide by ascetic precepts in exchange for a tax exoneration and the imposition of *corveé* (obligatary government service, such as military service or labor).

Su deemed the Chan doctrine with its "public case" (*gōng'àn* 公案, or kōan) practice—that is, describing an interaction between a Chan master and his student to demonstrate the master's insight—to be comprised of self-indulgent, absurd games of little intellectual value (Kong 1986, 12: 384–385). Ironically, soon after he came to Hangzhou, Su Shi became acquainted with some exceptionally intelligent Chan monks and participated in the "public cases" himself, as is shown in his witty poems from this period. Many of these monks were so-called "poet monks" whose poetry often betrayed a vivid interest in worldly affairs observed through the prism of a transcendental state of mind.

In addition to an elegant lifestyle, provincial tenures offered Su Shi the opportunity to observe first-hand the malpractice of the "New Policy" reforms. As vice governor of Hangzhou, and subsequently the governor of Mizhou (now Zhucheng, Shandong Province), and finally governor of Xuzhou (in modern Jiangsu Province), Su Shi was obligated to carry out policies that he was opposed to. Those were years of devastation. The countryside was affected by flood, drought, locusts, and bandits. But officials, promoted to implement the reforms, chose to cover up such desolation to window-dress the effect of the policies. In charge of relief works, Su Shi grieved over the miseries of the populace. Powerless to influence the situation, he satirized it. Poems he wrote during this period often openly or covertly criticize the reforms.

In 1076, Wang Anshi stepped down a second time and lived his remaining years in semi-reclusion in Nanjing. Years of political turmoil and of little accomplishment had weakened the emperor's trust in him, and natural disasters were often interpreted by his opponents as divine signs of disapproval over his measures. Conservatives sensed a chance for a comeback, but the remaining reformists at court fought harder still. Soon after Su Shi was transferred to Huzhou (in modern Zhejiang Province) in 1079, he sent a routine report back to the throne; in it he groused with obvious irony. A confident writer, he knew that the emperor enjoyed his prose. He forgot that less admiring readers were reading it too.

Under the Song, remonstrance officials were charged with reporting on any perceived or suspected crimes or misconduct by officials of any rank, without having to reveal their sources. Theoretically, even if their allegations were later found to be ungrounded, they were not to be punished for being "alert." In a time of factional strife, however, this system could be rigged to serve the dominant factions. The new chancellor Wáng Guī 王珪 (1019–1085), thinking his position to be insecure, sought to further damage the conservative's cause. Su Shi, who was broadly connected and whose satirical poems and essays were widely popular, was a perfect victim. A selection of his poems written during his provincial postings was judged to be libelous regarding the reforms and, consequently, the throne. Su was seized in Huzhou, moved to the capital, and imprisoned at Crow Terrace for interrogation. Many of those who had previously received these poems were implicated, demoted, or exiled. In the end, partly because the interrogators failed to produce sufficient evidence for conviction, partly because of the rescue efforts from many, including the Empress Dowager and Wang Anshi himself, Su Shi was spared a death sentence but was exiled to desolate Huangzhou (in modern Hubei Province).

It was in Huangzhou that Su Shi became Dongpo, or "East Slope"—the style name by which he is commonly still known—which refers to his farming on a piece of barren field east of the city wall. The ease with which he faced adversity is reflected in his "farming" poetry; however, it did not come without a painful period of transition. When Su first came to Huangzhou, he was tormented by a sense of guilt and shame. His rage against injustice turned inward and evolved into a form of self-censorship. He regretted that his unbridled urge to write had rendered him vulnerable and implicated those close to him. When he was not keeping to

A Poem by Su Shi: Water Tune Introduction

The following poem was written by Su Shi in Huangzhou on the eve of the Mid-Autumn Festival, or the Moon Festival, of 1076, and sent to his younger brother Su Che. It is a lyric song in the "Water Tune Introduction" 水調歌頭 *style.*

明月幾時有	When does the bright moon ever shine?
把酒問青天	Holding a cup of wine, I ask the dark blue sky.
不知天上宮闕	I wonder, in the celestial palaces,
今夕是何年	Which year will it be tonight?
我欲乘風歸去	I long to ride the wind and return,
又恐瓊樓玉宇	Yet fear, in those crystal terraces and jade towers,
高處不勝寒	Unbearable is the ethereal cold on high.
起舞弄清影	Now I dance to my own clear shadow,
何似在人間	How is it like in the realm of man!
轉朱閣	Turning around the vermillion loft,
低綺戶	Stooping to a silk-curtained window,
照無眠	Shining on this sleepless one—
不應有恨	You who should have no regret
何事悲向別時圓	Why do you always fully shine, on broken ties?
人有悲歡離合	At times men are sad or merry, apart or reunited;
月有陰晴圓缺	At times the moon is shadowed or clear, waxing or waning.
此事古難全	Since olden times, such things can never be perfect.
但願人長久	I only wish for a long, long life;
千里共嬋娟	That across a thousand miles, we share the lovely light!

Translated by the author. Source: Zou Tongqing 邹同庆 & Wang Zongtang 王宗堂 (Eds.). (2002). *Su Shi ci biannian jiaozhu* 苏轼词编年校注. Beijing: Zhonghua shuju, pp. 173–174.

himself indoors, he meditated in a Buddhist temple and read only *sutras* (Buddhist scriptures; from the Sanskrit for *thread*) for long moments. It seemed that he reached a state of mental tranquility first by transcending the glory and disgrace of the phenomenal world and subsequently via the catharsis experienced through physical labor and the immediate well-being that that effort engenders. Seclusion also provided him with quiet time for study. Having made remarkable progress in writing, scholarship, calligraphy, and painting, he witnessed his reputation rising in proportion to the harshness of the persecution he suffered. Some of his most famous poetic works were written during this period. A transcendent attitude toward the vicissitudes of life, most famously exhibited in the "Former Rhapsody on the Red Cliff" 前赤壁赋 written in 1082, came to define the image of Su Shi that has persisted since.

The Metropolitan Period

In the year 1084, Shenzong finally reprieved Su Shi by sending a "handwritten edict," a special form of edicts which circumvented the entire court bureaucracy, and had him transferred to Ruzhou (in modern Henan Province), a city close to the capital. Leery of the intricacies of court politics, Su petitioned for retirement in Changzhou (in modern Jiangsu Province), a request that was granted in the second Chinese lunar month of 1085. Just one month later, Shenzong died at thirty-eight *sui*. His teenage son Zhézōng 哲宗 (r. 1086–1101) ascended the throne. The custodian of the emperor was his grandmother, Empress Dowager Gāo Taotao (1032–1093), the widow of Yingzong (1032–1067).

The Empress Dowager admired the governance of Renzong—her father-in-law—and was determined to restore his more conservative policies. Sima Guang, by now an octogenarian, ended his retirement at Luoyang, returning to lead the court. Bearing in mind Renzong's high opinion of the Su brothers, she patronized Su Shi and promoted him swiftly. Within just a few months, he had already been promoted to Secretariat Drafter, a post that empowered him to draft imperial edicts or reject doing so when he deemed the matter improper. His meteoric ascension again made him a target of libel.

Politics during the Yuányòu 元祐 period (1086–1094) was marked by the swift upward and downward mobility of many of those involved in its deadly power clashes. It began with the dyarchy of Sima Guang, who was determined to completely dismantle the "New Policy" reforms, and Zhāng Dūn 章惇 (1035–1105), a beneficiary of those reforms. Zhang was soon expelled. Su Zhe, Su Shi's beloved younger brother, was now a member of the board of remonstrance. His vehement impeachments resulted in the dismissal of many high-ranking reformists. Their edicts of reprimand, moreover, were often drafted by the elder Su, whose rhetorical flair frequently added insult to injury. Yet Su Shi was in essence a moderate. His sympathy toward some measures of the reforms did not sway Sima Guang.

In 1086, with the restoration in full swing, Sima Guang died, a mere four months after Wang Anshi's death. The reformist court immediately splintered into more factions. Anecdotes circulated that Su Shi and Chéng Yí 程颐 (1033–1107)—a rising *lǐxué* 理学 (known today as Neo-Confucianism) scholar and new tutor to the throne—held each other in disdain. Su Shi was then a Hanlin Academician and would be appointed imperial tutor known as Reader-in-Waiting in 1087. Su Zhe soon joined the tutorial board. The Sus' scholarship, which recommended pragmatism and historicism, was in stark contrast to the moral philosophy of the Chengs—Cheng Yi and his elder brother, *Chéng Hào 程颢 (1032–1085). The constant tension between the two sets of brothers over issues of education and examination resulted in Cheng Yi's dismissal from the court in the eighth month of 1087. The Sus' increasing power had also unsettled some of Sima Guang's followers, dubbed the Shuo Faction 朔派, or "the Northerners." Though the Empress Dowager remained Su Shi's unfailing supporter, he was demoralized by the endless strife. So he again petitioned for a provincial post. In the fourth month of 1089, he left the capital to govern Hangzhou once again, an agreeable change for him.

Despite the vicissitudes of politics, Su Shi was enjoying the best period of his life. He took pleasure in the comfort and companionship he found there. He met with many younger protégés, the most prominent of whom were the "Four Scholars": *Huáng Tíngjiān 黄庭坚 (1045–1105), Qín Guān 秦观 (1049–1100), Cháo Bǔzhī 晁补之 (1053–1110), and Zhāng Lěi 张耒 (1054–1114), who were to become famous poets themselves. Huang would later initiate the highly influential "Jiangxi School" of poetry, representative of the Song style.

Su's successive provincial tenures were, seemingly, active and pleasant. In Hangzhou (1089–1091) he had silt dredged from the West Lake and built a causeway made of mud, which still bears his name, the Su Causeway. He spent a year (1091–1092) in Yingzhou (in modern Anhui Province) also to de-silt their West Lake. He tried to rid the area of bandits and organized famine relief. In early 1092 he was transferred to Yangzhou (in modern Jiangsu Province), but a mere half year later was again summoned to court, this time to be appointed Minister of War and Reader-in-Waiting.

Su Shi enjoyed governance more than politics. Even on his way back to court, he petitioned repeatedly for a provincial post—to no avail. He was soon appointed Minister of Rites, in charge of state ritual ceremonies, and was honored with two academician titles: Academician of Duanming Hall and Hanlin Academician Reader-in-Waiting. This was a rare honor. With his brother as vice director of the chancellery, both were one step removed from the chancellorship, and hence attracted vehement attacks. Su Shi's routine petitions for provincial posts were just as routinely ignored by the Empress Dowager, confident in her powerful patronage.

In the eighth month of 1093, his second wife, Wang Runzhi, died, leaving him two sons, Sū Dài 苏迨 (1070–1126) and Sū Guò 苏过 (1072–1123). One month later, Empress Dowager Xuanren also passed away, causing a political seism. The young emperor had long borne a grudge against his grandmother and was eager to assume control. The court was reshuffled: reformists flocked back, and conservatives were demoted. Su Shi's previous request to govern Dingzhou (in modern Hebei Province), a barren frontier prefecture, was granted.

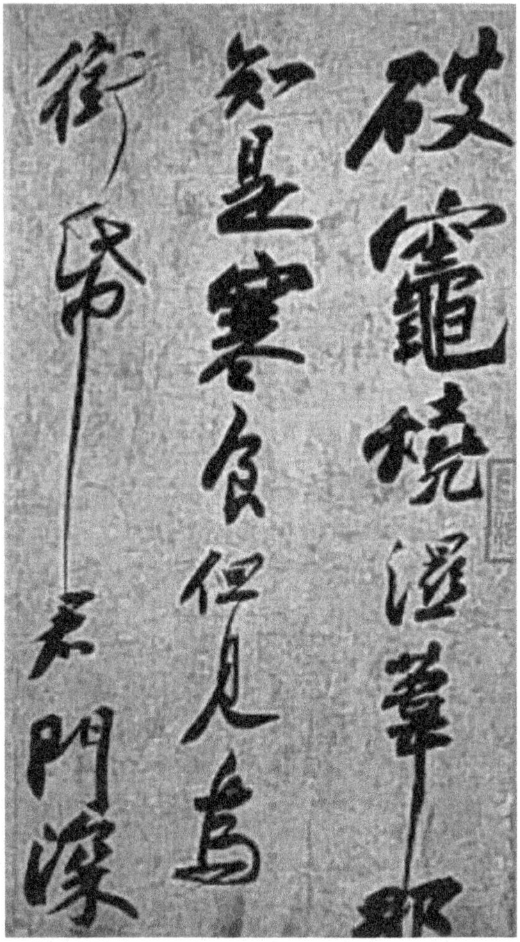

Calligraphy by the master Su Shi. National Palace Museum, Taipei, Taiwan.

Dingzhou was less a city than a fortress, perpetually on guard against Liáo 辽 (907–1125), the Khitan Empire. This nomadic neighbor had been causing trouble for the Song dynasty since its inception. By means of a treaty signed at Chanyuan (now Puyang, Henan Province) in 1004, the Song bought peace with annual tributes of silver and silk. Compared to the cost of warfare, this seemed a good bargain. But peace, as Su Shi discovered, had softened the Song troops. In response, he practiced military drills and discipline.

Meanwhile, a storm was gathering at court. The emperor decided to continue with his father's reforms. Zhang Dun again became Chancellor. In the intercalary fourth month of 1094, an edict arrived at Dingzhou, depriving Su Shi of his "academician" titles and demoting him to Yingzhou (now Yingde, Guangdong Province). Su Shi's last decade of exiles thus began.

Final Exiles to the Far South

Altogether one hundred and nineteen officials who served in the Yuanyou period were whisked off to remote corners of the empire. On his southward journey, Su Shi came across Su Zhe, who was traveling to Ruzhou. They decided to let Su Shi's son, Su Mai, bring most members of the family to Yixing (in modern Jiangsu Province). As he was still making his way, Su Shi received another edict banishing him even farther, to Huizhou (in modern Guangdong Province), a semi-barbaric miasmic region. Only his youngest son Su Guo and his faithful concubine, Wáng Zhāoyún 王朝云 (1062–1096), accompanied him. The latter would soon die of subtropical diseases caused by miasma (*zhàng* 瘴).

Curiously, amid his solitude, humiliation, and destitution, Su Shi found peace. Excluded from active governing, he participated in local charity works and sponsored bridge- and aqueduct-construction projects. He modeled himself after Táo Qián 陶潜 (c. 352–427 CE), a reclusive poet, and Gě Hóng 葛洪 (283–343 CE), a Daoist master. He wrote matching poems for the entire poetic corpus of Tao Qian, in the process reinterpreting his exile as not having occurred by force, but by choice—namely, in accordance with his natural inclinations. He practiced alchemy (for health reasons), and occasionally entertained the idea of becoming an "immortal." He eventually built a house on Mt. Luofu. In the second month of 1097, Su Mai brought the rest of the family to permanently reside with Su Shi. Barely two months later, however, another edict arrived that banished Su Shi, yet again, this time farther across the strait to Danzhou (in modern Hainan Province). Thinking that there would be no further chance to return from exile, he brought only Su Guo with him.

In the far-less civilized Danzhou, Su Shi filled his solitude with classical scholarship. In 1099 he finished a commentary on the *Classic of Changes* (*I Ching* or *Yìjīng* 易经), a project which had been started by his father, Su Xun, and was complemented later by Su Zhe, thus illustrating the full spectrum of the Su family's scholarship. The defining voice, however, is Su Shi's. Su Shi declared this work, together with a commentary on the *Analects* written during his exile in Huangzhou and a commentary on the *Classic of Documents* (*Shūjīng* 书经 or *Shàngshū* 尚书), to be the source of his greatest intellectual pride. For twenty-first century intellectual historians, Su's commentaries represent an alternative tradition to that of *lixue*, defined by the Chengs and later by the inimitable thinker, *Zhū Xī 朱熹 (1130–1200).

While enduring the isolation of Hainan, the poems Su Shi wrote there were nevertheless widely disseminated on the mainland. Their central theme was a celebration of his acceptance of his fate. But then, yet another wave from afar reached him: Emperor Renzong died in the first month of 1100, at the age of only twenty-five *sui*, leaving no heir. His brother Zhào Jí 趙佶 (1082–1135; r. 1100–1135) succeeded the throne, and would be known as Huīzōng 徽宗, a fine painter and calligrapher whose tutelage would bring the empire's downfall to the Khitans. In the general amnesty celebrating Huizong's enthronement, Su Shi returned from Hainan, taking his time to decide where to retire. His long-unseen hometown was too far away, so he finally opted for Changzhou, where he owned some estates. He followed the waterway from Jiangxi to Jiangsu, succumbing to the hot weather and difficult journey. He died of illness soon after he arrived at Changzhou, in August 1101.

Su Shi's Influence

Su Shi has left an impressive and diverse legacy in literature, classical studies, calligraphy, painting, and aesthetics.

High-register poetry since the Late Tang, generally speaking, had become increasingly reflective, referential, argumentative, and socially oriented. Su Shi's poetry is representative of this tendency and, because of its sheer *gravitas*, instrumental in its development. Yet he was also able to imbue a touch of freedom and spontaneity into such learned poetry, making it, at the same time, referential and expressive. Since his death, his poetry has continued to be broadly read throughout East Asia and from Mongolia to Korea and Japan.

Su Shi's talent was also one of breaking boundaries. This he also did in his lyric-song poetry, a genre traditionally written in a feminine voice intended to be sung by singing girls. Su Shi's discursive and masculine lyric songs therefore initiated the "heroic abandon" (*háofàng* 豪放) tradition in this genre, contributing also to an increase in its register.

His classical scholarship constituted a unique intellectual tradition that emphasized the pursuit of Dao (or "the Way") through a diversity of cultural accomplishments and empirical experiences, in contrast to the singular emphasis of the Song dynasty's *lixue* school on the moral learning.

Compared to his well-preserved corpus of writing, much of Su Shi's artwork, of equally important influence, did not survive. A dozen extant calligraphic works and two paintings are credited to him. These works seemingly testify to his aesthetic theory. Su believed that art was to be used as a means to pursue Dao, and that artistic spontaneity can be achieved only after the artist has first internalized rules and skills, and then, at the moment of execution, he sinks into active oblivion and creates in the seeming absence of intentionality. Su Shi's calligraphic works betray a temporality and seem to constitute an extension of their author's existence. His painting theory similarly emphasizes expression rather than representation. His ethical-aesthetics established the foundation for "literati art" that recommends learned simplicity and practiced spontaneity, a style that would fully mature only two centuries later.

Zhiyi YANG
Goethe University Frankfurt am Main

Further Reading

Bol, Peter K. (1982). *"This culture of ours": Intellectual transitions in T'ang and Sung China.* Stanford, CA: Stanford University Press.

Chaffee, John W. (1995). *The thorny gates of learning in Sung China: A social history of examinations.* Albany: State University of New York Press.

Egan, Ronald C. (1994). *Word, image, and deed in the life of Su Shi.* Cambridge, MA: Harvard University Press, Harvard–Yenching Institute Monograph Series.

Fuller, Michael A. (1990). *The road to East Slope: The development of Su Shi's poetic voice.* Stanford, CA: Stanford University Press.

Kong Fanli 孔凡礼. (Ed.). (1982). *Su Shi shiji* 苏轼诗集. Beijing: Zhonghua shuju.

Kong Fanli 孔凡礼. (Ed.). (1986). *Su Shi wenji* 苏轼文集. Beijing: Zhonghua shuju.

Kong Fanli 孔凡礼. (1991). *Su Shi nianpu* 苏轼年谱. Beijing: Zhonghua shuju.

Lin Yutang. (1947). *The gay genius: The life and times of Su Tungpo.* New York: John Day.

Watson, Burton. (1977). *Su Tung-P'o: Selections from a Sung dynasty poet.* New York: Columbia University Press.

Yoshikawa Kōjirō. (1967). *An introduction to Sung Poetry.* (Burton Watson, Trans.) Cambridge, MA: Harvard University Press.

Zou Tongqing 邹同庆 & Wang Zongtang 王宗堂 (Eds.). (2002). *Su Shi ci biannian jiaozhu* 苏轼词编年校注. Beijing: Zhonghua shuju.

Taizong, Emperor (of Song)

Sòng Tàizōng 宋太宗

939–997 CE—Second emperor of the Song dynasty (r. 976–997 CE)

Alternate names: birth name: Zhào Kuāngyì 赵匡义; reign names: Tàipíng xīngguó 太平兴国, Yōngxī 雍熙, Duāngǒng 端拱, Chúnhuà 淳化, Zhìdào 至道

•宋太宗•

Summary

The second emperor of the Song dynasty, Taizong grew up in the military-dominated Five Dynasties and Ten Kingdoms period. In contrast to those tumultuous years, the success of Taizong's reign lay in the unification of his empire, the establishment of fundamental institutions and policies, and the construction of a civil bureaucracy. An avid poet and calligrapher, he also ordered the compilations of three great encyclopedias and patronized the literary arts, which flourished under his reign. His efforts to consolidate the empire prevented the Song from becoming the next short-lived dynasty. With his contributions in the realm of culture, he also established the foundation for the intellectual and artistic flourishing of the Song dynasty.

The second emperor of the Sòng 宋 dynasty (960–1279), Zhao Kuangyi, grew up in the period of political division and social turmoil known as the Five Dynasties and Ten Kingdoms 五代十国 (907–960 CE), in which five dynasties (Later Liang, Later Tang, Later Jin, Later Han, and Later Zhou) rapidly supplanted one another in the north and more than ten regional military regimes were established in the south. Military governors held the political power during these turbulent years, and while it was the goal of the first Song emperor, Zhao's brother Zhào Kuāngyìn 赵匡胤 (927–976 CE), posthumously known as Emperor Tàizǔ 太祖 (r. 960–976 CE), to rectify this political fragmentation, it was during Zhao Kuangyi's reign that reunification of all of the states occurred.

After succeeding his brother to the throne, Zhao Kuangyi (whose posthumous temple name was Tàizōng 太宗) ruled for twenty-one years with the reign names Tàipíng xīngguó 太平兴国, Yōngxī 雍熙, Duāngǒng 端拱, Chúnhuà 淳化, and Zhìdào 至道 in succession. In addition to territorial unification, Zhao Kangyi was also deeply concerned about the centralization of the state and cultural affairs. He established the fundamental institutions and policies of the Song, and shaped China to be a civilian-dominated state by supplanting the military regime of the Five Dynasties and Ten Kingdoms with a civil bureaucracy. His major cultural achievements include the compilations of three great encyclopedias, entitled *Extensive Records of the Taiping Era* (*Tàipíng guǎngjì* 太平广记), *Imperial Readings of the Taiping Era* (*Tàipíng yùlǎn* 太平御览), and *Finest Blossoms in the Garden of Literature* (*Wényuàn yīnghuá* 文苑英华)

Childhood and Youth

Although there are few extant records about the youth of Zhao Kuangyi, he was known to have been born in the Junyi Prefecture of Kaifeng during the reign of the Later Jin, the third son of Zhào Hóngyīn 赵弘殷 (899–956), posthumously honored as Emperor Xuanzu, and Lady Dù 杜氏 (901–961). His father served as a military general under the Later Tang (923–936 CE), Later Jin (936–946 CE), Later Han (947–950 CE), and Later Zhou (951–960 CE) successively. In the Later Zhou period, Zhao Kuangyi's father and elder brother, Zhao Kuangyin, were both in charge of the imperial army.

As with many emperors, legend holds that there were auspicious signs upon Zhao Kuangyi's birth. It was said that his mother dreamed that an immortal endowed her with the sun and she became pregnant; during the night when she gave birth to Zhao Kuangyi, a bright red light flared up and the alley was filled with an extraordinary fragrance. As a child, Zhao Kuangyi was said to be outstanding, also that other children obeyed him from fear when they played together. Later, it was recorded that he became a serious student. When his father occupied counties, instead of demanding treasures, he asked for ancient books and presented them to Zhao Kuangyi. With such encouragement from his father, Zhao Kuangyi came to excel in the literary arts. These characteristics later made him a very different ruler than the military-minded Zhao Kuangyin.

Overthrow of the Later Zhou

Zhao Kuangyi served the Later Zhou in his early years. According to historical records, he played a crucial role in assisting his brother Zhao Kuangyin to usurp the throne by acting as an intermediary between Zhao Kuangyin and the troops in the coup at Chenqiao (*Chénqiáo bīngbiàn* 陈桥兵变) that led to the overthrow of the Later Zhou. Zhao Kuangyi also advised his brother not to harm the citizens during the overthrow, thus ensuring a peaceful and bloodless takeover. Due to inconsistencies in the records, however, some modern scholars doubt the importance of the role that Zhao Kuangyi played during the coup. They argue that it may have been made up by later historians to justify Zhao Kuangyi's succession to the throne.

After the founding of the Song dynasty in 960, Zhao Kuangyin (henceforth referred to as Emperor Taizu) gave Zhao Kuangyi the important position of palace inspectorate general and regent in the capital when Taizu went on military expeditions. Zhao Kuangyi's appointment as the governor of Kaifeng in 961 CE further elevated his status. It was in this position that Zhao Kuangyi took great pains to build up his power. He not only cultivated his own large staff, but also associated closely with the ministers at court. In 973, he was enfeoffed (i.e., given land and a title in exchange for a vow of fealty) as Prince of Jin.

Rise to the Throne

In 976 CE, Taizu died suddenly and Zhao Kuangyi immediately ascended the throne. From the time of the Song up to the present day, there have been disputes about whether Taizu's death was unnatural and why Zhao Kuangyi came to rule rather than Taizu's own sons. While some records implied that Taizu might have succumbed to sudden illness or alcoholism, the most popular version was that Zhao Kuangyi murdered Taizu in order to assume the throne. According to the tradition of primogeniture, Taizu should have been succeeded by his son rather than his brother. By the time of Taizu's death, moreover, his sons had already come of age: Zhào Dézhāo 赵德昭 (951–979 CE) was twenty-six years old, and Zhào Défāng 赵德芳 (959–981 CE) was eighteen years old. Zhao Kuangyi's impatience to change reign title (from Taizu's Kāibǎo 开宝 Reign to his own Taiping xingguo Reign) in the same year of Taizu's death also violated tradition and might imply his anxiety in supplanting Taizu.

Two popular early records concerning Zhao Kuangyi's rise to power can be found in Buddhist monk Wényíng's 文莹 *Inofficial Records from Mt. Xiang* (*Xù Xiāngshān Yělù* 续湘山野录) and the scholar and historian *Sīmǎ Guāng's 司马光 (1019–1086) *Sùshuǐ jìwén* 涑水纪闻. The *Inofficial Records from Mt. Xiang* recorded that Taizu knew that he would die on that snowy night from a prophecy by a Daoist (Taoist) priest, so he hurriedly called Zhao Kuangyi to the palace and drank with him. All the eunuchs and palace maids were asked to be outside, and they could only see that Zhao Kuangyi seemed to decline something

*People marked with an asterisk have entries in this dictionary.

in the shadow of the candlelight. After Taizu struck an axe-shaped tool (it may have been a stationery implement rather than a real axe) against the snow and said to Zhao Kuangyi, "Do it well! Do it well," then Taizu went to sleep, snoring like thunder. During the night, Taizu died. Zhao Kuangyi stayed in the palace and was able to succeed the throne immediately. This account has become known as "The Sound of the Axe in the Shadow of the Flickering Candle" ("Zhúyǐng fǔshěng" 烛影斧声).

In Sima Guang's version of events, Empress Song (952–995), upon hearing of Taizu's death, at once ordered the eunuch Wáng Jì'ēn 王继恩 (d. 999) to call Prince Zhao Defang to the palace. Wang Ji'en, however, thought that Taizu had long before decided to pass his throne to Zhao Kuangyi, and he went instead to Zhao Kuangyi. Empress Song was so shocked when she saw Zhao Kuangyi that she was cowed into accepting his succession. Though this version hints at an alibi for Zhao Kuangyi, it is still problematic. Later in the Southern Song, the *Long Draft of A Continuation of the* Comprehensive Mirror for Aid in Government (*Xù Zīzhì tōngjiàn chángbiān* 续资治通鉴长编, *juan* 17) also adopted these narratives by combining these two contradictory versions.

To further legitimize Zhao Kuangyi's (henceforth referred to as Emperor Taizong) accession, the story of the "golden box promise" ("jīnkuì zhī méng" 金匮之盟) eventually became popular. Recorded in an inconsistent way, two versions of this story prevailed: the one-step succession and the three-step succession. Both indicate that when Empress Dowager Du was on her deathbed in 961, she summoned the imperial advisor Zhào Pǔ 赵普 (922–992) to record her last words. She then asked Taizu why he was able to overthrow the Later Zhou, and pointed out that it was because the Later Zhou Emperor Shizong (Chái Róng 柴荣, r. 954–959) left a child as his heir. In order to avoid falling into the same trap, Empress Dowager Du required Taizu to leave the throne to his younger brother. This one-step succession meant that the throne would pass from Taizu to Taizong, while the three-step version was longer: the throne would pass from Taizu to Taizong to Taizong's younger brother Zhào Tíngměi 赵廷美 (947–984 CE), and only then to Taizu's son Zhao Dezhao. In this way, the Empress Dowager Du would guarantee an adult heir to the throne. She asked Zhao Pu to record this exchange and sign his name to it. The document was then to be kept in a golden box.

Not surprisingly, many modern scholars argue that the "golden box promise" is apocryphal. It was announced publicly only in 981 by Zhao Pu, and was not even mentioned when Taizong ascended to the throne. Since the controversy over his succession seemed to trouble Taizong, it is likely that the story of the promise was fabricated by Zhao Pu and Taizong to finally prove the legitimacy of his rule.

Consolidation of Empire

After witnessing some of the political turmoil of the Five Dynasties and Ten Kingdoms, Taizong strove to centralize the state throughout his reign. He established a civil bureaucracy and worked to reduce threats coming from within and outside of his realm of power.

Centralization of Authority

The foundation of Taizong's civic rule can be summed up like this: "taking preventive measures for everything, and preventing every wrongdoing" 事为之防，曲为之制 (Lamouroux and Deng 2005). This statement comes from Taizong's imperial edict of enthronement and, as the modern scholar Deng Xiaonan has pointed out, it was worshipped as the "Ancestors' Family Instruction" (*zǔzōng jiāfǎ* 祖宗家法) by the later Song emperors. The core of its meaning is precaution, and it emphasized vigilance over any danger or illegal activity in order to guarantee imperial authority. All of Taizong's policies, such as respect for civil officials, control over the military, and restraint of eunuchs and consort families, could be regarded as the embodiments of this statement.

A more concrete explanation of this statement was provided by Taizong: "If a state does not have internal troubles, it must have external worries; if it does not have external worries, it must have internal troubles. The external worries are no more than frontier affairs, all of which can be prevented. Only those treacherous are evil, and if they bring about internal worries, the situation is deeply fearful" (Yáng Yì 杨亿, *Tán yuàn* 谈苑). The precaution against domestic troubles was therefore a primary focus.

In consideration of the frequent army mutinies and regicides in the Five Dynasties and Ten Kingdoms, Taizong attached great importance to the restraint of military governors and the imperial clans. During Taizu's reign, the regional military commissioner (*jiédù shǐ* 节度使) was in charge of both the headquarter prefecture and several subordinate prefectures. Taizong first withdrew all the subordinate prefectures to the central government in 977; then gradually transferred the regional military commissioners to the capital, deprived them of their military power, and changed the *jiedu shi* to an honorific title.

To help control the generals, Taizong recruited and employed civil officials. The policy that "the general should obey the central command" (*jiàng cóng zhōng yù* 将从中御) was also applied by Taizong. He often imposed specific military plans and tactics on the generals who were in command at the frontier, which actually impeded the initiative of the generals. These policies weakened the strength and effectiveness of the Song army, but Taizong's goal to maintain internal stability was indeed achieved. For the duration of the Song dynasty, there were few domestic mutinies led by military governors.

Establishment of Civil Bureaucracy

While he restrained the power of military officials, Taizong also began to construct a civilian-dominated state. As a result, the Song are often considered a dynasty "emphasizing the civil and de-emphasizing the military" (*chóngwén yìwǔ* 崇文抑武). The most direct means to this end was the expansion of the imperial civil service examination system. In the first exam held by Taizong, in 977, a total of 109 people passed the *jìnshì* 进士 exam (presented scholar); during his twenty-one-year reign, 1487 would achieve the degree. In comparison, only 188 achieved the *jinshi* degree during Taizu's reign of seventeen years. Taizong selected a large amount of these *shì* 士 as civil officials, appointing them to positions in central and local government in order to replace military and clerical officials. This greatly raised the status of civil officials; furthermore, they were treated well and promoted rapidly. As scholars Edmund Worthy and Peter Bol point out, it was Taizong who helped bring about the re-emergence of the social class of *shi*. In this way, Taizong managed to establish a civil bureaucracy, which greatly influenced later dynasties.

Territorial Reunification

To centralize his political authority, it was indispensable for Taizong to achieve territorial unification. Taizu had almost subjugated all the kingdoms in the south, with only two regimes left independent. In 978, these two regimes surrendered to the Song without warfare: Chén Hóngjìn 陈洪进 (r. 964–978) gave up the Zhang-Quan area in modern Fujian, and Qián Chù 钱俶 (r. 948–978) submitted the Wu-Yue kingdom (907–978). All of the south was thereby pacified.

Taizong then focused on conquering the Northern Han kingdom (951–979). Both the Later Zhou Emperor Shizong and Taizu had attacked the Northern Han but failed. In 979, Taizong led his expeditionary troops in person. Forces from the Khitan Liao empire (907–1125) came from the north to reinforce their allies, but Taizong defeated them and then besieged the Northern Han capital of Taiyuan. After the ruler of the Northern Han, Liú Jìyuán 刘继元 (r. 968–979), surrendered, Taizong destroyed Taiyuan. The last kingdom in the Five Dynasties and Ten Kingdoms period was then incorporated into the territory of the Song, signaling the end of this period of political division.

Foreign Policy

In his dealings with foreign kingdoms, the most troubling for Taizong was that with the Khitan Liao. The focal point of Song-Liao relations was the ownership of "the Sixteen Prefectures of Yan-Yun" (Yān-Yún shíliù zhōu 燕云十六州), which covered the area from modern Beijing to Datong in Shanxi Province. In 937, Shí Jìngtáng 石敬瑭 (r. 936–942) ceded "the Sixteen Prefectures of Yan-Yun" to the Khitan in order to obtain their support when he founded the dynasty of Later Jin. In order to reclaim this territory, immediately after the victory against the Northern Han in 979, Taizong embarked on a campaign against the Khitan from Taiyuan. Though having an advantage at first and occupying the Zhuo and Yi prefectures easily, the exhausted Song troops failed during the siege of Youzhou (modern Beijing) and were defeated disastrously at the Battle of Gaoliang River. Taizong was even shot in the leg by arrows, and retreated by donkey cart in a panic. Within the same year, the Khitan attacked the Song to take revenge. The Song troops defeated them in the Battle of Mancheng, but in the following years, the Khitan initiated several small-scale battles against the Song, with the strengths of the two sides about equal.

A second large-scale military expedition against the Khitan, known as the Yongxi Northern Campaign, began in 986. Since the newly succeeded Liao emperor Shèngzōng 圣宗 (r. 982–1031) was young and the state affairs were in the charge of the Empress Dowager Xiao (953–1009), Taizong saw this as a new opportunity to seize the "the Sixteen Prefectures of Yan-Yun." This time Taizong stayed at court, sending three large armies to attack the Khitan. The eastern troops, led by Cáo Bīn 曹彬(931–999), were defeated in the Battle of Qigou Pass. Then the western troops, led by Pān Měi 潘美 (925–991) and Yáng Yè 杨业 (d. 986), also lost in the Battle of Chenjia Valley, during which General Yang Ye was captured and later died. The Khitan troops then took advantage of their victories to invade Song territory. The Song were defeated again in the Battle of Junzi Hall. These failures of the Yongxi Northern Campaign forced the Song into a defensive position against the Khitan.

Meanwhile, Taizong was also trying to reincorporate Giao Chỉ (Jiāozhǐ 交趾) or modern-day Vietnam. In 980, he launched an attack against Giao Chỉ, but his armies succumbed at the Battle of Baiteng River. At this point, the Song had to allow for the independence of Giao Chỉ. Toward the northwest in China, dealings with the Tangut also troubled Taizong. Though the Tangut leader, Lǐ Jìpěng 李继捧 (d. 1004), surrendered his land to the Song in 982, his younger brother Lǐ Jìqiān 李继迁 (963–1004) went on to revolt. Though his troops sometimes yielded to the Song, Li Jiqian continued to attack the Song in skirmishes, with the support of the Khitan.

Peasant Uprising

In 993, a peasant uprising broke out in Sichuan Province, the first since the establishment of the Song. Led by a local peasant Wáng Xiǎobō 王小波 (d. 993) with a slogan of equality for the poor and the rich, the uprising soon included tens of thousands of people. After Wang Xiaobo was severely injured and died, his brother-in-law, Lǐ Shùn 李顺 (died c. 994), continued to lead and proclaimed a Dàshǔ 大蜀 state in Chengdu in 994, giving himself the reign title of Yìngyùn 应运. Taizong sent out an army led by the eunuch Wang Ji'en to pacify Chengdu in 994, but it was only in 996 that the last remnants of this uprising were finally terminated.

Restoring Culture

While Taizu had focused on the unification by military forces, Taizong began to pay greater attention to the restoration of culture. He opened libraries and institutes, sponsored the compilation of vast encyclopedias, and promoted the traditional arts of poetry and calligraphy.

Establishment of Libraries and Institutes

The *guǎngé* 馆阁 (libraries and institutes) system started in the Táng 唐 dynasty (618–907 CE) but became prosperous during the Song. When Taizong visited the *sān guǎn* 三馆 (three libraries/institutes including Zhāowén Guǎn 昭文馆, Jíxián Yuàn 集贤院, and Shǐ Guǎn 史馆) in 977, he was dissatisfied with the narrow and humble buildings. He ordered the reconstruction of the *san guan* and incorporated them into an imperial library called the Institute for the Veneration of Literature (Chóngwén Yuàn 崇文院). It is said that Taizong even designed the buildings in person, and that the new Chongwen Yuan was gorgeous. Meanwhile, Taizong began to collect volumes for the institute. He issued an imperial decree to collect books throughout the whole country, and rewarded those who offered their holdings. As a result, the collection in the Chongwen Yuan became plentiful and rich. In 988, Taizong set up the Imperial Archives (Mì Gé 秘阁) in the Chongwen Yuan. The Mi Ge and Chongwen Yuan were known together as the *guange*.

In addition to collecting books, Taizong also strongly encouraged reading. He developed himself as an exemplary reader; the Chinese idiom "Opening the book is always rewarding" (*kāijuàn yǒuyì* 开卷有益) is derived from one of his speeches.

Compilation Projects

Taizong's greatest cultural achievement is the compilation of three enormous encyclopedias: *Extensive Records of the Taiping Era*, *Imperial Readings of the Taiping Era*, and *Finest Blossoms in the Garden of Literature*. In 977, he issued the edict for the compilations of *Imperial Readings of the Taiping Era* and *Extensive Records of the Taiping Era*, and appointed many talented scholars such as Lǐ Fǎng 李昉 (925–996) and Xú Xuàn 徐铉 (917–992) as compilers. *Extensive Records of the Taiping Era* was completed the next year, a large collection of pre-Song stories and tales. It contained 500 *juan*, or scrolls, and was arranged into 92 subject categories. *Imperial Readings of the Taiping Era* (originally titled *Tàipíng Zǒnglèi* 太平总类) was finished in 984. The contents of this general encyclopedia are extensive, with 1,000 *juan* and 55 sections. It is said that Taizong required of himself to read three *juan* of *Imperial Readings of the Taiping Era* each day, and thus finished reading the entire book in one year. When the project was almost completed, Taizong initiated the compilation of *Finest Blossoms in the Garden of Literature*, which was completed in four years. The 1,000-*juan* anthology aimed to be the continuation of the *Wénxuǎn* 文选 by Liang Crown Prince Xiāo Tǒng 萧统 (501–553 CE), and was divided into thirty-eight categories by genre. Included were literary works from the Liang dynasty to the Five Dynasties, though ninety percent of the volume was taken up by Tang works.

These three encyclopedias, together with the *Prime Tortoise of the Record Bureau* (*Cèfǔ yuánguī* 册府元龟) compiled during the reign of his successor, Emperor Zhēnzōng 真宗 (r. 997–1022), were known as the "Four Great Books of the Song" (*Sòng sì dà shū* 宋四大书). Since many original sources that these volumes cited are not extant, they have become a treasury of the pre-Song texts.

Taizong also became the patron of the compilation of *Model Letters in the Imperial Archives in the Chunhua Era* (*Chúnhuà gé tiè* 淳化阁帖). In 992, Taizong provided the imperial collections of ancient calligraphy to the imperial calligrapher Wáng Zhù 王著, and asked him to engrave them into model letters. This 10-*juan* collection is the earliest extant engraved model-letters compendia, regarded as "the ancestor of model letters" (*fǎtiē zhī zǔ* 法帖之祖).

Literary Writing and Calligraphy

Taizong himself was a poet as well as a calligrapher. He was said to have composed at least seven literary collections, but only three are still extant: *Xiāoyáo yǒng* 逍遥咏 (ten *juan*), *Yuán shí* 缘识 (five *juan*), and *Liánhuà xīnlún huíwén jìsòng* 莲华心轮回文偈颂 (twenty-five *juan*). The *Quán Sòng shī* 全宋诗 consisted of 18 *juan* with 562 poems by Taizong, many of which concern poetic interpretations of Daoism and Buddhism; also included were matched poems between Taizong and other literati.

Taizong's calligraphy was well known, and it was recorded that he was especially expert in cursive script and *fēibái* 飞白, a calligraphy style characterized by hollow strokes. Following Taizong's example, several Northern Song emperors also famously practiced *feibai*. The bestowal of *feibai* pieces to ministers became a political means of rewarding and inspiring officials.

Final Years

As Taizong neared the end of his life, the issues that had troubled the beginning of his reign came back to haunt him in the matter of his own succession.

Though the "golden box promise" had supported Taizong's legitimacy, at the same time it qualified Taizong's younger brother Zhao Tingmei, as well as Taizu's two grown-up sons, Zhao Dezhao and Zhao Defang, to be the future successors of Taizong. Though few historical records clearly declare that Taizong intentionally persecuted these successors, their unnatural deaths are indeed problematic. It seemed likely that Taizong plotted against them in order to pave the way for his own sons to ascend to the throne.

When Taizong led the military expedition against the Khitan in 979, Zhao Dezhao was serving in the army. One night, the troops could not find Taizong, and during the ensuing chaos some of the men schemed to support Dezhao as the new emperor. Taizong was not pleased when he heard of this later. Back at the capital, he delayed bestowing rewards for the conquest of the Northern Han on the grounds of the subsequent failure against the Khitan. When Dezhao remonstrated with him, Taizong became furious and said, "When you become the emperor yourself, it won't be too late to reward" 待汝自为之, 赏未晚也. Dezhao was so terrified by Taizu's rebuke that, after going back to his residence, he committed suicide. Two years later, Zhao Defang also died of an unidentified illness.

Though Zhao Tingmei had been elevated to the status of governor of Kaifeng and the Prince of Qin at the beginning of Taizong's reign, he was accused of conspiring for the throne in 982 and was demoted. Exiled to remote Fangzhou in modern-day Hubei Province, he died there in 984. After Tingmei's death, Taizong even claimed that Tingmei was actually his half brother, since he was the son of Taizong's wet nurse, Lady Geng 耿氏. By such means, Taizong ensured that his son would be his heir.

Taizong had nine sons and the eldest among them, Zhào Yuánzuǒ 赵元佐 (965–1027), was highly valued by his father. When Tingmei was accused and exiled, however, Yuanzuo was the only one to defend him. Hearing of Tingmei's subsequent death, Yuanzuo became so resentful that he went mad and often behaved violently. After he set his palace on fire, Taizong demoted his status to that of a commoner.

Taizong then focused on his second son, Zhào Yuánxī 赵元僖 (966–992), and appointed him governor of Kaifeng. Taizong was satisfied with Yuanxi, but in 992 he suddenly died. It's thought that he may have died of poisoning, that his concubine Lady Zhāng 张氏 might have schemed to poison Yuanxi's wife, with Yuanxi mistakenly drinking the poison. Taizong was extremely distressed, but finally installed his third son, Zhào Héng 赵恒 (r. 977–1022, originally named Zhào Yuánkǎn 赵元侃), as the crown prince in 995.

Taizong had suffered arrow wounds during the military expedition against the Khitan in 979, and he finally died of these wounds in 997 and was buried in the Yǒngxī 永熙 tomb. After his death, the eunuch Li Ji'en and Empress Li (960–1004) schemed to make Yuanzuo the emperor. The designated successor, Crown Prince Zhao Heng, posthumously known as Emperor Zhenzong, ascended to the throne only through the efforts of the prime minister, Lǚ Duān 吕端 (935–1000).

Lasting Impact

Taizong's reign was pivotal in making the transition from the military-dominated Five Dynasties and Ten Kingdoms period to the civil bureaucracy of the Song. He may have sprung from the last generation of elites who lived during the Five Dynasties and Ten Kingdoms period, but he went on to found the important and long-lasting institutions and policies of the Song dynasty. He ended a period of division and his great efforts to consolidate the empire prevented the Song from becoming the next short-lived dynasty. With his contributions in the realm of culture, he also established the foundation for the intellectual and artistic flourishing of the Song dynasty.

Yunshuang ZHANG
University of California, Los Angeles

Further Reading

Ang, Melvin Thlick-Len. (1983). Sung-Liao diplomacy in eleventh- and twelfth-century China: A study of the social and political determinants of foreign policy. (Unpublished doctoral dissertation.) University of Pennsylvania.

Bol, Peter K. (1992). *"This culture of ours": Intellectual transitions in T'ang and Sung China*. Stanford, CA: Stanford University Press.

Chaffee, John W. (1999). *Branches of Heaven: A history of the Imperial Clan of Sung China*. Cambridge, MA: Harvard University Asia Center: Distributed by Harvard University Press.

Cheng Kuang-Yu 程光裕. (1972). *Song Taizong dui Liao zhanzheng kao* 宋太宗考. Taipei, Taiwan: Taiwan shangwu yinshuguan,.

Chikusa Masaaki 竺沙雅章. (1975). *Sō no Taiso to Taisō* 宋の太祖と太宗. Tokyo: Shimizu Shoin.

Lamouroux, Christian, & Deng Xiaonan. (2005). The "Ancestors' Family Instructions": Authority and sovereignty in Medieval China. *Journal of Sung-Yuan Studies* 35, 79–97.

Deng Guangming 邓广铭. (1994). Song Taizu Taizong huangwei shoushou wenti bianxi 宋太祖太宗皇位授受问题辨析. *Zhenli zazhi*, 2 (1944). In *Deng Guangming xueshu lunzhu zixuan ji* 邓广铭学术论著自选集. Beijing: Shoudu shifan daxue chubanshe.

Deng Xiaonan 邓小南. (2006). *Zuzong zhi fa: Beisong qianqi zhengzhi shulue* 祖宗之法—北宋前期政治述略. Beijing: Sanlian shudian.

Kurz, Johannes L. (2001). The politics of collecting knowledge: Song Taizong's compilations project. *T'oung Pao 87*(4–5), 289–316.

Lau Nap-yin and Huang K'uan-chung. (2009). Founding and consolidation of the Sung dynasty under T'ai-tsu (960–976), T'ai-tsung (976–997), and Chen-tsung (997–1022). In Denis Twitchett and Paul Jakov Smith (Eds.). *The Cambridge history of China*. Volume 5. *The Sung dynasty and its precursors, 907–1279, Part 1*. Cambridge, UK: Cambridge University Press.

Li Tao 李焘. (2004). *Xu Zizhi tongjian changbian* 续资治通鉴长编 [Long draft of a continuation of the *comprehensive mirror for aid in government*] (*juan 17–42*). Beijing: Zhonghua shuju. (Original work published twelfth century)

Liu Anzhi 刘安志. (1995). Jinnian lai 'zhuying fusheng' yu 'jinkui zhi meng' yanjiu shuping 近年来"烛影斧声"与"金匮之盟"研究述评. *Shixue yuekan*, *1*, 25–28.

Liu Tzu-chien 刘子健 (James T. C. Liu). (1988/1990). Song Taizong yu Songchu liangci cuanwei 宋太宗与宋初两次篡位. *Shihuo yuekan*, *17*(3); *Zhongguo shi yanjiu*, *1*, 156-60.

Liu Tzu-chien 刘子健. (1962). An administrative cycle in Chinese history: The case of Northern Sung Emperors. *The Journal of Asian Studies*, *21*(2), 137–152.

McNair, Amy. (1994). The engraved model-letters compendia of the Song dynasty. *Journal of the American Oriental Society*, *114*(2), 209–225.

Qian Ruoshui 錢若水. (2005) *Taizong shilu* 宋太宗实录 [Veritable Records of Taizong] (*juan* 26–35, 41–45, 76–80). Gansu, China: Gansu renmin chubanshe. (Original work published tenth century)

Qi Xia 漆侠. (1992). Song Taizong Yongxi beifa 宋太宗雍熙北伐. *Heibei Xuekan*, *2*, 79–87.

Rossabi, Morris. (Ed.). (1983). *China among equals: The Middle Kingdom and its neighbors, 10th–14th centuries*. Berkeley: The University of California Press.

Tsang Shui-lung 曾瑞龙. (2003). *Jinglue You-Yan* 经略幽燕：宋辽战争军事灾难的战略分析. Hong Kong: The Chinese University Press.

Tao Jing-shen. (1988). *Two sons of heaven: Studies in Sung-Liao relations*. Tucson: University of Arizona Press.

Tuotuo 脱脱 (Toghto). (1977). *Songshi* 宋史 [History of the Song] (*juan* 4, 5). Beijing: Zhonghua shuju. (Original work published 1345)

Wang Huailing 汪槐龄. (1986). Lun Song Taizong 论宋太宗. *Xueshu Yuekan*, *3*, 61–68.

Wang Ruilai 王瑞来. (1987). Luelun Song Taizong 略论宋太宗. *Shehui Kexue Zhanxian*, *4*, 182–187.

Wang Yuji 王育济. (1993). 'Jinkui zhi meng' zhenwei kao "金匮之盟"真伪考—对一桩学术定案的重新甄别. *Shandong Daxue Xuebao*, *1*, 68–79.

Wang Yuji 王育济. (1994). Song Taizu chuanwei yizhao de faxian jiqi yiyi 宋太祖传位遗诏的发现及其意义. *Wen Shi Zhe*, *2*, 35–42.

Worthy, Edmund H, Jr. (1976). The founding of Sung China, 950–1000: Integrative changes in military and political institutions. (Doctoral dissertation, Princeton University).

Zhang Qifan 张其凡. (1987). Song Taizong lun 宋太宗论. *Lishi Yanjiu*, *2*, 96–109.

Zhang Qifan 张其凡. (1997). *Song Taizong* 宋太宗. Changchun, China: Jilin wenshi chubanshe.

Zhang Yinlin 张荫麟. (1941). Song Taizong jitong kaoshi 宋太宗继统考实. *Wenshi zazhi*, *8*, 26–31.

Wáng Ānshí
王安石

1021–1086—Statesman and reformer; rival of Sima Guang

Summary

Wang Anshi was a leading scholar-official in the Song dynasty who rose to become a chancellor under Emperor Shenzong. Known for his ambitious reform program called the New Policies, Wang sought to reorganize and fully integrate government and society, often removing office-holders opposed to his reforms. Among other innovations, he created the first truly national, government-run school system in human history. While he faced opposition—particularly from Sima Guang, who was taken aback by Wang's aim of removing the distinction between government and society—he is remembered as one of the most influential reformers in Chinese history, one who enjoyed almost unchecked power from the emperor to implement his policy platform. Wang has been utilized by some Chinese officials as a model for modern-day reform.

As a leading statesman in the Sòng 宋 dynasty (960–1279), Wang Anshi rose to serve as a chancellor in the administration of Emperor Shénzōng 神宗 (r. 1067–1085). During this period of service to Shenzong, Wang was given essentially a free hand to create, develop, and implement his own reform program, called the New Policies, which continues to rank as one of the most ambitious reform agendas in Chinese history. Wang's New Policies were far-ranging and sought to be total and universal in their scope, touching on economic, social, political, defense, and cultural policy. Wang's ambitious policy proposals won him supporters but also numerous political enemies, who eventually succeeded in dismantling much of his policies after his death. Nevertheless, Wang is today considered one of the most important reformers in Chinese history.

Early Life and Career

Born in 1021 in Linchuan, located in modern-day Fuzhou, Jiangxi Province, Wang Anshi came from a notable family who represented the new southern elite—educated scholar-officials who regarded southern China as their home and who built and developed their careers there. His family produced eight *jìnshì* 进士 ("presented scholar," the highest degree awarded in the civil service examinations system) from the start of the eleventh century to 1068. His father held local government positions, eventually rising to the post of vice-prefect of Jiangning in modern-day Nanjing, but it was Wang Anshi who became the first official in his family to ascend to a post higher than at the prefectural level.

Wang was born into a time of great cultural and intellectual development. The Song, divided into the Northern Song (960–1127) and the Southern Song (1127–1279), is regarded as a time of civil, sophisticated governance in which emperors did not generally act as depots but rather communicated with and consulted officials. Diversity of opinion at court was largely tolerated—the first Song dynasty emperor, Emperor Tàizǔ 太祖 (927–976), for example, promised never to execute anyone for disagreeing with him and urged later emperors to do the same. It was also a time of the full development of the scholar-official class that was recruited and appointed through the highly competitive civil service examinations; indeed, the Song recruited four to five times more *jinshi* scholar-officials than the Táng 唐 (618–907 CE) dynasty (Ebrey 2006, 160). Many historians consider the Song dynasty to be a period when the Chinese government came closer to matching the Confucian ideal, a time of great intellectual flourishing during which many leading scholars focused their energies on the revival of Confucianism. This eventually led to the development of the Neo-Confucian movement, which sought to imbue Confucianism with certain cosmological, metaphysical, and speculative qualities to supplant Daoism (Taoism) and Buddhism.

The cultural and intellectual renaissance of the Song dynasty notwithstanding, Wang was also born into a world of concern, uneasiness, and crisis. The Song dynasty was no longer the principal and most powerful empire in the region, a status its predecessors such as the Tang and Hàn 汉 (206 BCE–220 CE) dynasties had enjoyed. Rather, it was one state among many. The Song faced constant military threats from bordering peoples, namely the ethnic Khitans of the Liáo 辽 dynasty (916–1125) in the northeast and the Tanguts of the Western Xia Dynasty in the northwest; to deal with these threats, the Song oscillated between appeasement and military action. At court, many scholar-officials were genuinely concerned with improving the strength of the state and bettering the lives of the common people, but it was also a time of political factions as scholar-officials fought over differing reform programs and competed with one another for promotions and career advancement, given the increasing size of the bureaucracy.

In light of these crises and problems faced by the Song, certain officials attempted to push through reform agendas. In the 1040s, an ambitious national reform program was launched by Fàn Zhòngyān 范仲淹 (989–1052), a statesman and author in the Northern Song who served as a chancellor under Emperor Rénzōng 仁宗 (r. 1022–1063). In 1042, Fan submitted a ten-point memorial to the emperor which laid out his various policy proposals. Among his ideas, Fan wanted to reform the bureaucracy by rewarding competent officials and removing ineffectual ones, by reducing favoritism, and by shifting the content of the civil service examinations from poetry writing to practical issues relating to statecraft. Fan also wanted to improve salaries of officials, invest in agricultural development and infrastructure, and create local militias to improve local defense, especially in communities near the frontier-border regions.

Ink painting of Wang Anshi.

Fan's reform agenda met with heavy resistance—many bureaucrats who were weaned on the old system did not want changes to the examinations or personnel management, and the court was suspicious of the proposal to increase the power and strength of the militias, fearing a shift of military power from the center to localities (Mote 1999, 137–138). Eventually, Fan and his supporters were forced out of the capital. Although Fan's reform program failed, an awareness and foundation of reform, as well as a reformist impulse, had been set in place.

Some of Fan's supporters who remained in the central court continued to press for changes in the 1050s and 1060s. Eventually, this reformist spirit would be picked up by Wang Anshi.

This is the political and intellectual context in which Wang began his government career. Wang was a precocious student, placing fourth nationwide in his *jinshi* cohort in 1042. Given his scholarly prowess, he was offered positions in the capital, but he turned them down, choosing instead to serve in local posts in Jiangnan, where he could be closer to his family. In 1047, he served as magistrate of Yin County (modern-day Ningbo), where he devoted much of his attention to agricultural reform, including irrigation and land-reclamation projects, as well as creating an agricultural loan measure which provided farmers with grain during off-seasons and which farmers would pay back, with interest, during the harvest seasons (Smith 2008, 358). In 1058, he was appointed to the judicial intendancy of Jiangnan East circuit. (A circuit was a historical administrative division similar to a province.) This was also the same year Wang sent his "Ten Thousand Word Memorial" ("Wànyán shū" 万言书) to Emperor Renzong, laying out some of his reform ideas for the Chinese state accumulated during his numerous years of experience in local government.

The "Ten Thousand Word Memorial," one of Wang's most well-known writings, explains the various problems faced by the Song Dynasty. Wang laments that scholar-officials have deviated too much from the laws and institutions of the ancient kings and sage-kings. Scholar-officials themselves, according to Wang, were being selected not on their practical experience in state affairs but instead on literary ability (a concern shared by Fan Zhongyan). Wang himself was sympathetic to Fan's reforms, and he was also very close to one of Fan Zhongyan's allies, *Ōuyáng Xiū 欧阳修 (1007–1072), another leading statesman and author of the Song dynasty who had provided Wang with recommendations during the early part of his career. Wang's submission of the "Ten Thousand Word Memorial" brought him much fame, and he eventually was appointed to various positions in the capital, serving as a staff supervisor in the Finance Commission and as a draft official in the Secretariat. Wang remained in the capital until 1063, when his mother died and he returned to Jiangning for filial mourning. Wang's experience in local government, dealing with practical problems on a daily basis, would inform his later career and policy decisions.

Rise to Power and the New Policies

When the twenty-year old Emperor Shénzōng 神宗 (r. 1067–1085) ascended

*People marked with an asterisk have entries in this dictionary.

to the throne in 1067, he chose Wang as his chief advisor, appointing Wang as the vice chief councilor in charge of administration (Wang would eventually serve as the sole chief chancellor from 1075); in addition, ancillary officials friendly to Wang's ideas were also appointed. The young emperor delegated much power to Wang and gave him immense latitude to implement his reform agenda. Wang, in turn, sought to push through his ambitious reform program, collectively known as the New Policies (*xīnfǎ* 新法).

Theoretical Foundations of the New Policies

Wang based his New Policies on the classic canonical texts of the Chinese tradition, as well as on the actions of the sage-kings in Chinese antiquity. In particular, Wang focused much of his attention on *The Rituals of Zhou (Zhōulǐ* 周礼), a text believed to date from the fourth to third century BCE which purportedly sets forth the structure of the government of the Zhōu 周 dynasty (1045–256 BCE). Wang believed there was a universal system for the organization of state and society and that such a system could be discovered through the careful study and analysis of the classic texts and antiquity. He was not proposing that actions or models from Chinese antiquity should simply be applied mechanically in his time; rather, his goal was to discover and adapt the general principles expressed in the classic texts and the government institutions of the sage kings to the present situation. Wang sought to reorganize society on all levels, in particular the relationship between government and society, to match such principles. This was the theoretical foundation on which Wang based his New Policies.

The New Policies in Action

Wang's New Policies can be divided broadly into three groups: first, policies concerning state finance, trade, and the economy; second, policies concerning defense and social order; and third, policies concerning education and the civil service examinations (Mote 1999; Liu 1959). In the first group, those policies concerning state finance, trade, and the economy, Wang wanted to reduce unnecessary waste, increase economic efficiency, and increase the state's revenue. To achieve this, Wang focused on the common people and their economic situation, believing that they formed the basis of the state economy. Among Wang's first reforms was his restructuring of the makers of fiscal policy: Wang ordered that the Finance Planning Commission would be the sole institution to formulate and carry out the New Policies, taking authority away from the Finance Commission and the Council of State. He appointed investigating commissioners to conduct local inspections and provide policy recommendations, relying on young, lower-ranking officials. Wang also launched new government trade policies, creating offices to replace wealthy merchants as wholesalers, encouraging buying from and selling to smaller merchants, and instituting government loans to small merchants (Bol 1993, 169). Wang also abolished required local labor service in which the richest families had to undertake certain bureaucratic functions, such as collecting taxes, because the government lacked manpower and resources. Instead, Wang instituted a hired-service policy, so that a tax incurred on households would subsequently be used to hire personnel (Bol 1993, 169).

Wang also implemented numerous agricultural reforms, which, no doubt, can be traced to his previous agricultural work as magistrate of Yin County. In particular, the government provided "green shoot" loans of cash or grain to farmers at the time of sowing, which the farmers would pay back, at 20 percent interest, at the time of harvest (Lin 1934). Wang also ordered that land be resurveyed to make land taxes more equitable and expanded state monopolies on wine, tea, and salt (Ebrey 2006, 164). Although many of Wang's reforms in this area have a populist flavor to them, it is probably not fully accurate to say that Wang was driven to enact these economic reforms due to a populist bent. Wang was first and foremost motivated by his desire to strengthen the power of the state and state economy, and he saw attending to the needs of the common people and integrating them into government as the most effective way of realizing his desires.

Among Wang's second group of policies, those concerning defense and social order, the most well-known is the tithing (*bǎojiǎ* 保甲) policy. Households were organized into groups of ten, fifty, and five hundred; each household with two or more adult males would supply one who would receive training as a militiaman (Bol 1993, 168). These groups would be responsible for maintaining collective order and security within their communities and to form local militia corps to strengthen local defense. The *baojia* policy, perhaps more than any other of Wang's New Policies, most clearly represented Wang's desire to fully integrate government and society. He wanted to make farmers soldiers, not only because it was less expensive than keeping professional soldier regiments, but also to enhance the loyalty of the local population to the state. In Wang's view, these local residents, ideally, would eventually fulfill certain roles for the benefit of the state (in addition to serving as militia); indeed, by 1075, militia units were also helping the Song dynasty collect taxes and administering "green shoots" loans in their local communities (Bol, 176). In addition to the *baojia* policies, Wang also proposed methods for breeding more military horses by the frontier and enhancing military training to protect the Song state from its neighbors (Mote 1999, 140).

In Wang's third group of policies, those concerning education and the civil service examinations, he was spurred on by his belief that scholar-officials were being hired based on their literary rather than their governing talent. Wang reformed the civil service examination system by dropping various fields and promoting one single *jinshi* examination. He abolished the test on poetry; candidates instead would write on the classics and also prepare policy proposals (Bol 1993, 169). Tests in military, law, and medicine were also established to increase the range of practical expertise among the *jinshi* candidates. He also created the first truly national, government-run school system in human history. Wang's goal in this was to eventually turn over the civil service examinations to this graded school system, which would award degree certification after students passed the appropriate examinations (Mote 1999, 141). At the foundation of his educational reforms, Wang promoted a national, standardized curriculum, establishing a bureau for commentaries on the classics. Students preparing for the civil service examinations and studying in schools would have to learn the official commentaries to the classics that Wang himself had prepared.

Opposition to the New Policies

Wang's New Policies were polarizing. His "green sprouts" loans policy angered wealthy, landed families who had traditionally provided loans to farmers in their districts and who would foreclose on the farmers' land if they were unable to repay. His *baojia* policy also was seen as a threat by these wealthy families who traditionally wielded all the power and influence in their local areas. The hired service policy drew the ire of households who previously had control over local government through their providing of personnel. The established elite was suspicious of Wang's land resurveying reforms, and his educational and civil service reforms were controversial with many scholar-officials who had gotten ahead in their careers based on the old civil service examinations system. Wang, who represented the new elite from South China, was also disliked by the old Northern elite.

The primary leader of the anti-Wang faction (also known as the conservative faction) was *Sīmǎ Guāng 司马光 (1019–1086), a leading statesman in the Song Dynasty who would later serve as a prime minister in the court of Emperor Zhézōng 哲宗 (r. 1086–1101). Sima and his followers were taken aback by the New Policies and their aim of removing the distinction between government and society. For Sima, the state was best analogized as a static building—people are the foundation on which government is built, while proper hierarchy is maintained and clearly differentiated. Government and society were to be separated, as this would best preserve social stability. For Sima, there was no need to replace and rebuild the building, as Wang wanted to do; stability would be preserved by maintaining the existing building structure. Regarding the education system, Sima continued to prefer the recommendation system over Wang's examination policies, where candidates would be hired into government service largely based on the recommendations of existing officials (Bol 1993, 179).

Wang also faced resistance from *Sū Shì 苏轼 (1037–1101), a Song dynasty statesman and one of greatest writers in Chinese literary history. A renaissance man who excelled in writing prose, poetry, art, and gastronomy, Su was a relativist who detested what he saw as Wang's (and also Sima's) intense devotion to certain ideology and dogmas. For Su, literature and art—not political ideology—provided the best route to cultivation and good governance; independence of thought and the preservation of individualism was key.

Facing opposition from these various quarters, Wang was politically ruthless and sought to eliminate dissent to his New Policies, removing those who opposed him and his reforms from their offices.

Fall from Power and Later Life

In 1074, a famine struck north China that drove many farmers off their land; Wang and his "green shoots" loans policy were blamed and slandered at court. He was then appointed prefect at Jiangning by Emperor Shenzong, although he was asked back to serve in the court in 1075. The political environment was too vitriolic, however, as the anti-Wang faction continued to attack him and his policies. In 1076, Wang returned to Jiangning, where he remained and pursued literary endeavors until his death in 1086. After Emperor Shenzong's death, the empress dowager took power as regent for the nine-year-old Emperor Zhezong (r. 1086–1101). The empress dowager implemented anti-Wang policies and over the next eight years dismantled Wang's New Policies. After Zhezong was old enough to take power, he reinstated Wang's policies and hired a pro-Wang bureaucracy (Mote 1999, 142). The next ruler, Emperor Huīzōng 徽宗 (r. 1100–1126), generally agreed with Wang's policies, even banning the writings of Sima Guang and Su Shi (Ebrey 2006, 164), but his administration was marked by corrupt officials who further tarnished the reputation of the New Policies. Huizong's reign came to an end with the invasion by the Jurchens (originally a tribe of the Liao who later rebelled to form its own Jin Dynasty), which marked the end of the Northern Song. Following Huizong's death, Wang's New Policies essentially died out (Mote, 207).

Legacy

After his death, Wang generally did not have a very good reputation among later generations of Confucian scholar-officials.

He has continued to be influential in Chinese history, however. He was admired by many Chinese reformers in the late Qing dynasty and the early Republican period, such as *Liáng Qǐchāo 梁启超 (1873–1929), a Chinese scholar, philosopher, and reformer active in the late Qing, who wrote a full-length biography of Wang. Wang's thought and emphasis on the common people also influenced *Sun Yat-sen 孙中山 (1866–1925), the founder of the Nationalist Party (Guomindang, GMD) and the Republic of China. *Chiang Kai-shek 蔣介石 (1887–1975), the leader of the Nationalists after Sun, was also an admirer of Wang and adopted the *baojia* system. In the People's Republic of China, Wang has been traditionally portrayed as a good progressive, to be contrasted with Sima Guang, who has been portrayed as a bad conservative. In the past few decades, there have been more views; some mainland Chinese historians have attacked both Wang and Sima as representing the old feudal state against the interests of the people (Bol 1993, 135). Other historians have presented more nuanced views, eschewing traditional assessments of Wang and instead analyzing the New Policies and why they did not ultimately succeed.

Regardless of the varying views of Wang and his New Policies, one thing can be agreed upon: Wang arguably continues to be as polarizing and as important a figure today as he was during his lifetime. Given growing calls to address the growing problem of corruption and inefficacy in the Chinese Communist Party today, Wang has been utilized by some Chinese officials and also political commentators as a model and point of reference for modern-day reform.

Norman P. HO
University of Hong Kong

Further Reading

Bol, Peter K. (1993). Government, society, and state: On the political visions of Ssu-ma Kuang and Wang An-shih. In Robert P. Hymes & Conrad Schirokauer (Eds.), *Ordering the world: Approaches to state and society in Sung dynasty China*. Berkeley: University of California Press.

Bol, Peter K. (1992). *"This culture of ours": Intellectual transitions in T'ang and Sung China*. Stanford, CA: Stanford University Press.

de Bary, William Theodore, & Irene Bloom (Comp.). (1999). *Sources of Chinese tradition, Vol. 1: From earliest times to 1600* (2nd ed.). New York: Columbia University Press.

Ebrey, Patricia Buckley; Walthall, Anne; & Palais, James B. (2006). *East Asia: A cultural, social, and political history*. Boston: Houghton Mifflin Company.

Ebrey, Patricia Buckley. (1996). *The Cambridge illustrated history of China*. Cambridge, UK: Cambridge University Press.

Gracie, Carrie. (2012). Wang Anshi: The reformer beaten by the Mandarins. Retrieved August 24, 2012, from http://www.bbc.co.uk/news/magazine-19962432

Liang Qichao 梁启超. (2009). *Wang Anshi zhuan.* 王安石傳 [*Wang Anshi: A biography*] (Xie Xizhang

解璽璋, Ed.). Xi'an, China: Shaanxi shifan daxue chubanshe.

Lin Yu. (1934). Wang An-shish and his time. *The China Critic*. *10*(1), 10–12.

Liu, James T. C. (1959). *Reform in Sung China: Wang An-shish (1021–1086) and his new policies*. Cambridge, MA: Harvard University Press.

Mote, F. W. (1999). *Imperial China (900–1800)*. Cambridge, MA: Harvard University Press.

Smith, Paul Jakov. (2008). Shen-Tsung's reign and the new policies of Wang An-Shih, 1067–1086. In Denis Twitchett & Paul Jakov Smith (Eds.), *The Cambridge history of China (Volume 5, Part 1): The Sung dynasty and its precursors (907–1279)*. Cambridge, UK: Cambridge University Press.

Wei Xiaohong 魏曉虹 (Ed.). (2008). *Wang Anshi ji*. 王安石集 [A collection of writings by Wang Anshi]. Taiyuan, China: San jin chubanshe.

Williamson, Henry Raymond. (1973). *Wang An-Shih: A Chinese statesman and educationalist of the Sung dynasty*. Westport, CT: Hyperion Press.

Zhang Fan 張帆. (2001). *Zhongguo gudai jianshi* 中國古代簡史 [A Concise history of ancient China]. Beijing: Beijing daxue chubanshe.

Yuè Fēi
岳飞

1103–1142—Military leader

Summary

Yue Fei was a Song-dynasty military hero who fought against the invading Jurchen tribe from Manchuria during the early twelfth century. The troops under his command were famous for not plundering the villages they passed during battles, and were not allowed to accept gifts from local villages they had cleared of bandits and turncoats. He was praised after his death for his bravery and unwavering loyalty to the imperial court. Changes to the story of Yue Fei during the Ming and Qing dynasties illustrate developments in Chinese national identity and the ways in which historical memory can be manipulated. In the course of the twentieth century, Yue developed into one of the most famous historical figures and national heroes in Chinese history.

Yue Fei was the son of a farmer and a well-known fighter even in his youth. He was born in Tāngyīn 汤阴, in the prefecture Xiāngzhōu 相州 in today's Henan Province. When he participated in the imperial military examination in the capital, he defeated all other competitors and even turned down a rich reward offered by Cài Guì 蔡桂, the Prince of Liang, for renouncing his chance for a military degree. Yue's refusal to do so led to a private duel that resulted in the accidental killing of the prince. Yue was forced to flee from Kaifeng and shortly afterwards joined the Song army. Yue became famous for his combat skills as well as his military leadership, which played a significant role in hostilities between the Sòng 宋 dynasty and the invading Jurchen (Nǚzhēn 女真). The fighting resulted in the Song rulers and citizens retreating south, where the Southern Song 南宋 (1127–1279) dynasty was established. (The Song dynasty is divided into the Northern Song 北宋 [960–1127] and Southern Song based upon this migration and relocation of the state's capital.)

The Jurchen, a Tungusic tribe from northeast China (today's Heilongjiang Province), were the ancestors of the Manchu, who would go on to found the Qīng 清 dynasty in 1644. Historical accounts first mention them in 1069, and in the ensuing decades they enjoyed a quick rise, both militarily and politically. This resulted in the founding of the Jīn 金 dynasty (1125–1234) when the tribal leader Aguda proclaimed himself emperor of the Jin in Harbin and declared war on the neighboring Khitan (Qìdān 契丹) people (rulers of the Liáo 辽 dynasty, 916–1125). In 1120, the Jurchen joined forces with the Song dynasty rulers, and in 1122, the armies of both the Song and the Jin attacked the Liao Empire. The Jurchen were accepted as the overlords in northern China by the Xià 夏 in 1124 (when the Xia declared themselves vassals of the Jin), and by Korea in 1126. Shortly after the defeat of the Liao in 1125, the Jurchen broke their alliance with the Song and advanced to the provinces of Henan and Shandong. When they entered Kāifēng 开封, the capital of Song dynasty China, they took into custody both Emperor Huīzōng 徽宗 (r. 1100–1126) and his son Qīnzōng 钦宗, together with three thousand members of the imperial family (ending the Northern Song period). Prince Kāng 康, who would become Emperor Gāozōng 高宗 (r. 1127–1162, d. 1187), avoided capture and remained in southern China. At that time, the Song just managed to escape its demise, and continued to face a militarily superior opponent unwilling to accept the existence of the neighboring Song state in the south.

While the early twelfth century attacks by the Khitan Liao army never went further than the valley of the Huang (Yellow) River, the Jurchen destroyed most cities in the Yangzi (Chang) River valley and northern Zhejiang Province. In February 1126, they surrounded the Song capital Kaifeng, demanding that an imperial prince participate in peace negotiations in their camp. Emperor Qinzong asked his younger brother, Prince Kang, if he was willing to do so. The prince complied, but it was soon suspected in the camp that he was not the real successor of Emperor Huizong (who had stepped down in January 1126), and accordingly he was—at the demands of the Jurchen—replaced by another imperial prince. He thus escaped detention and returned to Kaifeng.

When Prince Kang departed for negotiations in December 1126, Chinese regional military officials—disappointed with the resistance of the Song against the invasion—convinced him en route that it would be wiser to join them and lead the resistance, whereby he became the nominal commander of all military forces in north China at the young age of twenty. When the Jurchen repeatedly attacked Kaifeng, Prince Kang moved his headquarters from place to place in the provinces of Hebei, Henan, and Shandong, thereby evading the enemy's attempts to capture him. His mobile court was under the management of Lǐ Gāng 李纲 (1083–1140), who commanded most of the local troops of 100,000 men that were eager to resist the Jurchen. Li Gang had been a prominent official, a grand secretary, and prefect of the capital city before the Northern Song collapsed. He favored an aggressive policy toward the Jurchen Jin, but due to the weak and shaky support of the emperor (even if the emperor was eager to ensure the population's continuous loyal support of military resistance), Li was soon forced out of the government by his political enemies.

By mid-1127, the Jurchen did not want to postpone their return to Manchuria, so left Kaifeng without having subjugated the Song. When returning to their homeland, they took with them—next to the precious loot from the Song palaces—Emperor Huizong and his eldest son, the later Emperor Qinzong, to Harbin where they remained in imprisonment. Both would never return to southern China: Huizong died in 1135, and Qinzong in 1161 in Manchuria.

In the years 1129–1130, the Jurchen armies returned to the south, crossed the Yangzi River, and advanced to Nanjing and Hangzhou, but withdrew due to heavy resistance. At that time, Yue Fei marched together with the vice-governor of Kaifeng, Dù Chōng 杜充 (d. 1141), to the south, after Yue had joined the fight against the invaders in 1126 under the commander of Xiangzhou near his home. At the same time, Prince Kang travelled through Xiangzhou while on his second mission as peace envoy, but did not complete the trip after the intervention of regional military officials who counseled that it would be wiser to resist than to negotiate. His change of attitude toward the Jurchen Jin is often assumed to be one of the reasons why Yue joined the resistance, even though the historical sources do not mention a meeting between them.

In the following years, Yue established a private army comprising more than 1,000 soldiers that served Liú Jia 刘韐 (1067–1127) whom he had joined forces with in 1122. Yue remained in Kaifeng during 1128 and early 1129 (after the Jurchen Jin had withdrawn to the north in 1127), until he was stationed in Jiànkāng 建康 (today's Nanjing). He drove back the advancing troops that were in pursuit of the Song emperor in 1129–1130, after which his reputation grew and he received numerous titles and commendations.

In 1131, he led his troops together with Zhāng Jùn 张俊 (1068–1154) to the Yangzi River to protect the region against attacks of the Jurchen military leader Tàlǎn 挞懒 (d. 1139). At that time, Yue defeated the troops of Lǐ Chéng 李成. Zhang Jun was summoned to the court, while he remained at the military headquarters in Jiāngzhōu 江州. With thousands of volunteer soldiers, Yue

Statue of a kneeling Qin Hui. Photo by Marc A. Matten.

successfully recaptured the fortress of Xiāngyáng 襄阳 at the Han River (Hànjiāng 汉江) in 1134/1135, and drove back the Jurchen along with their vassal Liú Yù 刘豫 (1073–1143).

By that time, Yue had already become a powerful warlord who commanded a large army of 30,000 elite soldiers. He then absorbed the naval forces of Yáng Yāo 杨幺, as well as about 50,000 defeated rebel troops, which made his "Yue family army" (*Yuè jiājūn* 岳家军), as it was commonly called, one of the most potent forces of the Southern Song. In 1138, when the Song founded their new capital in Hangzhou, and when Yue was on the verge of recapturing the former capital Kaifeng, Emperor Gaozong decided to negotiate peace with the Jurchen. Knowing that Yue Fei refused to engage in peace negotiations because he considered the Jurchen untrustworthy, the chancellor Qín Huì 秦桧 (1090–1155) convinced the Emperor to order Yue to withdraw his troops, and proposed to replace the Song generals with civilian commanders. In the late summer of 1140, Yue went to the court in Hangzhou and unsuccessfully protested against these plans. He received a new command one year later, but his success in driving back the Jurchen Jin led to a new order to withdraw, this time by sending an envoy to the front line that carried twelve golden medals (*shí'èr jīnzì pái* 十二金字牌), thus making the order inviolable and offering Yue no possibility to act in opposition. According to the *History of the Song Dynasty* (*Sòngshǐ* 宋史), he wept and wailed that the efforts of ten years were forfeit in one instance (*Shí nián zhī lì, fèi yú yīdàn* 十年之力, 废于一旦). The reason for the emperor to be obliged to do this was that the Jurchen Jin had told Qin Hui that Yue Fei had to be killed before peace negotiations started, and Qin convinced Gaozong that Yue had to be imprisoned for insubordination and malfeasance, because Yue was said to have remained in contact with his troops after having been removed from command. In the end, Yue Fei was killed in prison without having been properly trialed.

The negotiations resulted in an agreement with the Jurchen Jin that became the Treaty of Shaoxing 绍兴和议 in 1142. The treaty stated that the emperors of both dynasties coexist (defining the Song emperor as the elder brother of the Jin ruler), and that the Song had the duty to deliver yearly tribute payments to the Jin that were equal to the earlier tributes paid to the Liao. Traditional historiography reports that the decision to negotiate peace was influenced by Qin Hui, who was invested in peace negotiations based on personal interests aimed at maintaining his powerful post and profitable land. In order to be able to implement the treaty, it was necessary to get rid of those who were arguing for a continuation of war, among them the generals Hán Shìzhōng 韩世忠 (1089–1151), Zhāng Jùn 张俊 (1097–1164), and Yue Fei. Han and Zhang accepted bribes in the form of promotion to higher posts beyond direct troop command, but Yue—known for his incorruptibility—could not be bribed. Consequently, in 1142, Qin Hui had Yue falsely accused of treason and poisoned, which was the result of a plan devised by his wife Lady Wáng 王氏 as reported in a later novel entitled *Crime Plotted at the Eastern Window* (*Dōngchuāng shìfàn* 东窗事犯). His death was—as the legend tells—mourned throughout the whole country.

In 1161, Emperor Gaozong revoked the imprisonment of the families of Yue Fei and General Zhāng Xiàn 张宪, who had been executed together with Yue. His successor, Emperor Xiàozōng 孝宗 (1127–1194, r. 1162–1189) revoked the death sentence in 1162, presumably to appease public discontent. Additionally, Yue's body was moved to a formal tomb in the Zhìguǒ Temple 智果寺 (Temple of Wisdom) in Jiànmén Lǐnglǚ Tàishān 剑门岭履泰山, today's Xixiáling 栖霞岭, near West Lake 西湖 in Hangzhou. The tombs of Yue Fei and his son, Yuè Yún 岳云, are faced by four statues of approximately a meter in height that are depicted kneeling with their hands cuffed at their backs. Later historical accounts made these four persons responsible for removing Yue from his command, ending hostilities with the Jurchen, and finally sentencing Yue to death (thereby leading to the demise of the Southern Song dynasty). These persons were Qin Hui and his wife, who had convinced her husband to execute Yue; Judge Mòqí Xiè 万俟卨, who sentenced Yue Fei to death; and General Zhang Jun, who served under Yue, but withdrew his troops on orders of Qin Hui, which facilitated the advance of the Jurchen to the south. Judge Moqi had been a replacement for Zhōu Sānwèi 周三畏, who refused to hold the trial after seeing the tattoo on Yue's back: "to serve the country with utmost loyalty" (*jīngzhōng bàoguó* 精忠报国).

These statues did not exist when Zhiguo Temple was founded in 1221. Only in 1513 did the provincial governor of Zhejiang, Lǐ Lóng 李隆, order the casting of statues of Qin Hui, his wife, and Moqi Xie (Zhang Jun was added later). At that time, it was common practice among temple visitors to spit on the statues and otherwise maltreat them (as still happens today). This treatment caused the bronze statues to fall apart, so new statues were cast in 1594 (this time from iron). When the new statues disappeared a few years later, the commissioner of justice of the province of Zhejiang, Fàn Lái 范來, financed new ones and erected them opposite Yue Fei's tomb in 1602. In the ensuing centuries, the statues were regularly destroyed and re-erected in accordance with developments in the historical assessment of Yue Fei's story. The current statues date from 1979.

Assessment of Yue Fei in Ming and Qing Dynasties

Starting with the biographies of Yue Fei composed in the late Song dynasty, the first official biography was written sixty years after Yue's death by his grandson Yuè Kē 岳珂 (b. 1183). Later historical accounts made a great contribution in developing Yue Fei into a storybook hero, even allowing for the inclusion of mythic elements into the historical works. A central element of the hero narrative was the obvious opposition of a noble-minded and loyal fighter such as Yue and his treacherous enemy Qin Hui. History depicts Yue as a physically strong and honest man who valued righteousness and justice (the troops under his command were well known for not plundering and looting in the villages they passed during the battles, and were not even allowed to accept gifts from local villages they had cleared of bandits and turncoats). The biographies praise the discipline among his soldiers and his unshakable loyalty that was propagated by making use of flags that bore scriptures such as "the utmost loyal Yue Fei" (*jīngzhōng Yuè Fēi* 精忠岳飞). Qin Hui, on the other hand, appeared as a treacherous civil servant whose intrigues prevented Yue's final victory.

Because historiography in traditional China was not merely an act of describing what had happened, but also had a moral function in guiding human behavior in the eyes of the official historian whose duty it was to bestow praise and blame to the events of the past, it comes as no surprise that the biographies focus more on the figure of Qin Hui than on the fight against the invading Jurchen. Such a perspective continued to exist during the following Yuán 元 dynasty (1279–1368). The Yuan dynasty was founded by the Mongol leader *Khubilai (Qubilai) Khan 忽必烈汗 (1215–1294), so the new rulers were understandably interested in downplaying the conflict between the Chinese and the Jurchen—and of course the Mongols—because a discussion on this topic, and the implied celebration of opposition to foreign rule, would have put their legitimacy into question (after all, Khubilai Khan had established the Yuan dynasty after he had successfully conquered the territories of the Southern

*People marked with an asterisk have entries in this dictionary.

Song dynasty in the wake of his defeat of the Jin). For the same reason, Yue Fei is mentioned in the *History of the Song Dynasty*, but without explicitly referring to the conflict between the Chinese and the Jurchen Jin. The history simply reports that the Song dynasty collapsed due to the intrigue of Qin Hui and the capitulation of Emperor Gaozong on these accounts.

The conflict between the Han Chinese and the Jurchen was understood as an ethnic one only since the fifteenth century, when the founder of the Ming dynasty, Zhū Yuánzhāng 朱元璋 (1328–1398; r. 1368–1398 under the reign name of *Emperor Hóngwǔ 洪武), referenced the slogan "Exile the Mongols and Restore China" (*qū zhú Húlǔhuīfù Zhōnghuá* 驱逐胡虏恢复中华). This slogan seems to suggest that ethnic and/or racial categories were important when defining Chinese as a nationality. Initially, Zhu did not consider this question relevant: for him, the Mongols were part of China, and therefore ethnic and/or racial distinctions were negligible, and the figure of Yue Fei inconsequential. This changed in 1449 when the Crisis of Tumubao broke out (Tǔmùbǎo zhī biàn 土木堡之变; also known as the Tumu Crisis 土木之变), which greatly resembled the rebellion that took place during the reign of Emperor Gaozong when Mongol soldiers penetrated Chinese territory. The crisis, in which battle against Mongol soldiers led to the most severe military catastrophe of the Ming dynasty, and the abduction of Emperor Zhèngtǒng 正统, very soon led to the renewed popularity of Yue Fei: temples were built for him, poems composed, theater pieces written, and literary accounts published. Yue was mostly described as a frugal man who kept strict discipline among his soldiers, attached little value to wealth, and was concerned about the well-being of the people. The corrupt soldiers and generals of the Ming lacked these particular characteristics.

Scholarly discussion regarding the historical narrative of Yue Fei, as well as the literary treatment of his biography and influence, developed constantly during the Ming. The *Yongle Encyclopedia* (*Yǒnglè Dàdiǎn* 永乐大典, commissioned by *Emperor Yǒnglè 永乐 in 1403) mentions literary pieces such as *The Conspiracy Committed by the Imperial Tutor Qin at the Eastern Window* (*Qín tàishī dōngchuāng shìfàn* 秦太师东窗事犯); the *Flag of Utmost Loyalty* (*Jīngzhōngqí* 精忠旗), which was composed by Féng Mènglóng 冯梦龙 (1574–1645); and *The Romance of the Song Dynasty Revival* (*Dà sòng zhōngxīng tōngsú yǎnyì* 大宋中兴通俗演义), written by Xióng Dàmù 熊大木 in 1552. In the center of these presentations of Yue are still either his military activities or the intrigue of Qin Hui. Yue appears as a victim and his moral virtues are in the spotlight.

During the Qing dynasty, the official attitude toward Yue Fei became problematic. The Manchurian government was a government of foreign rulers that descended from the Jurchen, and as such, could not keep Yue in the official pantheon. At the same time, they could not change public opinion that continued to consider Yue an important role model. This view was propagated in public works such as the drama *Telling the Complete Biography of Yue Fei* (*Shuō yuè quán zhuàn* 说岳全传; date of publication unknown, either 1684 or 1744), which was composed by Qián Cǎi 钱彩, and enjoyed a broad circulation. In order to resolve this problem, Manchurian Qing rulers such as *Emperor Yōngzhèng 雍正 (1678–1735, r. 1722–1735) and *Qiánlóng 乾隆 (1711–1799, r. 1735–1795) emphasized the moral value of loyalty embodied by Yue, and thus were still able to harness his powerful symbolic capital. It was therefore necessary to suppress aspects of the historic narrative (particularly the fight against the Jurchen, which, ironically, had initiated Yue's strong sense of loyalty as well as his fighting spirit) without downplaying the intrinsic value of loyalty as a moral duty for all subjects of the Qing.

The "Creation" of Yue Fei as a National Hero

During the Qing dynasty, Yue Fei was not only a hero of the Han Chinese, but also a hero of the Manchus. When nationalist

Statue of Yue Fei in Hangzhao, China. Photo by Marc A. Matten.

sentiment began to rise in the years after the First Sino-Japanese War (1894–1895), the universal acceptance of the values embodied by Yue Fei was questioned. From this point until 1912 (i.e., the end of Qing rule), the story of Yue Fei was temporarily interpreted in a purely racial sense. This happened for two reasons: first, the influx of social Darwinism and other related ideologies that stressed race and racial descent as the most meaningful category in the determination of power and survival; and second, the growing criticism of the Qing dynasty as unable to implement necessary reforms. Consequently, Yue Fei became a national hero (*mínzú yīngxióng* 民族英雄) of the anti-Manchu movement and was understood as a symbol of the new nation-state to be established.

Although this reinterpretation of Yue Fei was based on traditional values like loyalty and steadfastness, his representation as a national hero was a successful recasting that proved to be useful in the fight against the foreign Manchu rulers of the Qing dynasty. This became obvious in numerous academic, revolutionary, and literary publications that appeared starting in 1903, notably "The First Chinese Nationalist: A Biographical Account of Yue Fei" ("Zhōngguó mínzú zhǔyì dì yī rén Yuè Fēi zhuàn" 中国民族主义第一 人岳飞传), published in the journal *Húběi Xuéshēng Jiè* 湖北学生界, which depicted Yue as the first national hero of China. In 1906, the poet Jiǎng Zhìyóu 蔣智由 (1866–1929) published an article titled "On the Psychology of the Chinese Worship of Yue Fei" ("Lùn Zhōngguórén chóngbài Yuè Fēi zhī xīnlǐ" 论中国人崇拜岳飞之心理) in the journal *Xīnmín Cóngbào* 新民丛报 that tries to analyze the reasons why the Chinese worship Yue and his spirit. Jiang argued that according to the findings of the contemporary Japanese historian Ichimura Sanjirō, traditional biographies of Yue like that in the *Official History of the Song Dynasty* should not be considered reliable sources due to many contradictions contained therein.

The only approach to understanding the historic figure of Yue Fei would therefore be to have a closer look at the nonmaterial reasons for his worship. In 1904, the scholars *Chén Dúxiù 陈独秀 (1879–1942; one of the founding fathers of the Chinese Communist Party), and Bó Wénwèi 柏文蔚 (1876–1947; a leading military figure in the Republican Era), founded the King-Yue-Society (*Yuèwánghuì* 岳王会) in Anhui Province. This revolutionary society propagated heroism and patriotism, and aimed at fighting against the autocratic Qing government.

After the successful Xinhai revolution 辛亥革命 in 1911 that resulted in the destruction of the Qing dynasty and the establishment of the Republic of China 中华民国 (1912–1949), the propagation of Yue Fei as a national hero became problematic because the new republic established on 1 January 1912 had to reintegrate the nationalities of the Mongols, Manchus, Tibetans, and Hui, in order to maintain territorial integrity. Yue Fei had to be reimagined as a non-ethnic national hero that could serve the necessities of a nation of five ethnicities (*wǔzǔ gònghé* 五祖共和). This process posed a considerable challenge for the multiethnic Republic of China. The historical drama writer Gǔ Jiànlù 谷剑鹿 described this struggle in his 1936 drama *The Death of Yue Fei* (*Yuè Fēi zhī sǐ* 岳飞之死). Gu stated that while Yue was intensively used as a historic role model in the fight against Japanese aggression:

> . . . It is irrefutable that it [the performance of this drama] is a very ungrateful job. If I characterize the figure of Yue Fei being too loyal, he resembles a national hero and this enables people to criticize me as a lackey of nationalism. Of course, there are also people who regard Yue as a military leader (like me when writing this piece) and want to repeat the past with a new and progressive worldview. This is surely the best intention, but what is the attitude of society towards Yue Fei? Would it not be better to characterize him otherwise, instead of being insulted as a lackey of nationalism? How could I accept such an ungrateful job? (Gu 1936, 12–13.)

The problem Gu mentions here is the fact that, writing in the twentieth century, Yue Fei has always been considered a national hero of the Chinese nation, but actually was a national hero of the Han Chinese who in the twelfth century fought against ethnic groups that were now part of China. If Yue's fight against the Jurchen Jin was emphasized too strongly in twentieth century China, it would do harm to national unity, and as such the application of the term *minzu yingxiong* should be reconsidered. It is questionable how far the term national hero can be dismissed if Yue Fei shall still be an important symbol for China today and in the future. If this is to be communicated successfully, the narrative of Yue Fei has to be made less contradictory and less politicized.

In late 2002, an attempt to depict Yue Fei's deeds in a politically correct context without reference to the term *minzu yingxiong* failed. In the winter of 2002–2003, the People's Education Press published a new guideline for history education in middle schools that emphasized that Yue Fei can no longer be worshipped as a distinct national hero (*minzu yingxiong*):

> Only outstanding persons like Qi Jiguang and Zheng Chenggong who fought against invaders from outside can be called national heroes. Outstanding persons like Yue Fei and Wen Tianxiang, although they have surely played an important role in the fight against ethnic exploitation and suppression, cannot be called national heroes. (Wang 2002)

It was argued that veneration of Yue Fei as a national hero (*minzu yingxiong*) would do harm to national solidarity (*mínzú tuánjié* 民族团结) and offend ethnic minorities, which historically were his enemies. Reports in the media strongly rejected this postmodern reinterpretation of Yue because it seemed on the one hand to diminish the importance of Yue's historic deeds, and on the other hand to distort history as it was customarily taught. The debate even went so far that Mongols and Manchus engaged in the discussion, and themselves criticized the new guidelines as distorting history. There were two major points of criticism. First, Yue had fought as a representative of the Southern Song dynasty against the Jurchen in order to maintain the independence and freedom of the Song state. Second, in the early twelfth century, there were already ethnic groups living in Song China for whom Yue also fought, thus he would not solely be a hero of the Han, but a hero of the multiethnic Chinese nation-state of the Song dynasty—who was later also venerated by the Mongols and Manchus. The unison of criticism finally led to a revision of the guideline. A representative of the Ministry of Education in Beijing stated in a press conference that the historic judgment on Yue would remain untouched. Possible reinterpretations of the national hero that had briefly been discussed were of a purely academic nature, and were not intended to be taught in school. Thus, Yue Fei maintained his classification of celebrated national hero without dishonoring the multiethnic Chinese nation-state or its history.

Marc A. MATTEN
Friedrich-Alexander-Universität Erlangen-Nürnberg

Further Reading

Anonymous. (1903). Zhongguo minzuzhuyi diyi ren Yue Fei zhuan 中國民族主義第一人岳飛傳 [The first Chinese nationalist—A biographical account of Yue Fei]. *Hubei Xueshengjie*.

Chida Daisuke 千田大介. (1997). Gaku Hi koji no hensen wo megutte—Chinkon monogatari kara eiyū monogatari e 岳飛故事の変遷をめぐって—鎮魂物語から英雄物語へ [On the Changes of the Yue Fei Story—From a requiem to a hero's saga]. *Chūgoku Bungaku Kenkyū*, *23*, 52–65.

Du Yingtao 杜穎陶. (1957). *Yue Fei gushi xiqu shuochang ji* 岳飛故事戲曲說唱集 [Collection of dramas and songs on the story of Yue Fei]. Shanghai: Gudian wenxue chubanshe.

Gu Jianlu 谷劍鹿. (1936). *Yue Fei zhi si* 岳飛之死 [The death of Yue Fei]. Shanghai: Zhonghua shuju.

Huang Donglan 黄东兰. (2004). Yue Fei miao: Chuangzao gonggong jiyi de chang 岳飞庙: 创造公共记忆的场 [The temple of Yue Fei: Creating a place of public memory]. In Sun Jiang 孙江 (Ed.), Shijian, *jiyi, xushu* 事件, 记忆, 叙述. [Event, memory, narrative]. Hangzhou, China: Zhejiang renmin chubanshe.

Ichimura Sanjirō 市村瓚次郎. (1904). Gaku Hi no panshi ni tsukite 岳飛の班師に就きて [On Yue Fei's withdrawal of his troops]. *Shigaku Zasshi 15*(2), 1–15; *15*(3), 42–51.

Jiang Zhiyou 蔣智由. (1906.) Lun Zhongguoren chongbai Yue Fei zhi xinli 論中國人崇拜岳飛之心理 [On the psychology of the Chinese worship of Yue Fei]. *Xinmin Congbao*, 72.

Kasai Naomi 笠井直美. (2002). Wareware no kyōkai—Gaku Hi koji no tsūzoku bungei no gensetsu ni okeru kokka to minzoku われわれの境界—岳飛故事の通俗文藝の言説における国家と民族. *Gengo Bunka Ronshū*, *23*(2), 13–48; *24*(1), 35–76.

Liu, James T. C. (1972). Yüeh Fei (1103–41) and China's heritage of loyalty. *The Journal of Asian Studies*, *31*(2), 291–297.

Matten, Marc Andre. (2009). *Die Grenzen des Chinesischen. Nationale Identitätsstiftung im China des 20. Jahrhunderts* [Borders of Chineseness—Creation of national identity in 20th century China]. Wiesbaden, Germany: Harrassowitz.

Matten, Marc Andre. (2011). The worship of General Yue Fei (1103–1142) and his problematic creation as a national hero in twentieth century China. *Frontiers of History in China*, *6*(1), 74–94.

Sun Jiang 孫江, & Huang Donglan 黄東蘭. (2004). Yue Fei xushu, gonggong jiyi yu guozu renting 岳飛敍述，公共記憶與國族認同 [The narrative of Yue Fei: Public memory and national identity]. *Ershiyi Shiji 86*, 89–100.

Wang En 王恩. (2005). *Yue Fei mumiao* 岳飞墓庙 [The tomb and temple of Yue Fei]. Hangzhou, China: Xinhua shudian.

Wang Xuejin 王学进. (2002). Pinglun: Cong Yue Fei Wen Tianxiang bu zai shi minzu yingxiong shuoqi 评论：从岳飞文天祥不再是“民族英雄”说起 [Commentary: Talking of Yue Fei and Wen Tianxiang no longer being national heroes]. *Jiangnan shibao*, 9 December 2002.

Wilhelm, Hellmut. (1962). From myth to myth: The case of Yüeh Fei's biography. In Arthur Wright & Denis Twitchett (Eds.), *Confucian personalities* (pp. 146–161). Stanford, CA: Stanford University Press.

Zhū Xī
朱熹

1130–1200 CE—Neo-Confucian scholar, philosopher, and official

Alternate names: courtesy names: Yuánhuì 元晦, Zhònghuì 仲晦; posthumous title: Wén 文, State Duke of Hui 徽国公

•朱熹•

Summary

Zhu Xi was a great thinker and educator in the Southern Song dynasty who synthesized a new system of Confucianism known in the West as Neo-Confucianism. A famous story told about him relates that one day when he was five years old, his father pointed to the sky and said, "That is sky." The young child's response was "What is beyond the sky?" His lifelong contribution to opening new horizons for Confucian orthodoxy as a scholar, philosopher, commentator, educator, and official has made him an exemplar of sincere and critical scholarship. He was also an official who realized the importance of the unity of theory and practice.

Zhu Xi was a great thinker of the Sòng 宋 dynasty (960–1279). A passionate commentator who re-consolidated the value of the Confucian classics, he was also an educator who exemplified the Neo-Confucian learning and reading curriculum he had worked to put into place. He was also an official who realized the importance of the unity of theory and practice, although the terms in which he actually held several official positions were very short. Even though there might be different attitudes of evaluation, no one would deny that he was one of the most influential philosophers. His philosophical system has been dominant in East Asian philosophy, politics, culture, and education.

His Life

The standard resources on the life stories of Zhu Xi are the *Record of Master Zhu's Life* (*Zhūzi xíngzhuàng* 朱子行状), written by Huáng Gàn 黄榦 (1152–1221 CE), one of Zhu Xi's best disciples and his son-in-law; the *History of the Song* (*Sòngshǐ* 宋史); and the *Chronological*

Biography of Master Zhu (*Zhūzi niánpǔ* 朱子年谱), written by Wáng Màohóng 王懋竑 (1168–1741 CE). As with most biographies of great historical figures, which contain stories that demonstrate greatness and talents at young ages, these records contain some interesting stories of Zhu Xi's youth. There are three particular stories about him that are the most famous: 1) One day when Zhu Xi was five years old, his father pointed to the sky and said, "That is sky." This young child's response was "What is beyond the sky?" 2) When Zhu Xi read the *Classic of Filial Piety* (*Xiàojīng* 孝经), he evaluated the book and wrote on a tree: "If one does not live in this way, one is not a man." 3) One day Zhu Xi was playing in a sandpit with a group of boys. He alone was writing something in the sand with his fingers. What he wrote was the eight trigrams (*bāguà* 八卦) of the *Classic of Changes* (*I Ching* or *Yìjīng* 易经). These three episodes demonstrate that already in his youth he showed the possibility of becoming a sincere Confucian scholar. They also demonstrate his philosophical curiosity and talents.

Although the surroundings of his youth were not quite desirable in an economic sense, they offered good opportunities for his education. In 1130, Zhu Xi was born in Youqi in the Fujian province, where his family was staying temporarily. His father, Zhū Sōng 朱松, was the first family member in three generations who served as an official. He was also a renowned poet and scholar, and held several official positions in both the central and local government of the Southern Song 南宋 dynasty. In 1140, Zhu Song was forced to resign from the positions of assistant director in the ministry of personnel and collator in the bureau of history, due to his opposition against the peace treaty led by Qín Huì's 秦桧 party. Zhu Song then retreated to Jianyang county, finally moving to the southern part of Jian'an. From this time, Zhu Xi learned from his father, but this home education didn't last long. In 1143, his father died at the age of forty-seven. He requested Liú Zǐyǔ 刘子羽 (Liu Zihui's brother), who was a retired high official and rich landowner, to take care of his family. Following his father's wish, Zhu Xi studied under Liú Zǐhuī 刘子翚 (1101–1147 CE), Liú Miǎnzhī 刘勉之 (1091–1149 CE), who later became Zhu Xi's father-in-law), and Hú Xiàn 胡宪 (1086–1162 CE), who were withdrawn but still great scholars. Although Zhu Xi never attended an official school system during his teenage years, he was fortunate to have stayed and studied with these scholars. There are no concrete records that show exactly what Zhu Xi studied with them, but it should be pointed out that he was influenced by the common characteristics of these three teachers, such as experience of the vicissitudes of the government and political powers, the secluded life, and the interest in Chán 禅 Buddhism (Zen in Japanese) and Daoism (Taoism).

Like many scholars of the day who were attracted by the simplicity of Chan Buddhist teaching, these teachers understood that the Confucian Dao (*dào* 道) and Chan Buddhist teachings had a great deal in common. Influenced by the life and scholarship of these teachers, Zhu Xi, who was a sensitive teenager, became interested in Chan Buddhism. After he had conversations with Dàoqiān 道谦, a leading Chan master of the day, he was even more attracted by Chan teachings. This was evident in his *jìnshì* 进士 degree (presented scholar) examination, where he submitted an answer that was inspired by Chan teachings. Although he thoroughly read the Confucian classics, his reading was not to prepare for any civil examination. At this time he set up his life's goal for not merely becoming a successful official, but mainly for becoming a sage. In 1148, at the age of eighteen, he passed the *jinshi* examination. He ranked 228 out of 330 examinees, which was impressive considering his age—he was one of only five successful eighteen-year-old examinees.

In 1151, he was appointed as Keeper of Records (*zhǔbù* 主簿) at Tong'an in South Fujian, and worked between the years 1153 and 1158. As a young and meticulous official, he worked in accounting and tax management. He also kept tax officials from possible usurpations. It is important to note that he always worked in the defense of the poor, against possible corruptions of officials and rich merchants. He also worked for school administration. He often invited famous scholars to the schools, and he rebuilt a library so that anyone could access the stored books.

When he was moving toward Tong-an, in 1153, Zhu Xi experienced an important moment in his life. He visited Lǐ Yánpíng 李延平 (1088–1163 CE), who had been highly regarded by Zhu Xi's father. Li, with Zhu Xi's father, learned from Luó Cōngyàn 罗从彦 (1072–1135 CE). Luo's teacher was Yáng Shí 杨时 (1053–1135 CE), who was a student of the Cheng brothers (*Chéng Hào 程颢 [1032–1085 CE] and Chéng Yí 程颐 [1033–1107 CE]). Li Yan-ping taught Zhu Xi about the Confucian classics and the difference between Confucianism and Buddhism, and he advised Zhu Xi to focus on the practice of Confucian teaching in daily life. His teaching motivated Zhu Xi to turn his attention to Confucianism and away from his interest in Chan Buddhism. Zhu Xi met with him in 1158, 1160, and 1162. In 1160 and 1162, he, as one of Li's disciples, was there to learn the teachings for months. In 1163, Li died, but his teachings, such as embodiment and recognition (*tǐrèn* 体认) of the unaroused state (*wèifā* 未发) of the mind-heart by quiet-sitting (*jìngzuò* 静坐), became important resources and questions of Zhu Xi's philosophical system. Zhu Xi recorded his learning with Li in the *Questions and Answers with Yanping* (*Yánpíng dáwèn* 延平答问).

---

*People marked with an asterisk have entries in this dictionary.

Zhu Xi also had important relationships with two other scholars during these years. In 1155, he met Lǚ Zǔqiān 吕祖谦 (1137–1181 CE), who was a renowned scholar and official of the day. He later edited the book *Reflections on Things at Hand* (*Jìnsī lù* 近思录) with Zhu Xi, and broadened Zhu Xi's relationships with other leading scholars of the day, including Lù Xiàngshān 陆象山 (personal name is Jiǔyuān 九渊 [1139–1193 CE]), who is often grouped with *Wáng Yángmíng 王阳明 (1472–1529 CE) as leading "School of Mind" thinkers.

In 1163, when Zhu Xi was summoned by Emperor Xiozong and stayed at Lín'ān 临安 (modern-day Hangzhou), he heard about Li Yanping's death, and met Zhāng Shì 张栻 (1133–1180 CE), who was a scholar of the School of Hunan 湖南学. Through discussions with Zhang Shi and other scholars in the School of Hunan, Zhu Xi interpreted the implication of *zhōnghé* 中和 (equilibrium and harmony) and the *wēifā* 未发/*yǐfā* 已发 (unaroused/aroused) state of the mind-heart. He also established his "old theory of *zhonghe*" (*zhōnghé jiǔshuō* 中和旧说) in which he understood nature as *tǐ* 体 (substance) and the mind-heart as *yòng* 用 (function). He continued to examine his old theory of *zhonghe*, and, in 1169, constructed his "new theory of *zhonghe*" and the unaroused/aroused (*zhōnghé xīnshuō* 中和新说), in which he interpreted the mind-heart as embracing and commending nature and emotions (*xīntǒng xìngqíng* 心统性情), with nature as *ti* and emotions as *yong*. He developed his new theory with the notion of *jìng* 敬 (reverence, seriousness, reverential attention) as a core idea of self-cultivation.

In 1175, Zhu Xi, with Lu Zuqian, compiled important statements of the preceding Neo-Confucians in the Northern Song 北宋, which they interpreted as the most important passages demonstrating the Neo-Confucian visions. The result is the book *Reflections on Things at Hand*. Lu Zuqian also prepared a meeting with Zhu Xi and the Lu brothers (Lù Jiǔlíng 陆九龄 and Lu Xiangshan) at É Hú Sì 鹅湖寺 (Goose Lake Temple). Although Lu Zuqian suggested this meeting with the hope that they would have a meaningful discussion and reconcile the keen difference between their theories, it resulted in a reconfirmation of the difference between their philosophical perspectives through their exchanged poems. Especially on the issue of inquiry and study (*dàowènxué* 道问学) and honoring the moral nature (*zǔndéxìng* 存德性) in the *Zhongyong* (chap. 27), Lu Xiangshan maintained the priority of honoring the moral nature. Zhu Xi regarded both of them as equally necessary, but focused more on the importance of inquiry and study.

In 1179, Zhu Xi finally accepted the appointment of prefect/governor in Nánkāng 南康 after he had refused the position several times. During this term, he built a memorial hall for Zhōu Dūnyí 周敦颐 (1017–1073 CE), a scholar of the School of the Way (*Dàoxué* 道学) in the

Northern Song, and rebuilt the Academy of White Deer Grotto (*Bái Lù Dòng Shūyuàn* 白鹿洞书院), where he educated students himself. In 1181, he opened a granary market for helping people. In 1180, Zhu Xi's respected friend, Zhang Shi, and Lu Xingshan's brother, Lu Jiuling, both died. In the second month of 1181, Lu Xiangshan visited Zhu Xi to request that he write an epitaph for the tomb of his brother. Zhu Xi invited Lu to deliver a lecture for his students at the Academy of White Deer Grotto while he was there. Lu Xingshan lectured on righteousness and profit (*Analects* 4.16). The lecture, summarized by Lu Xiangshan himself upon Zhu Xi's request, was recorded and carved on stone. In the same year, another of Zhu Xi's long-term friends, Lu Zuqian, died. Since 1178, he had requested to be appointed as a temple guardianship, but the request was still not accepted.

Although Zhu Xi suffered greatly from the loss of his mother (1169) and wife (1176), during the ten years before he accepted the position of governor in Nankang, his production of scholarly works peaked. He published the majority of his works in this period. These works include *Surviving Works of the Two Chengs* (*Èr Chéng yíshū* 二程遗书, 1168), *Additional Works of the Two Chengs* (*Èr Chéng wàishū* 二程外书, 1173), *Essentials of the Analects and the Mencius* (*Lún Měng jīngyì* 论孟精义, 1172), *Explanation of Zhang Zai's Western Inscription* (*Xīmíng jiěyì* 西铭解义, 1172), *Commentaries of Zhou Dun-yi's the Diagram of the Supreme Ultimate Explained* (*Tàijítú Shuōjiě* 太极图说解, 1173), *Explanation of Zhou Dunyi's Interpretation of the Book of Changes* (*Tōngshū jiě* 通书解, 1173), and the aforementioned *Reflections on Things at Hand* (1175).

He was able to continue writing his passionate scholarly works by requesting sinecure positions. In 1190, as a result of his long-term strenuous study and commentary works, Zhu Xi published the *Collection of Commentaries on the Four Books* (*Sìshū Zhāngjū jízhù* 四书章句集注). He added the Four Books (Sìshū 四书)—the *Analects* (*Lúnyǔ* 论语), the *Méngzi* 孟子, the *Doctrine of the Mean* (*Zhōngyōng* 中庸), and the *Great Learning* (*Dàxué* 大学)—to the Five Classics, that is, the *Classic of Changes* (*I Ching* or *Yìjīng* 易经), the *Classic of Poetry* (*Shījīng* 诗经), the *Classic of Documents* (*Shūjīng* 书经), the *Records of Rituals* (*Lǐjì* 礼记), and the *Spring and Autumn Annals* (*Chūnqiū* 春秋), which had been regarded as the core Confucian classics. Zhu Xi set up these four books with his commentaries as the core textbooks of the Confucian learning curriculum.

Throughout his whole life, the time he actually held official positions was very short (around nine years). He declined numerous positions including (since the term of governor of Nankang) a position in the imperial archives (1181), judicial intendant of Jiangnan West (1182), director of the army ministry (1188), assistant regional finance commissioner of Jinghu South (1191), and pacification and planning commissioner of Guangnan West (1192).

While he held official positions, however, he attempted to complete his services in diverse and revolutionary ways. For example, besides his service as keeper of records at Tong'an and governor of Nankang, in 1181, when he was appointed as superintendent for ever-normal granaries, tea, and salt in Eastern Liangzhe, he enforced the system of a community granary (*shècāng* 社仓) so that peasants could get grain loans at a low rate of interest. In 1190 and 1191, when he took the position of prefect of Zhangzhou, he attempted to renovate the system of taxation and land, and even impeached himself because an ordered measure of land was not completed. In addition, his commitment to the realization of the Confucian ideals and his political conviction against the policy of peace with Jīn 金 had been expressed through three sealed memorials to the emperor and three audiences with the emperor.

Instead of pursuing political power and fame, Zhu Xi repeatedly requested the position of temple guardianship because such a sinecure would allow him to focus more on scholarly works. On the other hand, it seems that, from his own experiences based on the cases of his father, teachers, and colleagues, he worried that ever-changing political situations could keep a Confucian scholar from commitment to a true realization of the Confucian vision. His worry came true. In 1182, he impeached Táng Zhòngyóu 唐仲友 (1135–1187 CE) for his corruption in office. Because Tang was the prefect of Taizhou and a relative of the prime minister, he was supported by many officials in the government who had high political power and were close with the prime minister. For this reason, Zhu Xi became a target of their political attacks. In 1194, Zhu Xi was recommended to be lecturer-in-waiting at court by the prime minister, Zhào Rǔyú 赵汝愚 (1140–1196 CE), and he lectured the *Great Learning* for Emperor Níngzōng 宁宗. Because his lecture contained an attack against Hán Tuózhòu 韩侂胄 (1152–1207 CE), who was an ambitious imperial relative, he sparked the political conflict between Zhao Ruyu and Han Tuozhou. Consequently, Zhu Xi, Zhao Ruyu, and even defenders of them were removed from the government. When Zhao died, Zhu Xi wrote a memorial for him that contained his defense of Zhao with his critique of the despotism of some officials, but he decided not to send it because of a divination, which even led him to change his literary name to Dùn Wēng 遯翁.

The political group of supporters of Han Tuozhou continued to attack Zhu Xi and the scholars of *Daoxue* in more severe ways. In 1196, the investigating censor Shěn Jìzǔ 沈继祖, who held the position because he criticized the teaching of Cheng Yi and led the proscription of *Daoxue* as *wěixué* 伪学 (false learning), impeached Zhu Xi for ten crimes, including *weixue*. The letter for impeaching Zhu Xi was originally written by Hú Hóng 胡纮

(1105–1161 CE), who, as investigating censor before Shen Ji-zu, had impeached Zhao Ruyu and moved to the position of vice-president of imperial sacrifice. Hu couldn't impeach Zhu Xi as a result of the new position. In 1196, even Cài Yuándìng 蔡元定 (1135–1198 CE), whom Zhu Xi respected as his friend even though he was one of his disciples, was exiled to Daozhou.

Through these historical facts, it is clear that, before and after his death, in the vortex of political struggles, Zhu Xi's lifelong efforts toward reconsolidation of the Confucian vision were attacked and dishonored by the government's denouncement of his teaching as *weixue*. Fortunately, after Han Tuozhou was executed in 1207 because of his political failure in dealing with Jin, the political atmosphere then changed so that political attacks against *Daoxue* became weak.

By his own record of later life, Zhu Xi revealed that he was suffering from many diseases, but because he was truly a sincere and diligent scholar he tried to revise the chapter of sincerity and will of the *Great Learning* a few days before he died. In 1209, Zhu Xi was finally honored by being given the posthumous title of Wén 文. In 1230, he was given the title of State Duke of Hui 徽国公, and his tablet was placed in the Confucian temple in 1241.

His Philosophy

The scholarly works Zhu Xi completed in his life covered a wide range of disciplines such as philosophy, literature, history, education, and commentaries, in which he demonstrated his strenuous, rigorous, and critical attitude toward learning, writing, and teaching. After he died, his teaching and discussions with disciples and colleagues were collected in 140 chapters of *Classified Conversations of Master Zhu* (*Zhūzǐ yǔlèi* 朱子语类, 1270) and in 121 chapters of *Collected Literary Works of Master Zhu* (*Zhūzǐ wénjì* 朱子文集, 1532). Selected excerpts from these two works were compiled in the *Supplement to the Reflections on Things at Hand* (*Xù Jìnsī lù* 续近思录, 1710) and in 66 chapters of *Complete Works of Master Zhu* (*Zhūzǐ quánshū* 朱子全书, 1714). Through these numerous resources we can grasp how he systemized and consolidated the Confucian vision in a new way by inheriting the so-called *Dàotǒng* 道统 (the orthodox transmission line of the Confucian *Dao* between Yao and Shun, *Confucius 孔子, *Mencius 孟子, and the Cheng brothers) and synthesizing his predecessors' key concepts, such as Zhou Dunyi's *tàijí* 太极 (supreme ultimate), Zhāng Zǎi's 张载 (1020–1077 CE) *qì* 气 (material force, matter-energy), and the Cheng brothers' *lǐ* 理 (principle, pattern, coherence). He thus completed a new system of Confucianism known in the West as Neo-Confucianism.

One of Zhu Xi's major contributions to Neo-Confucianism was his construction of a sound metaphysical foundation, on which he accounted for the goodness of human nature, the origin of evil, and the need of self-cultivation. The key notions in his metaphysics are *li* and *qi*. He claimed that everything in the world is composite of *li* and *qi*. In order to clarify the relationship between *li* and *qi*, Zhu Xi accepted Cheng Yi's notion of two realms, "above/before physical form (*xíng ér shàng* 形而上)" and "within/after physical form (*xíng ér xià* 形而下)." The notion of *li*, which belongs to the realm of *xing er shang*, means both the rule/law by which a thing should be and the reason it should be so. Zhu Xi also incorporated Zhang Zai's concept of *qi* as the basic element of reality. The notion of *qi*, which belongs to the realm of *xing er xia*, embraces both psychological and physical aspects, which constitute all things in this universe. The difference between human beings and other things, and between different characters and talents of human beings, is due to the different quality and purity of their *qi*.

Zhu Xi emphasized that *li* and *qi* shouldn't be separated or alloyed. When we talk and think about *li* and *qi*, they seem to be distinguishable, but they are not separable in reality. *Li* exists right in *qi*. Without *qi*, *li* has nothing to adhere to. As many commentators agreed, however, *li* may be considered to be logically prior, while *qi* may be considered ontologically fundamental. For further elaboration, he interpreted Zhou Dunyi's idea of *taiji* as *li* of Heaven and Earth and the myriad things. Each of the myriad things has been endowed with *taiji* and each in itself possesses *taiji* in its completeness. So *taiji* is one universal *li* and, at the same time, each individual *li*. In this sense, Zhu Xi accepted Cheng Yi's statement that *li* is only one and its manifestations in things are many (理一分殊). For a better explanation of this claim, Zhu Xi borrowed an analogy that was originally a doctrine of the Huàyán 华严 school of Buddhism: "there is only one moon in the sky, but because its light is scattered on different rivers and lakes, there can be seen many moons" (Zhu 1994, chap. 94, sec. 203). It does not mean, however, that the moon has been split.

Zhu Xi's notions of *li* and *qi* as metaphysical foundation serve mainly for his ethical perspective. *Li* is not only a cosmological order or pattern, but also a normative principle. Therefore, Zhu Xi felt no conflict in defining *li* as moral goodness, and the question of moral badness, evil, or failure was discussed only in terms of *qi*. This aspect also affected his way of dealing with human beings. Concerning human beings and human mind-heart (*xīn* 心), Zhu Xi used the word, *xìng* 性 (nature). *Li* is considered to be the original human nature and the concrete embodiment of the Way, and *qi* constitutes human psychophysical form. The different capabilities and characters of human beings are due to the different turbidity and purity of the *qi* that they receive. Such a relationship between human nature and *qi* was also expressed by the distinction between the original nature (*běnrán zhī xìng* 本然之性) and the nature that is in each endowed (*qìzhì zhī xìng* 气质之性). His analogy of a precious pearl immersed in impure water represents well the original goodness of human nature and potentiality of badness by *qi*. He also examined the human mind-heart in terms of the quality and purity of *qi*. The mind-heart is the most refined and refreshing part of *qi*.

In order to grasp the system of Zhu Xi's Neo-Confucian moral philosophy, it is necessary to understand his view of the relationship between human nature, mind-heart, emotions (*qíng* 情), and self-cultivation in terms of the *li-qi* foundation. Before he established his matured new theory of *zhonghe*, he was struggling to understand the notion of *zhong* (equilibrium, centrality), *he* (harmony), *weifa* (unaroused), and *yifa* (aroused), the states of the human mind-heart in the *Doctrine of the Mean* in terms of self-cultivation. Concerning these issues, he remembered that, following the way of meditation suggested by one of his teachers, Li Yan-ping, he had attempted to practice quiet-sitting in order to experience the equilibrium in the *weifa* state of the mind-heart, which was not successful. Later, through discussions with Zhang Shi, who learned from Hu Hong and thus was a scholar in the School of Hunan 湖南学派, he understood the implication of *xìng tǐ xīn yòng* 性体心用 (nature is substance and the mind-heart is function). Unlike Li Yan-ping, who highly regarded the unaroused state and meditation as a way of experiencing the unaroused state, one of the main claims by Chang Shi and the School of Hunan is that the aroused state is more important because it is only the aroused state that we actually experience in daily life. Thus, we need to examine the beginning of our conscientiousness first, and then preserve and extend it. Following Zhang Shi's ideas, Zhu Xi completed his old theory of *zhonghe*, which was developed in his four letters sent to Zhang Shi between 1166 and 1167. In his old theory of *zhonghe*, he identified the unaroused state as nature and the aroused state as the mind-heart, by accepting Zhang Shi's claim of *xing ti xin yong*. The unaroused state was understood to be present in the aroused state. Therefore, there is no need for quiet-sitting as a way to seek the unaroused state.

In 1169, when Zhu Xi had a discussion with Cai Yuanding, he found some mistakes in the works of Cheng Yi and thus realized that, although his old theory of *zhonghe* works for the relationship of human nature and mind-heart, it does not fit for the meaning of the unaroused and aroused because there is no foundation (本领) on which one practices self-cultivation in daily life. If the mind-heart is regarded only as the aroused state, then it is not possible to realize self-cultivation before the mind-heart is in the aroused state, which may lead to problems. In his new theory of *zhonghe* he recognized nature as *ti* and the unaroused state, and emotions as *yong* and the *yifa* state (性体情用). In other words, whereas nature means the state before activity begins (*wèidòng* 未动) and thus it is passive, the emotions are the state after activity has started (*yǐdòng* 已动) and thus they are active. The mind-heart is now regarded as embracing and commending the nature and emotions, and thus are both passive and active.

With his new theory of *zhonghe*, he interpreted one of the Confucian core ideas, *rén* 仁 (benevolence, human-heartedness, humanity), as the character/virtue of the mind-heart (*xín zhī dé* 心之德) and *li* of the specific emotion, love (*ài zhī lǐ* 爱之理). In the same way, he read Mencius' concept of four beginnings or sprouts (the feeling of commiseration, shame and dislike, modesty and yielding, the sense of right and wrong) as the manifestation of the mind-heart and the corresponding core virtues (*rén* 仁, *yì* 义 righteousness, *lì* 礼 propriety, *zhì* 智 wisdom) as nature. Zhu Xi also supported the Confucian conviction of the connection of Heaven and human beings by reinterpreting the notion of *ren* as the mind of Heaven and Earth that produces things. This new theory of the unaroused and aroused state and his interpretation of four beginnings and seven emotions with the *li-qi* foundation have been an important resource for the much later long and active Four-Seven debate (四端七情论), developed by Korean Neo-Confucians such as Yi Hwang 李滉 (1501–1570 CE) and Yi Yul-gok 李栗谷 (1536–1584 CE).

In order to point out the ethical importance of the mind-heart in terms of the *li-qi* foundation, Zhu Xi provided some core distinctions such as the distinction between the *dào-xīn* 道心 (the mind-heart of the Way) and *rén-xīn* 人心 (human mind-heart), and between the Heavenly *li* and human desires. The *dao-xin* refers to the mind-heart that completely receives and actualizes *li*. In this sense, the *dao-xin* means the ideal and perfect state of the mind-heart. The *ren-xin* refers to the mind-heart that is never stable and thus has always the potentiality of errors. With these distinctions, Zhu Xi could argue effectively that, while human nature as *li* and the *dao-xin* is originally good, human mind-heart, emotions, and desires can be either good or bad depending on how much they actualize their *li*.

His long philosophical struggle with the meaning of *zhonghe* and the *weifa/yifa* state, along with such detailed distinctions, was important because, in doing so, he established the foundations for his theory of self-cultivation. In his old view of *zhonghe*, he supported Zhang Shi's claim that examination and appreciation come first and then preservation and nourishment. After he criticized his old view because it provided no foundation for self-cultivation in daily life, he intended to develop his theory of self-cultivation for both the unaroused and aroused state. In this context, the traditional concept of *jìng* 敬 (seriousness, reverence, reverential attention) as affective and volitional virtue was incorporated into Zhu Xi's system of human nature and mind-heart. This single term came to connote many implications such as "concentrate on single-mindedness and freedom from distraction," "keep mindful alertness," "examine oneself," "be attentive," and "keep an attitude to be orderly and dignified," which point out the constant awareness of human mind-heart's tendency toward immorality. The way of abiding in *jing* was Zhu Xi's answer to the question of how the precarious mind-heart can keep its *ti* as moral goodness and how it manifests the goodness fully and properly in its activities.

While Zhu Xi dealt with the role of *jing* as the unique way of unifying the unaroused and aroused state of the mind-heart, he paid attention to the way of investigating *li* to the utmost (*qióngl*ǐ 穷理) with respect to the aroused state. He systemized the way of the investigation of things (*géwù* 格物) and the extension of knowledge (*zhìzhī* 致知) in the *Great Learning* as self-cultivation for the aroused state. For Zhu Xi, the investigation of things meant investigation of the *li* of things and events, and the only way to investigate *li* to the utmost is to pay attention to everything in our daily reading of books and handling of affairs. He believed that, although in the beginning of the learning process there might not seem to be progress, one would suddenly be able to find oneself in possession of extensive insight, if one exerts oneself and accumulates knowledge for a long time. For this work, he recommended not only a broad and thorough reading of the classics, but also critical examination and sincere discussion of them.

Regarding the aforementioned debate with Lu Xiangshan at Goose Lake Temple, it is obvious that Zhu Xi emphasized *both* honoring the moral nature as well as the path of inquiry and study as two wings or wheels of self-cultivation, which is contrasted to Lu Xiangshan's emphasis on the priority of the former. Now their difference is clearer. Lu Xiangshan claimed the mind-heart as *li* and thus believed that pursuit of study makes no sense without realizing the priority of honoring the moral nature. Based on his theory of the relation between human nature and mind-heart, Zhu Xi was concerned with an objective curriculum and criteria of learning and reading, so that students could exert themselves in order to progress in the way of self-cultivation without a simple subjective performance and evaluation.

The investigation of things and the extension of knowledge as a self-cultivation are to be completed by reading the classics, because the classics are the primary sources of the Way. This is also the reason Zhu Xi continued to do commentary works on the classics. In this sense, for Zhu Xi, the literary works, prose or poetry, in the classics are not merely aesthetic products, but, more importantly, instruments for carrying the Way. This view was applied to both reading and writing of literary works. Zhu Xi left many literary works such as preface, letters, poetry, and so on. Both writing and reading literary works were, after all, a way of self-cultivation. His main concern was with the articulation of what he intended to argue, clarity of concepts, and argumentative structure. It should be noted, however, that, unlike the Cheng brothers and other scholars of the School of Dao who regarded literary works as harmful to realization of the Way, Zhu Xi admitted literary works as a natural product of human mind-heart and thus did not wholly ignore the pure aesthetic pleasure and beauty derived from formal style and diverse expressions.

In 1313, his commentaries of the Four Books were authorized as the standard reading of the classics, and they continued to be the basic resource for all educated people who prepared for civil service examination until 1905, when the examination system was finally abolished. This historical record is simply an evidence of the greatness of his scholarship. His lifelong contribution to opening a new horizon of the Confucian orthodoxy as a scholar, philosopher, commentator, educator, and official, has made him an exemplar of sincere and critical scholarship, and of the unity of theory and practice in the intellectual history of East Asia.

CHOI Suk
Towson University

Further Reading

Angle, Stephen C. (2009). *Sagehood: The contemporary significance of Neo-Confucian philosophy*. Oxford, UK: Oxford University Press.

Chan, Wing-tsit. (1989). *Chu Hsi: New studies*. Honolulu: University of Hawaii Press.

Chan, Wing-tsit. (1987). *Chu Hsi: Life and thought*. Hong Kong: The Chinese University Press.

Chan, Wing-tsit (Ed.). (1986). *Chu Hsi and Neo-Confucianism*. Honolulu: University of Hawaii Press.

Chan, Wing-tsit. (1966). *Reflections on things at hand: The Neo-Confucian anthology complied by Chu Hsi and Lu Tzu-ch'ien*. New York: Columbia University Press.

Ching, Julia. (2000). *The religious thought of Chu Hsi*. Oxford, UK: Oxford University Press.

De Bary, W. Theodore (Ed.). (1989). *Neo-Confucian education: The formative stage*. Berkeley: University of California Press.

De Bary, W. Theodore. (1981). *Neo-Confucian orthodoxy and learning of the Mind-and-Heart*. New York: Columbia University Press.

De Bary, W. Theodore. (Ed.). (1975). *The unfolding of Neo-Confucianism*. New York: Columbia University Press.

Gardner, Daniel K. (2007). *The Four Books: The basic teachings of the later Confucian tradition*. Indianapolis: Hackett Publishing.

Gardner, Daniel K. (2003). *Zhu Xi's reading of the Analects: Canon, commentary, and the classical tradition*. New York: Columbia University Press.

Gardner, Daniel K. (1990). *Learning to be a sage: Selections from the conversations of Master Chu, arranged topically*. Berkeley: University of California Press.

Gardner, Daniel K. (1986). *Chu Hsi and the Ta-hsueh*. Cambridge, MA: Harvard University Press.

Huang, Siu-chi. (1999). *Essentials of Neo-Confucianism: Eight major philosophers of the Song and Ming periods*. Westport, CT: Greenwood.

Kim, Yung Sik. (2000). *The natural philosophy of Chu Hsi (1130–1200)*. Philadelphia: American Philosophical Society.

Metzger, T. (1977). *Escape from predicament: Neo-Confucianism and China's evolving political culture*. New York: Columbia University Press.

Tillman, Hoyt Cleveland. (1992). *Confucian discourse and Chu Hsi's ascendancy*. Honolulu: University of Hawaii Press.

Tillman, Hoyt Cleveland. (1982). *Utilitarian Confucianism: Ch'en Liang's challenge to Chu Hsi*. Cambridge, MA: Harvard University Press.

Zhu Xi. (1994). *Zhūzǐ yǔlèi* 朱子语类 [*Classified Conversations of Master Zhu*]. Beijing: Zhonghua shuju. Original work published 1270.

Jurchen Jin Dynasty

女真金朝

1115 – 1234 CE

A Jurchen man hunting from his horse, from a 15th century ink and color painting on silk.

The Jin dynasty was founded in the north of China by Jurchen chieftain Wányán Āgǔdǎ 完颜阿骨打, known posthumously as Emperor Taizu. The Jurchen were a forest-dwelling people from the northeast of China (Manchuria) who conquered the territory of the nomadic Khitans. The Khitans had earlier established the Liao dynasty (907–1125) after taking over north China from the Song dynasty. The Jurchens attempted to rule their Jin dynasty, which coexisted with the Southern Song, through a combination of tribal vigor and Chinese-style government. After signing a treaty with the Song wherein the Song would provide annual tribute to the Jin, the Jin dynasty was in turn conquered by the Mongols (along with much of the rest of Eurasia), whose great leaders, including Chinggis (Genghis) Khan, Batu Khan, and Ögödei Khan, were already active during the Jin rule, and who founded the Yuan dynasty.

List of Entries

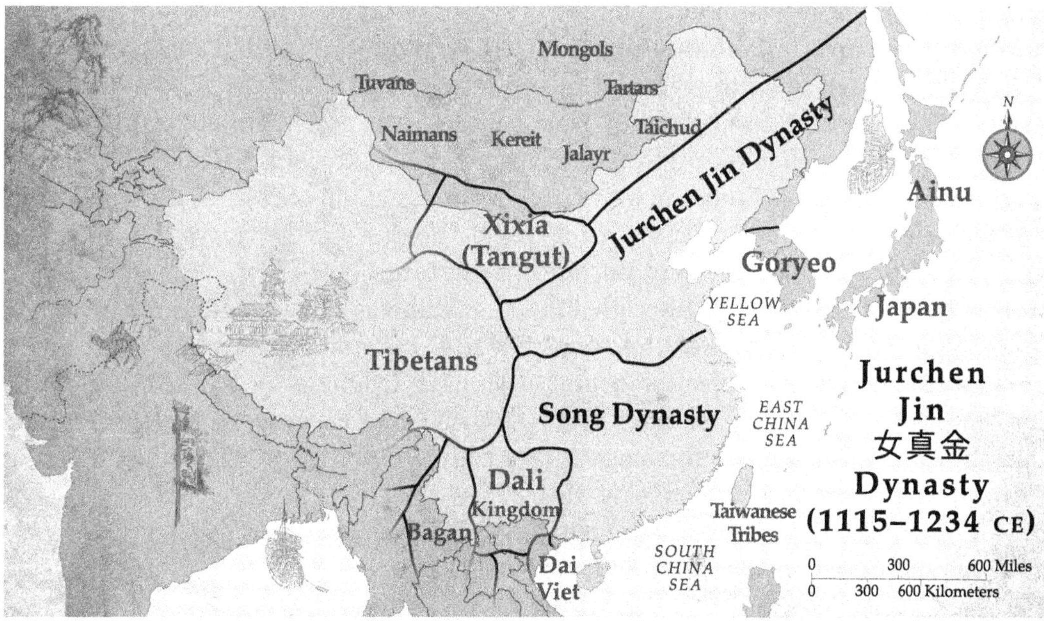

Batu Khan

Bádūhán 拔都汗

c. 1205–1255—Conqueror of much of Eurasia; Great Khan of the Golden Horde

Batu Khan on the throne, from Rashid-al-Din's *History of the World*.

Summary

Batu Khan, a grandson of Chinggis (Genghis) Khan, led ruthless conquests across Eurasia that allowed him to control a vast territory stretching from present-day Kazakhstan to the Danube. Batu's army, "the Golden Horde," crushed resistance so thoroughly that "No eye remained open to weep for the dead." Their use of fire-belching war machines was the first recorded use of gunpowder in Europe. Only the news of the Great Khan Ögödei's death in faraway Karakorum saved Western Europe from further destruction. Although his joint reign (with Möngke) of the Mongol Empire was without question brutal, the empire connected East and West through commerce, setting the stage for China's Yuan dynasty, which saw the development of rich cultural diversity and was a relatively peaceful period.

The Mongol ruler Batu (Bádū 拔都, sometimes given as Bádūhán 拔都汗, or Bádūkèhán 拔都可汗), whose name literally means "firm" in Mongolian, was born circa 1205 and died in 1255. He was the second son of Jochi (Zhúchì 朮赤) (1185–1225), himself the eldest son of *Chinggis Khan 成吉思汗 (1162–1227, and often spelled Genghis Khan). When Jochi died in 1227, Chinggis made Batu, the younger of his grandsons, his successor, to inherit the lands to the west, "as far in that direction as the hoof of the Tartar horse had penetrated."

Batu was a major figure in the Mongol world. He ruled the empire jointly with Möngke (Měnggē 蒙哥) (1209–1259), the fourth Great Khan of the Mongol Empire, from 1 July 1251 to 11 August 1259. In

*People marked with an asterisk have entries in this dictionary.

fact, at the time of Möngke's accession to the Great Khanate, Batu was a virtual kingmaker.

Batu founded the Golden Horde (Jīnzhàng Hánguó 金帐汗国) (1227–1255), a sub-khanate and one of the successor states of the Mongol Empire; the name comes from the Mongolian word *ordon* (palace). Under its auspices Batu launched numerous campaigns against the medieval powers of Poland, Kiev, Hungary, and miscellaneous tribes of more loosely organized peoples. As a result, he came to rule over a vast territory which at its apex stretched from today's Kazakhstan to the Danube. Batu's rule corresponded with the westernmost extension of the Mongol Empire, which in 1242 reached the outskirts of Vienna.

Extremely violent and merciless, Batu's assault on Europe was unanimously described by the peoples conquered as an absolute disaster. In retrospect, however, scholars acknowledge that the Mongol Empire at the time of his rule connected East and West, facilitating commerce and administration across Eurasia, and bringing a period of relative peace.

Background

After the collapse of the Táng 唐 dynasty (618–907 CE), anarchy was prevalent in China. A number of ephemeral imperial dynasties succeeded one another in northern China, while southern China was broken up into several provincial ruling houses. Eventually a great national dynasty, the Sòng 宋 dynasty (960–1279 CE), ascended the imperial throne. Batu lived during the Song, which was later followed by the Yuán 元 dynasty (1271–1368 CE), the only dynasty established by the Mongols and considered both as a division of the Mongol Empire and as an imperial dynasty of China.

During the twelfth century, after fighting a long war against the Song dynasty, a group called the Jurchens (Nǚzhēn 女真) captured Kaifeng from the Song. From this time on, Song hegemony was confined to the area south of the Yangzi (Chang) River, and the dynasty became known as Southern Song. North of the river, the Jurchens founded a new dynasty, the Jīn 金 (1115–1234 CE). In northwest China, however, there was another state called the Western Xia, or Xī Xià 西夏, ruled by the Tangut (Dǎngxiàng 党项), a north Asian ethnic group most likely related to Tibetans. Chinggis Khan understood that Xi Xia had to be his first objective because the Tangut could threaten his flank when he moved against the Jin. The battle against them was the Mongols' first victory against a sedentary state.

The Mongol invasion of China lasted over six decades and particularly involved the defeat of the Jin dynasty, Western Xia, the Dali Kingdom, and the Southern Song, which finally fell in 1276. The Mongol-Jin

Dynasty War (*Mĕng-Jīn zhànzhēng* 蒙金战争) lasted over twenty-three years and the Jin dynasty fell in the year 1234.

The Jin Empire had its capital at Zhongdu, the site of present-day Beijing. Previously named Yanjing, the town had been a secondary capital of the Liáo 辽 dynasty (916–1125) founded by the Inner Mongolian Khitan (Qìdān 契丹). In 1153 the Jurchens renamed the city Zhongdu, or "Central Capital." In 1215 the Mongols besieged, sacked, and burnt the city to the ground. An eyewitness reported several months later that the bones of the slaughtered formed white mountains and that the soil was still greasy with human fat. Later, in 1264, in preparation for the conquest of all of China to establish the Yuan dynasty, *Khubilai (Qubilai) Khan 忽必烈汗 decided to rebuild the city slightly north to the center of the Jin capital, and in 1272, he made it his capital, renaming it Dadu. For the Mongols, this city was known as Khanbalik (spelled as Cambaluc in Marco Polo's accounts). Prior to that date, Karakorum (Kharkhorin in Mongolian), had served as the capital of the empire. When Dadu became the new capital, Karakorum remained the administrative center for Mongolia for a further hundred years.

The Song was the first government in world history to issue paper money, and the first Chinese government to establish a permanent standing navy. Social life during the Song was vibrant and cities had lively entertainment quarters. The spread of literature and knowledge was enhanced by the earlier invention of woodblock printing and the eleventh-century invention of movable-type printing. Premodern technology, science, philosophy, mathematics, engineering, and other intellectual pursuits flourished over the course of the Song. Philosophers such as Chéng Yí 程颐 and *Zhū Xī 朱熹 reinvigorated Confucianism (*rúxué* 儒学) with new commentary infused with Buddhist ideals, and they emphasized a new organization of classic texts that brought out the core doctrine of Neo-Confucianism.

The later part of the Song dynasty, however, was dominated by war against northern nomadic tribes. To repel the Jurchens, and later the Mongols (Měnggǔ 蒙古), the Song developed revolutionary new military technology supplemented by the use of gunpowder. Gunpowder would later be used by Batu's army in his campaigns against Europe.

The legacy of Chinggis Khan, particularly with regard to military organization, had turned the Mongols from a group of warring tribes into a successful war machine. The army was organized into *arvans* (interethnic groups of ten), and the members of an *arvan* were loyal to one another regardless of ethnic origin. Ten *arvans* made a *zuun*, or a company; ten *zuuns* made a *myangan*, or a battalion; and ten *myangans* formed a *tümen* (*wànhùzhì* 万户制), or an army of ten thousand. *Tümens* were considered a practical size, neither too small for an effective campaign nor too big for efficient transport and supply. Indeed, this decimal-system organization of Chinggis Khan's military would prove very effective in conquering, by persuasion or force, the many tribes of the central Asian steppe.

These troops were made especially effective by a large supply of sturdy and robust horses. Of smaller stature than European horses, the Mongolian horses were able to cover vast distances in difficult conditions and with very little food. Such an advantage, combined with expert archers capable of shooting arrows while galloping at full speed, meant that the Mongols were capable of crushing the enemy despite being frequently outnumbered.

By the time of his death, Chinggis's armies had conquered northern China, part of Siberia, and Central Asia. His successors were to continue his campaigns, notably to Europe. Before he died, Chinggis Khan prepared his succession and divided his patrimony between the four sons borne to him by his principal wife Börte Üjin (Bèi'értiē 孛兒帖, c. 1162–1230): Jochi (Zhúchì 朮赤, c. 1180–1227), Chagatai (Chágětái 察合台, c. 1185–1241/42), *Ögödei (Wōkuòtái 窝阔台, c. 1186–1241), and Tolui (Tuōléi 拖雷, 1192–1232).

An assembly, or *quriltai* (*kùlìtái dàhuì* 库力台大会), was convened for the most prominent Mongol nobles to elect the new khan on the basis of collective judgment that the candidate was the most talented or competent. Although Chinggis Khan had designated Ögödei as his successor and left him the territory of central Siberia and eastern Xinjiang, it took two years after the death of Chinggis Khan before Ögödei assumed power as new khan. In 1229, a compromise was reached, which eventually resulted in the first territorial division of the Mongol domains. Following nomadic Mongolian tradition, the youngest son, Tolui, received northern China as well as the home territory of Mongolia as *ochigin,* "prince of the hearth," while Chagatai received Central Asia. The eldest son, Jochi, was given the lands furthest away from the homeland, in accordance with nomadic Mongol tradition.

Chinggis's wife Börte had been abducted by the Merged (Miè'érqǐ 蔑儿乞) tribe and liberated shortly before giving birth to Jochi, a situation that caused lingering uncertainty about whether Chinggis was his real father. Nonetheless, Chinggis always accepted Jochi as his first-born son. Jochi was thus favored as rightful heir to the Mongolian empire, but when Chinggis named Ögödei as his rightful successor, Jochi rebelled against his father. Chagatai and Ögödei were sent against Jochi, who died in February 1227 before any physical hostilities occurred, and only several months before Chinggis died.

Because Jochi had passed away before the death of his father, his appanage was transmitted to his two sons, Orda (Wò'érdā 斡儿答, c. 1204–1280) and

Batu. The traditional steppe nomad practice of granting the grazing lands furthest away from the home camp to the eldest son was thus upheld, though in this instance the pastures available would prove to be unusually extensive. Orda, the eldest, received western Siberia from the River Irtysh to the River Ural, and Batu, the second, was given the territories west of there. The fact that the territories given to Batu still remained to be conquered reveals the supreme confidence of the Mongols that he and his generals and troops would prove equal to the task.

The territories in question, geographically corresponding to western Kazakhstan, southern Russia, and southern Ukraine, had already been reconnoitered by the Mongols in 1223. But it was not until 1238–1240 that Batu carried out the real conquest, valiantly supported by such commanders as *Subatai Ba'adur (Sùbùtái 速不台; in Mongolian, Sübedei, 1176–1248). If Batu was nominally in charge of the westward conquest, the actual leader was in fact Subatai, then around sixty years old. Subatai had been the primary military strategist and general of Chinggis Khan and Ögödei Khan. He had directed more than twenty campaigns in which he conquered thirty-two nations and won sixty-five battles, and during which he conquered or overran more territory than any other commander in history. He gained victory by means of imaginative and sophisticated strategies and routinely coordinated movements of armies that were hundreds of kilometers away from each other. The campaigns against Russia were extremely successful, despite dissension and hostilities between Batu and Tolui's son Möngke, on the one hand, and Ögödei's son Güyüg (Guìyóu 贵由) (c. 1206–1248) and Chagatai's son Büri (Bùlǐ 不里) (d. 1252), on the other.

Moving Westward

As early as 1223, Subatai had led a reconnaissance force of three *tümens* through Qipchaq (Qīnchá 欽察) territory, a confederation of pastoralists and warriors who occupied a vast territory in the Eurasian steppe, stretching from north of the Aral Sea westward to the region north of the Black Sea (now in Ukraine and southwestern Russia). The election of Ögödei as Great Khan in 1235 led to the decision to renew the war against them and against the Russian principalities that lay beyond. The year 1236 saw a successful attack against the Volga Bulghars (Fúěrjiā Bǎojiālìyà 伏尔加保加利亚), a historic Bulgar state that existed between the seventh and thirteenth centuries around the confluence of the Volga and Kama rivers in today's southern Russia. The following year, the Qipchaqs were conquered.

Crossing the Urals, Batu's army swept over the plains of southern Russia, crushing resistance so mercilessly that, as a Russian chronicler put it, "No eye remained open to weep for the dead." In

November of the same year, the Mongols launched an attack against the Russian principalities. The fact that these territories were parceled into small principalities and dukedoms made it easier for Mongols to conquer them. Furthermore, throughout the campaign Russians princes showed neither unity of purpose nor any sense of the enemy they were facing. None of them surrendered to the Mongols, and they frequently fled when it became clear resistance was futile. The main Mongol force, headed by the Jochid princes Batu and Hordu—the future great khans Güyüg and Möngke—and several others, arrived at Ryazan' in December 1237. Once Ryazan' refused to surrender, the Mongols sacked it and massacred the whole population. In February 1238, Moscow, then a small town, was sacked. Suzdal and Vladimir were next. Vladimir in particular was the scene of terrible events. The population was massacred in the churches where they had sought refuge. Other Mongolian detachments attacked and sacked Yaroslav and Tver'. It was only thanks to the spring thaws that Novgorod managed to escape the same fate.

The siege of Kiev, in December 1240, represented the final blow in the Mongol conquest of Russia. The entire Mongol army camped outside the city, under Batu's command. Catapults were used against the city and after eight days of relentless bombardment the walls were finally breached. The whole city was destroyed and the population butchered. John of Plano Carpini (Bóláng jiābīn 柏郎嘉宾) (1180–1252), one of the first Europeans to enter the court of the Great Khan of the Mongol Empire, visited the town in 1246. He described how the entire countryside around the city was littered with skulls and bones, while the whole town was reduced to rubble with scarcely two hundred houses left standing.

Encounter with Europe

In 1241 the Mongols launched attacks on both Poland and Hungary. A detachment of Mongolian troops, under the commandment of Baidar (Bàidā'ér 拜答儿) and Qaidu (Hǎidū 海都) (1230–1301) attacked Poland. In March, Krakow was attacked and burnt. On 9 April, the town of Legnica, in Silesia, southern Poland, was raided. The town was the scene of untold massacres: European chroniclers recorded that the Mongols cut off an ear from each slain soldier and sent them to Batu Khan, filling nine sacks with the grisly proof of victory. After Moravia, that part of the troops joined the rest of the Mongolian army, under Batu's command and Ögödei's directions, which gathered in Pest on 2–5 April. On 7 April, greatly outnumbered, the Mongolian troops feigned retreat, thereby luring the Hungarian troops out of the city. This was a common tactic of the Mongols to achieve decisive victory: they would lure the enemy away from their base by a brief attack, followed by a feigned retreat of several days' duration. If the enemy followed, the Mongols, after giving battle at a place of their own choosing, were then able to wipe out the defeated soldiers as they fled back to their base. After two days of such pretense, the Mongols camped at Muhi, downstream from today's Miskolc. The battle that took place there on 11 April 1241 ended in total victory for the Mongols over the Hungarian army, led by King Béla IV (1235–1270). As the Hungarian troops crowded together at night in a laager (an encampment circled by wagons), Batu and Subatai, Batu's primary military strategist and general, encircled them.

Comparing the Hungarian troops to sheep in a pen, Batu and Subatai attacked with giant catapults and fire-belching war machines. It was the first recorded use of gunpowder in Europe, and this new weaponry contributed significantly to the Mongols' shock tactics and psychological warfare. Eventually, the Mongolian army deliberately left their circle open to allow Béla's soldiers to escape. As the whole Hungarian troops fled westward, Mongolian soldiers hunted them down as they ran. Despite some heavy losses, the Mongols emerged successful and crushed the Hungarian armies. Batu's share of the booty included Béla's magnificent golden tent. It became the symbol of Batu's prowess, and when he eventually settled down in southern Russia at Sarai, on the Caspian Sea, his Qipchaq-Mongol state was named the Golden Horde after Béla's golden tent.

If Batu went down in history as victor of the battle of Muhi, the real champion was his commander Subatai. In fact, Batu was later criticized for the irresolution he showed at Muhi, and he also had to live down the embarrassment of having struggled for two months against the Russian town of Kozel'sk which his cousins Qadan (Hādān 哈丹) and Büri stormed in merely three days.

After the battle of Muhi, the Mongolian troops continued their assault on Hungary. They burnt Pest, where in order to frighten into submission the people living on the other side of the Danube, they heaped the bodies of the butchered multitudes on the embankment while others skewered little children on their lances and carried them along the dykes. In Esztergom, the Mongols bombarded the city's wooden fortifications with thirty catapults to make a breach, and filled in the ditch using sacks of earth. When the city was entered on Christmas Day 1241 the inhabitants set fire to their own homes and buried their valuables so that the Mongols would not have them. Many people were roasted over slow fires to make them disclose where they had hidden their treasures.

In the ensuing months the whole Hungarian population was subjected to extreme violence. When a few months later King Béla succeeded in returning to

A fourteenth-century image of a young Batu Khan.

his country, he was met by scenes of death and destruction of such vast proportions that he despaired of his country. In regions which previously had been densely populated, he rode for days on end without seeing a living soul. Everywhere he saw hideously mutilated and half-decomposed bodies lying by the thousands, slowly disposed of by packs of wolves and other wild animals.

After Hungarian cities all fell one by one, there were no more barriers between the Mongols and Western Europe. Batu's army was poised to continue its assault on Europe when news arrived of Ögödei's death.

Death of Ögödei and Return to Mongolia

The news of Ögödei's death reached Batu at the end of June 1241. As Batu was literally about to unleash his horsemen for the final assault on Western Europe, an imperial messenger arrived from Karakorum, bringing the news from far away that the Great Khan Ögödei had died in December. Eager to compete for the throne, he knew that his presence in Karakorum was vital but, with the entire European continent virtually within his grasp, he hesitated. Having quarreled with his cousins Güyüg and Büri during the European campaign, he knew that he could not afford to be away from Karakorum if he was to stand a chance. Güyüg and Möngke had already gone back to Mongolia. The Yasaq, the body of laws and practices decreed by Chinggis Khan and his successors, which gradually came to form a sort of constitution of the Mongol Empire, required that every member of Chinggis's clan must attend the *quriltai* that elected the new Khan. The importance of the *quriltai* unequivocally trumped his quest for glory, and Batu decided to interrupt his campaign.

The campaigns of 1236–1242 increased significantly the territories of the House of Jochi. As commander of these campaigns, at least nominally, Batu was the legitimate ruler of this vast domain. Nevertheless, important tensions between Güyüg and Batu had emerged during the conquest of the Russian principalities. Güyüg, the eldest son of Ögödei, and Büri, Chagatai's grandson, were jealous of Batu's prominence and dissension rose in the Mongolian army. As Batu and his commanders sat down to enjoy a banquet after a victory against a Russian principality, Batu took a drink before the others. Güyüg and Büri begrudged this and left the feast without sharing it. As Büri rode away he is reported to have said: "Batu is our equal, how dared he drink first? He is just like an old woman with a beard." Möngke, Tolui's son, also left Batu's army but he remained in good terms with Batu, and this friendship was to have significant consequences for the history of the Mongols.

After Ögödei's death in 1241, the regency was entrusted to his widow, Töregene Khatun (Zhāocí huánghòu 昭慈皇后), who ruled as regent until the succession was settled in 1246. Eager to have her son Güyüg elected as Great Khan, she extended the regency period for several years. Güyüg was elected Khan in August 1246, but his reign was to be short-lived. Early in 1248, Güyüg started to move west, allegedly for health reasons. But Sorghaghtani (Suōlǔhétiění 唆鲁禾帖尼), Tolui's widow, suspected his real intention was to attack Batu, and she sent him a warning. This cemented the Jochid-Toluid alliance against the Ögödei and Chagatai lines. The showdown never happened, since Güyüg died en route suddenly, possibly of poisoning. A number of historians have disputed this, however, some believing he died of natural causes, and others believing he died a result of a violent brawl. His widow Oghul Qaimish (Qīnshū huánghòu 欽淑皇后) took over as regent but was ultimately unable to keep the succession within her branch of the family. After Güyüg's death in April 1248, Batu became the clear leader among the Mongol princes, despite the gout that kept him bedridden.

Möngke's Reign

In July 1251 Batu called a *quriltai* in his own territory in a place called Ala-Qamaq, in the mountains south of the Ili River. Sorghaghtani sent Möngke, while other attendees included leaders of the families of Chinggis Khan's brothers as well as several important generals. Güyüg's sons attended briefly but then left, and the only remaining representatives of the Ögödei and Chagatai families were outsiders with little influence in their families. The *quriltai* rejected the idea that only descendants of Ögödei could be khan and first offered the throne to Batu. Rejecting it, Batu instead nominated Möngke. Despite vehement objections from Oghul Qaimish's delegate, a Uygur scribe called Bala, the *quriltai* approved Möngke. One supporter of Möngke even threatened to execute anyone who opposed Batu's choice.

Undoubtedly this was nothing less than a coup d'état, organized by Batu (who himself declined election) in collaboration with the Toluids. An extensive purge of the families of Ögödei and Chagatai ensued, and from that date the Great Khanate remained a perquisite of the house of Tolui. All of Batu's surviving tormentors, such as Yesü Möngke (Yěsù Ménggē 也速蒙哥), son and first successor of Chagatai, who had publicly ridiculed his battlefield ineptitude, were executed.

In return for his support of Möngke, Batu was conceded virtual autonomy in his own territory of the Golden Horde. Möngke became Great Khan but Batu remained in charge of the Golden Horde. Moreover, as kingmaker and supporter of Möngke, Batu enjoyed great prestige. As quoted by William of Rubruck (Lǔbùlǔqǐ 鲁不鲁乞) (c. 1220–c. 1293), a Flemish Franciscan missionary and explorer, Möngke is reported saying, "As the sun sends its rays everywhere, likewise my sway and that of Batu reach everywhere."

A vast territory, the Golden Horde stretched from the Irtysh in the east to the Danube in the west. Jochi's fourteen sons divided the steppe into longitudinal strips, nomadizing north to south along the main rivers. Of all the successor states of the Mongol Empire, the Golden Horde was the first territory to emerge as a separate entity. The family's early separatist tendency reflected Jochi's alienation from his father, Chinggis Khan. Furthermore, Jochi's son and successor, Batu, was an immense distance from Mongolia and his suffering from gout reinforced his reputation as a coward. As a result, he preferred to defend his autonomy rather than compete for rule in Mongolia.

Batu is said to have had twenty-six wives and four sons. Of the latter, two were to play a historic role: Sartaq (Sǎlǐdā 撒里答) (d. 1256), who succeeded Batu as Khan of the Golden Horde, and Toqoqan (Tūhǎn 秃罕) (c. 1220–c. 1256), whose son Möngke Timur (Mánggē Tiēmù'ér 忙哥帖木儿) (d. 1280), was khan of the Golden Horde from 1267 to 1280. Both Sartaq and his son Ulaghchi (Wūláhēichì 乌剌黑赤) (died 1257), Batu's successors, died in quick succession, possibly through poisoning, and were succeeded by Batu's brother Berke (Bié'érgē 别儿哥) (d. 1266).

Batu is also credited with the foundation of the town of Sarai (Sàlái 萨莱), on the Volga, near today's village of Selitrennoye in Russia, about 120 kilometers north of Astrakhan. Its construction did not, however, imply that he took to a settled existence or abandoned the characteristic Mongol preference for living in tents, or *ger* (sometimes called *yurts;* in Chinese, *měnggǔbāo* 蒙古包). Sarai was the capital of the Golden Horde and was a prosperous and cosmopolitan city. When Ibn Batutta (Yīběn Báitútài 伊本白图泰) (1304–1368 or 1369), an Islamic scholar and traveler, visited in 1323, numerous ethnic groups resided in Sarai: Mongols,

Russians, Qipchaqs, Circassians, and Greeks, as well as Egyptian, Iraqi, Iranian, and Italian merchants. He noted in particular the peaceful coexistence of various religious practices. The capital was later relocated to a second town of Sarai, New Sarai (Xīn Sàlái 新萨莱), 65 kilometers east of today's Volgograd, which flourished until 1395 when it was sacked and effectively disappeared.

Batu's Influence

Batu's Mongol contemporaries praised him as a just and sagacious ruler, bestowing upon him the posthumous title of Sayin Khan (i.e., the Good Khan). According to Ala ad-Din Ata-Malik Juvayni (1226–1283), a Persian historian who wrote an account of the Mongol Empire, Batu did not subscribe to a particular faith or religion, but he recognized a belief in God, namely Tengriism (*ténggélǐ* 腾格里), the worship of the sky traditionally practiced by Mongols. Not all his contemporaries, however, saw him in such a positive way, and because of his performance at the Battle of Muhi and especially at Kozel'sk, he earned the reputation of coward among some of the Mongol army commanders.

This contrasted drastically with the perception Russians and other vanquished peoples had of him. They unanimously viewed him as a cruel and ruthless conqueror. In fact, because of his campaigns, the Mongols were destined to be a synonym of terror to most of the inhabitants of Eurasia for hundreds of years. In Europe, they were also commonly known as Tartar, which was a deformation of the ethnonym "Tatar," a group of Mongolized Turks, which recalled for Europeans the name "Tartarus" (i.e., the "hell" in Greek mythology).

Undoubtedly, the European experience of the Mongol army was traumatic. In battles, Mongols showed no mercy, massacring the whole population of any town that had refused to submit to the khan. Even after a victory, the Mongolian army would frequently carry out wholesale massacre and indiscriminate destruction in order to ensure complete security. As Chinggis Khan had warned, "when the enemy is vanquished, it does not mean that he is pacified." Characteristically, the Mongols systematically devastated vast tracts of land on the Hungarian plains following their victory in Muhi and Esztergom. China narrowly escaped the same fate. When Chinggis's generals, not knowing what to do with the vast urban population of conquered China, decided to massacre them all, obliterate their towns, and turn their well-tended fields into grazing land for the Mongol horses right down to the Huang (Yellow) River, Yēlǜ Chǔcái 耶律楚材, advisor and administrator during the reign of Chinggis Khan and that of his successor Ögödei, successfully convinced the Khan that it was in his own interest to use the industrious Chinese as a source of regular tax revenue rather than as fertilizer.

Pax Mongolica

If, undeniably, the Mongol assaults on Eurasia were extremely destructive, later generations of historians have sought to highlight its more beneficial outcomes. The conquests of Chinggis Khan and his successors effectively connected the Eastern world with the Western world, ruling a territory from Korea to Eastern Europe and Siberia to Southeast Asia. The Silk Roads, linking trade centers across Asia and Europe, came under the sole rule of the Mongol Empire. That "a maiden bearing a nugget of gold on her head could wander safely throughout the realm" was a common aphorism of the time. In fact, the phrase "Pax Mongolica" was coined by Western scholars to describe the stabilizing effects of the conquests of the Mongol Empire on the social, cultural, and economic life of the inhabitants of the vast Eurasian territory that the Mongols conquered in the thirteenth and fourteenth centuries. The term is used to describe the eased communication and commerce the unified administration helped to create, and the period of relative peace that followed the Mongol's vast conquests. The Mongols are also credited with setting up a postal system and stimulating cultural exchanges throughout Eurasia and beyond. Furthermore, if the period of the Mongol conquests had been merciless and brutal, the Mongol Empire itself was comparatively tolerant and liberal. While Europe was in the throes of religious persecution, complete freedom of religion reigned in the Golden Horde and the rest of the Mongol Empire.

In China as well, initial negative evaluations were later reassessed. Genghis Khan and his successors are recognized by a number of twenty-first century scholars as Chinese heroes who conquered Europe and unified China by founding a new dynasty In 1272 Khubilai Khan (23 September 1215—18 February 1294), the fifth Great Khan of the Mongol Empire from 1260 to 1294, issued an edict posthumously pronouncing his grandfather Chinggis Khan founder, or Tàizǔ 太祖, of the new dynasty which he called "Yuán" 元 (i.e., "the origin"). The title is said to have been suggested to Khubilai by his Chinese advisor Liú Bǐngzhōng 刘秉忠 (1216–1274), and it marked a departure from Chinese precedent in that previous dynastic titles had tended to have a geographical derivation, referring to the dynasty's own place of origin. As in the rest of the Eurasian landmass, the process of unification initiated by the Mongols brought peace in China, and led to the fostering of commercial and cultural contacts with Europe and the Islamic world. As a result, the Yuan dynasty witnessed the development of a rich cultural diversity, notably the development of drama and the novel, as well as an increased use of the written vernacular.

Franck BILLÉ
University of Cambridge

Further Reading

Allsen, Thomas T. (2001). *Culture and conquest in Mongol Eurasia*. Cambridge, UK: Cambridge University Press.

Atwood, Christopher P. (2004). *Encyclopedia of Mongolia and the Mongol Empire*. New York: Facts On File, Inc.

Grousset, René. (1941). Histoire de l'Asie. *Que sais-je? Série* [Asian history. What do I know? Series]. Paris: Presses Universitaires de France.

Khrustalëv, D. G. (2008). *Rus' ot nashestvia do "iga"* [Rus' from the invasion to the "yoke"]. Saint Petersburg: Evrazia.

Morgan, David. (1986). *The Mongols*. Oxford, UK: Blackwell.

Ronay, Gabriel. (2000). *The Tartar Khan's Englishman*. London: Phoenix Press.

Soucek, Svatopluk. (2000). *A history of Inner Asia*. Cambridge, UK: Cambridge University Press.

Chinggis Khan

Chéngjísīhán 成吉思汗

c. 1162–1227—Mongol leader and world conqueror

Alternate name: birth name: Temüjin

Fourteenth-century image of Chinggis (Genghis) Khan. National Palace Museum, Taipei, Taiwan.

Summary

Chinggis (often spelled Genghis) Khan was an illiterate nomad who created a world empire that is still remembered today. Chinggis Khan's later success as a world conqueror was based on his skills in organizing men in the nomadic society into which he was born. He was seeking political and commercial relations with the large Islamic state of Khwarazm when he sent a delegation to the shah in 1218; unfortunately the entire trade delegation—except one—was murdered on the way, thus bringing on the full wrath of Chinggis Khan. That event heralded the first full push by Chinggis and his sons westward to extend his nascent empire, which only ended at the gates of Europe and not by any military defeat experienced by the Mongols.

Most people probably know something about the battles fought by Chinggis (Genghis) Khan (c. 1162–1227), or his infamy as a world conqueror. Examples abound, such as the five-month siege of the city of Otrar and the razing of the famed city of Samarkand. Less well known is the world into which he was born that shaped his views and actions. To get a better understanding of how an illiterate nomad with few resources created—in the space of twenty short years—a world empire that is still remembered today, one must look at the steppe and its tribes from which Chinggis Khan emerged. He was above all a supreme organizer and pragmatist who tapped the best parts of his nomadic, tribal society in creative ways to form one of the most efficient military and administrative organizations the world has ever known.

The Mongol Tribes

The people who would become known as the Mongols (Měnggǔ 蒙古) emerged out of the forested area of northeastern Asia known as Manchuria. According to Chinese sources, these tribal peoples migrated southwest from their original homeland to eventually settle in northeastern Mongolia, between the Onon and Kerulen rivers. Since this new area was mixed forest and steppe, the former forest dwellers took up herding. What prompted these forest tribes to migrate away from their homeland? It may well have been the consolidation of Khitan (Qìdān 契丹) tribes to form the Liao Empire in northern Asia. The Khitan confederation resulted in the dispersal or rearrangement of many tribal units in northern Asia at that time, and the Mongols were only one among many groups to feel the effects of that imperial project.

The history of the Mongol tribes in the tenth century is not easy to disentangle from that of other tribes in the area, not least because the sources are not consistent in which tribes or groups were known as or claimed the name of "Mongol." We know considerably more about the identity and role of the Mongols by the early twelfth century when the Manchurian Jurchen (Nǚzhēn女真) peoples had replaced the Khitans as lords of northern Asia with their Jīn 金 ("Golden") dynasty (1127–1234). Around the 1120s many tribes, including the Mongols, had become members of that new empire, serving to keep the peace in the steppe. It was around that time that the first leader of the united Mongol tribes was known; Khabul Khan was bound to the Jurchens in a type of tributary relationship by 1147, where Jin supplied the Mongols with supplies and an official title to Khabul Khan.

All were not happy, however, among the various tribes that served the Jin state; in particular, the Jurchens were all too happy to promote differences between the Tatars and Mongols, and by the 1160s the Mongols were again divided among themselves as a result of partisan infighting and Jurchen-Tatar alliances. It was also this fratricidal atmosphere that had a great impact on the future of Chinggis Khan when he eventually formed his own tribal confederation. One aspect of that tribal infighting was the fact that the most promising young men often left their natal tribes to seek out an up-and-coming leader of another tribe, who appeared to be the best bet for upward mobility. Once found, they attached themselves to that leader by means of a vow to become a companion and servitor, performing all sorts of functions that included household duties, administrative tasks, and military service as the chief's bodyguards. In return for their loyal service, these companions (Mongolian *nököd*) would receive a share of all booty captured in raids, as well as the leader's favor. By this means a capable tribal leader could attract the best and brightest from other tribes, who would otherwise not naturally lend their loyalty to him. This was the nucleus of any successful tribal confederation.

The Young Temüjin

Chinggis Khan's father was a descendant of the twelfth century Mongol leaders, their "royal clan" the Borjigin clan. Yesügei was actually the descendant of the eldest son of that clan's ancestor, so he had a true claim to leadership of the Mongol tribes. Yesügei's wife, Ho'elun, gave birth to their first son somewhere near the Onon River, and some sources report that the boy was born with his fist around a blood clot. In Asian folklore this is commonly seen as a sign that the child will grow up to be a great warrior. The baby boy was named Temüjin because Yesügei had just captured a Tatar chief named Temüjin Öge. This probably occurred sometime between 1162 and 1167. Temüjin was eventually joined by four siblings who were born to Yesügei's first wife, his brothers Khasar, Khachi'un, and Temüge Otchigin, and a sister named Temülün. Yesügei's second wife also provided two brothers, Begter and Belgutei.

When his son Temüjin was about nine years old, Yesügei decided that it was time for him to be married. Marriages were commonly arranged with other tribes to secure providential alliances, and this one was no exception; Yesügei had it in mind to marry off his eldest son to a daughter of his first wife's tribe. Along the way, however, Yesügei and Temüjin happened to stop with a chieftain of another tribe, the Onggirat, named Dai Sechen, who had a very attractive and lively daughter named Börte (Bèi'értiē 孛兒帖), and was probably a year older than Temüjin. According to the custom, Yesügei left Temüjin in Dai Sechen's camp to work for his future father-in-law as a bride price. This was also providential for Yesügei, since it enabled him to renew a tribal alliance with the Onggirat.

While traveling back to his own tribe after depositing young Temüjin into the hands of Dai Sechen, Yesügei stayed with some Tatars as steppe hospitality demanded. By the time he reached home he was deathly ill, presumably from food poisoning by his Tatar hosts. That, at any rate, was the story related to Temüjin, who was brought back home. This disaster brought on a lot of suffering for Temüjin and his family, but was also the crucible that forged Temüjin's qualities as a leader of his tribe and family.

When Yesügei died, the tribal alliance he headed broke up, and the chieftain of a rival tribe, the Tayichi'ut, assumed leadership. Some sources state that Ho'elun was cut out of Yesügei's family by the Tayichi'ut tribe after his death, while others assert that one of

Yesügei's brothers stayed with Ho'elun, following the custom of levirate marriage that demanded a younger brother or son by another wife of the deceased marry the widow. What we do know is Ho'elun worked very hard under trying circumstances and with minimal resources to keep her family together, and the children grew up on various wild plants and animals as they scrounged for a living near the Onon River.

Temüjin was not to remain there for long. The leader of the rival Tayichi'ut tribe, Tarkhutai, rode into Ho'elun's small camp one day and demanded that she hand over Temüjin to him. This was undoubtedly his attempt to forestall Temüjin's claim of leadership over the united tribes from his dead father and on behalf of his father's tribe, the Borjigin. That claim was made stronger by the fact that Temüjin and his small family had survived being left alone by the Tayichi'ut. Temüjin was taken back to Tarkhutai's camp where he was held prisoner. He was lucky, however, since a man from another tribe—who were subjects to the Tayichi'ut—named Sorkhan Shira, helped him escape. Sorkhan and his sons would one day become loyal followers of Temüjin when he began his imperial project.

The matter of Temüjin's bride had not yet been settled, and after returning to his mother's encampment, he then returned to Dai Sechen's camp to claim Börte. Temüjin was by that time about sixteen years of age, and this marriage would further support Temüjin's newly reclaimed leadership of his father's tribal alliance. One story about the marriage bears repeating; after the new bride had returned to her husband's camp she presented her mother-in-law with a gift of unusual value, a black sable coat. This was a gift that far exceeded normal expectations and it confirmed to the Borjigins Börte's importance as Temüjin's first wife.

Emergence of Chinggis Khan

Once his marriage was settled, it was time for the young Temüjin to start building alliances with other tribal leaders and a set of followers on whom he could depend. At this point Temüjin and his small family were living deep in the Hentai Mountains on a mountain called Burkhan Khaldun, near the Onon River. It is in this mountainous area that the steppe rivers Kerulen, Tula, and Onon have their headwaters. West of these mountains lies the great Lake Baikal and lands controlled by the Naiman, Merged (Miè'érqǐ 蔑儿乞), and Kereit tribes. East of this location roamed the Tatar tribes, and south of the area was controlled by Onggirat tribes. Much further south and east lay the Jin and Song empires. While Temüjin's gaze may not have stretched that far, he certainly was mindful of the need to reunite all of the tribes that had once been led by his father. One obvious alliance was to be had with one of his father's old sworn blood-brothers (Mongolian *anda*), Toghril Khan, who headed the Kereit group of tribes. At that time Toghril was camped on the Tula River west of Temüjin. Temüjin went to Toghril's camp and presented him with a reminder that Toghril and Yesügei were sworn blood-brothers. On that basis Temüjin presented the black sable coat to Toghril, in effect becoming his adopted son. Toghril thereupon promised to help Temüjin reunite the people formerly led by his father.

Now Toghril was not the most trustworthy man, as events show. Temüjin's subordination to this strong player in steppe politics, however, was a canny move that certainly provided what Temüjin was seeking: followers. One important man to join Temüjin at that time was Jelme, the son of a tribal chief who had been a subordinate to Yesügei. Jelme would eventually become one of Chinggis Khan's most fierce and loyal warriors. Another *anda* was the young man Bogurchi, who had helped the young Temüjin recapture several horses that thieves had stolen from his camp some time earlier. It was also about this time that Börte was taken captive by the Merged tribes in a raid on Temüjin's camp. Temüjin avoided them by hiding on Burkhan Khaldun, a place he would later come to view as sacred. The Merged tribe took her to their camp and made her the wife of the chief. Temüjin

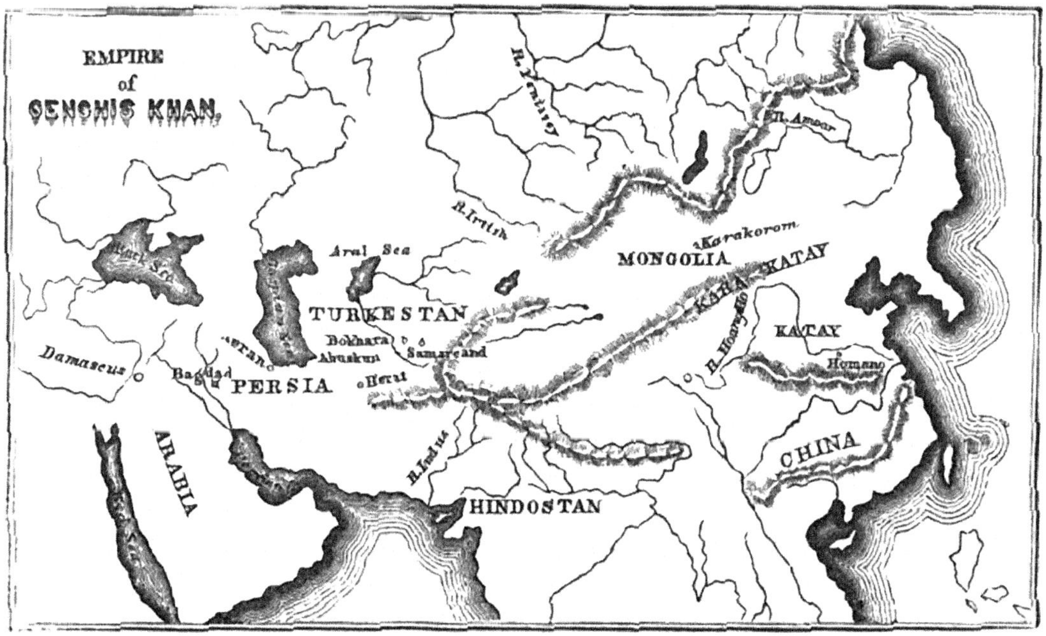

Historical map showing Chinggis Khan's empire. From *Ghengis Khan* by Jacob Abbott.

appealed to his newly adopted father, Toghril, for help in retrieving Börte, and he was happy to help. Toghril also brought with him another childhood friend of Temüjin's, a man named Jamukha. The three led a combined force to the rescue, and a now-pregnant Börte was reunited with her husband.

This action, probably in the early 1180s, had several long-ranging consequences for the future Chinggis Khan. First, Börte's pregnancy by a rival chieftain did not pose a personal threat to Temüjin. It did, however, throw into question the legitimacy of his eldest son, Jochi (Zhúchì 朮赤, c. 1180–1227), whose descendants were never considered successors to the leadership of the united Mongol tribes after Chinggis Khan's death. Second, this affair began the fateful relationship between the three men Temüjin, Toghril, and Jamukha. The eventual breaks in their friendship would prove critical to Temüjin's election as grand khan of the Mongol tribes.

The precise break came a couple of years after the combined campaign against the Merged to rescue Börte. While Toghril was obviously the strongest man in terms of loyal troops at the time, he chose to place Jamukha in charge of the whole campaign. The battle plan laid out by Toghril called on each of the three to provide for ten thousand men; while this was easy for him, it is far less clear how either of the two younger men, especially Temüjin with his still-small group of family and retainers, could have done so. In any case, Toghril and Temüjin were late in arriving at the meeting place, whereupon Jamukha became petulant. The outcome, as already observed, was a good one, and the Merged possessions and women were divided among the three men as spoils. Thereafter Temüjin and Jamukha joined forces while Toghril returned to his usual grazing grounds on the Tula River. A year or so later, as the combined group was setting out for their summer grazing grounds, Jamukha made an odd remark about where to strike camp for the night. Börte suggested that his remarks showed that he had grown tired of them, and that Temüjin and his company should part ways with Jamukha. This uneasiness was undoubtedly due at least in part to the fact that Jamukha had in his company the same Tayichi'ut tribes that had treated Temüjin's mother so badly after his father had died. It could also have been a strategy put into play by Börte to make sure that her husband did not end up the loser in a potential rivalry between these two strong, young leaders. In any event, Temüjin took this opportunity to set out on his own. Shortly after, Temüjin's followers and allies elected him as their Grand Khan.

Building the Mongol Confederation

We do not know precisely when Temüjin was elected to the position of Grand Khan, but it was most likely between

1184 and 1189, and he was about twenty-eight years of age. He likely did not receive or assume the title Chinggis Khan until 1206, so this election by his small group of family and followers set the stage for his full election to lead the larger confederation of Mongol tribes in 1206. The immediate outcome was resentment within Jamukha's camp.

One of the first things that the Grand Khan Temüjin did was to organize his followers into a rudimentary administrative group, as a household staff. The titles and duties of this group included cooks, quiver bearers, herders, provisioners, guards, and secretaries, all essential tasks to support the nomadic khan and his royal clan. This system did not distinguish civil from military functions and authority, and was common in nomadic confederations. It was adopted in all of the states they conquered and ruled.

Toghril was still, at that time, nominally in authority over both Temüjin and Jamukha, and he does not appear to have been disturbed by Temüjin's election as leader by his close followers. Soon, however, the incipient rivalry between the two young leaders came out into the open. The sources are divided over who started the fight and what specific actions each side took (claims of boiling in oil and cannibalism are attributed to both men). The immediate outcome was a growing rivalry between the two leaders. At that same time, Toghril was overthrown by his brother with support from the Naiman tribes. Toghril fled into the Gobi Desert and sought Temüjin's help, which was readily forthcoming. Then the Jurchen Jin emperor brought Toghril and Temüjin together to fight another old enemy, the Tatar tribes, who were causing trouble on Jin's northern frontier zone. Naturally, this proved a golden opportunity to Temüjin since he could eliminate one of his longstanding enemies. Jin attacked from the southeast while Toghril and Temüjin attacked from the west, and the Tatar chief was captured and executed in 1196. As a result, the Jin conferred the high honorary title of Prince (*wáng* 王) on Toghril, and gave Temüjin a lesser honorary title (in Jin eyes Temüjin was a subordinate and vassal to Toghril). Feeding on their joint success, Toghril and Temüjin continued their alliance for the next several years, attacking and defeating rival tribes such as the Naiman and the Tayichi'ut (even killing Targhutai in 1200). This provoked some envy among neighboring tribal units, who formed a confederation led by none other than Jamukha to bring down this successful operation. Jamukha's alliance disintegrated in 1201 after a brief engagement with the Toghril-Temüjin forces that was halted by a snowstorm. Jamukha then fled to the Kereit tribes to bide his time.

By that time Toghril was quite old and looking to secure his successor. All indications are that he favored Temüjin, which did not sit well with his natural son, Senggüm, who was beholden to

Jamukha. In an effort to secure his association with Toghril, Temüjin in 1203 proposed that his eldest son, Jochi, be married to one of Toghril's daughters, and that one of his daughters marry a son of Senggüm, which he refused. Senggüm and Jamukha were both now allied with the Kereit tribes, and they accused Temüjin of arranging an attack on Toghril's camp. Toghril sided with his son and Jamukha, who was put in charge of the army of his followers, which had joined the Kereit. After one unsuccessful attempt to lure Temüjin into a trap, Jamukha and Senggüm led a major force to attack Temüjin and his army. There were too many men for the Mongols to handle, and Temüjin and some loyal followers fled—after retrieving his severely wounded son, Ögödei—into a marshy area in southeastern Mongolia. Encamped by a lake called Baljuna, several leading figures who had followed Temüjin all swore an oath of allegiance to defeat the Kereit forces by drinking of the bitter Baljuna water. It is unclear whether this oath-swearing actually occurred, but it quickly developed into a potent myth that was used by later writers to enhance the prestige of these same men.

By the summer of 1203 Temüjin and his followers had left the Baljuna area for their traditional grazing areas at the Onon River. Temüjin put out the word for his friends and allies to join him. He also took the opportunity to organize his military forces into groups of thousands, hundreds, and tens. This decimal system of organization had been used successfully by other nomadic leaders and, in fact, Toghril's Kereit forces were so organized. It was a most successful way to quickly dispatch orders from top down, and to ensure the complete loyalty of everyone. Mongol cavalry were divided into light and heavy units. The latter used lances and axes, and wore full body armor, while the former relied on the bow and their mobility. At the same time, Temüjin was reorganizing his rudimentary household and administrative staff to better prepare for the coming conflict and potential for great enlargement of his numbers. He reorganized some of his personal staff into a system of day and night bodyguards. These guards (Mongolian *keshig*) were recruited from the sons of chiefs of the allied tribes and eminent military men, and they served as the core of his growing military machine.

In May of 1204, the newly reorganized and strengthened Mongol army rode west along the Kerulen River to confront their enemies. By this time, Jamukha and company had made no less than three separate attempts to assassinate Toghril, each of which was foiled. Temüjin and his troops first marched on Toghril's group, who were located near to the headwaters of the Kerulun River. Most of the Kereit troops were trapped on a narrow cliff and perished there, but Toghril and his son, Senggüm, managed to escape the onslaught and fled further west to find shelter with the Naiman tribes. Jamukha had yet again fled the scene of battle rather than fight. He joined up with the Merged tribes. As mentioned earlier, it was the Merged who had kidnapped Temüjin's wife, Börte, and its chief was undoubtedly the biological father of Jochi, their eldest son. So Temüjin now had two potent scores to settle.

Temüjin never got the opportunity to mete justice to his former chief, however, since Toghril was killed as he was entering Naiman tribal territory by a tribesman who did not recognize him. Senggüm kept going west, hoping to find protection among the settled Uygurs who lived in the Tarim Basin area in present-day Xinjiang. He was eventually killed there. The deaths of both men occurred in late 1203, by which time Temüjin held the eastern part of present-day Mongolia in his power. The most important tribes that he still faced were to his west, the Naiman, Oirat, Merged, and Onguts. Temüjin had integrated the remaining Kereit into his own growing tribal alliance, distributing them among these other tribes. The Ongut realized their position and made an alliance with Temüjin and the Mongols, while the Naiman, Oirat, and Merged tribes allied to fight Temüjin. The two forces met in battle in 1204, and the Mongols were the victors. It actually took several more years, however, to completely wipe out the Merged and Naiman holdouts; another successful battle against remaining Naiman and Merged units occurred in 1208, and it was not actually until about 1218 that the last Naiman leader was tracked down and killed.

There are different accounts of the end of Temüjin's former *anda* and nemesis Jamukha. By that time he had descended to leading a roving band of robbers and ne'er-do-wells. His followers actually handed him over to Temüjin, who, according to the *Secret History of the Mongols* (De Rachewiltz, 2004) account, even pled with Jamukha to join him again as an ally. Jamukha refused and instead begged to be put to death because he had broken his oath to his blood-brother. He was then either killed without shedding his blood, the normal style of execution reserved for nomadic nobility, or was hacked to death by Temüjin's youngest brother. This probably occurred in 1205, which left Temüjin free to consolidate his power over the tribes on the Mongolian plateau.

Chinggis Strikes Out on His Imperial Project

In 1206 the successful Temüjin summoned his tribe, his close companions, and the commanders and leaders of all of the tribes who had come into an alliance with him as subordinates to a *quriltai* (*kùlìtái dàhuì* 库力台大会) at the Onon River, where they all elected him as their grand khan. It was at this time that he was given, or claimed for himself, the name Chinggis (Mongolian *fierce*), and exclusive use of a white standard with streamers of nine yak tails (some sources report earlier usage of this name by Temüjin). In fact, this latter device was a most important symbol of his legitimacy as supreme tribal leader, since the color white and number nine are both ancient auspicious symbols to steppe peoples. Most of the sources relate that a Mongol shaman named Teb Tenggeri actually coined the name Chinggis for Temüjin. The 1206 *quriltai* culminated a long process of tribal consolidation under Temüjin's power, and signaled to everyone that this man was now the ruler of "all tribes living in felt tents" (De Hartog 1999, 24–34) and the true start of his imperial project, the Great Mongol Nation (Mongolian *Yeke Mongol Ulus*).

It is unlikely that Chinggis Khan at this point had in mind the conquest of China and other great settled states, but his immediate task of consolidating and unifying all of the remaining tribes in the northern steppe brought him naturally to confront the Jurchen Jin state. It is interesting to see how quickly other tribes fell in line with Chinggis's growing power after 1206. Along with tribes such as the Kirgiz and Oirats to the west, one of the most important results was the voluntary submission to Chinggis by the Uygur state in 1209. The literate and multicultural Uygurs were perhaps the epitome of high civilization as experienced by tribal peoples, and their acquisition brought Chinggis a good deal of cultural capital, not least because he had adopted the Uygur writing system to represent spoken Mongolian by the year 1204.

Along with this consolidation of power, Chinggis expanded the ranks of his military and administrative machinery after 1206. He inducted several recently submitted tribes into his army, creating regiments of one thousand men in three separate divisions (Right Wing, Left Wing, Center). Most of these peoples were distributed among new military formations to bolster the growing Mongol army, and to create new loyalties to Chinggis and his own tribe. He also increased his personal guard troops to ten thousand. It was also at this time that the Mongols first began to use written documents, which were necessary as the Mongol administration grew to accommodate the peoples who had been, and would continue to be, folded into the growing Mongol empire. The first such written tools were a court record that included legal declarations and official records of imperial decisions called the "Blue Book" (Mongolian *kökö debter*), and a compilation of legal pronouncements of Chinggis known as the *Yasakh* (the existence of this set of sayings in written form is still questioned). It is important to note here that the famous *Secret History of the Mongols* was produced long after Chinggis's death by writers who wanted to enhance the heavenly ordained nature of Chinggis Khan's rulership.

Chinggis Khan's first adventure beyond the steppe came with an attack on the Tangut (Dǎngxiàng 党项) state to his southwest in 1209. The Mongols penetrated as far as the Tangut capital, Zhongxing (present-day Yinchuan City, Ningxia), which they tried to capture. The siege did not go as planned, however, when the intended flood of the city flooded their own camps instead. After negotiations, the Tangut emperor (Li Anquan, r. 1206–11) in 1210 essentially agreed to become a vassal of Chinggis, giving a daughter in marriage to Chinggis Khan and promising to provide supplies to the Mongol armies in future. Chinggis then turned to his real target, the Jin state.

Ever since taking part in the raids on the Tatar tribes in 1198, Chinggis had been considered by the Jin court as a vassal. By 1211 he was ready to renounce that relationship, and convened a *quriltai* to plan the coming war. His reasons for going to war were, first to avenge the murder of two of his clan members by the Jin, and second, to avenge the defeat of the Khitans by the Jurchens. It was cast as the first national war of the united Mongol tribes. Initial advances into Jin territory occurred in 1211, as far as the main Jin capital at present-day Beijing. Then Chinggis withdrew his troops to the steppe for resupply. The attack recommenced in late 1212, and a year later the Mongols had the Jin capital blockaded. The Jin emperor only got the siege lifted by providing one of his daughters to Chinggis in marriage as well as tribute gifts. Chinggis and his main army then returned north. When the Jin emperor and court fled south to the Jin southern capital Kaifeng, Chinggis ordered his troops back to their main capital. Another siege was commenced in late 1214, Chinggis himself took charge of the assault in 1215 and the city surrendered in May 1215. Mongol troops burned and looted the city for a full month. At the same time, Mongol troops had occupied Manchuria and the rest of north China that had been in the Jin state. By 1216 events further west claimed Chinggis Khan's attention, and he left the finishing up of Jin to his trusted general, Mukhali. It took another twenty years to fully conquer Jin.

Chinggis was really looking for good political and commercial relations with the large Persian state of Khwarazm when he sent a delegation to the shah of that state in 1218, in response to an earlier visit by Khwarezmian envoys in 1215. Unfortunately for the Khwarezmian state, the entire trade delegation—except one—was murdered by the governor of Otrar, the first place for the delegation to enter Khwarezmian lands. Not only was it an international crime to kill an imperial envoy, but Muhammad II, the Khwarezm shah, brought on himself and his people the full wrath of Chinggis Khan. That event also heralded the first full push by Chinggis and his sons westward to extend his nascent empire, which only ended at the gates of Europe and not by any military defeat experienced by the Mongols.

In late 1218, Chinggis began to plan the conquest of the Khwarezmian state.

The siege of Zhongdu (Beijing) in 1215 CE by Chinggis Khan and his troops as depicted in the historical chronicle *Jami' al-tawarikh* by the scholar Rashid-al-Din Hamadani (1430).

The combined Mongol forces, now greatly strengthened with Chinese, Khitan, Uygur, and other peoples, and led by Chinggis and his sons Jochi, Tolui, Chaghadai, and *Ögödei (Wōkuòtái 窝阔台, c. 1186–1241), set out in 1219 to the center of the Khwarezm state in Transoxania, present-day Uzbekistan and parts of the surrounding nations. This Islamic state was a fusion of Turkic and Persian cultures, but the people there had only recently come under Muhammad's rule, and he was not especially liked. The first city in the Mongols' path, Otrar, fell after a five month siege, and the centerpieces of that state, the cities of Bukhara and Samarkand, fell within a year. This opened up eastern Persia to Chinggis, into which he advanced in 1220. After a series of successful campaigns over the next two years, Chinggis Khan and his armies had reunited with other Mongol forces and returned to

*People marked with an asterisk have entries in this dictionary.

the steppe to rest, to visit with an invited Daoist (Taoist) adept from China, Cháng Chūn 长春, and to plan his next move on the Tanguts.

Chinggis Khan's End

The Tanguts were obligated to supply Chinggis's troops when called upon, but in 1222 a contingent of Tangut troops sent to help the Mongols in northern China rebelled. This coincided with a new alliance between the Jin and Tangut courts, which further eroded Chinggis's confidence in the reliability of the Tanguts to his own cause. It was to quell this possible trouble spot that Chinggis finally set out in 1226 with his army towards the Tangut realm. Late in 1226 they began their siege of important Tangut cities on the east bank of the Huang (Yellow) River in present-day Ningxia. The Mongol campaign stopped in winter, and was resumed in February 1227. Sometime in 1227 Chinggis's horse bolted and he fell in battle, subsequently falling into a high fever. His generals wanted to call off the attack, but Chinggis refused, and the campaign continued. By summer of 1227 the Tangut king knew his situation was hopeless and he bargained with Chinggis for a month to collect tribute and surrender, which was granted. By the time he arrived in September of that year Chinggis had died, but this was not revealed to the Tangut king, whose execution had been ordered by Chinggis on his deathbed. It was also shortly before he died that he instructed his son, Tolui, about the best way to finish the campaign against the Jin state, since his eldest son, Jochi, had already died earlier in the year.

All accounts report that Chinggis Khan's body was taken to the sacred mountain, Burkhan Khaldun, where he was buried. The site is now the focus of intensive expeditions in Mongolia. It is fitting that it has never been found; this great leader of men and empire builder went out the way he came in, a nomad who was comfortable in the wide expanse of the steppe where the water runs clear and the grazing is good.

Michael C. BROSE
University of Wyoming

Further Reading

Allsen, Thomas T. (1994). The rise of the Mongolian Empire and Mongolian rule in North China. In Herbert Franke & Denis Twitchett (Eds.), *The Cambridge history of China, Volume 6. Alien regimes and border states, 907–1368* (pp. 321–365). Cambridge, UK: Cambridge University Press.

Allsen, Thomas T. (2001). *Culture and conquest in Mongol Eurasia*. Cambridge, UK: Cambridge University Press.

Amitai, Reuven & Biran, Michal (Eds.). (2005). *Mongols, Turks and others*. Leiden, The Netherlands: Brill.

Barthold, Wilhelm. (1968, 1988). *Turkestan down to the Mongol Invasion*. Taipei, Taiwan: Southern Materials Center.

Brent, Peter. (1976). *Genghis Khan: The rise, authority and decline of Mongol power*. New York: McGraw-Hill.

Brose, Michael C. (2007). *Subjects and masters: The Uyghurs in the Mongol Empire*. Bellingham: Western Washington University Press.

Cleaves, Francis W. (1995). The historicity of the Baljuna Covenant. *Harvard Journal of Asiatic Studies, 18*, 357–421.

Dawson, Christopher. (1955, 1980). *Mission to Asia*. Toronto: University of Toronto Press.

Dunnell, Ruth. (2010). *Chinggis Khan: World conqueror*. Boston: Longman.

Golden, Peter. (1992). *An introduction to the history of the Turkic peoples*. Wiesbaden, Germany: Otto Harrassowitz.

De Hartog, Leo. (1999). *Genghis Khan, conqueror of the world*. New York: Barnes & Noble.

Juvaini, Ata-Malik. (1997). *Genghis Khan: The history of the world conqueror*. (J. A. Boyle, Trans.). Seattle: University of Washington Press. First published 1958.

Kahn, Paul. (1998). *The secret history of the Mongols: The origin of Chingis Khan*. Boston: Cheng & Tsui.

Lamb, Harold. (1940). *The march of the barbarians*. New York: The Literary Guild of America.

Lane, George. (2004). *Genghis Khan and Mongol rule*. Westport, CT: Greenwood Press.

Lindner, Rudi Paul. (1982). What was a nomadic tribe? *Society for the Comparative Study of Society and History, 24*(4), 689–711.

May, Timothy. (2007). *The Mongol art of war*. Chicago: Westholme Publications.

Morgan, David. (1991). *The Mongols*. Cambridge, MA: Blackwell.

De Rachewiltz, Igor. (2004). *The secret history of the Mongols: A Mongolian epic of the thirteenth century*. Two volumes. Leiden, The Netherlands: Brill.

Rashid al-Din. (1998, 1999). *Jami'u't-tawarikh* (*Compendium of Chronicles*) (W. M. Thackston, Trans.). Boston: Harvard University, Department of Near Eastern Languages and Civilizations.

Ratchnevsky, Paul. (1991). *Genghis Khan, his life and legacy* (Thomas Nivison Haining, Trans.). Oxford, UK: Basil Blackwell.

Song Lian (Comp.). (1978). *Yuanshi* 元史 [History of the Yuan]. (15 vols). Beijing: Zhonghua shuju.

Spuler, Bertold. (1972). *History of the Mongols*. (Helga and Stuart Drummond, Trans.). New York: Dorset Press.

Ögödei Khan

Wōkuòtái 窝阔台

c. 1186–1241—Second Great Khan of the Mongol Empire; r. 1229–1241

Summary

A son of Chinggis (Genghis) Khan, Ögödei Khan helped to expand the empire across China, Central Asia, and Eurasia during his reign. Under his rule administrative structures were improved, a capital city established, and a postal system was expanded to facilitate empire-wide communications. While many attribute the Mongol vision of world conquest to his father, Ögödei Khan was responsible for the successful advancement of Chinggis Khan's policies. Sedentary territories were conquered and taxes were imposed; administrative policies were put into place to facilitate permanent rule. Ögödei Khan actively promoted the notion that the Mongols held the Mandate of Heaven, which lent to their legitimacy as world conquerors. His death heralded an era of succession struggles that would eventually divide the loyalties of the imperial family.

Ögödei Khan was the second ruler of the Mongol Empire, which was founded by his father, *Chinggis (Genghis) Khan (c. 1162–1227), in 1206. During Ögödei's reign the empire was significantly expanded with territorial holdings consolidated in China, Central Asia, and Russia. The Jīn 金 and Khwarazmian Empires were overthrown, many princes of Rus were reduced to vassal status, and eastern Europe came under threat as well.

Under the leadership of Ögödei Khan, Mongol prerogatives had shifted. Previously, under the rule of Chinggis Khan, Mongol goals centered on uniting the nomadic tribes of Central Asia and merely raiding sedentary polities. By the time of Ögödei Khan's reign, however, expansion policies had turned toward actual conquest and permanent rule over

*People marked with an asterisk have entries in this dictionary.

sedentary societies. Ögödei Khan's military actions indicate that he promoted a vision of Mongol world conquest. Furthermore, he also stabilized administrative structures that were necessary to govern a territorially expansive empire, while simultaneously undertaking measures to expand commerce and improve communication networks across the empire. Ögödei Khan's policies went beyond typical expectations for a steppe ruler, especially when he established and built a capital city at Karakorum. Ögödei Khan's reign resulted in improved administrative stability within the empire as well as significant territorial expansion. The succession struggles that occurred upon his death in 1241, however, foreshadowed the political divisions and strife that would eventually wreak havoc among the imperial family.

Early Life

Ögödei Khan was born to Chinggis Khan of the Borjigin clan and his first wife Börte (1161–1230) of the Onggirat clan before his father rose to his highest office as the founder and ruler of the Mongol Empire. Ögödei was the third of four sons born to his parents and, while not much is known of Ögödei's early life, his childhood was probably typical for one born into a nomadic Mongol society of the thirteenth century. Unlike neighboring China, where agriculture and sedentarism dictated ways of life, the Mongols were steppe nomads whose homelands were centered on the pasturelands of Inner Asia. As pastoralists, Inner Asian nomadic groups migrated seasonally to meet the needs of their herd animals, while also hunting and trading with settled societies along the borderlands of their territories. Inner Asian pastoral nomads faced harsh environmental conditions, as well as the constant threat of intertribal warfare and raiding. It was in this setting that Ögödei's father fought to conquer and unite all of the indigenous nomadic tribes of Inner Asia under his rule.

Ögödei would have learned to ride on horseback during early childhood and would have been trained extensively in hunting and archery. These skills were necessary for survival on the steppes of Inner Asia, where pastoralism, migration, harsh environmental conditions, and intertribal warfare defined life. The survival skills of daily life, such as hunting and archery, easily translated into military skills. In contrast to sedentary societies, where many peasants were engaged in agriculture as a primary pursuit, and where military training was a specialized activity, the Mongol way of life prepared every man to serve as a warrior. In this way, the entire male population could be mobilized for military service. Ögödei's experience was no different and he was actively involved in his father's military campaigns by the time he was a teenager. In 1203, during the early period of Mongol expansion, Chinggis Khan was still consolidating power and fighting to conquer the neighboring nomadic tribes of the

Inner Asian steppes. At this time Ögödei was wounded in battle fighting against his father's prime rival for power in Inner Asia, Jamukha (d. 1206). The Mongols were defeated in this skirmish and it was initially believed that Ögödei had been lost in battle; he was rescued, however, and fully recovered from his injuries.

Marriage

In 1204 Ögödei married Töregene (r. 1244–1246), who was the former wife of the leader of the Merkit tribe. After the Merkits were defeated by the Mongols, Chinggis Khan awarded Töregene to his son. This was not an uncommon phenomenon since in Mongol society marriages often served as a means to cement political alliances, to reinforce loyalties, and to establish familial connections. Such alliances, however, were not merely symbolic in nature. Women held high status in Inner Asian pastoral nomadic society and were active participants in tribal affairs. This meant that marriage alliances within the imperial Mongol family often led to actual positions of political power and influence for elite women such as Töregene, especially in the form of regencies during periods of interregnum after the death of the khan. In this way, Ögödei's wife would eventually go on to act as regent after his death in 1241.

Rise to Power

In 1206 a *quriltai*, or consultative assembly, was held and Chinggis Khan was elected as leader of the united Mongols. *Quriltais* were meetings where Mongol elites (including both men and women of high status) gathered as a tribal consultative body to make important decisions, namely that of electing leaders. While candidates for leadership were usually preselected, with various powerful political factions present to support their candidacy, formal election via the *quriltai* process served as a means for bestowing the highest level of political legitimacy. During his lifetime, Chinggis Khan had made it clear that he wished for Ögödei to succeed him as ruler of the empire so that there would be no controversy or dispute in this matter, ensuring a peaceful and smooth transition of power. After the death of his father, Ögödei was confirmed as his father's successor and awarded the title of the Great Khan at the *quriltai* held near the Kerülen River in 1229.

Early Military Activities

Ögödei, along with his brothers, had always been actively involved in the military pursuits of his father that resulted in the establishment of the Mongol Empire. After the nomadic tribes of Inner Asia were united under the singular rule of Chinggis Khan, attentions were turned toward the conquest of sedentary societies, China in particular. Both before and after the era of the Mongol Empire, nomadic tribes bordering Chinese territories had continually engaged in raiding activities along frontier borderlands. For such nomads, life revolved around pastoralism, so that subsistence needs were generally met by obtaining milk and meat from their herds of sheep, horses, goats, yaks, and camels. Yet, they were not completely self-sufficient. The pastoral nomads of Inner Asia valued a variety of commodities produced in sedentary societies, such as grain, textiles, and other luxury goods, which could be traded for horses. The benefits of trade were bilateral since horses were an essential commodity for sedentary societies who relied on nomads for their supplies of horses to accommodate their military needs. When favorable trade agreements could not be reached, raiding and warfare often ensued.

Early Mongol incursions into China emulated this pattern. The Mongols made a habit of raiding to obtain booty, followed by retreats back to their steppe homelands. During these early raiding ventures the Mongols did not have the siege technology to fully conquer walled cities, nor did they have the desire to do so. The Mongols, however, were beginning on a path of military exploits in China that would eventually lead to outright conquest. The strategies and desires of the Mongols began to change over time, making their conquests quite distinct from those of any other previous steppe empires emanating from Inner Asia. The Mongols began to turn from a military ideology fueled by raiding toward one driven by outright conquest. The conquest of China was the result of years of prolonged fighting, mainly in the form of raiding, gradually shifting toward an ideology of permanent conquest. This process began with Chinggis Khan's conquest of Xi Xia, the nearest western neighbor to the Mongols, in 1209. Repeated raids and assaults against the Jin followed this victory beginning in 1211, so that the Jīn court was eventually forced to move their capital to K'aifeng in 1215. Prior to this, in 1213, Chinggis Khan divided his forces in China into three groups, with one of these groups led jointly by three of his sons; Jochi (1181–1227), Chagatai (d. 1241), and Ögödei. While the brothers did succeed in taking several cities, these military exploits represented typical Mongol raids and not necessarily attempts at permanent conquest. The eventual induction of Chinese siege engineers into the Mongol army, however, radically changed the military situation on the ground, so that now the Mongols could feasibly begin to attack walled cities with more success than they had been able to achieve in the past.

Mongol expansion during this period was not only oriented toward their eastern frontiers. Ögödei also actively participated in his father's conquest of the Khwarazmian Empire, which was situated in Central Asia along the Syr Daria River in Transoxiana (parts of modern-day Uzbekistan, Tajikistan, Kyrgyzstan, and Kazakhstan) and was ruled by the Khwarazm Shah. The troubles between the Mongols and the Khwarazmians began in 1218 when a Mongol caravan was confiscated, with merchants and envoys put to death on the suspicion that they were spies. Chinggis Khan demanded compensation for these affronts and when his demands were rebuffed he promptly declared war. In 1219, with a division commanded by Chinggis Khan's sons, Chagatai and Ögödei, the Mongol army penetrated the city of Otrar, even though they took the town only after a prolonged siege. Consequently, most of the town's inhabitants were either massacred or enslaved, and the region was decimated.

Ögödei Succeeds His Father

Following the death of Chinggis Khan in 1227, Ögödei Khan ascended to power as the second ruler of the Mongol Empire. Fortunately, he had been nominated as his father's successor so that the transition of power occurred without causing a political crisis. It took two years, however, before the official *quriltai* was held in 1229, which confirmed the legitimacy of his succession. Ögödei's family branch ruled until the succession shifted to his brother's Toluid line in 1251, which culminated in family squabbles and outright warfare as Ögödeid and Toluid imperial descendants vied for succession and supremacy.

With the death of his father, the territories of the Mongol Empire were distributed among Ögödei and his brothers. Ögödei inherited the territory east and northeast of Lake Balkhash, with the Ögödeid camp being near the Emil River. Even though the territories of the Mongol Empire were divided among Chinggis Khan's sons after his death, the empire was not divided in terms of supreme rule. All territories were deemed to be united under the authority of one khan, the Great Khan, Ögödei. Even though Ögödei had been chosen by his father to rule, this did not mean Ögödei's inherence was inevitable or automatically determined by traditional Mongol succession practices. Initially, Chinggis Khan preferred to pass his authority to his eldest son, Jochi. His second son, Chagatai, however, objected on the grounds that Jochi's paternity was questionable since their mother Börte became pregnant with him around the time that she had been kidnapped by Merkit tribesmen. In order to make peace, Chinggis Khan selected his third son Ögödei as his successor, since he was capable and well liked by both brothers.

There was a two-year interregnum after Chinggis Khan's death when his youngest son Tolui acted as regent from 1227–1229. Yet, this time lapse between Chinggis Khan's death and Ögödei's investiture was not representative of any political discord among the Mongols. In such a vast empire it simply took time to recall leaders and elites to convene a *quriltai* that would formalize the transfer of authority. Acting as regent, Tolui did not go against his father's wishes or

The coronation of Ögödei as Great Khan of the Mongol Empire after the death of his father, Chinggis Khan.

attempt to usurp power from Ögödei, and he readily relinquished control after his brother's succession was legitimized at the *quriltai.* Ögödei's appointment as supreme khan rested on the support of his brothers and other relatives, and also on their respect for Chinggis Khan's personal wishes. This was because of the fact that in Mongol society there were a variety of ways to handle issues regarding succession. There were precedents for lateral succession, when a ruler's brothers inherited power. Precedents also existed for eldest sons to inherit power. Furthermore, Mongol customs also allowed for the youngest son to inherit his father's personal property, army, and camp, giving them access to power as well. Ögödei's selection and confirmation ultimately supported the practice of tanistry, or the notion that the khan had the right to choose his own successor during his lifetime. His formal legitimization as ruler via the *quriltai* process illustrated the continued importance of Turko-Mongol notions of shared familial power and also emphasized the importance of consensus in deciding who had the right to rule.

Reputation

Ögödei had a reputation for both generosity and tolerance. For example, water was religiously significant for Mongols and taboos were in place that forbade bathing and washing in rivers. Despite such taboos, Ögödei took pity on a man who was caught breaking them. To ensure that the offender would escape punishment, Ögödei had gold placed in the river, providing a valid reason for the taboo to be broken. He was also known for his generosity toward the merchants and diplomats who came to court for the purposes of trade and to pay their respects. His father chose him for the succession due to the fact that he was skilled in keeping peace among his brothers.

When Chinggis Khan sent Jochi, Chagatai, and Ögödei to attack the Khwarazmian city of Otrar, it was Ögödei who led the assault since his older brothers often quarreled. He was able to make peace between them during the campaign, so that in working together the conquest was a success. Historical accounts record that Ögödei Khan's younger brother Tolui actually sacrificed himself in order to save The Great Khan's life. Ögödei Khan had fallen ill and was being attended by shamans. Tolui believed that his brother was being punished for sins committed during their conquests in China. To this end, Tolui prayed for the gods to take him and spare Ögödei. Tolui died soon after, but in reality, he most likely died of alcoholism, which would have been a common occurrence among the Mongol imperial family since they were known to be heavy drinkers. In any case, the more romanticized account serves to illustrate the strong bond and affection between the brothers. Outside of his popularity within the imperial family, Ögödei was also renowned for other good deeds, such as providing dowries for poor women, generously reimbursing a herder whose sheep had been killed by a wolf, and rewarding a courtier with a gift of priceless pearls.

Not all of his deeds were praiseworthy, however. Most notably, Ögödei Khan had demanded possession of all the marriageable girls over the age of seventeen from the Oirat tribe. The Oirats disobeyed by marrying their daughters to others and, consequently, were severely punished. In retaliation,

Ögödei ordered that these four thousand daughters be assembled, where they were raped by Mongol troops. Some women were sent to the imperial harem; others were married off to commoners or sent to brothels. These descriptions of Ögödei Khan's character illustrate that, while he was known for his generosity and peacemaking abilities within the imperial family, he was still a ruthless ruler when faced with disobedient subjects.

Expansion of the Empire

Under Ögödei Khan's leadership the empire continued to expand and during his lifetime warfare was waged across the continent of Asia, as Mongol armies conquered territories from China all the way into southern Russia, occasionally even venturing into eastern Europe. During this period of expansion some of the empire's most well-known generals and princes were dispatched by Ögödei to the eastern and western frontiers of the empire in efforts to expand Mongol territory and solidify power. Even though Ögödei and his brothers had already conquered the Khwarazmian Empire under the orders of Chinggis Khan, Ögödei Khan faced an attempted restoration of the previous ruling dynasty by its heir to the throne, Jalal al-Din (d. 1231). To squash this unrest, in 1230–1231 Ögödei sent thirty thousand troops into Persia commanded by the general Chormaqan (d. 1241). Jalal al-Din fled from the Mongols to Transcaucasia and despite his best efforts to outrun his enemies, he was eventually murdered by Kurdish peasants in 1231. These conquests in central Asia led the Mongols further east toward the borders of the Abbasid-controlled territories of Persia and the Christian territories of Armenia and Georgia, and eventually led to the seizure of the coveted pasturelands of Azerbaijan. Throughout this period many Central Asian cities were ravaged and destroyed. In the wake of Mongol destruction, many rulers submitted to Mongol and became tribute paying vassals in order to save themselves and their people from destruction. For example, the city of Tabriz submitted to their authority and placated the Mongol general Chormaqan by sending precious fabrics to Ögödei's court in 1233. In 1236 the Mongols invaded Georgia and in 1239 they invaded Armenia under the authority of Chormaqan. By 1244, King Hetum I of Armenia submitted to Mongol authority.

In 1231 Ögödei's troops invaded Korea taking the capital city, Kaesŏng. Yet, in 1232, by order of the Korean king, all resident Mongols were massacred. Consequently, a new army was dispatched to occupy mainland Korea in 1236. The result was that in 1241 Korea became a vassal kingdom of the Mongol Empire. This relationship was solidified through political marriages, allowing the Korean royal family to maintain a high degree of prestige during this period as a son-in-law kingdom with close ties to the imperial Mongol family.

Mongol conquests in China persisted during Ögödei Khan's reign. Even though Chinggis Khan had raided and attempted to conquer the Jīn many times throughout his reign, their ultimate conquest was achieved under the rule of Ögödei Khan. In 1232 he was able to capture the city of Hochung and then his army circled around to meet with the army of his younger brother Tolui at Henan (Ho-nan). While the Jin fought vigorously against the Mongols, they could not hold out indefinitely. In March 1232 Ögödei ordered his general, Subotai (1175–1248), to besiege K'aifeng, the Jīn capital, and it was finally taken in 1233. Ögödei wished to destroy the capital city and allow the land to revert back to pasture but was persuaded by his main advisor, Yel-ü Ch'u-ts'ai, to refrain from destroying the land. This advice was based on Yel-ü Ch'u-ts'ai's rationale that more profit could be made through taxation of the people. This change in policy marked a turning point for Mongol activity in China, as they planned to implement taxation and tribute rather than rely on their previous strategies of raiding and destruction. With the capital city taken, the Jīn emperor Aizong (1198–1234) fled in order to regroup, although he ultimately committed suicide during the final Mongol assault in March of 1234. Consequently, the Mongols definitively conquered the Jīn Empire in northern China and Manchuria in 1234. The Chinese Sòng 宋 dynasty (960–1279) had assisted the Mongols in their efforts and they were rewarded by being allowed to retain certain districts in the southeastern point of present-day Henan Province. Still, the Song Emperor Lizong (1205–1264), angry over not possessing the whole of Henan, attacked the Mongols. These hostilities allowed the Chinese to reoccupy Kaifeng and Luoyang in July–August of 1234, even though they were ultimately driven out by the Mongols. The end result was disastrous for the Song Empire, since at the *quriltai* held at Karakorum in 1235 the Mongols agreed to conquer the Song. This began a protracted period of war between the Mongols and the Song Empire that would last for more than four decades.

In 1235 Ögödei called a *quriltai*, where military attentions were again directed westward. The Great Khan sought to accomplish the task of conquering the lands that already been given by Chinggis Khan to his eldest son, Jochi. Despite Jochi's premature death, his territorial inheritance and rights of conquest passed on to his son *Batu Khan (Bádūhán 拔都汗, c. 1205–1255). Under the command of Batu, the Mongol army ruthlessly conquered Russian territories, often leaving no survivors and establishing what became known as the Golden Horde. (The name refers to the ornate golden tent seized from the king of Hungary.) With this western push, armies were even campaigning in Europe as far away as Hungary. With the death of Ögödei in 1241, however, the army was forced to withdraw from Hungary, never to return in full force again, perhaps saving Europe from a full-scale Mongol invasion.

While many attribute the Mongol vision of world conquest to Chinggis Khan, the military actions ordered by Ögödei Khan illustrate the actual advancement of this policy. Rather than merely raiding sedentary neighbors in search of goods or slaves, sedentary territories were conquered and taxes were imposed on these populations. Administrative policies were put into place to facilitate permanent rule. Perhaps most tellingly, Ögödei Khan actively promoted the notion that the Mongols held the Mandate of Heaven, which lent to their legitimacy as world conquerors.

Establishment of the Capital City of Karakorum

Ögödei Khan also broke new ground, as the ruler of a pastoral-nomadic people, when he established a fixed capital at Karakorum. The city was situated on the open steppe of the Orkhon valley of central Mongolia in the former territories of the Naiman tribe, and it served as the first stationary Mongol city. This site was historically significant since it was situated in the upper Orkhon region where previous steppe empires had also established their capitals. The site was initially used as a Mongol encampment, but eventually a city was built and walled in 1235. The impetus for establishing a walled capital city was not merely for the purpose of illustrating imperial prestige and power, it was a necessity for the management of the empire. Covering an immense amount of territory, and experiencing rapid expansion, the Mongols were collecting taxes, tribute, goods, and slaves from across Asia. Essentially, they needed a storehouse for these goods and an administrative center for the management of this wealth. Karakorum was founded to meet these needs, so that it became a center for commerce and tribute as well as imperial administration. This did not mean, however, that Ögödei became a strictly sedentary ruler. He had many pavilions and palaces built within the vicinity, and moved among these seasonally.

Contributions to the Empire

While the Mongol conquests were often destructive for those who refused to submit and surrender, the stabilization of Mongol rule also brought about some improvements. The reign of Ögödei Khan gave rise to a variety of developments, especially in terms of infrastructure, commerce, and communications. For example, the Great Khan ensured that wells were dug and walled in the Gobi Desert. While this helped facilitate trade in an area that was previously difficult to traverse and gave greater access to pasture lands, these advancements also had practical purposes that benefitted the state. Wells ensured that the Mongols now had an easy route for their armies to enter China when necessary. Ögödei Khan also ensured the commercial viability of

Karakorum by paying merchants top prices for their goods, only to give them away as gifts. Such activity attracted merchants, caravans, and diplomats to the city. These practices allowed the Great Khan to build a reputation for excessive generosity. While he was not thrifty, his spending did much for improving the vitality, importance, and economic health of the city. The importance of merchants in Karakorum was also due to the economic significance of trade on the Silk Roads. The high status of merchants in Mongol society allowed their influence to rise throughout the empire and they had close dealings with the imperial family, often serving as advisors. While relationships between merchants and the imperial family were beneficial in the short-term, this was not to prove true in the long-term. Eventually, the rising power of merchants led to corruption and interference in the economic management of the empire.

The success of Ögödei Khan's reign can also be attributed to his employment of wise advisors. Exploitation and destruction during his conquests were limited, to a degree, due to the influence of a sinicized Khitan advisor named Yel-ü Ch'u-ts'ai, who served as a bridge between Mongol and Chinese culture. This made him an invaluable consultant since he was able to familiarize Ögödei Khan with the practices of sedentary administration and politics. Under Yel-ü Ch'u-ts'ai's advisement, Chinese, Tangut, Uygur, and Persian departments were set up within the Mongol chancellery, representative of some of the various conquered populations that had been incorporated into the empire. Grain storehouses were set up along courier routes and a fixed budget was established for the empire whereby the Chinese paid taxes in silver, silk, and grain, and Mongols contributed 10 percent of their horses, cattle, and sheep. Conquered portions of China were organized into ten districts in 1230 and they were administered by both Mongol and Chinese officials. During this period many Chinese were recruited into Mongol civil service and Confucian schools were also set up to educate Mongols for administrative posts.

Ögödei Khan's attention to administrative concerns was a prime factor in maintaining the stability of the empire during his reign. The *yam*, or postal relay system, instituted by Chinggis Khan was greatly extended by Ögödei Khan in 1234 with post stations spaced evenly across the empire, approximately a day's journey apart. This greatly facilitated communication, which was of vital importance in a vast empire with ever-expanding frontiers. The yam system was restricted to official imperial business and required an imperial authorization pass, or *paiza*. These posts were operated by the army and were initially intended to provide horses and provisions for those carrying out imperial orders. In time, however, both merchants and elites abused *paizas* and the *yam* system, using them for personal benefit.

Such abuses took a heavy toll on the local populations who were responsible for provisioning these stations, as they faced continually increasing demands on their resources.

Death of Ögödei Khan

Known to be a heavy drinker, Ögödei Khan died from excessive alcohol consumption in December of 1241. He was fond of wine and often drank to excess, and his health was in decline. Although many sought to intervene and control his alcohol intake, it was to no avail. A minister was even appointed by Ögödei Khan's brother Chagatai to oversee and limit his alcohol intake. The Great Khan was only allowed to drink a certain number of cups per day. Yet, these measures were sidestepped when Ögödei decided to simply drink from a larger cup. Despite attempts to limit his drinking, in the end his alcohol intake remained the same until, after a night of excessive drinking, he was found dead in his bed. Conspiracy theories related to his death circulated, with accusations falling upon servants and relatives, but in the end reason prevailed and the accusations were eventually dismissed.

Interregnum

Ögödei's death in 1241 led to a prolonged period of interregnum and political struggles concerning who should be his successor. This was not a struggle among brothers since his eldest brother Jochi had died even before their father, Chagatai lived only a few months more than Ögödei, and Tolui, the youngest brother, died early during Ögödei's reign. This meant the field was now open for succession squabbles among cousins who were the grandsons of Chinggis Khan. In the meantime, Ögödei Khan's widow, Töregene Khatun (r. 1241–1246), ruled as regent until the succession was settled. While she was not Ögödei's senior wife, she was the mother of his eldest son and this swayed other Mongol elites to support her claim to the regency.

It was common practice for royal widows to act as interim regents and during such periods they were able to exercise varying degrees of independent authority and many, as mothers of contenders for the throne, wielded significant influence over the outcomes of *quriltai* elections. Despite the fact that Töregene Khatun's regency was considered to be a period of disorganization and chaos, she successfully influenced popular opinion in favor of her own choice for the khanship, her son Güyüg (1206–1248). She achieved this feat by offering gifts to nobles in exchange for supporting her son's candidacy and gained the reputation of being a shrewd woman. She also had the support of senior Prince Chagatai, and this political alliance helped to further her aims. She antagonized many officials and alienated many Mongol elites, however, making it difficult to call a *quriltai* since the

Mongol nobles whose presence was required to confer legitimacy on the proceedings had refused to attend. As a result, she ruled as regent until she could ensure that the succession would fall upon her own favored son.

Ögödei Khan's death ushered in a period of turmoil and tension within the imperial family that would only continue to grow with time. His widow Töregene Khatun was known for her deviation from standard political protocol, even to the point of abandoning the wishes of her late husband who, before his death, had suggested his own choice for the succession. Ögödei Khan had originally wished for the succession to fall upon his third son Kuchu, but he was killed fighting against the Song in 1236. Chinggis Khan had suggested that Ögödei's second son Köten should be next in line for the throne; he suffered from poor health, however. Ögödei Khan's next preference was for Kuchu's son Shiremun to succeed him, but when the time came he did not have enough political support. With the support of Töregene Khatun, Ögödei's eldest son Güyüg was eventually able to secure election to the khanship in 1246. Although he did not live long, dying in 1248. Upon Güyüg's death, his widow Oghul Qaimish acted as regent, with a reign more unpopular than that of her mother-in-law Töregene Khatun. Ultimately Oghul Qaimish was executed in a Toluid coup, so that she served as the last of the Ögödei branch to hold power. In the end, the tensions surrounding the succession crisis that began with Ögödei Khan's death illustrated the growing divisions within the imperial family that would eventually wreak havoc on the stability and unity of the empire under the rule of future khans.

Donna HAMIL
Georgia State University

Further Reading

Barfield, Thomas. (1989). *The perilous frontier: Nomadic empires and China, 221 BC to AD 1757.* Cambridge, MA: Blackwell Publishers.

Grousset, René. (2010). *The empire of the steppes: A history of Central Asia.* (Naomi Walford, Trans.). New Brunswick, NJ: Rutgers University Press.

Juvaini, 'Ala-ad-Din 'Ata-Malik. (1997). *Genghis Khan: History of the world conqueror.* (J. A. Boyle, Trans.). Seattle: University of Washington Press.

Lane, George. (2006). *Daily life in the Mongol Empire.* "Daily Life through History" Series. Westport, CT: The Greenwood Press.

May, Timothy. (2012). *The Mongol conquests in world history.* London: Reaktion Books.

de Rachewiltz, Igor (Trans.). *The secret history of the Mongols: A Mongolian epic chronicle of the thirteenth century,* Vols. 1–2. (2004). Leiden, The Netherlands: E. J. Brill.

Rashidduddin Fazlullah. (1998). *Jami'u't-tawarikh: A history of the Mongols,* Vols. 1–3. (W. M. Thackston, Trans.). Cambridge, MA: Harvard University of Department of Near Eastern Languages and Civilizations.

Subatai Ba'adur

Sùbùtái 速不台

c. 1176–1248—Mongol general and strategist

•速不台•

Summary

A renowned general during his own time, having vanquished over thirty nations, Subatai Ba'adur served under Chinggis (Genghis) Khan and his son Ögödei Khan. An intrepid strategist, he helped the Mongols to conquer a huge land mass stretching from the northern regions of China through Central Asia, and even led forces into Europe. Subatai's fame did not last, however, and today he is largely forgotten.

Subatai Ba'adur (also spelled as Subedei, Subetai, Subodai, or Tsubotai) was a legendary figure in his lifetime, known for his daring, his military genius, and his great efficiency on the battlefield. He was the victor in over sixty battles and the vanquisher of over thirty nations. It was largely because of his celebrated achievements that the Mongols were called "the storm from the east." Subatai's glory has entirely faded, however, so that today he remains largely unknown outside of specialized academy circles. This disregard by the modern world in no way diminishes his unrivaled feats and successes.

Subatai was born sometime in 1176, likely somewhere near the Kherlen River, or along the banks of the Onon River in Mongolia. He belonged to the nomadic Uriankhai tribe, who were Oirat-speakers, and his family was traditionally linked with the clan of Temüjin (later known by his more famous name, *Chinggis, or Genghis, Khan). Indeed, it is through his close association with the world-conqueror that Subatai achieved his renown, along with his brother Chaurkhan and his uncle Jelme. As Chinggis Khan (c. 1162–1227) struggled to win supremacy over the various Mongolian tribal confederacies, Subatai's capable military

*People marked with an asterisk have entries in this dictionary.

leadership ensured Chinggis Khan of success. By the time that Chinggis Khan became ruler of all the Mongols, sometime in 1206, Subatai was to be found among the warrior elite, commanding a hundred archers (a *jaghun*); that year, he led a thousand men (a *mingghan*). It is likely at this time that he became one of the "Four Hounds" (*dörben noqas*) of Chinggis Khan, commanders who were deemed faithful and capable. Promotion in the Mongol military system under Chinggis was solely dependent on merit; this virtue was likely exhibited by Subatai, since by 1212 he was in charge of an entire *tumen,* which comprised ten thousand men. It is also likely that at this time he acquired his honorific title, *ba'adur* ("the valiant").

Military Campaigns under Chinggis Khan

From 1209 to 1211, Subatai was sent by Chinggis to destroy the troublesome Merkits tribe, his traditional enemies. Subatai chased them westwards, well into the Persian Khwarezm territory in Central Asia, where he clashed briefly with Muhammad II before withdrawing, since he did not want to start a conflict without the consent of Chinggis. Instead, Subatai withdrew and went back to Mongolia.

In 1218, because of provocations by Muhammad, which included the killing of Mongol emissaries, Chinggis ordered an attack. By 1220, the Khwarezm Empire had been annihilated and the capital city of Urgench was obliterated by the Mongols. Muhammad fled, with Subatai and another commander pursuing him right up to the shores of the Caspian Sea. The pursuit ended when Muhammad became ill and died in a village.

Before returning to join the rest of the Mongol army, Subatai probed further westwards, towards the Caucasus Mountains, subduing the Cumans, Kipchaks, and Alans. He also made incursions into modern-day Georgia, defeating an army of the East Slavic tribes of Kievan Rus before wheeling eastwards, where he was repulsed, for the first time, by the Bulgars, a Turkic people of the steppe in Eastern Europe. Thereafter, he rejoined the main Mongol army, which now began invading the northwestern parts of China, and played crucial roles in the subjugation of the Western Xià 西夏, also known as the Tangut empire.

Incursions into China and Europe

During this time, Chinggis died, in 1227, and Mongol leadership fell to his son, *Ögödei Khan (Wōkuòtái 窝阔台, c. 1186–1241), who continued the policy of his father and pressed further into the territory of the Jurchen Jin (Nǚzhēn Jīn 金女真) dynasty (1125–1234). Subatai played a crucial role in the conquest of the Jin. The Mongols then entered into an uneasy accord with the (Southern)

Mounted Mongolian warriors pursue enemies. Illustration from the historical chronicle *Jami' al-tawarikh* by the scholar Rashid-al-Din Hamadani (1430). Staatsbibliothek Berlin.

Sòng 宋 (960–1279), but this did not last long, since both had greater ambitions. Hostilities broke out in 1235 and would continue until the decisive battle of Yamen, some forty-four years later. Meanwhile, the Mongols had already veered further south and begun attacking Korea.

At the same time, Ögödei looked westwards and sent his nephew *Batu Khan 拔都汗 (c. 1205–1255), along with Subatai to bring more territory under his control. The Mongols already controlled Central Asia and Persia and had also reached south into Kashmir and northwestern India. This time, Subatai quickly overcame the Bulghars and then turned his attention on the various East Slavic Kievan Rus principalities. He conquered Ryazan and Vladimir-Suzdal in Russia;

by 1240, Chernigov, Kiev, and Vladimir fell under his assaults. All of Europe now lay before him.

In 1241, Subatai attacked Poland and Hungary, and emerged the victor in five decisive battles that brought the Mongolian Empire deep into Europe. Soon Subatai was knocking at the gates of Vienna itself, with nothing to stop him and his victorious army. In 1241, however, before he could deliver the much-planned death blow to the Holy Roman Empire (962–1806), word came that the Great Khan Ögödei was dead. Subatai had to return to Mongolia in order to participate in the process of selecting the next emperor. Western Europe was thus spared the wrath of the Mongols, who would never return to complete their conquest.

Final Years

The new emperor, Güyüg Khan (Guìyóu 贵由; c. 1206–1248), son of Ögödei Khan and his wife Töregene Khatun (who had ordered that the news of her husband's death be carried across the steppes), sought to consolidate his hold in China and, in 1246, put Subatai charge of subduing the Song, which Subatai effectively did for a year. By 1248, however, he grew weary of incessant campaigning and requested to return to Mongolia. He was seventy-two years old. He moved to the north and lived along the banks of the Tuul River until his death sometime later in 1248.

As one of the "Four Hounds" of Chinggis Khan, a brilliant general who led troops enormous distances across deserts and steppes and deep into another continent, Subatai was arguably one of the most effective generals in history.

Nirmal DASS
Wilfrid Laurier University

Further Reading

Allsen, Thomas T. (2004). *Culture and conquest in Mongol Eurasia*. Cambridge, UK: Cambridge University Press.

Biran, Michal. (2005). *The empire of the Qara Khitai in Eurasian history. Between China and the Islamic world*. Cambridge, UK: Cambridge University Press.

Buell, Paul D. (1993). Sübötei Ba'atur. In Igor de Rachewiltz (Ed.), *In the service of the Khan*. Wiesbaden, Germany: Otto Harrassowitz Verlag.

Buell, Paul D. (2003). *Historical dictionary of the Mongol world empire*. Lanham, MD: The Scarecrow Press.

Lane, George. (2004). *Chinggis Khan and mongol rule*. Westport, CT: Greenwood Press.

Taizu, Emperor (of Jin)

Jīn Tàizǔ 金太祖

1068–1123—Leader of the Jurchens and founder of the Jin dynasty

Alternate names: birth name: Wányán Āgǔdǎ 完颜阿骨打; Wányán Mín 完颜旻

Summary

Taizu, born Wanyan Aguda, was the powerful leader of a nomadic Jurchen tribe who occupied the north and east of Manchuria. After defeating the reigning Mongol-speaking Khitan Liao, he conquered all of north China and founded the Jin dynasty (1115–1234). As a ruler, Taizu depended on a strong military, but he also undertook political and cultural reforms, based upon Jurchen traditions, which laid the foundation of the dynasty's success until it was overthrown by the Mongols. The ascendancy of the Jin became apparent when, in 1123, the Song signed a treaty agreeing to pay the Jin an annual tribute; Aguda died in that same year.

A hereditary ruler of the Wanyan, a Jurchen (Nǚzhēn 女真) tribe, Wanyan Aguda succeeded in creating a federation of the Jurchen people, with himself as its head. This power-base allowed him eventually to destroy the Khitan Liáo 辽 dynasty (916–1125) and establish his own empire, the Jin, in 1115, which lasted until the Mongol conquest of 1234.

Aguda was born the second son of Helibo, the chieftain (*tàishī* 太师) of the Wanyan clan. The family traced its origins back to Hanpu in the early parts of the tenth century, whose legendary deeds were integral to Wanyan tribal identity. The family's right to leadership was granted by the Khitan Liao emperors, who saw in them able and potent governors who could maintain Liao influence over an area that was often wild and lawless due to family feuds and tribal vendettas. The Wanyan, like the rest of the Jurchen people, were hunters and gatherers who lived in the forests of Manchuria. They were a patriarchal society, made up of loosely structured kinship groups, often small in number, that battled over resources with other clans. The bonds of kinship were often stronger than any notions of national identity, which in turn meant that there was little or no political cohesion other than that imposed by a foreign power, such as the Liao Empire of the Khitan people.

Rise to Power

Upon the death of Helibo in 1092, his brother Yingge became chief in 1094 and ruled until 1103. Yingge did not have a son of his own, and so the chieftainship went to Wuyashu, Helibo's eldest son, who took up the leadership of the Wanyan in 1104. Under his rule, the tribe increased greatly in number because it began to take in and adopt those members of other clans who were destitute and often on the verge of starvation. This policy of Wuyashu ensured that the Wanyan tribe eventually became the largest and the most powerful among the Jurchen. Strengthened in this way, Wuyashu undertook a series of campaigns against other Jurchen clans and tribes in order to bring them under Wanyan sway. He was successful in this policy, until some of the Jurchen sought help from the Goryeo, the powerful dynasty that ruled most of Korea. In this way, the Wanyan became engaged in a protracted war with the formidable Goryeo.

Despite setbacks, however, Wuyashu proved to be an able military leader, although the Goryeo eventually won, under the leadership of their general Yun Gwan. Thereafter, the Goryeo built nine fortresses in the northern parts of Korea, which successfully contained the Wanyan. Because of court intrigue, however, in 1108 Yun Gwan was sacked and imprisoned (he died a broken man in 1111); the nine fortresses were turned over to the Wanyan. In this way, the Wanyan were ensured supremacy among the Jurchen, and their influence now reached far along the Suifen River basin in north China. When Wuyashu died in 1113, he was succeeded by his very able younger brother, Aguda, who transformed Jurchen regional power into an empire.

Conquering the Liao and Song

One year after his ascension to chieftainship, Aguda began to test the might of his overlords—the Khitan Liao. He based his military might on the cavalry, which gave him great mobility to carry out hit-and-run tactics. In 1114, he took up rebellion against the Liao and struck where Liao power was the weakest—the city of Ningjiangzhou (now Fuyu, in Jilin Province), which he quickly captured. Then he met a Liao army at Chuhedian and soundly defeated it. This emboldened him to press forward further into Liao territory. By 1115, he had won enough land to have the confidence to declare himself the ruler of a new empire, which he named Jīn 金, or golden (a color sacred among the Jurchen). In the summer of that year, he attacked and captured the important city of Huanglongfu (now Nong'an in Jilin Province). When the Liao gathered a large force to destroy the Jurchen, Aguda's cavalry quickly won the day at the Battle of Hubudagang. Thereafter, Aguda undertook a systematic attack on all the principal Liao cities and succeeded in capturing them.

These strikes at Liao power brought Aguda a powerful ally—the Northern Sòng 宋 (960–1127), who saw in Aguda a natural ally who, like them, sought to destroy the Liao. This soon led to negotiations, begun in 1115, which led to the Alliance on the Sea of 1119. The terms of the agreement stipulated that the Song and the Jin would jointly attack the Liao, and neither side would unilaterally enter into a peace accord with the mutual enemy. The Jin were far more successful in their attacks than the Song were, and by 1121 Liao power was broken. They were driven into Central Asia by 1123, where they would establish the Kara-Khitan Khanate the next year.

The ascendancy of the Jin was now apparent when, in 1123, the Song signed a treaty agreeing to pay an annual tribute. It was at this high-point that Aguda died, in August of that year. He had taken a regional power and forged it into a formidable and robust empire, which would eventually be strong enough to destroy the Song and take control of northern China. This would be accomplished by Aguda's brother, Wuqimai, who succeeded him as the next Jin emperor, and who soon turned his attention on the Northern Song and added their territory to that of Jin.

Aguda laid the foundation of this success not only by formulating a solid Jurchen military, but by undertaking political and cultural reforms, based upon Jurchen traditions. Thus, he brought in a system of government based upon feudal structures, and he instituted the collectivization of agriculture in order to control economic disparity. Aguda also had a great cultural influence, in that he established a writing system specifically for the Jurchen language—the Jurchen large-character script, which was created by Xīyǐn 希尹, his chief advisor.

Aguda's family, who would continue to rule the Jin Empire in northern China, bestowed upon him the throne name of Tàizǔ 太祖 of Jin. The empire would last over a hundred years, until driven from the throne by the Mongols in 1234.

Nirmal DASS
Wilfrid Laurier University

Further Reading

Franke, Herbert, & Chan Hok-Lam. (1997). *Studies on the Jurchens and the Chin dynasty*. Farnham, UK: Variorum Ashgate.

Mote, F. W. (2003). *Imperial China 900–1800*. Cambridge, MA.: Harvard University Press.

Peterson, Willard J. (2003). *The Cambridge history of China*. Cambridge, UK: Cambridge University Press.

Tao Jing-shen. (1976). *The Jurchen in twelfth-century China*. Seattle: University of Washington Press.

Yuán Dynasty

元朝

1279 - 1368 CE

Detail from *Autumn Colors on the Que and Hua Mountains* by Zhao Mengfu (1254–1322). National Palace Museum, Taipei, Taiwan.

The Yuan dynasty was founded after the Mongol leader Khubilai Khan (Hūbìlièhàn 忽必烈汗; r. 1260–1294) conquered the Jurchen Jin 女真金 (1115–1234) dynasty in the north and the Southern Song 南宋 (1127–1279) dynasty in the south. The Mongol rulers adapted some Han Chinese customs, but many Han still felt discriminated against. Since getting an official position in the government was nearly impossible for Chinese men, many turned to visual arts and literature instead, contributing to its flourishing cultural legacy. The Yuan dynasty moved its capital north, to Dàdū 大都 (modern-day Beijing) and initially expanded its territory. The final years of the empire were characterized by rapid inflation, popular revolts, and natural disasters, which led to the eventual decline of the Yuan.

List of Entries

Guàn Yúnshí 贯云石 (1286–1324)
Guō Shǒujìng 郭守敬 (1231–1316)
Khubilai Khan 忽必烈汗 (1215–1294)
Luó Guànzhōng 罗贯中 (c. 1330–1400)
Wáng Zhēn 王祯 (fl. c. 1290–1333)
Zhào Mèngfǔ 赵孟頫 (1254–1322)

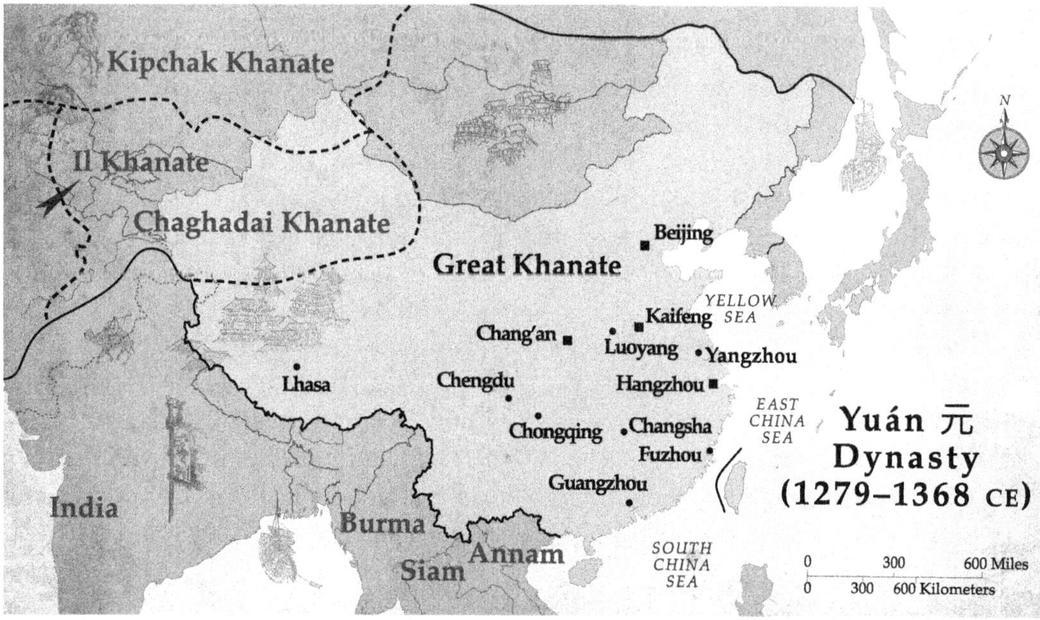

Guàn Yúnshí
贯云石

1286–1324 CE—Uygur scholar-official, songwriter, and poet

Alternate names: Uygur name: Sewinch Qaya/ Xiǎoyún Hǎiyá 小云海涯; style name: Guàn Suānzhaī 贯酸斋

Summary

As a literary figure, Guan Yunshi exemplified a cosmopolitanism shared by a multiethnic group of writers active in the political capital of Beijing and the cultural capital of Hangzhou under the Mongol-led Yuan dynasty. He transformed the previously considered trivial genre of *sanqu* songs into an independent and respected literary form and wrote the preface for the seminal anthology of this free-spirited form. He excelled in both military and literary pursuits, and was often compared to a very fine horse. Guan embodied an ideal form of elite masculinity in the eyes of his contemporaries.

An offspring of the Uygur service elite, Guan Yunshi exemplifies the cosmopolitan outlook that is beginning to be recognized by recent scholarship in English and Chinese as a hallmark of cultural elites under the rule of the Mongol-led Yuán 元 dynasty (1279–1368). Guan's particular contribution to this cultural, sophisticated diversity lay in the literary domain. Together with a group of Chinese and non-Chinese writers, he turned a song genre, the so-called *sǎnqǔ* 散曲 songs, from a convivial and colloquial genre for private banquets and festive occasions at the Yuan court into an independent literary form with a permanent afterlife.

To the extent that we can reconstruct it, Guan's literary practices defied precedent in several regards. He was the first official to include such songs in the manuscript of the collected works that he circulated as a literary calling card among the leading academicians of his day. After becoming a member of the literary academy himself, he resigned the post in order to pursue songwriting in earnest in concert with other writers in Hangzhou. As a culmination of his efforts, he not only created a distinctive body of songs that was neither purely ceremonial nor a simple continuation of conventional poetry in another literary form, but he authored the critical preface for the seminal, printed anthology of the genre. This was not just the first time in the history of Chinese literature that a recent immigrant launched a literary form, but in the preface, he privileged the writing of songs over having served at the court's most prestigious literary institution. Guan thus belongs among China's earliest voices to advocate for literary creation in the vernacular as an activity that surpassed the traditionally more highly regarded activity of public service. Finally, insofar as Guan wrote in Chinese, his corpus contributed to the transformation of colloquial Chinese into a literary lingua franca among a pan-Asian elite, ultimately expanding the social uses of a new facet of the Chinese language through print. Thus Guan's oeuvre forms an important milestone in the acceptability of colloquial writing in print; it also constitutes an important chapter in the career of Chinese as a world literary language.

The Cosmopolitan Yuan Context

Rather than interpreting Guan's career in the context of an attempt to sinicize himself, this essay suggests that Guan belonged to a cosmopolitan elite that selectively hybridized current cultural practices drawn from Uygur, Chinese, and Mongol repertoires. Guan was the descendant of a Uygur diaspora elite that originated in Central Asia. Guan's forebears had a tradition of administrative service and multilingualism dating back to at least the eighth century. In 1209, the Uygurs from Gaochang were the earliest Central Asian kingdom to voluntarily surrender to *Chinggis (Genghis) Khan (c. 1162–1227). Hence, they enjoyed a prominent position in the khan's multiethnic service corps. As we shall see, Guan's family is a case in point.

In important ways, however, everyone in that corps to some degree became an outsider to the communities that they had previously belonged to, no matter whether they were Uygurs, Mongols, Muslim, or Chinese. This alienation from their roots—through physical migration, shifting political alliances, or new professional commitments—appeared to create remarkable cohesion among the members of this service corps. At the same time, many among them gravitated toward cultural pursuits in the scholarly, literary, or artistic domain. Such lofty cultural activities also served to differentiate these elite transplants from forcibly relocated, socially less-privileged denizens of the Yuan empire.

In contrast to the traditional Chinese service elite with its pronounced preference for the civil arts, however, the Yuan court favored dual accomplishments in military and civilian pursuits. In reading

*People marked with an asterisk have entries in this dictionary.

Temple mural in Shanxi Province, depicting a Yuan-style theater performance (1324).

over posthumous commendations for distinguished members of the Yuan service corps, one cannot help but be struck by the reiteration of the idea of dual proficiency in the military and civil arts. In this context, the fine stallion became a salient image in both the literary and visual arts that bridged the dual domains of war and peace. As we shall see, Guan Yunshi excelled in both military and literary pursuits, and was often compared to a very fine horse. Guan thus embodied an ideal form of elite masculinity in the eyes of his contemporaries. His multiple talents, together with his family pedigree and his own irrepressible temperament, generated a social space in which he was free to defy convention and create his own momentum for literary innovation within a broader Yuan context of ongoing cultural improvisation and hybridization.

The Arc of Guan's Life

In keeping with the multiple social and cultural locations that he traversed in his short life, Guan Yunshi was a man of many names. In keeping with his Uygur ancestry, his Uygur name was Sewinch Qaya 小云海涯. In contemporary sources, it was often remarked that Guan was the grandson of Arigh Qaya (Ālǐhǎiyá 阿里海涯) (1227–1286), one of the legendary generals and administrators of the early Yuan conquest regime. Originally hailing from Beshbaliq, the capital of Uyguristan, Arigh Qaya had brought the family to the Chinese heartland after a successful campaign against the Southern Song 南宋 dynasty (1127–1279). Guan Yunshi grew up under the tutelage of his father Guàn Zhǐgē 贯只歌, who served as the head of a military garrison in the Chinese interior, as well as that of his mother, who herself hailed from another eminent Uygur family with both military and literary inclinations, the Lian clan. In his teens, Guan distinguished himself through his daring mastery of military arts such as horse riding and archery. At first, he followed in the footsteps of his father and served as a garrison commander, but then one day he abruptly ceded his post to his younger brother, Hūdù hǎiyá 忽都海涯. This was to be the first abrupt change in Guan's aspirations.

After moving to the capital, Guan became a student of Yáo Suì 姚燧 (1238–1313), one of the leading men of letters of his age. As a member of the Hanlin Academy, Yao, himself the nephew of an early influential advisor to Chinggis Khan, Yáo Shū 姚枢 (1203–1280), had presided over the training and appointment of a large number of young men of letters to the academy, which performed literary functions for the court. When Yao Sui read Guan's literary writings—including his essays, songs, and old-style poetry—he marveled at their boldness. Partially under Yao's guidance, Guan prepared his own annotated version of the *Classic of Filial Piety* (*Xiàojīng zhíjiě* 孝经直解) (1308), a primer in Confucian ethics that would have been suitable reading material for a prospective emperor. From the extant version of that text, we know that Guan at this point in his career had adopted the name of Chéngzhāi 成斋, "Studio of Mature Attainment." He signed the preface as "Commander of the Lianghuai Division, the General Sewinch Qaya, known under the sobriquet Chengzhai." From the interlinear commentary, it is apparent that Guan followed in his teacher's footsteps and adopted Confucian tenets, including the idea that music could act as a morally transformational force. Around the same time, Guan wrote *sanqu* songs that lauded the glory of dynastic rule in no uncertain terms, praising both its military and civil achievements.

If the goal of writing at this point in his career was to draw the court's attention to himself, Guan succeeded beautifully, undoubtedly assisted by Yao Sui's powerful patronage. Before long, Guan was chosen to serve as a tutor for Shidebala, the future Emperor Yīngzōng 英宗 (r. 1320–1323), a post he held until 1313. During this period, he married, a union that produced several children. Under Emperor Rénzōng 仁宗

(r. 1311–1320), Shidebala's father, Guan was promoted in 1313 to reader-in-waiting (*shìdú xuéshì* 侍读学士) at the Hanlin Academy, where he drafted imperial memorials and contributed to the compilation of the historical records. He was among the men who drafted the regulations for the first civil service examinations to be held under the patronage of the Yuan dynasty in 1314–1315, an important milestone in the ongoing debates as to whether the court should rely on the Mongol practice of hereditary appointments or on the Chinese tradition of impartial examinations to aid in the selection of its service corps. During his years at the academy, Guan befriended many fellow academicians, some of whom ranked among the dynasty's most distinguished literati: *Zhào Mèngfǔ 赵孟頫 (1254–1322), the dynasty's most eminent painter; Yú Jí 虞集 (1272–1348), the dynasty's most noted poet; and other notables such as Ōuyāng Xuán 欧阳玄 (1258–1329), Chéng Jùfū 程巨夫 (1239–1318), and Dèng Wényuán 邓文原 (1258–1329), among others. After submitting a memorial on sensitive topics in 1317, however, Guan became deeply disaffected with court politics and under the pretext of illness, he took his leave of the court and moved to Hangzhou, the cultural center in south China.

The second major turn in his life, however, neither spelled the end of the friendships that he had formed with other members of that academy, nor did it stop him from forming intimate bonds with men without any official credentials. During this period, he deepened his interests in the cultivation of both Daoism (Taoism) and Buddhism through friendships with religious figures as well as through contacts with commoners. He was reported to have sought out the company of ordinary folks such as butchers, wine sellers, and shepherds, a gesture that suggested overtones of him seeking to attain higher levels of Daoist cultivation. Moreover, he was also said to hang out a shingle in the market of Hangzhou, pretending to be buying and selling goods, only to impress upon prospective sellers that amidst the hustle and bustle, they should wake up to the metaphysical underpinnings of it all—the grand void signified by his empty hands. Such eccentric behavior straddled the boundaries between a comic act and Buddhist instruction, earning him several other nicknames among his contemporaries.

At the same time, Guan kept in close contact with his former colleagues at the Hanlin Academy. One Hanlin member, Deng Wenyuan, originally a refugee from Sichuan, was among the people he met in 1318 in Hangzhou, a contact that may well have opened doors to other members of the Sichuanese diaspora in Hangzhou. In addition, Guan befriended many songwriters during his time in Hangzhou, including Zhāng Kějiǔ 张可久 (1270–1348), the most prolific of all Yuan *sanqu* writers, and Ālǐ xīyìng 阿里西映 (fl. 1317), a Muslim *sanqu* writer, one of whose songs became something of a hit among the local songwriting community. Guan formed one of his closest literary friendships with another songwriter, Yáng Zhāoyīng 杨朝英 (fl. 1324–1351), a likely member of the Sichuan diaspora community that had been displaced by the early Mongol conquest and who had settled in Hangzhou. In a reversal of the anecdotes where Chinese literati bestow names on their foreign-born friends, in Guan and Yang's case, Guan gave Yang the name "Mild-mannered Studio" (Dànzhāi 淡斋) after adopting for himself in what appears a tongue-in-cheek reversal of his first studio name at court, the literary name "Bitingly Sour Studio" (Suānzhāi 酸斋). It was under that latter name that Guan would acquire a reputation of as one of the preeminent songwriters of his day.

Two song anthologies would grow out of the collaboration between Yang and Guan, the seminal *Songs, Newly Edited in the Spirit of the Cloud-Stopping Melodies of Old* (*Yuèfǔ xīnbiān Yángchūn báixuě* 乐府新编阳春白雪) (c. 1324), and *The New Sounds of Songs of Great Peace Gathered from All Over the Land* (*Cháoyě xīnshēng Tàipíng yuèfǔ* 朝野新声太平乐府) (preface 1351). Between them, these anthologies launched *sanqu* songs—hitherto mostly an oral genre deployed on festive occasions—as a literary form around which literati, and to a lesser degree courtesans, from different geographic, social, and religious backgrounds coalesced. Both anthologies featured large numbers of songs produced by different groups under the sway of the Yuan empire—Jurchen from northern China, Muslims, Mongols, Chinese, and others from Central Asian background. It is the first time in Chinese literary history that a group of people from very diverse backgrounds can be shown to have had a hand in turning a song form into an aesthetic artifact that aided in the formation of abiding ties between those whose communities had been at war just a couple of generations prior. Through their editorial practices, the two anthologies cultivated a form of literary cosmopolitanism nurtured by the friendship between Guan and Yang.

In his dual commitments to administrative and cultural pursuits, Guan is typical of the most visible members of the Uygur service elite. Guan's career spans multiple milieus and is characterized by continuous improvisation that is neither reducible to "Uygur" nor "Chinese" practices. It is not clear, for example, at what point Guan Yunshi adopted "Guan" as a Chinese-style surname, but for those who want to read this gesture as a sign of sinicization, one would have to caution that Guan chose part of his father's name as his surname; such a surname was not common among the standard Chinese surnames and hence remained recognizably foreign. Furthermore, even after he adopted this particular name, he did not use it to the exclusion of his original Uygur names, as is evidenced by extant specimens of his calligraphy. In addition, none of his children adopted Guan as their surname. Despite

Guan's self-professed distance to the court in his later years, thanks to his enduring friendships with the members of the Hanlin Academy, Guan was posthumously enfeoffed, or bestowed land in exchange for fealty; granted the posthumous name of Wénjìng 文靖 ("one whose literary patterns are consummately balanced"); privately commemorated by one of his fellow academicians, Ouyang Xuan; and officially commemorated in the histories of the Yuan.

Significance of Guan Yunshi's Writings

Guan's life unfolded in three different major stages, each with a different emphasis: growing up as a military prodigy in Yongzhou, a small town in modern-day Hunan Province; serving as an exponent of Neo-Confucian thought and imperial tutor at the Yuan court in Beijing; and becoming a free spirit given to Daoism, Buddhism, and feasting in Hangzhou, the old capital of the Southern Song dynasty. Throughout these different phases, however, Guan cultivated an interest in songs. He first encountered songs as part of military culture, then came into contact with them as an aspect of court ritual, and finally he fashioned them into a literati pursuit together with similarly inclined literary enthusiasts.

Compared to other traditional song genres in the Chinese repertoire, the assimilation of *sanqu* into elite culture happened relatively quickly in the course of the second half of the thirteenth century. The musical patronage of the Yuan court played a major part in this process through the interweaving of the rural, urban, and imperial musical repertoires. Members of the conquest elite of military men, some with ties to Central Asia, some with roots in the Jin dynasty's political and cultural establishments, as well as northerners and southerners, were charged with the fashioning of the imperial musical program, where songs came to play an important role. Some of these men derived inspiration for such songs from oversight over training musicians in the context of military training; others were said to be personally acquainted with an urban courtesan culture that prized singing skills. With different components of the imperial musical repertoire in place by the 1280s, the Hanlin Academy was eventually put in charge of writing lyrics for ceremonial music. By the 1310s at the latest, *sanqu* songs had become the climax of the musical program of imperial occasions such as imperial birthday celebrations, New Year's festivities, court audiences, and Buddhist festivals. It was only with Yang Zhaoying and Guan Yunshi's foundational anthology, however, that such songs were recast as literature worth preserving for future generations.

Significantly, rather than following Chinese precedent for writing prefaces to anthologies, Guan's preface to *Yangchun baixue* reflects new priorities. Guan pointed to the stylistic capaciousness of *sanqu* in the hands of successive generations of *sanqu* writers. From the "blandness" to the "melodious elegance" to the "bewitching qualities" to the "boldness," Guan commended it all, thus highlighting the stylistic universality of the songs. Guan also sought to differentiate *sanqu* from *cì* 词 song lyrics as well as traditional *shī* 诗 poetry by emphasizing the new genre's inherent versatility. Perhaps he was aware of the newer and well-received Yuan anthologies of *ci* and critical writings on *ci* that began to privilege a "delicate" sensibility over a "bold" one. In marked contrast to such a partial and particularized aesthetic vision, Guan defined a boldly conceived stylistic space for *sanqu* that defied conventional binaries between north and south, elegant and plain, bold and delicate. In addition to pluralizing the possibilities of style, Guan also allowed for the comparable legitimacy of different subjects, ranging from matters of the heart to songs on history, landscape, travel, officialdom, and reclusion. In contrast to earlier prefaces that either included an elaborate apologia for or a repudiation of songs dealing with love, Guan thus treated them matter-of-factly as equally worthy of attention, a fact also borne out by the many love songs in his own oeuvre.

In another break with prefatorial traditions, Guan downplayed the merits of office holding in the pursuit of excellence in songwriting rather than highlighting official rank as a necessary prerequisite to defend against the threat of vulgarity hovering over sung forms. Guan noted how his own official duties had left him without enough time to live up to the exemplars among the ranks of the songwriters, and that he felt ashamed as a result of his merely rudimentary grasp of songwriting. In contrast to many prefaces to vernacular works that emphasize how the writer pursued this form in their spare time from official duties or during a protracted illness, Guan thus portrayed office holding as a liability that interfered with rather than aided in the pursuit of learning about the "complexities" of songwriting. Hence, the act of songwriting demanded neither apologies nor defense. It was a worthy pursuit, one that he began in his childhood, but believed he still had not exhausted in his mature years. In many of several dozens of songs of his that survive, he praised the benefits of a life dedicated to the pursuit of unencumbered leisure that would be conducive to songwriting:

> 競功名有入車下坡。驚險誰參破。
> 昨日玉堂臣。今日遭殘禍。
> 爭如我避風波走安樂窩。

> Striving for public glory is like getting on a cart that is careening downhill
> Who discerns how precarious of a journey that is?!
> One day an esteemed public servant in the Hall of Jade

Another day struck by a calamity!
What better course of action than mine:
Seeking shelter from the vagaries of wind and waves
In this tranquil happy lair!

Influence of Guan's Work

Literati of the Yuan dynasty were unanimous in their favorable assessment of Guan Yunshi. Yao Sui characterized him as a "someone whose brilliance was such that, despite his tender age, his words deserved to be anthologized among the representative writings of the age" (Deng 1972, 1/55A). Deng Wenyuan thought that "his writing moves at the swift pace of a heavenly horse from Ferghana that has thrown off its bridle and covers a thousand miles in a single jump," noting that among those who were just versed in the literary arts such as himself, none could match Guan with his consummate mastery of both the civil and military arts (Deng 1972, 1/55B). Comparing Guan to the auspicious and rare phoenix and unicorn, Ouyang Xuan echoed Deng, wondering "how we can ever do justice to his exalted character?" (Ouyang 1919, 9/21B). Others commended a particular talent of his. In commenting on his calligraphy, Táo Zōngyí 陶宗仪 (1316–after 1368), one of the most broadly learned men of the Yuan dynasty, commented that the words that "have flowed from the tip of his brush are so singular and strange that their ethereal nature appears to defy their own materiality" (Tao 1980, 7/21A). Another critic observed: "He was an elegant and dashing young man, and no matter whether he wrote long or short *sanqu*, they were spirited and untrammeled and belonged to the very best of their kind" (Yao 1991, 13). To cap it all, the leading poet of the fourteenth century, Yáng Wéizhēn 杨维桢 (1296–1370), believed that Guan figured among the six most important songwriters of his time.

By contrast, when the early Ming prince, Zhū Quán 朱权 (1378–1448), a major patron of the arts and theater, reevaluated the world of Yuan song and drama, he gave preference to Chinese writers, particularly those who wrote operatic lyrics for the stage. Neither foreign writers nor those who exclusively wrote songs fared all that well in his estimation. In Zhu's hierarchically organized list of Yuan songwriters, he thus relegated Guan to a second tier of writers. Given that Zhu's work would go on to become the most widely circulated critical work on the subject of Yuan songwriting, Guan's reputation suffered accordingly. Furthermore, Guan's role in defining the critical framework for the work was also obscured. Despite two Yuan printings, the *Yangchun baixue*, the seminal anthology for which Guan had authored the preface, became a rarity during the first half of the Míng 明 dynasty (1368–1644). Two manuscript versions of the text appeared, perhaps in response to the general shortage of books characteristic of the period between 1360 and 1500. Strikingly, however, even though these editions contained most of the same songs as the print edition and retained the other paratexts, Guan Yunshi's preface was missing. Some later editions retained the preface, but the unreliable transmission of his critical thought also undoubtedly deflected attention from Guan's accomplishments.

It is only now when scholarship on the Yuan period has begun to emancipate itself from the constraints of nativism and nationalism that it has become possible to imagine that an entire genre might owe its incorporation into the literary canon, however precariously, to the cosmopolitan practice of Guan Yunshi and other Yuan literati.

Patricia SIEBER
The Ohio State University

Further Reading

Brose, Michael C. (2007). *Subjects and masters; Uyghurs in the Mongol Empire*. Bellingham: Center for East Asian Studies, Western Washington University.

Deng Wenyuan 邓文原. (1972). *Bāxī jí* 巴西集 [The collection of Western Sichuan). Taipei, Taiwan: Taiwan Commercial Press.

Lynn, Richard John. (1980). *Kuan Yün-shih*. Boston: Twayne Publishers.

Mair, Victor H. (2005). Vernacular paraphrases of the classics for the Mongol rulers. In Victor H. Mair, Nancy S. Steinhardt, & Paul R. Goldin (Eds.), *Hawai'i reader of traditional Chinese culture* (pp. 437–439). Honolulu: University of Hawaii Press.

Ouyang Xuan 欧阳玄. (1919). *Guīzhāi jií* 圭斋集 [The collection of the Gui Studio]. SBCK edition. Shanghai: Commercial Press.

Smith, Paul J. (1992). Family, landsmann, and status-affinity in refugee mobility strategies: The Mongol invasions and the diaspora of Sichuanese elites, 1230–1330. *Harvard Journal of Asiatic Studies, 52*(2), 665–702.

Sui Shusen 隋樹森. (1989). *Quán Yuán sǎnqǔ* 全元散曲 [The complete *sanqu* songs of the Yuan dynasty]. (2 vols., Rev. ed.) Beijing: Zhonghua shuju.

Tao Zongyi 陶宗仪. (1980). *Shūshǐ huìyaō* 书史会要 [The essential guide to the history of calligraphy]. Taipei, Taiwan: Taiwan Commercial Press.

Watt, James C. Y. (Ed.). (2010). *The world of Khubilai Khan: Chinese art in the Yuan dynasty*. New Haven, CT: Yale University Press.

Weitz, Ankeney. (2002). *Zhou Mi's* Record Of Clouds and Mist Passing Before One's Eyes*: An annotated translation*. Leiden, The Netherlands: E. J. Brill.

West, Stephen H. (2010). Literature from the late Jin to the early Ming, ca. 1230 ca. 1375. In Kang-i Sun Chang & Stephen Owen (Eds.), *Cambridge history of Chinese literature* (pp. 557–650). Cambridge, UK: Cambridge University Press.

Yang Jian 杨镰. (1983). *Guàn Yúnshí píngzhuán* 贯云石评传 [A critical biography of Guan Yunshi]. Urumqi, China: Xinjiang renmin.

Yao Tongshou 姚桐寿. (1991). Lèjiāo sīyǔ 乐郊私语 [Whispers from the Realm of Happiness]. Beijing: Zhonghua shuju.

Xu Jinbang 许金榜 (Ed.). (1991). *Yángchūn báixuě zhùshì běn* 阳春白雪注释本 [Annotated edition of *Yangchun baixue*]. Zhengzhou, China: Zhongzhou guji.

Guō Shǒujìng

郭守敬

1231–1316—mathematician, astronomer, hydraulics engineer, and statesman

Summary

Guo Shoujing designed the waterways of the Yuan dynasty, which enabled the capital Dadu (present-day Beijing) to flourish, and connected China with the West in significant ways. He came of age during the chaotic transition to Yuan national rule under the conquering Mongols, and quickly caught the attention of the Yuan founder, Khubilai Khan, who allocated to Guo increasingly significant projects, including the creation of a new calendar that would become the standard for centuries after Guo's death. Guo's work was part of Khubilai Khan's strategy to win the hearts and minds of the people of his newly conquered lands by putting their skills to good use on massive projects.

Guo Shoujing was born into a poor family in Xíngtái 邢台, Hebei Province, where education was valued, and where, as a child prodigy, he was given great encouragement. His paternal grandfather, Guo Yong, who was primarily responsible for the upbringing of his grandson, was renowned as a master of hydraulics, astronomy, and mathematics and he exerted a great influence on the developing child. Records of his life note that as a young child and teenager, Guo Shoujing would watch his grandfather at work, and learned much from his observations of the old man. He followed Guo Yong carefully as the scientist worked on developing a water clock, and upon obtaining the blueprint, the young Guo was able to understand the principles of the device's operation. After mastering the construction of water clocks, especially lotus clepsydra types often associated with astronomy (*liánhuā lòu hú* 莲花漏壶; a water clock named after its lotus-shaped upper receiver into which the water drops), the young prodigy was able to start the study of mathematics at the age of sixteen. This then led him into the world of both astronomy and hydraulics.

Historical Background

During Guo's early lifetime, the political situation in the north of China was stabilizing after decades of turmoil as the Mongols under *Chinggis (Ghengis) Khan 成吉思汗 (c. 1162–1227) and then under his son *Ögödei Khan (c. 1186–1241), established and consolidated power in the lands formerly ruled by the Jurchen Jīn 金 dynasty (1115–1234). The Jurchens officially ceded power in 1235, whereupon the Chinggisid armies concentrated their resources into undermining the Sòng 宋 dynasty (960–1279) emperors of the south. In 1251, following a bloody coup, the Chinggisid crown passed to the House of Tolui as Möngke Khan (r. 1251–1259) ascended the throne, heralding great change throughout much of the empire. Möngke Khan quickly dispatched his two brothers to the east and to the west to consolidate his hold on power and to establish his vision of a global, multicultural empire based on trade and the accumulation of wealth. In the west, Hulegu Khan (d. 1265) founded the Ilkhanate (1258–1335): a culturally rich Turko-Persian trading nation, which was a forerunner to the re-birth of Iran as a political and mercantile world player. In the east, Möngke's other brother, *Khubilai (Qubilai) Khan 忽必烈汗 (1215–1294; r. 1260–1294), sought to win over his Chinese subjects of the Yuán 元 dynasty (1279–1368), which was to become the wealthiest and most powerful state on Earth at the time. This was a fortuitous time for the talented, opportunistic, and entrepreneurial, as the old order was swept away while the Toluid brothers and Chinggisids rebuilt the world in their own fashion.

*People marked with an asterisk have entries in this dictionary.

Career

In 1251, at the age of twenty, Guo Shoujing was working for the government as a hydraulics engineer repairing an old bridge over the river Dáhuóquán 达活泉 near the town of Xīnzhōu 忻州 in his home province of Hebei. Because he was a skilled engineer, and a man of many talents and great potential, Guo quickly came to people's attention. One of those whose interest he stirred was his friend and fellow government employee, Zhāng Wénqiān 张文谦 (1216–1283), who in 1260 asked his talented friend to accompany him to Dàmíng 大名 in southern Hubei Province on a mission for Khubilai Khan. During this mission, Guo was able to demonstrate not only his engineering skills but also his ability to devise and construct instruments used for astronomical measurements. He knew that accurate observations depended on very precise instruments, and it was during this period that he began to construct various elaborate mechanisms including water clocks crucial for precision timing, and armillary spheres (an instrument consisting of a framework of rings that show the positions of objects within the celestial sphere, such as celestial latitude and longitude) that represent the celestial globe.

Khubilai was a visionary who realized that defeat of the mighty Song dynasty was unlikely to be achieved solely through military means. He knew that he would win hearts and minds by example, and already former servants of the Jurchen rulers were flocking to his cause as it became clear that the Chinggisids came not to destroy and plunder, but to build and to develop. Khubilai needed artisans and engineers in order to realize a number of prestigious projects that he hoped to implement. Guo Shoujing quickly came to his attention as he was strongly recommended by his friend, Zhang Wenqian, who emphasized Guo's intelligence and skills as a hydraulics engineer. Guo was granted an audience with the Chinggisid emperor in 1262, in which he was asked to suggest possible improvements to the irrigation and waterways in the region south of Yànjīng 燕京 (modern-day Beijing) and north of the Huang (Yellow) River. Guo presented six original plans, whereupon Khubilai immediately appointed him superintendent of waterways for the region, and implemented the first of his suggestions.

Khubilai Khan knew that population growth in the new capital, Khanbaliq (known as Dàdū 大都 in Chinese), was inevitable as his empire consolidated and trade routes became entrenched. He quickly realized that he would have to secure a reliable water supply to facilitate this growth. Consequently, Khubilai tested out Guo Shoujing's growing reputation, and throughout the 1260s, awarded him various projects associated with water management, such as flood control, the transportation of essential supplies, and irrigation. Among the projects that Guo oversaw was the exploitation of the Bǎifù 百富 spring in the Shenshan Mountains, the water of which he was able to harness and bring to the people of the capital by means of an eighteen-mile (twenty-nine-kilometer) channel. The success of this project in particular put Guo firmly in Khubilai's sights, and he was increasingly asked to act directly for the emperor. In 1264, Guo was commissioned to carry out extensive repair work to the irrigation system in Gansu Province that had been devastated by decades of war between the Chinggisids, the Song rulers, and other Inner Mongolian groups in the area. Guo, accompanied by Zhang, compiled an extensive report for the attention of the Khubilai himself that covered all aspects of the damage done, repairs needed, and future work recommended.

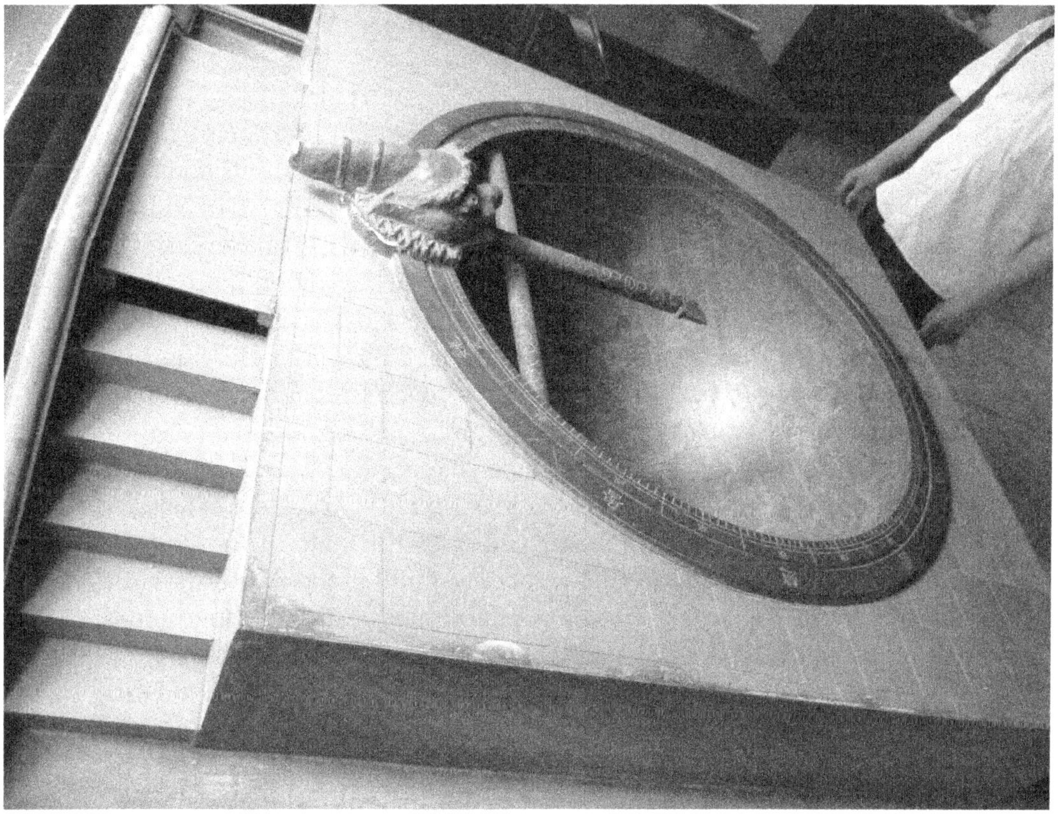

An instrument invented by Guo Shoujing. It measures the position of the sun and the process of a solar eclipse, using shadows that fall upon the bronze cauldron, which has hours and directions carved into it. Photo by George Lane.

In 1276, Khubilai Khan's general, Bayan Noyen, oversaw the peaceful takeover of the Song capital, Hangzhou, after which Emperor Gōng 恭 (r. 1274–1276) and the Empress Dowager Quán 全 were sent to Khubilai's capital, Dadu. Bayan Noyan was charged with establishing an administration and incorporating the Song metropolis into the dynamic new Yuan Empire. This involved extending the Grand Canal system to join the political capital of Dadu in the north with the cultural capital of Hangzhou in the south.

Thus, Guo Shoujing's theories and successful methods of water hydraulics assured his reputation in perpetuity. Due to Guo's careful planning and ability

Calculating Dates and Times

Chinese calendars were constructed along scientific principles from the time of the Han dynasty, and were subject to routine revisions; such "calendars" were not designed solely for the purpose of controlling the calendar date, but were in fact complete astronomical systems, and included the node and apogee of the moon, and all the planetary parameters. Guo Shoujing reviewed the earlier systems and derived a new system by combining their parameters and his own careful observations. This new approach probably arose under the influence of systems of Islamic origin.

Guo Shoujing worked with others, especially Wang Xun, to produce the new calendric system, the *Shòushí Lì* 授时历. Here at last was a Chinese system which agreed well with the state of the heavens over a long period, and in that respect resembled the Western (that is Islamic) systems. In fact it continued to be used in the Ming period, although with a change of name to *Dàtǒng Lì* 大统历.

Guo Shoujing also made a very precise determination of the time of the winter solstice, a time which is as important to the Chinese system as the Spring Equinox is in the contemporary Islamic systems (based on Greek astronomy). To determine the exact time of the winter solstice, a forty-foot (twelve-meter) gnomon (*gāobiǎo* 高表) was erected, at the top of which was placed a horizontal bar whose noon shadow was projected on a scale at ground level with the use of a particularly clever device, the "shadow definer" (*yǐng fù* 景符). In order to determine the time of the winter solstice numerous measurements were made of the sun's altitude on days within about a week of the solstice, and from these, by linear interpolation, the precise time of minimum altitude was derived, i.e., the time of the winter solstice.

—Raymond MERCIER, *University of Cambridge*

to anticipate areas of concern, the port of Tianjin and the Imperial Granary (*huángjiā liángcāng* 皇家粮仓) were incorporated into the water system despite complex difficulties and obstacles involved in the smooth and regular flow of water through these areas. Guo's greatest feat of engineering may be the vast manmade reservoir, Kunming Lake (Kūnmíng Hú 昆明湖). Kunming provided water to the entire population of the Yuan capital, and it remains the primary geographical feature of the present-day Summer Palace (Yíhé Yuán 颐和园) in Beijing. The merits of Kunming Lake motivated Khubilai to appoint Guo to the position of chief imperial advisor on hydraulics, astronomy, and mathematics, after which he was assigned to similar projects throughout the empire. In the realm of mathematics, Guo Shoujing is particularly remembered for his work in spherical trigonometry, which he was able to apply to complex astronomical calculations, as well as the construction of instruments that utilized these calculations. Khubilai is said to have listened attentively from morning until afternoon when Guo demonstrated these devices before him. When Khubilai decided that his empire needed a new calendar, he ruled that Guo should design its framework and implementation. In 1279, Khubilai ordered the construction of an observatory in Dadu based on designs submitted by Guo. This complex is still standing in present-day central Beijing. Zhang Wenqian became the observatory's first director and on his death in 1283, Guo was appointed his successor. Using the various astronomical machines and tools that he had devised, Guo in collaboration with Wáng Xún 王恂 was able to calculate the year to within twenty-six seconds of modern-day calculations, which was accurate enough to establish a new calendar that would last for the next 364 years. In all, some twenty-seven observatories were built throughout China during the Yuan period; many designed by Guo Shoujing. In 1292, in addition to his directorship of the observatory, Guo was appointed head of the Water Works Bureau and charged with extending the water system nationwide. In 1303, all civil servants of seventy years or more in age were ordered to retire, however Guo was asked by Khubilai's successor, Emperor Chéngzōng 成宗 (r. 1294–1307), to remain at his post and start work on a new project to extend the Grand Canal network to the Yuan summer capital of Shàngdū 上都, in present-day Inner Mongolia.

Later Years and Legacy

Despite his official position, Guo's later years were spent in isolation. He did, however, devise a few new clocks: the cabinet incense clock, the movable door-screen incense clock, and a portable clepsydra for use by the emperor in ceremonial rites while traveling. Many scholars have now challenged Guo's reputation as a mathematician and as an astronomer with claims that his theories and calculations were based on unacknowledged Western sources. The Yuan dynasty had unprecedented close contact with the Ilkhanid regime in Iran, and many Persian and Arab scholars ventured to the East just as

Chinese scholars and scientists travelled to the Islamic world trading ideas and knowledge and expanding cultural exchange between East and West. Nasir al-Dīn Tūsī (1201–1274) established his own observatory in the Ilkhanid capital, Maragha, where his seat of learning, the *Rasad Khaneh*, became a haven for an international collection of the empire's most active and learned minds.

In 1267, Khubilai invited the Persian astronomer, Jamāl al-Dīn (fl. c. 1255–1291), to China to share his ideas and knowledge, and to advise on the observatory (that Guo designed) soon to be built in Dadu. Though there is no evidence that Guo himself ever travelled to Iran, he must have had some communication with Islamic scholars, and he most certainly would have been aware of Islamic and Persian scholarship, and would have therefore been influenced by these new ideas and theories. He must also have used and examined the various astronomical instruments brought over from Iran by Jamāl al-Dīn.

Regardless of how much he was influenced by Islamic and Persian scientists, Guo Shoujing had a major influence on the development of science in China and is highly regarded to this day. He even had an asteroid named after him in the late Míng 明 dynasty (1368–1644). His mathematical and astronomical methods are described in the calendrical chapters of the *History of the Yuan* (*Yuánshǐ* 元史) and the *History of the Ming* (*Míngshǐ* 明史): two of the Twenty-Four Histories of China, which were commissioned by the succeeding dynasty of each period covered to act as both a record of events and a guide to model citizenship.

Yet it was the profound social and economic impact of his work as a hydraulics engineer that assured his reputation among his contemporaries. Khubilai credited his work in water management as a significant factor in social stability, and called for his assistance in instances of social unrest in which Guo's intervention brought food shortages to a halt and ensured grain supplies for unstable communities. Guo Shoujing continues to be an esteemed role model for the number of his ingenious and original devices and schemes, and for his invaluable contributions to hydrology and astronomy.

George LANE
School of Oriental and African Studies, University of London

Further Reading

Bai Shouyi. (2002). *An outline history of China.* Beijing: Foreign Language Press.

Ho, Peng Yoke. (2000). *Li, Qi, and Shu: An introduction to science and civilization in China.* Mineola, NY: Dover Publications.

Ho, Peng Yoke. (1993). Kuo Shou-ching. In Igor de Rachewiltz Hok-lam Chan, Hsiao Ch'i-ch'ing, & Peter W. Geier (Eds.), *In the service of the Khan: Eminent personalities of the early Yuan Mongol period (1200–1300).* Wiesbaden, Germany: Harrassowitz Verlag.

Hockey, Thomas. (Ed.). (2007). Guo Shoujing. In *The biographical encyclopedia of astronomers* (pp. 450–451). New York: Springer.

Needham, Joseph. (1986). *Science and civilisation in China. Volume 3: Mathematics and the sciences of the heavens and the earth*. Taipei, Taiwan: Caves Books, Ltd.

Ng Say Tiong, (2000/2001). *Calendars, interpolation, gnomons and armillary spheres in the work of Guo Shoujing (1231–1314)*. Retrieved December 12, 2013, from http://www.math.nus.edu.sg/~mathelmr/projects/nst-urops.pdf

O'Connor, J. J., & Robertson, E. F. (2003). *Guo Shoujing*. Retrieved December 12, 2013, from http://www-history.mcs.st-andrews.ac.uk/Biographies/Guo_Shoujing.html

Rossabi, Morris. (2008). The reign of Khubilai Khan. In Herbert Franke and Denis Twitchett (Eds.), *The Cambridge history of China* (vol. 6, pp. 414–490). Cambridge, UK: Cambridge University Press.

Shea, Marilyn. *Guo Shoujing* 郭守敬. Retrieved December 12, 2013, from http://hua.umf.maine.edu/China/astronomy/tianpage/0018Guo_Shoujing6603w.html

Khubilai (Qubilai) Khan

Hūbìliè Hán 忽必烈汗

1215–1294—Fifth Great Khan of the Mongol Empire; founder of the Yuan dynasty

Alternate names: Qubilai Khan (Mongolian: Хубилай хаан); given name: Kublai; temple name: Shìzǔ 世祖

Summary

Khubilai (Qubilai) Khan was the fifth Great Khan of the Mongol Empire from 1260 to 1294 and the founder of the Yuan dynasty in China after defeating the previous Song dynasty. The grandson of Chinggis (Genghis) Khan, he transcended his steppe origins and created a multiethnic, multicultural administration, which united China and incorporated a greater Iran. His mother ensured that he and his brothers had the traditional Mongol skills of riding, hunting, archery, and combat, and also schooled him in literature, the arts, and sciences. Khubilai's remarkably long reign on the throne of China oversaw a period of comparative prosperity and reasonable stability, and was a rare period of unity.

The remarkable rise to power of the Toluid brothers, Möngke (d. 1259), Khubilai (d. 1294), Hulegu (d. 1265), Ariq Buqa (d. 1266), grandsons of *Chinggis (Genghis) Khan 成吉思汗 (c. 1162–1227), owes much to the dedication and ambition of their mother, Sorghaghtani (Sorqaqtani) Beki. Her resistance to remarriage after the death of her husband, Tolui Khan, the youngest son of Chinggis Khan, in 1233, and her exploitation of family connections along with her willingness to become involved in political intrigue and rivalry, allowed her sons to reap rich political rewards. Her determination was evident in the letter she wrote to the great *Ögödei Khan (1186–1241), resisting his wishes to marry her to his son and successor, Güyüg Khan. She was the daughter of Jagambo, the brother of the Kerait ruler, Ong Khan, and therefore had already had a formidable political background by the time she was married into the royal family through her union with Chinggis

*People marked with an asterisk have entries in this dictionary.

Khan's youngest son, Tolui. Her upbringing had been steeped in political intrigue and she ensured that her sons were likewise fully cognizant of political reality as they grew up. By remaining single after her husband's death in 1233, she was able to concentrate on developing political and personal connections and building cross-family networks, which might have been difficult had she been married to a major political player. While her husband Tolui had been alive and busy campaigning, she had been left alone to educate and raise her four sons. After his death she concentrated on ensuring that her sons benefited from the connections she was forging. She kept a low profile and during the reign of Töregene Khatun (1241–1246), she began to "cultivate the goodwill of the nobles through gifts and beneficence," she "planted love and affection in everyone's heart and soul," and "through generosity and favors she kept the troops and foreigners obedient and on her side" (Rashīd al-Din, Roushan, and Musavi 1994, 823). She was an astute political operator, a consummate politician, and a formidable opponent.

Sorghaghtani Beki is credited with arranging the enthronement of her eldest son, Möngke, as Great Khan of the Chinggisid Empire. She accomplished this feat through a timely warning of an imminent attack and assassination attempt on *Batu Khan (Bádūhán 拔都汗 c. 1205–1255) by Güyüg Khan, which was delivered to the empire's kingmaker and ruler of the Golden Horde via his wife, an act that if uncovered could have cost Sorghaghtani her life. Batu's gratitude was eventually translated into solid support for Möngke's claim on the throne and the inevitable bloodletting that followed. Batu's support was crucial and without his backing the Touid dynasty could not have become so firmly entrenched. According to William of Rubruck (1220–1293), the Pope's representative who had traveled east in time to witness Möngke's coronation, Batu and Möngke appeared to have divided the vast empire between them, ruling as equals, Möngke in the east and Batu in the west. With Möngke Khan now preoccupied with matters of state, the business of the continuing war of attrition in China was left in the hands of his younger brother, Khubilai Khan.

The Kingdom of Dali

After having successfully absorbed northern China and the Jurchen administration into the empire, often with the aid and tacit support of the Sòng 宋 dynasty (960–1279), the Chinggisids now under Khubilai began slowly to erode the confidence of the Song emperors and the trust of their subjects. For four decades from 1235 until 1276, Khubilai used military confrontation, harassment, financial inducements, propaganda, and political machinations to undermine the Song state at every opportunity and at all levels.

In the 1250s, Khubilai directed a military campaign with his leading general, Uriyangqadai Noyan (1199–1271), against the kingdom of Dali, in modern-day Yunnan Province. His aim was to split the Song defenses and force them to divert manpower to the south. The province of Dali was inhabited by non-Han tribe people who harbored little loyalty or attachment toward their oppressive Chinese neighbors, the very people whom Guo Baoyu, a Han Chinese strategist and advisor to Chinggis Khan, had advised employing against the Song. "The bravery and fierceness of the tribes of the southwest should be put to use by first subjugating them, and then using them to surround the territory" (Armijo-Hussein 1996, 151). Khubilai had heeded his Chinese advisors and began moving his forces south. His strategists, Yao Shu and Liu Ping-chung, cautioned him against using excessive force to subdue the native population. They were adamant that he should resist all provocation and desist from any general massacres. Khubilai was receptive to this message, just as he had been receptive previously to the wise words of his mother. Yao Shu narrated the story of the successful Song general, Cao Bin, who had launched an assault on the city of Nanjing. The general had captured the city without bloodshed or even killing "so much as a single person; the markets did not alter their opening, and it was as if the proper overlord had returned" (Mote 2003, 452).

The Dali Stele, erected in 1304 outside Dali's city walls opposite the western gate to commemorate Khubilai's conquest of Yunnan, is a testament to the success that those policies achieved. The kingdom of Dali was absorbed into the Yuan Empire. Retribution for the murder of the first Chinggisid envoys sent to negotiate peace with the king, Duan Zhishan, was limited to the official deemed responsible, Gao Taixiang, who alone lost his head. Eventually the renowned Sayyid 'Ajall Shams al-Dīn 'Omar Bokhari [d. 1279] was appointed governor of the province, which he integrated into the empire. He introduced irrigation and agricultural policies, and set up a network of schools, mosques, and temples. Sayyid 'Ajall was so successful that he is revered throughout Yunnan, now an integral part of China, to this day. Yunnan was Khubilai's first opportunity to practice those administrative and imperial policies that he had learned from his mother and that he had been practicing in those lands originally assigned to him. His successes were interrupted by the premature death of his brother, struck down by pestilence, and his own elevation to the imperial throne. His successful campaign in the southwest is a testament to his mother's perseverance and emphasis on education and learning.

Khubilai's Formative Years

Khubilai's military victories in Yunnan would have pleased his father, Tolui Khan. His father was "a great winner of battles" whose reputation as a warrior was legendary. The thirteenth-century

Persian physician and historian, Rashīd al-Din (1247–1318), reported that no other prince had conquered as many countries as Tolui Khan, the supreme compliment for any Mongol. His mother, Sorghaghtani Beki, carried an equally impressive reputation, as reported by Atā' Malik Juwaynī (1226–1283), Persian historian and author of the famous historical account about the Mongol empire, and echoed by many other diverse voices. "If I were to see among the race of women another woman like this, I should say that the race of women is far superior to that of men" (Bar Hebraeus 2003, 398). So intoned Mutanabbi, a poet invoked both by Bar Hebraeus and Juwayni, though Juwayni is also effusive in his own praise:

> Now in the management and education of all her sons, in the administration of affairs of state, in the maintenance of dignity and prestige and in the execution of business, Beki, by the nicety of her judgement and discrimination, constructed such a basis and for the strengthening of these edifices laid such a foundation that no turban-wearer (*kulāh-dār*) would have been capable of the like or could have dealt with these matters with the like brilliance. (Juwayni 1997, vol. 3, 550)

The second son of this remarkable woman and Ulugh Noyan Tolui Khan, Chinggis Khan's youngest son, was Khubilai, who was a favorite of his mother. She closely monitored his education and ensured that curiosity and a love of learning informed all of his early experiences. She successfully resisted formidable pressure to marry the Great Khan, Ögödei's son and successor, Güyüg Khan, and concentrated instead on her appanage, or estate bestowed to younger children of an heir, Chen-ting in Hebei Province, educating her sons through example in the art of statecraft and administration. She taught her sons to respect and nurture the land and their subjects, and ensured that the boys received a comprehensive education.

The earliest reference to Khubilai concerns a coming-of-age ceremony, *yaghlamishi* (Doefer 1963, 1863–1875), performed by his grandfather after his first hunting expedition near the Ili River in 1224, Bechin Yil the Year of the Monkey, with his brother, Hulegu. The brothers had made their first kill, an antelope and a rabbit, near the Ili River in what is today northern Xinjiang Province. Their grandfather, following Mongol tradition, smeared fat from the dead animals onto the boys' middle fingers and greased their thumbs. Rashid al-Din recounts this tale claiming that during the anointing Khubilai held Chinggis Khan's thumb gently, but the young Hulegu grabbed his grandfather's proffered digit and squeezed it hard, eliciting a cry from the old man (Rashīd al-Din, Roushan, and Musavi 1994, 260). This early anecdote makes plain that the young boys' links with the steppe and Mongol traditions were encouraged and kept alive by, among others, their grandfather. What also becomes clear, however, is that these boys were very aware and influenced by the wider world beyond the steppe, and that their mother Sorghaghtani Beki ensured that her sons had mastered the

Image of Khubilai Khan on a hunting trip (1280) by the artist Liu Guandao. National Palace Museum, Taipei, Taiwan.

traditional Mongol skills of riding, hunting, archery, and combat. She also had them schooled in literature, the arts, and sciences, a task for which she employed Chinese scholars, a Persian tutor from the northern Iranian city of Qazvin, and an Uygur named Tolochu to teach them Mongolian literary skills. Her boys were well versed in those skills and they were learning what would enable them to flourish in the lands south of the Eurasian steppe lands of their forefathers.

Khubilai's First Appanage

Sorghaghtani Beki guided Khubilai in the administration of his own appanage (i.e., gift of land) of Hsing-chou in northern China, aware that any experiences from these formative years of his youth could well determine the style of governance he would adopt in later years. She firmly believed that the successes and failures that Khubilai endured now would determine the choices and decisions he would make later in life. She instilled a strong sense of tolerance and appreciation of multiculturalism in her son from the beginning, even appointing a Buddhist Tangut wet nurse, a woman who the young boy was not to forget.

After the final surrender of the Jurchen Jin in 1236, the Great Khan, Ögödei, awarded the Toluid boys and their mother some lands in Hebei Province to which eighty thousand tents were attached. These eighty thousand families would of course be supportive of their new masters and would look to them for support against the indigenous settled communities of Khitans, Jurchens, and northern Chinese. Most of these tents would be traditionalist Turko-Mongols generally harboring the biases and prejudices of their steppe upbringing expressed by distain for, ignorance of, and lack of interest in the indigenous, settled inhabitants of the province, whether rural peasants or urban sophisticates. These settled people and their communities were viewed as a source of income, and their towns and farms as ripe for the picking and ready for exploitation. Settled people themselves had traditionally been viewed from the steppe as simply slaves for labor, servitude, or sex. The potential that artisans might possess was recognized, however, therefore such skilled workers were beginning to be prized for their craftsmanship and for their resale value.

Now that the Turko-Mongols were arriving as settlers rather than invaders, attitudes were expected to change. Change was slow, however, and such chauvinist attitudes were deeply entrenched. Such a profound transformation was generational and would also have to have demonstrable advantages. The generation to which Khubilai belonged was at the vanguard of this metamorphosis. Their fathers and grandfathers had been the warriors. They had been born into the hardship of the steppe and they had had to fight their way out of it. Now they wanted their reward, and they enjoyed feasting on the prizes that they felt they had earned. Khubilai and his generation had been born into power and luxury. They had not experienced the depravation of the steppe. They had grown up with the trappings of "civilization." They had enjoyed education and learning, and the company of the empire's elite. Their attitudes had been formed and cultivated in a different cultural petri dish than that of their fathers, and for the most part different than that of most of their subjects.

To cite but one example: Ata Malik 'Ala al-Din Juwayni, personal assistant to Hulegu Khan and subsequent governor of Baghdad, is possibly the epitome of Persian sophistication and erudition. His eloquent and learned history of the Chinggisids is a testament to a classical education and reflects his knowledge of languages, of literature, of history, and of theology. Juwayni was highly erudite, and he had the scholar's arrogance and disdain for the less well-read and for those not as well versed as he in Persian learning. The contempt that he felt for his predecessors at court is captured in his dismissal of those who "consider the Uygur language and script to be the height of knowledge and learning" (Juwayni 1997, vol. 1, 4). What is not so widely appreciated, however, is that Juwaynī acquired his enviable education in a Mongol ordu, or court. His father Baha' al-Dīn entered Chinggisid service after leaving Jalāl al-Dīn Khwarazmshāh's court when his sons were still boys. Both sons would therefore have been educated taking advantage of the resources available in the royal ordu. Ata Malik traveled east to China at least three times in his youth and these journeys took years rather than months. It must be assumed that the young Juwaynī boys would have received their education along with other children of the elite, and that the books and scholars would have been traveling along with the rest of the royal household. Records identify that a scholar from Qazvin tutored the Toluid boys, including Khubilai. It must be assumed that the enviable education enjoyed by the Juwaynī brothers must have been available to Khubilai Khan and his brothers as well.

Khubilai received ten thousand tents, but his early attempts at administering his land and people resulted in a disastrous abandonment of the lands and a general exodus by the farmers and peasants. The farms and the peasantry had not necessarily been sacked and plundered but the tax regime imposed on them was far too harsh and it was imposed without consultation or cooperation. The basic predatory attitude had not been abandoned and therefore the Chinese had reacted in a wholly predictable fashion, as they fled southward out of reach of the Mongol hordes. It was only the timely intervention of Khubilai's mother that prevented bankruptcy as his tax returns steadily dwindled. Sorghaghtani Beki sent her son, Khubilai, Chinese officials who enacted tax and administrative reforms. They taught him lessons that were to remain with him the rest of his life and that would go on to inform his subsequent principles and ideas of government and conquest. Any attempt to impose a pastoral economy on the Chinese was forgotten. With an army of Chinese, Tibetan, Muslim, and Mongol councilors, Khubilai set up an administration to help him govern, recognizing that he would have to accommodate the Chinese and assimilate their institutions and practices with those of his councilors. He therefore fostered an agrarian economy and set about building an irrigation system with a planned agricultural policy, which would make use of improved tools and imported seeds. What he began as a youth in northern China he would continue elsewhere whenever the opportunity arose, and the conquest of Dali was that welcome opportunity to translate his lessons and early experiences into reality.

Khanbaliq, a New Capital

To clarify his intentions and signal his own transformation, Khubilai established a new capital. Karakorum, Ögödei's capital, was a steppe capital, though in reality it had become a vibrant, dynamic, and very much multicultural and multiethnic city. Without a hinterland, however, the city's burgeoning population could not be provided for. Khubilai built his new capital on the plains southeast of the steppe lands of his birth, close enough to maintain his links with his past and far enough away to assure his Chinese subjects of his commitment to them. He allowed himself to be guided by the principles of divination in choosing an exact location. Geomancy, or *fengshui,* dictated the most propitious location for the placement of tombs, residences, and palaces, while a mixed team of nationalities undertook the actual construction, which started in 1267.

The capital's dual name, Turkish Khanbaliq and Chinese Dadu, reflects the powerful influences that were vying for supremacy in all aspects of the new state's administration and image. Khubilai had the layout of his city designed along traditional Chinese lines with symmetrical east-west and north-south axes, with eleven three-story tower gates allowing access. There was a clear separation between the imperial city where the royal family resided, and the rest of the subjects. Firstly there was an inner wall within which government officials lived and worked, and secondly there was an outer wall marking the area designated for ordinary citizens of the city. Such an urban layout would have been very familiar to his Chinese subjects, as would the buildings within the imperial city, such as the reception hall for foreign embassies and the royal palace with quarters for the khan himself, for his consorts, and for his concubines. The imperial city was crisscrossed by canals, bridges, lakes, and gardens, all features found in traditional Chinese grand residences, although the Turko-Mongols of the Eurasian steppe hardly had much experience with urban planning or the design of ornate gardens. Khubilai Khan, however, had certainly not abandoned his Mongol heritage, and within the confines of the imperial city he had traditional *gers* (Mongolian tent houses, sometimes called *yurts*) entrenched. His sons lived close to their father in their own *gers* adjacent to the palace, and when one of Khubilai's wives became pregnant he ensured that the last stages of the childbirth were experienced in the traditional felt-covered dwelling. In the Great Khan's sleeping quarters, curtains and screens made of ermine skins and animal pelts were hung as reminders of his nomadic past, though hunting was a pastime the khan enjoyed throughout his life. In modern-day Mongolia, the practice of erecting *gers* in the gardens or yards of the town houses is still widely observed.

Khubilai Khan in Literature

The mystique of Khubilai Khan spread to Europe after the Venetian merchant Marco Polo (1254–1324), who was a guest of the Great Khan for several years, brought often fantastical tales of his empire back to Europe. The following is an extract of the poem "The Ballad of Kublai Khan" by the British Romantic poet Samuel Taylor Coleridge (1772–1834).

"The Ballad of Kublai Khan"

In Xanadu did Kublai Khan
A stately pleasure-dome decree,
Where Alph, the sacred river ran
Through caverns measureless to man
Down to a sunless sea.

So twice five miles of fertile ground
With walls and towers was girdled 'round,
And there were gardens bright with sinuous rills,
Where blossomed many an incense-bearing tree;
And here were forests ancient as the hills,
Enfolding sunny spots of greenery. . . .

—*Samuel Taylor Coleridge*

If his capital had become largely Chinese, Khubilai made sure that Mongol traditions were kept alive and practiced in his original capital, Shangdu, in which he had first been proclaimed Khan on 5 May 1260. This was the city that Marco Polo (1254–1324) visited in the 1270s, and which subsequently achieved universal fame and acclaim as Xanadu. While Khanbaliq lay on the plains just south of the steppe lands of Chinggis Khan's childhood, Shangdu (until 1263 K'ai-p'ing) had a closer association with its nomadic past and continued to serve as a summer hunting preserve, with one source claiming as many as five hundred birds of prey.

Just as in the West where Hulegu had built an observatory, the *Rasadkhana,* which was overseen by Nasir al-DīnTusi, housing a library consisting of books "borrowed" from Baghdad and the Isma'ilis, Khubilai also had an observatory, still standing today, built in his new capital, Khanbaliq. Dispatched especially from Iran, Jamal al-Dīn cooperated with *Guō Shǒujìng 郭守敬 (1231–1316) in setting up this famous astronomical center, devising better maps with color coding, grids, and a new Chinese calendar.

Civil Service Examinations

Khubilai's remarkably long reign on the throne of China oversaw a period of comparative prosperity, of reasonable stability, and, perhaps most importantly, a period of long sought after and highly cherished unity. Just as in the West, where his brother Hulegu had received the cooperation of the indigenous people of Iran in recognition of his establishment of their ancient land of Iran within clear historically defined borders and his expulsion of the Arab occupiers, in the east Khubilai sought to heal some of China's damaging internal disputes and to exploit the euphoria engendered by the unity of north and south. He sought the close assistance of Liu Bingzhong, a Buddhist monk well versed in Confucianism, but skilled most notably in mathematics, astronomy, calligraphy, and painting. Liu assumed the task of governing Khubilai's lands in the north along traditional Chinese lines, restoring ancient Chinese ceremonial ritual and establishing the legal and financial institutions, including the tax regimes that underpinned the imperial system. Khubilai, however, refused to reintroduce the civil service examinations, which had dominated all aspects of Chinese government for centuries. By their very nature, such examinations would immediately exclude non-Chinese, and Khubilai wanted to integrate his new China into a global empire in which he would be able to reward those that had been loyal to his Chinggisid ideals.

Although the abolition of the civil service examination system has often been perceived as being an anti-Chinese measure designed to exclude native Chinese from local and national government, the reality simply meant that the entrance qualifications were opened to far more people than had previously even thought of applying. The abolition of these civil service examinations simply abolished the built-in Chinese bias and the blatant disadvantage that handicapped any non-Chinese sitting the exams. The much vaunted racial preference league table, which is often quoted in regards to employment policies under the Yuan, does not indicate any racial discrimination or favoritism. It reflects the growth of the empire and the degree of perceived loyalty based on length of service. It was the Turko-Mongol tribesmen who were the first to flock to Chinggis Khan's banner, and those early supporters were generously rewarded with positions of power and prestige. As his armies moved south, east, and west, Chinggis encountered the sedentary world, and he needed administrators and officials to deal with the new unfolding reality. Many of those who answered his call for help were the Uygurs, Muslims, and other Semeran, who subsequently held on to the top administrative positions. The same story occurred as lands fell to the Chinggisids and the people were incorporated into the growing administration. The result was the appearance of a roughly four-tier system of appointments, with the southern Chinese assigned to the lowliest ranks since they had been the last to join the swelling army of bureaucrats. A system apparently weighted in favor of the Muslims and Persians was also created by the Persian sources, which tended to concentrate on their co-religionists and fellow Persians and again created an impression of a society where these minorities held undue influence.

Khubilai, Mongol Khan, or Chinese Emperor

Khubilai has often been portrayed as a Chinese emperor attempting to reconcile his Mongol background to his new role and identity, while at the same time retaining the loyalty of his traditional Mongol following. This view, however, is to misunderstand not only Khubilai's considerable achievements but also his aims and aspirations. In his new capital, Khanbaliq, with his magnificent new palace, his garden containing a traditional Mongol tent has often been ridiculed. Again the contempt is misplaced and rebounds on the observer who exhibits only a failure to comprehend the nature of the Yuan vision. The Toluids, whom Khubilai led and epitomized, aspired to create a global empire encompassing the full extent of their rule. The Chinggisid armies patrolled the frontiers of Asian, Islamic, European, and maritime states. Their soldiers wore the dress of a multitude of different people. Their kitchens employed chefs from around the world and the cuisine that was served catered to every conceivable taste, as just a quick perusal of the magnificent pages of Togh Temur's culinary guide soon reveals.

The Toluids created a multiethnic and, more significantly, a multicultural empire, which combined, synthesized, and ultimately transcended any one culture to create a unique and richer culture reflecting all its constituent parts. Khubilai Khan did not preside over a Chinese court, a Mongol court, a Persian court, or a Muslim court. He was emperor of a Yuan court, which combined and grew from out of the many parts that constituted the whole. Khubilai presided over a court of many colors, and he saw his job as to maintain harmony and peace, and to reconcile the many conflicts that would inevitably arise.

Buddhist and Daoist Rivalry

The festering rivalry between Buddhist and Daoist (Taoist) monks had undermined many attempts at governing the north, and the disputes between the two sides frequently erupted into violence. Möngke Khan had originally charged his younger brother with solving this intractable problem, and Khubilai was able to demonstrate his political skills in tackling this issue. The two religions shared some basic beliefs, and the Buddhists had made liberal use of Daoist terminology when translating very basic religious concepts from their Buddhist texts into Chinese. The disputes were not essentially over doctrine but concerned far more practical matters, such as land rights, ownership of property, and access to government patronage. Power and access to power, rather than ideology or doctrinal disputes, were the cause of the violence that the religious leaders inflicted on one another. The appropriate doctrinal argument could always be found and invoked as an excuse for the violence. The Buddhists claimed that the historical figure of the Buddha predated *Lǎozǐ 老子 (fl. 500 BCE), Daoism's founder, and therefore he could claim superiority over the Chinese philosopher. These claims were dismissed since the Daoists countered that Laozi had in fact traveled to the "Western Regions," India, and Transoxiana in Central Asia, where he had assumed various emanations, one of which was the Buddha. The teachings that he then espoused, speaking through the mouth of the Buddha, were a simplistic form of his original wisdom, designed to be understood by the less sophisticated and less educated peoples of those regions.

In 1258, Khubilai forced the two sides together at a conference where their leading theorists could debate before him. Such religious debates had been a favorite pastime for generations of Chinggisid princes. By 1258, however, Khubilai had already formed strong religious leanings of his own, and the young Tibetan Buddhist monk, Phags-pa, was already installed at Khubilai's court where he and his chief wife, Chabi, received religious instruction. It was this highly influential monk who devised a script with which to write the Mongolian language, hitherto usually written down in Uygur script, and which actually became the official script of the state. With the two warring sides together under one roof, Khubilai charged the Daoists with demonstrating before the assembled audience the various magical powers that they professed to have. When they failed to change the weather, foretell the future, or even cure various diseases, Khubilai declared the Daoists the losers. As punishment, seventeen leading Daoists had their heads publicly shaved and they were then forced to convert to Buddhism. In addition, various Buddhist temples, which had been occupied by Daoists, were liberated, and a number of properties confiscated by Daoists from the Buddhists were returned to their rightful owners. No other action was taken and the Daoists were not banned nor restricted from practicing.

When Möngke Khan assumed the throne he presided over a united empire, but the factions had been forced into a marriage built on bloodshed. Möngke's first task had been to strengthen his power base and to build an unassailable Toluid state. He had sent his brother Hulegu west to quell any dissent in the Islamic world. To this end he was able to manipulate the Persian/Arab rivalry, which was already destabilizing the region. They were welcomed by Iranians eager to be absorbed into a greater trading market, which promised more than just commercial potential for its entrepreneurs, opportunists, and adventurers. The empire to which they were attached as a pariah state offered stability, security, and an end to the military rule and the anarchy that prevailed over much of the country. Iranians flocked to Hulegu's banner and willingly participated first in the destruction of the blasphemous Isma'ilis and then in the fall of Baghdad, replacing the weak and corrupt Arab Caliph with a Persian governor. In 1258 the fall of Baghdad saw the demise of the old order, the 'Abbasid Caliphate, and the rise of the new, the Ilkhanate (1258–1335).

In the East a similar movement took place though nearly two decades separated the two events. In 1276, Khubilai ordered the taking of Hangzhou and, like in Iran, the old order, the Song, gave way for the new, the Yuán 元 dynasty (1279–1368). Baghdad fell after a firefight, though pestilence accounted for most of the appallingly high death rate, whereas Hangzhou fell without a fight and there was a peaceful transition of power. In Iran, Hulegu was generally welcomed and the only military confrontation was with the despised Isma'ilis. Song China went down fighting, but not to the degree that has often been portrayed. In fact, other than some very famous confrontations—such as the battle for the city of Xiangyang, the gateway to the Yangzi (Chang) plain, which was defended by the Song general Cao Youwen until it capitulated in 1236,

Conquest of Baghdad by the Mongols in 1258. Illustration from the *Jami' al-tawarikh* by the scholar Rashid-al-Din Hamadani (1430). Staatsbibliothek Berlin.

and the battles in Sichuan Province—many of the Mongols' victories were the result of defections. Jia Sidao's timely defection led to the final submission of Changdu, which opened the road to Dali. Political infighting, peasant revolts and uprisings in the region of modern Fujian led by Yan Mengbiao and Hunan, and the importation of new military technology from Persia expertly deployed by Khubilai, all led inexorably to the slow collapse of the Song. With the establishment of the Ilkhanate following the fall of Baghdad in 1258, Persian opportunists and adventurers had flocked to the east and eagerly signed up to help Khubilai in his wars with the Song and with the Ogodaid traditionalists under Qaidu fighting for Turkestan.

Bayan Noyan, a Loyal General

Bayan Noyan was the young general and court favorite whose string of military victories had ensured that he was awarded the prestigious task of overseeing the surrender of the Song capital.

Bayan Noyan (1236–1295) was born and raised in Persian Turkestan, and he accompanied his father when he moved west with Hulegu's armies. He served Hulegu in Iran until he was dispatched east by Abaqa to assist Khubilai. After the success of his campaign against Xiangyang, he was appointed commander of Khubilai's forces coinciding with the official founding of the Yuan dynasty in 1273. After dispatching the Empress Dowager northward to Khubilai's capital, Khanbaliq, in 1276, he was faced with the problem of appointing a city administration for the Yuan's cultural capital. It is probable that he recruited many Iranian notables to positions of power and influence in the city as the establishment of the Phoenix Mosque in 1281, and a number of Persian tombstones would seem to suggest this as well (Lane 2011c).

Foreign Adventures

If Khubilai achieved comparative success at home, his adventures abroad did not reflect this flush of triumph. In as early as 1256, his entanglement in the jungles of Annan spelled early disaster just as his concurrent absorption of the kingdom of Dali into the Yuan state became an enduring success. Three raids on Burma, in 1277, 1283, and 1287, eventually saw Mongol rule in the Irrawaddy delta, and a puppet king in Bagan, the capital of the Pagan Kingdom. Failure to even land successfully in Japan became a costly humiliation and a perceived defeat that undermined the cultivated image of the Chinggisid military machine as an almost irresistible force of nature.

The erosion of that image of invincibility had begun with the defeat by the armies of the Mamluk commander, Qutuz, in 1261 at the Battle of Ayn Jalut. Although the battle did not involve Hulegu's main military forces and the defeat in no way altered the military balance in the area, the symbolic impact resounded globally and the image of a vanquished Chinggisid army was powerful and compelling. Syria quickly became a battlefield, and it was evident that the unstoppable had now been stopped.

Ayn Jalut coincided with the Chinggisid civil war, pitting brother against brother as those deeply entrenched ideologies, which had long been maturing, erupted in violence. Crowned by a quriltai (a Mongol assembly of tribe leaders) hastily convened in Karakorum and encapsulating the aspirations of the traditional beliefs, values, and practices of the steppe, Ariq Buqa, the youngest of the Toluid brothers, had the backing of the Golden Horde of Russia as well as the disgruntled and vengeful Chaghadaids and Ogodaids. Against these reactionary forces, Khubilai was able to call forth the wealth and might of China. Even in these early years, the Chinese were able to recognize a friend and they knew that their interests lay with a triumphant Khubilai, and that a victorious Ariq Buqa would be disastrous for China's future. Once again the

Song lent their support to the Chinggisids and Khubilai soon accepted the surrender of his brother with apparent magnanimity. When in 1266 his youngest brother died in questionable circumstances, however, many assumed Khubilai to be responsible. Ariq Buqa's challenge to Khubilai was serious and has been greatly downplayed by the Toluid historians of Iran.

After Khubilai's victory Chinggis Khan's empire was irrevocably split. The split was not just between ambitious princes greedy for wealth, land, and power, but had far deeper roots. The war had been for the soul of the empire and with Khubilai Khan's victory, it was the progressive, dynamic forces that wedded the cultures of Iran, China, Turan, and the steppe, and that wove an intricate cultural weft with a commercial warp, and a pile of a diverse and dynamic population. Ariq Buqa had united those forces, which viewed the direction their leadership was moving in with distaste and alarm. They viewed the sedentary world as there to service their needs and to be exploited. The Toluids saw the Chinese and Persians as partners rather than as expendable subjects. This dichotomy not only divided the greater empire but would remain an issue and a bone of contention within the Toluid ranks as well.

After Ariq Buqa's death in 1266, the "Back to Basics" banner was raised by a prince from the very much weakened house of Ögödei. Originally Kaidu Khan (1230–1301) (Kaidu or Qaidu; Mongolian: Хайду, Khaidu) took up arms against Khubilai not to challenge his right to be Great Khan or indeed to claim that honor for himself, but to restore the ancestral rights of his humiliated forefathers who had suffered so cruelly at the hands of Khubilai's brother, Möngke. Kaidu Khan wished to claim those lands and rights that his "family" felt they had wrongly and unjustly been deprived off. Kaidu's cause, however, was soon subsumed under the greater cause and all those who resented the ascendancy of the house of Tolui. They deemed that the Toluid accommodation for the settled, sedentary empires amounted to a blasphemous betrayal of the ideals and beliefs of Chinggis Khan and the Yasa of the Mongols.

Kaidu's rebellion effectively split the Toluid Empire in two, separating the Ilkhanate from the Yuan state with a region of instability and lawlessness, which was dangerous for merchants and inadmissible to government officials or diplomats. When Marco Polo traveled east to return with his father to the court of Khubilai Khan, he was forced to travel along the high and very inhospitable passes of the Pamirs along the Wakkan corridor. On his return in 1292, taking with him his valuable human cargo of a princess and blushing bride, Marco Polo, like so many others traveling between the Yuan and the Ilkhanate, was forced to brave the treacherous seas of the Spice Route. Although the Song's former superintendent of shipping, Pu Shoukeng, had

A compilation of six Mongol Empresses of the Yuan dynasty. National Palace Museum, Taipei, Taiwan.

happily jumped ship and now served Khubilai's interests throughout the Indian Ocean, those shipping lanes remained extremely hazardous, time-consuming, and an unsatisfactory alternative to the Silk Roads through Turkistan.

Between 1278 and 1294, Khubilai managed to force commercial cooperation on some parts of the Malay Peninsula, southern India, and the Khmer kingdom. It was his attempts at conquest of Java, however, that preoccupied Khubilai, where he committed twenty to thirty thousand men to a punitive raid against the Javanese kingdom of Singhasari (1293). His forces were compelled to withdraw by the Majapahit king, however, at a cost of three thousand lives. At the time of his death, all Khubilai had to show were the two Thai vassal kingdoms of Sukhotai and Chiangmai. The historian Waṣṣāf records the attraction that Java held for the Emperor:

> It is a portion of the portions of the ocean full of accumulated curiosities and abundant wealth, with plenty of all kinds of treasures and precious jewels, and charming products of ingenuity, and honourable gifts of merchandise, displaying the contrivances of the incomparable one. That country and all around it is fragrant with the odours of aloewood and cloves, and plains and precincts are vocal with the notes of parrots, saying, "I am a garden, the shrubs of which are envied by the freshness of the garden of Paradise," etc., and so forth. (Wassaf 1853, 22–23)

One reason for the adventures in the southern seas was the ongoing war against his cousins in the north and west. Trade was the lifeblood of the empire and if one artery was blocked another one must be started. If the merchants could not forge a way through the deserts of Turkestan, then their ships must brave the dangerous seas of the southern oceans. Hostile forces that were disrupting trade along the ancient Silk Roads held Transoxiana. The justly famous Yam system of interlinked caravanserais, postal relay stations, and fresh camels, horses, and couriers, spread right across Eurasia and Persia, linking the antagonistic Golden Horde and the allied Ilkhanate with Karakorum and Khanbaliq, but security could no longer be guaranteed as once it had under the domination of the *Pax Mongolica*.

As soon as word of the fall of Hangzhou and the surrender of the seals of the Song emperors had reached the south, the superintendent of the imperial fleet, a Muslim with family connections with the western Islamic world, Pu Shoukeng, offered his fleet and his services to the Chinggisid khans. His vessels opened up the Spice Route to the eager ortaqs and merchants of Khubilai Khan.

The administration that was introduced by Khubilai when he assumed power was essentially the same form of government that remained throughout the period of Yuan rule until 1368. The one major change was the reintroduction of the state exams that had been abolished as soon as Khubilai assumed power. It would have been blatantly unrealistic to have expected the many foreigners who flocked eastward in search of fame and fortune to have studied such specialist subjects demanded by these state exams. The Chinese classics and Confucianism are not widely known subjects outside of China. When in 1313 the examinations were reinstated, however, a sufficient cross section of society must have achieved access to education to feel able to take these grueling tests.

Later Years and Decline

Khubilai probably also oversaw the apex of his dynasty's rule, and his successors unfortunately had a hard, if not impossible, task to follow. Khubilai not only built the dynasty's new capital, Khanbaliq or Dadu, but with the help of Persian hydraulic engineers, he also created a new water supply for the city, which eventually became the Grand Canal between Khanbaliq and Hangzhou. This canal linked north and south China in a very real sense, allowing trade to flourish along its eleven hundred miles, the transport of rice in particular. But the slow descent into chaos and unraveling of Yuan rule allowed much of the Chinggisid legacy to be absorbed and assimilated with the Chinese psyche. Khubilai's final years were marred by ill-health and depression brought on by family tragedy. In 1286, there was the premature death of his heir apparent, Zhenjin, while the two were involved in an acrimonious and unresolved squabble. The death of his beloved wife Chabi Khatun also deeply affected the emperor, who subsequently withdrew from direct contact with his courtiers. On Chabi's suggestion, Khubilai married her younger niece, Nambui, who became his mouthpiece to the outer world. He sank into depression haunted by his military failures in Japan and Vietnam, and he also succumbed to the vice of so many Mongol khans, alcohol. The traditional Mongol diet so rich in meat combined with heavy drinking and his general despondency and lack of any exercise, resulted in gout and chronic obesity. A famous painting from 1280 by the Chinese court artist Liu Guandao captures the emperor dressed in distinct Mongolian-style furs over Chinese silk brocades showing early signs of weight problems, which would later contribute to his death from ill-health.

Khubilai appreciated the fine arts and retained court painters, the most famous of whom is *Zhào Mèngfǔ 赵孟頫 (1254–1322)—although initially the artist resisted attempts to coopt him to the Yuan court. Like many of the other intellectual elite who considered themselves Song loyalists, Zhao thought the Yuan emperors were very liberal and tolerant as far as the intellectual elite were concerned, and the literati were free to develop and express themselves without government interference. The Yuan century saw landscape painters and the dramatic arts in particular as experiencing what has been described as a golden age. There are some who credit this spirit of tolerance and liberalism to disinterest and plain ignorance, but this is not borne out by the evidence. Khubilai himself was a generous and appreciative patron of the arts, while such avowed Song loyalists and passive resisters as Zhou Mi, the art collector and journalist of Hangzhou, included Yuan administrators, Muslims, and Semerun among his closest intimates.

Khubilai was succeeded by his grandson, Zhenjin's son Temür. The empire had enjoyed its heyday under Khubilai and after his death the Yuan went into gradual, slow decline. When the Mongol army withdrew and retreated north to Karakorum, this armed camp did not comprise all the descendants, the defenders, and the core administration of the Yuan state. It comprised merely the core upholders of the emperor's power while the vast majority of those who had defined themselves as subjects of the Chinggisid khans had long reconciled themselves to serving whoever would best serve their interests. It is revealing that one of the earlier rebellions that shook Quanzhou, the empire's gateway to the Indian Ocean, was instigated by local Persian malcontents.

George LANE
School of Oriental and Asian Studies, University of London

Further Reading

Allsen, Thomas. (2001). *Culture and conquest in Mongol Eurasia*. New York: Cambridge University Press.

Armijo-Hussein, Jacqueline Misty. (1996). Sayyid 'Ajall Shams al-Din: A Muslim from Central Asia, serving Mongols in China, and bringing civilization to Yunnan. (Unpublished Doctoral Dissertation). Harvard University, Cambridge, MA.

Atwood, Christopher. (2004). *Encyclopedia of Mongolia and the Mongol Empire*. New York: Facts on File Inc.

Bar Hebraeus. (2003). *The chronography of Gregory Ab'lFaraj the son of Aaron, Hebrew physician commonly known as Bar Hebraeus. Being the first part of his political history*. Piscataway, NJ: Gorgias Press. (Original work published thirteenth century)

Bartol'd, V. V. (1968). *Turkestan down until the Mongol invasion* (H. A. R. Gibb, Trans.). London: Gibb Memorial Series.

Biran, Michal. (1997). Qaidu and the rise of the independent Mongol state in Central Asia. London: Routledge.

Bretschneider, Emil. (1888). *Mediaeval researches from Eastern Asiatic sources*. London: Trübner Oriental Series, 2 vols.

Bretschneider, Emil. (2005). *Archaeological and historical researches on Peking and its environs*. Shanghai: Elibron Classics. (Original work published 1876)

Doefer, Gerhard, (1963). Türkische und Mongolische Elemente im Neupersischen. In *Mongolische Elemente im Neupersischen* (pp. 51–105). Wiesbaden, Germany: Franz Steiner Verlag.

Eliot, Sir H. (1867–1877). *History of India, as told by its own historians: The Muhammadan period*. In John Dawson (Ed.), Vol. III. London: Trubner Company.

Haw, Stephen G. (2006). *Marco Polo's China: A Venetian in the realm of Khubilai Khan*. London: Routledge Studies in the Early History of Asia.

Haw, Stephen G. (2008). *Beijing—A concise history*. London: Routledge Studies in the Modern History of Asia.

Herman, John. (2002). Mongol conquest of Dali: The failed second front. In Nicola di Cosmo (Ed.),

Warfare in Inner Asian history (500–1800). Leiden, The Netherlands: Brill.

Juwaynī,'Atā' Malik. (1997). *Genghis Khan: The history of the world-conqueror* (John Andrew Boyle, Trans.). Seattle: University of Washington Press. (Original work published thirteenth century)

Khwandamir. (1994). *Habib as-Siyar* (Wheeler Thackston, Trans.). Cambridge, MA: Harvard University Press.

Lane, George. (2003). *Early Mongol rule in thirteenth century Iran*. London: RoutledgeCurzon.

Lane, George. (2011a). The Dali Stele. In Nurten Kilic-Schubel & Evrim Binbash (Eds.), *Horizons of the world: Festschrift for IsenbikeTogan / Hududü'l-Alem: İsenbikeTogan'aArmağan*. Istanbul: Ithaki Press.

Lane, George. (2011b). Jovayni, 'alā'-al-din. *Encyclopaedia Iranica*. Retrieved January 30, 2013, from http://www.iranicaonline.org/articles/jovayni-ala-al-din

Lane, George. (2011c). The Phoenix Mosque. *Encyclopaedia Iranica*. Retrieved January 31, 2013, from http://www.iranicaonline.org/articles/phoenix-mosque

Lane, George. (2013). Whose secret intent? In Morris Rossabi (Ed.), *Eurasian influences on Yuan China* (pp. 1–40). Singapore: National University of Singapore Press.

McCausland, Shane. (2011). *Zhao Mengfu: Calligraphy and painting for Khubilai's China*. Hong Kong: Hong Kong University Press.

Morris Rossabi. (1988). *Khubilai Khan: His life & times*. Berkeley: University of California Press.

Mote, Frederick W. (2003). *Imperial China 900–1800. Cambridge* MA: Harvard University Press.

Rashīd al-Dīn; Jāmi' al-Tavārīkh, Mohammad Roushan; & Mustafa Musavi (Eds.). (1994). Jāmi' al-Tavārīkh (4 vols.). Tehran: Nashr Elburz. (Original work compiled between 1307 and 1316)

Song Lian (Comp.). (1978). Biography of Guo Baoyu. In *Yuanshi* 元史 [History of the Yuan] (15 vols) (*juan* 149, pp. 3521). Beijing: Zhonghua shuju.

Thackston, Wheeler. (Trans.). (1999). *Jami'u't-Tawarikh: Compendium of chronicles* (3 vols.). Cambridge, MA: Harvard University Press.

Waṣṣāf, 'Abd Allāh ibn Faḍl Allāh Shirāzī. (1853). *Tajziyatalamṣār watazjiyat al-acṣār, Tārīkh-i- Waṣṣāf* [The allocation of cities and the propulsion of epochs] (Reprint). Tehran: IbnSīnā.

Yule, Henry. (1914). *Cathay and the way thither* (3 vols.). London: Hakluyt Society.

• 忽必烈汗 •

Luó Guànzhōng
罗贯中

c. 1330–c. 1410—Fiction writer and playwright; supposed author of *Romance of the Three Kingdoms*

Alternate names: Luó Běn 罗本; Luó Guàn 罗贯; nickname: Húhǎi Sànrén 胡海散人

Summary

Luo Guanzhong was most likely born during the Yuan dynasty, with his life spanning the Yuan-Ming transition. While many of the details of his life remain unclear, his status as a prolific writer, especially of fiction, is unquestionable. It is generally accepted that Luo authored the historical novel *Romance of the Three Kingdoms*, which draws from official historiography as well as oral and popular traditions, and tells the story of the final decades of the Later (Eastern) Han and the ensuing Three Kingdoms period, over a thousand years before Luo's time. By "fictionalizing" history, Luo Guanzhong was among the writers responsible for the gradual shift in Chinese narrative from history writing to fiction writing.

Among all writers of late imperial Chinese vernacular literature, there are few names associated with so many works as Luo Guanzhong's. While Luo is known to have authored a number of plays, he is remembered primarily as a fiction writer. Among the fictional works attributed to him, the most prominent ones are *Romance of the Three Kingdoms* (*Sānguó yǎnyì* 三国演义, or simply *Three Kingdoms*) and *Water Margin* (*Shuǐhǔ zhuàn* 水浒传, also translated as *Outlaws of the Marsh*, *All Men Are Brothers*, or *Marshes of Mount Liang*). They are the earliest two of the four full-length works of vernacular fiction of the Míng 明 dynasty (1368–1644) that are generally known as the Four Masterworks of the Ming (*sìdà qíshū* 四大奇书), the other two being *Journey to the West* (*Xīyóu jì* 西遊记, also known as *The Monkey and the Monk*) and *The Plum in the Golden Vase* (*Jīn Píng Méi* 金瓶梅, or *Golden Lotus*). Unfortunately, little is known about Luo Guanzhong's life apart from the consensus reached by most modern scholars that Luo was born during the Yuán 元

dynasty (1279–1368). The consequence of this lack of biographic data is ironic: the man who deserves to be called the father of late imperial Chinese vernacular fiction has remained largely a shadowy figure.

There are accounts of Luo Guanzhong's life in different Ming sources, but they are not only scanty but also inconsistent. In his *Xīhú yóulǎn zhìyú* 西湖游览志余, a volume of anecdotes about the city of Hangzhou and the nearby lake of Xihu, Ming-dynasty scholar Tián Rǔchéng 田汝成 (1503–1557) called Luo Guanzhong a native of Qiántáng 钱塘, present-day Hangzhou. Several other Ming scholars, including Láng Yīng 郎瑛 (1487–1566), Gāo Rú 高儒 (fl. 1540), Wáng Qí 王圻 (1529–1612), and Hú Yīnglín 胡应麟 (1551–1602), agreed with Tian Rucheng on Luo's nativity, but they did not agree with each other on Luo's name. Lang Ying and Hu Yinglin believed that Luo Guanzhong had another name as Luó Běn 罗本, while Wang Qi put Luo's name as Luó Guàn 罗贯.

Not surprisingly, these scholars also could not reach a consensus on the dates of Luo Guanzhong's life. Tian Rucheng dated Luo's lifetime as early as the Southern Song period (1127–1279). According to Hu Yinglin, Luo was a "disciple" of Shī Nài'ān 施耐庵, to whom alone Hu ascribed *Water Margin*. Since Hu called Shi a man of the Yuan, the alleged master-disciple relationship may suggest a later dating for Luo's lifetime, possibly straddling the late Yuan and early Ming. Wang Qi went along the same lines as Hu Xinglin about Luo's lifetime but was more unequivocal, as he called Luo one of the people with "political aspirations" during the period of the Yuan-Ming transition.

Among all the Ming sources about Luo Guanzhong, a biographic note on Luo included in *A Sequel to the Registry of the Ghosts* (*Lùguǐbù xùbiān* 录鬼簿续编), a bibliographic work on popular drama and dramatists of the Yuan and early Ming periods, seems most reliable. According to the writer, Luo was from Taiyuan and nicknamed Húhǎi Sànrén 胡海散人 (Loafer of Lakes and Seas), which may suggest Luo's status as a scholar with no official position. While calling Luo an "aloof man with few friends" 与人寡和, the writer considered his own personal relationship to Luo one of "friendship despite a gap in age" 忘年交. Given his lamentation in the note that he did not know how his friend's life had ended, it is reasonable to assume that Luo was at least ten years his senior.

Most importantly, the writer claimed that he had personally met Luo in 1364, only four years before the demise of the Yuan and founding of the Ming. As the writer stated that "Over sixty years have passed since we parted from each other," the date for *A Sequel to the Registry of the Ghosts* should not be earlier than 1424, more than a half century into the Ming period. While *A Sequel to the Registry of the Ghosts* is an anonymous work, its writer was probably the early Ming dramatist Jiǎ Zhòngmíng 贾仲明, as most modern scholars tend to agree. As Jia was born in 1343, he would have been twenty-one years old when he met Luo Guanzhong for the last time in 1364. That would suggest that Luo, even though considerably older than Jia, was in the prime of life in 1364, which would in turn corroborate the conjecture that Luo's life straddled the Yuan-Ming transition.

Modern scholars, however, have repeatedly challenged the statement in *A Sequel to the Registry of the Ghosts* that Luo Guanzhong was a native of Taiyuan. The challenges are well grounded: among all Ming editions of the fictional works attributed to Luo Guanzhong, many denote Luo's place of nativity to be Dōngyuán 东原, present-day Dongping in Shandong Province, and none has Taiyuan as his place of origin. To reconcile the conflict between these two place names, some modern scholars have suggested that the written symbol of *tài* 太 in Taiyuan 太原 in *A Sequel to the Registry of the Ghosts* might have been an inadvertent scribal deviation from the *dong* in Dongyuan. Indeed, such a scribal error was possible, as the earliest extant copy of this text is dated to the sixteenth century, after a process of textual transmission lasting at least a century following its original composition in 1424 or slightly after.

No doubt, uncertainties remain about Luo Guanzhong's life, but a synthesis of the available information from different Ming sources seems to allow this surmise: Luo Guanzhong was born in the late Yuan, possibly around 1330. As he was an extremely prolific writer, it is reasonable to assume that he lived a long life, living perhaps about four decades into the Ming. Most likely, he was from Dongping of Shandong, but, like many other men of letters in northern China of his time, migrated to the south at a certain point of his life and lived in Hangzhou for a number of years.

Romance of the Three Kingdoms (Sanguo Yanyi)

Romance of the Three Kingdoms is by far the most read historical novel in China. Its enormous popularity had long spilled into China's East Asian neighbors before it was translated into different Western languages. The novel chronicles the major events over approximately one hundred years that cover the ending decades of the Later (Eastern) Han (27–220 CE) and the ensuing Three Kingdoms 三国 period (220–265 CE). Drawing from sources in official historiography as well as oral and popular traditions, the novel mingles history with legends in a narrative, which is, in the estimation of the eighteenth-century scholar Zhāng Xuéchéng 章学诚 (1738–1801), "with seven-tenths in facts and three-tenths in fabrications." It dramatizes the military conflicts and diplomatic intrigues among the numerous warlords, which eventually led to the tripartition of China into the kingdoms of Wei, Shu, and Wu before the country became once again reunified under the Jìn 晋 dynasty (265–420 CE).

The earliest known edition of *Romance of the Three Kingdoms* is actually titled *Sānguó zhì tōngsú yǎnyī* 三国志通俗演义 (literally, *An elaboration of the Meaning of the* Records of the Three Kingdoms *to Reach the Masses*). The front page features a legend that reads "*Hòuxué Luó Běn Guànzhōng biāncì*" 后学罗本贯中編次, or "Compiled by the humble student of a later age, Luo Ben, styled Guanzhong." The edition has two prefaces, penned by the pseudonymous writers Yōngyúzǐ 庸愚子 and Xiūránzǐ 修髯子 and dated 1522 and 1494 respectively. Judging from the dates for the prefaces, this edition could have been published in 1522, possibly following a late fifteenth-century precursor. No textual exemplars of *Romance of the Three Kingdoms* prior to 1522 are extant, but it is almost certain that the process of the textual evolution of the novel had started much earlier.

While modern scholars have questioned the attributions of some other works to Luo Guanzhong, Luo's authorship or his compilation of *Romance of the Three Kingdoms* seems most firmly established and least challenged. If Luo was indeed responsible or at least partially responsible for the composition of the novel, the date of his lifetime and the date of the earliest text of the novel would be mutually corroborative. Once again, the most relevant source is the biographic note on Luo Guanzhong in *Luguibu xubian*. If *Romance of the Three Kingdoms* was written during the Yuan, the writer of *Luguibu xubian*, who met Luo only four years before the end of the dynasty, would have known and mentioned it, especially because he was particularly generous in commending his fellow playwrights for their literary and cultural accomplishments outside the field of drama. Instead, it seems he was completely unaware of such a work. Even at the time of his compilation of *A Sequel to the Registry of the Ghosts*, when he took Luo Guanzhong's death for granted, he still could not associate Luo's name with any version of *Romance of the Three Kingdoms*. On the other hand, however, it is stated in Yongyuzi's 1522 preface to *Sanguo zhi tongsu yanyi* that once the manuscript of the novel was completed, literati scholars "vied with each other to copy it out." Obviously, if such massive textual transmission of the novel had taken place prior to 1424, the author of *A Sequel to the Registry of the Ghosts*, as a central figure in the field of popular literature, would have noted it.

These available sources do not constitute any indisputable evidence, but they provide a solid ground for this conjecture: without completely ruling out the possibility of its initiation in the final few years of the Yuan, one finds good reason to believe that the earliest manuscript version of *Romance of the Three*

Pages from a fifteenth-century edition of Luo Guanzhong's *Romance of the Three Kingdoms*.

Kingdoms was composed in the early decades of the Ming. The manuscript remained in relative obscurity for some time before it became popular in certain circles of literati readers, probably during the late fifteenth century, and the growing demand for textual transmission eventually led to the print of the novel toward the end of the century, followed by another print in 1522 known as *Sanguo zhi tongsu yanyi*.

Water Margin (Shuihu Zhuan)

While *Romance of the Three Kingdoms* appears in a language that is largely a mixture of vernacular language (*báihuà* 白话) with simplified classical or literary language (*wényǎn* 文言), *Water Margin* is generally considered China's earliest full-length fictional work in the full-fledged written vernacular. The novel is about the 108 bandit heroes in the half-historical and half-legendary twelfth-century uprising in Liangshan, their gathering in the lair from different places, their repeated battles against the government forces, their voluntary surrender to the imperial court, and their subsequent expeditions against other rebels. Prior to the novel, the Liangshan rebellion had long been an extremely popular subject matter in oral storytelling and popular performance. In the storytellers' repertoires from the Southern Song period (1127–1279), several tales, judging by their titles, could have belonged to an oral complex centering on the Liangshan bandits, although none of them is extant. During the Yuan and the Ming, the Liangshan bandit heroes were featured in paintings and, even more often, in drama. While it is impossible to figure out exactly the specific ways in which *Water Margin* is connected to its antecedents in oral and popular Liangshan cycles, it seems safe to say that the novel agglomerated a large number of tales from multiple sources and assembled them into a narrative of epic dimensions.

Since the Ming period, *Water Margin* has always been attributed to either or both of these two names: Shi Nai'an and Luo Guanzhong. Among the Ming scholars who made references to *Water Margin*, some, including Lang Ying, Tian Rucheng, and Wang Qi, believed Luo Guanzhong to be the lone compiler of the novel. Tian Rucheng even suggested that three generations of Luo's offspring were dumb as a retribution for his compilation of *Water Margin*, a book that "corrupted people's minds by teaching them treachery and treason." Gao Ru, on the other hand, stated in his bibliographical work *Books of One Hundred Streams* (*Bǎichuān shūzhì* 百川书志) that *Water Margin* was based on "the authentic script by Shi Nai'an" and "edited by Luo Guanzhong." That assertion assigns Luo only a secondary role in the compilation of the novel, but it did not say anything about the personal relationship between Shi and Luo. Without citing any sources, Hu Yinglin called Luo Guanzhong a "disciple" (*ménrén* 门人) of "a Shi fellow of the Yuan from Wulin," presumably Shi Nai'an, whose *Water Margin* was "exceedingly popular." Interestingly, despite his tone of indisputable certainty on the master-disciple relationship, Hu Yinglin actually did not acknowledge any role by Luo Guanzhong in the compilation of *Water Margin*. Unfortunately, the additional name of Shi Nai'an and his possible personal tie with Luo Guanzhong provide no further clues to Luo's life. The reason is simple: despite occasional scholarly efforts to prove otherwise, there is virtually no verifiable information about Shi's life.

To compound the nebulosity about its authorship, *Water Margin* has an extremely convoluted history of textual evolution. In 1975, a fragment of an edition of *Water Margin*, entitled *Jīngběn Zhōngyì zhuàn* 京本忠义传, was discovered in the Shanghai Municipal Library, which is believed to be an early sixteenth-century print. That is the earliest known edition of the novel. But it was another edition perhaps slightly later, the so-called Wǔdìng 武定 edition—named after its alleged sponsor Guō Xūn 郭勋 (1475–1542), the Earl of Wuding—that had a great influence on the later editions. While the historical existence of the Wuding edition is generally accepted, no textual exemplar of it is extant. A sixteenth-century fragment, consisting of eight chapters and one additional page, was once believed to be part of a copy of the Wuding edition, but that theory has met challenges in the late twentieth century. In the late sixteenth and early seventeenth centuries, several editions appeared in print, with different numbers of chapters—100, 110, 115, and 120—in them. Around 1640, *Jīn Shèngtàn's 金圣叹 (1608–1661) truncated seventy-chapter edition emerged, which supplanted all earlier editions and remained as the standard version of the novel for at least two and a half centuries. To further complicate the situation, all these editions belonged to two different lineages, the so-called *fánběn* 繁本 (full text) recension (i.e., revised edition) and *jiǎnběn* 简本 (simple text) recension. Modern scholars differ in their views of the relationship between these two textual traditions: while some believe the *jianben* editions to be abridged versions of their *fanben* counterparts, others argue that the *jianben* versions represented an earlier stage of the textual evolution and therefore must be closer to the earliest prototype of the novel.

If Luo Guanzhong lived in the late Yuan and early Ming, as the available sources of information seem to suggest, obviously his lifetime was considerably earlier than the dates of the earliest known editions of *Water Margin*. Given the textual volatility among the sixteenth- and seventeenth-century editions of the novel—in contrast to the relative stability among different editions of *Romance of the Three Kingdoms* during the same period—it is impossible to know exactly what the prototype text by Shi Nai'an and/or Luo Guanzhong was like and how it was related to the *fanben* and *jianben* traditions, if such a prototype text had indeed existed.

Other Works

Among the other fictional works that are traditionally attributed to Luo Guanzhong, *The Three Sui Quash the Demons' Revolt* (*Sān Suì píng yāozhuàn* 三遂平妖传) tells a supernatural tale adapted from the oral and popular sources about the eleventh-century rebellion led by Wáng Zé 王则. A late sixteenth-century twenty-chapter "reprint" (*chóngkān* 重刊) edition of the novel is extant, which claims to have been originally "compiled by Luo Guanzhong of Dongyuan." In the early seventeenth century, a forty-chapter

*People marked with an asterisk have entries in this dictionary.

version of the novel came into existence, which denominates Luo Guanzhong its original author and Féng Mènglóng 冯梦龙 (1574–1646) the one responsible for its expansion. A sixty-chapter novel titled *A Popular History of the Late Tang and Five Dynasties Periods* (*Cán Táng-Wǔdài shī yǎnyì zhuàn* 殘唐五代史演义传) is preserved in a number of editions, each with Luo Guanzhong's name affixed on the front page as Luo Ben. Extant in an early seventeenth-century edition, *Suí-Táng liǎng cháo zhìzhuàn* 隋唐两朝志传 (*A Popular History of the Sui and Tang Dynasties*) carries a legend that denotes Luo Guanzhong as the compiler. In addition to these fictional works, titles of three plays are listed under Luo Guanzhong's name in *Luguibu xubian*, among which *The Gathering of Emperor Taizu of the Song and Other Heroes* (*Zhào Tàizǔ lónghǔ fēngyún huì* 赵太祖龙虎风云会) is the only one that is extant. As the writer of *A Sequel to the Registry of the Ghosts* claims that he had no knowledge of Luo's whereabouts after he met Luo for the last time in 1364, we can assume that all three plays were written in Luo's early years, before he switched from dramatic composition to fiction writing.

Obviously, all the fictional works attributed to Luo Guanzhong are, to different extents, based on history. For centuries, historiography was the predominant and most prestigious genre in Chinese prose narrative. By "fictionalizing" history, Luo Guanzhong was among the writers responsible for the gradual shift of the gravity in Chinese narrative from history writing to fiction writing. Another salient feature of these works is their affinity and proximity to oral and popular story cycles, which may have been the reason that they are among the earliest fictional works in the written vernacular. To be sure, these works are by no means comparable, even in their literary values, as *Romance of the Three Kingdoms* and *Water Margin* are immeasurably superior in comparison with any of the others. In terms of the writing styles, they are indeed so varied and diverse that one wonders over the possibility that Luo's name was simply borrowed for commercial reasons. Yet, even if that were true, it would only speak to Luo's enormous fame and popularity at the time. Different scholars may have different assessments of any particular work attributed to Luo Guanzhong, but Luo's status, as a towering figure in the early stage of Chinese vernacular fiction, is simply unchallengeable.

Liangyan GE
University of Notre Dame

Further Reading

Fusek, Lois. (Trans.). (2010). The Three Sui Quash the Demons' Revolt: *A comic novel attributed to Luo Guanzhong*. Honolulu: University of Hawaii Press.

Ge Liangyan. (2001). *Out of the margins: The rise of Chinese vernacular fiction*. Honolulu: University of Hawaii Press.

Hanan, Patrick. (1971). The composition of P'ing-yaochuan. *Harvard Journal of Asiatic Studies 31*, 201–219.

Hegel, Robert E. (1998). *Reading illustrated fiction in late imperial China*. Stanford, CA: Stanford University Press.

Hegel, Robert E. (1994). Traditional Chinese fiction—The state of the field. *The Journal of Asian Studies* 53(2), 394–426.

Hsia, C. T. (1968). *The classic Chinese novel: A critical introduction*. New York: Columbia University Press.

Huang, Martin W. (1990). Dehistoricization and intertextualization: The anxiety of precedents in the evolution of the traditional Chinese novel. *Chinese Literature: Essays, Articles, Reviews* 12, 45–68.

Idema, Wilt L. (1974). *Chinese vernacular fiction: The formative period*. Leiden, The Netherlands: Brill.

Irwin, Richard G. (1953). *The evolution of a Chinese novel: Shui-huchuan*. Cambridge, MA: Harvard University Press.

Plaks, Andrew H. (1987). *The four masterworks of the Ming novel*. Princeton, NJ: Princeton University Press.

Roberts, Moss. (Trans.). (1991). *Three kingdoms*. Berkeley: University of California Press and Foreign Languages Press.

Shapiro, Sidney. (Trans.). (1976). *Outlaws of the marsh* (2 vols.). Bloomington: Indiana University Press and Foreign Languages Press.

Wáng Zhēn
王祯

fl. 1290–1333—Agronomist and inventor

Alternate name: Wáng Bóshàn 王伯善

Summary

Wang Zhen was an inventor and scholar-official during the Yuan dynasty. His book *Agricultural Treatise* used descriptions of agricultural tools to respond to the numerous intellectual and political problems of his times. Assuming posts in different regions put Wang in a position to help the common people still suffering from the aftermath of the Mongolian conquest. By advocating reforms through the use of innovative technologies, Wang created a unique source for modern historians with far-reaching implications for China's intellectual history. His detailed descriptions remain a valuable contribution to contemporary historians of ecology and technology; his work is emblematic of how Chinese intellectuals thought of their role within society at times when conditions at court were not in their favor.

Little information about the inventor and scholar-official Wang Zhen has survived beyond his official career record. A native of Dōngpíng 东平 (in Shandong Province) he held posts in Jīngdé County 旌德县 (Anhui Province) in 1295, and subsequently in Yǒngfēng County 永丰县 (Jianxi Province). Wang wrote the *Agricultural Treatise* (*Nóngshū* 农书, hereafter: *Treatise)* in which he describes methods for using wooden moveable types for printing and gives a comprehensive account of farming tools and practices. Previous works on agriculture failed to match the comprehensiveness of the *Treatise,* its innovative use of diagrams, and the technological inventions surrounding its production process. Wang's enthusiastically reproduced work shaped the debate on agricultural tools in China, and to a lesser extent the treatment of technical subjects in general. The *Treatise* allows the modern reader a glance at agricultural practices that seldom leave traces within the historical record. It remains a valuable piece of documentation for thirteenth- and fourteenth-century practices that would otherwise have been lost.

Confucian Ethics under Mongol Rule

Wang's work sits at the intersection of political, intellectual, and regional tensions that the downfall of the Southern Sòng dynasty 南宋 (1127–1279) and the establishment of Mongol rule by the Yuán 元 dynasty (1279–1368) brought into focus. The *Treatise* responds to the conflicting demands encountered by generations of Chinese literati—for example, loyalty to the ruler versus serving the people, the need for literary refinement to attain official positions versus the need to administer local affairs during one's tenure, and the cultural barriers that office holders could encounter when assuming randomly assigned posts throughout a geologically vast and diverse empire.

The *Treatise* is more than just an illustrated book of agricultural equipment and technological innovations, however, and it is important to understand the appeal it had to Wang's contemporaries.

Questions of Loyalty

The Confucian notion of four hierarchical relationships (ruler-subject, father-son, husband-wife, and older-younger brothers) posed peculiar problems to Chinese literati at the beginning of Mongolian rule. In addition to the limited number of available positions compared to previous dynasties, the demands of piety to the former dynastic rulers in principle remained unbroken. How to best fulfill one's obligation towards the peoples' well-being thus becomes a pressing issue, as Wang describes in this passage from his *Treatise* on the rake (*yúndàng* 耘荡):

> I personally observed farmers in Jiandong and elsewhere weeding their fields by hand, crawling between grain stalks on their knees. . . this is truly a pity. . . I hope that humanitarians [愛民者] will disseminate [the rake] to make its use more common.
>
> (For a full translation of this passage, see Hammers 2013, 287t.; Wang 1981, 233)

Assuming posts in different regions put Wang in a position to best understand and elevate the plight of the common people who were still suffering from the aftermath of the Mongolian conquest. He primarily addresses fellow members of the elite to act on their humanitarian duties by joining his cause. He uses quotations from ancient texts that are central to the Chinese cultural identity to convince those in doubt about public service within the new regime. Using sagely practices of antiquity, which are in contrast to the nomadic roots of the Mongolian rulers, agricultural education offers possibilities for

Two watermills from Wang Zhen's *Agricultural Treatise* (1313).

serving the public even outside the state administration. Emperor Chéngzōng's 成宗 (1265–1307) decree from 1304 to publish the *Treatise* shows that Wang successfully addresses his superiors about the role of agriculture for the functioning administration of the Yuan territory (Hammers 2013, 294; Wang 1981, 446).

Art historian Roslyn Lee Hammers recently showed commonalities between Wang's ideas and those of the controversial Song reformer *Wáng Ānshí 王安石 (1021–1086) (Hammers 2013). Both Wang Anshi's reforms and the administration efforts of the Yuan dynasty involve officials in charge of agriculture, and Wang Zhen firmly positions himself in favor of such policies (Kuhn and Needham 1988, 13).

Wang presents his topic with a keen awareness of regional differences between the dry-land farming practiced in his native regions in the north and the methods of irrigation used in the south where he assumed his official posts (Bray 2007, 538). The *Treatise* thereby offers a glance at the role that Wang envisions for

*People marked with an asterisk have entries in this dictionary.

officials in spreading agricultural knowledge. Knowledge about tools from each region can benefit each other and thereby the empire as a whole. Scholar-officials have access to written accounts, and the freedom to travel to different regions, which puts them in an ideal position to instruct the people. In this way, Wang takes a highly localized form of knowledge and shows that people like himself can play a role in unifying the empire by disseminating knowledge across regional boundaries.

Behind Wang's choice of topic lies a larger theoretical discourse about the state's role in respect to agriculture within a correlational worldview, in which political and cosmological events are intertwined. The necessity of food production was never in question, but the role of government officials in relation to it was, since disparate events such as solar eclipses or famines could both be signs of bad governance. Wang's work refuses to be reduced to strictly pragmatic concerns about useful activities for elite families as well as to purely theoretical debates regarding the cosmological role of agricultural policies. Agricultural tools did not figure prominently in other writings circulating among members of the elite. The didactic purpose of the *Treatise* tries to overcome the stigma of applied knowledge as less valuable than literary knowledge. Wang implicitly criticizes bookish approach to farming by encouraging his readers to engage with technological innovations and make first-hand observations. According to Wang, within the field of agriculture, more recent technological innovations appeared as an equally valid (or even better) path for the continuation of the Chinese cultural heritage. Familiarity with artisanal knowledge would thus lead to better governance, and ultimately greater cosmological harmony.

Publishing and Printing: Wang the Innovator

Two innovations figure prominently in the current discourse on Wang: his description of wooden moveable-type printing, and the *Treatise's* unique use of diagrams. Ironically, neither innovation gained much traction in China before contact with Western printing techniques made them appear obsolete.

Wang uses images and text to give detailed instructions on the use and production of a wide range of tools. As the social anthropologist Francesca Bray argues, this use of images as technical drawings might be Wang's most far-reaching innovation (Bray 2007). While the potential for reproducing unknown tools based on Wang's descriptions is invaluable to modern historians, it failed to inspire authors of later periods to imitate his methods. Literal copies of loosely associated sections from the *Treatise* regularly substituted the kind of applicable instructions Wang provided, so that many subsequent innovations are lost to us.

Finally, Wang mentions his experiments with using wooden types for printing a local gazetteer (Carter and Goodrich 1955, 214–217). While he intended to use this technology for printing the *Treatise*, since production of woodblocks, where dual pages are carved and printed from a single block, had already begun, it was no longer economically feasible to use types. Wang's personal experience holds true for most of Chinese history, where moveable type printing did not become the dominant form of producing books. Wang made significant advances compared to the ceramic types used by the inventor *Bì Shēng 毕升 (c. 990–c. 1051) during the Southern Song dynasty, in retaining ink, and lowering material costs. Wang included a description of a revolving type table in which characters where sorted based on phonetic rhyme-schemes in his *Treatise* (See image below).

Without any surviving Yuan editions of the *Treatise*, the exact design and layout of Wang's diagrams have been lost. It remains undisputed, however, that Wang intended his text to be accompanied by diagrams. Following the editorial work by the Chinese scholar Wáng Yùhú 王毓瑚 (1907–1980) there is evidence supporting an original publication

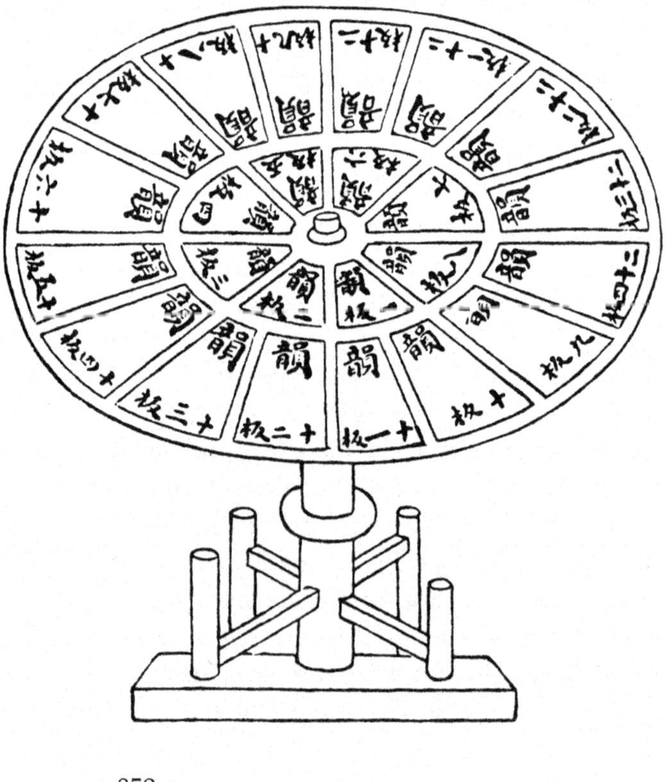

Image of Chinese movable type, as described by Wang Zhen in his 1313 *Agricultural Treatise*. The individual moveable characters are arranged by a rhyming scheme.

date of 1303 as well as a foreword from 1313 preserved as part of a compilation from 1407 (Wang 1981). There are little textual variances between this edition and another edition with higher quality diagrams (from 1530), which remains the basis for modern reproductions.

Legacy

Most information about Wang is related to his official life and his *Treatise*, and we assume that he died in the second decade of the fourteenth century, after retiring from office (Kuhn & Needham 1988, 11). The *Treatise* is a fitting expression of Wang's intellectual endorsement of artisanal knowledge. His detailed descriptions remain a valuable contribution to contemporary historians of ecology and technology. They allow us to see how one ingenious official responded to the challenges that resulted from the fall of the Song dynasty. In doing so, his work goes beyond the specifics of China at the beginning of the fourteenth century. It is part of a much longer narrative of how Chinese intellectuals thought of their role within society at times when conditions at court were not in their favor, and the new possibilities of circulating ideas through print continue to play an integral part of this response. The *Treatise* is one of the most striking examples of how printing shapes the formation of knowledge, and serves as a reminder to modern readers to explore the complex networks of meaning in which early prints are located.

Duncan PATERSON
Heidelberg University

Further Reading

Bray, Francesca. (2007). Agricultural illustrations: Blueprint or icon? In F. Bray, V. Dorofeeva-Lichtmann, & G. Métailie (Eds.), *Graphics and text in the production of technical knowledge in China: The warp and the weft* (pp. 521–567). Leiden, The Netherlands: E. J. Brill.

Bray, Francesca, & Needham, Joseph. (1984). *Science and civilisation in China: Biology and biological technology: Agriculture* (1st ed, Vol. 6 Part 2). Cambridge, UK: Cambridge University Press.

Carter, Thomas Francis, & Goodrich, Luther Carrington. (1955). *The invention of printing in China and its spread westward* (2nd Ed.). New York: Ronald Press Co.

Hammers, Roslyn Lee. (2013). Picturing tools for a perfect society: Wang Zhen's "Book of agriculture" and the northern Song reforms in the Yuan dynasty. *Journal of Song-Yuan Studies, 42*(1), 279–308. doi:10.1353/sys.2013.0013

Kuhn, Dieter, & Needham, Joseph (1988). *Science and civilisation in China: Chemistry and chemical technology: Textile technology—Spinning and reeling* (Vol. 5 Part 9). Cambridge, UK: Cambridge University Press.

Wang Yuhu 王毓瑚. (1981). *Wáng Zhēn nóngshū* 王禎農書 (1st ed.). Beijing: nongye chubanshe.

Zhào Mèngfǔ

赵孟頫

1254–1322—Official, painter, calligrapher, and poet

Alternate names: style name: Zi'áng 子昂; pennames: Sōngxuě 松雪, Sōngxuědàoren 松雪道人, Shuǐjīnggōngdàoren 水晶宫道人, Ōubō 鸥波

Summary

Zhao Mengfu was a leading painter and calligrapher during the Yuan dynasty. A pivotal figure in the development of Chinese art, Zhao's painting and calligraphic style impacted generations of artists. Zhao's various government posts allowed him to travel widely, which exposed him to different landscapes and gave him the means to collect antique objects and paintings. He assumed several significant roles in his lifetime, including poet, scholar, and musician, and he held several posts in the court of Khubilai Khan. Upon his death, a biographer wrote, "other people when painting landscapes, bamboos, rocks, figures, horses, flowers and birds, if they excel in one field are likely to be weak in another, but he was able to (re)create all their subtleties and rendered to the full their Heaven-sent qualities."

Dubbed "champion of the Yuan" (Yuán rén guān miǎn 元仁冠勉), in reference to the Yuán 元 dynasty during which he lived, Zhao Mengfu was famous for his talents across different media: painting, calligraphy, poetry, the creation of seals, and music. Within each medium, his subject matter or styles were also diverse. Zhao synthesized painting styles developed prior to his time, and paved the way for a great number of stylistic possibilities and techniques for generations to come.

Biography

Zhao Mengfu was born in Wúxīng 吴兴 (present-day Húzhōu 湖州), Zhejiang Province during the Southern Sòng 宋 dynasty (1127–1279). His ancestral lineage went back to Tàizǔ 太祖 (r. 960–976), the founding Song emperor; he belonged to the eleventh generation of this imperial line. Zhao had a large family: he was the seventh son of Zhào Yǔyín 赵与訔 (1213–1265), who had ten sons and fourteen daughters. Skillful in poetry, Zhao Yugao was also Deputy Minister of Revenue (*hùbù shìláng* 户部侍郎), and held various local government posts during the Southern Song. (The Song dynasty is divided into the Southern Song and Northern Song based on the geographical location of its capital due to incursions from Mongolia.) His father's pedigree gave Zhao Mengfu access to an extensive family library, and it is said that he was incredibly smart from the very beginning of his life. Zhao Mengfu "could recite a passage after one perusal, and quickly finish a writing once starting it" (*Yuanshi* 172). Zhao Mengfu's family fortune reversed after his father died in 1265, when the child was only eleven years old. At age fourteen, Zhao Mengfu was appointed a minor official because of his late father's governmental services.

When Zhao was in his twenties, he witnessed the conquest of the Southern Song by the formerly nomadic Mongols. His political aspirations seemingly crushed, Zhao retired to his hometown of Wuxing, not far away from the Southern Song court in Hangzhou. Zhao stayed at home and focused on studying classical writings in history, poetry, music, and painting. He soon was known to be one of the "Eight Talents of Wuxing" (Li 1965). The conquering Mongols initially were quite hostile toward Han scholars. (Hàn 汉 is the majority ethnic group in China, and is used to refer to the population and rulers of imperial dynasties not ruled by conquering foreigners such as the Mongols.) Within just a few years, however, the Yuan court realized the necessity of drawing talents from the highly educated Han scholars who had spent many years studying Confucian literature and art. In 1286, *Khubilai (Qubilai) Khan 忽必烈汗 (1215–1294; r. 1271–1294) decreed that southerners be recruited to the Yuan court in the capital of Dàdū 大都 (present-day Beijing). Zhao accepted this official offer along with some two dozen of his peers, and went to the capital. This acceptance provoked bitter feelings among many Han Chinese, who regarded service for the Yuan (the dynasty that ruled from 1279–1368) as a dishonorable collaboration with the Mongolians.

In Dadu, Emperor Khubilai Khan gave Zhao an audience, and was impressed by his "flourishing countenance and otherworldly manner" (*History of the Yuan* [*Yuánshǐ* 元史]). The emperor seated Zhao ahead of the chancellor of the right, which was the most significant civil post in the Yuan dynasty. Zhao's imperial Song lineage caused uneasiness among some Mongolian officials, who questioned whether it was wise to place him within reach of the emperor's confidence. The emperor, however, was not concerned,

*People marked with an asterisk have entries in this dictionary.

This and following page: *Autumn Colors on the Qiao and Hua Mountains* by Zhao Mengfu (1254–1322). National Palace Museum, Taipei, Taiwan.

and would not be disappointed in Zhao's performance. Zhao's subsequent advice and numerous drafts of imperial decrees were well liked by the emperor. In the same year that Zhao started serving in the Yuan court, he married Guǎn Dàoshēng 管道升 (1262–1319), a noted artist. In 1290, Zhao was appointed Auxiliary Member of the Mandarin House (*Jí xián zhí xuéshì* 集贤直学士); in 1292, he became Lieutenant Governor of Jinan Prefecture (*Jǐnán lù zǒngguǎn fǔ shì* 济南路总管府事), where he was known for his clear and straightforward governance. Shortly thereafter, he was promoted to Administrator of Fénzhōu 汾州, and later Tàizhōu 泰州, although he did not assume either post. In 1299, Zhao became Supervisor of Confucianism in his hometown of Zhejiang, and held this post for over ten years. In 1310, Zhao was summoned back to the capital, and there held several positions:

- Reader in Waiting of the Imperial Academy (*Hànlín shì dú xuéshì* 翰林侍读学士),
- Lecturer in Waiting of the Mandarin House (*Jíxián shì jiǎng xuéshì* 集贤侍讲学士),
- Grand Master of Middle Reverence (*Zhōngfèng dàfū* 中奉大夫),
- Lecturer in Waiting of the Imperial Academy (*Hànlín shì jiǎng xuéshì* 翰林侍讲学士),
- Grand Master of Augmenting Virtue (*Zīdé dàfū* 资德大夫),
- Director of the Imperial Academy (*Hànlín xuéshì fèngzhī* 翰林学士奉旨),

- Grand Master of Glory and Emolument (*Rónglù dàfū* 荣禄大夫)

Most of these posts were honorary, but nonetheless held high political status.

After serving more than five emperors, Zhao Mengfu died in 1322 at the age of sixty-eight. Three years prior, in 1319, his wife, Guan Daosheng, passed away. Zhao was posthumously promoted to Duke of the Wei (*Wèi Guógōng* 魏国公), and given the title of Cultured and Acute (*wénmǐn* 文敏).

Painting

Zhao's various posts in local and central governments gave him a unique opportunity to travel frequently in both northern and southern China. As a result, he was exposed to different landscapes and had opportunity to collect antique objects and paintings of different subjects. Combined with his keen interest in learning and synthesizing different styles and mediums, such diverse exposure must have contributed to the versatility of Zhao's art.

Zhao Mengfu painted a wide range of classical Chinese subject matter, including landscape, human figures, bird and flower painting, bamboo and rocks in monochrome ink, horses, goats, and sheep. The techniques he used also varied, including *gōng bǐ* 工笔 (*refined brush*, or literally, "meticulous"), *xiě yì* 写意 (*broad brushstrokes*, literally "freehand"), blue green landscape (*qīnglǜ shānshuǐ* 青绿山水), and ink plum (*mòméi* 墨梅, paintings of plums done with simple strokes in calligraphy ink). His bamboo and plums denote a sense of purity, freshness, and grace; his horses are lively and portray deeper meaning through their abstract, often round, shapes that counterbalance other characters in the scene.

One of Zhao Mengfu's most famous landscape paintings, *Autumn Colors on the Que and Hua Mountains* (*Què huá qiūsè* 鹊华秋色; handscroll, ink and color on paper, 1296, National Museum, Taipei, 11.25 × 36.75 in.), was based on his visit to Hua Hill (Xiyuè 华山) and Que Hill (Quèshān 鹊山) in Shandong province while he was the lieutenant governor in Jǐnán 济南. Upon returning to his hometown of Wuxing, Zhao painted the piece from memory for his friend Zhōu Mì 周密 (1232–1298), a famous writer and connoisseur of the late Song and early Yuan dynasties, who had his ancestral home in the Jinan area, but lived most of his life far away from his hometown.

Autumn Colors has an open landscape of marshy land, water, and trees, populated by fishermen, villages, and goats. To the right sits the triangular Hua Hill with twin pointed peaks. Que Hill, by contrast, balances the angularity of Hua Hill with a bread loaf-like shape at the left. Both rise in the far distance, painted in dark blue. Greenish mist separates the two mountains and the trees in the foreground. This is a calm and serene autumn day. Some of the trees are already barren, while the leaves on others are turning red, yellow, or a shade of brown. The initial focal point is Hua Hill at the right. Moving from there to the foreground, the viewer sees a group of some twenty pines in dark green with two smaller groups of trees dotting the middle ground. One tree branches out as if forming an arch to link with the arm of one of the nine trees in the middle inlet. These nine trees are arranged diagonally from the background to the foreground, their trunks painted rather uniformly with identical shapes of ferns growing around their bases. Moving toward the left are four large, gnarled willow trees framing and fronting a cottage at the left section. Toward Que Hill in the background, still in diagonal arrangement, are groups of trees flanking three cottages, two of which form a compound. Mist permeates these trees, and goats roam along the riverbank while fishermen tend to their business (Li 1965).

In brushwork, *pī má cūn* 披麻皴 (hemp-fiber wrinkles) texture strokes made with the tip of the paintbrush rendered the roundness, masses, and textures of mountains and strips of land. By comparison, most trees and houses were painted using a medium brush, while very thin, fine brushstrokes painted reeds, boats, human figures, and fishnets.

The painting is far from being naturalistic, however: the mountains in the back are diminished in scale compared to the adjacent houses and trees in front of them. This may be taken as a direct reference to the Southern and Northern Dynasties (Nánběicháo 南北朝) (420–589 CE), when such painters as Gù Kǎizhī 顾恺之 (c. 345/348–405) were still experimenting with spatial relations among human figures, trees, rocks, and flowers.

The archaism in Zhao's painting is more pronounced when compared with works of Táng 唐 dynasty (618–907 CE) painters, as well as the work of Dong Yuan (early tenth century CE) and Li Cheng (919–c. 967), two landscape painters of the Sòng 宋 dynasty (960–1279) and Five Dynasties and Ten Kingdoms 五代十国 (907–960 CE) period, respectively.

Among Tang dynasty painters, Zhao Mengfu held *Wáng Wéi 王维 (699–759), a high court official best known for his poetry on landscapes and country life, in particularly high regard. Because of the Southern Song movement among literati artists who were more withdrawn from civil service than their Northern Song counterparts were, Wang Wei's painting virtuosity was gradually recognized for its simplicity, freshness, and spontaneity. He was posthumously promoted as the founder of the Southern School of painting that valued exactly these characteristics, and historians have maintained this view of his contributions. Zheng's *Autumn Colors* can be seen as a tribute to the practices of Wang Wei and the Southern School of painting. Compared to Wang's painting, *Wăng Chuān Villa* 辋川图, *Autumn Colors* also takes liberty in assigning scale to objects. The ground in both works appears tilted upward so that the audience can view the pictures from a vantage point. Mountains are formed by layers, and spatial clarity is maintained throughout. Compartmental organization is used to group buildings, trees, and mountains. Both paintings show variety in tree types, attention to tree trunks.

There also is obvious difference between the two scrolls. In particular, Wang Wei's painting is grounded in masses of solid rocks and buildings, while Zhao's *Autumn Colors* balances voids and solids. Although Zhao's painting revived Wang's style, he was still indebted to the compositional schema of open spaces and *píng yuăn* 平远 (level distance) popular among Southern Song painters. An excellent example of this style is *A Dream Journey on the Xiao-Xiang Rivers* by an anonymous twelfth century painter known as Li *sheng* (Mr. Li) (Tokyo National Museum, ink on paper). In *Autumn Colors*, the ground plane recedes gradually and continuously from the near to the far distance, typical of the *ping yuan* schema.

The other notable feature of the painting was its many seals and colophons, authenticating or eulogizing *Autumn Colors*. Foremost among such inscriptions were by Dǒng Qíchāng 董其昌 (1555–1636), the great painter, calligrapher, and theorist of the Míng 明 dynasty (1368–1644), and the powerful *Emperor Qiánlóng 乾隆 (r. 1736–1795), the major patron of the arts during the Qīng 清 dynasty (1644–1911/1912). These colophons gave the painting an almost complete, uninterrupted history from the time of its execution to the modern-day.

Zhao's painting also differs from Southern Song landscapes. In another of his highly praised paintings, *Water Village* 水村图 (1302, Palace Museum, Beijing,

9.8 × 47.4 in.), there is clear recession of near to far ground planes. Rather than Southern Song's void spaces to fill in the middle ground, Zhao Mengfu introduced huge marshy lands as a main component of the middle ground (Li 1965). The prominence of treetops and huge boulders that dominated the corners of Southern Song paintings are gone. Rather, Zhao painted a panoramic view of the water village with trees, riverbanks, and mountains for its setting. Gone were the ink wash and axe-cut texture strokes (a type of broad-brush stroke used to represent elements of nature) preferred by Southern Song painters; instead Zhao used the *cun* wrinkle texture strokes. Zhao was thus totally negating the Southern Song painting style. Zhao himself stated that he tried to reject Song styles, and his simple and seemingly rough painting would be viewed by future audiences as modeled after the excellent pre-Song ancients. Zhao's painting thus marked a decisive move from the idealization and lyricism of the Southern Song painting practice.

With the syntheses of established styles and new modes, Zhao Mengfu paved the way for the next generations of painters—most notably the Four Masters of the Late Yuan: Huáng Gōngwàng 黄公望 (1269–1364), Wú Zhèn 吴镇 (1280–1354), Ní Zàn 倪瓒 (1301–1374), and Wáng Méng 王蒙 (1308–1385)—to explore compositions, brushstrokes, and the use of space. In addition, the famous Ming dynasty Wu or Wumen School (*Wúmén huàpài* 吴门画派) of the fifteenth to sixteenth centuries in the adjacent Jiangsu area, was deeply impacted by Zhao's style.

Zhao Mengfu's bird and flower paintings often used abbreviated brushwork. Conversely, his *Elegant Rocks and Sparse Trees* (*Xiùshí shū lín* 秀石疏林; handscroll, ink on paper, Palace Museum, Beijing, 21.3 × 11.1 in.) was executed in broad and cursive brushstrokes to depict the rough texture of rocks, which is typical of his painting in calligraphic style. A huge rock dominates the picture, surrounded by a blossoming plum tree, bamboo leaves, and pine trees: three of the favorite Confucian literati themes that symbolize purity and perseverance. Zhao's own colophons on the painting state, "Rocks as in flying white (script), trees as in seal script," and "calligraphy and painting have always been the same." Landscape, then, becomes a tool to express his brushstrokes, which are objectified.

Zhao's horse paintings are also archaic. *Man Riding a Horse* 人骑图 (handscroll, ink and color on paper, 1296, Palace Museum, Beijing) depicts a red-coated civil official riding a horse. The official's left arm reins the horse gently while the other hand rests on the right leg. The horse's body is in grayish white. It has skinny legs and the left front leg steps forward. The painting was dated and titled by Zhao in an inscription placed just above the horse. The accompanying inscriptions to the left side of the painting state, "I have loved painting horses since childhood. Recently I was able to see three authentic scrolls by *Hán Gàn 韩干

[706–c. 783, a specialist in horse paintings], and began to discern his message." In associated subject matter and brushwork, Zhao Mengfu's horse was similar to that of Han Gan. While Han Gan's horse in *Night-Shining White* 照夜白图 (handscroll, ink and color on paper, Metropolitan Museum of Art) is more rounded in torso and appears agitated in strong emotion, Zhao's horse has a more slender torso and is quieter in mood. Han Gan's depiction of the horse seems to allude to the tragic constraint of Tang dynasty court life. Zhao's picture, by contrast, speaks about the calmness, elegance, and intelligence of a scholar-official.

Zhao completed *Horses Drinking in the Suburbs in Autumn* 秋郊饮马图 (handscroll, Palace Museum, Beijing, 10.4 × 39.4 in.) in 1312 when he was 59 years old. It begins with two playing horses at the right corner. A red-robed official rides on a dark-haired horse, with a staff in his right hand. The official is looking back to the right, thus encouraging the viewer to imagine more horses beyond the painting frame. Moving to the left, five horses of different colors and hair texture wade in the water, some drinking. One is curiously looking up to the front. In the middle to far distance, one horse is chasing the other. The water is tan colored, tree trunks gnarled, the bank blue, and foliage red, gray or gray yellow. There are horses and human figures, each differing in complexion, gesture, movement, and bone structure. Fine

Horse and Groom in the Wind (ink on paper) by Zhao Mengfu. The delicate brushstrokes convey the power of the wind. National Palace Museum, Taipei, Taiwan.

lines are used to paint human figures, while wash, *cun* wrinkles, and delineation are intermingled to depict rocks and waterfronts. Relative scale is clear: the two chasing horses in the back are smaller than those in the near ground. At the same time, a masterful use of foreshortening is in place: the body parts of horses in different angles are proportionally shorter or smaller the farer away they are from the viewers. Level, high advantage, and low angle viewing points are all used to depict trees and horses in the back, horses and officials in the front, and tree tops in the foreground. Overall, this painting combines ease with beauty, fine detail with literati rawness, and elegance with balance. This is a world of peace and playfulness.

Some of Zhao Mengfu's other paintings include *Groom and Horse* 人马图 (1296, ink and color on paper), *Twin Pines, Level Distance* 双松平远图 (c. 1300, ink on paper), both at the Metropolitan Museum of Art; *Recurring Rivers and Peaks* 重江叠嶂图卷 (1303, Palace Museum, Taipei), and *Monk in a Red Robed* 红衣罗汉 (1304, color on paper, Liaoning Museum).

Zhao Mengfu's writing on painting theory appears sporadic, but he clearly emphasized archaism and the *qì* 气 spirit (the basis of life force and the underpinning of many Chinese philosophical ideals), a combination of literature and ink, and the correlation of poetry, calligraphy, and painting. Perhaps the official biography of Zhao Mengfu, written in the year he died (1322), best described the versatility of his abilities: "other people when painting landscapes, bamboos, rocks, figures, horses, flowers and birds, if they excel in one field are likely to be weak in another, but he was able to (re)create all their subtleties and rendered to the full their Heaven-sent qualities" (Yang Zai, 112-b).

Calligraphy

Zhao Mengfu was a very influential calligrapher, particularly on formal scripts and running scripts. He was considered to be the only scholar since the Tang dynasty to match the talents of Ōuyáng Xún 欧阳询 (557–641), Yán Zhēnqīng 颜真卿 (709–785), and Liǔ Gōngquán 柳公权 (778–865). These three masters plus Zhao have been formally grouped as the "Four Great Masters of the Formal Scripts." Indeed, Zhao Mengfu's calligraphy was often considered comparable to that of *Wáng Xīzhī 王羲之 (303–361) and his son Wáng Xiànzhī 王献之 (344–386), two of the most respected calligraphers in the history of China. His calligraphic style, called the "Zhao Style," is characterized as elegant and flying in structure.

Although particularly noted for the *xiǎokǎi* 小楷 small formal style, Zhao Mengfu was also memorialized as superior in other styles in the *History of the Yuan* (*Yuánshǐ* 元史), which is part of the *Twenty-four Histories of China* that were recorded during the Ming dynasty. These styles included seal scripts, official scripts, and cursive style. Unlike Song and Yuan masters who mostly specialized in running or cursive styles, Zhou was very versatile in writing styles. His renowned calligraphy even became popular in Korea and Japan.

The inscription that he wrote on *Autumn Colors* was in the *xiaokai* style. The characters are well spaced, finely controlled, and clearly lineated in each stroke. The coordination among different strokes is closely interlinked and correlated. Together, they appear graceful, fluent, and focused, regardless of whether individual strokes are horizontal, vertical, diagonal, or curved. Their structure is stable and powerful. The flow between characters is fluent, and the whole paragraph or section of words is rhythmic and harmonious.

Another notable example of Zhao Mengfu's formal style is his version of the *Dàodéjīng* 道德经 (*Classic of the Way and Its Power,* an important set of Daoist doctrines; ink on paper, 9.57 × 60.4 in., Palace Museum, Beijing). Copying classic works in one's own calligraphic style was a common practice thought to assist the calligrapher in embodying the ideals of the work at hand. Zhao Mengfu made a copy of the Daodejing in 1316 at the age of 63. The movement of brushstrokes is fluent, indicating Zhao's confidence and relaxed mind. Between characters, the thickness of characters varies; within each stroke, the lines are generally consistent in thinness or thickness.

His extant works display mastery of several styles. *Nymph of the Luo River* 洛神赋 and *Odes to the Red Cliff* 前后赤壁赋 (also called *Two Lyrics of the Red Cliff* 赤壁二赋贴), *Thirteen Postscripts of Orchid Pavilion* 兰亭十三跋, and *O, Come Back Home* 归去来兮辞 are in the running style; the *Danba Tablet* 胆巴碑, *Modeling Classics of the Yellow Court* 临黄庭经, are in the formal scripts; and *1000 Characters* 千字文 is in cursive style. Zhao Mengfu's theory on calligraphy had far-reaching impact. According to Zhao, one has to learn calligraphy in both strokes and character structure. If the strokes are not well, the writing appears pretentious; if the structure is not elegant, the character looks rather tenuous. Zhao Mengfu also emphasized the importance of understanding *gǔ yì* 古意, or archaic meaning, by ancient calligraphers.

Zhao was excellent in poetry and connoisseurship. Emperor Rénzōng 仁宗 (r. 1311–1320) once compared Zhao Mengfu's literary achievements to those of *Lǐ Bái 李白 (701–762) of the Tang dynasty, and *Sū Shi 苏轼 (1037–1101) of the Song dynasty, two of the most famous poets and lyricists in Chinese history.

Music

Two short writings on music, attributable to Zhao Mengfu, are *On Violin* (*Qínyuán* 琴原), and *On Music* (*Lèyuán* 乐原). He covered music principles, measurements, the tones of violins, and the alignment between music principles and the lunar calendar. Once again consistent with his emphasis on *gu yi,* these compositions demonstrate Zhao's understanding of the *yin* and *yang* balance, Daoist diagrams, traditional cosmology, temperament, and musicology. His music guiding principle is order, structural harmony, and ritual function.

Views of Social Economics

Zhao was not particularly known as an economist, but *History of the Yuan* records his advocating for less harsh punishments on alleged crime perpetrators, and his criticism of the use of previous coin standards in the contemporary context because the weak economy of his day made pre-existing standards unfair. He was vigorously against excess taxes. In 1290, an earthquake struck the capital, which caused hundreds of thousands of deaths and injuries. Zhao advised that heavy taxes be lifted to stabilize society and comfort citizens. Relieved of this burden, the Yuan population was said to regain its economic footing.

Zhao's Artistic Family

Zhao Mengfu had a family full of artistic and literary achievements. His wife, Guan Daosheng, was a renowned painter, calligrapher, and poet. Her favorite subjects included ink bamboo, plum, and orchid flowers, while her *Theories on Ink Bamboo* touched upon many painting techniques, particularly on how to paint ink bamboos. Zhào Yōng 赵雍, Zhao Mengfu's son, painted a landscape titled *Modeled after Dong Yuan*, and specialized in figure and horse paintings. His other son, Zhào Yì 赵奕, was a fine painter and calligrapher as well. Zhao Yong's son, Zhào Fèng 赵凤 had a style of painting orchids and bamboo so similar to Zhao Yong's that often such paintings were mistaken to be created by the father. Zhao Yong's other son, Zhào Lín 赵麟, was equally skillful in horse and figure paintings.

Zhao Mengfu's brother, Zhào Mèngyù 赵孟籲, who also became a high rank Yuan civil official, was famous for his figure and bird and flower paintings, as well as his calligraphy. His noted works included *Scrolls of the Eighteen Luohan Arhats* 十八罗汉卷 (c. 1301). Another brother, Zhào Mèngyí 赵孟颐, was a professor of Confucianism in the Hangzhou Prefecture. Wang Meng, who is mentioned above in the paragraph on the Four Masters of the Late Yuan, was noted for his *cun* texture strokes, and was one of the foremost late Yuan painters. He was a grandson of Zhao Mengfu.

Impact on the Literati Class

Zhao Mengfu's life was characterized by fluctuations in family fortune and political/professional advantage, primarily caused by the backlash from many of his Han Chinese peers after Zhao accepted an official post in a non-Han court (the Mongol Yuan dynasty). Yet Zhao persisted, and his talents in so many artistic mediums made him arguably the most accomplished artist of the Yuan dynasty.

Although viewed unfavorably by many of his Han peers, Zhao's art does not reveal bitterness. Rather, his works convey peace, ease, clarity, and graciousness. If Zhao had not answered the emperor's call to serve in court, he would not have had the opportunity to travel widely and gain exposure to a broad range of mediums and subject matter. Thus, Zhao's many artistic achievements may not have been possible without his service in the Yuan court. At the same time, Zhao Mengfu's acceptance by Yuan emperors and his high political status, although more honorary than practical, must have improved the Mongolian court's perception of ethnic Han scholars, and indirectly elevated the status of Han Confucian scholars during the Yuan dynasty.

Yu JIANG
Xavier University of Louisiana

Further Reading

Cahill, James. (1997). The Yuan dynasty (1271–1368). In Yang Xin (et al.), *Three thousand years of Chinese painting* (pp. 138–195). New Haven, CT, & London: Yale University Press.

Fong, Wen (Ed.). (1992). *Beyond representation: Chinese painting and calligraphy, 8th–14th century*. Princeton Monographs in Art and Archaeology, No 48. New Haven, CT: Yale University Press.

Li, Chu-Tsing. (1965). *The Autumn Colors on the Ch'iao and Hua Mountains:* A landscape by Chao Meng-Fu. *Artibus Asiae, Supplementum 21*, 4–7, 9–85, 87, 89–109.

Song Lian 宋濂, et al. (fourteenth century CE). *Yuanshi* 元史 *Lie zhuan* 列传 [*History of the Yuan*. Biography), no. 59.

Vinograd, Richard. (1978). River village: The pleasures of fishing and Chao Meng-'fu's Li-Kuo style landscapes. *Artibus Asiae, 40 (2/3)*,121–142.

Wu, Hung. (1997). The origins of Chinese painting (Paleolithic period to Tang Dynasty). In Yang Xin (et al.), *Three thousand years of Chinese painting* (pp. 79–81). New Haven, CT, & London: Yale University Press.

Yang Zai 杨载. (1322). *Zhao Wenmingong xing zhuang* 赵文敏公行状 [Biography of Master Zhao Wenmin].

Zhi Jinping 支金平. (2013). Zhao Mengfu: Guanzhi cong yi pin di kai shu da jia 赵孟頫: 官至从一品的楷书大家 (Zhao Mengfu: Master of formal scripts who attained the deputy 1st rank) *Wenshi Tiandi* 文史天地, 7. Retrieved November 1, 2013, from http://collection.sina.com.cn/cjrw/20130926/0648128407.shtml

Míng Dynasty

明朝

1368 - 1644 CE

Leaf album painting of flowers, a butterfly, and a twisted rock sculpture, by Ming dynasty artist Chen Hongshou (1598–1652).

The Ming dynasty, founded by a poor peasant turned rebel leader, became an era of Chinese cultural revival (*wén yì fù xīng* 文艺复兴). The founder, Emperor Hongwu, restored many Chinese customs that were abandoned during the Mongol-ruled Yuan dynasty, including Confucian values, marriage, dress code, social hierarchy, rituals, and the civil service examination. The capital was redesigned and renamed Běijīng 北京 ("Northern Capital"). Popular culture and the arts flourished, the population grew, and many industries expanded into major enterprises. Interactions with Europeans increased, both for trade and for intellectual and religious reasons. Large parts of the Great Wall (*cháng chéng* 长城; started during the Qin dynasty) were reconstructed and connected to keep foreigners (such as the Mongols) at a distance. The Ming also embarked on the most extensive maritime explorations (*hǎiyáng tànsuǒ* 海洋探索) in Chinese history. The dynasty was faced with peasant rebellions and the influence of corrupt eunuchs (*tàijiàn* 太监) at court during its final decline.

List of Entries

Altan Khan (1508–1582)
Hǎi Ruì 海瑞 (1514–1587)
Hóngwǔ 洪武, Emperor (of Ming) (1328–1398)
Jīn Shèngtàn 金圣叹 (1605–1661)
Koxinga 郑成功 (1624–1662)
Lǐ Shízhēn 李时珍 (1518–1593)
Lǐ Zhì 李贽 (1527–1602)
Lǐ Zìchéng 李自成 (1606–1645)
Nurhaci 努尔哈赤 (1559–1626)
Qiú Yīng 仇英 (1494–1552)
Ricci, Matteo 利玛窦 (1552–1610)
Tāng Xiǎnzǔ 汤显祖 (1550–1616)
Wáng Yángmíng 王阳明 (1472–1529)
Wànlì 万历, Emperor (of Ming) (1563–1620)
Wèi Zhōngxián 魏忠贤 (1568–1627)
Wú Chéng'ēn 吴承恩 (c. 1505–1580)
Xú Guāngqǐ 徐光启 (1562–1633)
Xú Xiákè 徐霞客 (1587–1641)
Yǒnglè 永乐, Emperor (of Ming) (1360–1424)
Yuán Chónghuàn 袁崇焕 (1584–1630)
Yuán Hóngdào 袁宏道 (1568–1610)
Zhèng Hé 郑和 (1371–c. 1433)

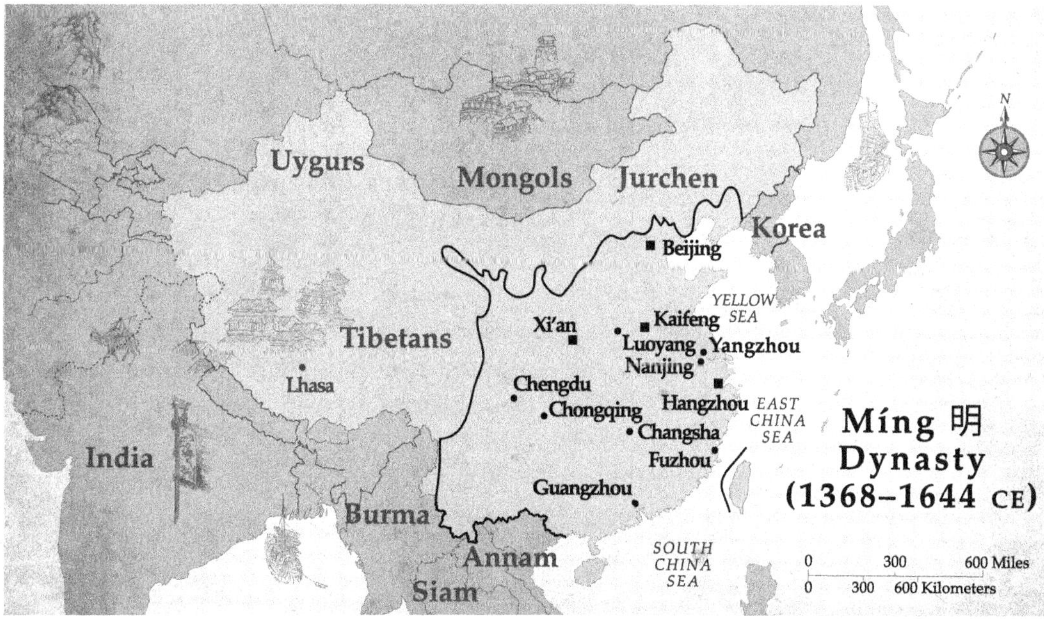

Altan Khan

Ālātǎn Hán 阿拉坦汗

1508–1582—Mongol ruler

阿拉坦汗

Summary

Altan Khan was born in 1508 in Ordos, in Inner Mongolia, where his father was ruler. Following a tumultuous political situation, Altan became the most powerful Mongol ruler in the late sixteenth century, ruling the Tümed of southwestern Inner Mongolia. Although he tried many times to initiate trade with the Ming dynasty in China, his attempts at establishing ongoing relations with them ultimately failed. He is perhaps most famous for meeting with the Dalai Lama in 1578, thereby setting in motion the conversion of the Mongols to Buddhism.

Altan Khan was the most powerful Mongol ruler of the sixteenth century. He not only signed a peace deal with the Míng 明 dynasty (1368–1644) in 1571, but also met with the Dalai Lama in 1578, thereby setting in motion the conversion of the Mongols to Buddhism.

Altan ("Golden") and his twin sister, Mönggön ("Silver"), were born on 20 January 1508 to the Mongol nobleman Barsubolod Sain Alag in Ordos, the area within the great bend of the Huang (Yellow) River that is now southwestern Inner Mongolia. At the time this area was not only ruled by Altan's father, the *jinong* (viceroy) of Ordos, but it was also in open revolt against his grandfather Dayan Khan (c. 1480–c. 1517); namely, while Dayan ruled over eastern Inner Mongolia, he was once again trying to unify all the Mongols under one ruler, and it was this unification project that the Ordos Mongols were resisting. Nevertheless, against all odds Dayan Khan succeeded. After conquering all the Mongols he therefore divided them among his sons, creating the so-called Six Tümen. Yet this newly unified Mongol state was not to last because Altan, the ruler of one of these Tümen, was to both convert to Buddhism and become the most powerful Mongol ruler, which changed forever the religio-political structures of Mongol society. Moreover, these developments were in turn to change not only Sino-Mongol relations, but also pave the way for the rise of the Manchu Qīng 清 dynasty (1644–1911/1912).

The Mongol Empire

To make sense of these interlocking developments it is necessary to take a longer view of Chinese and Inner Asian history, beginning with the Mongol Empire in the thirteenth century. In particular, rather than thinking of this empire as a unified whole stretching from Korea to the borders of Europe, as is often the case, let us see it as four virtually autonomous units operating under an ideological concept of Mongol unity. These four were the Golden Horde (Jīnzhàng hánguó 金帐汗国) in Russia, the Ilkhans in the Middle East, the Chaghataids in Central Asia, and finally the Yuán 元 dynasty (1279–1368) in China, which was conceived as the supreme ruler over the other three, especially during the reign of *Khubilai (Qubilai) Khan 忽必烈汗 (1215–1294, r. 1260–1294 as Shìzǔ 世祖). Yet after his death, the relations between the four units began to fray and eventually they largely went their separate ways. The Golden Horde was eventually conquered and incorporated into czarist Russia; the Ilkhans morphed into the Timurids and then the Mughals of India; the Chaghataids became the Moghuls of Inner Asia; and the ruling elite of the Yuan became the Mongols when they were expelled from Beijing in 1368 by the forces of *Emperor Hóngwǔ 洪武 (born Zhu Yuánzhāng 朱元璋; 1328–1398; r. 1368–1398), the founder of the Ming dynasty.

The Mongols, however, were not able to return to their old imperial capital of Karakorum on the Mongolian plateau because it was already occupied. Indeed, their ancestral homeland had been captured by the Oirad, an overarching designation for a group of peoples that had taken control over the plateau as the Mongols had become more and more embroiled in the affairs of China during the Yuan dynasty. The Mongols were therefore in limbo; they eventually established themselves, however, in the no-man's-land between the Great Wall and the Gobi Desert, which is now the Inner Mongolia Autonomous Region of the People's Republic of China. Nevertheless, two years after arriving as a refugee in this environmentally and politically marginal buffer zone, the last Yuan emperor, Togon Temür (1320–1370; r. 1333–1368, posthumous title Shùndì 顺帝), died of dysentery.

While his ignominious death symbolizes well the waning fortunes of the Mongols in the post-Yuan period, they were not completely powerless. Much of this had to do with the fact that they

*People marked with an asterisk have entries in this dictionary.

controlled the trade in Central Asian horses, which were essential for both the Ming military and its larger economy. Without them the Ming would quite literally have ground to a halt since Chinese soil lacks selenium, a vital mineral for the raising of strong horses. And the immensity of this trade is well reflected in the fact that annually the Ming bought nearly two million horses from the Mongols. Of course, for the Ming court it was intolerable that their national security was in the fickle hands of their enemies, and thus it had to be dealt with. The initial option was invasion and conquest, but every campaign of both emperors Hongwu and *Yǒnglè 永乐 (r. 1402–1424) were resounding failures. In response to these failures the Ming court adopted a two-pronged strategy. The first was to find another source of horses, which they did by reestablishing the tea-for-horse trading network with Tibet. The second was to trade with the Mongols, but on their own terms. Their plan was to funnel all this trade through the small independent city-state of Hami, which in 1406 had been brought into the Ming system of frontier garrisons.

The Mongol khan Gülichi (r. 1402–1408), however, did not agree with these terms and he poisoned the Prince of Hami, who had made the deal with the Chinese. At this turn of events the Ming court was bewildered, but they still hoped to salvage the trade negotiations. Yet when their envoys were executed at the command of the new Mongol ruler Punyashri, the Ming court finally decided to circumvent the Mongols entirely. They therefore made contact with the Mongols' archrival, the Oirad, and then not only bestowed titles and privileges upon the Oirad ruler but also opened up direct trade relations. The immediate consequence of this was that any power the Mongols had over the Ming simply evaporated, and both their wealth and power rapidly collapsed, while the Oirad rose in their place. Their power would reach its apogee during the reign of Esen (d. 1455), who in 1449 even captured Emperor Yīngzōng 英宗 (r. 1320–1323) at Tumu Fort 土木堡, fifty miles (eighty kilometers) northwest of Beijing; this event profoundly rattled the Ming court but emboldened Esen. He thus proclaimed himself khan and the rightful ruler of all the Mongols in 1453. While the Ming court hesitantly approved this move, the Mongols saw this action as a gross violation of the Chinggisid principle, which held that only direct descendants of *Chinggis Khan (1162–1227; often spelled Genghis Khan) could ever become a true khan and hold the Mongol throne, and Esen was an Oirad. They therefore violently resisted, and after Esen's death in 1455, the power of the Oirad weakened.

In their place rose the Mongols. Yet how the Mongols were actually able to rally themselves at this particular point in time is little understood. One factor in their favor, however, was the environment. Chinese sources recorded that on account of poor climatic conditions, northern China suffered severe famine during the 1450s and 1460s. The same conditions must clearly have affected both the Mongols and the Oirad, yet because the Oirad were on the Mongolian plateau, which has far greater weather extremes than Inner Mongolia, it is very likely that they were far worse off during these decades than the Mongols. Moreover, being closer to China, the Mongols could not only trade with the Chinese, but if need be they could also raid over the border. Regardless, it was during this time that the Mongol ruler Mandagul became khan and reigned briefly in the late 1470s. Upon his death, Bayan Möngke became khan, and upon Mongke's death in 1484 his seven-year-old son, Batu Möngke, was married to Mandagul Khan's widow, which enabled him to be recognized as the rightful ruler of all the Mongols.

Once the fortunes of the Mongols began to turn under this young ruler's direction, he became as famous as Dayan Khan. His meteoric rise to power began with his consolidation of the Mongols living in eastern Inner Mongolia and his reorganization of them into the Three Eastern Tümen (Chakhar, Khalkha, and Uriyangkhan). Next came his greatest military achievement, the conquest of the Mongols of Ordos, who had taken advantage of the Tumu incident to occupy the area within the great bend of the Huang River. Having only recently moved into and taken over this territory, the Ordos Mongols did not initially want to ally themselves with Dayan Khan. Instead they violently resisted Dayan Khan's project of unification. Ultimately, however, Dayan was victorious, and the Ordos Mongols were then organized into the Three Western Tümen (Ordos, Tümed, and Yüngshiyebü). And it was on account of this organizational reformulation of the Mongols into the Six Tümen under the authority of the Chinggisid ruler Dayan Khan that they were able to reassert their power against the Oirad.

Yet none of Dayan Khan's children, who each ruled over one of these separate Tümen, had either the iron fist or the political savvy to keep the fractious Mongols together, thus devolving the political situation into a virtual civil war. Within this infighting, however, Altan was to rise to the top; but because he was the second child of Dayan Khan's third son, he had no legitimate claim to the Mongol throne. He was instead simply the local ruler of the Tümed in the Ordos. But like Chinggis and Dayan Khan before him, he was ambitious, politically astute, and a military genius.

Altan Khan's Rise to Power

Altan Khan recognized that the linchpin of his future success would be his relations with China and access to its markets. To this end he initially put all his military energy into consolidating control of Mongol territory, which ran all along the Ming dynasty's northern border, so that he could use it as a launching pad to raid the riches of China. In so doing he not only forced the Mongul ruler Daraisun (r. 1548–1557) to recognize him as khan, but also pushed Daraisun and his people out of their traditional pastures, thereby setting in motion a massive migration. Most notably the Khalkha Mongols moved into the territory that was formerly occupied by the Oirad, which is now Outer Mongolia. The Oirad in turn were pushed farther west into the pastures north of the Tian Shan mountains where they came upon the remnants of the Moghuls and other nomadic groups, with whom they eventually forged the powerful empire of the Zünghars, which the Qing dynasty conquered in 1757.

Long before then, however, Altan was trying to deal with the Ming. At first Altan and his belligerent older brother, Mergen Jinong (1506–1542), thought the best strategy was simply to raid over the border and take what was needed. Although such a strategy provided the brothers with resources they could use to pay troops and forge alliances, Altan soon came to realize that it was shortsighted. To wit, while such raids provided certain immediate rewards, they also hardened the Chinese court's determination to defend the border from such depredations. Altan therefore wanted to normalize trade relations by establishing markets along the Sino-Mongol border where goods could be bought and sold. Such a free market system, however, was not only potentially beyond the ever hypervigilant control of the Chinese state, but it was also antithetical to the traditional Chinese tribute system, in which trade with foreign countries was never simply an economic transaction; instead it was an elaborate piece of the imperial ideology to keep alive the illusion of China as the center of the universe. All trade was therefore imagined as being tribute presented to the Chinese emperor by subjects from afar, and the Chinese goods sold in return were simply the magnanimous gift of the Chinese sovereign. Since the Chinese market was so valuable, most foreign traders through history had been willing to put up with this charade, but Altan did not. He wanted open markets.

To this end, once his older brother passed away in 1542, Altan began sending envoys to the Ming court to discuss the possibilities of opening border markets. But the Chinese refused. Even when Weng Wanda (1498–1552), the military commander of the region just west of the capital and a key imperial advisor, wrote petitions in 1546 and 1547 in favor of opening trade with Altan, the emperor refused. Of course, the proper response to these overtures was an issue that greatly divided the Ming court. Nevertheless, Emperor Jiājìng's 嘉靖 (r. 1522–1567) position of military containment and no-trade relations prevailed throughout the 1540s. Even in the face of growing

Sixteenth century image of Altan Khan as icon of Bhuddism.

dissent among court officials, the emperor's personal animosity toward the Mongols—he even mandated that the characters for the word *barbarian* should be written in the smallest possible characters in all official records—continued to shape Sino-Mongol relations. In fact, it was within this context that the Ming dynasty began in earnest to build the Great Wall, perhaps the world's greatest monument to xenophobia and trade protectionism ever built.

Even so, Altan tried to normalize trade relations throughout the 1540s. He persisted even after his trade envoys were publicly executed. After a decade of this one-sided and failed diplomacy, however, Altan launched an audacious attack on China. Yet it was not only the trade dispute that drove Altan to undertake this rash act: it also had not rained for 155 days, and the situation was dire. The Mongols were facing a severe famine, and the Ming court still refused to talk. Altan Khan thus invaded China, and by September he had surrounded Beijing and forced the Ming court to capitulate to his demands. The emperor agreed to the normalization of relations, and he allotted 100,000 taels of silver to purchase goods at two border markets at Datong in Shanxi Province and Xuanfu in today's Xuanhua, Hebei Province.

These markets were seemingly a success; several leading Mongols, however, complained about the fact that only horses could be exchanged for satin and cotton fabrics at these markets. As a result, the markets excluded all but the nobility (which Chinese policy supported, because they believed the enriched nobles would in turn control the actions of the overwhelmingly poor majority). Following up on these suggestions, Shǐ Dào 史道, the official in charge of the markets, sent a memorial to the court requesting that sheep and cattle also be allowed to be traded for grain. The court, however, argued that Mongols do not eat grain, and thus this idea was simply a ruse to help feed the Chinese who had settled in Altan Khan's territory. Shi Dao was therefore recalled in disgrace, and the markets closed, though a few sporadic markets continued to held through 1552. Yet after the Mongols began raiding again, the emperor abolished all border markets and forbade the matter ever to be brought up again for discussion. Nevertheless, in February 1553, Altan once more sent six envoys to request markets. The Ming court arrested all of them. Four were to die in jail, and two survived and were released in 1573.

Altan therefore realized that his ambitious plans for relations with China were over, and thus he turned his attention to securing his position on the Mongolian plateau. To this end he launched a massive campaign in 1558. He first marched through Ningxia and Gansu, where he conquered the Yellow Uygurs, and then turned north to present-day Xinjiang. There he first established relations with the Muslim rulers of Turpan and Hami. Then he campaigned against the Oirad in the Ili Valley and western Mongolia, which eventually resulted in the two sides establishing marriage relations and in the Oirad chiefs recognizing Altan as khan.

Dealing with the Chinese

After Altan Khan had secured his power across Inner Asia, he returned to Ordos, where his first course of action was to engage with the local Chinese community. Initially this group was comprised of members of the Buddhist White Lotus sect, which the Ming state ruthlessly persecuted. But over time it had come to include many other Chinese as well, such as those fleeing economic hardship or military service. Either way, the Mongols realized that such migrants were an economic boon and supported them by establishing twelve large and thirty-two small settlements where they could live and farm. Thus by the early 1560s there were fifty thousand Chinese in Altan Khan's territory.

While Altan's court recognized the value of these migrants, especially on account of their introduction of agriculture, the Mongols also wanted to entice educated Chinese who could help them deal with the Ming court. To this end the Mongols posted a sign: "All graduate scholars of the second rank who kindly join the barbarians will be treated very well and be my equals," which elicited such a response that all the applicants had to be screened (Serruys 1959, 69). For the Mongols this brain drain was another boon since these scholars knew not only the "Ming system" (language, military, trade, etc.), and could therefore help Altan Khan's court deal with China, but they also brought with them Chinese culture. Many of these Chinese were therefore brought into Altan Khan's inner circle of advisors. Several became successful military leaders fighting against the Ming; others became teachers for the children of the Mongol elite, who studied the Chinese classics, and some became the architects and builders of Altan Khan's palace, which was based on Chinese imperial precedent and constructed in the 1560s. It even had Chinese inscriptions over the two main gates reading *kāi huà fǔ* 开化府 (civilizing and developing government) and *wēi zhèn huá yí* 威震华夷 (overawe Chinese and barbarians).

But these Chinese literati were not the only ones promoting the power of Altan Khan. There was also a charismatic preacher and adept fortune-teller named Lǚ Hè 吕鹤, who not only acquired a large following of Ming Chinese by preaching a messianic message that claimed a massive Mongol invasion would result in the death of 70 percent of the Chinese population, but he also claimed to have an elixir that enabled one to survive without grain. Such a technological edge was clearly something that intrigued Altan Khan's court, and, as with all the other recent Chinese technologies they had obtained, the Mongols also wanted this elixir—yet so, too, did the Ming court. As evidenced in the market disputes that arose in the early 1550s, the Ming court knew that grain was the key commodity in Sino-Mongol trade relations, and if this elixir worked, they would no longer have any leverage with Altan Khan and his growing Chinese community. Thus when they captured Lü He in Beijing in 1564, he was summarily executed.

The situation between the Ming and Altan Khan was therefore growing tense. In many ways it could easily have spiraled out of control as it had in 1550. Yet rather than descending into violent confrontation, the two sides signed a peace treaty in 1571. Of course, how and why this happened at this particular juncture in time has been much debated. Nevertheless, to explain this development, two factors need to be taken into consideration. The first was the Chinese community in Altan's territory, which helped the Mongols to better understand how to deal with the Ming court; the second factor was the Ming court itself. After forty-five years on the throne the rabidly anti-Mongol Jiajing emperor had died, and during the transition period before the *Emperor Wànlì 万历 (r. 1572–1620) was enthroned, many old debates were revived including how to best deal with the Mongols. The long-standing wisdom at the Ming court had been to isolate the Mongols and keep them at bay with both the Great Wall and a vast array of border garrisons, yet through the decades this strategy had always been questioned. Many had pointed out that maintaining border security was not only bankrupting the government but also was ineffective. As a result, they argued that opening up border markets and expanding the tribute system would ensure peace. Upon the death of the Jiajing emperor, this argument was given a new hearing.

One of the most prominent voices in this regard was Wáng Chónggǔ 王崇古 (1515–1589), who had made a name for himself as a young official by fighting piracy along China's coast. The Jiajing court saw the Mongol situation in much the same light; therefore in 1559 they sent Wang to Shaanxi Province. Upon arriving, however, he quickly realized that the Sino-Mongol situation was not a question of piracy. Moreover, to resolve the escalating tensions on the border, Wang realized that the Ming strategy needed to change. But policy was set in Beijing, thus Wang's options were limited. He could not, for example, unilaterally open border markets.

Even so, he did as much as possible to establish a relationship with Altan Khan by petitioning the court to agree to his sporadic requests. In particular, he was especially forceful in arguing that the Ming court should support Altan's interest in Buddhism. Beginning in the 1550s, Altan had petitioned the court for Buddhist texts, statues, and even craftsmen to build temples, all of which had been rejected. Wang argued, however, that granting such requests would not only decrease border tensions but that the Mongol conversion to Buddhism would pacify their warlike tendencies. While this peace-through-Buddhism strategy was a pipe dream, Wang's more engaged strategy was effective. And as the situation on the border improved, both Wang's reputation and rank increased. By 1570 he was governor-general of Shanxi Province and in a perfect position to take advantage of the situation that unfolded when Altan Khan's son defected to the Ming.

Daiching Ejei surrendered with his family at Báihú Fort 败胡堡 on 18 October 1570 because he felt wronged by his father. Altan had married a young woman named Noyanchu Jönggen, who had previously been promised to somebody else, and therefore another wife needed to be offered to the offended Mongol nobleman in order to ameliorate the situation. Altan thus offered him a granddaughter who was previously promised to Daiching Ejei, which in turn enraged Daiching and ultimately made him flee to China. Wang then realized that Daiching Ejei's defection could be used to forge a Sino-Mongol peace accord. In particular, he aimed to use Daiching Ejei as not only bait for Altan to sue for peace but also as a lever to change the policies of the Ming court. In both cases he succeeded; on 13 June 1571 Altan Khan and representatives from the Ming court met just north of Datong to ratify a peace deal. In return for ceasing hostilities against China and handing over the leaders of the White Lotus for execution, the Ming granted Altan Khan the title Shùnyì Wáng 顺义王 (Obedient and Patriotic King), which allowed him to present tribute in Beijing, and opened several horse markets on the Ordos border. In addition both sides signed a thirteen-point agreement that dealt with issues of refugees and deserters, and in particular judicial matters concerning the punishment of Chinese and Mongols who committed crimes in the other's territory.

A Crisis of Faith

The meeting between Altan Khan and the Dalai Lama in 1578 on the shores of Lake Kökenuur in the northern reaches of the Tibetan plateau has become an iconic moment in Eurasian history. Indeed, because the meeting was to become so important in later Mongol, Tibetan, and Qing imaginings of themselves, their religion, and their state, this meeting has often been presented as less an historical event than a powerful symbol. It is therefore important to recognize that the meeting of Altan Khan and the Dalai Lama was nothing unique; it was simply one of many such meetings. In fact, contrary to the common narrative of Gelukpa (the Yellow Hat sect of Tibetan Buddhism) exclusivity that this meeting entails, it is vital to recognize the pluralistic nature of Mongol religiosity—namely, the Dalai Lama and his Gelukpa order had no exclusive claim to the Mongols' hearts and minds. They were simply one of a hodgepodge of religious specialists who provided their services at the Mongol court. With the subsequent rise of the Gelukpa during the Qing dynasty, however, this diffuse religiosity of Altan Khan's court was to be readily forgotten. Instead, all that was to be remembered was that Altan Khan met the young Sonam Gyatsho, gave him the title of Dalai Lama, and thenceforth the Mongols were Gelukpa Buddhists.

The reality was slightly different. When Altan Khan passed away, for example, his funeral took place on the southern side of a mountain according to shamanic practices, and a Buddhist astrologer and Chinese *feng shui* master deduced his burial site. Such a pluralistic

The Third Dalai Lama, Sonam Gyatso, received that title from Altan Khan. His predecessors received the titles of First and Second Dalai Lama retroactively.

vision needs to be kept in mind when dealing with Altan Khan's multifaceted approach to religion. Altan Khan, for example, had relations with numerous Tibetan lineages, including the Kagyü, which was the archrival of the Dalai Lama's own Gelukpa order. Moreover, as seen earlier in this chapter, Altan Khan was interested in more than just Tibetan Buddhism. He had been a great supporter of the Chinese White Lotus Buddhist order, which offered him not only spiritual succor but also claimed to possess a mantra so powerful it could shatter the walls of a Chinese city. Yet their secret weapon did not fare much better than the grain-defying elixir of Lü He. When Altan Khan took the Chinese

Buddhists out into the field, their mantras had no effect, and when the Chinese fortifications still stood after two days of chanting, Altan Khan apparently gave up on the White Lotus. Their future among the Mongols was therefore sealed when the Ming asked for their extradition in 1571; Altan acquiesced.

The same kind of failure had also turned Altan Khan away from his shamans. They had advised him that 1547 was an auspicious year to inaugurate trade relations with the Ming, therefore Altan had tried to present one black-headed white horse, seven camels, and three thousand geldings. He also provided intelligence to the Ming court about another Mongol ruler's impending attack on the garrison of Liaodong in present-day Liaoyang, in Liaoning Province. But the shamans were wrong. The Ming court still refused to open trade relations.

It was at this time that Altan turned to the White Lotus, but they too had failed, and now Altan Khan faced another crisis. In particular, the increased Sino-Mongol intercourse ushered in by the 1571 peace accord had been a double-edged sword. While it had brought normalization in trade relations and improved the economic situation among the Mongols, it had also enabled the urban diseases of China, especially smallpox, to run rampant across the steppe with devastating consequences. Indeed, these epidemics not only put a halt to the upsurge of the Mongols at this time and enabled the Manchus to rise in their place, but they also opened the door for Tibetan lamas and their vast repertoire of medical lore and tantric rituals to be invited back among the Mongols.

There were no doubt other reasons why Altan Khan turned to the Tibetans and their tantric Buddhism at this time, such as his definitive break with the White Lotus after the 1571 peace accord. The conventional narrative, however, has it that Altan's turn toward Tibet happened on account of Asing Lama, a monk from the sacred mountain of Wutai Shan who appeared at the Mongol court in 1571. Asing supposedly not only introduced Altan and Noyanchu Jönggen to tantric Buddhism, but he also recommended that they that invite Sonam Gyatsho to Mongolia. While the later may be true, it is clear that Altan Khan did not need an introduction to Buddhism. Indeed, as noted above, he had long had contact with the lively tantric Buddhist scene that the Ming court supported in Beijing. Even so, it was probably the case that Altan's interest in Tibetan Buddhism was furthered at this time since he had recently campaigned and conquered large areas of Amdo in Tibet. Thus his turn to the lamas and their Buddhism was not without political overtones.

By meeting with various Tibetan lamas, however, Altan Khan was not trying to unify the Mongols by harking back to the iconic meeting of Khubilai

Khan and Pakpa Lama during the Yuan dynasty. This is precisely how later historians framed this meeting, but Altan Khan's ambitions were always more local. As the second son of Dayan Khan's third son, he could never claim to the rule the Chinggisid throne. He could not even claim to rule the Three Western Tümen of Ordos. He could only claim to be the ruler of the Tümed, his hereditary appanage in southwest Inner Mongolia. And even though he was the most powerful ruler among the Mongols during the late sixteenth century—and recognized as such by the Ming court—he never claimed to be anything other than the ruler of Tümed. Yet by consolidating his power over and against the rightful Chinggisid heir, and by having his local authority ritually recognized by Buddhist hierarchs, he changed the nature of Mongol society by putting an end to the Chinggisid principle of primogeniture. By abandoning the Chinggisid principle of one Mongol ruler enshrined by his grandfather Dayan Khan, the numerous descendants of Dayan Khan could thereby follow Altan's lead, and by allying themselves with a Tibetan lama be proclaimed khan. And this is invariably what happened.

The particular religio-political model that Altan Khan had forged—one whereby local authority was conferred by Tibetan Buddhist hierarchs—was subsequently emulated by the Mongol leaders of the six different Tümen. Thus, in the wake of Altan Khan's reign, rather than there being a unified group of Mongols, there instead came to be numerous independent Mongol groups that in turn came to fight not only with the Ming but also among themselves. But the subsequent Mongol civil war was only one consequence of Altan Khan's particular innovations: on account of these competing khans allying themselves with different Buddhist orders, they were also drawn into competing sides in Tibet's civil war. Chogtu Taiji of the Khalkha, for example, had allied himself with the Karmapa and his Kagyü lineage and launched an invasion of Tibet against the Dalai Lama and his Tümed allies.

On account of these competing religious and political alliances, the situation in Inner Asia quickly spun out of control in the beginning of the seventeenth century. Yet the crisis was not contained to this area. Indeed, much as the Ming dynasty's economic and political weakness in the mid-sixteenth century had played an important role in setting these events in motion, it was subsequently the Ming that would suffer the ultimate fate of this deteriorating situation on the northern border. In 1644 the Ming would be conquered by the Manchus, who before the invasion had made alliances with several of the now independent local Mongol rulers as well as agreements with Tibetan lamas as Altan Khan had done. And this would continue throughout the course of the Qing dynasty. The legacy of Altan Khan, who had passed away in 1582, thus continued to profoundly shape

Chinese history even though more often than not he is remembered for simply having met the Dalai Lama.

Johan ELVERSKOG
Southern Methodist University

Further Reading

Elverskog, Johan. (2003). *The* Jewel Translucent Sūtra: *Altan Khan and the Mongols in the sixteenth century*. Leiden, The Netherlands: E. J. Brill.

Elverskog, Johan. (2007). Tibetocentrism: Religious conversion and the study of Mongolian Buddhism. In Hildegard Diemberger & Uradyn Bulag (Eds.), *The Mongolia-Tibet interface: Opening new research terrains in Inner Asia* (pp. 59–81). Leiden, The Netherlands: E. J. Brill.

Serruys, Henry. (1959). Chinese in southern Mongolia during the sixteenth century. *Monumenta Serica, 19*, 1–95.

Serruys, Henry. (1960). Four documents relating to the Sino-Mongol peace of 1570–1571. *Monumenta Serica, 19*, 1–66.

Serruys, Henry. (1974–1975). Two remarkable women in Mongolia: The Third Lady Erketü Qatun and Dayicing-Beyiji. *Asia Major, 19*(2), 555–613.

Hǎi Ruì
海瑞

1514–1587—Incorruptible scholar-official

Alternate name: posthumous name: Zhōngjiè 忠介

海瑞

Summary

An iconic scholar-official of the Ming dynasty, Hai Rui was noted for incorruptibility and the courage to stand up for his convictions regardless of the risks to his career and life. Hai Rui dared to criticize corrupt officials and even the moral failings of the emperor, for which he was tortured and imprisoned (but not executed); he reportedly said farewell to his family and had bought a coffin in preparation for the worst. During the Cultural Revolution of the twentieth century, his name reemerged as someone who dared to speak out against authority, a dangerous proposition at that time.

Hai Rui has achieved fame as an irreproachable scholar-official of the Míng 明 dynasty (1368–1644), who dared to stand up to two emperors and faced torture and prison (and the distinct possibility of execution) for his belief in the morality of officials and rulers. His efforts earned him the posthumous name, Zhōngjiè 忠介 ("Loyal and Incorruptible") given to him by the dynasty under which he served.

Born in 1514 into a family of Confucian scholars from Qiongshan, on Hainan Island near Guangdong Province (Qiongshang is in the environs of modern-day Haikou), Hai Rui's widowed mother took charge of his early education and had an important impact on both his Confucian education and his character.

Career in the Civil Service

Hai entered the imperial civil service in 1549 by passing the provincial-level examination (*xiāngshì* 乡试) upon which he earned the official designation of *jǔrén* 举人 (selected man). He sat for the metropolitan examination, the highest level and the most prestigious degree, in 1550 and 1553, but was not successful. During the Míng 明 dynasty (1368–1644), it was not typical for a scholar of Hai Ru's status to receive positions within the central government, but Hai Rui was no ordinary man. He stood out among his contemporaries as an official who took his responsibilities to imperial service very seriously.

Hai Rui began his career as a lowly instructor at a Confucian school in Nanping, Fujian Province in 1554 and ended it in 1587 as censor-in-chief of the imperial Censorate. During the Ming dynasty, the Censorate was one of the top organizations of the government, in charge of supervising and disciplining all scholar-officials. This was a remarkable achievement for someone who had not achieved the highest degree in the imperial civil service examination system.

Modern historians are in agreement that Hai Rui was one of the moral exemplars of the Ming dynasty, but there is debate about what influences defined him as a person and official. The historian Ray Huang (1918–2000) called Hai Rui an "eccentric" for his unusual behavior. One popular anecdote related Hai Rui's extreme frugality. He supposedly celebrated his mother's birthday by splurging on just two "catties" of pork for her banquet (equivalent to a little more than two pounds, or one kilogram). Hai Rui insisted that the cheapest paper be used for documents related to his position. He also did not allow officials to greet him outside the walls of a city when he was on an inspection tour, and he set a strict (and low) limit on the amount of money that local officials could spend on food to entertain him (Huang 1981).

The author and researcher Joanna Handlin Smith views Hai Rui's behavior as an indicator of his moral standards. She referred to Hai Rui as an administrator-sage influenced by the philosopher *Wáng Yángmíng's 王阳明 (1472–1529) School of Mind-and-Heart, which sought to unify the impulses of thought and action, and points out that, for Hai Rui, the goal of imperial service included the quest for moral perfection for himself and others (Handlin 1983). At every appointment, from regional to central government postings, Hai Rui insisted on following correct procedures and holding himself and all those who worked for him to high and exacting standards. He was not afraid to stand up to powerful families, fellow officials, or even emperors.

The historian Harry Miller does not question Hai Rui's commitment to moral governance, but describes Hai Rui's approach as a matter of strict application of Confucian "fundamentalism." Miller also seems to be less impressed with the legend of Hai Rui's frugality and stresses his role not just as an official but also as a member of the gentry (Miller 2009, 22).

Accounts of Hai Rui's career in Ming dynasty history stress that he began his

*People marked with an asterisk have entries in this dictionary.

tenure in a position by publically stating his intentions to root out corruption and apply policies to all under his jurisdiction. Hai also used the power of law to correct human behavior. His beliefs earned him both admirers and detractors at every level of Ming bureaucracy.

One way to understand Hai Rui's dedication to moral action is to put him into the context of a long-standing tradition of remonstrance associated with the Confucian scholar-official class (*shì* 士 or *shì dàfū* 士大夫). The remonstrance ideal expected officials to come forward to provide guidance and even criticism to a superior when necessary, regardless of the risks that included the very real possibility of death. Officials accepted the risk as part of their professional and personal identities.

In the *Analects* (*Lúnyǔ* 论语), attributed to *Confucius 孔子 (551–479 BCE), the single most important philosopher in China history, the roles and responsibilities of rulers, scholars, and subjects were established. Confucius referred to a group he called the *jūnzǐ* 君子 ("noble person") to provide moral leadership to society (de Bary and Bloom 1999, 44). Members of the scholar class had the greatest opportunity to become *junzi* because they were able to study the past. Confucius therefore expected a great deal from them: "The scholar, who perceiving danger, is prepared to sacrifice his life; who, seeing the possibility of gain, thinks of rightness; who, in sacrificing, thinks of reverence; who, in mourning, thinks of grief, is worthy of approval" (*Analects* 19.1; de Bary and Bloom, 63).

Confucian considered remonstrance an essential part of the scholar-officials' role in government, especially in regards to helping the ruler maintain his virtue (*dé* 德). Their motivation was based on righteousness (*yì* 义) and loyalty (*zhōng* 忠). These terms all focus on the models of behavior, which all Confucian scholars would understand and be expected to emulate. The philosopher *Mencius (Mèngzǐ) 孟子 (c. 372–c. 289 BCE), Confucius's most significant successor, took the role of the scholar an important step further. He established remonstrance as a key role and responsibility of the scholar-official.

The concept of remonstrance thus became embedded in the intellectual tradition and was an essential part of the moral duty of the scholar-official. Confucian scholar-officials instructed the emperor, and when necessary spoke up to rectify the ruler's behavior. In the ideal expression of remonstrance, they would not seek to attack the ruler for their own purposes. They would explain their concerns in moral terms, drawing references from China's past. They should take their roles as moral leaders seriously.

To come forward to stand up for a principle, especially with the ruler, was dangerous for scholar-officials throughout Chinese history, and in some periods, such as the political environment of Hai Rui's time, this could easily result in death. Among the terms for remonstrance, the one that most clearly addresses these dangers is *jiànsǐ* 谏死, "risking one's life in remonstrance" because it indicates the level of commitment scholar-officials were willing to make in order to fulfill their Confucian duty to the ruler.

Although they might die for their principles, courageous officials such as Hai Rui still came forward to offer remonstrance. Standing by his convictions was more important to Hai Rui than his life.

Criticizing the Emperor

Hai Rui's first appointment in the Ming capital of Beijing came in 1564 when he received the post of secretary in the Ministry of Revenue. It was from this vantage point that Hai Rui assessed the emperor, Zhu Houcong, who reigned as the Jiajing ("Excellence and Serenity") emperor from 1521 to 1566. Hai Rui saw much that he thought was wrong with the way the emperor handled not only affairs of state but also his personal behavior.

In 1565, Hai Rui submitted a scathing memorial to the Jiajing emperor. Hai Rui's actions were remarkable for his candor about the emperor's personal failings. He could not have been the only high-ranking official to notice what the emperor was doing, but he was the only official to take the emperor to task for his behavior. In doing so, he used the most direct and unambiguous terms:

> Criticizing him for his failure as sovereign, father, and husband, and for his inattention to the public business in the previous twenty years. This he said resulted in the prevalence of injustice, corruption, military weakness, heavy taxation, and destitution among the common people, as shown in the popular pun on his reign title, Chia-ching [Jiajing], rendered as "every family cleaned out." He found fault with the emperor for his vanity as shown by his search for longevity, for his senseless involvement of the court in Taoist [Daoist] prayer ceremonies, and for his eccentric ways of constructing building on the palace. (Fang 1976, 475)

Hai Rui's accusations reputedly enraged the emperor, but surprisingly, he took no immediate action. There is much speculation about why the Jiajing emperor delayed his official response. For his part, Hai Rui expected the harshest of punishments; accounts stress that he had already said goodbye to his family and purchased a coffin.

The emperor finally ordered Hai Rui's imprisonment in February 1566 and subjected him to torture. He was supposed to be executed by means of strangulation for his disrespect to the emperor. The Ministry of Justice equated the tone of Hai Rui's indictment with that of a son cursing his father, demonstrating a complete lack of filial piety. The Ming dynastic law code of 1397, the *Great Ming Code* (*Dàmíng lǜ* 大明律), referred to such a crime as one of the "Ten Abominations," considered to be so serious that they were punished by the most painful and extreme forms of capital punishment (Jiang 2005, 18).

The conflict between Hai Rui and the Jiajing emperor suggests that at least on one level, the two understood each other. Hai Rui's memorial was harsh and direct, but this made sense coming from a scholar-official who sought moral perfection for himself and his ruler. He called for the emperor to reform himself in order to restore his virtue. True to his belief in remonstrance, Hai took it upon himself to help the emperor realize the error of his ways, doing so out of righteousness and loyalty. It is significant that Hai Rui did not call upon the emperor to step down. Neither did he call upon anyone to overthrow him.

Even more curious is the emperor's response to Hai Rui's memorial. Even after the Ministry of Justice recommended the death penalty, the emperor once again delayed meting out the punishment. Fortunately for Hai Rui, the sentence was never carried out, as the Jiajing emperor died in 1566. For Hai Rui, the consummate It would be best to keep this line to the left column, if possible, so that the heading starts at the top.

Career under a New Emperor

Upon his release from prison in 1567, Hai Rui was able to take up his former rank in the civil bureaucracy. Between 1567 and 1570, he received promotions several times, including that of governor of Nan Zhili, (the Southern Metropolitan Region), headquartered in Yingtian, modern-day Nanjing.

Hai Rui felt it necessary to act on behalf of commoners who could not speak for themselves in dealings with the rich and powerful. His intervention in 1567 in a local land tenure dispute for those who lost their property to money lenders and landowners with ties to highly placed officials proved to be his undoing, and resulted in his ouster from public service in 1570. He spent the next fifteen years in forced retirement.

Finally, in 1585, Hai Rui was called back into service and was named assistant head of the Censorate in Nanjing, where he served as vice minister. Hai Rui's last promotion brought him to the highest position of his career, censor-in-chief at Nanjing 1586, in which he confronted another Ming emperor, Zhu Yijun, who reigned as *Emperor Wànlì, 万历 (1563–1620; r. 1573–1620). Hai Rui was among the many officials who came forward to remonstrate about the emperor's behavior during the latter part of his long reign.

Punishments for Corrupt Officials

Before Hai Rui took up his post in the imperial Censorate, he submitted a most unusual memorial to the Wanli emperor in which he called upon him to take action against the rampant corruption of officialdom. As a solution to the problem, Hai Rui promoted the use of extremes measures such as flaying the skin from the bodies of offenders, employed by Zhu Yuanzhang, who established the Ming dynasty and reigned as the *Hóngwǔ emperor 洪武帝 (1328–1398; r. 1368–1398). Such punishments were not specified in the *Great Ming Code*, but were a type of "extra-legal punishment" (*fǎwài zhīxíng* 法外之形) used by Hongwu.

The Hongwu emperor was a harsh ruler, who had little trust for the officials who served him. He meted out harsh punishments for real and imagined crimes he believed were committed by officials—employing a number of statutes, including the *Great Warnings* of 1385–1387 (one of the major documents associated with his autocratic vision for Ming society)—especially when he sought punishments more severe than those called for by the *Great Ming Code*. The "extra-legal punishments" appeared with great frequency in the articles of the *Great Warnings*. They did not apply to commoners, but were used as retribution for the treachery of officials that the emperor saw at every turn.

Among the types of "extra-legal punishments" were death by "slow slicing," wearing of a wooden cangue (a board fitted around the accused's neck), tattooing of the face and body, severing of hands or fingers, castration, removal of knee-caps, and amputation of legs. Although technically considered corporal rather than capital punishment, mutilation often caused the death of the accused. The intent of such punishments seems to have been two-fold: to prolong an offender's pain and to make an example of the mutilated offenders for all to see.

Hai Rui's call in 1586 for the Wanli emperor to use such violent methods to punish officials in his own time may seem curious, but it demonstrates Hai's pursuit of moral perfection and his frustration with the degree of corruption he encountered at all levels of the imperial bureaucracy. He believed in law and relied on it to deal with offenders. Yet his motivation for using these punishments was very different from that of the Ming founder. The Hongwu emperor distrusted officialdom as a whole and assumed they naturally engaged in evil behavior. In contrast, Hai Rui's own career was a model of decorum and morality; it was the behavior of other officials he condemned. The great irony was that there was no guarantee that Hai Rui himself would escape the same sort of punishment he called for, not for wrongdoing but for his acts of remonstrance, first with Jialing in 1565 and then with Wanli in 1586.

It is indeed fortunate for Hai Rui that it was Wanli and not Hongwu who decided his fate in 1586. The Wanli emperor's reply to Hai Rui's memorial was nevertheless surprising: "His [Hai Rui's] suggestion for cruel punishment contradicts our sense of good government. Furthermore, he has made some personal criticisms of myself; the wording silly and inept, even though I have decided to ignore it" (Huang 1981, 154). Other remonstrators in this period were not so lucky and the emperor had them beaten.

When Hai Rui died in 1587, he had only a modest estate and his funeral was paid for by contributions. Yet word of his integrity and courage had spread during his lifetime and he became a legendary model for officials after his death. There was a great public outpouring of appreciation for his dedication and service. His name became widely known through legend, as well as through the literary works that celebrated his courage during the Ming dynasty and the Qīng 清dynasty (1644–1911/1912) that followed.

There are few historical figures in China who are better known and admired than Hai Rui, both as an exemplary official and one who could be counted on to stand up against corruption and injustice wherever it existed in government. Popular appreciation for Hai Rui's character and policies in China has resonated over the centuries with commoners in need of a champion. Officials admired his determination, his promotion of good government, and his courage in standing up to rulers in dire need of reform.

Hai Rui as Political Allegory in Maoist China

In twentieth-century China, during the political era dominated by Chinese Communist Party leader, *Máo Zédōng 毛泽东 (1893–1976), Hai Rui's name arose again in the public realm, this time in a way he could never have expected.

Between 1959 and 1961, Wu Han (1909–1969), the deputy mayor of Beijing and a Ming dynasty specialist, wrote a number of works featuring Hai Rui, including the controversial play, *Hai Rui Dismissed from Office*. The play focused on Hai Rui's role as the loyal and upright official, who was unjustly punished by the emperor for his criticisms.

The subsequent political downfall of Wu Han in 1965 is generally regarded as the opening salvo of the Cultural Revolution (1966–1976), a period of great turmoil for China. The allegorical play had praised Hai Rui for bravely trying to criticize mistaken imperial policies. The Chinese Communist Party leaders close to Mao's wife, *Jiāng Qīng 江青 (1914–1991), assumed that the play was a thinly disguised criticism of Mao's dismissal of *Péng Déhuái 彭德怀 (1898–1974), the former minister of defense. Peng had spoken up about the failures of the 1958 Great Leap Forward, a disastrous campaign of industrial and agricultural "reforms," at the Chinese Communist Party conference of 1959. Mao's response to Peng and his subsequent dismissal set off a barrage of criticism of Mao for his unfair treatment of Peng. Among the reactions to this controversial play is the implication that if Peng Dehuai represented a modern-day Hai Rui, then the "emperor" figure in the play must be Mao Zedong, despite the fact that Wu Han himself denied the comparison.

Many Chinese Communist Party leaders interpreted Wu Han's play as a criticism of how harshly Mao dealt with one of his own upright officials. Not surprisingly, the play was denounced in 1965, beginning the devastating political upheaval of the Cultural Revolution. Hai Rui's tomb on Hainan Island was attacked. Wu Han was arrested and imprisoned; he committed suicide in 1967.

After the Cultural Revolution, the issue of Hai Rui's place in Chinese history and politics again resurfaced. In 1979, Wang Ruoshui, deputy editor of the *People's Daily* and leading Marxist reformer in the *Dèng Xiǎoping 邓小平 era (1978–1997) kept alive the link between Hai Rui and the Maoist era in a speech Wang gave to the Chinese Communist Party Central Committee. Wang stressed in his speech that Peng Dehuai "was also a Hai Rui" (Wang 1979).

Wu Han, deputy mayor of Beijing, specialist on the Ming dynasty, and author of the play *Hai Rui Dismissed from Office,* which was denounced in 1965 and in some ways marks the beginning of the Cultural Revolution under Mao Zedong.

Hai Rui in Contemporary China

Popular interest in Hai Rui is evident in a historical drama series for Chinese television aired in 2007 about the Jiajing emperor, called *Ming Dynasty: 1566.* In the series, Hai Rui demonstrates his courage as the best example of an official from the past, who is also the model for the leaders China needs in the future.

The Chinese government has sponsored a number of current Internet sites that highlight Hai Rui's importance as a cultural symbol of China. These include a video for children sponsored by China's Confucius Institute, the cultural arm of the People's Republic of China: "Hai Rui: An Upright and Incorruptible Official" (http://kid.chinese.cn/en/article/2009-09/01/content_51099.htm). One of the most curious recent treatments of Hai Rui's role as moral exemplar is a reference on the Chinese government's English-language website: "Hai Rui. 'The Lord Bao in the South'" (http://characters.cultural-china.com/chinaWH/html/en/33History2378.html). (Lord Bao was an incorruptible judge during the Song dynasty who has often been used in contemporary China as a symbol of social protest.) The linkage of Hai Rui and Bao Zheng, two "pure officials" (*qīngguān* 清官), first occurred in the Hundred Flowers Campaign of 1956–1957, when intellectuals were invited by Mao to offer criticisms of the Chinese Communist Party. It is unclear why the current Internet site refers to Hai Rui in this way, but it seems to suggest that Hai Rui is once again relevant to Chinese politics.

Anita M. ANDREW
Northern Illinois University

Further Reading

Andrew, Anita M., & Rapp, John A. (2000). *Autocracy and China's rebel founding emperors: Comparing Chairman Mao and Ming Taizu.* Lanham, MD: Rowman & Littlefield Publishers.

Asia for Educators. (n.d.) *Selections from the Mencius: On the duty of ministers to reprove a ruler*. Columbia University. Retrieved December 16, 2013 from http://afe.easia.columbia.edu/ps/cup/mencius_reproving_ruler.pdf

Dardess, John W. (2012). *Ming China, 1368–1644: A concise history of a resilient empire*. Lanham, MD. Rowman & Littlefield.

de Bary, W. Theodore, & Irene Bloom. (Comps.). (1999). *Sources of Chinese tradition, Vol. 1, From earliest times to 1600*. New York: Columbia University Press.

Fang Chao-Ying. (1976). Hai Rui. In L. C. Goodrich & Chao-Ying Fang (Eds.), *Dictionary of Ming biography, 1368–1644 (Vol. 1)* (pp. 474–479). New York: Columbia University Press.

Fisher, Tom. (1993). The play's the thing: Wu Han and Hai Rui revisited. In Jonathan Unger (Ed.), *Using the past to serve the present: Historiography and politics in contemporary China* (pp. 9–45). Armonk, NY: M.E. Sharpe.

Handlin, Joanna F. (1983). *Action in Late Ming thought—The Reorientation of Lu K'un and other scholar–officials*. Berkeley and Los Angeles: University of California Press.

Huang, Ray. (1981). *1587: A year of no significance, The Ming dynasty in Decline*. New Haven, CT: Yale University Press.

Hucker, Charles O. (1985). *A dictionary of official titles in imperial China.* Stanford, CA: Stanford University Press.

Jiang Yonglin. (2005). *The great Ming code, Da Ming lu.* Seattle: University of Washington Press.

Miller, Harry. (2009). *State versus gentry in late Ming dynasty China: 1572–1644.* New York: Palgrave Macmillan.

Mote, Frederick W., & Denis Twitchett. (Eds.). (1988). *The Cambridge history of China, Volume 7, The Ming dynasty, 368–1644, Part I.* Cambridge, UK: Cambridge University Press.

Robinson, David. (Ed.). (2008). *Culture, courtiers, and competition, The Ming court (1368–1644).* Cambridge, MA: Harvard University Press.

Wagner, Rudolf G. (1993). In guise of a congratulation: Political symbolism in Zhou Xinfang's, *Hai Rui submits his memorial.* In Jonathan Unger (Ed.), *Using the past to serve the present* (pp. 46–103). Armonk, NY: M. E. Sharpe.

Wan, Maggie C. K. (2009). Building an immortal land: The Ming Jiajing emperor's West Park. *Asia Major* (3rd series), *22*(2), 65–99.

Wang Ruoshui. (1980). "The greatest lesson of the Cultural Revolutions is that the personality cult should be opposed," Joint Publications Research Service (JPRS) 75291 (March 12, 1980): 78–100.

Hongwu, Emperor (of Ming)

Hóngwǔ 洪武

1328–1398—Founder of the Ming dynasty (r. 1368–1398)

Alternate names: birth name: Zhū Yuánzhāng 朱元璋; courtesy name: Guóruì 国瑞; temple name: Tàizǔ 太祖

Summary

Zhu Yuanzhang rose from poverty to become Emperor Hongwu, founder of the Ming dynasty. In his youth his family was so poor they had to give up two of his brothers for adoption; he later had to leave a Buddhist monastery after the monastery ran out of food. As emperor, he forced the Mongol rulers to flee and established his court in Nanjing. His sympathizers argue that as a pragmatic ruler, Hongwu quickly restored order after a chaotic civil war through the establishment of institutions that effectively governed China for almost six hundred years. His cruelty toward his perceived enemies, however, led to thousands being put to death and contributed to his reputation as a cruel despot.

As founder of the Míng 明 dynasty (1368–1644), Emperor Hongwu was one of the most influential rulers in all of Chinese history. His reputation, however, has been the subject of various controversies over the last few centuries. He has been fiercely attacked for the liberal use of harsh punishments, for deadly purges of top officials, and for the autocratic institutions he installed to stabilize his rule but which consolidated too much power in the hands of the emperor. His sympathizers argue that as a pragmatic ruler, Hongwu quickly restored order after a chaotic civil war through the establishment of institutions that effectively governed China for almost six hundred years. They also argue that, after the rule of the Mongols during the Yuán 元 dynasty (1279–1368), he revitalized Chinese Han civilization by emphasizing the Confucian classics, civil service examinations, the laws of the Táng 唐 (618–907 CE) and Sòng 宋 (960–1279) dynasties, and by removing Mongol customs from local societies.

Early Life

Born Zhū Yuánzhāng 朱元璋 into a poor peasant family in what is now Fèngyáng 凤阳, Anhui Province, the first Ming emperor experienced a life more dramatic than most rulers. He endured bitter battles and bloody power struggles to rise from a beggar-monk all the way to the throne of the most vast and wealthy empire of his time. Because of his humble origins, information about Zhu's life before his seventeenth year can only be found in the emperor's autobiographical accounts. We are told that Zhu was the youngest among four boys and two girls of a poor family whose financial situation was so bad that the second and third sons had to be given up for adoption. In 1344, his region was hit by a plague that took the lives of the entire Zhu family except for his second brother, the son of his eldest brother, Zhū Wénzhèng 朱文正, and Zhu Yuanzhang himself. The burial of the dead was made possible only after a charitable neighbor donated a piece of land. In desperation, the teenaged Zhu entered the nearby Buddhist monastery at Huangjue Temple (Huángjuè Sì 皇觉寺) as a novice. He stayed at the monastery for only fifty-six days before the abbot disbanded all of the disciples because of lack of food. Having no other choice but to wander as a mendicant, the future emperor begged for food in the western Anhui region, and then returned to stay at the monastery for four years.

The Fall of the Yuan

The signs of the fall of the ruling Yuan dynasty were increasingly obvious during the 1350s. The Red Turbans, a peasant rebellion led by the followers of Míng Jiào 明教, a Chinese version of Manichaeism (a dualist religion founded in Iran and concerned with the struggle between good and evil), and by the White Lotus Buddhist sect (which worshipped an Eternal Mother and was outlawed by the Mongols) developed rapidly in central and south China. (The Red Turbans rebellion should not be confused with the much earlier Yellow Turbans rebellion, discussed in the article in Volume 1 on the Han-dynasty warlord and general *Cáo Cāo 曹操.) Although a physically strong young man, Zhu Yuanzhang was not yet adventurous enough to join either the government forces nor any of the rebels at this early stage. Only after his monastery was burned by the Mongols, and its members forced to take sides to survive, did Zhu make up his mind to join the rebels after repeated divination. In 1352, he became a soldier

*People marked with an asterisk have entries in this dictionary.

under the command of a local Red Turban leader Guō Zǐxīng 郭子兴 (d. 1355) and began the path toward toppling the Mongols. Guo was so impressed by Zhu's appearance as well as his bravery in battles that he promoted him to be a member of Guo's bodyguards. He also offered his foster daughter, whose surname was Mǎ 马, in marriage to Zhu; she would become Empress Ma (1332–1382) of the Ming empire. After winning battle after battle, Guo was killed by rival forces in 1355, and Zhu took command. He expanded his realm quickly and recruited several hundred followers from his native region. Among these new recruits, twenty-four, including Xú Dá 徐达 (1332–1385) and Tāng Hé 汤和 (1326–1395), became the core of his military elite fighting force.

Zhu Yuanzhang soon captured Nanjing and made this his capital. He then advanced to Níngguó 宁国, Huīzhōu 徽州, and Yángzhōu 扬州. In 1361, Zhu assumed the title of Duke of Wu and over time became one of the three most powerful warlords in south China. Zhu's strategic position, however, was not as favorable as those of his main rivals, Chén Yǒuliàng 陈友谅 (1320–1363), who ruled the Húguǎng 湖广 region of the middle course of the Yangzi (Chang) River, and Zhāng Shìchéng 张士诚 (1321–1367), who controlled the Suzhou area, since Zhu's realm was located between the two areas.

Zhu decided that he had to defeat the more powerful Chen first. He believed that Zhang Shizheng would remain neutral in order to let the other two fight to the death, and in this way a two-front war could be avoided. In 1363, Zhu took the initiative to attack the superior navy of Chen Youliang at Lake Poyang. This became one of the greatest water battles in history, with both sides suffering extremely heavy losses. Several times, Zhu Yuanzhang was almost killed or captured, but eventually it was Chen Youliang who was shot in the head with an arrow, by accident, while retreating. Chen's force eventually collapsed after its commander in chief was killed.

Zhu then concentrated his powers on Suzhou. After defeating his rival in 1367, he took the title of Prince of Wú 吴王, which Zhang Shizheng had once conferred upon himself. In early 1368, at age forty, Zhu proclaimed himself Emperor Hongwu and his dynasty as the Ming, meaning "clear." When the rule of the south was almost consolidated, Zhu sent a large expedition force led by Xu Da and Cháng Yùchūn 常遇春 (1330–1369) to drive out the Mongols in the north. In September 1368, the Ming army captured Beijing and forced the last Yuan emperor, Togon Temür (r. 1333–1368), to flee to the steppe.

Establishing a Dynasty

As emperor of a new dynasty, Hongwu's first task was to legitimize his rule and assert Han Chinese dominance. Even while conquering China, he had been keen to cultivate close links with the Chinese literati, schooled in Confucian classics; as ruler he turned to them for strategic planning and institution formation.

Hongwu had studied classics, history, and literature under the close instruction of the most prominent scholars of the time, such as Sòng Lián 宋濂 (1310–1381) and Liú Jī 刘基 (1311–1375), so he was well versed in Confucianism when his dynasty was established. Among many possible choices of ideology, he abandoned Buddhism, Daoism (Taoism), and the White Lotus doctrine for populist Confucian tradition. In order to erase any connection with the Red Turban movement and to maintain the stability of his new dynasty, he soon issued a decree to prohibit unorthodox religious sects, especially the White Lotus sect and the Ming Jiao.

Forming Institutions

Emperor Hongwu wanted to establish a dynasty that would last forever, so he carefully designed institutions inspired by such Confucian classics as the *Classic of Documents* (*Shūjīng* 书经 or *Shàngshū* 尚书) and the *Records of Rites* (*Lǐjì* 礼记). For example, he installed the *lǐjiǎ* 里甲 census system all over the country: every eleven households formed a *jia*; ten *jia* made a *li*. All households had a chance to be the chief of a *jia* or a *li* by annual rotation, and everyone in a *li* was supposed to know each other and guarantee the behavior of the fellow members. A doorplate was put on each household, indicating the names, ages, and registered professions of its members. This institution was responsible for taxation and labor services. Zhu later added a judicial function, so that civil disputes were settled by these units.

Zhu Yuanzhang also drafted a set of codes guaranteeing stability and promoting Confucian virtue. He promulgated the "August Ming Ancestral Instruction" (*Huáng Míng zǔxùn* 皇明祖训), which prescribed rules for his household and princes. Most of his sons, grandsons, and nephews were assigned principalities at strategic points of the country. Each of the princes received a palace, a generous annual revenue, and a guard of three thousand to twenty thousand soldiers. They were expected to protect China in the borderlands and support the court whenever needed.

This system was not successful in the long run, as many of the princes committed serious crimes that invited heavy punishments and even the death penalty. Soon after Hongwu's death, his fourth son, the Prince of Yān 燕 (Zhū Dì 朱棣, 1360–1424), went even further by usurping the throne of his nephew Emperor Jiànwén 建文 (r. 1399–1402) and proclaiming the reign name *Yǒnglè 永乐 (r. 1403–1424) as the third Ming emperor.

Hongwu was also deeply involved in the legislation of the *Great Ming Code* (*Dà Míng lǜ* 大明律), the foundation of the Ming legal system. It was revised at least seven times during his reign, and

One of a pair of guardians that line the Sacred Way, a path leading to the Thirteen Ming Tombs in a valley outside Beijing, the largest of which belongs to Emperor Yongle. Emperor Hongwu's tomb is located near modern-day Nanjing. Photo by Joan Lebold Cohen.

Zhu made it a rule that not a single character of the code could be altered after his death. The succeeding Qīng 清 dynasty (1644–1911/1912) inherited a large part of this code, and its influences on the daily life of the Chinese extended well into the twentieth century.

Purging Enemies and Rivals

While the punishments found in the *Great Ming Code* are relatively moderate, Zhu has been portrayed as a ruthless tyrant due to the harsh measures he took during political struggles. Certainly there were times when Zhu resorted to heavy punishments to cope with serious social disorder and to suppress challenges to his rule. There were in fact four major purges, or "great cases," that took a heavy toll during his reign and cast a dense pall over his rule.

The first purge is known as the Prestamped Document case and occurred in 1376, when Zhu executed hundreds of local officials and underlings who were found guilty of simplifying reporting procedures by "prestamping" fiscal documents. This was an old practice of the Yuan, in which officials stamped their official seal on uncompleted report forms of tax revenue shipments to Nanjing so that the exact amount of materials arriving in the capital could be correctly recorded, notwithstanding any possible loss during transportation. Zhu maintained that this was a hidden form of corruption and a continuation of what he considered barbarous Mongol practices. This case could be seen as a sign that Zhu had started to distrust the literati officials, perhaps suspecting them of despising his humble origins, since in the early years of Ming rule many Confucian scholars had preferred to live in seclusion when called upon to serve at court.

The second purge is known as the Hu Weiyong case, and involved Hú Wéiyōng 胡惟庸 (d. 1380), the prime minister under Hongwu. Hu was charged with the crime of high treason for plotting to seize imperial power. Alongside the councilor and his associates, thousands of their alleged followers were executed. Hongwu's infamous secret police, the Jinyiwei (Embroidered-Uniform Guard), continued the purge over the following fourteen years, putting to death as many as forty thousand people. In his wrath toward treason and his fear of losing power, the emperor abolished the position of prime minister permanently to concentrate power and responsibilities in his own hands. The Six Ministries of the central government—namely, the Ministries of Personnel, Revenue, Rites, War, Justice, and Works—were now under the direct coordination of the emperor. It thus became an extremely demanding position to be the emperor, as shown in the records that state that Zhu needed to make decisions on over ten thousand matters over several days' time. In exhaustion, his successors developed an advisory body, the Grand Secretariat, which played a similar role to that of the grand councilors but with a much weaker institutional foundation.

The third purge is known as the Guo Huan case, and it involved the Vice Minister of Revenue Guō Huán 郭桓 (d. 1385). Guo was charged with the crime of stealing over seven million *piculs* (one *picul* equals about 130 pounds, or 60 kilograms) of government grain. He was put to death with hundreds of tax collectors and minor officials. Realizing that corruption was widespread, the astonished emperor started to issue his series of *Grand Pronouncements*, which recorded measures to punish both commoners and officials for corruption and other misdeeds. It expressed his personal standards of right or wrong and served as an instruction of exemplary cases supplementing the code in judicial judgments.

Among other rules, the *Grand Pronouncements* allowed local people to capture corrupted officials and send them straight to the palace for trial, permitted the commoners to communicate with Zhu in person, and gave more control to local society, at least in the capital region near Nanjing.

The fourth major purge is known as the Lan Yu case. As a victorious commander who repeatedly defeated the Mongols, General Lán Yù 蓝玉 was reportedly an arrogant and self-willed man. In 1393, he was prosecuted for plotting a mutiny. This was followed by a purge of over fifteen thousand nobility and military officers, in a similar fashion to the Hu Weiyong case. The real reason for this massacre is unclear, but it is generally believed that Hongwu seized upon this trial as an excuse to eliminate possible threats by senior military leaders to his grandson and heir apparent, Zhū Yǔnwén 朱允炆 (1377–1402), whose father, the original crown prince Zhū Biāo 朱标 (1355–1392), died prematurely the previous year.

Legacy and Interpretations

Emperor Hongwu died in 1398 at seventy years of age. Although imperial power had been consolidated under his well-designed institutions and the purges of possible enemies, the elimination of experienced generals resulted in the vulnerability of the court against the later coup d'état led by the Prince of Yan. Many of Hongwu's original institutions were maintained by the usurper, however, in order to claim his own legitimacy, thus further enhancing the founding emperor's impact on the later course of the Ming dynasty.

Hongwu undoubtedly gave no mercy to those he categorized as his enemies or rivals. During his long rule, however, he generally paid more attention to the common people than did most Chinese emperors. Even in the realm of law, in which he is bitterly criticized, it is obvious that his harsh legal policy was short-lived and that his legal attitude underwent many developments over time. Many cases of amnesty and mercy, as well as policies of redemption, illustrate that the steel-minded emperor's attitude toward punishment might have undergone revisions in response to his social reality. He could be harsh in order to eliminate what was evil in his own eyes, but he could also be lenient to achieve his goals.

Hongwu is also criticized as being inconsistent in many of his policies. It is understandable, however, that in founding a dynasty, the emperor might experiment in order to find the right form of institutions. Indeed, during the thirty-one years of his rule, he continuously improved his policies and legal codes to cope with new problems and to try to achieve perfection. Consequently, the Ming shaped the style of Chinese government and its legal system even after the fall of the dynasty, so much so that the effects can still be felt in the modern era.

Some historians suggest that the policies instituted by Hongwu were aimed at increasing his personal power. This may well be correct, but it is worthwhile reconsidering whether or not this was actually his purpose or simply the means to accomplish higher ideals. Given the extraordinary path of the emperor's rise to power, and also the strokes of good luck at many turning points of his life, it just might be that Hongwu believed that he was chosen by the heavens to rule China, and that he must keep to this mandate at all costs and fight any oppositions to the divine will that had put him on the throne.

TAM Ka-chai
Hong Kong Baptist University

Further Reading

Chu, Hung-lam 朱鴻林. (Ed.). (2010). *Ming Taizu de zhiguo linian jiqi shijian* 明太祖的治國理念及其實踐 [*Ming Taizu's ideas on statecraft and their implementation*]. Hong Kong: The Chinese University Press.

Dreyer, Edward L. (1982). *Early Ming China*. Stanford, CA: Stanford University Press.

Farmer, Edward L. (1995). *Zhu Yuanzhang & early Ming legislation: The reordering of Chinese society following the era of Mongol rule*. Leiden, The Netherlands: E. J. Brill.

Jiang Yonglin. (2011). *The Mandate of Heaven and the* Great Ming Code. Seattle: University of Washington Press.

Langlois, John D. (1988). The Hung-wu reign, 1368–98. In Frederick W. Mote and Denis Twitchett (Eds.). *The Cambridge history of China: Vol. 7. The Ming dynasty, 1368–1644: Part 1* (pp.107–181). Cambridge, UK: Cambridge University Press.

Tam Ka-chai 譚家齊. (2001). *Ming Taizu dui xingfa qingzhong de taidu shangpian: Taizu yongxing taidu de yanbian guiji* 明太祖對刑罰輕重的態度(上篇)—太祖用刑態度的演變軌跡 [Ming Taizu's (r. 1368–1398) attitudes towards punishment (part 1): The track of Taizu's changing attitudes]. *Journal of Chinese Studies, 41*, 87–109.

Tam Ka-chai 譚家齊 (2002). *Ming Taizu dui xingfa qingzhong de taidu xiapian: cong shezui kan Taizu dui xingfa qingzhong de taidu* 明太祖對刑罰輕重的態度(下篇)—從赦罪看太祖執行刑罰輕重的態度 [Ming Taizu's (r. 1368–1398) attitudes towards punishment (Part 2): Taizu's attitudes on punishments as revealed in his application of amnesties]. *Journal of Chinese Studies, 42*, 213–245.

Tam Ka-chai 譚家齊. (2004). *Cong Taizu Huangdi qinlu kan Ming Taizu xiuding Zuxun lu de yuanyin*

從太祖皇帝欽錄看明太祖修訂祖訓錄的原因 [A re-examination on Ming Taizu's reasons for revising the *Zuxun lu* in the light of the *Taizu Huangdi Qinlu*]. *Journal of Chinese Studies, 44,* 83–103.

Tam Ka-chai 譚家齊. (2007). *Ming Taizu Yuzhi da gao zai Hongwu chao yihou xingyong qingkuang xin-tan* 明太祖御製大誥在洪武朝以後行用情況新探 [An-examination on the legal authority of Zhu Yuanzhang's *Grand Pronouncement (Dagao)* after the Hongwu reign]. *Journal of Chinese Studies, 47,* 73–91.

Teng, Ssu-yü. (1976). Chu Yüan-chang. In L. Carrington Goodrich & Chaoying Fang (Eds.), *Dictionary of Ming biography, 1368–1644* (Vol.1, pp. 381–392). New York: Columbia University Press.

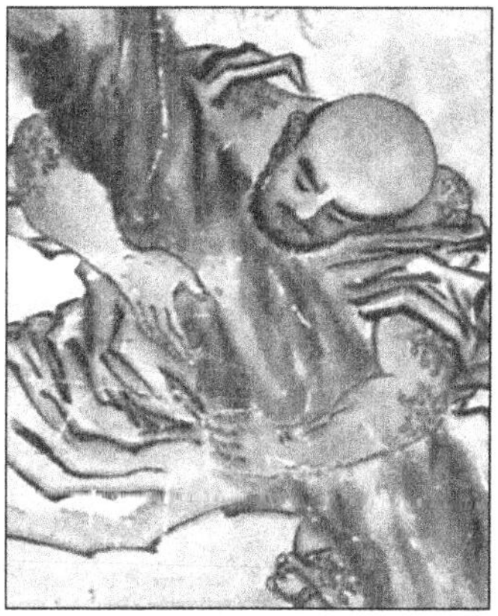

Jīn Shèngtàn

金圣叹

1608–1661—Literary critic

Alternate names: Jīn Cǎi 金采, Rénruì 人瑞; courtesy names: Ruòcǎi 若采, Shèngtàn 圣叹

Summary

Jin Shengtan was a major innovative force in Chinese language and literature during the late Ming and early Qing dynasties. His critical works on popular fiction and drama, most notably on *Water Margin* and *The Story of the Western Wing*, promoted the writing of commentary into a literary genre in its own right; both became the definitive versions of these highly popular works of literature until the twentieth century. His promotion and use of vernacular (spoken) language helped pave the way for the literary modernization in the twentieth century.

Jin Shengtan's literary achievements capped two centuries of dramatic economic, social, and cultural change. In the sixteenth century, as the Chinese economy became the destination for over two-thirds of the world's silver, the attendant commercialization and urbanization profoundly disrupted traditional social hierarchies. Confronted with the growing impact of monetization, Chinese thinkers, writers, and critics struggled to make sense of this brave new world of silver. The most daring among them advocated for moral renewal in the face of what they identified as rampant profiteering and political opportunism, placing a premium on the individual—irrespective of the person's social background—as a locus for morally genuine action. Such new approaches to Confucian and Buddhist concepts gained traction, thanks to a burgeoning print commerce.

At the same time, in a quest for cultural authenticity, literati turned to folk sources that they frequently refashioned. As part of an unprecedented literati interest in literary works written in vernacular rather than classical Chinese, Jin Shengtan produced new editions of two popular works, *Water Margin* (*Shuǐhǔ zhuàn* 水浒传), a story about a group of outlaws, and *The Story of the Western Wing* (*Xīxiāng jì* 西厢记), a love story about two talented, beautiful, and respectable youths.

Illustration by Chen Hongshou to *Story of the Western Wing*. Jin Shengtan commented upon this work by the Yuan dynasty playwright Wang Shifu.

Synthesizing elements from Buddhist literature, Confucian examination culture, and the literary marketplace, Jin Shengtan amplified the original stories with his own extensive commentary embedded throughout the text. Despite the existence of prior commentaries on fiction and drama, Jin's project was arguably the first that turned the writing of commentary into a literary genre in its own right. Through his literary thought and practice as exemplified in his two blockbuster commentaries, Jin Shengtan popularized new notions of the self, community, and literary value that were to have an enduring impact on Chinese literature ever after.

A New Literati Life

Jin Shengtan's novel approach to self and community is apparent in his naming practices. Originally he was known as Jīn Cǎi 金采, with the courtesy name of Ruòcǎi 若采. According to some records, he changed his name during the

Míng 明 dynasty (1368–1644) in order to sit a second time for the civil service examination after a spectacular failure in his first attempt. According to others, he adopted that name upon the inception of the Qīng 清 dynasty (1644–1911/1912). Irrespective of the precise timing, his new personal name was Rénruì 人瑞, and his courtesy name, Shèngtàn 圣叹 ("the sage sighed"); the latter was a highly symbolic choice. When asked about the meaning of his new name of Shengtan, Jin referred the interlocutor to two passages in the *Analects* (*Lúnyǔ* 论语). Through the allusion, Jin hoped to evoke one of *Confucius's 孔子 (551–479 BCE) favorite disciples, the free-spirited Zēng Diǎn 曾点; however, Jin's adoption of this name went beyond a symbolic gesture of invoking a historical exemplar. In due course, Jin Shengtan transformed his new name into an all-encompassing public persona that commanded attention. First, in the spirit of social iconoclasm, he adopted this epithet to refer to himself, thus leveling the customary distinctions between honorific and humilific (or anti-honorific) self-referents. Second, his contemporaries began to call him Shengtan or Master Shengtan, as though the name itself signaled that he had become a local celebrity. Finally and most importantly, in an era when most literati were reluctant to publicly disclose their involvement with popular literature, Jin visibly deployed Shengtan as the primary authorial person of his vernacular commentaries. In fact, so enduring has Jin's coinage proven to be that even modern scholars refer to him exclusively by that name rather than by his personal names of Jin Cai or Jin Renrui.

Jin's bold outlook on life and literature was undoubtedly shaped by the city of his birth and lifelong residence, Suzhou. Located on the Grand Canal, by the sixteenth century Suzhou had become the empire's most important commercial city. Not only was it Ming China's premier center for the manufacture of silk and cotton and of all manner of sophisticated handicrafts, but it also assumed pride of place among the major cultural centers in China. This cultural emphasis was palpable for the young Jin as he grew up in a scholarly family. By all accounts, the family's pursuit of learning did not yield much wealth, but it engendered an abiding devotion to the world of book learning and education. Young Jin observed that his father recited the Confucian classics at night in what appeared to be a state of happiness. Jin developed a similarly deep affection for books, but in his case, his most enduring affinities were reserved for titles outside the bounds of the standard Confucian canon. He attended school at the relatively late age of nine, and while he was alternately puzzled and bored by the teacher's lectures on the Confucian classics, he later, as part of the fashioning of his public persona, fondly reminisced about all the books that he discovered on

*People marked with an asterisk have entries in this dictionary.

his own. Among the volumes that he singled out among his early literary enchantments, we find what modern scholarship has identified as some of the masterpieces of literature in Chinese, namely the *Lotus Sutra* (*Fǎhuá jīng* 法华经), *Qū Yuán's 屈原 (c. 339–c. 278 BCE) "Encountering Sorrow" ("Lísāo" 离骚), and *Sīmǎ Qiān's 司马迁 (c. 145–86 BCE) *Records of the Grand Historian* (*Shǐjì* 史记). With the exception of the first, all of the others figured among the titles of what Jin later famously termed the "books by/for/about geniuses" (*cáizǐ shū* 才子书).

Early in life, in what was the fiercely competitive environment of Suzhou, Jin aspired to succeed through the conventional route of the civil service examination. He attained the rank of a licentiate, the lowest rung of the official ladder of success, perhaps as early as his late teens, but eventually, with further progress evidently stalled, he poured his energy in the pursuit of other, newly fashionable pursuits among literati. For one, perhaps in keeping with family tradition and as part of his preparations for the civil service exams, Jin built a library of fine editions. For another, he began to style himself as a teacher for the members of his own immediate family and may have tutored others as well. As was the case with other talented men who routinely failed the examinations, his own lack of progress did not stop him from compiling model writings for others to study. To that end, he put together a posthumously published prose anthology, *The Must Read Writings by and for Geniuses in the World* 天下才子必读书. Decidedly more unconventional was the choice of another text he believed capable of instilling the art of attentive reading and resulting good writing. In the last of his lengthy and highly rhetorical prefaces to *Water Margin*, Jin addressed his ten-year-old son to introduce him to what Jin postulated as the ultimate method to comprehend not just *Water Margin*, but all prose texts old and new. Inspired by his own abiding fascination with the trials of *Water Margin*'s bandit-heroes, Jin thought that his edition would tap into a boy's natural curiosity while ultimately honing superior writing skills. Flying in the face of official and parental injunctions against *Water Margin*, Jin's "Fifth Book of Genius" appeared in 1644 and became instantly notorious.

Jin's second major work, the *Western Wing* commentary published under the title "Sixth Book of Genius," may well have taken its inspiration from Jin's other major social circle—his friends—many of whom shared Jin's abiding interest in Buddhism. He formed close and lifelong friendships with other Suzhou men such as Wáng Zhuóshān 王斫山 (fl. 1656). Jin also cultivated enduring bonds with Hán Zhù 韩住 (fl. 1644–1656), Xú Zēng 徐增 (1612–c.1661), and other lay Buddhists. In one surviving work, Jin Shengtan and a number of his dharma friends test each other's acumen and wit with koans (*gōng'àn* 公案), the kind of riddles commonly deployed in Zen

(Chán 禅) Buddhism to assess a person's progress on the path to enlightenment. If the many poems addressed to Buddhist masters are any indication, Jin also entertained close relationships with eminent monks. Furthermore, Jin himself mastered the art of the oral explication of Buddhist texts. In 1644, he was said to have taught the dharma in one of the major temples of Suzhou. In 1648, he lectured to audiences in his friend Han Zhu's studio, the Guanhua Hall on an elevated platform, with friends, disciples, Buddhist monks, and some skeptical strangers in attendance. Having read widely in all manner of Buddhist texts, Jin even composed his own, now-lost Buddhist treatise on enlightenment, which he expounded on such occasions. According to Xu Zeng, Jin abhorred conventional socializing, but always accepted two kinds of invitations, namely, lecturing on the dharma and drinking with friends. While such a conjunction of activities may seem contradictory—after all, one of the vows for Buddhist laymen and monks alike was to abstain from alcohol—to Jin, they may well have both represented viable means to realize an authentic and free-spirited existence, a view born out by Jin's enthusiastic endorsement of the iconoclastic monk Lǔ Zhìshēn 鲁智深, a character in *Water Margin* who disregards his monastic vows of abstinence but is an otherwise admirable man. As we shall see, it was Jin's *Western Wing* commentary, published in 1656, that most explicitly drew on Buddhist rhetoric to produce a novel understanding of the meaning of that work.

After the successes of his *Fifth and Sixth Books of Genius*, Jin was still engaged with commenting on other works in his prospective canon of six new classics as well as on other titles when his life came to an abrupt end. In 1661, the Shunzhi Emperor (r. 1644–1661) died. On the occasion of the public mourning for his passing in Suzhou, a city with a history of protest against unjust governance going back at least two hundred years, a group of literati demonstrated against the harsh reign of the local magistrate, an episode that became known as the "Case of the Lament at the City Temple" (*Kūmiào'àn* 哭庙案). The newly established Qing dynasty, intent on consolidating its control of southern China, turned this local protest into a means to cow the local elite into submission. Perhaps Jin Shengtan's notoriety was partly responsible for being singled out as a ringleader among the hundreds of participants. In what has been termed a show trial of the young Qing state, Jin, along with nearly twenty other men, was condemned to death. Thus, as he was to lament in his testamentary poem, his life's work, the annotation of other "works of genius," would be left unfinished. Despite Jin's unfortunate end, the common people of Suzhou sympathized with his plight and ultimately, despite the hateful glee of some staunch traditionalists who reveled in Jin's untimely demise, his literary legacy survived intact.

Lu Zhishen, one of the characters from *Water Margin*, uprooting a tree. Jin Shengtan wrote an influential commentary upon the novel. Mural in the Long Corridor in the Summer Palace in Beijing.

Jin life's work became synonymous with the idea of "books of genius"; in other words, Jin had instantiated the idea that a literary work could be defined primarily through literary skill rather than by virtue of the extraliterary, social criteria that had previously dominated the evaluation of literature. In short, literary technique trumped such measures as the social status of the author, the prestige of the genre, the use of classical language, or the presence of morally uplifting content. So influential was Jin's legacy that even when the modern reformer *Liáng Qǐchāo 梁启超 (1873–1929) famously called for new fiction to rejuvenate the Chinese people, among the examples of good writing that he held up for emulation was none other than Jin's *Water Margin*. The following sections examine how print commerce, reformist philosophy, and Buddhist rhetoric served as intellectual and practical resources that enabled Jin Shengtan to lastingly redefine the popular literary canon despite strong resistance from conservative quarters favoring traditional social and literary hierarchies.

Print Commerce and Literary Innovation

The expansion of private and commercial publishing from the mid-sixteenth century onward proved to be one of the transformative aspects of literati life during the next century. After a lull in publishing in the fifteenth century that mirrored the broader economic and cultural slump of that period, several regions within the Ming empire began to distinguish themselves through a renewed vigor in both the quantity and quality of their publications. Located at the heart of major trade routes, Suzhou emerged as an important publishing hub where commercial publishing houses as well as private literati publishers redefined the literary landscape. The most eminent proponent of popular literature, Féng Mènglóng 冯梦龙 (1574–1646), hailed from greater Suzhou. Other critics from Suzhou were equally influential in the field of examination essay anthologies, assuming the role of a vanguard that began to contest the judgments of the government appointed examiners. Eventually, through the literary societies such as the Restoration Society (Fùshè 复社), Suzhou critics created pressure on official examiners to pass their talented members in greater numbers. Thus, the aura of Suzhou as the home of literary arbiters with an empire-wide following undoubtedly helped underwrite Jin's new approach to literary works.

Amid the increase of qualified candidates, regional quotas, and a stagnant number of official positions, literati from the south found it increasingly difficult to pass the civil service examinations. Many educated men turned to publishing as an alternative career that made use of their knowledge and commanded some respect. In some cases, Suzhou literati such as the playwright Zhāng Fèngyì 张凤翼 (1527–1613) acknowledged the flagrantly commercial nature of their publication ventures, but most others framed their publishing activities in more subtle terms irrespective of whether or not they earned their livelihood in this manner. By the time Jin Shengtan began publishing in the 1640s, he echoed the misgivings of many literati about outright commercial publishing as a form of "book burning." At the same time, he hoped that his own editions of *Water Margin* and *The Story of the Western Wing* would be so successful as to eclipse the many earlier and parallel editions of these popular works. Thus, like many of his peers, Jin sought to capitalize on ready access to skilled printers and bookshops, on lack of official oversight over publishing, and on his own literary reputation to harness the power of the burgeoning print commerce to disseminate his ideas. In short, even for a man with limited means at his disposal and with a willful contempt for the ways of the world, printing allowed Jin to make his mark.

Water Margin

One of the four Chinese classic novels of the Ming and Qing dynasties, *Shui hu zhuan* is based on historical events. The novel tells a tragic story of 108 people of different backgrounds who are forced to become rebel leaders on the lakeside Mount Liang. The book begins with treacherous officials of the Song court bullying their subordinates and their families, driving them into the camp of the Mount Liang rebels, led by Song Jiang. After many a successful battle against the government army, Song Jiang and his men surrender after the emperor makes them believe that they are being offered amnesty. The emperor then dispatches them to repulse the invasion of Liao, a kingdom established by the Nurchens north of Song, and to put down a series of peasant uprisings; many of the rebels die. The rest are then killed with poisoned wine "gifted" them by the emperor.

Water Margin is based on a true event that took place from 1119 to 1121, when Song Jiang led his thirty-five fellow rebels in fighting the government. Stories about the event later found their way into other compilations. The original text of *Water Margin* is long lost, but different block-printed editions, both simplified and detailed, remain. The detailed editions are more popular, and better known among them are the 120-chapter edition compiled and supplemented by Yang Dingjian around 1614, the 70-chapter edition edited by Jin Shengtan (1608–1661), and the 100-chapter edition published by Guo Xun during the reign of the Jiajing Emperor (1522–1566).

Water Margin has been interpreted differently by different people in different times. It has been either dismissed as advocating banditry or welcomed as singing the praises of heroism. In the 1950s the book was regarded as an ode to peasant uprisings. In the 1970s, however, Mao Zedong condemned it for setting a negative example, even though it had been one of his favorite childhood books. The stories from *Water Margin* are so popular that many efforts have been made to adapt them into dramas, films, and television series.

—Haiwang YUAN, *Western Kentucky University*

For Jin, the work that launched his career as a controversial critic and turned him into something of a local legend was not standard examination-related fare, but his edition of *Water Margin*, a novel that, on account of its theme of banditry, had been proscribed just two years prior to the appearance of Jin's version in 1644. Jin radically revised, streamlined, and reimagined *Water Margin* and published it under the title of *Fifth Book of Genius* 第五才子书. From its initial appearance, Jin's edition elicited very contradictory responses. Some seventeenth-century critics charged Jin with outright plagiarism; others criticized him for excessive meddling with the original by cutting out fifty chapters; others heralded him for turning an undervalued text into an instant classic. *Water Margin* had evolved over many centuries on an oral-literary continuum, but Jin's version unambiguously recruited it as a member of a new canon of texts, his self-styled "Books of Genius." In contrast to the moral exemplariness of the sages of old that defined the hallowed Confucian classics, in Jin's view *Water Margin* distinguished itself through its literary achievements: those of an alleged original author (created through Jin Shengtan's many unacknowledged revisions and fabrications); those of its perceptive and omnipresent commentator, Jin Shengtan; and those of the equally savvy prospective readers. In the deployment of a noisy, pervasive, and highly personal form of commentary, Jin singlehandedly fashioned a new social compact between author, commentator, and readers: everyone who was able to recreate and engage with Jin's interpretation stood the chance of becoming part of a circle of genius-like initiates capable of good writing and authentic moral action. This new approach to literature was developed with even more sophistication in Jin's second masterpiece, *The Story of the Western Wing* (1656). In treating the reading process as an interior process of unlocking hidden meanings within two controversial texts and within oneself to attain both greater writing skills and a genuine understanding of self and reality, Jin synthesized both Confucian and Buddhist notions of textuality in strikingly new ways.

Buddhist Rhetoric and Literary Modernity

Jin's socioliterary innovation was indebted to the broader philosophical trends that shaped the literary thought of the most famous late Ming figures. Beginning with *Wáng Yángmíng 王阳明 (1472–1529), a neo-Confucian philosopher and official, literati rethought the locus of experiential authority. Rather than locating what was morally authoritative in a universe that was external to the subject, Wang proposed a new synthesis between Confucian and Buddhist thought. According to this view, each person could discover what was morally authentic within him- or herself. Iconoclastic thinkers like *Lǐ Zhì 李贽 (1527–1602) took this moral leveling of the playing field in favor of "everyman" even further and advocated that it was the socially marginal figures that exemplified the untainted goodness that he called "the child's mind" (*tóngxīn* 童心). Importantly, Li Zhi singled out *Water Margin* and *The Story of the Western Wing* as literary works that represented this "genuine quality" in textual form. Thus in Li's scheme, texts that had been popular for centuries, but had been widely understood as pure entertainment, now advanced to the status of morally serious, if not exemplary, literature.

At the same time that Wang Yangming was reimagining Confucianism after his own intense engagement with Buddhism and Daoism (Taoism), a group of eminent monks revitalized Buddhism through monastic reform and extensive engagement with lay people. Among them, four men known stood out—namely, Yúnqī Zhùhóng 云栖袾宏 (1535–1615), Zǐbó Zhēnkě 紫柏真可 (1543–1603), Hānshān Déqīng 憨山德清 (1546–1623), and Ǒuyì Zhìxù 藕益智旭 (1599–1655). These monks made lay practice a foundation for their own understanding of Buddhism, setting the groundwork for lay Buddhists in later centuries.

What allowed these monks to attract followers among the literati class was that they portrayed Confucian virtue as a specialized case of a more universal principle of Buddhist truth. Moreover, they advocated means of religious cultivation that were accessible to Buddhist lay practitioners and downplayed the need for monastic affiliation in order to attain enlightenment: the recitation of the name of the Amitabha Buddha (*niànfó* 念佛), the release of animals originally destined for human consumption, the promotion of ledgers to keep track of merits and demerits, and the publication of Buddhist scriptures. Just as Confucian practice was taking a turn toward commoners, Buddhism attracted many lay followers during this period as the large number of biographies of eminent lay practitioners put together by Péng Shàoshēng 彭绍升 (1740–1796), the most prominent lay Buddhist of the Qing dynasty, attests. Thus large number of laymen participated in Buddhist practice as proponents of a worldview that emphasized compassion for all and advocated detachment from worldly possessions and success.

Jin Shengtan developed his own idiosyncratic uses of Buddhist thought, literature, and practice. Jin noted that he began studying Buddhism when he was very young. As noted earlier, he claimed to have discovered the *Lotus Sutra* amid his precocious readings as a young teen. In his adult years, his Buddhist reading encompassed many scriptures associated with the Chan tradition, such as the *Sutra of Perfect Enlightenment* (*Yuánjuéjīng* 圆觉经), the *Surangama Sutra* (*Lèngyánjīng* 楞严经), and the *Great Compassion Dharani Sutra* (*Dà bēi āluóní* 大悲阿罗尼), among others. He read extensively in the different koan collections, creating an anthology with his own commentary on twenty-five famous cases. In the manner of the Chan masters of old, he and his Buddhist lay friends also created a "spoken record" (*yǔlù* 语录) of their own attempts at trying to show their understanding of famous koans. Most significantly, perhaps, Jin innovatively blended Buddhist concepts, language, concepts, and community with the vernacular tradition of fiction and drama.

Jin's engagement with Buddhism was particularly apparent in his commentary on *The Story of the Western Wing*. In this commentary, Jin Shengtan perfected the art of writing as though he was giving a Buddhist-style lecture in informal spoken language to a group of fellow initiates, admirers, and like-minded spirits. In the opening preface, someone asked Shengtan why he felt compelled to annotate and print *The Story of the Western Wing*. Then, in answer to that interlocutor, it is noted that "Shengtan said," with the answer that followed being couched in the highly unusual, casual "I" form (*wǒ* 我) that colors much of the remainder of the text.

The very fact that the question was addressed to the persona of "Shengtan" suggests that Jin assumed the role of a serious yet chatty master at the onset of the text, treating what had been an amusing love comedy as a profound text that demonstrated at least two major Buddhist-flavored teachings. On the one hand, the written words allowed the reader to capture an internal vision of each individual character as if they represented the visualization of particular Buddhist deities commonly found in Buddhist sutras. On the other hand, the immersion into the characters' states of mind, their perceptions of themselves and others, and their actions were meant to enable the reader to vicariously experience their intense feelings, but with a view toward being able to transcend the illusory dream of existence. In his introductory essay, Jin drew upon several famous koans to invoke the parallels between the real yet illusory nature of fiction on the one hand and the illusory, yet seemingly real, nature of reality on the other. It was a point that would elaborated much more explicitly in China's novelistic masterpiece, *Cáo Xuěqín's 曹雪芹 (c. 1724–c. 1766) *The Dream of the Red Chamber* (*Hónglóumèng* 红楼梦), also known as *The Story of the Stone* (*Shítóujì* 石头记).

The Afterlife of Jin Shengtan

In terms of the success of Jin's commentaries, his wildest hopes were realized. His versions of *Water Margin* and *The Story of the Western Wing* became the definitive versions of these highly popular works of literature until the twentieth century. As his contemporaries were quick to point out, everyone who took on the newly fashionable pursuit of bringing other popular fiction and plays to the fore through comprehensive commentaries modeled themselves in one way or another on Jin's example. Among these, we may mention the father and son team of Máo Lún 毛纶 and Máo Zōnggāng 毛宗岗, responsible for highly influential commentaries on the play *The Lute* (*Pípá jì* 琵琶记) and *The Romance of the Three Kingdoms* (*Sānguó zhì yǎnyì* 三国志演义), Zhāng Zhúpō's 张竹坡 commentary on *Jin Ping Mei*; and Wāng Xiàngxù 汪象旭 and Huáng Zhōuxīng's 黄周星 commentary on *Journey to the West* (*Xīyóu jì* 西游记), to name just some of the most prominent. Thus even though Jin had not completed his roster of alternative masterpieces before his death, other men in Suzhou and in other parts of the empire followed in his footsteps and fleshed out this new canon with other old and new stalwarts of the fictional repertoire.

Thanks to such commentaries, fiction became upwardly mobile, reaching readers from the court to the urban literati to those residing in the hinterland. These and other annotated versions increasingly bound together readers in the far-flung corners of the Qing empire, drawing people from many social status groups into the ambit of their influence. Furthermore, in dramatizing well-meaning, ordinary protagonists in conflict with the two primary institutions of Chinese life—namely, local and imperial government and the extended family—the works opened up new ways of what it meant to be an individual in the sprawling landscape of late imperial China. Arguably, Jin's championing of a novel and a drama as the *Fifth and Sixth Book of Genius* pioneered the possibility of a common language beyond the classics that would find its ultimate realization in the context of the literary modernization of the twentieth century. Even though most proponents of the early twentieth-century May Fourth movement (a movement to cast off traditional Confucian values and call for cultural rejuvenation and a more modern worldview) decried Jin Shengtan's alleged conservatism, it was, ironically, Jin who had helped usher in the adoption of the vernacular language as a subtle, versatile, and vigorous medium of communication. Retrospectively, his new canon had laid a foundation for yet another new form of written Chinese to be rapidly popularized between the 1910s and the 1930s, which in turn enabled new forms of state building, community, and self not anticipated by the otherwise visionary Jin.

Patricia SIEBER
The Ohio State University

Further Reading

Chow, Kai-wing. (2004). *Publishing, culture, and power in early modern China*. Stanford, CA: Stanford University Press.

Jin Shengtan. (1990). How to read the *Fifth Book of Genius* (John C. Y. Wang, Trans.). In David L. Rolston (Ed.), *How to read the Chinese novel* (pp. 124–145). Princeton, NJ: Princeton University Press.

Rolston, David L. (1997). *Traditional Chinese fiction and fiction commentary: Reading and writing between the lines*. Stanford, CA: Stanford University Press.

Sieber, Patricia (2003). *Xixiang ji* editions, the bookmarket, and the discourse on obscenity: Wang Jide (d. 1623), Jin Shengtan (1608–1661), and the creation of uncommon readers. In Patricia Sieber, *Theaters of desire: Authors, readers, and the reproduction of early Chinese Song-drama, 1300–2000* (pp. 123–161). New York: Palgrave Macmillan.

Koxinga

Zhèng Chénggōng 郑成功

1624–1662—Sea lord, military folk hero, and conqueror of Taiwan

Alternate names: childhood name: Fukumatsu 福松; courtesy name Zhèng Sēn 郑森

Summary

Zheng Chenggong, better known as Koxinga and nicknamed the "Attila of the East," was the son of a Chinese sea lord and a Japanese mother. Like his father before him, Koxinga squeezed the East Asian trade routes to supply his military forces, which grew from a few hundred to more than 100,000 soldiers at their peak. Years of mutual slaughter between Koxinga and the new Qing dynasty led the Qing to depopulate the coast to cut off Koxinga's sources of supply. His conquest of the Dutch colony of Taiwan in 1662 brought the island into Chinese history for the first time, and he remains a controversial hero in both mainland China and Taiwan. Koxinga's image is split between those who regard him as a hero of Taiwan's independence from China and those who cite Koxinga as a symbol for Taiwan's reunification with China.

Koxinga: a sea lord, a pirate king; a half-Japanese marauder and fierce Chinese patriot; an anticolonial hero; a ruthless romantic; a mad tyrant; conqueror of Taiwan; savior and butcher; a benevolent god. Rarely has a historical figure earned such stormy epithets, and in truth all of these contradictory images are vital parts of the man, the myth, and the legend that is Koxinga.

The historical Koxinga left behind no diary and few personal records; what we know comes from scattered sources (mostly from his enemies). Even portrait artists from Europe to Asia never seemed to agree on what he looked like. Still, darkly as we might see him through the glass of time, what a spirited individual he must have been to incite such passions! In his brief thirty-eight years of life, Koxinga ruled a vast maritime trading empire, warred up and down the Chinese coast for fifteen years, and finally defeated the Dutch in one of their largest and richest colonies, Taiwan. Koxinga's conquest of Taiwan in 1662 brought the island firmly into Chinese history for the first time and became his lasting legacy.

Who was Koxinga, this sea lord, this man for all seasons and storms? We must begin with his family and with a place called Fujian Province. Although Koxinga was born in 1624 in Japan, his destiny was tied to the exploits of his father, Zhèng Zhīlóng 郑芝龙 (1604–1661), who was the first sea lord and an ambitious son of a remarkable province of China.

Fujian: The Other China

Fujian was the Portugal of imperial China. This southeastern province (with a land area larger than the country of Portugal) was home to China's finest sailors and shipwrights. If we look closely at a map of Fujian, its complex coastline is full of coves, bays, and great protective harbors. There are about a thousand islands, big and small, off its shores. A hundred miles (180 kilometers) across the sea lies the great island of Taiwan, which the Portuguese called Ilha Formosa ("beautiful island").

Historical Fujian, too, was beautiful and green, but life was hard even in the best of times. Fujian had very little farmland (only 7 to 8 percent arable land, including hill terraces) and was densely populated in a narrow strip along the coast. About 90 percent of Fujian was covered by mountains and hills that disrupted landward communications. Thus the people of coastal Fujian had a long history of depending on the sea for their food and livelihood.

Fujianese mariners built and navigated the largest wooden ships in history: the Ming "treasure fleets" that sailed from China to India and Africa from 1405 to 1433. After the Míng 明 dynasty (1368–1644) canceled its great ocean voyages in the fifteenth century, Fujian became known as a rogue province of smugglers and pirates. The coastal Fujianese, especially the Hokkiens (Mǐnnánrén 闽南人) of the south, were fiercely independent and defied government efforts to limit their mobility. Most coastal residents made a living from seasonal patterns of fishing, salt making, trading, and raiding. Some sons and daughters of Fujian, however, dreamed bigger and made their own rules. They did not simply sail across the sea—they lived on it until the land came home.

One such intrepid sailor was Zheng Zhilong, leader of the Zheng clan. Zheng was a man of the sea who huckstered, bribed, and battled his way to become a maritime overlord and one of the richest men in the world. All around the rise and fall of this man lay the dizzy world of maritime East Asia in the 1600s. Portuguese *fidalgos* (noble adventurers), Spanish galleon captains, Jesuit priests, and Dutch rogues, officers, and gentlemen were trying hard to break into this world dominated by Chinese and Japanese networks of trade and piracy. The Europeans soon met their match.

The Sea Lord

During his lifetime, the wily and dashing Zheng Zhilong was also known as Nicholas Iquan, Jasper (or Gaspard), Tei Shiryû, Ytcuam, or even Chinchillón. His many names matched a colorful career. The Spanish missionary Victorio Riccio (1621–1685) called him "Nicolas the apostate, a marvel of human fate, who rose up by most despicable chance to challenge kings and emperors" (Borao Mateo 2001, 586–587).

Zheng Zhilong was born in 1604 into the family of a minor Fujianese bureaucrat. As a teenager, he ran away from his hometown of Anhai and hustled around the docks in the Portuguese enclave of Macao, where he picked up some street Portuguese, a smattering of trade skills, and even a little Catholicism—he was baptized Nicholas Gaspard or Nicholas Iquan, though he never gave up worshipping his own sea gods. Zheng probably first visited Japan around age eighteen (c. 1622) and was captured by pirates, who let him go because he was too pretty and charming to kill. His sweet-talking skills soon served him well. He was taken under the wing of the wealthy Lǐ Dàn 李旦 (also known as Captain China, d. 1625), a master con man and leader of the Chinese merchants in Hirado (near Nagasaki in far western Japan).

It was also in Hirado that Zheng Zhilong met and married his first love: Lady Tagawa Matsu 田川松, whose name and lineage are disputed but who was possibly the daughter of a low-ranking samurai family. Zheng returned to Fujian to do business, leaving the pregnant Lady Tagawa to bear their child alone in Hirado. In late August (possibly the twenty-eighth) of 1624, the boy was born. Little else is known about the boy's early life, but storytellers would later spin miraculous yarns about howling storms and a gigantic whale with glowing eyes that leapt from the ocean before Lady Tagawa gave birth on Hirado's Senrigahama Beach (a stone pillar marks the supposed spot). The boy was given the Japanese childhood name of Fukumatsu 福松, officially named Zhèng Sēn 郑森, and later renamed Zheng Chenggong—but the world would eventually call him Koxinga.

Meanwhile the proud new father's star was rising. Zheng Zhilong's career in the 1620s took him far afield to work for the Dutch VOC (Vereenigde Oostindische Compagnie, or East India Company) as a translator, then a privateer, and then an independent pirate. By age twenty-seven, Zheng was popular with the Dutch in Taiwan—who, strangely enough, called him "Daddy." He learned from early setbacks and clawed his way up from pirate to sea lord, trounced Ming fleets in 1627, defeated a Dutch fleet in 1633, and smashed his last great pirate rival, Liú Xiāng 刘香, in 1635. The Ming state tried to buy him out with honors and admiralty. By age thirty-six (c. 1640), only a few years before fall of the Ming dynasty, Zheng Zhilong was the supreme commander of Fujianese military forces and the most important man in Fujian.

As a sea lord, Zheng was a maritime monopolist and an internationalist without equal. Among the sixty thousand men under his command, his loyal Black Guard of hundreds of African musketeers stood out for their size and skill. His fleet combined Fujianese pilots, Dutch muskets, Portuguese cannons, and Japanese steel. Hundreds of ships flying the Zheng flag carried silver, tea, silk, porcelain, guns, and spices across the trading networks from Japan to Southeast Asia. At his hometown of Anhai, Zheng built a personal castle ringed by waterways that allowed ships to sail directly into a special dock beneath his domicile. It was to this magnificent headquarters, in 1630, that he called his wife and firstborn son, whom he had not seen for years. Lady Tagawa was unable to travel but sent the seven-year-old boy on a lonely journey across the seas to Anhai. There, atop the battlements where his family banner fluttered, Zheng Zhilong embraced the young Koxinga for the first time and promised him that this brave new water world would one day be his.

Betrayal

This rich and corrupt world, however, came crashing down in 1644 with the collapse of the Ming empire. The Ming dynasty had been in decline since the mid-1500s, but when it finally fell to domestic rebellion, China was engulfed by decades of war and civil war. Rebels captured the imperial capital of Beijing in 1644, the last Ming emperor committed suicide, and the Manchus (a vigorous frontier people from beyond the Great Wall of China) invaded from the north to build a new empire: the Qīng 清 (1644–1911/1912). Loyalists fled south to carry on a Southern Ming resistance, and Zheng Zhilong and his province of Fujian were now threatened by dangers on all sides.

At first, Zheng generously supported the Southern Ming loyalists, donating silver and soldiers to prop up the exiled prince Zhū Yùjiàn 朱聿键 (1602–1646), who called himself Emperor Lóngwǔ 隆武. In gratitude, Emperor Longwu gave Zheng's firstborn son an honorary adoption into the imperial family, and so the young man was called Guó xìng yè 国姓爷 ("Lord of the Imperial Surname), pronounced "Kok-seng-ia" in the Hokkien dialect. The Dutch wrote this down as Cocksinja in 1653 and as Koxinga in 1670, and later English, French, and Spanish writers sought to improve upon it with bastardizations like Coxinga, Coccenyà , Cotsen, Cogseng, Con-seng, Kuesim, Cogsin, Coseng, Kue-sing, Quoesing, Coxiny, Quesin, Cocxima, and even the Latinized form Quaesingus (Keene 1951, 45; Borao Mateo 2001, 584). Zheng Zhilong, the original international man of mystery, would have been proud if he had lived to see his son's later fame.

Zheng quickly became disillusioned with the pompous Southern Ming ministers who wanted to rush into a reckless crusade against the Qing invaders. Was he now to throw away his naval and marine forces as cannon fodder? Would it not be more prudent to use Fujian's advantages in seaborne commerce to finance a network of strongholds in south China, contain the Qing onslaught, and plan a future counteroffensive, perhaps with the help of potential foreign allies like the Japanese, Portuguese, and Dutch? So Zheng argued in 1645, but his advice fell on deaf ears.

Then, in September 1646, Emperor Longwu and his court of quixotic ministers charged inland and were captured and killed. Zheng played no small role in this fiasco, since he had already withdrawn his border guards and decided to abandon the Ming court to its fate. The Qing forces, represented by Manchu Prince Bolo 博洛, made Zheng a grand offer: Fujian would be spared the horrors of war, and Zheng would be made viceroy of the seaboard provinces of Guangdong and Fujian. On 21 November 1646, Zheng accepted and traveled to Fuzhou (the capital of Fujian) to offer his fealty to the Manchus.

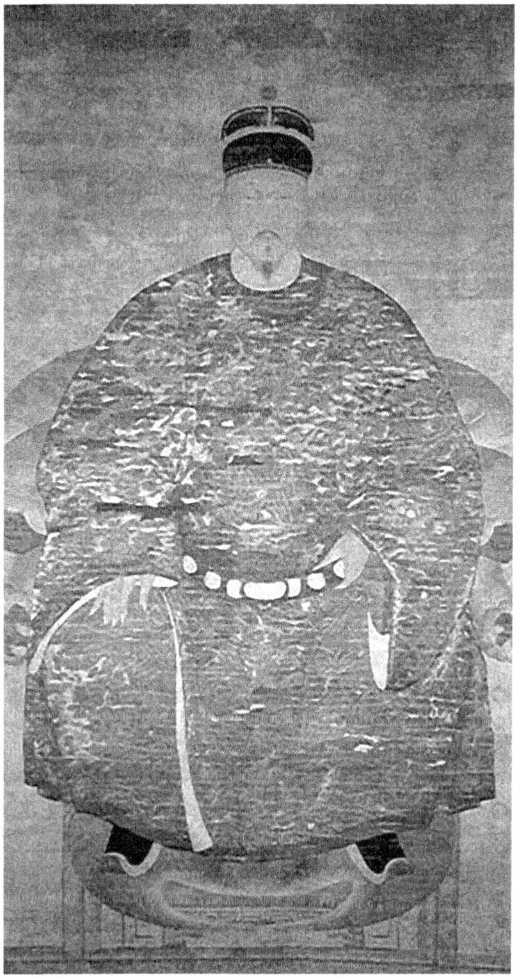

Portrait of Koxinga. Portraits of him disagree on what, exactly, he looked like. He was an heir to the maritime power structure built by his father, Zheng Zhilong.

Some hostile commentators (who can be very brave by proxy) have been quick to label Zheng a traitor to his country and his race. His own son Koxinga begged him not to join the Qing empire, saying that "a tiger cannot leave the mountain; a fish cannot leave the water," to which Zheng retorted that Koxinga was a mere boy who knew nothing of power and politics (Jiang 2004, 71–72). Koxinga had grown up with wealth, education, and honor by dint of his father's power as sea lord; he had not seen the ugliness of the world that his father had fought so hard to master. When Zheng had hugged the seven-year-old Koxinga for the first time atop Anhai castle, he had not been able to explain to his son just what it had taken to build it all.

Zheng Zhilong had been a risk taker all his life, but this last gamble tore his family apart. Koxinga pledged loyalty to the Southern Ming; a powerful nephew named Zhèng Cǎi 郑彩 also held off; and Zheng Zhilong's trusted brother Zhèng Hóngkuí 郑鸿逵 (alias Zhīfèng 芝凤) deserted him by putting out to sea with a good part of the fleet. These betrayals crippled Zheng's bargaining power, and Prince Bolo became suspicious that the sea lord was playing both sides in the Ming-Qing war. After days of hard feasting and hard drinking in Fuzhou, Prince Bolo abruptly ordered his soldiers to seize Zheng Zhilong. Too late, Zheng cried out to his faithful African musketeers, his Black Guards; many were cut down as they tried to rescue their lord, singing the name of St. James (who was their patron saint after they converted to Catholicism while enslaved by the Portuguese) as they fell (Boxer 1941, 437). Zheng was dragged to Beijing under armed guard; he would never see his homeland or the sea again.

Koxinga's Crusade

All of this, of course, only confirmed for Koxinga and the rest of the Zheng clan that the Manchus had planned treachery all along. (It did not occur to them—or they did not admit it to themselves—that their betrayals had helped to seal the downfall of Zheng Zhilong.) Not long after abandoning his father, Koxinga tragically lost his mother, who had finally joined him in China in 1645 only to commit suicide in early 1647 when Qing troops overran southern Fujian. Koxinga swore revenge against the Qing and seized control of the clan after a violent struggle for authority with his uncles and cousins. This was no mean feat for a man who was only twenty-two at the time of his father's fall and his mother's death, but Koxinga was a zealot who literally whipped his men into shape. By about 1651, at the age of twenty-seven, he overpowered his rivals and took complete control of the Zheng enterprise.

Over the next decade, Koxinga rebuilt his father's empire into a complex organization that warred for stockpiles and stockpiled for long-term war. To his father's musketeers, fireships, and men-of-war, Koxinga added cannoneers, pikemen, and a class of "iron men"—fearsome fighters clad from head to knees in bulletproof steel plate and wielding those polearms that the Dutch called "soap knives": battle swords lashed to staves as long as a man. These last iron giants were marvels to friends and foes alike and were said to be the strongest men in Fujian. Nationalist Japanese writers (both historical and dramatic) of the nineteenth and twentieth century would promote a different myth: the "iron men" must have been Japanese samurai, not Chinese soldiers, rallying behind the half-Japanese Koxinga.

Like his father before him, Koxinga squeezed the China–Japan–Southeast Asia trade routes to supply his military forces, which grew from a few hundred to more than 100,000 soldiers at their peak. His sailors also terrorized and looted coastal residents for grain and money. Trained by Zheng Zhilong and whipped by Koxinga, the seamen of Fujian were nearly indomitable in their own element.

From 1651 to 1654, Koxinga's armies attacked major ports and blockaded the cities of central and southern Fujian. In 1657, Koxinga sent a fleet of some five thousand ships and sixty thousand men northward to probe the coastal defenses of Zhejiang Province and the Yangzi (Chang) Delta region (near present-day Shanghai), the richest areas in China. And then, in the campaigns of 1658–1659, Koxinga's armada burst out of Fujian in an audacious strike at the economic heartland of the Qing empire.

His goal was Nanjing, the traditional southern capital of China, and Koxinga wanted an epochal showdown. Confident, even arrogant now, Koxinga moved deliberately and slowly so that the final battle would be as big as possible. With over eighty-five thousand infantry and a total invasion force numbering probably between 150,000 and 200,000, Koxinga felt that time was on his side. The Qing defenders barricaded the wide mouth of the Yangzi (the third longest river in the world) with massive chains, shipwrecks, cannon barges, and shore guns. Despite this, Koxinga's assault smashed through the Qing defenses in what was no doubt one of the largest amphibious maneuvers of the seventeenth century.

On 24 August 1659, the invasion force arrived at the high walls of Nanjing, and Koxinga seemed within an ace of a huge symbolic victory. Instead he made the blunder of his career: for two weeks, presuming that Nanjing would surrender to his overwhelming numbers, Koxinga did not launch any serious attacks. His generals urged him to storm the city immediately, but Koxinga took his time and even allowed his troops to celebrate his birthday by drinking themselves into oblivion. To his dismay, on 9 September, Qing soldiers charged out of Nanjing, bolstered by fresh cavalry and crack reinforcements. Koxinga's troops were routed, his navy was kept busy transporting the surviving troops to safety, and Gān Huī 甘辉, his best general and friend, was captured and killed. Koxinga wept.

The sea lord returned to his headquarters at Amoy Island (present-day Xiamen) in Fujian in October 1660. Morale had been damaged by the debacle at Nanjing, and the pressing concern was to defend against an imminent Qing counterstrike. "The island is a gunshot away, separating the sea from the dry land of this empire," wrote Victorio Riccio, who led the small Amoy church in the 1660s (Borao Mateo 2001, 589). On 17 June 1660, the Qing navy attacked. "Thus broke out the fiercest and most dreadful battle ever fought in the Orient seas," wrote Riccio, our eyewitness:

> This terrible struggle made the sea turn blood red, with the dead and the dying. . . . Masts snapped in two, destroying ships; there was a heavy rain of arrows; lances and cannons fell; mountains of fire exploded. Combatants howled, the dying cried out; there was the chaotic blare of bugles, the rumble of war drums, the clanging of bassinets; add to this the volley of gunfire. It was a picture of a real life hell, filled with repulsive fumes, desperate screams and grotesque and frightful confusion of men. (Borao Mateo 2001, 597)

Koxinga's forces beat back the attack, and for weeks the beaches of Amoy were littered with rotting bodies and wreckage. Koxinga challenged the Qing to do better next time; but in truth, Koxinga knew that his offshore bases could not hold out forever. He needed a stronger, safer base, and he set his eyes on the big island across the sea where his father had once worked: Taiwan.

Lonely Are the Brave

In 1660, while Koxinga was making his decision to conquer Taiwan, his father's house arrest in Beijing went from bad to worse. The Qing government had repeatedly tried to negotiate with Koxinga from 1647 to 1654, sending gifts and offering noble ranks and coastal territories in Fujian if he would peacefully submit; and as a show of good faith, Zheng Zhilong had been treated courteously and given freedom to write letters to his son. When the talks broke down in 1654, Zheng Zhilong was imprisoned and pitiably chained—cold, alone, and destitute.

Koxinga's defeat at Nanjing in 1659 turned the tide of the war, and this time it was Koxinga's turn to send an emissary to Beijing to negotiate—but the Qing court was no longer willing to compromise. At last, the court ruled that Zheng Zhilong should die.

Differing accounts claimed that Zheng was cruelly sliced to death, or that he was killed by a saber blow, or that he was poisoned. A Spanish work offered an explosive hypothesis: Zheng was "blown to the skies by gunpowder with all his men, to fall miserably into hell. A death well deserved for his atrocious faults and sins, and specially for having apostatized from the Holy Faith that he professed in Baptism" (Borao Mateo 2001, 588). More likely he was simply strangled or beheaded, quickly and without ado. No doubt Zheng's persona, "like that of his more famous son, was of such interest that

Painting of Koxinga by the seventeenth-century painter Huang Zi. National Museum of China.

people chose to invent incidents rather than state the insufficient facts known to them" (Keene 1951, 65).

On 24 November 1661, Zheng and eleven family members, including two sons, were removed from their prison cells and executed in Beijing. Few mourned him; some reviled him; most had neither sympathy nor time for grief. But Ruǎn Mínxī 阮旻锡, who served by Koxinga's side, recorded the young sea lord's reaction. Near the end of 1661, while locked in combat with the Dutch in Taiwan, Koxinga heard the news of his father's death. "He shouted that it must be a false rumor, but in the middle of the night he sobbed with grief, and thereafter he passed his days in sorrow" (Ruan 1982, 47). The boy who had hugged his father for the first time atop Anhai castle, who had grown under his father's stern but twinkling eyes—and who became a hardened thirty-seven-year-old patriot who denounced his father for the sake of a dying cause—had never really forgotten the most important man in his life.

Last Conquest

Many of Koxinga's generals protested the move to attack Taiwan. They wanted to attack west, not east, and they were reluctant to leave their familiar home coast for an island that had never officially been part of China. Most had never been to Taiwan. But Koxinga's stubbornness and choler were legendary, and he had made up his mind.

Qing moves also forced his hand. Fifteen years of mutual slaughter and rapine between Koxinga and the Qing had convinced the Qing government to take a drastic measure: to depopulate the coast and cut off Koxinga's sources of supply. Experiments in the forced evacuation of coastal towns in late 1660 grew into a scorched earth policy known as "coastal depopulation" (*qiānjiè lìng* 迁界令), which lasted from 1661 to 1683. Fujian was the main target of this policy, but other coastal provinces suffered as more than fifteen hundred kilometers of coastline were laid to waste, and hundreds of thousands of people were killed or burned out of their homes.

Koxinga's growing supply problems and the loss of coastal allies hardened his resolve for the Taiwan campaign. On 21 April 1661, he assembled his fleet of hundreds of ships and twenty-five thousand men and embarked. A storm nearly upset the expedition midway, but Koxinga pushed defiantly through the downpour, saying that Heaven was on his side. What later commentators saw as Koxinga's faith in Heaven was really a calculated knowledge of the waters, as Koxinga rushed to reach the Bay of Taiwan (present-day Tainan City) in time for the spring tide. On 30 April, Koxinga's ships arrived and safely crossed the shallow Deer's Ear Gap (Lù'ěrmén 鹿耳门) into the Bay of Taiwan, thanks to the high tide.

The two forts in Taiwan, Zeelandia and Provintia, could not prevent the landing, but the 1,200 Dutch soldiers grimly prepared for war. For nine months the two sides were locked in battles, yelling, bluffing, and intermittent diplomacy. The most serious battle was hunger, as Koxinga's large army lacked the food supplies to carry a long campaign so far from home. Both the Chinese attackers and the besieged Dutch suffered from malnutrition, scurvy, beriberi (a nutritional deficiency common in areas where polished rice is the staple diet), malaria, and other ailments (Andrade 2011, 188–193).

The war's outcome turned on the questions of supply, leadership, and technology. The Dutch held some technological advantages but squandered them with poor leadership. During the first shots of the war, the bombastic Captain Thomas Pedel sallied forth with 240 musketeers, calling the Chinese effeminate cowards and believing that one Dutchman was worth more than twenty-five Chinese combined. Instead, it was the famed Dutch soldiers who dropped their guns and ran in panic as the Chinese officers outsmarted and smashed Pedel's company. Governor Frederick Coyet ordered a foolish naval attack that was equally beaten by Chinese tactics. For his part, Koxinga's numerical advantage was plagued by logistical problems and starvation; furthermore, although Koxinga captured Fort Provintia, he was stymied by the strong renaissance fortress at Fort Zeelandia, which withstood his siege for nine bitter months (Andrade 2011).

In the end, Koxinga's adaptability won him the war. "Within a nine-month span, he learned siege tactics that had taken Europeans centuries to perfect," and although this required help from European defectors, it was

Koxinga's willingness to listen that truly distinguished him from the Dutch, who had not heeded Chinese advice (Andrade 2011, 325–326). The final battle of 25 January 1662 ended with Koxinga's capture of a strategic hill that forced Fort Zeelandia into submission. On the evening of 1 February 1662, Frederick Coyet signed a treaty of surrender to Koxinga. They were allowed to sail away unmolested, leaving behind their castle, their treasure, and their colony.

Koxinga had been born in 1624, the same year that the Dutch began building their Taiwan colony. Thirty-eight years later, he took it. He did not know that this victory would be his last.

King of Taiwan

On 23 June 1662, barely seven months after his father's death, Koxinga perished in Taiwan. Many accounts claimed that he went mad and clawed at his own face; others pointed to fever. Plans were left undone. He had just begun to build his new capital in Taiwan. He had just threatened to conquer the Spanish colony in the Philippines. He had also issued orders to execute his oldest son, Zhèng Jīng 郑经 (1641–1681), on charges of incest, but his orders were disobeyed. He still dreamed of retaking Fujian.

Like his father's case, Koxinga's death inspired fanciful and hyperbolic stories. But whether he died of madness, rage, malaria, syphilis, overwork, a severe cold, or grief, by biting off his own tongue or gnawing off his fingers, or haunted by the ghosts of slain enemies (Keene 1951, 68–75), Koxinga's untimely death at age thirty-eight was a turning point. A succession struggle erupted and nearly tore the Zheng clan in pieces. Zheng Jing, the oldest son of Koxinga, won the power struggle in 1663 and secured himself in Taiwan, where he focused on making Taiwan a wealthy and independent kingdom and elevating Koxinga as the island's dynastic founder. Agents of the British East India Company signed a trade contract in 1670 with Zheng Jing, the "King of Tywan," taking special care to tell him, "wee would have your Majesty know, that wee are Englishmen and a distinct Nation from Hollanders—some people of which Nation about ten years since were driven out of your Land by his Majesty your Renowned Father" (Campbell 1903, 501).

Zheng Jing made one last hurrah during the massive Rebellion of the Three Feudatories (1673–1681). His forces returned to the Chinese coast and captured territories in Fujian, but six years of seesaw warfare ended in smoke when Qing armies drove the sea lord off the Chinese coast once more. In 1680, Zheng Jing sailed back to Taiwan in defeat and fell into wine, women, and song—and finally perished in 1681.

In July 1683 the Qing government resolved to end the conflict by sending Admiral Shī Láng 施琅 (1621–1696), who had once served in Koxinga's navy, with a Qing armada to defeat the Zheng forces in Taiwan. Shi Lang won the sea battle, and on 8 October, Zheng Jing's teenage son Zhèng Kèshuǎng 郑克爽 (1669–1707) formally surrendered to Qing rule. The mainland coast was reopened to trade, and the island was absorbed into the Qing empire as part of Fujian Province. Taiwan had become Chinese.

Contested Memory

Once upon a time, "every Dutch schoolchild learned that in 1662 the cruel pirate Coxinga robbed his [or her] ancestors of their beautiful colony, Formosa" (Blussé 1981, 90). By contrast, Chinese schoolchildren learned that the great hero Koxinga expelled the evil Dutch and recovered Taiwan for the motherland. These are but pieces in the roller coaster of Koxinga's memory.

Koxinga was first admired by the Ming loyalists, and after he was safely dead even his former Qing enemies honored his bravery. In 1875, the Qing emperor officially renamed him a "paragon of loyalty" (*zhōngjié* 忠节). Local shrines and temples in Fujian and Taiwan burned incense to Koxinga, who had become a very god. Koxinga's fame in Japan flowered in the eighteenth century when the puppet play *Kokusenya kassen* (*The Battles of Coxinga*) by Chikamatsu Monzaemon 近松門左衛門 (1653–1725) made him a tragic hero. Pictures of Watonai 和藤内 (Koxinga's name in Japanese) taming tigers became a popular artistic trope. When Japan conquered Taiwan and ruled it from 1895 to 1945, Koxinga's half-Japanese heritage helped legitimize Japan's colonial rule; when China reclaimed Taiwan

Image (1850) based on the 1715 play *The Battles of Coxinga* by Chikamatsu Monzaemon. Koxinga is the figure on the far left.

in 1945, Koxinga's Chinese identity was emphasized. People in southern Fujian disdained such crude national attempts to claim him: he was their own Fujianese folk hero.

The historical waters are further muddied by the legacy of the Chinese civil war (1945–1949) between the Nationalists and the Communists. When Nationalist leader *Chiang Kai-shek 蒋介石 (1887–1975) was defeated in China and retreated to Taiwan with a million troops and loyalists, the parallels with Koxinga were striking. Chiang Kai-shek resolved to his dying day that he would fight his way back to the mainland. His successors developed Taiwan into an economic success story, and today Taiwan remains a thriving and self-governing democracy. Consequently, Koxinga's image is split between those who regard him as a hero of Taiwan's independence from China (the "Father of Taiwan") and those who cite Koxinga as a symbol for Taiwan's reunification with China. The mainland Chinese government maintains that Koxinga planted the flag and that Taiwan will forever be part of the motherland.

As if to drive home the point, a gigantic stone statue of Koxinga stands today in Xiamen, China, looking eastward toward Taiwan. Meanwhile, in the ruins of Fort Zeelandia in Tainan City, Taiwan, a modest sculpture of the god-king gazes benignly on all worshippers, including high school students and their parents, who pray to him for success in the grueling college entrance examinations. In 2012, China and Taiwan celebrated the 350th anniversary of Koxinga's conquest of Taiwan—each in its own way.

Warped memories of Koxinga as a political symbol will likely continue, as will Asian movies and dramas that celebrate and twist his memory. And are they wrong? During his lifetime, Koxinga cultivated a romantic image of passionate intensity and manifest destiny; after his death, the mythmaking continued. To remove the stories is to remove half of his living memory. As the historian Tonio Andrade has said, "It's impossible to resist the dramatic stories about him because his life *was* dramatic" (Andrade 2011, 60).

Loved or hated, the man, myth, and legend endure because people choose to see what they want to see in the mercurial hero, Koxinga.

Dahpon D. HO
University of Rochester

Further Reading

Andrade, Tonio. (2011). *Lost colony: The untold story of China's first great victory over the West.* Princeton, NJ: Princeton University Press.

Andrade, Tonio. (2008). *How Taiwan became Chinese: Dutch, Spanish, and Han colonization in the seventeenth century.* New York: Columbia University Press.

Blussé, Leonard. (1981). The VOC as sorcerer's apprentice: Stereotypes and social engineering on the China coast. In W. L. Idema (Ed.), *Leyden studies in sinology* (pp. 87–105). Leiden, The Netherlands: E. J. Brill.

Borao Mateo, José Eugenio. (Ed.). (2001). *Spaniards in Taiwan: Documents, vol. II, 1642–1682*. Taipei, Taiwan: SMC Publishing Inc.

Boxer, Charles R. (1941). The Rise and fall of Nicholas Iquan (Cheng Chi-Lung). *T'ien-hsia Monthly, 11*, 5, 401–439.

Campbell, William. (1903). *Formosa under the Dutch: Described from contemporary records, with explanatory notes and a bibliography of the island.* London: Kegan Paul.

Clements, Jonathan. (2005). *Coxinga and the fall of the Ming dynasty*. Phoenix Mill, UK: Sutton Publishing.

Croizier, Ralph C. (1977). *Koxinga and Chinese nationalism: History, myth, and the hero.* Cambridge, MA: Harvard University Press.

Jiang Risheng 江日昇. (2004). *Taiwan waiji* 台湾外志(外记) [Historical novel of Taiwan] (Liu Wentai 刘文泰, Ed.). Jinan, China: Jilu shushe. (Original work published 1700s)

Keene, Donald. (1951). *The battles of Coxinga: Chikamatsu's puppet play, its background and importance*. London: Taylor's Foreign Press.

Ruan Minxi 阮旻锡. (1982). *Haishang jianwenlu dingben* 海上见闻录定本 [Personal record of the maritime resistance] (Xiamen Zheng Chenggong jinianguan, Ed.). Fuzhou, China: Fujian renmin chubanshe.

Struve, Lynn A. (1984). *The Southern Ming, 1644–1662*. New Haven, CT: Yale University Press.

Tang Jintai 湯錦台. (2002). *Kaiqi Taiwan diyiren Zheng Zhilong* 開啟台灣第一人鄭芝龍 [Zheng Zhilong: The pioneer of Taiwan]. Taipei, Taiwan: Guoshi.

Terao Yoshio 寺尾善雄. (1986). *Minmatsu no fūunji tei seikō* 明末の風雲児鄭成功 [Koxinga: Last hero of the Ming]. Tokyo: Tōhō Shoten.

Wakeman, Frederic, Jr. (1985). *The great enterprise: The Manchu reconstruction of imperial order in seventeenth-century China* (Vols. 1–2). Berkeley: University of California Press.

Wills, John E., Jr. (1974). *Pepper, guns, and parleys: The Dutch East India Company and China, 1622–1681*. Cambridge, MA: Harvard University Press.

Yang Ying 楊英. (1995 [1968]). *Congzheng shilu* 從征實錄 [Records in the service of Koxinga, by Yang Ying, Chief Financial Officer] (Taiwan Wenxian Congkan 32, Rep.). Taipei, Taiwan: Taiwan sheng wenxian weiyuanhui.

Lǐ Shízhēn

李时珍

1518–1593—Pharmacist and physician; compiler of medical encyclopedia

Alternate name: courtesy name: Dōngbì 东璧

Summary

Li Shizhen was a sixteenth-century physician, natural scientist, and pharmacist who made his mark during the late Ming dynasty with the towering *Compendium of Materia Medica*. Based on firsthand knowledge of herbal and local remedies that he gathered while travelling around several provinces, as well as research into some eight hundred medical books, it took more than thirty years to complete and was regarded as China's foremost medical encyclopedia for centuries. His comprehensive classification of 1,900 herbal components, along with some 1,600 illustrations, remains a valuable contribution to traditional Chinese medicine.

Li Shizhen was a notable herbalist, acupuncturist, and scholar-turned-doctor of the late Míng 明 dynasty (1368–1644). His father and grandfather were traditional Chinese physicians, but Li initially aspired to be a scholar before apprenticing himself to his father. He went on to become China's most famous physician, pharmacist, and herbalist, far surpassing his father's reputation as a physician-scholar. Li's book, *Compendium of Materia Medica* (*Běncǎo gāngmù* 本草纲目), is a masterpiece in the literature of herbal medicine and has had a profound influence on later research in medicine, natural history, and botany. So important was Li's work to the discipline of medicine that more than four hundred years after his death, his portrait continues to grace the halls of traditional Chinese medical colleges in China.

Life and Career

Born in Qízhōu 蕲州 (now Qichun County, Qizhou Township, Hubei Province), Li was also known as Dōngbì 东璧, though in later years he referred to himself as Bīnhú shānrén 濒湖山人

("Mountain Person Living Near the Lake"). Living in the late Ming era, when the dynasty was already starting to decline, Li witnessed political turmoil in the courts during the reign of four emperors, spanning from Zhengde (1491–1521) to *Emperor Wànlì 万历 (1563–1620). The dynasty would come to an end within fifty years of Li's death.

Li was strongly influenced by Neo-Confucianism, which had reinterpreted and revived the ideas of *Confucius 孔子 (551–479 BCE) beginning in the Sòng 宋 dynasty (960–1279). Early in life and in line with his father's expectations, Li walked the path of the Confucian-influenced civil service examinations (*kējǔ* 科举). He became, at age fourteen, a *xiùcái* 秀才 (elementary scholar), but he failed three times in the subsequent examinations at the provincial level and could not fulfill his desire to attain the *jǔrén* 举人 (selected men) degree.

Throughout his academic quest, he maintained a keen interest in medicine. When it became clear to him that, because of his poor performance in the examinations, he was not suited to a career in government, he approached his father with the intention to follow his ancestral path and practice medicine: "With my body like a boat in the counter current, my heart is harder than rock or iron. I wish Father would allow me to follow my dream, and I will follow it till death" (Tang 1991, 21).

*People marked with an asterisk have entries in this dictionary.

Convinced of his son's sincerity, his father then took him on as an apprentice; by then, Li was in his early twenties (hardly the young apprentice), and his father was seventy-eight years old.

After abandoning the Confucian career path of scholar-official, with its built-in political career and social status, Li became a doctor, following in the footsteps of his ancestors. Chinese society held the examination system in such high regard that those who passed the exams could expect a life of upward mobility and social status, while physicians were deemed to be of lower status. Nevertheless, once he had made up his mind, Li put considerable time and effort into his study of medicine and medical research, just as he had done when studying for the examinations.

By the time Li reached his thirties, he had become a renowned local physician; by age thirty-eight he came to the notice of the Prince of Chu and was hired as *fèng cízhèng* 奉祠正 (a position in charge of medical affairs). In 1558, Li was hired for a position in the Tàiyīyuàn 太医院 (Imperial Medical Center). He was based in the capital, Beijing, but resigned from his position after a year, as he was dissatisfied with what he believed to be his colleagues' inefficiency and incompetence, blaming them for contaminating his work environment.

Li then returned to his hometown of Qizhou and built a new house on the northern shore of Lake Yu. He named it *Hóng huāyuán* 红花园 (Red Flower Garden), and it was here that he spent some

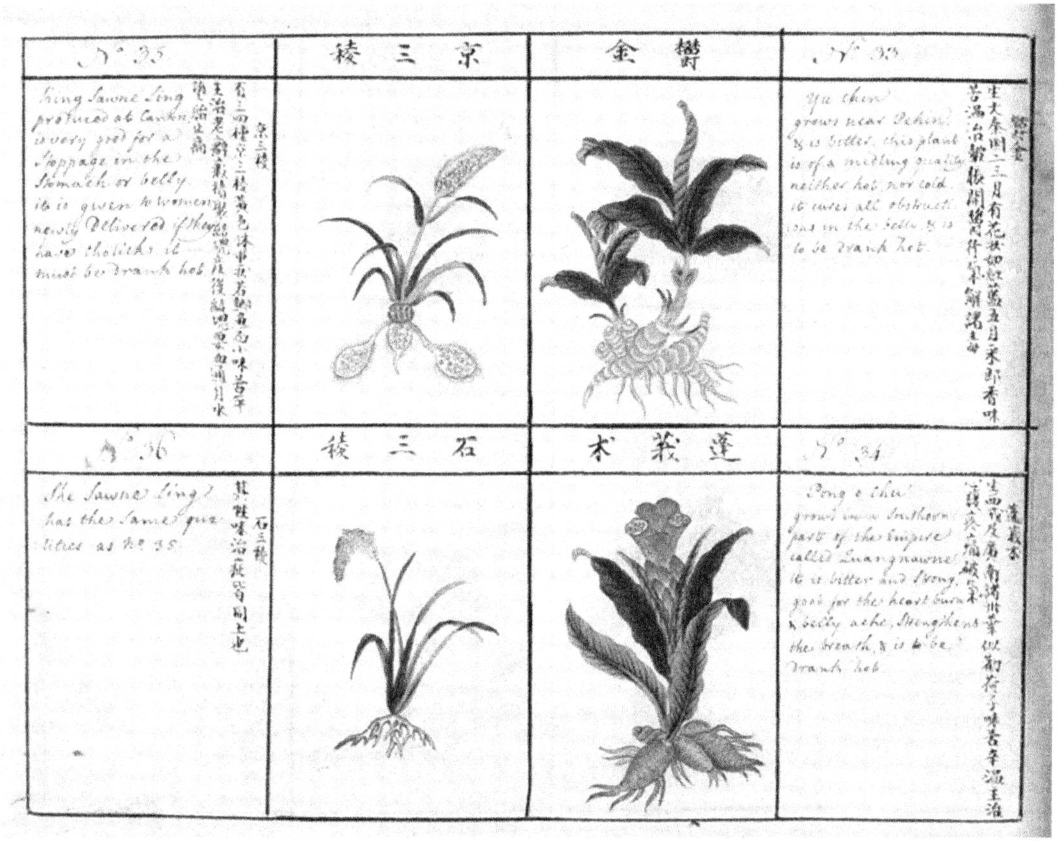

Page from *Account of 814 Plants & Insects, Most of Which Are Reckoned Medicinal by the Chinese*. A book based on the *Bencao Gangmu* by Li Shizhen.

of his best years in the dogged pursuit of medical and herbal knowledge and the practice of medicine. His quest to learn all he could about Chinese medicine resulted in the *Compendium of Materia Medica*, his multivolume work that took nearly three decades to write, and another twelve years and three rounds of revisions to complete. By then, his health had deteriorated. Li died in 1593, the twenty-first year of Emperor Wanli's rule, and he was buried near the shore of Lake Yu in Qichun County, Qizhou Township, Hubei Province.

Compendium of Materia Medica

The *Compendium of Materia Medica* is edited and collated mainly from the *Classified Materia Medica* of Táng Shènwēi 唐慎微, compiled in the Song dynasty. The

Compendium comprises fifty-two volumes and contains 1,892 types of drugs (among which 374 different varieties were added by Li). The *Compendium* contains 190 million characters; 1,109 illustrations; 11,096 prescriptions (among which more than 8,000 were first collected or proposed by Li); and is divided into sixteen sections (water, fire, earth, stone, grass, grain, vegetables, fruit, wood, apparel and instruments, insects, fish, crustaceans, birds, mammals, people) and sixty classes. Each drug is listed in multiple entries, which include designation (determining the name); records (stating the origins); corrections (correcting mistakes in the literature); preparation (preparation methods); odor, targeted symptoms, and inventions (these three deal with analysis of drug functions); and other prescriptions (including folk prescriptions).

Li's work on the *Compendium of Materia Medica* was prompted by several observations and events. In his practice of medicine, Li noted that ancient herbal books "came in a huge number and complex names. They sometimes broke down one substance into several, or mistook two for one." In particular, many toxic substances were described as "longevity promoting with continuous usage" (Luo 2003, preface), when in fact they could cause fatal harm. Li repeatedly petitioned the court to require a reorganization and collation of data in the medical literature; unfortunately, the court did not accede to his request. He then decided to undertake the task of reorganizing and collating medical and herbal substances himself, utilizing the comprehensive and encyclopedic knowledge of medical literature he had accumulated when he worked in the local court and the capital.

During his compilation of *Compendium of Materia Medica*, Li realized that there was much confusion about the names, classification, and the functions of various herbs. Despite their repeated explanations, previous herbal books actually added to the confusion, since much of their information was based on hearsay or commonplace understanding; the authors had not carried out any in-depth research but had merely copied from other sources. With so many contradictions in the books, physicians and herbalists did not have a basis upon which to agree or disagree, nor could they make informed decisions based on the information they found there. Li, along with his son, Jiàn Yuán 建元, and apprentice, Páng Xiàn 庞宪, trekked across mountains and into the wilderness, observing and collecting extant specimens of medicinal herbs.

In addition to his tireless collecting and testing of herbs, Li also visited other famous physicians, as well as commoners such as fishermen and farmers to gather folk remedies. He started by interviewing people in his home area, and subsequently took his interviews farther afield, traveling to Huguang (modern-day Hubei and Hunan provinces), Jiangxi, Jiangsu, and Anhui provinces. He also visited Mount Tàihé 太和 in Jūnzhōu 均州, known today as Wudang Mountain. He left his footprints in places with abundant herbal resources, such as Lúshān 庐山 Mountain in Jiangxi, as well as Mount Shè 摄山, Mount Máo 茅山, and Mount Niúshǒu 牛首山 in Nanjing.

The physician Zhào Xuémǐn 赵学敏, from a much later generation, noted in *Compendium of Materia Medica Supplements* that the drugs listed in Li's book are "products from untraveled places; essence from fairy mountains," which reflect Li's life of unceasing treks and interviews. Unfortunately, his three-decade dedication to working on *Compendium* took a toll on his health, and he died before it was published.

In 1596, three years after Li Shizhen's death, *Compendium of Materia Medica* was officially published in Nanjing. Wáng Shìzhēn 王世贞, a leading literary figure and Li's contemporary, described his work as "golden valley with iridescent colors; legendary King's palace with untold treasures." Much later in the West, Darwin evaluated it as "the sixteenth-century Chinese encyclopedia," which provided information and methodologies for scientific research in his own era (Needham 1976, 216).

Reinterpretations of Li Shizhen

Modern interpretations of Li Shizhen and his significance are changing with the times, the most critical offered by researchers after the founding of People's Republic of China (in 1949). They admonished him for his philosophy, which they viewed as lying in the tradition of simple materialistic thinking. Admittedly, Li started from the idea that *qì* 气 (vitality or energy) is the origin of everything. It gives credence to the cycle of *yīn-yáng* 阴阳 and the five elements, the interaction between things with different physicality (e.g, water and air, earth and sky), and finally reaches its conclusion about the unity of Heaven and humans, as well as the power of humans over nature, Li developed his thinking along the lines of traditional philosophy. At the same time, however, other researchers have countered that studying his ideas by viewing them in the ahistorical and narrow way is somehow gradually out of favor.

In addition to the continuous attention on his *Compendium of Materia Medica*, more recent research tries to situate Li within the larger context of medical history and the social environment of his time. For example, the relationship between his thoughts and the comprehensive political backdrop has been studied. During Li's time, a sociopolitical crisis was brewing within the courts, leading statesmen such as Grand Secretary Zhāng Jūzhèng 张居正 to start a pseudo-political reform movement. Previous studies suggest a tenuous link between this reform movement and Li's innovation in the field of medical

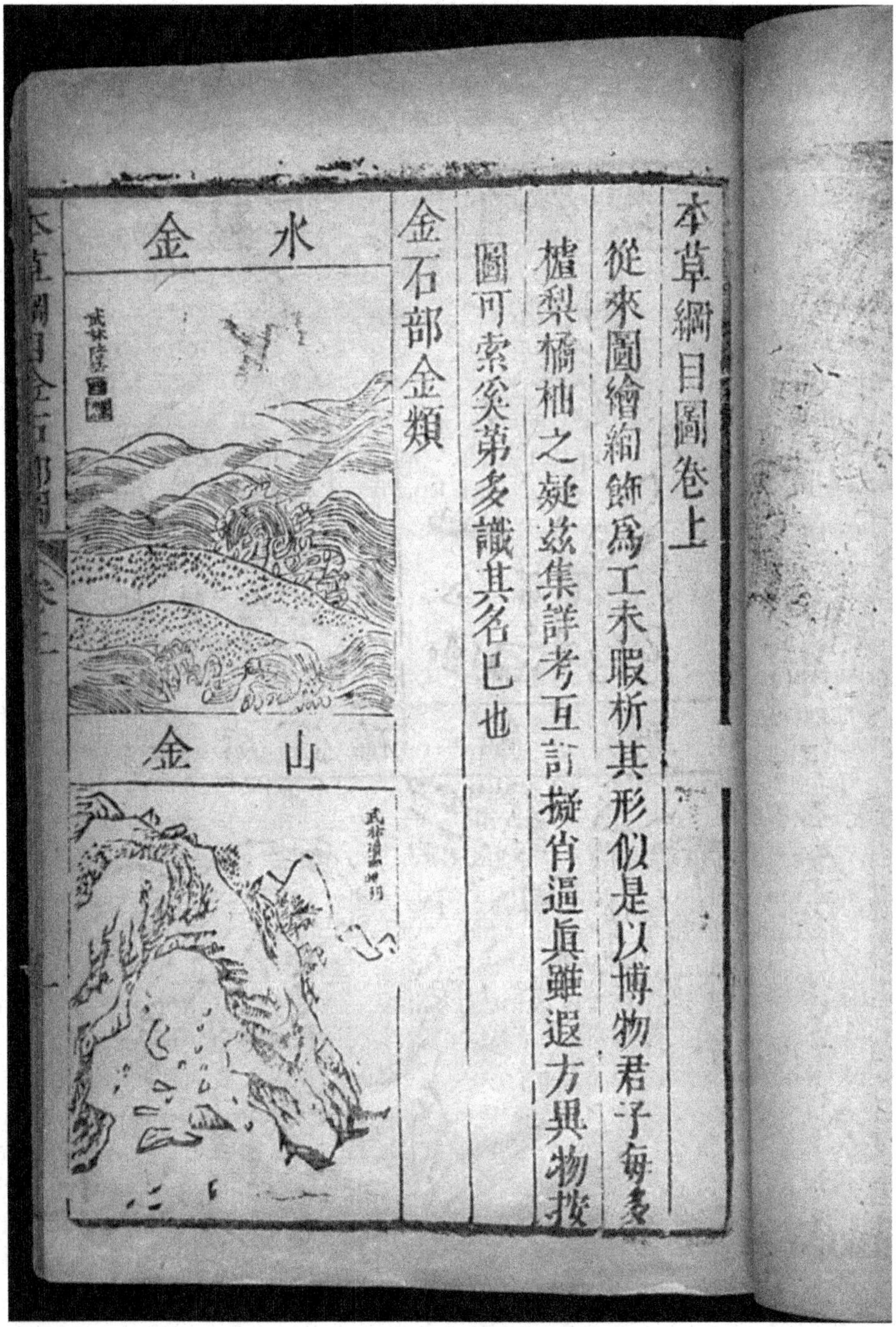
本草綱目圖卷上

從來圖繪綃飾爲工未暇析其形似是以博物君子每多

櫨梨橘柚之疑茲集詳考互訂擬肖逼眞雖遐方異物搜

圖可索奚第多識其名已也

金石部金類

水金

山金

A page from an eighteenth-century edition of the *Compendium of Materia Medica.*

science. This trend is also reflected in the development of "Philosophy of the Mind" and vernacular literature, as well as scientific and technological innovations during the late Ming era.

Increasingly, more attention is also being paid to his literary accomplishments, personal life, and interactions with other scholars. In the eyes of modern scholars, not only was Li Shizhen a towering figure in medical, cultural, and intellectual history; he was also a *wénrén* 文人 (a literati or intellectual), who experienced ups and downs in his career but nevertheless had excellent literary training and who played an active role in Chinese civil society.

HE Yanran
National University of Singapore

Further Reading

Chang Hui-chien. (2005). *Li Shih-chen: Great pharmacologist of ancient China*. Honolulu, Hawaii: University Press of the Pacific.

Li Shih-Chen. (2003). *Chinese medicinal herbs: A modern edition of a classic sixteenth-century manual* (Porter Smith & G. A. Stuart, Trans.). New York: Dover Publications.

Li Shizhen. (2003). *Compendium of Materia Medica (Bencao gangmu)* (6 vols.) (Luo Xiwen, Ed.). Beijing: Foreign Language Press. (Original work published 1596)

Lu, Gwei-Djen. (1960). China's greatest naturalist: A brief biography of Li Shih-Chen. *Physis*, 13, 382–392.

Needham, Joseph. (1976). *Science and civilisation in China: Vol. 5, Pt. 3*. Cambridge, UK: Cambridge University Press.

Tang Mingbang 唐明邦. (1991). *A critical biography of Li Shizhen*. Nanjing, China: Nanjing University Press.

Lǐ Zhì
李贽

1527–1602—Critic of Confucian orthodoxy

Alternate names: given name: Zǎizhì 载贽; courtesy names: Hóngfù 宏父, Zhuōwú 卓吾; alternative/style name: Wēnlíng Jūshì 温陵居士

Portrait of Li Zhi. Image by 曳杖行歌意欲仙.

Summary

Li Zhi was one of the leading thinkers in Ming intellectual history, known in particular for his criticism of Confucian orthodoxy and his re-evaluations of famous historical figures. In Li Zhi's eyes, scholars of Confucianism during his time were hypocrites and sycophants who did not demonstrate the true qualities of Confucian learning. He was a controversial figure during his lifetime who received both scorn and adulation from his contemporaries among the scholar-elite. His tragic suicide in prison reflects the difference between reality and the ideal for a Chinese intellectual of the times.

Li Zhi is a familiar subject in Chinese history for both Chinese and Western scholars, as well as one of the most prominent thinkers in Míng 明 dynasty (1368–1644) thought. Ming and Qīng 清 dynasty (1644–1911/1912) scholars, however, hold divergent views in their appraisal of Li Zhi since his philosophy was seen (and even self-proclaimed) as heretical during his lifetime, but was later recognized as a forebear to intellectual developments. The poet and essayist *Yuán Hóngdào 袁宏道 (1568–1610), for instance, wrote in *Readings on Meigong's Reflections* (*Dú méigōng dúshū jìng* 读眉公读书镜) that: "The writings of Zhuōwú 卓吾 [Li Zhi's style name] hold ultimate truth. Literary works abound, but Zhuowu's works have been most uplifting" (Pan 1977, 3/5b). In his Ming dynasty history, *Unofficial Matters from the Wanli Reign* (*Wànlì yěhuò biān* 万历野获编), Shén Défú 沈德符 (1578–1642) stated that "Wenling Li Zhuowu is an ingenious man with incisive arguments, yet he is quick to speak and persuasive in debate, beneficial to the mind of

*People marked with an asterisk have entries in this dictionary.

others. Philosophical masters, Jiāo Ruòhóu 焦弱侯 of Mòlíng 秣陵, and Liú Jìnchuān 刘晋川 of Qìnshuǐ 沁水, both regard him as a sage" (Shen 1959, 27.691).

Such opinions or remarks were not baseless. Li Zhi had contributed to his generation during the late Ming period through so many exceptional works that they prompted the comment: "whether it is the city or the village, anyone who could read would scramble for his writings in the same way that water is eager to put out a fire" (Zhu 1975).The penetrative influence of Li Zhi's writings was so immense that "men no longer read the *Four Books* and *Five Classics*, turning instead to Li's *A Book to Conceal* (*Cángshū* 藏书) and *A Book to Burn* (*Fénshū* 焚书), which have become prized possessions of their owners" (Zhu 1975, 69).

Li Zhi's ideas were groundbreaking. As Shén Zàn 沈瓒 explained in the *Remnants of Current Affairs* (*Jìnshì cóngcán* 近事从残), "[Li Zhi] excels in making startling arguments, aiming to refute *daoxue* [the learning of the Way] of the Song Confucians . . . the objective of his sayings is to break free of dogma and be direct, so that many of the young and talented admire him. Later torrents of learning [because of Li Zhi's influence] have prevented Confucian thought from collapsing and released it from the shackles of many standards and rules" (Shen 1975, *juan* 1, 84).

Shen's comments on Li Zhi leave room for debate, but it was an undisputable fact that Li Zhi had broken new ground by formulating his own rendition of existing Confucian dogma. Whether or not Li Zhi's ideas gained wide acceptance was a different matter. During the Ming-Qing period, numerous scholars rejected Li Zhi's thought. For example, Gù Yánwǔ 顾炎武 (1613–1682) argued that "from time immemorial, the most unabashed and treacherous of all men had to be Li Zhi" (Gu 1975/1976, *juan* 18, 84). Qing literatus Jì Yún 纪昀 (1724–1805) even said in the *Annotated Catalog of the Complete Imperial Library* (*Sìkù quánshū zǒngmù tíyào* 四库全书总目提要) that:

> Li Zhi was not a sage but an outlaw, for he had brazenly proposed heterodox ideas. Although his ideas resulted in his imprisonment and later suicide, scholars such as Jiao Hong extolled him for his views, and his arguments were so popular that mediocre scholars would wholeheartedly embrace them. The one irrefutable fact is that Li Zhi's thought has had a lasting impact, negatively or positively. (Ji et al. 1933, 178.3901)

Gu Yanwu's criticism reflects the general sentiments of Ming-Qing era thinkers who had aspired to make a difference in their context of political change and upheaval. Ji Yun was an example of traditional *daoxue* Confucian scholars who had reproved Li Zhi. From the perspective of the traditional *daoxue* scholars, Li Zhi's ideas were regarded as raging floods and ferocious beasts, and held in direct opposition to what they had known. Li Zhi's ideas were an assault on traditional Confucianism, so it is understandable that the *daoxue* scholars saw Li Zhi as an antagonist. In the twenty-first century, however, scholars should aim to see Li Zhi in an impartial light. Ming Confucianism, subject to the dominance of the Neo-Confucians, had become a rigid set of doctrines that hindered philosophical development. Li Zhi was resilient enough to withstand the censure of his views and break the Confucian mold, seeking a breakthrough in intellectual history. He hoped to construct a free and realistic intellectual system, which would widen the horizon of Ming thought. Such was Li Zhi's contribution to Chinese intellectual history. He recognized the value of self-worth, and was a proponent of individuality: an idea that had flourished in the late Ming period because of him (de Bary 1970).

Life and Career

Li Zhi was a native of Jìnjiāng 晋江, Fujian Province, born in 1527, in the sixth year of the Jiājìng 嘉靖 emperor (r. 1521–1567). In 1522, Li received the status of *jŭrén* 举人 (a title conferred when one passes the second tier of the civil service examination system required to become an official in the bureaucracy). He was unable to pursue the higher *jìnshì* 进士 degree (presented scholar) due to financial difficulties. Thus, he was forced to choose from the limited posts available to *juren*, and in 1555, assumed the post of Education Director of Gòngchéng 共城 in Henan province. In 1560, he was promoted to Erudite of the National University in Nanjing, a principal teacher at the National University, but had to return home to observe mourning rites a few months later because of the death of his father (mourning rites required a strict set of observances that often lasted for three years after the death of close relations). In 1561, he brought his family to the northern capital of Beijing, and waited two years for his new post at the National University. His career at the capital was also short-lived, however. His grandfather passed away, and he had to relinquish his job in order to observe the mourning rites at home. He returned to Beijing in 1566 to assume the post of office manager at the Ministry of Rites. From 1571 to 1576, Li Zhi acted as the vice director in the Ministry of Justice in Nanjing. During his stay in Nanjing, he met the Gĕng 耿 brothers and Jiāo Hóng 焦竑, who later became his close friends and intellectual soul mates.

Li Zhi's last official appointment was in 1578, as the prefect of Yáo Ān 姚安 in Yunnan Province. He resigned after serving the three-year term and devoted himself completely to intellectual pursuits. Later, he moved to Huáng Ān 黄安 to stay with the Geng brothers and to help educate their sons. He had intellectual disputes with one of the brothers, scholar-official Gěng Dìngxiàng 耿定向, and decided to leave.

In 1585, he sent his wife and daughter back to Fujian and moved to the Hubei Province city of Máchéng 麻城, a neighboring district southeast of Huang An. Here he found shelter in a Buddhist temple on the shores of the Lóngtán 龙潭 (Dragon Lake) with his son and younger brother. Misfortunate struck shortly thereafter: his only son drowned at the lake, which caused Li Zhi great grief, and influenced his attitude and philosophy toward life. In 1588, he shaved his head to show his determination to leave his family and the materialistic world, and devoted most of his time to writing and teaching.

In 1590, he published his first collection of work, *A Book to Burn*, in Macheng. His second work, *A Book to Conceal*, a personal evaluation of historical figures and episodes from the Warring States 战国 period (475–221 BCE) to the Yuán 元 dynasty (1279–1368), published nine years later in Nanjing. A supplement to each book was published in 1618 and 1602 respectively. His writings soon became very popular among intellectuals, which antagonized many of the conservative Confucians and scholar-officials. In 1600, a mob of locals from Macheng chased him out and demolished the temple in which he lived. The local censor (*yùshǐ* 御史; a civil position charged with superintendence of members of the bureaucracy) Mǎ Jīnglún 马经纶, took him in and provided him with shelter. In 1602, however, Zhāng Wèndá 张问达 (d. 1625), a supervisor censor in Tōngzhōu 通州, impeached Li Zhi, requested his arrest, and ordered his writings destroyed. Li's life ended when he slashed his throat with a razor in prison. His last words before death were, "What more could an old man of seventy ask for?" (Li 1974c, 5)

The True Confucian

Recent scholars have regarded Li Zhi as "non-Confucian, anti-Confucianism" (Li 1974, Introduction), or a "staunch anti-Confucian against the conventional trend" (Department of Chinese 1974, 260–272). Such statements exaggerate, rather than reflect, historical realities. Although Li Zhi's ideas have been seen as heretical, he was certainly not seeking a clean break with Confucianism. The arguments put forth in Li Zhi's *A Book to Conceal* support the idea that the teachings of Neo-Confucian philosopher Chéng Yí 程颐 (1033–1107) were "axioms that hold true for millennia," (Li 1974, 32.533). Li Zhi also eulogized the work of Yáng Shí 杨时 (1053–1135), who was responsible for recording and transmitting the foundational teachings of Neo-Confucianism, as illustrative of "great talent and sagacity, practical *daoxue* (Learning of the Way)" (Li 1974, 32.536). Hence, Li Zhi's critique of Confucianism was not unequivocally negative. Moreover, Li Zhi's *Collections of Chu Tan* (*Chūtán jí* 初潭集) followed the

Confucian writing format by dividing its text into the four parts of virtue, speech, affairs, and literature, of which virtue is the most important. Li Zhi also stated that "writing Confucian books prioritizes the writing of virtue, but the person who could both write a Confucian book and practice Confucian virtues is me" (Li 1974d, 1). This demonstrates that Li Zhi was a self-professed Confucian, and his thinking was endowed with strong Confucian tendencies. The censor, Ma Jinglun, put forth the following:

> Relish in the Way, interpret the sayings of the sages; Li Zhi's [writings] have their origins in the teachings of Fuxi, King Wen of Zhou, Confucius, and Mencius, and they match the intellectual standards of Zhou [Dunyi 周敦颐], Shao [Yong 邵雍], Chen [Xianzhang 陈献章, 1428–1500], and Wang [Yangming 王阳明], among other great Neo-Confucian scholars. (Ma 1977, 4.18a–18b)

Therefore, Li Zhi was not anti-Confucian. What he vehemently opposed were distorted or false *daoxue* teachings and their bearers, the alleged Confucians who did not practice what they preached.

Li Zhi wrote, "If a *daoxue* scholar asks whether I can eulogize Confucianism, he would not understand it [i.e., Confucianism] regardless of whether or not I can do so" (Li 1974d, 20.346). He also criticized "false" Confucians:

> They usually do nothing but adulate one another, sit a whole day like sculptures, and liken themselves to great sages if their distractions and temptations do not act up. If a crisis arises, they would look at one another in bewilderment and shirk their responsibilities to protect themselves from harm. (Li 1974c, 4.156)

According to Li Zhi's castigation, these false scholars performed Confucianism only in theory and never in practice, and their teachings were false *daoxue*. In Li Zhi's eyes, scholars of Confucianism during his time were hypocrites and sycophants who did not demonstrate the qualities of Confucian learning. In the context of the Ming intellectual milieu, the ossification of Confucian thought was a product of the state promulgation of the Cheng-Zhu school of thought (*Chéngzhūlǐxué* 程朱理学), which argued that human nature was essentially good, but required training and purposeful action to attain purity. Li Zhi instead regarded the Yangming School (*Yángmíngxué* 阳明学, which would lead to the *Tàizhōu* 泰州 School) as the orthodox *daoxue*. This school was founded upon the teachings of *Wáng Yángmíng 王阳明 (1472–1529), who believed in self-cultivation of goodness as an intuitive process of the mind.

In *Collections of Chu Tan*, Li Zhi offered a more incisive analysis of the grandiloquent *daoxue* scholars, making a distinction between *xuédào* 学道 and *dàoxué* 道学. On *xuedao* scholars, he said, "The learning of the Way lies in its essence"; on *daoxue* scholars, he said, "*Daoxue* lies in its name. Men who pursue fame would definitely discuss *daoxue* and depend on *daoxue* to make their name. Mediocre men would surely talk about *daoxue* so as to use *daoxue* for their purposes. Those who deceive the world would certainly speak of *daoxue*, for *daoxue* serves their aim of deceiving the world" (Li 1974, 20.345). This analysis shows Li Zhi's critical attitude toward *daoxue* scholars. Li Zhi was unbiased against the Cheng-Zhu School; what he did was to argue that the literati of his time acquired the rhetoric of the sages but did not perform the sages' actions and deeds to back their words up.

Citing the ancient sages as examples, Li Zhi stated that "The words of the sages can definitely be acted upon, and these actions would definitely match the words. The words may be different, but there has been no instance where actions are taken without the words" (Li 1975, Introduction). Li Zhi revered scholars whose actions matched their words. These great philosophers included Cheng Yi, Yang Shi, and Wang Yangming. He berated "false" Confucians whose practices deviated from what they preached. This illustrates that he opposed so-called false Confucians and Confucianism, rather than Confucians or Confucianism in general.

Accused of being a "traitor of Confucianism," Li Zhi received much condemnation in history. Zhāng Nài 张鼐 once wrote, "We can reprove Zhuowu [Li Zhi] for his ideas but not for his intentions . . . . In sum, he wants people to discard the rhetoric and see the true heart of themselves and others: loyal as an official, filial as a son, devoted as a friend, and resilient as a warrior. This is the principle that the best men should accept and believe in. An extraordinary man is one well versed in Zhuowu's books and knows how to distinguish the right from the wrong" (Zhang 1976, 126).

Conversely, one may ask whether Li Zhi proposed anti-Confucian philosophy in his *A Book to Conceal*, where he suggested that scholars should "not regard Confucius's distinction of right and wrong as a universal one" (Li 1974a). Li Zhi recognized the contributions and status of Confucius in the context of his own time. In the section of *A Book to Conceal* titled "Discussions on Le Ke" (*Lèkè lùn* 乐克论), Li explains that, "if the world did not have Confucius, it would not know what is right and what is wrong" (Li 1974a, 32.522). Li Zhi's philosophy considers Confucius correct in highlighting *shìfēi* 是非 (literally "is this/not this")—or the right and wrong of human behavior that was thought to promote order—within the context of the chaotic Spring and Autumn 春秋 period (770–476 BCE) in which he lived.

Li sensed conflict in the intentions of later generations that had made Confucius's teachings into a rigid set of doctrines, and yearned to promulgate them as universal doctrines for the world in posterity. He interpreted this as "dogmatic," and believed that "dogma harms the Way."

Li Zhi incisively criticizes *daoxue* scholars for relying on the principles in Confucius's original teachings when determining punishment and reward. His intention was to point out the temporality of *shifei*, and the fact that ethical standards change with time, such that *shifei* of yesterday does not equate with that of today. Therefore, Li Zhi did not criticize Confucius. He criticized the misappropriation of Confucian teachings for selfish or inappropriate purposes.

Perhaps one of the most distinctive dichotomies between Li Zhi's thought and that of the Neo-Confucians that rallied against him is Li's value of results and recognition of the existence of egoism and desire. Within his published works, Li praised accomplished rulers and officials, and plainly stated that:

> It is natural that men harbor selfish hearts. Men must have selfishness before they have a heart for things, so if there is no selfishness, there is no heart. Farmers desire a copious harvest in autumn, so they strive to toil in the fields. Householders desire wealth in their family, so they strive to manage the household. Scholars desire progress in their studies, so they strive to make a name for themselves. This is why if no fortune exists in officialdom, no man would come forward to become officials. Without [the promise of] official titles, men would not come forward to serve. (Li 1974a, 32.544)

Men are inherently selfish, and harbor desire, so when *lǐxué* 理学 (the *teaching of principle;* another term for the *daoxue* of the Cheng-Zhu school of thought) scholars argue that a gentleman does not discuss rewards and results, their rhetoric does not match reality. On the premises of stressing industry and recognizing human desire, the doctrines and teachings that the *daoxue* Neo-Confucians had enacted seem meaningless. Li Zhi's thought stood in opposition to Neo-Confucian doctrines and teachings, so *daoxue* scholars had branded it as a *corruption of the norm.*

Ideal and Reality

Li Zhi was a man of ideals, as well as a tragic figure. In the context of modern scholarship, it matters little that he was condemned by *daoxue* scholars as a "heterodox" figure. Within sixteenth century imperial Chinese society of which Li was a contemporary, however, his ideas were unlikely to ever gain wide acceptance and currency. He sought a breakthrough in intellectual development on the basis of Confucian thought, searching for new knowledge based on the ancient works of sages, but he was destined to fail in his endeavor. The pressures of traditional society had caused him to drift away from his ideals.

In the words of one of the inaugurating authors of literary prose in post-imperial China, Zhōu Zuòrén 周作人 (1885–1967) the reason behind this outcome is that "the most dangerous act to perform in the world is to offer unconventional arguments, and many confinements and censorship of thought and words have arisen as a result. In the first place, it is not difficult to agree with conventions, and when an unconventional figure interferes in the norms, danger befalls the person" (Zhou 1944, 124). Ultimately, in the thirtieth year of the reign of the Wanli emperor (1602), Li Zhi committed suicide in prison, embodying eternal freedom and emancipation. Li Zhi was utterly disappointed with his time, but he did not feel any regret. His own words echo in this last act: "A great man does not fear consequences, and so he succeeds in whatever he does" (Li 1974, 224).

Li Zhi was one of the more insightful thinkers of sixteenth century China following the emergence of Wang Yangming and the development of the Taizhou School. Although his philosophical positions were never accepted by his mainstream contemporaries, Li Zhi challenged late Ming thought. He enjoyed an unambiguous standing in the history of Ming thought, because he sought to blaze a new path in thought and to pursue truth in learning. Li Zhi's quest for knowledge reflected the trends and realities of Ming intellectual development, and also uncovers the reasons behind the gradual ossification of late Ming philosophy. On the other hand, Li Zhi's tragedy illustrats the price that literati had to pay in their pursuit of independence of thought. Although Li Zhi had failed to make an immense impact during his lifetime, his process of pursuing the truth became a form of reality for later philosophers, and secured his significance in Ming-Qing intellectual history.

LEE Cheuk Yin 李焯然
National University of Singapore

Further Reading

Chan Hok-lam. (1980). *Li Chih 1527–1602 in contemporary Chinese history: New light on his life and works.* New York: M. E. Sharpe.

Chan Kam-chiew 陈锦钊. (1974). *Li Zhi zhi wenlun* 李贽之文论 [The literary theories of Li Zhi], Taipei, Taiwan: Jiaxin shuili gongsi.

Chiu Ling-yeong 赵令扬. (1973). Li Zhi zhi shixue 李贽之史学 [The History Writings of Li Zhi]. *Journal of Oriental Studies*, *XI*(1), 122–142.

de Bary, Wm. Theodore. (1970). Individualism and humanitarianism in late Ming thought. In Wm. Theodore T. de Bary (Ed.), *Self and society in Ming thought.* New York: Columbia University Press.

Department of Chinese, Nanjing University. (1974). Li Zhi de zuifa fanru sixiang he douzheng jingsheng. In *Lun fajia ho rujia douzheng* (pp. 260–272). Beijing: Beijing renmin chubanshe.

Goodrich, Carrington, & Chaoying Fang. (Eds.). (1976). *Dictionary of Ming biography, 1368–1644.* New York: Columbia University Press.

Gu Yanwu. (1975/1976). *Rizhi lu* (*juan* 18). In Xiamen University Department of History (Ed.), *Li Zhi yanjiu cankao ziliao* 李贽研究参考资料 [Reference materials on the study of Li Zhi (p. 84). Fuzhou, China: Fujian renmin chubanshe.

Hsiao Kung-ch'uan. (1938). Li Chih: An iconoclast of the sixteenth century. *T'ien-hsia Monthly, 6*(4), 317–341.

Ji Yun, et al. (Eds.) (1933). *Siku quanshu zongmu tiyao* (summary of *Li Wenling ji*) (*juan* 178, p. 3901). Shanghai: Commercial Press.

Jung Chao-tsu 容肇祖. (1973). *Li Zhuowu pingzhuan* 李卓吾评传 [A critical biography of Li Zhi] (Reprint). Taipei: Taiwan Commercial Press reprint.

Li Zhi 李贽. (1974a). *Cangshu* 藏书 [A book to conceal], Beijing: Zhonghua shuju.

Li Zhi. (1974b). *Xu Cangshu* 续藏书 [Supplement to *A Book to Conceal*], *Zaiban shuoming*. Beijing: Zhonghua shuju.

Li Zhi. (1974c). *Fenshu* 焚书 [A book to burn]. Beijing: Zhonghua shuju.

Li Zhi. (1974d). *Chutan ji* 初潭集 [Collections of Chu Tan]. Beijing: Zhonghua shuju.

Li Zhi. (1975). *Mozi pi xuan* 墨子批选 (2 vols.). Taipei, Taiwan: Chengwen chubanshe.

Li Zhi. (2000). *Li Zhi wenji* 李贽文集 [Collected works of Li Zhi] (Zhang Jianye, Ed.) (7 vols.). Beijing: Shehui kexue chubanshe.

Lin Haiquan 林海权. (1992). *Li Zhi nianpu kaolue* 李贽年谱考略 [A Study of the annalistic biography of Li Zhi]. Fuzhou, China: Fujian renmin chubanshe.

Lin Qixian 林其贤. (1992). *Li Zhuowu zhi foxue yu shixue* 李卓吾的佛学与世学 [Li Zhuowu's Buddhist and human thought]. Taipei, Taiwan: Wenjin Press.

Ma Jinglun. (1977). Yudang daoshu. In Pan Zenghong 潘曾纮 (Ed.), *Li Wenling waiji* 李温陵外纪 [Biographical materials of Li Wenling] (4:18a–18b). Taipei, Taiwan: Wei-wen Books reprint.

Mote, F. W. (1979). Forward to Li Chih (1527–1602): New light on his life and works by Hok-lam Chan. *Ming Studies, 9*, 31–32.

Pan Zenghong 潘曾纮 (Ed.). (1977). *Li Wenling waiji* 李温陵外纪 [Biographical materials of Li Wenling] (Ming edition). Taipei, Taiwan: Wei-wen Books reprint.

Shen Defu 沈德符. (1959). *Wanli yehuo bian* 万历野获编. Beijing: Zhonghua shuju.

Shen Zan. (1975/1976). Jinshi congcan (*juan* 1). In Xiamen University Department of History (Ed.), *Li Zhi yanjiu cankao ziliao* 李贽研究参考资料 [Reference materials on the study of Li Zhi] (p. 84). Fuzhou, China: Fujian renmin chubanshe.

Wu Ze 吴泽. (1949). *Rujiao pantu Li Zhuowu* 儒教叛徒李卓吾 [Li Zhi: A rebel against Confucianism]. Shanghai: Huaxia shudian.

Xu Jianping 许建平. (2005). *Li Zhi sixiang yanbian shi* 李贽思想演变史 [History of the Development of Li Zhi's Thought]. Beijing: Renmin chubanshe.

Xiamen University Department of History (Ed.). (1975/1976). *Li Zhi yanjiu cankao ziliao* 李贽研究参考资料 [Reference materials on the study of Li Zhi] (First & Second series). Fuzhou, China: Fujian renmin chubanshe.

Yan Leishan 鄢烈山 & Zhu Jianguo 朱健国. (2000). *Li Zhi Zhuan* 李贽传 [Biography of Li Zhi]. Beijing: Shishi chubanshe.

Ye Xiansi. (1974). Luelun Li Zhi zunfa fanru de sixiang. *Zhongshan daxue xuebao, 3*, 18–23.

Yue Qingsi. (1974). Li Zhi de zunfa fankong sixiang 李贽的遵法反孔思想. *Wenwu, 5*, 21–27.

Zhang Jianye 张建业. (1981). *Li Zhi pingzhuan* 李贽评传 [A critical biography of Li Zhi]. Fuzhou, China: Fujian renmin chubanshe.

Zhang Nai. (1976). Baomutang chuji. In Xiamen University Department of History (Ed.), *Li Zhi yanjiu cankao ziliao* 李贽研究参考资料 [Reference materials on the study of Li Zhi] (p. 126). Fuzhou, China: Fujian renmin chubanshe.

Zhou Zuoren. (1944). Du chutan ji 读初潭集. In Zhou Zuoren, *Yaotang zawen* 药堂杂文 (p. 124). Beijing: Xin minyin shuguan.

Zhu Guozhen. (1975). *Yongzhuang xiaopin* (*juan* 16). In Xiamen University Department of History (Ed.), *Li Zhi yanjiu cankao ziliao* 李贽研究参考资料 [Reference materials on the study of Li Zhi (p. 69). Fuzhou, China: Fujian renmin chubanshe.

Zhu Weizhi 朱维之. (1935). *Li Zhuowu lun* 李卓吾论 [An appraisal of Li Zhi]. Fuzhou, China: Fujian Christian University.

Zuo Dongling 左东岭. (1997). *Li Zhi yu wanming wenxue sixiang* 李贽与晚明文学思想 [Li Zhi and late Ming literary thought]. Tianjin, China: Tianjin renmin chubanshe.

Lǐ Zìchéng
李自成

c. 1606–1645—Late Ming peasant rebel and founder of the Shun dynasty

Alternate name: given name: Lǐ Hóngjī 李鸿基

Li Zicheng on a Chinese 5-yuan coin.

Summary

Though capable of acts of great brutality, Li Zicheng has come down in history as the most militarily competent and politically savvy of the late Ming peasant rebel leaders, and the one most concerned about the welfare of ordinary peasants. As such, he earned a place as a romantic champion of the masses in the early Communist era, a reputation which has endured. On the first day of the lunar new year of 1644, Li proclaimed the establishment of his Shùn state in Xi'an, taking the reign title of Yǒngchāng, though he refrained from assuming the title of emperor.

As might be expected, owing to his humble background, little is known of Li Zicheng's youth other than stories that circulated later in his life, some of which clearly seem to have been intended to contribute to his growing legend and reputation. According to some accounts, Li Zicheng was the nephew of Gāo Yíngxiáng 高迎祥 (d. 1636), one of the prominent peasant rebel leaders who first emerged in the late 1620s in northwest China. Li's hometown—Mǐzhī 米脂, Shaanxi Province—was in dry and dusty country, prone to heavy winds and populated by sturdy people with short lifespans. Li's childhood name was Lǐ Hóngjī 李鸿基, and he was the second son of Li Shouzhong. His brother was twenty years older than him, and they were born of different mothers. Li's father was much older than his mother, and he died when Hongji was just a few months old. His stepfather, however, reportedly stressed education, and Li started learning characters at the age of six *sui* (a traditional Chinese way of recording age, counting the number of calendar years somebody had been alive). Li apparently never fit in his dull village. He was bright and inquisitive and was always asking questions. But he was also known as a rowdy and a troublemaker, and he often skipped school, earning frequent beatings. One of his favorite pastimes was mounted archery, at which he excelled.

Because his family was impoverished by repeated droughts, Li became a shepherd at the age of ten. It is said that even though his boss often beat him, Li did not complain. His mother died three years later, but despite his harsh life, Li grew up tall and strong, "with eyes that sparkled like lightning and the spirit of a tiger" (Xie 2007, 24).

His closest companions were his nephew Li Guo, who was just one month younger than Li, and his cousin Liu Guolong. While his companions dreamed of rising to military glory, Li Hongji realized the value also of literary achievement. He took the name Zicheng, which means "achieving on one's own," after he moved a huge incense burner at a temple to Guāndì 关帝, the Chinese god of war.

Adult Life

Li first tried to join the army at the age of sixteen but was turned down because of his youth. He was, however, allowed to join a few months later. At the age of eighteen he married a celebrated local beauty named Han Jin'er, supposedly to help take care of his aging stepfather. He then seems to have left the army and worked in a variety of odd jobs and in a family wine shop until he got a job with the postal service in 1626. The pay was low, and it was difficult to support his family. Matters were made worse by the fact that his superior beat him and denied him food and water for extended periods on account of loafing.

While Li supposedly swallowed his bitterness at these indignities, he became an outlaw when, after returning from an extended business trip, he killed a man whom he found in bed with his wife. Li protested that killing a cheating wife was perfectly within the limits of propriety, but his protests were ignored, and he was imprisoned while awaiting trial. Li was freed through the efforts of his nephew Li Guo, who had apparently bribed the jailer, but the two then killed the official who had sentenced Li in the first place, and they had to flee the area.

They went to Suide, where they again ran afoul of the law, so they moved on, traveling to Ningxia and then to Gansu Province. In Gansu, Li again joined the army and, by virtue of his military talents, soon became a squad commander of fifty men. Li's squad was among those sent to suppress the uprising of the "Dashing Prince," Gao Yingxiang. One version of events holds that Li found that he sympathized with the rebels (but recall that Gao may have been related to Li) and joined their cause. Another suggests that he was charged with stealing rations, so he decided to cast his lot with the rebels. Still another references a challenge of combat wherein neither Li nor his foe could gain the upper hand, so they stopped, had drinks, and joined forces. No matter the exact circumstances, Li would soon emerge as one of the smartest and most talented peasant rebel leaders, his own rise somewhat echoing that of the august founder of the Míng 明 dynasty (1368–1644), Zhu Yuanzhang (*Emperor Hóngwǔ 洪武, 1328–1398; r. 1368–1398).

Rebel Leader

For the next several years Li would serve under Gao Yingxiang as he ascended to a more prominent position among the rebel leaders following the death of Wang Jiayin at the hands of his own followers in the sixth month of 1632. At this time the Ming government was still grappling with the most effective means of quelling the peasant rebels. The high official initially dispatched to handle the problem, Yang He, had advocated a policy of appeasement, hoping to settle affairs with as little bloodshed as possible by distributing famine relief and resettling peasants on vacated lands. But this policy had proved fruitless as many leaders were inclined to accept government offers out of expediency, only to rebel again when left alone. The government's credibility was further eroded by the inconsistent application of policy; in some cases peasant rebels who surrendered were in fact slaughtered at "reconciliation banquets." Moreover, the Ming state had pressing problems in the northeast. In 1631 the Latter Jin (Manchu) had besieged and eventually captured the strategically important city of Dalinghe. A force sent to help relieve that siege under the commander Kong Youde had mutinied in Shandong and seized several key cities and fortresses in that province. These concerns forced the government to pull some troops from the northwest and allowed the peasant rebellions to expand outside their Shaanxi base into the neighboring provinces of Shanxi and Henan.

But the appointment of Hóng Chéngchóu 洪承畴 to the position of overall commander of anti-bandit operations signaled a new period of aggressiveness on the part of the Ming; in conjunction with the official in charge of bandit suppression Chén Qǐyù 陈启玉, they made significant progress in weakening bandit power in the northwest. Chen eventually bottled up many of the leading rebel bands in the Chexiang Gorge in western Henan in the summer of 1634. The rebels were short on food and supplies, and heavy rains had ruined their weapons. This prompted them to offer to surrender; Li Zicheng allegedly hatched a plan and took the lead by symbolically binding himself in ropes before Chen. For reasons that are still debated, Chen accepted the surrender, and the rebels were marched back toward Shaanxi, ostensibly so that they could resume their lives as farmers. Along the way, however, a dispute arose between the surrendered rebels and local officials, which resulted in the deaths of several

*People marked with an asterisk have entries in this dictionary.

dozen rebels and caused them to reignite their movement. They emerged with a vengeance, and rebel numbers swelled dramatically over the next several months.

In 1635 some thirteen rebel groups in seventy-two divisions held a great conclave to decide a common strategy for pursuing their ends. The conclave was held near Rongyang, a county in central Henan near the Huang (Yellow) River. Li Zicheng assumed a prominent role in the planning at this conference despite the fact that he was still considered at least a nominal subordinate of Gao Yingxiang. In the wake of these discussions, a joint force under Gao and Zhāng Xiànzhōng 张献忠, who would later emerge as Li's most significant rival, managed to plunder the Ming ancestral tombs at Fengyang, releasing many political prisoners and burning hundreds of ancient pine trees and dwellings. While not militarily significant, this act severely damaged Ming imperial prestige and caused great consternation at the Ming court. But in the wake of this triumph, the rebels' unity collapsed, and they found themselves increasingly pressured by the effective counterinsurgency operations of Hong Chengchou and Lu Xiangsheng.

Li eventually moved back into his native Shaanxi but found himself reduced to hit-and-run activities due to the new vigor of Ming field commanders. He also suffered the loss of perhaps his most able lieutenant, Gao Jie, who had initiated an affair with one of Li's concubines and therefore decided to defect to the Ming side rather than risk Li's wrath. Li fought a series of inconclusive skirmishes over the next year until Gao Yingxiang was captured and executed by Sūn Chuántíng 孙传庭, the Ming dynasty's defense minister, in the summer of 1636. This action forced Li to retreat in the short term, but also gave him the opportunity to take control of Gao's erstwhile forces and adopt the mantle of "Dashing Prince" for himself, which Li did in due course.

The next couple of years marked a decline in the power and influence of the rebellions as the Ming government took advantage of a brief lull in their war with the newly proclaimed Qīng 清 dynasty (1644–1911/1912) to redouble their efforts against the peasant rebels by implementing the so-called ten-sided net strategy of Minister of War Yáng Sìchāng 杨嗣昌, who was in fact the son of the previously disgraced Yang He. Yang's plan appeared to bear fruit initially as the Ming obtained the surrender of Zhang Xianzhong and later the prominent rebel commander Luo Rucai, who both declared their desire to become loyal subjects once again. In the interim, Li laid low in central China, biding his time until Zhang formally rebelled again in the spring of 1639. Many scholars believe that the failure to wipe out the peasant rebels at this juncture marked perhaps the last good opportunity for the Ming to eradicate them, but in fact even a few years later the tide might have been reversed had better strategies under more competent commanders been adopted. In any case, after the failures of his subordinates, Yang Sichang himself took the field against the peasant rebels but concentrated his initial efforts against Zhang Xianzhong, whom he deemed more dangerous at that time. Li, for his part, retained a low profile as his forces were greatly reduced and he had fallen ill, so he retreated to Shaanxi for much of 1639 and 1640.

Li's fortunes would revive in 1640, as continuing famine in western Henan drove new masses of peasants to his cause. Most significantly he acquired the services of two minor officials, Lǐ Yán 李岩 and Niú Jīnxīng 牛金星, who would aid him greatly in planning and propaganda efforts over the next several years. A third important figure to join Li around this time was the dwarf sorcerer and fortune-teller Sòng Xiàncè 宋献策, who lent Li's retinue a mystical aura that impressed many of Li's followers and marked him as a man of destiny. In the spring of 1641 he was poised to reascend the national stage. Li did this in spectacular fashion, capturing the towns of Yongning and Yiyang before advancing to take the city of Luoyang in Henan Province. In Luoyang, Li killed the local Ming Prince of Fu and butchered him, mixing his blood with wine and consuming his flesh alongside his men. The prince was hated by the locals for his greed, and they reportedly welcomed his demise. Li plundered his coffers, distributing some of the wealth among the local populace. Acts such as this, coupled with the efforts of Li Yan to sell Li's "programs" on their behalf, gained Li a considerable degree of popular support and distinguished him from the other rebel leaders. Around the same time, Zhang Xianzhong killed the Ming Prince of Xiangyang. These two disasters drove Yang Sichang to despair, and he committed suicide soon thereafter.

The Sieges of Kaifeng

At this point Li's aspirations rose and he looked toward entrenching himself more firmly in Henan. He then moved to besiege the provincial capital of Kaifeng, which could serve as an important springboard for further operations. But the city proved to be better defended than Luoyang, and with the efforts of the local Ming Prince of Zhou and the military commander Chen Yongfu, Li was turned back after a week-long siege. Li also suffered a personal tragedy when his left eye was shot by an arrow fired by either Yongfu or his son, Chen Ce, but the loss of the eye would add further to Li's growing mystique. Li retreated for the time being but remained in Henan, attracting more followers as the Ming scrambled to contain him, with Ding Qirui being appointed to succeed Yang Sichang as Supreme Commander. In late 1641 Li took Xiangcheng and then Nanyang, the latter city being the most important one in southern Henan. He then resolved to go after Kaifeng again, besieging it in January 1642.

This time the fighting lasted much longer and involved a number of stratagems and counter stratagems. The rebel leader Luo Rucai was also present in a supporting role. Li tried to both scale and tunnel through the 120-foot (36-meter)-thick walls. Artillery and all manner of noxious substances were employed by both sides. There was even a bizarre exchange whereby the rebels tried to goad the defenders into attacking by parading naked female captives before the city walls. This prompted the Ming forces to put their own naked monks atop the walls; the hapless monks were killed. In the end the rebels were defeated when the explosive charges they detonated to destroy the walls exploded backward and inflicted heavy casualties upon their own ranks. Li withdrew, but he continued his operations in southern and eastern Henan. He returned to besiege Kaifeng again in May 1642.

This time Li decided upon a more defensive strategy of a protracted siege. Ming forces within the city girded themselves for the siege, but Ding Qirui favored more aggressive countersiege operations. Ming commander Zuo Liangyu, stationed south of the city, was defeated by Li, allowing the rebels to establish a stronger cordon around the city. In late summer Ming relief columns scored a few minor victories but proved unable to lift the siege. The rebels then considered cutting the Huang River dikes north of the city to flood it, though for the time being they refrained from implementing the plan. By late summer morale within the city was plummeting, and there were reports of cannibalism as grain speculation and price gouging ran rampant. Eventually the government side decided to cut the Huang River dikes, hoping to engulf the rebel camps surrounding the city. Their initial efforts to do so may have been thwarted by the rebels or finished by them; the sources are unclear. In any event the dikes were cut, and water from the river rushed into the city. Initially, however, water levels were not that high, and they actually helped the defenders by bringing in fish and water creatures from the river for the consumption of the populace. But about a month later, the dike was cut again by the rebels at another point, and the city was entirely deluged by the river that had been swollen by autumn rains.

Kaifeng was inundated and utterly destroyed. Ming officials tried to rally the defenders and ferried some survivors out on boats, but hundreds of thousands died according to some Ming records, though such figures are probably exaggerated. Looters did more damage, and by the time Li captured the city, it was empty and bereft of military or strategic value. This great city, which had once been the capital of all of China, never recovered its former glory. Li had hoped to use it as a strategic springboard for attacking Beijing, but instead he left it empty. Its loss was significant in the sense that it increased the chaos in Henan and denied the Ming a base from which to continue their own struggle against Li. Li subsequently moved to attack Nanyang, which he eventually secured, driving the Ming commander Sun Chuanting back toward Tong Pass on the Shaanxi border. At this juncture, Li could have strengthened his position in Henan, but he instead decided to expand his operations into Húguǎng 湖广 Province (modern-day Hubei and Henan provinces).

Conquests and Defeat

Thus in early 1643 Li captured several towns in Huguang, most significantly Xiangyang, and first evinced his dynastic aspirations by renaming it Xiangjiang and assuming first a military and later a princely title. He set up a skeletal civil administration and appointed his followers to official posts. He would soon thereafter execute several of his erstwhile allies, most notably Luo Rucai. Through the summer of 1643, Li's forces fought skirmishes with Ming units and tried to determine their next course of action. After considering several plans, Li decided for an attack upon Beijing via the northwest. This would entail engaging Sun Chuanting at Tong Pass. Sun himself recognized the strategic import of his position and resolved to defend the pass. But bowing to pressure at court for more forceful government action, the emperor ordered Sun into the field against Li in the autumn of 1643. Sun eventually led his forces forth and enjoyed several minor victories in the first weeks of the campaign. But bad weather and overstretched supply lines soon compromised Sun's position, and he was forced to fall back. One of his subordinates was routed, and Li's armies took advantage of the situation to press the attack. Sun desperately tried to reorganize the Ming units at Tong Pass, but they were defeated, and Sun was killed in battle in November 1643.

Soon thereafter Li occupied Xi'an, another of China's ancient capitals, without a fight. On the first day of the lunar new year of 1644, Li proclaimed the establishment of his Shùn 顺 state in Xi'an, taking the reign title of Yǒngchāng 永昌, though he refrained from assuming the title of emperor at this time. He would then devote his efforts to building his military strength and consolidating his political control over Shaanxi in preparation for his final assault upon Beijing. By this time the Ming government had been severely discredited in the eyes of the masses, and Li enjoyed considerable support for his endeavors. Many local officials flocked to Li's banner, and most cities surrendered to his armies without a fight. Over the next three months, Li's forces would fan out over Shaanxi and Shanxi, encountering only isolated resistance, most notably at

Ningwu Pass. Even the very defensible Juyong Pass, the access point for Beijing through the Great Wall, was yielded to Li without a fight.

The desperate Ming Emperor Chóngzhēn 崇祯 (r. 1628–1644) considered and rejected several plans, including one to abandon the capital for Nanjing in the south. A last-ditch effort to save the Ming launched by Grand Secretary Li Jiantai ended in an utter debacle as his hastily raised troops deserted. The emperor ennobled several Ming generals, most notably Wú Sānguì 吴三桂, then stationed at Ningyuan in Liaodong, and ordered them to come to the rescue of the capital, but none answered. Li's forces surrounded Beijing on 23 April 1644. He tried to negotiate with the emperor, even offering to help fight the Manchus in exchange for a degree of recognition of his independent power, but his entreaties were refused. The demoralized defenders of Beijing put up minimal resistance, and Chongzhen hanged himself on Coal Hill behind the Forbidden City on the morning of 24 April. Li and his retinue entered the capital the next day.

The peasant rebel forces were initially welcomed by the populace, who burned incense in their honor and held placards proclaiming themselves "subjects of Shun." But matters soon turned ugly as it became clear that the vast majority of Li's followers had no interest in governing the empire but saw the whole adventure as a way to plunder and enrich themselves. Officials and commoners alike were brutalized, and women were raped throughout Beijing. While some officials sought to curry favor with the new regime, others fled or killed themselves. Though Li took rudimentary steps to appoint officials for his government, he delayed formally ascending the throne, most likely because of the still-looming threat of the Ming general Wu Sangui, then entrenched at Shanhaiguan in the east, and the Manchus, who were still advancing toward China proper. Li made several overtures toward Wu but did not receive the desired responses, so he eventually resolved to engage Wu in the field of battle.

Meanwhile Wu had opened his own negotiations with the Manchus, eventually coming to an accord with Prince Dorgon, who was then acting as the de facto regent for the child emperor Shunzhi. The Manchus agreed to support Wu's military operations against Li and thereby help him avenge the defeat of the Ming, which would in turn enhance their own legitimacy as they moved to take Beijing for themselves. In late May 1644, the two forces clashed outside Shanhaiguan Pass. Li's forces were fairly successful early in the battle and started pushing Wu's troops back toward their fortifications. But then the wind shifted, blowing dust into the eyes of the peasant armies. Soon thereafter two wings of Manchu cavalry swept into the field, bolstering Wu's troops in the vanguard and routing the peasant armies, most of which were led by defector commanders whose loyalty to Li Zicheng was tenuous at best.

Li's armies retreated to Beijing, where Li finally belatedly enthroned himself. His armies then looted the capital and fled before the advance of the combined armies of Wu Sangui and the Qing. The Qing would occupy Beijing on 6 June 1644. Li fled west to Shaanxi, seeing his armies crumble as he retreated to Xi'an. Over the next six months his authority would disintegrate throughout the areas he had formerly captured, as Ming loyalists, semi-independent warlords, and Qing forces captured districts and towns from Li's appointees. Li's close advisers also turned against one another as Niu Jinxing intrigued to have Li Yan executed in the summer of 1644. Taiyuan fell to the Qing in the fall of 1644, and Tong Pass was breached after heavy fighting at the start of 1645. Li's remaining commanders and forces regrouped at Xi'an, before retreating southeast into Henan before the Qing advance. Li's armies dispersed further at this point, and Li finally ended up in the vicinity of Mount Jiugong with a mere twenty followers in midsummer 1645, hotly pursued by the Manchu prince Ajige.

The exact circumstances of Li's death remain a matter of some dispute. One account maintains that Li hanged himself after being surrounded by a band of angry peasants from whom he stole food, but by the time his corpse was recovered, it had decayed beyond recognition. Another version of events relates that Li was beaten to death by angry peasants who did not know who he was (presumably also after he stole food), but they identified him later by his seals, fine clothes, and missing left eye. His body was then turned over to Southern Ming authorities, who decapitated it. Still another account relates that Li's men scattered, and no one knows what became of him. The only one among Li's followers who survived was his nephew Li Guo, who, ironically like Zhang Xianzhong's former subordinates, eventually defected to the Southern Ming and served them as a military commander.

Li's Legacy

Li has continued to enjoy a fair reputation since his death, particularly in Chinese Communist history annals. Even today he continues to be the subject of novels, comic books for children, films, paintings, and the like. There is a great statue of Li near the freeway between the Ming Tombs and Beijing, and the palace he had built for himself in his hometown of Mizhi has been restored as a tourist attraction.

Li was regarded as the most righteous of the late Ming peasant rebel leaders and the most sincerely committed to the cause of peasant revolution. Certainly, while he was not a revolutionary in the social sense, he was sensitive to the plight of his fellow peasants and seemed to have been at least somewhat interested in ameliorating their condition. He was much more reserved in his personal conduct than most of his fellow peasant leaders, and though he could be ruthless, his general pattern of behavior was less violent and erratic than that of Zhang Xianzhong. Li also seems to have had an appreciation for honor and integrity, and there are numerous accounts of his favorable recognition of loyal Ming officials and acts of magnanimity. As might be expected of someone who commanded the loyalty of hundreds of thousands of men at the height of his influence, Li was also smart and charismatic. He appears to have been competent as a field commander but perhaps somewhat limited as a strategist. Indeed it is indicated that much of the planning of his operations was carried out by others, most notably his sometime-ally Luo Rucai. Many of his most significant victories can be ascribed more to the incompetence of his adversaries than to his own acumen. His abilities as a judge of character are also suspect as he surrounded himself (in part no doubt due to circumstance) with many who did not share his vision for a new state but instead only sought to aggrandize themselves. And his avowed plans to remit taxes, while certainly attractive to the masses, did little to endear him to the official stratum whose support was essential for establishing a stable government.

In the final assessment Li certainly took advantage of the opportunities presented him, but committed too many mistakes to secure his position and establish his regime for the long haul. As the common saying goes, he could conquer the realm from horseback, but not rule it from there. There seems to have been no coherent plan in place for what his state would do after they seized Beijing. Perhaps had they done a better job of consolidating their power in Xi'an and gained more administrative experience, things would have been different. This should not detract from the scope of Li's achievements, however. He remains an important symbol of the age, one of the most important commoners in the annals of Chinese history, and an icon in modern China.

Kenneth M. SWOPE
University of Southern Mississippi

Further Reading

Dai Li 戴笠, & Wu Qiao 吴乔. (Comps.). (1991). *Liukou changbian* 流寇长编 [Compilation of materials on the wandering bandits] (2 vols.). Beijing: Shumu wenxian chubanshe.

Des Forges, Roger V. (2003). *Cultural centrality and political change in Chinese history: Northeast Henan in the fall of the Ming*. Stanford, CA: Stanford University Press.

Li Guangtao 李光濤. (1965). *Mingji liukou shimo* 明季流寇事末 [The complete story of the wandering bandits of the late Ming]. Taipei, Taiwan: Zhongyang yanjiuyuan lishi yuyan yanjiusuo.

Liu Yinan 柳义南. (1983). *Li Zicheng jinian fukao* 李自成紀年附考 [Annotated supplemental chronological biography of Li Zicheng]. Beijing: Zhonghua shuju.

Parsons, James B. (1993). *Peasant rebellions of the late Ming dynasty* (Rep.). Ann Arbor, MI: Association for Asian Studies.

Swope, Kenneth M. (2013). *The military collapse of China's Ming dynasty, 1618–1644*. London: Routledge.

Xie Chengren 謝承仁. (2007). *Li Zicheng xinzhuan* 李自成新传 [New biography of Li Zicheng]. Beijing: Beijing tushuguan chubanshe.

Zeng Buxian 曾步贤, et al. (Eds.). (2001). *Li Zicheng xunnan Tongcheng ziliao xuanyi* 李自成殉难通城资料选辑 [Historical materials pertaining to Li Zicheng's martyrdom at Tongcheng]. Tongcheng, China: Tongcheng xian shizhi xuehui.

Nurhaci

Nǔ'ěrhāchì 努尔哈赤

1559–1626—Jurchen chieftain, conqueror, and state builder

Alternate name: Nǔěrhāqí 努尔哈齐

Summary

The Jurchen chieftain Nurhaci began in 1583 with less than a hundred followers and proceeded to unite the Jurchen tribes. After defeating and consolidating the various tribes, as well as many of the surrounding Mongols, he attacked Ming China and took over the Liaodong area, establishing the Aisin ("Golden") Empire. Nurhaci could well be called the father of the Manchus because it was he who gathered the many disparate peoples of Manchuria and formed this new ethnic identity, establishing a Manchu written language and a form of government that embraced both military and civilian society. The boundaries of the modern Chinese nation owe their existence to the descendants of Nurhaci, who expanded the borders to include all these lands.

Nurhaci was of tremendous importance in the history of China even though he was non-Han, the dominant ethnic group of modern China. He was a Jurchen leader who established the Later Jin (936–946 CE) dynasty at the beginning of the seventeenth century, which was later to expand into the Manchu-ruled Qīng 清 dynasty (1644–1911/1912) that enveloped all of the territory covered by traditional China as well as Mongolia, Tibet, and much of Turkestan. The boundaries of the modern Chinese nation owe their existence to the descendants of Nurhaci, who expanded the borders to include all these lands. Nurhaci could well be called the father of the Manchus because it was he who gathered the many disparate peoples of Manchuria and formed this new ethnic identity. He also developed a simultaneously military and civilian system of governance that made possible the enormous conquests conducted by his sons and grandsons, called the banner system; the Manchus are often referred to as "Bannermen" (*qírén* 旗人)

after Nurhaci's system. There are interesting parallels in the life of Nurhaci with the great Mongol leader Chéngjísīhán 成吉思汗 (c. 1162–1227), known in the West as *Chinggis (Genghis) Khan. Although Chinggis/Genghis is a household word throughout the West, Nurhaci is scarcely known at all.

Much has been written in Asia about Nurhaci, but because he is a larger-than-life and polarizing figure, it is difficult at times to sort out what is reliably historical and what is legend and fancy. Also, sources from close to the time he lived often betray a bias, either for or against him. Perhaps the most reliable source is a collection of documents written in an early form of Manchu produced at or about the time he was coming into power. These were translated into Japanese and given the title *Mambun Rōtō,* later translated into Chinese with the title *Mǎnwén lǎodàng* 满文老档 (*Old Manchu Annals*). Unfortunately the earliest of these doesn't record anything before 1606. A fuller Manchu document that traces the life of Nurhaci, called the *Yargiyan kooli* 满洲实录 (*Manchu Veritable Records*) was produced during the long reign of the Kāngxī Emperor 康熙 (1662–1723; r. 1661–1722) and later revised during the reign (nearly as long) of *Emperor Qiánlóng 乾隆 (1711–1799; r. 1736–1795); it contains such things as a fanciful myth on the origin of the Manchus and appears to have expunged anything from earlier records that was considered damaging to the reputation of Nurhaci. Many claim it also exaggerates some of Nurhaci's victories. Nevertheless, in most cases it appears to be a fairly reliable, if slightly biased account. There are a couple of contemporary accounts of Nurhaci and his capital at Fe Ala, written by Korean ambassadors to his nation, that are found in the annals of the Korean Yi dynasty (1392–1910). There are also a few scattered early references in Chinese, although most of the Chinese materials are from later periods and often of questionable validity, indiscriminately recording folklore tales and legends that had grown up around him. It seems the most reliable way to trace Nurhaci's history is to allow the Manchus to tell their story through the *Yargiyan kooli,* checking it, of course, with Chinese and Korean sources where possible.

The Jurchens

Nurhaci was a Jurchen (*Nǚzhēn* 女真). The Jurchen people once lived in what is now Jilin, Heilongjiang, and parts of Liaoning provinces in northeast China, as well as adjoining lands in Russian Siberia. They lived along the banks and tributaries of the Sungari, Nonni, Mudan, Tumen, Sahaliyan (Heilong), Ussuri, and parts of the Liao rivers. The word "Jurchen" comes from the name these people used to identify themselves: *jušen* ("the people"). A number were descendants of the Jurchens who had several centuries earlier formed a great empire: the

*People marked with an asterisk have entries in this dictionary.

Aisin ("Golden") Empire (Jīn金). This empire existed alongside the Chinese Southern Song (Nán Sòng 南宋; 1127–1279) and covered all of what is now northern China south to the banks of the Yangzi (Chang) River. It lasted until 1234, when the Jurchens were defeated and became subject to the Mongols. The Mongols in turn controlled this area until 1368, when they were defeated by the newly emerging Míng 明 Empire (1368–1644) of the Chinese and retreated back to the north.

After the defeat of the Mongol Yuán (1279–1368) dynasty, the Jurchen homeland became somewhat complex politically. The Mongols still had a great deal of influence, but the Koreans to the east attempted to capitalize on waning Mongol power to exert some influence of their own. Of course the Chinese Ming Empire also wished to extend their own influence into the area to maintain much needed trade for frontier products, mainly horses from the Mongols and Koreans but also ginseng from the mountain forests as well as animal furs, freshwater pearls, and foodstuffs such as mushrooms, chestnuts, and pine nuts. The Ming also wished to use the Jurchens as a buffer between themselves and the Mongols. Jurchen tribes were in flux. Some aligned themselves with the Mongols or Koreans for a time, others with the newly powerful Chinese. But they essentially attempted to maintain as much of their autonomy as they could.

The Ming Chinese distinguished the various Jurchen tribes into three major groups. Two were identified by the names of commanderies set up by the Chinese: the Haixi Nuzhen, who lived in the region of the Sungari (Haixi) River; and the Jianzhou Nuzhen, who were tribes originally living near the Jianzhou Commandery to the north but later moved to the western foothills of the Changbai Mountains. (A commandery was a historical administrative division similar to a prefecture.) They were sandwiched between the Koreans to the east beyond the mountains and the Chinese to the west, in the Liao River basin. The third group was called the Yeren Nuzhen ("Wildman Jurchens"). These were the Jurchens who lived in the northern reaches along the Sahaliyan (Amur), Ussuri, Tumen, and Mudan rivers, and had little exposure to Chinese "civilizing" influences.

The Jianzhou Jurchens originally lived farther to the north but migrated south and west to be closer to the Chinese markets upon which they depended for trade. The Chinese had established a number of "horse markets" in frontier towns such as Kaiyuan and Tieling to conduct trade. During Nurhaci's time a branch of the Jianzhou Jurchens, who were living along the Suksuhu River (a tributary of the Hunhe), traded downriver in a Chinese frontier town called Fushun. Living in close proximity to the Chinese, they had also begun to engage somewhat in agriculture, mainly carried on for them by Chinese they had captured and made their slaves.

Birth and Early Years

Nurhaci was born in the town of Hetu Ala in the year of the Yellow Sheep, the thirty-eighth year of the Jiajing emperor of the Ming dynasty (1559), to a Jurchen named Taksi and a woman of the Hitara clan. His grandfather, Giocangga, was one of the *ningguta beile*, the six chieftains of the people of the Suksuhu River. The six chieftains were brothers who established themselves, together with their people, along the Suksuhu in the mid-sixteenth century. They were nominally all under the control of a *jušen* named Wang Gao, who had the Chinese title of Commandant of the Left Protectorate of the Jianzhou Jurchens. Nurhaci's father, Taksi, was the fourth son of Giocangga, but he seems to have shared some in Giocangga's rule, at least according to the later Manchu sources. Being part of the ruling class, we can assume that Taksi's household was relatively well off.

Nurhaci's birth mother died when Nurhaci was around nine (or ten *sui*, a traditional Chinese way of recording age, counting the number of calendar years somebody had been alive), and Taksi took another wife, this time from the Nara clan (one of the most prestigious of the Jurchen clans), named Kenje. She disliked her stepsons, and Nurhaci and Surgaci, his younger brother, likely left their family compound and went to live with Wang Gao, a relative by marriage.

Wang Gao had a stormy relationship with the Ming Chinese. The Ming only had nominal control over the affairs of the frontier. When it served his needs, Wang Gao would align himself with the Ming, but when it did not, he had no scruples acting against the Ming to further his own interests. So it happened that in 1576 Wang Gao lured a Chinese official to his stronghold and had him killed. As a result, a frontier general of Korean ancestry who was serving the Ming, Li Chengliang, attacked Wang Gao and took his compound. Wang Gao fled to the Hada, another Jurchen tribe, but was eventually turned over to the Ming and executed. Li Chengliang may have captured Nurhaci and Surgaci at that time. According to some later Chinese sources, the young boys defiantly asked to be put to death, but Li Chengliang, admiring their courage, instead took them into his service to be his personal servants.

Some write that Nurhaci showed courage and ambition while he was serving with Li Chengliang, always volunteering to be in the vanguard in battles. It is also said that while with the Chinese he grew very fond of the stories from the historical novels *Romance of the Three Kingdoms* (*Sānguó yǎnyì* 三国演义) and *Water Margin* (*Shuǐhǔ zhuàn* 水浒传). None of this is found in the Manchu histories, however, and it is doubtful that he was ever able to read Chinese. We cannot know for sure the relationship he had with Li Chengliang, but from all that happened between the two men, there is ample evidence that there was perhaps a close relationship.

When Nurhaci was about eighteen years old (nineteen *sui*) he married a woman from the Tunggiya tribe of the Hitara clan. At that point he returned to his father's house to claim his inheritance, but his father, Taksi, due to the influence of Nurhaci's stepmother, Kenje, refused to give Nurhaci what should have been his due. He was given a very small portion of what he was entitled to and had to make do with it. Later Taksi repented of his stinginess toward his eldest son and offered him his full inheritance, but Nurhaci refused it, showing it was not in his character to overlook a slight to his dignity.

In 1583 Li Chengliang came back, this time to attack the sons of Wang Gao, Ahai and Atai. They had taken over the position of their father, and their hatred toward the Ming for killing their father soured their relationship with the Chinese. Ahai's stronghold was soon overrun, but Atai's was more formidable. Nurhaci was about twenty-four (twenty-five *sui*) at the time.

Li Chengliang first attacked Ahai and killed him in his fort called Šaji, then attacked Atai in his fortifications at Gure. The Chinese gave one account of the battle, but the Jurchens gave a different one. According to some Chinese accounts, Nurhaci's father and grandfather served as guides for Li Chengliang's army. When they arrived at Gure and the Ming troops were unable to take the fortifications, they sent Giocangga and Taksi into the fort to try to convince Atai and his people to surrender. Atai refused and retained Giocangga and Taksi inside the fort. When the Ming troops stormed the fort in the subsequent attack, Atai and his people were killed as well as Giocangga and Taksi.

The Jurchens have a different version of the story. They say a Jurchen man with the nickname of Nikan Wailan ("Official of the Chinese") led the troops of Li Chengliang. Nikan Wailan, who had a nearby fortification called Turun, saw his chance to eliminate the sons of Wang Gao and take their place as a leader of the Jianzhou Jurchens, so he approached the Ming armies and offered to guide them to Gure. When Giocangga and Taksi found out the fort at Gure was being attacked, they rushed there to save Giocangga's granddaughter, Taksi's niece, who was married to Atai. First Giocangga entered the fort to persuade Atai to let him take his daughter out of harm's way, but Atai refused. When Giocangga did not return, Taksi entered the fort and was retained as well. Meanwhile, the battle was not going well for Li Chengliang's troops. The compound was well fortified, and Atai would occasionally launch attacks from the fort, killing the Ming troops. Calling on Nikan Wailan, Li Chengliang said this trouble was his fault since he was the one that incited them to come and attack the fortress. Nikan Wailan was alarmed at the turn of events and told Li Chengliang he would devise a plan to take the fort. He went himself up to the fort and called out to the inhabitants, saying that once the Ming troops had come, they were not about to go away until they had destroyed the compound. But if someone would kill Atai for them, they would make him head of the fortress in Atai's stead. The people believed Nikan Wailan, and Atai was killed. Li Chengliang then said that all who wished to surrender to him were to open the gates of the compound and come out, and he would then spare them. It was a trick, however, and as soon as they opened the gates and began to come out, the Ming troops slaughtered them all. When Li Chengliang's troops subsequently stormed the fort and set fire to it, Taksi was shot and Giocangga was burned to death in the confusion of the battle.

War of Revenge against Nikan Wailan

Nurhaci, when he learned of the death of his father and grandfather, went to the Ming leader to demand an explanation. The Ming claimed it was a mistake that his father and grandfather had died, returned the corpses to him, and gave him thirty oxen and thirty horses to recompense his loss, but Nurhaci was not satisfied. He demanded they turn over Nikan Wailan to him for his treachery, which had resulted in the killing of his grandfather and father, but the Ming would not acquiesce. They considered it a challenge to their authority and said they would instead raise Nikan Wailan to be chief over the Suksuhu people—Nurhaci's tribe—and declare Nurhaci a rebel. But Nurhaci could never be subject to Nikan Wailan, a man who had once been a subject of his father and now had brought on his father's death by his betrayal. Although his father left him precious little, only thirteen sets of armor and a small band of faithful followers, he would wage a war of revenge against Nikan Wailan. But Nikan Wailan had the upper hand. The Chinese supported him, and the rest of Nurhaci's clan knew it. Instead of aiding Nurhaci in his fight, they vowed to destroy him. This was a turning point in Nurhaci's life.

Nurhaci, with a troop of about one hundred followers (only thirteen of whom were armored), attacked Nikan Wailan's fortified town of Turun, but Nikan Wailan abandoned the town and escaped with his family and slaves before Nurhaci was able to take it.

Some of the Jianzhou tribes also had an enmity toward Nikan Wailan and gravitated to Nurhaci's side. Among them were two brothers: Nomina and Naikada of the town of Sarhu. Even though they swore their allegiance to Nurhaci, when they heard a rumor that the Ming were going to support Nikan Wailan to be the leader of the Jianzhou Jurchens, they reneged on their oath to Nurhaci and did not come to the staging ground to go to battle. They secretly sent messengers to Nikan Wailan informing him of Nurhaci's movements, allowing him to escape. Nurhaci told Naikada and Nomina to attack the people of Hunehe, but they countered that he should first attack the Dunggiya and Barda tribes, which were at war with the brothers. Nurhaci conceived a plan to rid himself of these false friends. He said, "Let us both go up and attack Barda." When Nomina declined, Nurhaci said, "If you won't attack Barda, give me all your weapons so my troops can use them to fight" (*Yargiyan kooli* 35). Nomina turned them over, thinking he had fooled Nurhaci into fighting his battles for him, but as soon as Nurhaci obtained the weapons he attacked and killed Nomina, his brother Naikada, and all their troops. Nurhaci was not a man to be trifled with.

There are many episodes in the early life of Nurhaci that serve to show his resourcefulness under pressure, his disregard for danger, and his doggedness in pursuing his goals. In this early period, many of Nurhaci's own tribe allied themselves with Nikan Wailan and swore an oath to kill Nurhaci. Some men once attempted to break into his house and do him harm, but Nurhaci's dog began to bark and awakened his master. He quickly hid his daughter and two young sons, grabbed his long-handled sword, and shouted, "Who is that outside! Why don't you come in?! If you don't come in, I'm coming out!" (*Yargiyan kooli* 38–39).Then he banged on the window frame, pretending he was going to come out through the window but instead kicked open the door and charged. They all fled, managing to kill only one servant in Nurhaci's household who had been sleeping outside at the time.

In the year of the Green Monkey (1584), Nurhaci went to battle against one of his own tribe who had treacherously led a troop of the Hada against him. It was winter and the traveling was difficult; in addition, Lidai, his relative, expected the attack. Some of Nurhaci's troops thought they should give it up, but Nurhaci would not retreat, so they attacked and took the city. Lidai fully expected to be executed, but Nurhaci pardoned him of his crimes and returned home.

Despite his success against Lidai and his magnanimity toward a vanquished foe, many of his own tribe continued to hold out against him. At one point his friend Gahašan Hashu, to whom he had given his own sister to be his bride, was ambushed on the road and killed. When he went to get the body, his family would not go with him, since they were complicit in the crime. Outside the walls of his family's town, he rode back and forth, brandishing his weapon saying, "Let those who want to kill me come out together," then he went and recovered the body, taking some his own clothes to prepare it for burial (*Yargiyan kooli* 42).

Other members of his tribe staged an assassination attempt. One very dark night Nurhaci again heard the sound of someone outside. He woke his wife and said to her, "Pretend to go out to the toilet and I will slip out with you" (*Yargiyan kooli* 43); he remained behind when she returned to the house. When the assassin, not knowing Nurhaci was there, came close, Nurhaci knocked him down and had the servants come bind him. His household wanted the man killed, but Nurhaci reasoned, "If I kill him, with so few men on my side, his master will simply take that as an excuse to come against me and destroy me." So aloud he said, "This man probably just came to steal one of my cows, let him go." (*Yargiyan kooli* 43–44). Others continued to come against him at night, but by luck or divine providence, he was aware of them and repulsed them all.

In the sixth month of that same year, Nurhaci took his small army up against the stronghold of Mardun, those who had killed his friend and brother-in-law. His small contingent, advancing behind shielded carts, was pounded by rocks catapulted toward them, and eventually they were pinned down. Nurhaci, standing behind a stump, shot and killed Nesin, the leader of the city. He also killed four others on the wall, allowing his soldiers a chance to retreat. They besieged the fortress for three days; on the fourth night he had his troops scale the cliff leading to the city barefoot, and they took the fortress by surprise.

Not only were there challenges from within his tribe, but neighboring tribes also tested Nurhaci's rise to power. The Donggo tribe had an enmity against Nurhaci's grandfather for allying with the Hada and attacking them, so they prepared for war against Nurhaci. Nurhaci staged a preemptive attack against them, although his small troop had misgivings about traveling so far afield. While he was fighting the Donggo, the chieftain of the Wanggiya tribe came and asked him to attack the Onggolo. Nurhaci sent his troops against their town. While he was attacking them, Nurhaci, in a position far in advance of his troops, was struck twice with arrows, seriously wounding him. The blood ran from wounds in his head and neck to the soles of his feet. His soldiers wanted to rescue him, but fearing they would expose themselves to enemy fire Nurhaci said no, he would return to their lines on his own. Once he was back among his troops, he lost consciousness several times from the loss of blood; it was a long time before he recovered his strength. That was one of the few battles Nurhaci engaged in where he returned without taking the city.

In the fourteenth year of the Wanli emperor of the Ming (1586), Nurhaci attacked Nikan Wailan's city of Eregun and took it. Nikan Wailan fled again to the Ming, but this time the Ming refused him sanctuary. Nurhaci's troops killed him and presented his head to Nurhaci, who set it on the altar of his deceased father and grandfather as an offering.

Nurhaci Builds His Nation

By this time in his battle of revenge against Nikan Wailan, Nurhaci had managed to take over his own clan as well as some neighboring clans. This was the time to lay claim to the leadership of the Jurchens of the Suksuhu. At a place called Hulun Hada ("Smokestack Ridge"), he built his fortress called Fe Ala ("Old Hill"). The fortified town had an inside and an outside wall, as well as an interior palisade that housed his family and that of his brother Surgaci. Within the outer wall was a space for about one hundred families. Outside of these walls there were about four hundred more families. Here he promulgated a few rudimentary laws: no stealing, no rebellion, and so forth. The location was not far from his hometown, Hetu Ala.

The Nikan (Chinese) recognized that Nurhaci was now the local power to deal with, so they made him their commander of the left protectorate of the Jianzhou Jurchen. Nurhaci displayed his own allegiance to the Nikan by traveling to their capital of the north, Beijing, to present tribute. Such success was alarming to the other tribes of the Jianzhou federation. The mighty Hulun confederacy of the Haixi Jurchens in the north was also concerned.

The Hulun confederacy was made up of four major tribes. At one time the tribe of the Ula River was preeminent. The people of this tribe were originally from the land called Hulun and belonged to the powerful Nara clan. The tribe of the Hada land was an offshoot of the Nara clan. The tribe of the Yehe River was originally Mongol but took on the name of the Nara and soon became very powerful, rivaling the Ula. The tribe of the Hoifa River originally were of the Ikderi clan, part of the Nimaca tribe who lived on the banks of the Sahaliyan (Amur) River. But when they aligned themselves with the Hulun, they also became Nara and settled on the banks of the Hoifa.

In the nineteenth year of Wanli (1591), the leader of the Yehe sent a messenger to Nurhaci demanding some of his land for their tribe. Nurhaci told the messenger that land was not like cattle that could be given to another. His land was his land just as the land of the Yehe was their land. He could not go on their land, and they could not come on his. The Yehe summoned all their allies: the Ula, the Hada, the Hoifa of the Hulun confederacy as well as the Khorcin Mongols, the Sibe, the Guwarcha, and two tribes of the Far White Mountains, the Jusheli, and the Nayin. These nine federated tribes amassed a mighty army of thirty thousand warriors and marched against one of Nurhaci's towns, conquering it easily and taking their cattle and goods. When Nurhaci learned of it, he set out with his small army to challenge them. As they approached the enemy's camp he sent out his spies. They reported back that the enemy's campfires on the opposite bank were as numerous as the stars in the sky. But Nurhaci was not afraid. He encouraged his troops saying: "Here at Gure there is a very strategic stronghold, one that they will have a hard time overrunning. We will lure them here to fight and rain logs and stones on their heads. Though they are a huge army, they are formed from many different tribes and do not work as a single body. If we can kill a few of their leaders it will throw the army into confusion and we will take them" (*Yargiyan kooli* 95).

The battle unfolded just as Nurhaci said it would. In a dangerous encounter on horseback, Nurhaci himself engaged and killed Bujai, the leader of the Yehe, and Bujantai, the Ula leader, was taken captive. The federated troops were thrown into disarray, and the victory went to Nurhaci.

Nurhaci immediately attacked the tribes of the Far White Mountains who had taken part in the fight against him and destroyed them. But to the large tribes of the Hulun confederacy, he was conciliatory. He did not kill Bujantai, but kept him at Fe Ala and married one of his brother Surgaci's daughters to him. The Khorcin Mongols also made their own peace with Nurhaci.

At the end of the twenty-third year of Wanli (1596), the Ming granted him the title of dragon and tiger general. He attacked and defeated the Hoifa in the twenty-sixth year of Wanli (1598). That same year, Menggebulu of the Hada asked for his aid against the Yehe, who were trying to annex his territory. Menggebulu even sent a couple of his children as hostages. Nurhaci sent a couple of generals and troops to aid him, but the Yehe, learning of this, convinced Menggebulu to return to their alliance.

In the twenty-seventh year of the reign of Emperor *Wànlì 万历 (1599), Nurhaci decided to attack the Hada because of their treachery vis-à-vis the Yehe. This same year Wangga and Jangga from the Forest tribes of Donghai came to present tribute and marry into the Jianzhou Jurchens. In this year, Nurhaci had two of his advisors, Erdeni and Hegai, develop a new script for the language of the Jurchens, basing it on the Mongol script they had been using heretofore. Nurhaci also opened a mine and began ironworking activities.

In the twenty-eighth year of Wanli (1600), Nurhaci killed Menggebulu, but because the Hada were allies of the Ming, he soothed the Ming court by returning Menggebulu's son to lead the Hada, as well as giving his daughter to be his wife. The Hada were in the midst of a devastating famine, and Menggebulu's son, since he could obtain no help from the Ming, had no choice but to return and throw his lot in with Nurhaci and the Jianzhou Jurchens. So the Hada tribe ceased to exist (Chen 2003, 65).

In 1601 Nurhaci organized the people under his control into fighting, social, and economic units, using the old "arrow companies" of the Jurchen as a model (the old companies consisted of ten men with an "arrow leader" [*nirui ejen*]). Now he made permanent arrow companies of kinship-related fighting groups with, ideally, up to three hundred fighting men and their families. Several arrow companies were grouped into *gūsa* ("banners") represented by different banner colors, first five then reduced to four. In the forty-third year of Wanli (1615), these were expanded to eight (Roth Li 1975, 19–30). (Please see sidebar below for more information on the Eight Banners.)

In the thirty-first year of Wanli (1603), Nurhaci built a new capital city near Hetu Ala, the land of his birth, and in the thirty-third year of Wanli (1605), he developed a way to dry ginseng so it could be preserved and sold when the Jurchens wanted (Roth Li 1975, 32–33).

The Eight Banners

The Eight Banners (*jakūn gūsa, bāqí* 八旗) are perhaps the most distinctive feature of Manchu society during the Qing dynasty. It was an all-encompassing system, overseeing the military, economic, governmental, and social aspects of Manchu society. What began as a way to organize military raids morphed into the complex ordering of a society. Nurhaci is credited with this system of organizing the people under his control.

Up until their conquest of China, hunting was the mainstay of economic livelihood for the Jurchens. Relatively large-scale organized hunts called *aba* were a common event. The participants would spread themselves out into a large circle and in an organized way slowly move inward, trapping all the game in the area within that circle. These hunts were put together by organizing groups of approximately ten men under a leader. The leader was charged with meting out the arrows used for the hunt for the people in his charge and for directing their actions so they were in coordination with the entire hunting party. The leaders of these groups were called *nirui ejen,* or "arrow masters" and the groups themselves became known as *niru* ("arrows"). The composition of the *niru* was generally men of the same family or lineage (*mukūn*). Indeed these lineage groups would generally stay together as a collective and the word *mukūn* most likely first meant simply a group or band—later it became synonymous with "village."

Nurhaci took over the organization of the Jurchen hunting parties once his band of raiders became large enough to need more than just rudimentary organization. As his army increased and there was a need for a higher-level organization he looked to the military organization used during the earlier Jurchen Aisin (Jin) dynasty.

At first, for the most part, the lineage and village groups were left intact and became single *niru*. Most of them would not reach the ideal of three hundred fighting men per *niru*. Later, as Nurhaci began to take more belligerent peoples under his control, he did not allow them to stay in their original village and/or lineage groups and instead parceled them out to various *niru* that were perhaps short of the full complement of three hundred soldiers. Thus the *niru* became more regularly units of three hundred fighting men and the family, lineage, and village allegiances began to be replaced by allegiances to his government.

On a higher level, a certain number of *niru* were organized into five *gūsa* (banners), each represented by a different color flag or banner: blue, yellow, red, white, and black. (The black banner was eventually eliminated, perhaps because the black banner was too hard to see at night when they made raids.) All this organizing of *niru* and *gūsa* became regularized on the eve of the establishment of Nurhaci's Aisin Empire in 1616. The *niru* were regularized as companies of three hundred households. Five *niru* were grouped to form a *jalan* (regiment) and five *jalan* were grouped into a *gūsa*. The original four banners of yellow, white, red and, blue were increased to eight, the four new banners being represented by bordered versions of the original four plain-colored banners. Each of the banners was led by *gūsa-i ejen* "banner leader." Each banner was also the charge of a *beile* (chieftain), in a way becoming a tribe unto itself, though not made up this time of lineages but an artificially produced governmental hierarchy. The *beile* of the banners were members of Nurhaci's own family, hence the term *beile* is sometimes translated as "prince."

—Stephen A. WADLEY

In 1606, at approximately forty-four years of age (forty-five *sui*), the Khalka Mongols gave Nurhaci the title of Kundulun Han ("Revered King"). This is the first time Nurhaci, who prior to this time was known by his followers as Sure Beile ("The Wise Chieftain") was proclaimed a "king" (*han*).

The Final Conquest of the Jurchen

In the thirty-fifth year of Wanli (1607), Nurhaci took the stronghold of the Hoifa by stratagem and destroyed them. The Warka, a tribe by the Tumen River, petitioned to come to Jianzhou and be under Nurhaci's command, so Nurhaci sent his brother Surgaci and his two sons Daišan and Cuyen to accompany them back. Along the way the Ula blocked them.

Nurhaci had courted the Ula to be friends. At the battle of Gure he had spared the Ula leader Bujantai's life and kept him at Hetu Ala for four years. When the Ula chief Mantai died, he sent Bujantai up to be chief of the Ula, also marrying his daughter and a niece to him. But instead of being loyal to Nurhaci, Bujantai expanded his power by attacking the tribes of the Tumen River and resisting Nurhaci's efforts to bring them under his rule. In the event the Ula troops attacked Nurhaci's troops at Wu'aiyan, Surgaci, saying he had seen a bad omen on their way there, held his own troops back from the battle. Daisan and Cuyen, however, went forward and killed three thousand Ula troops, also capturing five thousand horses and three thousand sets of body armor. When they returned to Hetu Ala and Nurhaci learned of this, he took away much of Surgaci's military power and had two of his military advisors killed. Surgaci himself died or was killed in 1611 at the approximate age of forty-seven (forty-eight *sui*) (Roth Li 1975, 15–16).

In 1608 Nurhaci sent Cuyen and Amin to attack the Ula city. They killed a thousand of the enemy, got three hundred pieces of body armor as well as livestock, and then returned. With Ula power broken, Nurhaci turned his attention to the Donghai tribes, the "Wildmen Jurchen." He first attacked the Forest tribes (Weji). The next year he sent his general Eidu to attack and absorb the tribes of the Mudan and Sufen rivers. In 1611 he sent his sons Abatai, Fiodon, and Fiyanggu to attack up into the Ussuri River drainage.

In 1612 he led an army with his fifth son Manggutai and eighth son Hong Taiji to attack the Ula. They first attacked and captured six of the Ula cities before arriving at the capital. When they got there they camped on the opposite bank of the river and waited, capturing Ula grain and livestock. Manggutai and Hong Taiji wanted to attack, but Nurhaci said, "This is like chopping down a tall tree. You can't fell it with one chop but must keep hacking away at it until it falls" (*Yargiyan kooli* 150). So he burned the six cities he captured, with all their grain. Bujantai came out in a boat to the middle of the river and petitioned for peace, but Nurhaci rode into the river on his white horse and enumerated Bujantai's crimes. Nevertheless, he didn't take the capital after all, but he left a detachment of a thousand men there in a fort and returned to his capital.

The next year he came again against the Ula. The Ula, with Bujantai leading, arrayed their forces of thirty thousand troops. Nurhaci and his small army defeated them, however, killing six or seven out of every ten. Bujantai escaped with barely a hundred troops and went over the Yehe. The Ula were no more.

Cuyen's Rebellion

During all this time Nurhaci was giving more and more power to Cuyen, his eldest son, assuming he would succeed him as leader. But Cuyen did not get along with Nurhaci's five faithful ministers or his other sons. He threatened to have any of them killed who crossed him and took increasingly larger shares of the conquest spoils. Finally the ministers and other sons summoned the courage to report his misdeeds to Nurhaci, who at that point no longer trusted Cuyen. Nurhaci didn't take Cuyen along on the attacks against the Ula in 1612 and 1613, and he confined him after the Ula campaigns. In 1615 Nurhaci had Cuyen killed. Cuyen was about thirty-five years old (thirty-six *sui*).

The Aisin (Later Jin) Dynasty

During the spring festival in the year of the Red Dragon, the forty-fourth year of Wanli (1616), Nurhaci declared the beginning of the Aisin Empire (sometimes called the Later Jin to distinguish it from the Aisin or Jin dynasty of the Jurchens of the twelfth century).

The four *beile* (princes) of the banners were there: second son Daišan, nephew Amin, fifth son Manggultai, and eighth son Hong Taiji. Adun was on his right and Erdeni on his left. In this year he established a hierarchy of government. The *jarguci* ("judges") were the first layer, next the five *amban* ("ministers"), next the eight *beile*, and finally Nurhaci himself, acting as supreme head of the government.

Conquest of the Ming

In 1618, the third year of Abkai Fulingga ("Blessed by Heaven"), as Nurhaci's reign over the Aisin Nation was known, Nurhaci openly came out against the Ming dynasty stating, "The Ming has inflicted on me *nadan amba koro* 'seven great wounds' [generally translated as 'grievances'] and thousands of small ones" (*Mambun rōtō* I: 86). The seven great wounds were (1) the Ming killed Nurhaci's father and grandfather for no reason; (2) the Ming allied with the Yehe against him; (3) he killed Chinese who encroached on his border in accordance with the treaty negotiated with the Ming, but they pressed him for recompense; (4) because they had the backing of the Ming, the Yehe gave a princess who had been promised to Nurhaci to the Mongols instead; (5) the Ming wanted to change the negotiated borders and expel Jurchens from the Chaihe, Sancha, and Fu'an areas; (6) the Ming conspired with the Yehe to insult and degrade Nurhaci; and (7) the Ming pressed him to reestablish the Hada after he had defeated them, but then allowed the Yehe to take them over (*Mambun rōtō* I: 86–89).

In the fourth month he began his attack on the Ming. He divided his forces into two routes. Four of the banners were to form the left wing and attack Dongzhou and Magundang, while he would take the remaining four banners and attack Fushun directly, but the Fushun commander Li Yungfang surrendered before an attack was made (Roth Li 1975, 60).

The Ming set up a counterattack from four directions. With the help of Yehe and Korean troops, they would attack Nurhaci's banner troops from Kuangdian in the southeast, Qinghe in the southwest, Shenyang in the west, and Kaiyuan in the north. Nurhaci, after discussing strategy with his ministers and princes, said, "However many directions they attack me, I will attack them in one direction" (Yan 1993, 266). His plan was the right one under the circumstances. The Ming armies from the southeast and north were bogged down in their advance. Only Du Songyi's army from Shenyang came in rapidly, with the bulk of their forces camped at Sarhu. Nurhaci sent six of his banners there to attack, assuming that if the Sarhu force was beaten, the other Ming troops would lose heart, making it easy to conquer them.

In the event the western route of the Ming armies was indeed defeated, the northern route then came next, and finally the eastern route, and they were defeated each in their turn. The southern route (led by Li Chengliang's son) was so slow in coming that the other three groups were defeated before they even reached the battlefield. Learning the other three routes had been defeated, they retreated without fighting. In the war, over three hundred of the Ming leaders and nearly forty-six thousand troops were killed. The Aisin reported a loss of only two hundred troops.

Nurhaci followed up on his victory over the Ming troops by cutting off the Ming from his Jurchen rivals, the Yehe, in attacking and taking the two outposts of the Ming, Kaiyuan and Tieling. Neither was heavily guarded at the time, and attacking them served a double purpose: in eliminating them, it isolated the Yehe from their allies the Ming; and, being trading towns, there was an abundance of foodstuffs and other supplies. It was said that it took three days for the Aisin to haul all of the stuff out of Kaiyuan once it was taken. They looted all the material out of the outposts, then set the outposts ablaze.

In the fourth year of Abkai Fulingga (1619), Nurhaci came against the Yehe. Two chieftains traditionally led the Yehe; at the time Buyanggu held the Western City, and Gintasi held the Eastern City. In the battle, Daišan led his forces against Buyanggu, while Nurhaci led his troops against Gintasi. The Eastern City was strategically located and hard to attack. Gintasi was also well prepared with large stones and timbers to roll out on the attacking forces and a large contingent of archers raining arrows down on them. Nurhaci's troops suffered many casualties while trying to set up siege ladders. He finally had them dig into the wall, fill it with gunpowder, and blow open a breach. Gintasi sealed himself in the eight-sided tower in the city. Nurhaci sent for his eighth son Hong Taiji to try to talk him into surrender, since Gintasi was brother to Hong Taiji's birth mother, but it was to no avail. Gintasi didn't want to be subject to Nurhaci, so he killed his retainers and tried to set fire to the tower and to himself. Nurhaci's troops braved the flames to capture him alive, but he was subsequently hanged by Nurhaci. Meanwhile, Daišan had an easy time getting into the Western City. Buyanggu blockaded himself inside as well, so Daišan swore an oath that he would not kill him if he would surrender. He finally did surrender, but Nurhaci, fearing the Ming could well make use of Buyanggu, had him killed later as well.

In the sixth and seventh year of Abkai Fulingga (1621–1622), Nurhaci defeated the Ming at Shenyang and Liaodong and moved his capital to Liaodong City. Nurhaci was prepared to move the Chinese occupying the newly conquered Liaodong area north to take them away from the front and possible collaboration with the enemy, as well as to provide room for his own troops. The Chinese, mainly farmers, convinced Nurhaci instead to allow them to remain and let his troops room with them in their homes. Thus an experiment of co-occupant (Jurchen and Chinese) living began sometime around this time; it did not go well, however. Despite repeated admonitions that the occupying army was not to harass the local population or feel free to use their lands and goods, the conquering troops felt that the people were the spoils of battle and treated them as such. At this point the Chinese opposition to Jurchen rule began to express itself in such things as the poisoning of wells or of the Jurchen's food. The eighth year of Abkai Fulingga (1623) saw a major land redistribution, as well as a widespread Chinese revolt that began around the Guangning area (Roth Li 1975, 71–76). The practice of co-occupation was phased out as the relationship between Jurchen and Chinese deteriorated. Nurhaci, who was brilliant in the conquest and consolidation of the Jurchen tribes, had much more trouble attempting to govern an intransigent Chinese population.

In the tenth year of Abkai Fulingga (1625), Nurhaci moved his capital to Mukden (Shenyang), and the most serious Chinese rebellion yet broke out (Roth Li 1975, 85).

In the beginning of the eleventh year of Abkai Fulingga (1626), Nurhaci attacked Ningyuan on the coast and suffered a defeat, the only major defeat of his career. He was wounded during the battle by Portuguese-made cannons. Half a year later, on the eleventh day of the eighth month of the eleventh year of Abkai Fulingga (1626), he fell ill and died outside of his capital of Mukden. Nurhaci is buried in an imperial tomb on the east side of his capital. Although he encouraged his sons to rule by consensus in the long-standing tradition of the Jurchens after he was gone, his eighth son, Hong Taiji, consolidated power and eventually became ruler, continuing the Aisin conquest of the Ming. It is difficult to say how far Nurhaci was intending to pursue his own conquest, but his descendants eventually took over all of China from 1642 to 1644 and expanded its borders to produce the largest "Chinese" dynasty that ever existed, reigning for nearly three hundred years, to 1911.

Stephen A. WADLEY
Portland State University

Further Reading

Chen Jiexian 陳捷先. (2003). *Nu'erhaqi xie zhen* 努爾哈齊寫真 [Portrait of Nurhaci]. Taipei, Taiwan: Yuan liu chubanshe ye gufen youxian gongsi.

Chen Jiexian 陳捷先. (2005). *Nu'erhaqi shi dian* 努爾哈齊事典 [Encyclopedia of Nurhaci]. Taipei, Taiwan: Yuan liu chubanshe ye gufen youxian gongsi.

Ch'en Wen-shih. (1981). The creation of the Manchu Niru. *Chinese Studies in History, 14*(4), 11–46.

Crossley, Pamela Kyle. (1990). *Orphan warriors: Three Manchu generations and the end of the Qing world*. Princeton, NJ: Princeton University Press.

Crossley, Pamela Kyle. (1997). *The Manchus*. Cambridge, MA: Blackwell Publishers.

Elliott, Mark C. (2001). *The Manchu way: The eight banners and ethnic identity in late imperial China*. Stanford, CA: Stanford University Press.

Gimm, Martin. (2005). Nurgaci versus Nurhaci: An annotation to P. Adam Schall. *Central Asiatic Journal, 49*(2), 204.

Jiang Xiusong 蔣秀松, Li Zhiting 李治亭, & Zhang Xuanru 张璇如. (1986). *Qing chao kai guo huangdi Nu'erhachi* 清朝开国皇帝努尔哈赤 [First emperor of the Qing dynasty, Nurhaci]. Shanghai: Shanghai renmin chubanshe.

Manbun rōtō 滿文老檔. (1955–1963). *Tongki fuka sindaha hergen i dangse* [The secret chronicles of the Manchu dynasty, 1607–1637] (Kanda Nobuo, et al., Trans.) (7 vols.). Tokyo: Tōyō Bunko.

Manwen laodang 滿文老檔 [The old Manchu annals] (2 vols). (1995). Beijing: Zhonghua shuju.

Pang, Tatiana, & Stary, Giovanni. (2010). Manchu versus Ming: Qing Taizu Nurhaci's "Proclamation" to the Ming dynasty. *Aetas Manjurica 14*. Wiesbaden, Germany: Harrassowitz Verlag.

Rossabi, Morris. (1998). The Ming and Inner Asia. In Denis Twitchett & Frederick W. Mote (Eds.), *The Cambridge history of China* (Vol. 8, pp. 221–271). Cambridge, MA: Cambridge University Press.

Roth Li, Gertraude. (1975). *The rise of the early Manchu state: A portrait drawn from Manchu sources to 1936.* (Doctoral dissertation, Harvard University)

Roth Li, Gertraude. (2002). State building before 1644. In Willard J. Peterson (Ed.), *The Cambridge history of China* (Vol. 9, pp. 9–72). Cambridge, MA: Cambridge University Press.

Wakeman, Frederic. (1985). *The great enterprise: Vol. I.* Berkeley: University of California Press.

Yan, Chongnian 阎崇年. (1983). *Nu'erhachi zhuan* 努尔哈赤传 [Biography of Nurhaci]. Beijing: Beijing chubanshe.

Yan Chongnian 阎崇年. (1993). *Tianming Han* 天命汉 [Emperor Blessed by Heaven (*Abkai Fulingga*)]. Changchun Shi, China: Jilin wenshi chubanshe.

Yargiyan Kooli. (1985). In *Qing Shilu* 清实录 [Qing veritable records]. Beijing: Zhonghua Shuju.

Qiú Yīng
仇英

c. 1494–1552—Painter

Alternate names: style names: courtesy name: Shífù 实父; pseudonym: Shízhōu 十洲

• 仇英 •

Summary

Though counted as one of the Four Great Masters of the Ming dynasty, Qiu Ying is lesser known than the other three, and in fact the details of his life are quite sparse. A versatile painter who used a variety of techniques to paint an array of subjects, he possessed the unique ability to depict reality in his artwork, which was in high demand. He was repeatedly called upon to participate in the production of commemorative and presentation works for a wide circle of patrons from the aristocracy and the gentry, as well as from families on the rise in the sixteenth century. The life of Qiu Ying, however, is known only through his art.

Qiu Ying, an artist who lived in Suzhou, Jiangsu Province, is one of the Four Great Masters of the Ming (*Míng sì dàjiā* 明四大家) dynasty along with Shěn Zhōu 沈周 (1427–1509), Wén Zhēngmíng 文征明 (1470–1559), and Táng Yín 唐寅 (1470–1524). Shen, Wen, and Tang, all members of the elite, literati gentry class, engaged in the gentlemanly pursuits of painting, poetry, wine parties, and calligraphy. Each of the three left a corpus of written materials; all three are frequently mentioned in the social writings of the era; and all three received full biographical treatment by their contemporaries.

In contrast, Qiu Ying's life is enigmatic. Although he evidently could write his name, there is no evidence that he composed poetry or prose of any kind, as practiced by cultured Chinese gentlemen. Qiu left no collection of literary works. He established and maintained lasting associations with most of the cultural leaders in Suzhou and its neighboring towns, but he could not participate in their social world as an equal, so his name never appears in their social writings. No one prepared a full biography or a tomb inscription for him, the normal sources of information about a prominent individual in China.

Despite his widespread reputation, contemporaneous written documentation for his life is exceedingly sparse.

Consequently, Qiu Ying is known only through his art, upon which he relied for his living. His artistic life experiences are not remarkable. Like other professional artists, he relied on selling his art for his living, often working on commission. He painted in the same genres as did other artists, professional and otherwise, especially commemorative pictures so sought after in the Suzhou area, as well as contributing to composite scrolls of calligraphy, literature, and painting. Qiu, like other painters, supplied the facsimile copies of older compositions solicited by collectors. Because of a lack of written documentation, Qiu Ying's "life story" is embedded in his artistic career.

Problems in Finding Information

The study of Qiu Ying and his art is fraught with problems and issues, and is hampered by the lack of a formal, full-length biography composed by a contemporary as well as by minimal biographical information dating from the sixteenth century. This gap has left much room for conjecture. Over the past two decades nearly fifteen scholars, seemingly intent upon filling the vacuum created by this scarcity of data in older records about Qiu Ying, have written about this artist. Among the assertions is that Qiu Ying began as a craftsman. One claim is that he was a ceramic decorator. Another speculation is that he began as a lacquer artisan who also painted colorful decorations in houses. Because none of these assertions can be verified through contemporary sources, it is doubtful that Qiu was either a ceramic or a lacquer ware artisan.

The few acceptable facts about Qiu Ying's life come from brief statements about him in sixteenth-century collections of biographies of painters and from short statements inscribed by contemporaries or near contemporaries on his paintings. Two sixteenth-century accounts, one by Wáng Zhìdēng 王穉登 (1535–1612) and one by Wáng Shìzhēn 王世贞 (1526–1590), are the most reliable sources for accurate information about Qiu. These two men played leading roles in Suzhou area literary circles. Wang Zhideng was a calligrapher and connoisseur. In his record of Suzhou painters from the fourteenth century until his own time, he gives minimal factual information, preferring to concentrate on artistic appraisal. About Qiu Ying, he says:

> Qiu Ying, *zi* [courtesy name] Shifu, was from Taicang and moved his family to the prefectural city [Suzhou]. In painting, he studied with Zhōu Chén 周臣 [ca. 1500–1535], but did not come up to Zhou's skill. He was especially good at making copies [*lín* 临 and *mó* 摹], and making draft pictures on yellow [tracing] paper;

> his brushwork could be confused with the originals. As for his moss greens, hair-thin golds, silken reds and thread-like whites, they were delicate, exquisite and extremely beautiful; he had no reason to defer to the ancients. Even if he occasionally changed his methods and altered his movements [to improve on the originals], he could not avoid adding feet when painting a snake. (Wang 1962)

A few decades later, Wang Shizhen's collection of colophons (identifying marks or emblems) that he inscribed on Táng 唐 through Míng 明 dynasty paintings provides a few more fragments about Qiu Ying. In particular, giving his pseudonym (*hào* 号) as Shizhou, mentioning that Qiu came from humble beginnings and that Zhou Chen considered him unusual and taught him. Wang Shizhen repeats that Qiu Ying copied all the famous masters of the Tang and Sòng 宋 dynasties and adds that his copies could be confused with the originals (Wang 1976).

Taicang, in Jiangsu Province, is located approximately twenty miles (thirty-two kilometers) northeast of Suzhou. In view of his artistic talents, Qiu's transfer to Suzhou was a wise choice. Suzhou, a much larger city than Taicang, is sited on the Grand Canal, near Lake Tai and even closer to Stone Lake; at the end of the fifteenth century it exceeded Taicang in general prosperity, wealth, history, and culture.

Qiu Ying's Art

In a late seventeenth-century compendium of artists' biographies, the authors present a sanguine view of Qiu Ying's accomplishments:

> Although Qiu Ying's landscapes were based on Song styles, Qiu himself established his own style; he excelled in the blue-and green heavy color mode. His figures and ladies were mostly of palace types, with the demeanor of the wealthy; his ruled drawing of towers and terraces, his carts, horses, boats and oars all were fine and exact. Once he copied a Northern Song painting, with one-inch figures and bean-sized horses, hair, eyebrows, and all objects, the composition and color, deep and light were perfect. In his album leaves and handscrolls, the smaller, the more beautiful. In the past, he can be compared with the ancients, in the future, no one will be able to succeed him. (Lan & Xie late seventeenth century, 1:2a)

The accuracy of these observations is confirmed by evaluations and analyses of some of Qiu Ying's extant works.

Qiu was immensely versatile, commanding a wide range of styles and subjects. He worked in all the accepted techniques, formats, and media. For landscapes, he employed both the opaque blue-and-green palette originating in the Tang dynasty and the more recent, lighter blue-and green technique. For figures, he used *báimiáo* 白描 ink outline without color, ink and light color, as well as *gōngbǐ* 工笔, the meticulously drawn and detailed, brightly colored approach. His figures were set in extensive landscape or architectural surroundings, or sometimes without any background at all. He depicted private gardens, illustrations to traditional stories and legends, flowers, beautiful women, and portraits. He created customized presentation pieces celebrating birthdays or other personal events and made copies of ancient paintings, mostly of the Song dynasty.

It is conventional in studies of an artist to group and discuss the master's oeuvre on a chronological basis as a means of charting the progress of his career: stylistic development, modifications in types of themes or subjects depicted, sequences of patrons, or personal events that affected his art. Chronologies are put forward upon the examination of a corpus of genuine paintings which, preferably, bear a date in the artist's own hand. Unfortunately, few of Qiu Ying's paintings are dated by him. The range and nature of Qiu's art is further obscured by a host of fakes, imitations, re-constructions, and dubious attributions, some of which are the products of the later, lucrative art forgery industry which flourished in Suzhou and numerous other centers throughout China. The general situation thus renders it impossible to generate a neat, firm, clear-cut, step-by-step stylistic chronology for Qiu Ying.

Lacking positive dating, approximate dates may be derived from reliable external evidence. A genuine inscription, written directly on the painting by an individual known to have predeceased the artist provides a *terminus ante quem*. The time span during which the painting might have been created, however, can be lengthy, and so the dating is imprecise. Another type of secondary evidence is a statement by someone of the period providing information about the subject or recipient written on a separate piece of paper or silk, and mounted with the scroll.

Early Works

The appearance of writing by the local literatus, Wáng Chǒng 王宠 (1494–1533) on three of Qiu's paintings is of significance because Wang died in 1533; consequently, these works must have been created before that date. Wang Chong's inscription on *Bamboo Courtyard*, a fan painting in ink and color on gold-spattered paper, is dedicated to an unidentified monk (Museum für Ostasiatische Kunst, Berlin). In a simple landscape, a man sits decorously on a low rock in a bamboo grove near a stream. An album leaf in ink and light color on paper, inscribed by Wang Chong, shows a man sitting at the base of a pine tree (Kurokawa Institute of Ancient Cultures, Japan). The figure is scantily dressed; he wears a thin, transparent robe, pulled off one shoulder exposing his bare chest. The man's torso, arms, and upper legs are all clearly visible beneath the thin fabric. The man and the twisting pine dominate the picture, as the background is screened out with washed-in mountains. The poem inscribed by Wang Chong includes reference to the Qi Garden (Lacquer Garden) where the ancient Daoist (Taoist) philosopher *Zhuāngzǐ 庄子(c. 369–c. 268 BCE) is supposed to have lived. Perhaps the individual represented here is meant to be Zhuangzi. A third picture inscribed by Wang Chong is the hanging scroll in ink and light color on paper, *Thatched Hut under Bamboo and Wutong Trees* (Shanghai Museum). In his poem inscribed on this painting, Wang Chong refers to an unidentified individual, presumably the designated recipient. Inside the hut, surrounded by a grove of tall trees and located next to a mountain stream, a bare-chested man reclines in a lounge chair; he is surrounded by literati accoutrements: books, ink stone, water dropper, and a jar of brushes. The man in his mountain hut occupies the lower half of the vertical format; the mountain setting occupies the upper part of the scene. This compositional arrangement is frequently seen in paintings by sixteenth-century artists. It is noteworthy that two of these three early paintings are presentation pieces, indicating that early in his career, Qiu Ying was already recognized and in demand for creating special pictures.

A distinctive characteristic of Qiu Ying's art is evident in these three paintings: accurate depiction based on careful observation of reality, and an extraordinary ability to convey that reality through brushwork. His people look more "real" and "alive" than most figures rendered by other artists who relied extensively on brush stroke formulae rather than on careful visual observation.

For the most part, gentlemen depicted by Qiu Ying and other artists are fully dressed and in discreet, formal poses. Consistent with Qiu's reliance upon observed reality is his willingness to depart from this idealized norm to present partially-clad men in informal situations. This is already evident in his two early paintings of bare-chested men (*Zhuangzi* and *Thatched Hut under Bamboo and Wutong Trees*). In later times, Qiu continued his "slice of life" scenes in at least three paintings. In the undated handscroll *Picking Lotus* (present location unknown), a man reclines in a thatched kiosk at the edge of a lotus pond; he is barefoot, one leg is propped on the other knee; his chest and belly are exposed and the sleeve of his robe is rolled up to bare his arm. A neglected lute lies nearby. A servant wearing thin summer garb cools the master with a gauze fan. The lotus pickers, three

*People marked with an asterisk have entries in this dictionary.

women in a skiff (small flatbottom boat), are far out on the lake. In the hanging scroll in ink and light color on paper, *Fisherman's Flute Heard over a Lake*, a gentleman in a lakeside pavilion listens to the music played by a fisherman in the distance (formerly in the Crawford collection, now in the Nelson-Atkins Museum, Kansas City). The gentleman's chest is bare, as are his feet, and he sits relaxed with one leg drawn up at an angle. In the ink on paper hanging scroll *Fishing by a Willow Bank*, the subject is not actually fishing, but relaxes, seated on the edge of his boat. His open robe exposes his somewhat portly torso and the skirt of his garment is pulled up so he can dangle one bare foot in the cooling water (National Palace Museum, Taipei). In these five paintings, through the informal, casual, and lazy poses of the men and their casual attire, Qiu Ying not only captures a bit of real life, but also conveys a sense of the heavy, muggy climate of south China.

Qiu Ying and His Patrons

Qiu Ying attracted consumers from throughout south China, including Nanjing, Kunshan, Wuxi, and Yixing, but it is unknown exactly when he worked for these mostly lesser, one-time clients. On the other hand, Qiu had three major patrons who invited him to become a "painter in residence." Although Qiu Ying is considered a Suzhou painter, the three patrons with whom he lived, perhaps for several years at a time, were all located outside the city. Chén Guān 陈官 (d. after 1577) may have had a country estate to the northwest, Zhōu Fènglái 周凤来 (1523–1555) resided in Kunshan, some sixty kilometers northeast of Suzhou, and Xiàng Yuánbiàn 项元汴 (1525–1590) lived in Jiaxing, some sixty kilometers south of Suzhou. It is not known in exactly what sequence Qiu stayed with these patrons.

The relationship between Qiu Ying and Chen Guan is unclear. A laudatory comment composed in 1552 by Péng Nián 彭年 (1505–1566), a Suzhou poet and calligrapher, is attached to a long handscroll of *Tribute Bearers*, in ink and color on silk, dedicated in Qiu Ying's inscription to Chen Guan (Palace Museum, Beijing). In his comment of high praise, Peng states that the scroll was painted in the home of Chen Guan and that Qiu Ying lived in Chen's mountain retreat for several years, but Peng does not say when, nor does he tell us where the mountain retreat was located. Another painting bearing Chen's seals, a large hanging scroll in ink and color on silk, depicting travelers crossing a stream signed by Qiu Ying is believed to represent the *Emperor Guang Wu of the Eastern Han Dynasty and His Entourage Fording a River* (National Museum, Ottawa). The landscape elements in both scrolls are in opaque blue-and-green pigments and are major examples of Qiu's command of this archaic colored landscape mode. In *Tribute Bearers*, eleven delegations from foreign lands wend their way toward the capital. The miniature figures are rendered with extraordinary precision with exacting details of clothing, banners, exotic animals, and precious, luxury goods. There is much for the viewer to explore and admire.

The compositional arrangement of *Emperor Guang Wu of the Eastern Han Dynasty and His Entourage Fording a River* is one often used by Qiu Ying and other Ming painters. Somewhat similar to *Thatched Hut under Bamboo and Wutong Trees*, the large vertical space is divided into the lower part where miniscule but finely described figures on foot and horseback travel through the landscape, and the upper part is occupied by towering sheer peaks. Typical of Qiu Ying's artistry are the additional narrative vignettes, such as the lone horseman, half hidden by escarpments, moving away from the imperial group and perhaps journeying to the elaborate villa composed of three large separate buildings in the mid-distance. The depiction recalls the famous blue-green rendition of *Emperor Minghuang's Journey to Shu*, perhaps of Song dynasty date (National Palace Museum, Taipei).

***Towers and Pavilions in Immortal Mountains* (c. 1550) by Qiu Ying.** National Palace Museum, Taipei, Taiwan.

Much more is known about Zhou Fenglai, Qui's second major patron. He was born into great luxury, a son of a scholarly family residing in Kunshan. Although he was a National University student, he preferred to live in his retreat, studying Buddhism, and amassing collections of books, antiquities, and paintings. One of his acquisitions was a poem written by the famous Yuán 元

(1279–1368) dynasty artist, *Zhào Mèngfǔ 赵孟頫 (1254–1322), about the exchange of tea for his writing of a Buddhist sutra. But Zhao's original calligraphy of the sutra was long ago lost. Consequently, Zhou requested Wen Zhengming to provide a transcription of the sutra to replace the lost Zhao Mengfu writing and Qiu Ying to contribute a pictorial rendition of the event. The result is the handscroll in ink and light color on paper *Zhao Mengfu Writing the "Heart Sutra" in Exchange for Tea* (Cleveland Museum of Art). Wen Zhengming's sutra text is dated 1542. Qiu's painting is believed to have been done in the same year. Qiu stages the meeting of Zhao Mengfu and a monk in a pine grove, with the trees placed along the two sides of a "v," so that the two men, seated at a long table are immediately the center of viewer attention. The two men are accurately described, as is typical of Qiu's figural style. True to his bent for including narrative elements, Qiu Ying poses the calligrapher holding his brush in readiness for inscribing the scroll in front of him; he looks toward a servant bringing a basket of tea leaves for approval, and further to the left, another boy fans a brazier (metal container for hot coals); tea utensils and other paraphernalia are set on a low table. Further to the left, another boy approaches with scrolls of paper.

Xiang Yuanbian, Qiu Ying's third sustaining patron, lived in Xiushui (Jiaxing), Zhejiang province. He was born into a family of degree holders and officials, but he failed in the provincial civil service examination. He turned to business and owned a pawn shop. Xiang became a collector, housing his collection in his Tianlai Pavilion 天来阁; he himself was a painter of note. An inscription dedicating an exceptional floral depiction by Qiu Ying, *Narcissus and Winter Plum Blossoms* to Xiang Yuanbian is dated "second month of winter 1547" (National Palace Museum, Taipei). Qiu Ying possibly began his residence with Xiang in this year. In this hanging scroll in ink and color on silk, the differences between the two plants are beautifully conveyed. The angular, thin branches of the leafless plum with its meager, tiny blossoms in the upper portion of the scroll contrast with the long, tapered, gently twisting leaves of two narcissus plants below. One vertical stalk bears single narcissus blooms, the other the double cultivar.

The significance of this floral combination is twofold. The Chinese like to decorate their homes with flowers at the New Year season. Narcissus plants were forced into bloom in time for this festival because it is believed that narcissus will bring good fortune in the coming year. The plum is the floral symbol of the first lunar month when its tiny blossoms begin to appear. Because the flowers appear on apparently lifeless branches, they are also considered symbols of longevity. In an extended interpretation, the combination of narcissus (*shuǐxiān* 水仙) and plum (*méihuā* 梅花) evokes the expression: *tiānxiān gòngshòu* 天仙供寿, meaning:

"May the heavenly immortals honor you with longevity" (Bartholomew 2006). The painting might have been a gift expressing wishes for a prosperous upcoming New Year for the Xiang family in general, and perhaps, more personally, wishing Xiang Yuanbian a long life.

When living with Xiang, Qiu Ying filled at least one commission: a portrait of Xiang's older brother, Yuánqí 元淇 (1500–1572), titled *Thatched House in the Peach-blossom Village* (Palace Museum, Beijing). Yuanqi never passed the *jìnshì* 进士 (presented scholar) civil service degree that led to a coveted official position, but did hold a minor bureaucratic position; he preferred to write poetry and practice calligraphy. The *Peach-blossom Village* probably refers to a particular area of the Xiang estate. The large hanging scroll rendered in ink and color on silk features a small figure in white in an extensive landscape including a small thatched hut surrounded by peach trees and occupied by servants bearing scrolls and washing inkstones. It is a primary example of Qiu's ability to combine the ancient blue-and-green color scheme with descriptive detail revealing the subject's personal preference.

Qiu Ying's Copies of Earlier Paintings

In Xiang's home, Qiu Ying had access to older paintings, and for Xiang, he copied ancient paintings presumably in Xiang's collection. An album of copies, known as the Tianlai Pavilion album, is published as by Qiu Ying, although there is neither signature nor seal to that effect (Shanghai Museum). The album includes genre scenes, illustrations to stories, children playing, and bird and flower motifs. Two leaves depict large, elaborate pavilions occupied by people, all drawn in the exacting technique known as *jièhuà* 界画 "ruled or measured painting" used in rendering architecture.

A set of six paintings in ink and color by Qiu Ying are copies of Song and Yuan landscapes (National Palace Museum, Taipei). The album bears a colophon by Xiang Yuanbian, but there is no evidence that Xiang commissioned the copies. Qiu's remarkable sensitivity to the nuances of earlier landscape traditions is evident. These scenes are exceptional for their striking and perceptive descriptions of times of day and night, and for unusual treatments of the sky. One leaf is a moonlight vista wherein a blue patch set in a broad sweep of yellow surrounds the moon in the sky above as it appears reflected in a lake below. The most stunning is a view of a farm villa at dusk. In a rustic environment, miniscule farmers are still at work and a lone fisherman is in a skiff. The time of day is dusk, the hues of the landscape are muted, those of the sky darkening. The brightest spot is near the center where two gentlemen sit in conversation in a villa, its lighted buildings and compound aglow in the subdued surroundings. A third

Spring Morning in the Han Palace, by Qiu Ying. National Palace Museum, Taipei, Taiwan.

leaf depicts a man enjoying a sunset: the mountains are flooded with colored light and a red sun setting beyond a ridge casts a pink flush throughout much of the sky, a tint of which merges imperceptibly into blue grey surrounding barely visible clouds. The landscape itself is suffused with sunset radiance reflected from golden-pink spires and cliffs. Song dynasty painting was relatively faithful to real nature. As such, these album leaves must have appealed to Qiu Ying, who was so attuned to conveying reality in many of his paintings.

Perhaps the most famous of Qiu Ying's paintings is the long handscroll in careful brushwork and bright color, the *gongbi* meticulous outline and color fill technique, *Spring Morning in the Han Palace* (National Palace Museum, Taipei; pictured above). Executed in ink and color on silk, it bears ownership seals of Xiang Yuanbian, but was apparently made for someone else and then purchased by

Xiang. It was common for artists to include motifs borrowed from ancient pictures. Throughout Qiu's long scroll there are dozens of mostly female figures in palace buildings and courtyards. In one passage, there is a heavy reliance upon earlier figure groupings, with allusions especially to Tang and Song dynasty depictions of court ladies. Two damsels playing a board game could have been derived from the well-known *Ladies Playing Double Sixes* (Freer Gallery of Art, Washington, DC); an ironing scene from *The Silk Beaters* (Museum of Fine Arts, Boston); and the embroidery vignette from *Ladies Holding Fans* (Palace Museum, Beijing). In Qiu's scroll, a section showing women playing with infants is based upon a Song dynasty composition familiar from a number of interpretations, including that copied by Qiu and included in the Tianlai Pavilion album of copies of Song paintings, once owned by Xiang Yuanbian mentioned above (Shanghai Museum). With its variety of activities and its antiquarian allusions, this section of *Spring Morning in the Han Palace* provides the knowledgeable viewer with a unique opportunity to savor the recycling of ancient figures, once placed against a blank ground, now revitalized and incorporated into a fully developed palace setting.

Other Paintings by Qiu Ying

In contrast to the neat descriptive drawing and colorful *Spring Morning in the Han Palace* is Qiu's ink on paper handscroll depicting a gentleman watching a servant tugging on the rope of an obstinate donkey (Arthur M. Sackler Gallery, Washington, DC). This is an example of the outline without color technique known as *baimiao*. The scroll was created to commemorate the subscription list of contributors to a fund to purchase a donkey for the scholar Zhū Cúnlǐ 朱存理 (1444–1513), a noted, but poor, Suzhou author, bibliophile, and calligrapher. The painting was not commissioned for presentation to Zhu, but rather to accompany the calligraphic text of the subscription list. The drawing of the scholar is based on the brushwork of the Song dynasty painter, Lǐ Gōnglín 李公麟 (1049–1106). The scroll has a distinctive Qiu Ying realistic touch: the donkey, with lowered head, is clearly stubborn and unwilling to be led by the servant.

Two large hanging scrolls in ink and light color on paper are exceptional paintings in Qiu Ying's oeuvre (National Palace Museum, Taipei). One depicts two gentlemen enjoying music, *Passing a Summer Day in the Shade of Banana Palms*, the other shows two men in *Conversation in the Shade of Firmiana Trees*. Both represent the quiet, leisure pastimes pursued in a peaceful, isolated location favored by the literati. Qiu's usual tight and careful brushwork is here abandoned in preference of more loosely applied brushwork, giving the paintings a sense of great immediacy.

What must have been one of Qiu Ying's last paintings is the ink and color on paper hanging scroll *Towers and Pavilions in Immortal Mountains* (National Palace Museum, Taipei; shown on page 976). Above the picture and on the same piece of paper, Lù Shīdào 陆师道 (1511–1574) inscribed the lengthy *Immortal Mountains Prose-poem* composed by Cài Yǔ 蔡羽 (1457–1541), a well-known Suzhou writer and friend of many Suzhou cultural luminaries. Lu's inscription is dated 1550, and it is believed that the painting must have been made in this year or perhaps somewhat earlier. The isles of the immortals and mountains of the immortals were perennial subjects for artists. Qiu Ying's version is unique. It is as delicate and almost as ephemeral as the fabled locale itself: a fastidious depiction of extravagant buildings located deep in a mountain stronghold. The architecture is impeccably rendered, recalling the *jiehua* leaves in the Tianlai Pavilion album of copies of Song paintings by Qiu. All parts of the buildings are clearly legible yet integrated into a logical structure. The pavilion is securely anchored on a stone foundation and nestled in a grove of flowering trees. The inhabitants of this magical hideaway are barely visible. In the background a palisade of mountains is composed of thin, insistently vertical peaks, and includes a waterfall and a temple-like structure among pines, typical of the narrative elements Qiu Ying liked to include in his paintings. Interwoven among the towering peaks are horizontal strips of white clouds. The landscape is in a light version of the ancient blue-green approach lending an unreal aura to a completely imaginary, truly other-worldly, paradise.

Qiu Ying's Descendants

One facet of Qiu's life that has been ignored is the fact that he was the ancestor of three generations of talented artists. Qiu's son, whose personal name is unknown, had no repute in the art world, but his son, Shìxiáng 世祥 (dates unknown), Qiu Ying's grandson, had a modest reputation; his *Peach Blossom Spring* is extant. One of Qiu's daughters, Qiú Zhū 仇珠, an artist in her own right, continued her father's style. Another daughter, apparently without artistic bent, married Yóu Qiú 尤求, (active c. 1550–1590). You worked in Qiu Ying's manner, and moved from Suzhou to Taicang where he was a close friend of the great literatus, Wang Shizhen (one of the first to provide brief factual information about Qiu Ying), perhaps even living in Wang's residence in Taicang. You's relationship with Wang was close. Wang repeatedly mentions You in his writings; sometimes You was asked to produce a painting for Wang or one of his colleagues; sometimes You was invited to literary parties. You's son, Dàohéng 道恒 (dates unknown), was a calligrapher of minor note. You's daughter (name unrecorded) was a painter as well as a poet; she married Zhōu Fèngyí 周凤仪 (dates unknown). They both wrote poetry and painted for a living. Thus, Qiu Ying's family moved into the lower levels of the literati world, where, with them, the questions of literacy and ability to compose poetry were moot points.

Conclusion

Given Qiu Ying's outstanding command of painting techniques and subjects, it is no wonder that he and his work were in demand. He was repeatedly called upon to participate in the constant production of commemorative and presentation works for a wide circle of patrons who came from the aristocracy and the gentry, as well as from families on the rise in the sixteenth century. Qiu Ying may also have sold his paintings through local painting shops. It is no wonder that he was widely imitated and copied, and it is no wonder that he was lauded as one of the Four Great Masters of the Ming Dynasty.

Ellen Johnston LAING
University of Michigan

Further Reading

Bartholomew, Terese Tse, & Asian Art Museum—Chong-Moon Lee Center for Asian Art and Culture. (2006). *Hidden meanings in Chinese art*. San Francisco: Asian Art Museum of San Francisco.

Fu, Marilyn, & Fu, Shen. (1973). *Studies in connoisseurship: Chinese paintings from the Arthur M. Sackler collection in New York and Princeton*. Princeton, NJ: Princeton University Press.

Gugong bowuyuan 故宫博物院. (1990). *Mingdai Wumen huihua* 明代吴门绘画 [Paintings of the Ming dynasty Wu school]. Beijing: Gugong bowuyuan & Hong Kong: Shangwu yinshu guan.

Guoli gugong bowuyuan 国立故宫博物院. (1970). *Guoli gugong minghua xuancui* 国立故宫名画选萃 [Masterpieces of Chinese painting in the National Palace Museum]. Taipei, Taiwan: Guoli gugong bowuyuan.

Guoli gugong bowuyuan 国立故宫博物院. (1989). *Qiu Ying zuopin zhan tulu* 仇英作品展图录 [Exhibition of paintings by Qiu Ying]. Taipei, Taiwan: Guoli gugong bowuyuan.

Ho, Wai-kam, et al. (1980). *Eight dynasties of Chinese painting: The collections of the Nelson Gallery-Atkins Museum, Kansas City and the Cleveland Museum of Art*. Cleveland, OH: Cleveland Museum of Art in cooperation with Indiana University Press.

Laing, Ellen Johnston. (1991). Sixteenth century patterns of art patronage: Qiu Ying and the Xiang family. *Journal of the American Oriental Society, 111*(1), 1–7.

Laing, Ellen Johnston. (1996). Erotic themes and romantic heroines depicted by Ch'iu Ying. *Archives of Asian Art, 59*, 68–91. doi:10.2307/20111266

Laing, Ellen Johnston. (1997a). Five early paintings by Ch'iu Ying. *Taida Journal of Art History, 4*, 223–251.

Laing, Ellen Johnston. (1997b). Qiu Ying's delicate style. *Ars Orientalis, 27*, 39–66.

Laing, Ellen Johnston. (1997c). Qiu Ying's late landscapes. *Oriental Art, 43*(1), 28–36.

Laing, Ellen Johnston. (1997d). Qiu Ying's other patrons. *Journal of the American Oriental Society, 117*(4), 686–692.

Laing, Ellen Johnston. (1999). Problems in reconstructing the life of Qiu Ying. *Ars Orientalis, 29*, 69–89.

Laing, Ellen Johnston. (2000). *Suzhou Pian* and other dubious paintings in the received *oeuvre* of Qiu Ying. *Artibus Asiae*, *69*(3–4), 265–295.

Lan Ying 蓝瑛 & Xie Bin 谢彬. (1962). *Tuhua baojian xuzuan* 图画宝 鉴续纂 [Supplement to precious mirror of paintings]. In Yu Anlan 于安澜 (Ed.), *Huashi congshu* 画史丛书 [Series on painting history]. Shanghai: Renmin meishu chubanshe. (Original work published late seventeenth century)

Lee, Sherman E. (1991). Emperor Guang Wu of the Eastern Han Dynasty and his entourage fording a river. In Jay A. Levenson (Ed.), *Circa 1492: Art in the age of exploration* (p. 453). New Haven, CT. Yale University Press.

Little, Stephen. (1985). The demon queller and the art of Qiu Ying (Ch'iu Ying). *Artibus Asiae*, *46*(1–2), 5–128.

Rogers, Howard, & Lee, Sherman E. (1988). *Masterworks of Ming and Qing painting from the Forbidden City*. Lansdale, PA: International Arts Council.

Wang Shizhen 王世贞. (1976). *Yanzhou shanren sibugao* 弇州山人四部稿 [Drafts of materials by Yanzhou shanren]. Taipei, Taiwan: Weiwen tushu chubanshe. (Original work published 1577)

Wang Zhideng 王稚登 (1962). Wujun danqing zhi 吴郡丹青志 [Records of paintings in Wu]. In Yu Anlan 于安澜 (Ed.), *Huashi congshu* 画史丛书 [Series on painting history]. Shanghai: Renmin meishu chubanshe. (Original work published 1563)

Weng, Wan-go. (1978). *Chinese painting and calligraphy: A pictorial survey: 69 fine examples from the John M. Crawford, Jr. collection*. New York: Dover.

Young, Martie W. (1976). Ch'iu Ying. In L. Carrington Goodrich & Fang Chaoying (Eds.), *Dictionary of Ming biography, 1368–1644.* (pp. 255–257). New York: Columbia University Press.

Ricci, Matteo

Lì Mǎdòu 利玛窦

1552–1610—Italian-born Jesuit missionary to China; polymath

Detail of Matteo Ricci from a seventeenth century text. Beinecke Rare Book and Manuscript Library, Yale University.

• 利玛窦 •

Summary

Matteo Ricci was an Italian-born Jesuit priest credited with bringing Catholic missions to China. Arriving at a time when all foreigners were regarded with suspicion, Ricci gained access to the court by bestowing gifts of new technologies, such as chiming clocks, on Chinese emperors. His contributions were valued more for their practical, scientific applications; he made less progress in religion conversion. In his gifts, in his desire to explain China to Europe, in his translations of Western works into Chinese, and in his promotion of the study of the Chinese language and philosophy, Ricci set the tone for much subsequent contact with China.

The Jesuit missionary Matteo Ricci (1552–1610) is generally described as the founder of the Catholic missions in China. He was born in Italy, in Macerata in the Marche, into a family of pharmacists. Educated at first in Macerata, where he studied at a new Jesuit college for seven years, he was then sent to Rome in 1568, where he studied law for two years before applying to enter the Society of Jesus. He was accepted into the noviciate in 1571. In 1577, he applied to join a Jesuit mission to India. Preparation for the mission took place in Lisbon, where Ricci was ordained in 1578. He arrived in Goa, India, in the company of fathers Rudolphe Aquaviva, Michele Ruggieri, Nichola Spinola, and Francisco Pasio in September 1578 and began teaching rhetoric there. Father Alessandro Valignani (1538–1606) requested that Ricci and Ruggieri be transferred to Macao and there, in 1582, Ricci began his study of Chinese.

The Jesuit mission to China was not the first Christian contact with China. Several missionaries were sent out from Europe in the mid-thirteenth century as Christian rulers sought Mongol support for their crusades in the Holy Land, but most got no further than the Mongol capital of Karakorum, the ruins of which are in present-day Mongolia. In 1291, the Franciscan John of Montecorvino (1247–1328) arrived in Beijing and built a church, complete with spire, in 1299, but no lasting mission was established. Impetus was given to Catholic missionary work by the pioneering sea voyages of Vasco da Gama and Christopher Columbus, which made possible the foundation of the trading establishments of the Dutch in the East Indies and the Portuguese in Goa (a small state in western India) and Macao. In addition, the Catholic Church, hard-pressed by opposition from the Protestant Reformation in Europe, felt the need to go out to the rest of the world and convert. In this, the Catholic Church led the way, for, despite the Dutch presence in the East Indies, the Protestant Church did not begin to send missionaries to the Far East until the beginning of the nineteenth century.

The founder of the Society of Jesus (the term "Jesuit" was first used in 1544) was St. Ignatius Loyola (1491–1556). His religious order differed from others in that it did not have choirs, it did not require wearing a distinctive habit or uniform, it stood aside from religious office, it increased the length of probation or training, and it was the first order to undertake foreign missions, at the order of the Pope. It was also notable for a stress on education. St. Francis Xavier (1506–1552), who had met Loyola, was sent eastward by King Joao III of Portugal and spent ten years in India and Japan, always conscious of the need to establish a mission in China. In 1551, he was to join an embassy sent from the Viceroy of the Portuguese Estado da India to the emperor of the Míng 明 dynasty (1368–1644) but the embassy was cancelled by the Admiral of Malacca (Vasco da Gama's son) and when, in 1552, Xavier found a Portuguese merchant willing to drop him on the Chinese coast, he died on a rocky outcrop near the mouth of the Pearl River.

Early Influences in Guangzhou and Beijing

As can be seen from St. Francis Xavier's failure, the Chinese authorities did not welcome outsiders during the sixteenth century. Portuguese traders were, however, beginning to arrive in the city of Guangzhou (Canton), in Guangdong Province. The local authorities allowed Portuguese residence on the Macao peninsula, but access to the mainland was severely restricted. Portuguese traders were permitted to enter Guangdong twice a year for trade in tea, silks, and porcelain but were not allowed to spend a night on the mainland, and were forced to return to their ships at dusk. Ruggieri went to Guangzhou and tried to persuade the local authorities to allow priests greater latitude; in the winter of 1582 he received permission to travel to Zhaoqing (then the capital of Guangdong Province) with Father Pasio, but they were expelled shortly after. The

Chinese authorities seemed to treat them as rather elevated merchants, without understanding their desire to preach, not trade. In 1583, however, Ricci and Ruggieri returned with local government permission to build a house and a church. Though they managed to baptize two local literati in 1584, a new local governor seized their fine house in 1587, and Ricci was forced to move to Chaozhou, on the Jiangxi border. In 1594, he was encouraged to travel to Beijing, which he did dressed in Chinese robes, a dress style approved by the pope. This adoption of Chinese clothing was part of Ricci's grand plan for acceptance, although his first decision, to adopt Buddhist dress, was perhaps a mistake since at the time Buddhism was a religion followed mainly by the poor, and many Buddhist monks were regarded with some suspicion. Ricci then chose to adopt the robes normally worn by scholars or literati for he felt these placed the Jesuits in a position of respect in the Chinese social context, somewhere between the educated literati and officials.

On his way north, he stayed for some time in Nanchang, Jiangxi Province where, in 1595, he published two works, *Jiāoyǒu lùn* 交友论 (*On Friendship*), and *Xīguó Jìfǎ* 西国记法 (*The European Art of Memory*). The first was an essay in imitation of Cicero, setting out Western philosophical and religious views of friendship, the latter a description of how to create hierarchies of objects and ideas in order to retain information. The purpose of this memory system was to master complex religious texts and systems but it was of considerable interest to educated Chinese whose education system, designed to lead to official positions, was rooted in the memorization of vast reams of Confucian texts needed to pass the examinations required of those who hoped to obtain official government positions. Both Ricci's works were greatly admired by the local literati. One of his most significant converts was *Xú Guāngqǐ 徐光启 (1562–1633), an official who eventually rose to the position of Grand Secretary and whose memory is still preserved in the Catholic Church in Shanghai, built in Xujiahui on land donated by the Xu family.

Despite his local success, Ricci was determined to pursue his trip to Beijing and set out with the support of a local official who was going to the capital to take up an appointment as Head of the Lǐbù 礼部, or Bureau of Rites. Although an imperial eunuch greeted Ricci upon arriving in Beijing in 1598, threats of war with Japan exacerbated the suspicion of foreigners and forced Ricci to leave almost immediately for Suzhou. In 1601, he returned to Beijing, accompanied by the Spanish Jesuit Father Diego de Pantoja (1571–1618). While Ricci entertained visitors in his hope of getting to the court, de Pantoja traveled through the surrounding countryside baptizing

---

*People marked with an asterisk have entries in this dictionary.

converts (and after Ricci's death, supervised the production of the imperial calendar in 1611).

Ricci's return to Beijing was not without its difficulties. He and de Pantoja were held up for six months in Tianjin before they and the presents they had brought for the emperor were allowed to proceed. Their gifts were taken to court where, according to a Jesuit source, "the emperor admired the images of Our Lady but was above all captivated by the clocks" (Pfister 1976, 29). The emperor in question was the *Emperor Wànlì 万历 of the Ming who reigned from 1573 to 1620. Though he never gained access to the court and never met the emperor, Ricci remained in Beijing until his death in 1610 and he was buried in land given by the emperor, which is now in the grounds of the city's Communist Party School.

Ricci and His Legacy

The Wanli emperor's interest in Ricci's chiming clocks and in de Pantoja's astronomical skills demonstrate one of the great ambiguities of the Jesuit enterprise in seventeenth- and eighteenth-century China, the problem of being accepted not for its faith but for its practical skills. Valignani, who had called Ricci to China, recognized the enormous importance of learning Chinese in order to convert, and Ruggieri, de Pantoja, and Ricci left publications in Chinese that demonstrated their mastery of the language. Ruggieri's *Shèngjiào Shílù* 圣教实录 (*True Record of the Sacred Teaching*), printed in Guangzhou in 1584, was the first Chinese catechism and the first work written in Chinese by a European, composed in the form of a dialogue between a European and a Chinese. Ricci's earliest publications in Nanchang included *On Friendship* and *The European Art of Memory* which were not exclusively religious in nature, but he also published *Tiānzhǔ Shíyì* 天主实意 (*The Truth of God*) in Nanchang in 1595, which, like Ruggieri's *Shengjiao Shilu*, took the form of a dialogue between a European and a Chinese designed to "refute the principal errors current in China."

In Beijing in 1604, he published *Èrshíwǔ Yán* 二十五言 (*Twenty-Five Moral Maxims*) on the essentials of Christianity, in 1609 the *Jīrén Shípiān*畸人十篇 (*The Ten Paradoxes*), which sought to challenge Buddhist ideas, and the *Biànxué Yídú* 辫学遗牍 (*Dispute with Idolatrous [Buddhist] Sects*).

Pursuing one of his principles, that the Jesuits could prove themselves useful to the Chinese court because of their modern European scientific skills, he was associated with several works published by his Chinese disciples such as the *Tóngwén Suànzhǐ* 同文算指 (*Practical Mathematics*), 1614, *Cèliáng Fǎyì* 测量法义 (*Practical Geometry*), *Gōugǔ yì* 勾股义 (*On the Triangle*), *Yuánróng Jiàoyì* 圜容较义 (*On Isoperimetrical Forms*), 1614 and *Húngài Tōngxiàn Túshuō* 浑盖通宪图说 (*On the Celestial Sphere*) 1607. He also produced a significant world map, *Wànguó Yútú* 万国舆图,

drawn in Zhaoqing in 1584, corrected and published in Nanjing in 1598. With Ruggieri he compiled a Portuguese-Chinese dictionary, the first ever European-Chinese dictionary, probably when they were in Zhaoqing between 1583 and 1588. Deposited in the Jesuit Archive in Rome, the dictionary was only rediscovered in 1934 and first published in 2001.

Ricci's stress on scientific expertise as a way into the Chinese court did not lead to more than a handful of converts there but it had an effect on the Jesuit mission in China that lasted for nearly 150 years as both the Ming court and that of the conquering Qīng 请 dynasty (1644–1911/1912) used Jesuit experts as astronomers, mathematicians, map makers, clock repairers, painters, and craftsmen. Johann Adam Schall von Bell 汤若望 (1591–1666) successfully predicted eclipses more accurately than the official court astronomers, and worked on the production of the official imperial calendar as well as creating bronze astronomical instruments. In 1645, he was made Director of the Astronomical Bureau, the first of several Jesuits to hold the post, such as Ferdinand Verbiest 南怀仁 (1623–1688) whose second set of instruments can still be seen on the observatory tower in Beijing.

The *Emperor Qiánlóng 乾隆 of the Qing (r. 1736–1795) was the last Chinese emperor to appreciate Jesuit skills. His grandfather, the *Kāngxī 康熙 emperor (r. 1661–1722) had studied mathematics and surveying with the Jesuit fathers Jean-Francois Gerbillon 李明 (1654–1707) and Verbiest, and had mathematical and astronomical instruments constructed in the palace workshops under their supervision. The Qianlong emperor made some use of Jesuit painters such as Guiseppe Castiglione 郎世宁 (1688–1766), who painted him on horseback as if he were a European king-emperor.

The *Emperor Yōngzhèng 雍正 (r. 1722–1735) temporarily exiled the Jesuits in 1724 and though some, like Castiglione, returned to court, their dominance was effectively over as court patronage declined and serious problems developed back in Europe. Dominicans and Franciscans, jealous of Jesuit success, stirred the controversy over the "Chinese rites," accusing the Jesuits of excessive accommodation to the Chinese and misrepresenting Chinese practices in the argument over whether ancestor worship was permissible to Chinese Christian converts. The order was suppressed in 1773.

It can be argued that the Jesuits had very little effect on China as the number of converts was never large, and therefore that Ricci had little impact. They did have a greater effect on the late Ming and early Qing courts, but primarily as scientists and experts along the lines pioneered by Matteo Ricci, who thought that by ingratiating themselves with the court the Jesuits could make converts at the top of society and the populace would follow. Instead, success at court led to jealousy and was part of the reason for suppression. Nevertheless, the effect of the Jesuits' China mission on Europe was enormous. For from the early period, not only did they publish Christian and scientific works in China, but they began to publish very widely on China in European languages. As one scholar put it:

> One way to gauge the impact of the Jesuits' propaganda efforts is to imagine an empty European bookcase from 1590 and watch it fill up with books large and small over the course of the following hundred years. The first works on the Jesuits in China would be the printed Annual Letters from the East Indies, which contained sections on Macao and the Guangdong Province residences. These small books would be dwarfed by Nicholas Trigault's account of the heroic deeds of Matteo Ricci and his colleagues, *De Christiana Expeditione apud Sinas* (Augsberg 1615). Seven other editions of this work appeared in just over a decade in translations into French, German, Spanish, Italian and English . . . By the middle of the seventeenth century, the pace of publication of Jesuit texts on China quickened. (Brockey 2007, 152–153)

Ricci himself left some of the earliest European eyewitness descriptions of China in his letters, the forerunners of the famous *Lettres Edifiantes et Curieuses* [Interesting and Uplifting Letters] first published in 1704, in which Jesuit missionaries described their places of work from all aspects, providing European readers with a very broad coverage of the history, politics, beliefs, and physical aspects of India, China, and other far-flung places. Ricci wrote about tea, picked in spring, dried in the shade and served throughout the day, not only with meals but whenever a visitor arrived. He described Chinese fireworks, "representing trees, fruits, fights and balls of fire turning in the air. It seemed to us when we lived in Nanking that on the first day of the year which is their special celebration, they use as much gunpowder as in ten years continuous warfare."

He wrote on printing, noting that printing in China was "a little older" than in Europe, but very different, owing to the nature of the language. In the earliest description of woodblock production, he noted that the woodblocks for printing were made from pear, apple, or jujube wood and that the written text was placed face down on the block and very gently rubbed so that only the characters remained visible. The rest of the block was carved away so that only the characters stood out. They then print out their pages with great speed. "Sometimes, one printer could produce 1,500 sheets in a day. And they also carve their blocks as fast as a [European] printer could compose and correct a page [of

A print showing the Jesuit missionary Matteo Ricci (left) and the Chinese scholar Xu Guangqi (right), who was among his first converts. Printed in 1669 by John Macock. Collection of the Beinecke Rare Book and Manuscript Library, Yale University.

movable type]" (Boothroyd and Detrie 1992, 117–119, author's translation). The work of Chinese printers was of interest to Ricci for the production of his own books and subsequently the multitude of primers as well as the religious and scientific texts put out by the Jesuits.

Ricci approved of the use of fans made of reeds, wood, ivory, ebony, paper, silk, and sweet-smelling straw—round, oval, or pleated and folded and sometimes decorated with a painting or a line of calligraphic verse. Though he noted some differences between Chinese and Europeans, he concluded that they were very similar, despite the geographical separation, in their way of eating, sitting, and sleeping, for they had tables, chairs, and beds, unlike the neighboring peoples (of Southeast Asia and India) who sat on mats on the ground, where they also ate and slept.

Ricci left a description of Beijing, "in the north of the country, only 100 miles from the famous walls built against the Tartars. In terms of size, street layout, great buildings and defenses, it is in truth, inferior to Nanking, although it has a greater population and a greater number of officials and soldiers. It is encircled by great walls, wide enough for 12 horses to ride comfortably abreast" (Boothroyd and Detrie 1992, 122–123). As few streets were paved, Ricci described the difficulty of walking through mud in winter and dust in summer, dust which got everywhere inside houses. He was pleased to note that the way to avoid the dust hazard was, then as now, four hundred years later, to wear a silk veil, which was greatly appreciated by the bearded European Jesuits who could walk through the streets unrecognized in their veils.

Ricci's descriptions of the warm reception of European striking clocks in the imperial palace set the tone for imperial presents for hundreds of years, with succeeding embassies such as that of Lord Macartney in 1792–1794 taking ornate clocks and watches as gifts, items that can still be seen in the exhibition galleries of the Forbidden City.

In his gifts, in his desire to explain China to Europe, in his translations of Western works into Chinese and his promotion of the study of the Chinese language and philosophy, Ricci set the style for much subsequent contact and his legacy in Europe was the foundation of the scholarly study of China, taken up by European thinkers like Leibniz and Voltaire.

Frances WOOD
British Library

Further Reading

Boothroyd, Ninette, & Détrie, Muriel. (1992). *Le voyage en Chine* [Trip to China]. Paris: Robert Laffont.

Brockey, Liam Matthew. (2007). *Journey to the East: The Jesuit mission to China, 1579–1724.* Cambridge, MA: Belknap Press.

Mungello, David E. (1989). *Curious land: Jesuit accommodations and the origins of sinology.* Honolulu: University of Hawaii Press.

Mungello, David E. (1999). *The great encounter of China and the West, 1500–1800.* Lanham, MD: Rowan and Littlefield.

Krahl, Regina; Murck, Alfreda; Rawski, Evelyn S.; & Rawson, Jessica. (2006). *China: The three emperors 1662–1795.* London: Royal Academy of Arts.

Spence, Jonathan D. (2008). *The memory palace of Matteo Ricci.* London: Quercus.

Ruggieri, Michele, & Ricci, Matteo. (2001). *Dicionário Português-Chinês* [Portuguese-Chinese dictionary]. Witek, John W. (Ed.). Lisbon, Portugal: Biblioteca Nacional.

Wood, Frances. (1996). *Did Marco Polo go to China?* Boulder, CO: Westview.

Tāng Xiǎnzǔ
汤显祖

1550–1616—Dramatist, author of *The Peony Pavilion*

Summary

Tang Xianzu was the foremost Chinese dramatist of the Ming dynasty. His four main works are all based on dreams, and his masterpiece, *The Peony Pavilion,* was a tender love story with a happy ending. An actress was reportedly once so moved by her part as Du Liniang in *The Peony Pavilion* that she died on stage. Tang's main contribution to dramatic theory is his emphasis on love or emotions, as opposed to reason. Although he himself held several official positions, he was an outspoken critic of power holders and may have retired from public life because of this, focusing instead on his writing.

Tang Xianzu was the most important playwright of the Míng 明 dynasty (1368–1644), with a major place in Chinese literature. Many have called him "China's Shakespeare" because of his distinction and because he lived almost exactly contemporaneously with the English bard. Tang completed four major dramas, all of them about dreams and entitled *The Four Linchuan Dreams* (*Línchuān sìmèng* 临川四梦). By far the most significant drama was *The Peony Pavilion* (*Mǔdān tíng* 牡丹亭), completed in 1598. His style was notable for its emphasis on feeling (*qíng* 情), as opposed to theory or reason (*lǐ* 理).

Background Career

Tang came from Línchuān 临川, Jiangxi Province, hence the collective name of his four dramas. He was from a prosperous family, and his father was a conventional Confucian scholar who expected Tang to follow an official career. After several unsuccessful attempts, he passed the metropolitan examinations and became a *jìnshì* 进士 (presented scholar) graduate in 1583. Tang then held various posts from 1584 to 1598, most notably secretary in the Ministry of Rites (Lǐbù 礼部) in Nanjing.

Despite the posts he held, Tang refused to kowtow to officials more powerful than he and, in particular, was no admirer of Grand Secretary (*Nèigé dà xuéshì* 内阁大学士) Shēn Shíxíng 申时行 (1535–1614), for which reason his official career was drastically less successful than it might otherwise have been. In 1591, Tang even wrote a memorial accusing Shen of corruptly ignoring a late-1580s famine, and indirectly criticizing the emperor himself. As a result, he was exiled to a minor post in Guangdong Province. Although later reinstated and appointed to a post in Zhejiang, he continued to be an outspoken critic of power holders.

In 1598, Tang retired from officialdom altogether, being stripped of all his titles in 1600. He spent the rest of his life in retirement in his hometown. Although he was quite poor, his studio, the Yùmíng Táng 玉茗堂, was popular with learned and literary friends and housed many historical and literary texts. Tang himself converted to Buddhism and became increasingly philosophical and mellow with age.

Theatrical Context

Tang lived during the late Ming Wànlì 万历 period (1573–1620). Apart from the first decade or so of his reign, the ruling emperor was venal and selfish, turning a blind eye to state problems and official corruption, meanwhile spending large sums of money on his own concerns, such as promoting his relations and building grand palaces. The Wanli reign and following period saw fiscal bankruptcy, natural disasters, and increasing eunuch power at court, factors that led in 1644 to the collapse of the Ming.

In terms of drama, the sixteenth century was the period when the traditional genre called *chuánqí* 传奇 (literally "transmitting the marvelous"), which had reached a zenith in the south in the fourteenth century, was evolving into the *Kūnqǔ* 昆曲 form. This genre came from Kūnshān 昆山 in Jiangsu Province and developed from a little-regarded folk style called *Kūnshān qiāng* 昆山腔. Despite this, it became the exclusive preserve of the educated elite, sometimes being termed "elegant parts" (*yǎbù* 雅部). Although originally southern in feel and origin, it spread all over China. Scholars and officials frequently ran their own *Kunqu* troupes in their mansions, with performances being a standard part of a banquet or similar entertainment. Guests could select favorite scenes from very long dramas, which, if performed complete, might last several days. *Kunqu*'s main musical characteristics are a regular four-four time and a softness and elegance not found in most regional styles, with the *dízi* 笛子, or side-blown bamboo flute, usually dominating.

The sixteenth century also saw the growth of various styles of regional theater (*dìfāng xì* 地方戏), most of them belonging far more to the category of "popular theater" and not in the least "elegant." In the south, the most important system of popular theater was the *Yìyáng qiāng* 弋阳腔, which was already fairly widespread by the middle of the sixteenth century. Its musical accompaniment lacked wind or string instruments, being dominated by percussion, especially drums. In a temple stele in Yíhuáng 宜黄, Jiangxi Province, Tang Xianzu mentions the prevalence of *Yiyang qiang* theater in his own time, adding that the rhythm was beaten out with a drum. Another important feature was parenthetical texts inserted into original *chuanqi* or *Kunqu* texts, a major function of which was to explain difficult allusions and classical language to illiterate audiences.

Role in Ming Dynasty Thought

Despite his family origins, Tang was somewhat unconventional in his ideas from early in his life. His education put some weight on spontaneous learning, as opposed to the rote learning that was normal at the time for those hoping to pass the civil service examinations and gain entry into the bureaucracy. Tang declared that the major influence on his thinking in his early life was Luō Rǔfāng 罗汝芳, and in his mature years, Dáguān 达观 (Zhang and Guo 1992, 541–542).

Luo was one of the main scholars of the Tàizhōu 泰州 School, located in a town in the economically and culturally prosperous lower Yangzi (Chang) Valley. This philosophical school emphasized the intrinsic value of all people and has justly acquired the reputation for being extremely progressive in the context of traditional China, and for promoting social fluidity. As a boy, Tang studied under Luo, the focus of whose ideas was vitality. As one specialist has written, Luo saw "as the animating principle of the universe the phenomenon of life itself, or the endless process of birth and growth" (Hsia 1970, 249). Tang adopted this notion in his own thinking strongly enough that, when in exile as a minor official in Guangdong in 1591–1592, he called an academy he established Guìshēng 贵生, which means "reverence for life." Tang explained,

> the education of a great man starts with "knowing life." Knowing what life is, he knows how to respect himself. Then he will also know how to hold in reverence all forms of life in this universe. (Hsia 1970, 250)

Tang's emphasis on feeling as against reason, to which we return in discussing his drama theory, springs from his concern for vitality.

Daguan, acknowledged as influencing Tang's later years, was a Buddhist philosopher, yet also was politically radical enough to suffer government persecution, dying in prison in 1603. Tang first met him in 1590, but they corresponded frequently and saw each other in Linchuan at about the time *The Peony Pavilion* was completed. Although they did not always agree, it appears to have been Daguan's influence that converted Tang to Buddhism. Daguan's anti-government ideas and activities were most likely a factor influencing Tang to withdraw from the world.

As a political thinker, Tang Xianzu was undoubtedly on the reformist and radical side. A study from the People's Republic of China calls him "a front-ranking progressive thinker in the period since the mid-Ming" (Zhang and Guo 1992, 541). The influences of the Taizhou School's individualistic Luo Rufang and the anti-state Buddhism of Daguan already position him in a hostile relationship with the government. His willingness to take the personal risk implicit in his memorandum against Shen Shixing shows him as a passionate opponent of corruption. Tang is on record as saying that officials "must not want money nor begrudge death" (Zhang and Guo 1992, 544).

Chinese Theater: Tang Xianzu's Role and Ideas

Coming at a time when *chuanqi* was well advanced in evolving into a new form, Tang Xianzu played a significant role in the development of Chinese theater. Although classified as a *chuanqi* author, his plays were adapted into *Kunqu* and usually performed in that genre. There are also adaptations of his plays into various styles of regional theater, but their delicacy and emphasis on the civil (*wén* 文) as opposed to the military (*wǔ* 武) make them particularly well suited to *Kunqu*. Ironically, given the importance of *Kunqu* in the history of Tang's dramas over more than four centuries, Tang himself did not welcome alterations in his work. He is on record as insisting that performers must follow his original version, fearing that adaptations would fail to preserve his original idea.

Not long after the rise of *Kunqu*, bitter debate arose on modes of expression. The most important issue was where to place the emphasis in drama: feeling or love (English renderings of the Chinese original *qíng* 情) as against reason or theory (both renderings of *lǐ* 理). Tang was the main proponent of the "feeling" school; he believed that the overwhelming function of drama was to give play to the characters' emotions. In his Yihuang temple stele, Tang writes,

> Feelings can be expressed through chanting and singing and through body movements. Sometimes they are completely poured out, and sometimes they are pent up for such a long time that they make one restless. (Tang trans. Fei 1999b, 55)

And in the preface of *The Peony Pavilion*, he writes of the power of love (*qing*):

> Love is of a source unknown, yet it grows ever deeper. The living may die of it; by its power the dead live again (Tang trans. Fei 1999b, 55) 情不知所起, 一往而深. 生者可以死, 死可以生.

The alternative point of view was that restraint was the best artistic principle. The chief proponent was Shěn Jǐng 沈璟 (1553–1610). He and his followers considered that allowing feelings to be given too free a rein would be ruinous to theater, and to the public; morality they believed should be upheld.

The Yihuang temple stele, which is actually a paean of praise for a theater god, contains several other ideas Tang developed on theater. One of them is the power of theater to create illusion:

> Several actors on a stage, performing with all the ease, brilliance, rhythm, and grace, may show spectators the illusions of people a thousand years from now or scenes from any dream. (Tang trans. Fei 1999b, 55)

It is perhaps no accident that Tang's plays put so high a priority on the world of dreams.

Despite this need to escape from the world, a path Tang indeed finally chose, he retains some Confucian ethics in his approach to theater. He expresses the ability of theater to improve people and society, though we still find a focus on love and emotion. In the Yihuang theater stele, he writes as follows:

> Theater reinforces the order between the emperor and his subjects, strengthens the tie between fathers and sons, improves the affection between the old and the young, and enriches the love between husbands and wives. Theater can express friendship, relieve conflict, soothe anxiety, and amuse the common people. (Tang trans. Fei 1999b, 56)

We can see a development in Tang's dramas. The earlier works represent the acme of the praise of love and the outpouring of emotions, with *The Peony Pavilion* the most passionate expression. His last two plays retain the emphasis on love, but give a larger role to religious thought, and appear much less positive about love in its worldly and sensual form. One modern scholar sees the dramas of Tang Xianzu as "a study of the human condition under the curse of time" (Hsia 1970, 252). The dream of *The Peony Pavilion*'s heroine "depicts a timeless condition where love is seen as the sole reality." On the other hand, the dreams in the last two plays "contract time and dramatize the transience of life" (Hsia 1970, 279). For Tang Xianzu, time apparently gains dominance as it itself proceeds.

Tang Xianzu's Works and the Four Dreams

Tang Xianzu began writing dramas before he earned his *jìnshì* degree. This was an activity frowned upon for somebody seeking success in the bureaucracy and, although he was already an aspiring dramatist and believed in the "feelings" idea that was to characterize his work, his early output was hardly enormous. Most of his work dates from a period of just a few years at the end of the sixteenth and beginning of the seventeenth centuries. This was the part of his life when his official career was becoming a source of increasing bitterness to him, and just after he finally retired.

Tang Xianzu's writing style combines an elegant literary flavor with an earthy colloquialism. Tang did not act on the stage. He did, however, direct performances of his own plays and worked closely with professional actors.

The Purple Hairpin

In 1577, Tang Xianzu began a drama called *The Story of the Purple Flute* (*Zǐxiāo jì* 紫箫记). A love story, it was based on a tale written in the Táng 唐 dynasty (618–907) called "The Story of Huo Xiaoyu" ("*Huò Xiǎoyù zhuàn*" 霍小玉传), Huo Xiaoyu being the name of the female protagonist. In the original, Huo's lover is a treacherous figure; indeed, famous as such in Chinese literature, but Tang Xianzu portrays him much more sympathetically as a victim of circumstances. On the stage the play was initially successful, Tang himself claiming that it was in great demand from accomplished performers who sang the lyrics to enormous audiences.

The fate of this drama is unclear. Despite Tang's satisfaction with its popularity, it was never published in complete form. There may have been manuscripts of the whole drama, but only thirty-four scenes survive. The full manuscript could well have succumbed to a fire that in 1613 also destroyed Tang's collection of calligraphy and painting. The reason why no full text was ever released is also unclear, but it may have contained satire about current Ming politics that made publication dangerous.

In 1586 and 1587, Tang rewrote the drama using the title *The Story of the Purple Hairpin* (*Zǐchāi jì* 紫钗记), although he did not hand it to the printer for publication until 1595 (Xu 1958, 217–226). The story and characterization are similar to the earlier version: Huo Xiaoyu is still obsessed with love and loyalty, while her lover is well-intentioned but much less passionate and colorful. Love and feelings are still dominant as dramatic themes. In line with *chuanqi* convention, the ending is a happy one. There is dark satire, however, in an evil official who comes between the lovers, possibly a representation of Shen Shixing or another of Tang's powerful enemies. The new version is much more elaborate in structure, much longer (having fifty-three scenes), and much more in the tradition of the *chuanqi* than the old. *The Story of the Purple Flute* has the general reputation as the weakest of Tang's plays, while it is *The Story of the Purple Hairpin* that was accepted among *The Four Linchuan Dreams*.

The Peony Pavilion

Also known as *The Return of the Soul* (*Huánhún jì* 还魂记), *The Peony Pavilion* is set in the Southern Sòng 南宋 dynasty (1127–1279). It tells the story of blossoming love and sexuality in a young lady from a highly sheltered background and the triumph of love over social convention. The main protagonist is Dù Lìniáng 杜丽娘, daughter of a stern Confucian bureaucrat, Dù Bǎo 杜宝, who insists on controlling her life and marriage. She falls asleep after a walk in a garden, and dreams of the young scholar Liǔ Mèngméi 柳梦梅, who is himself already in love with her. In the dream they make love in a pavilion set in a peony garden. Liniang later dies of love and is buried, together with a self-portrait. During a journey to the capital for the examinations, Liu finds the portrait and disinters Liniang's body, and she comes back to life. Meanwhile Du Bao establishes his reputation further by defeating a rebellion. He also flogs Liu for disrespect to Liniang's grave. Eventually, however, all ends happily when Liu Mengmei scores at the top in his examinations, leading Du Bao to accept the younger man as his son-in-law.

Tang shows himself a master of characterization. In many scenes he portrays the development of love in Du Liniang with great sensitivity. A highlighted scene is "The Interrupted Dream" (*Jīngmèng* 惊梦), in which she and her maidservant Chūnxiāng 春香 wander in a garden, Liniang falls asleep and Liu Mengmei visits her in a dream and makes love to her. The portrayal of Du Liniang is superb, and this is one of the scenes that have led two authorities to write that Tang has created "the most moving image of a lovelorn girl ever presented on the Chinese stage" (Birch and Cuadrado 1986, 753). Liu Mengmei is the archetypal lover, willing to defy the stern Confucian bureaucrat and suffer for the sake of his beloved and, most important of all, the scholar who does well in the official examinations and wins his beloved and career success. The character of Chunxiang is famous in Chinese literature and theater as a maidservant role, much less serious-minded and constrained than her mistress, sometimes disrespectful and pert, but always loyal.

Among Tang's works, *The Peony Pavilion* is the one that best illustrates his mastery of language. Several factors show this. Du Liniang's lyrics and those relevant to her love are expressive and tender, in some places containing a very appealing eroticism. The language is rich in allusion, with frequent references

From *The Peony Pavilion*, "The Interrupted Dream"

This is the passage that leads up to the dream that is central to the drama, where Liu Mengmei appears to Du Liniang, declares his love, and makes love to her.

Du Liniang:

Though born and bred of a noted line of holders of office, I have reached the age to "pin up my hair" without plan made for my betrothal to a suitable partner. The green springtime of my own life passes unfulfilled, and swift the time speeds by as dawn and dusk interchange. *(She weeps)* O pity one whose beauty is a bright flower, when life endures no longer than leaf on tree!

From turbulent heart these springtime thoughts of love will not be banished

—O with what suddenness
comes this sudden discontent?
I was a pretty child, and so
of equal eminence must the family be
truly immortals, no less
to receive me in marriage.
But for what grand alliance
is this springtime of my youth
so cast away?
What eyes may light upon my sleeping form?
My only course this coy delaying
but in secret dreams
by whose side do I lie?
Shadowed against spring's glory I twist and turn.
Lingering
where to reveal my true desires!
Suffering
this wasting,
where but to Heaven shall my lament be made!

I feel rather tired, I shall rest against this low table and drowse for a while. (*She falls asleep and begins to dream of Liu Mengmei)*

Source: Tang Xianzu. (1980). *The Peony Pavilion: Mudan ting*. (Cyril Birch, Trans.). Bloomington: Indiana University Press. 46–47.

showing deep knowledge of China's history and literature. The words are full of imagery and symbolism, a prime example being the peony as the late-blossoming maiden. There is also plenty of comic relief. The language shows abundant puns, while many of the less important characters are figures of fun or involved in humorous situations, for example, the scene in which Chunxiang teases Liniang's tutor. There is also much bawdy humor and the scholar who writes that "Sex in *Mudan ting* runs the gamut from sublime eroticism to farce" (Swatek 2002, 15), is not alone in her view among commentators.

The image of Du Liniang has proved very popular over the centuries, especially among young women. Unrealistic as the dream may be, it gives play to erotic love and to emotions more intense than those the Confucian ethic permits. According to Chen Meilin, who adapted Tang Xianzu's original into novel form, the publication of this drama "had a great influence on society and there were repercussions among women who had been ruled by feudal ethics." He claims that one woman wept so bitterly after reading it as to bring on her death, and a Hangzhou actress was so moved that she died on stage (Tang, adapted by Chen 1999, n.p. introductory section "About the Original Play *The Peony Pavilion*"). It is tears of emotion that have resulted in these deaths, not misery.

The Story of Handan

The first of Tang's final two plays was *The Story of Handan* (*Hándān jì* 邯郸记). Completed in 1600, it has forty-four scenes and is based on a Tang dynasty story by Shěn Jìjì 沈既济 (c. 740–c. 800), *Inside a Pillow* (*Zhěnzhōng jì* 枕中记). The story is about Lú Shēng 卢生, a man who while asleep dreams an entire lifetime, resting his head on a porcelain pillow, waking to find that the reality had lasted only a few minutes.

In Tang's drama, a Daoist (Taoist) immortal suggests that Lu Sheng go to sleep, which results in his dream. Lu is presented as a selfish and slightly dishonest official, who struggles against a more powerful and even more corrupt bureaucrat. His only concern is for success in life. Lu experiences various vicissitudes in his career, including marriage to a rich man's daughter, a period of exile to Hainan Island, long and distinguished service at court, and rewards from the emperor. Meanwhile, his main enemy ends up exposed and executed. Mainly loyal to his wife, Lu engages in Daoist sexual practices late in life. Aiming thereby to bring about immortality, these practices actually end up shortening Lu's life. Yet he dies happy and feeling that he has achieved a successful career and good life. After he wakes up, the Daoist immortal accepts Lu as a disciple, taking him to the Pénglái 蓬莱 Islands, in Chinese mythology a place of eternal youth and paradise.

There is a great deal of politics in this drama. In his dream Lu has no wish to leave politics, and although he suffers greatly from exile in Hainan, he ends up happy with his life overall and is victorious over his main enemy. Lu Sheng is a political opportunist, and has periods of suffering, but this dream does not overall suggest the need for withdrawal from politics or the uselessness of human life or the world. Daoism has a positive role in the sense that a Daoist immortal takes the main character to paradise, even though the sexual regimen it recommends is ultimately a failure. There are still strong emotions portrayed in the drama, but in fact Tang gives them less emphasis in this play than in his others.

The Story of Nanke

Tang Xianzu's last play was *The Story of Nanke* (*Nánkē jì* 南柯记), completed in 1601 in thirty scenes. Like *The Story of Handan*, it is based on a story of the Tang dynasty, in this case "The Governor of Nanke" ("*Nánkē tàishǒu zhuàn*" 南柯太守传), by Lǐ Gōngzuǒ 李公佐 (c. 770–c. 848). Its central figure is Chúnyú Fén 淳于棼, a former military officer who has become an alcoholic. In his dream he is in an ant kingdom where he marries a princess and receives an appointment to run the province of Nanke. He repels the invasion of another ant kingdom, but despite doing his job well, he suffers calumny at court and is advised to return to the human world. The world of ants turns out to be a swarm under a tree on his own property. He turns away from the world, giving up wine and sex, and becomes a recluse, achieving Buddhahood but dying three years afterward.

Tang still believed strongly in the importance of emotions. There are some differences, however, in this drama in comparison with his earlier works. The human body is pitiful and worth nothing. The play ends with its main character giving up sex and other pleasures, almost as if the erotic world was something evil, not worthy and delicious, as it is portrayed in *The Peony Pavilion*. The moral is the transience of human life, which is no more important than that of ants. We can also see that Tang evidently laid much more weight on religion by this stage of his life. There is a figure in the drama similar to the Buddhist Daguan, and most likely modeled on him. In contrast to *The Story of Handan*, it is easy to relate Tang's last work to his own life, as discussed in this article in the section "Background Career." By this time, Tang had become convinced that official life was trivial and resistance to authority useless. His escape was in religion and literature.

Tang Xianzu in His Own Time and Afterwards

Tang Xianzu's plays attained a good degree of popularity in his own time. Both during his lifetime and after, *The Peony Pavilion* has enjoyed the reputation not only as Tang's masterpiece, but also as a landmark in Chinese drama and literary history.

Favorable mentions in the famous eighteenth-century novel *Dream of the Red Chamber* (*Hónglóumèng* 红楼梦) are among the factors showing *The Peony Pavilion*'s influence during the Qīng 清 dynasty (1644–1911/12), at least among the educated elite. Several famous and enduring *Kunqu* scenes from *The Story of the Purple Hairpin*, *The Story of Handan*, and, especially, *The Peony Pavilion* attest to the persistent popularity of Tang's corpus of plays.

The early People's Republic period from 1949 to the early 1960s saw excellent performances of scenes from *The Peony Pavilion*, including "a performance of the entire play . . . during a national festival in the mid-1950s" (Birch 1986, xiv). At about the same time, the scenes "Wandering to the Garden" and "The Interrupted Dream" ("Yóuyuán jīngmèng" 游园惊梦) were performed with the popular female impersonator Méi Lánfāng 梅兰芳 (1894–1961) in the role of Du

Images of Mei Lanfang, the immensely popular male actor who played the female role of Du Liniang from *The Peony Pavilion* in the early twentieth century. Illustration by Anna Myers.

Liniang. This was especially notable because Mei has had the reputation as the best and most famous actor China has ever produced. Scholarship about Tang Xianzu flourished, the most distinguished writer being Xú Shuòfāng 徐朔方. The Cultural Revolution of 1966 to 1976, however, saw the total suppression of traditional dramas, and Tang Xianzu's works were all banned.

This situation changed drastically after the Cultural Revolution was discredited in 1981, and traditional theater returned as if floodgates had opened, including performances of *The Peony Pavilion*. In 2001, UNESCO added *Kunqu* to its list of "Masterpieces of the Oral and Intangible Heritage of Humanity," assisting the revival of Tang Xianzu's greatest work. New productions of *The Peony Pavilion* have included one performed over three evenings by the Jiangsu Provincial Kunju Troupe (*Jiāngsū shěng Kūnjù yuàn* 江苏省昆剧院) at the Beijing Music Festival of 2004, and a two-hour version performed twice a week in the old Imperial Granary in Beijing since 2010.

The new popularity of *The Peony Pavilion* has also inspired international productions. The most notable was the 1999 avant-garde *Peony Pavilion* directed by American Peter Sellars with music by the Chinese US-based composer Tán Dùn 谭盾. Although Sellars knew Tang Xianzu's text, however, and his production is based on it, his version was very different from the original and "has been aptly characterized as contemporary American theater" rather than updated *Kunqu* (Swatek 2002, 14).

These revivals show Tang's reputation as high, both in his own country and internationally. As the author of dramas based on love and dreams, he is unsurpassed. He was "China's Shakespeare" only in relative terms, however. His output was much less than his English counterpart's and, even in China, he is not a household name in the way that Shakespeare is internationally.

Colin MACKERRAS
Griffith University

Further Reading

Birch, Cyril, & Yü Cuadrado, Clara. (1986). T'ang Hsien-tsu. In William H. Nienhauser, Jr. (Ed.), *The Indiana companion to traditional Chinese literature* (pp. 750–754). Bloomington: Indiana University.

Hsia Chih-tsing. (1970). Time and the human condition in the plays of T'ang Hsien-tsu. In William Theodore de Bary & the Conference on Ming Thought (Eds.), *Self and society in Ming thought* (pp. 249–290). New York: Columbia University Press.

Lu, Tina. (2001). *Persons, roles, and minds: Identity in* Peony Pavilion *and* Peach Blossom Fan. Stanford, CA: Stanford University Press.

Mao Xiaotong 毛效同. (Comp.). (1986). *Tang Xianzu yanjiu ziliao huibian.* 汤显祖研究资料汇编 [*Compilation of research materials on Tang Xianzu*] (Vols. 1–2). Shanghai: Shanghai guji chubanshe.

Swatek, Catherine C. (2002). Peony Pavilion *onstage: Four centuries in the career of a Chinese drama*. Ann Arbor: Center for Chinese Studies, The University of Michigan.

Tang Xianzu. 汤显祖 (1962). *Tang Xianzu ji 汤显祖集* [*Tang Xianzu's collected works*] (Vols. 1–4). Xu Shuofang 徐朔方 & Qian Nanyang 钱南揚, (Eds.). Shanghai: Zhonghua shuju.

Tang Xianzu. (1980). *The Peony Pavilion: Mudan ting*. (Cyril Birch, Trans.). Bloomington: Indiana University Press.

Tang Xianzu 汤显祖. (1999a). *The Peony Pavilion* 牡丹亭. (Chen Meilin 陈美林, Adapted). (Kuang Peihua 匡佩华 & Cao Shan 曹珊, Trans.). Beijing: New World Press.

Tang Xianzu. (1999b). Tang Xianzu on theater. In Faye Chunfang Fei (Ed., Trans.), *Chinese theories of theater and performance from Confucius to the present* (pp. 54–58). Ann Arbor: The University of Michigan Press.

Tang Xianzu. (2003). *A dream under the southern bough* (Zhang Guangqian, Trans.). Beijing: Foreign Languages Press.

Xu Shuofang 徐朔方. (1980). *Tang Xianzu nianpu 汤显祖年谱* [*Chronological biography of Tang Xianzu*]. Shanghai: Shanghai guji chubanshe. (Original work published in 1958. Beijing: Zhonghua shuju).

Xu Shuofang 徐朔方. (1983). *Lun Tang Xianzu ji qi ta 论汤显祖及其他* [*On Tang Xianzu and other things*]. Shanghai: Shanghai guji chubanshe.

Zhang Geng 张庚, & Guo Hancheng 郭汉城. (Comps.). (1992). Tang Xianzu ji qi "Simeng" 汤显祖及其 "四梦" [Tang Xianzu and his "Four Dreams".] In *Zhongguo xiqu tongshi* 中国戏曲通史 (*Comprehensive history of Chinese traditional drama*) (pp. 538–563). Beijing: Zhongguo xiju chubanshe.

Wáng Yángmíng
王阳明

1472–1529—Neo-Confucian philosopher and official

Alternate names: birth name: Wáng Shǒurén 王守仁; courtesy name: Bó'ān 伯安

Summary

The most important Confucian philosopher of the Ming dynasty, Wang Yangming also served in many government positions, including governor of Jiangxi Province, where he suppressed rebellions and re-organized the local government. He taught an interpretation of Neo-Confucianism that emphasized both the morality of understanding and service to society. All people, according to Wang, had the innate faculty of moral knowledge. Through ups and downs in his career, he attracted a large following as well as many detractors, and his influence in the realm of Confucian thought can still be felt today.

Known as a charismatic teacher, an innovative state official and community reformer, and a successful military strategist, Wang Yangming had an eventful life in which he overcame many personal and professional trials, including an unjust beating and exile. But it was in the realm of Confucian philosophy that he made his mark, especially in his interpretations of Neo-Confucianism and his ideas of the supremacy of innate moral knowledge, or *liangzhi*.

The social and ethical teachings of Confucianism, first gathered by *Confucius 孔子 (551–479 BCE), became government ideology beginning in the second century BCE, and remained the dominant underpinning of government and social mores until the end of imperial China in 1912. As a follower of Confucius, Wang Yangming was a passionate seeker of the truth who taught that each person contained innate moral knowledge and just needed to recognize and act on this. He insisted on putting his ideas into practice, teaching that knowledge is the beginning of action and action is the

*People marked with an asterisk have entries in this dictionary.

completion of knowledge. In addition to introducing the major arguments in Confucianism as a lived philosophy, his life story elucidates the elite culture and government organization of the Míng 明 dynasty (1368–1644) during which he lived.

Founded by a poor peasant turned rebel leader, the Ming overthrew the Yuán 元 dynasty (1279–1368) and became the only Chinese dynasty to rule all of China in the final eight centuries of imperial China. Many Chinese literati had not been allowed or chose not to serve the Mongol rulers, so there was great excitement at a Chinese dynasty, since Confucian teachings emphasized civil service to society. The first Ming emperor, however, set up a despotic system in which government officials were distrusted and treated harshly. In spite of the difficulties of state service, educated men flocked to join official ranks, attempting to pass the various levels of the civil service examination system. Wang Yangming was one of them.

Family and Youth

Wang was born southeast of Hangzhou in Zhejiang Province and was given the private name of Shouren and the courtesy name Bo'an. Wang chose the honorific name of Yangming during his time in retirement near Yangming Cave between 1502 and 1504. Wang Yangming enjoyed a privileged childhood as the son of an educated father who served as a government official after passing in first place the highest tier of the national civil service examination of 1481. Implemented in the second century BCE, this exam system had slowly gained traction until, by the time of the Ming, it served as the main route to official recruitment, social status, wealth and influence.

The curriculum for the exams consisted of the Confucian classics as interpreted by the great synthesizer *Zhū Xī 朱熹 (1130–1200), and required a successful candidate to spend years in "examination hell" memorizing, practicing essays, and passing exams at first the local, then the regional, and finally at the national and palace levels. The rewards for success were high, but failure rates were phenomenal. Thoughtful scholars bemoaned the narrowness and careerism of the exam curriculum, but in spite of these criticisms and the dangers of state service, the supply of young men wanting to enter official life always exceeded demand. So the examination system remained an important part of literati life.

Wang's family could provide him with the necessary leisure, books, and instruction, which also meant psychological pressure to work hard to try to continue the family prestige and financial security. In 1499, Wang Yangming passed the national level of the examinations in second place, on his third attempt, at the comparatively young age of twenty-eight. Wang's family had the additional advantage of living in Zhejiang Province in the lower Yangzi (Chang) region of south-central China, the most prosperous and educated part of China. By the mid-Ming period, this area was undergoing rapid commercialization and urbanization, and enjoyed a flourishing book publishing industry. Though the emperors were not fond of commerce and tried to control trade through the traditional tributary system, demand for Chinese silk and porcelain drew China into the developing international trading system. The influx of silver began to monetize the Chinese economy and the rapid social growth resulted in negative socio-economic dislocations which contributed to the demise of the Ming in the seventeenth century.

Wang spent much of his childhood near his father, even accompanying him to his post in the capital city of Beijing from the age of eleven to sixteen. His mother died when he was thirteen. His stepmother supposedly treated him harshly until he scared her by putting a lizard in her bed; after that she treated him more carefully. The young Wang enjoyed practicing martial arts, in particular swordplay and archery. His interest in physical pursuits was a bit unusual for the time, as in the previous few centuries the cultural ideal for elite males had become more bookish. (Similarly, female aesthetics underwent a similar shift at this time, so that delicate women with bound feet were admired.) Wang's early interest in martial arts may have informed his interest in and ability at military strategy in his official career.

The elite family of the Ming was patriarchal and polygamous, with emphasis on early marriage and many children. In line with other elite males, Wang entered into an arranged marriage at seventeen. This marriage did not produce a son, which was a major disappointment in a patrilineal society. *Mencius 孟子 (c. 372–c. 289 BCE), second only to Confucius as a revered ancient master, taught that the most unfilial act was to not produce a son to continue the family line and perform rituals to the ancestors. Near the end of his life, Wang fulfilled this duty by having a son with a concubine. Perhaps adding to the difficulties of producing children was the fact that Wang was often away from home on official duties and spending time with his many students. In fact, there is a famous story about Wang's wedding night. He stopped in at a Daoist (Taoist) temple and became so engrossed in discussions with the priest that he spent his wedding night away from his bride.

While studying Confucian texts to prepare for the civil service exams, Wang's main spiritual interest seems to have been in Daoism, China's other lasting and indigenous way of thinking. Every educated male read the Daoist classics and so was conversant with Daoist teachings of emptiness, non-striving, harmony with nature, and longevity. In contrast to the group orientation and emphasis on state service in Confucianism, Daoism insisted on a private life, and was often a resource for creativity. Daoist longevity techniques of breathing, diet, and sexual techniques may have appealed to Wang in part because he suffered from poor health throughout his life. There was also some family tradition in popular religious techniques, as his great-great-grandfather was a recluse skilled in divination. Wang's father, however, appears to have been a stern Confucian official who eschewed both Daoism and Buddhism.

In spite of his father's attitude, another interest of Wang Yangming's was in Buddhism and, in particular, in the practice of spiritual detachment. Buddhism entered China through travelers along the Silk Roads in the first century and gradually became sinified and an important part of Chinese culture. During his lifetime and after his death, Wang was sometimes seen by Chinese scholars as so influenced by Buddhism that many accused him of being a Chán 禅 Buddhist (Zen in Japanese) rather than a Confucian. Wang Yangming grew up in a society where Buddhism, Daoism, and Confucianism, the so-called Three Ways of Thinking, had mixed to a great extent. Syncretism has always been evident in China, in contrast to the exclusivity of the world's great monotheistic religions. Buddhism and Daoism both had great personal relevance for Wang, and he spent years studying them.

Official Career

After passing the national examination in 1499, Wang served in minor official posts for the next few years. In 1499, in response to semi-nomads invading northwest China, Wang submitted a memorial on national defense. Although the court did not follow his advice, his reputation as a military strategist grew among officials. In his early thirties, from 1502 to 1504, Wang retired due to ill health and removed himself from the world to practice Buddhist techniques of meditation and a Daoist regimen seeking longevity. Under pressure from himself, his family, and his society to succeed in a public career, Wang's withdrawal functioned as a safety valve and as nourishment. Wang was recalled to office in 1504 as the examiner for the Shandong provincial examinations. In his examination questions, he criticized Buddhism and Daoism as being selfish because they did not advocate bringing order to this world. He emphasized the social relevance of Confucianism, but criticized its decline. Even as a committed Confucian, Wang continued borrowing from Buddhism and Daoism what he found helpful for his own cultivation and that of his students.

The years 1506 to 1510 were trying but rewarding for Wang Yangming. After the eunuch Liu Jin wrestled control from a playboy emperor, Wang memorialized his support of officials imprisoned for their protests of Liu's usurpation. Liu had Wang beaten for forty strokes and exiled to Guizhou Province in southwest China to dispatch horses in the transit system. Wang lived among the Miao minority in rustic conditions. These years in exile forced Wang to contemplate his inner life, and he became convinced of the need to look inward to the mind/heart to recover one's innate moral knowledge (*liángzhī* 良知).

Wang's exile ended in 1510 and he became a magistrate in Jiangxi Province, after which he received several promotions to serve on the national level. From 1516 to 1520, he held high positions pacifying rebels and bandits. Putting his knowledge and interest in military affairs to use, he recruited and led soldiers, restored order, established schools, and reorganized local government.

In 1519, he captured the rebel Prince Ning, a nephew of the emperor. Due to official infighting, Wang was rumored to have conspired with the prince, and was not credited with putting down the rebellion. In 1521 Wang requested sick leave, returned home to Zhejiang and was out of office until 1527. Hundreds of disciples gathered around him, however, and he spent these years teaching. Recalled to suppress a rebellion in Guangxi Province in 1527, he was again successful and, as before, established schools and reorganized local society and government. During this time, Wang was coughing and had to oversee military matters from a carriage. He started home, only to die on the way.

Wang Yangming's Place in the Confucian Tradition

Wang Yangming had studied Confucianism, Daoism, and Buddhism, but after years of introspection and struggle, he dedicated himself to what he came to believe was the one true way: Confucianism. Like every Confucian, Wang considered himself a follower of Confucius but was especially drawn to the teachings of Mencius.

In order to place Wang within the Confucian tradition, it's important to understand Confucius's developing interpretations of such important concepts as the ideal community, human nature, self-cultivation, and the perfected human being, or sage. Confucius was responding to the growing disunity and violence he observed as the feudal order of the Zhōu 周 dynasty (1045–256 BCE) began to disintegrate with rulers of the various states under Zhou rule jockeying for central power and influence. Confucius's answer was to revive the teachings of the early Zhou (1045–770 BCE) in order to develop humane men who would be able to restore just and harmonious rule. He was conversant with the history and rituals of ancient China, and viewed the early Zhou period as a golden age when the Way (*dào* 道) was being practiced in the world.

Though he was in many ways revolutionary, Confucius claimed to be merely a transmitter of the wisdom of the ancient sages. Confucius travelled from state to state trying to convince a ruler to give him an official post and put his teachings into practice. He failed at this, but found his calling as a master teacher. He was persuasive and charismatic enough to convince a group of disciples to take up his ideas. Confucius's teachings were mainly aimed at making the world a more humane, orderly, and hierarchical place. The model for state and society was the reciprocal relationships within the ideal family. His appeal was to tradition and the need for people to return to the example of his idealized interpretation of a golden age in the past. Confucius did not discuss human nature. Self-cultivation for Confucius consisted of study of ancient texts and performance of rituals through which the individual could discover and embody the wisdom of the past. The quest for self-perfection should be carried out in community. The ultimate goal of self-perfection was sagehood. His view of sages (completely perfected human beings) was that sage-kings ruled during the golden age, but that sagehood was a distant and all but impossible goal. When his own disciples wanted to call him a sage, Confucius objected.

Mencius studied with Confucius's grandson and followed the example of gathering a group of disciples around him and traveling from state to state seeking a ruler to put his teachings into practice. Like Confucius, he taught a moral way based on the example of the harmonious, if hierarchical, ideal family. In the century after Confucius's death, China had descended into the greater violence and chaos of the Warring States 战国 period (403–221 BCE). Many thinkers were arguing over various interpretations of human nature. Mencius was no exception and presented an argument that human nature is good. He argued that there are fragile sprouts of goodness within the heart-mind (*xīn* 心) of each individual. If individuals would cultivate these incipient tendencies, their human nature could serve as fuel to help them progress toward realization of a Confucian utopia built on the example of the ideal family. For Mencius, Confucius was a sage. So, he brings the possibility of sagehood a bit closer to human possibility.

When we consider Wang Yangming's reinterpretation of Confucianism, we must remember that he lived about two thousand years after the death of Confucius and one thousand years after Buddhism had taken root in China. The context had shifted, but there was still enough resemblance in the questions asked and his vision of a harmonious, hierarchical society to place Wang within the Confucian tradition. Occasionally, Wang taught about the ideal family as the model for a peaceful, orderly society. More often, he used a metaphor which goes beyond the family to include the entire universe. Wang's metaphor was "forming one body with Heaven, Earth, and all things." For Wang, the universe is united in fundamental ways, including humans, animals, and plants. Though Mencius teaches that human nature is endowed by Heaven, his philosophy is still predominantly human-centered. Wang teaches not that humans should unite everything, but that everything is united and it is a matter of humans realizing this. In his views, Wang was influenced by the metaphysical underpinnings added to Confucianism by the Sòng 宋 dynasty (960–1279) thinkers.

Much of the re-evaluation and restoration of Confucianism occurred under the impetus of the strength and appeal of Buddhism, and also Daoism, from the late Hàn 汉 dynasty (206 BCE–220 CE) up to the Song dynasty. Confucianism had been installed as the state orthodoxy by the Han dynasty, but when the dynasty was overthrown in 220 CE, China descended into more than 350 years of disunity. Though Confucian ethics continued to inform human relationships, both elites and commoners were inspired by the sophisticated metaphysics and institutional organization of Buddhism. During this time a Daoist church was built under the influence of the Buddhist model. Buddhist ideas of the mind and emptiness, and Daoist concepts such as the Way as origin and progenitor, and the Supreme Ultimate (*tàijí* 太极) were incorporated into the Confucian synthesis during the Song dynasty. This reorientation and reinvigoration of Confucianism was so thorough that it received a new designation often translated as Neo-Confucianism.

In his analysis of human nature, Wang takes on the concept of sprouts of goodness or moral intuition taught by Mencius (*Mencius* 7A.15). This concept of *liangzhi* has been translated as innate moral knowledge or as pure knowing. In Wang's use of the concept, rather than a body of knowledge, *liangzhi* is a faculty which enables the mind to spontaneously respond to any stimuli with the appropriate response and/or action. For Wang, *liangzhi* is the ultimate authority. It is more important than the golden age of the past, sage kings, texts, or rituals in self-cultivation.

In placing himself within the Confucian tradition, Wang also developed his own lineage of the Transmission of the Way (*dàotǒng* 道统). This assertion of an intellectual lineage was developed by Confucians in the Song on the model of the Chan Buddhist genealogies of the mind-to-mind transmission from patriarch to patriarch. The Way thus passed from Confucius to Mencius, then to the Song philosophers *Chéng Hào 程颢 (1032–1085) and Lu Xiangshan, and then to himself. Both Cheng Hao and Lu Xiangshan emphasized the authority of the mind over externals, though not to the extent of Wang. Lu famously remarked that the Confucian classics were merely his footnotes. The accepted orthodox Transmission of the Way during the Ming period was through Song thinkers Cheng Yi and Zhu Xi, who together form the Cheng-Zhu school of Neo-Confucianism.

Wang came to view himself as an orthodox Confucian. To uphold this view, he had to reconcile his philosophy with that of Cheng Yi and Zhu Xi. As a *jìnshì* 进士 degree (presented scholar) recipient and government official, Wang was expected to have mastered the Cheng-Zhu interpretations of Confucianism that the state had adopted as the standard for the examinations. For many years Wang studied Zhu Xi's writings and tried, but failed, to put Zhu's method of self-cultivation and the investigation of things (*géwù* 格物) into practice. Zhu taught that principles should be sought in external things (mainly classical texts), but Wang came to the conclusion that principles were situated within the mind. While in exile in Guizhou, Wang tested and expanded his own philosophy. There he had an enlightenment experience, realizing that principle is found in the mind-heart (*xīn* 心). This contrasted with Zhu Xi's view that principle was found in the nature (*xìng* 性). Though rejecting both Zhu's method and object of self-cultivation, Wang satisfied his claim to orthodoxy in his own mind by asserting that Zhu Xi ultimately arrived at ideas similar to his own.

In common with other Neo-Confucians Wang taught that sagehood is a distinct possibility and that humans must strive to become sages. Even unlettered men and women have *liangzhi*, an innate capacity for goodness. This belief shows the influence of Mencius, as well as the Buddhist teaching of the Buddha-nature inherent in each person. Rather than developing this, it is more a matter of recognizing it.

The Song reorientation of Confucianism, the examination system, and the difficulties of state service were givens with which Wang grappled. He questioned the decision of many young men to study primarily to advance through the civil service examinations, and tried to persuade his students to focus on the larger goal of attaining sagehood.

Master and Disciples

Like Confucius and Mencius, Wang Yangming used the dialogic approach between master and disciples in the spiritual quest for self-perfection. Wang accepted his first disciple in 1505 and as soon as the 1510s, his teachings were becoming well-known and controversial. Many contemporary Confucians criticized him as misrepresenting Zhu Xi. In a 1520 letter to a critic, Wang stated his belief that the Way belonged to all and that the words of Zhu Xi, and even of Confucius, needed to be evaluated for their contemporary relevance. In this letter, Wang asserted that the Way and the teachings are public and belong to everyone. They should be discussed openly and "are not the private properties of Master Zhu or even Confucius" (Wang 1963, 164; *Instructions,* 176). Although Wang worked to reconcile his teachings with those of Zhu Xi, in his mature teaching there is a sense that he believed himself beyond any human standard of orthodoxy. As in the quote above, he wanted his students to question any authority, even Confucius, that did not conform to their own faculty of innate moral knowledge (*liangzhi*) when put into practice.

Wang Yangming's inspirational teaching, social reforms, and active government career were powerful models which drew students to him. Wang was a charismatic teacher, but he resisted writing down his ideas in a systematic way. Much of the problem for students arose from Wang's use of paradoxes, similar to Chan Buddhist koans. These were meant to awaken them from their old way of thinking, so they could achieve their own awareness of the innate goodness of the mind and of the mystical unity of man with heaven, earth, and the myriad things. For example, Wang stated "Mt. Tai is not as large as the level ground," and taught his students that it was all right to use the concepts of *wèifā* 未发 (the pre-stirred state of the mind) and *yǐfā* 已发 (the already issued state of the mind) if they realized that such states do not really exist; yet it was also all right to say they exist, since they do (*Instructions*, 204).

The same problem arose with any attempt at definition of his concepts. For example, innate moral knowledge (*liangzhi*) was identified with many different things when Wang attempted to explain it. He equated it with the Way, the heart of the Way (*dào xīn* 道心), the principle of heaven (*tiānlǐ* 天理), the mind-heart, the ultimate substance of the mind-heart (*xīn zhī běntǐ* 心之本体), and with sagehood (*shèng* 圣) (Ching 1976, 113, 123). This ambiguity would seem to emphasize his teaching that understanding is personal and difficult to express. It also fits with Wang's reluctance to write down his teachings and his insistence on face-to-face instruction between master and disciple. Even more than Confucius, Wang varied his teaching depending on the individual needs of his students. He would urge meditation on a student overly reliant on texts and vice versa.

Wang's reinterpretation of Confucianism did not eclipse state-supported Cheng-Zhu Confucianism, but for about a century the numerous followers of Wang and his teachings played a lively and important role in China's cultural life. Because Wang questioned older forms of authority such as texts, the authority of his teachings was tied to his personal example. Once he was gone, his many followers interpreted his teachings in their own ways so that several different branches developed. The Taizhou branch in the late Ming pushed Wang's ideas to extremes by insisting that since everyone contained *liangzhi*, there was no need for education or even literacy. Once a person realized this *liangzhi*, they had become a sage and were equal or better than others. It then followed that there was no room for social hierarchies or rules of etiquette. Confucianism and Chinese society were based on hierarchies of age, generation, and gender, but some Taizhou men argued that women should be considered equal to men, since both had the capacity to access their *liangzhi*.

In large part due to the logical extremes in which the Taizhou followers of Wang pushed his ideas, the seventeenth century saw a conservative turn away from Wang. Even in the sixteenth century, many Ming Confucians had decided that Wang was heterodox. During his lifetime, some of his students did not pass the civil service examinations when they espoused his interpretations.

Wang Yangming Remembered

After Wang's death, the minister of rites accused him of heterodoxy and deserting his final office as he had started home without official permission. Therefore, posthumous honors were not awarded, and his earlier titles were taken away. Only in 1567 did the new emperor grant a posthumous title (Wénchéng 文成, Completion of Culture), and restore Wang's other titles to him and to his son. In 1572, there was a debate at court over the memorials for and against Wang's inclusion in the Confucian temple. Wang's inclusion was agreed to, but the actual installation came only in 1584 after the death of its main opponent, Grand Secretary Zhang Zhuzheng. Enshrinement in the Confucian temple, an honor bestowed on only four men during the Ming, conferred state orthodoxy upon Wang. After 1584, Wang became part of the state religion and was worshipped in all Confucian temples throughout China. But enshrinement did not protect Wang from posthumous criticism. One of Wang's most prominent critics was the Qing scholar Gù Yánwǔ 顾炎武 (1613–1682), who blamed the fall of the Ming dynasty on what he interpreted as the useless speculation on mind and inattention to statecraft that Wang's teachings encouraged in his followers (Gu 1695, *Rizhi lu* 6/8/121).

Wang's closest disciples thus shaped his legacy by successfully urging the court to grant him posthumous honors and include him in the Confucian temple, by advocating an intellectual lineage from Confucius in which Wang revived the transmission of the Way, by editing and printing Wang's writings and biography, and by establishing shrines to him and participating in rituals at these shrines.

Although it's clear how Wang Yangming related to Confucianism in its various aspects of moral philosophy, familial ethics, political ideology, and education curricula, the religious import of his project is much more difficult to apprehend. In contrast to religions in the West, Chinese religion has lacked strong institutional organization (with the exception of Buddhism, for a brief period), and has been diffused through various agencies, primarily those of the state and the family. As discussed, the tension between learning for oneself and in order to achieve worldly success was apparent. The orientation of Confucianism, however, remained worldly. Questions about the ultimate meanings of life and death remained rooted in moral responsibilities to other people, rather than to a god or other elements of supernatural religion.

The ethico-religious elements within Confucianism did not teach that its adherents could attain a physical immortality, as the Daoist religion promised. In Confucianism, and in Chinese traditional beliefs, there was a rather vague concept of social immortality, expressed in the family's need for a male heir to carry on the family name and perform ancestral sacrifices. Adoption was often resorted to when there was no natural son to continue the family line. The dead were remembered, and if the family continued, the names of early ancestors would be recorded. These concepts were combined in the practice of ancestor commemoration.

Confucius countered questions concerning death with, "While you do not know life, how can you know about death?" Regarding social immortality, though, Confucius is reported to have said, "The superior man dislikes the thought of his name not being mentioned after his death." Confucius taught above all that morality must be pursued for its own sake and that pursuing his teachings would guarantee the student neither honor in this lifetime nor immortality after death. Likewise, Wang Yangming criticized the belief in physical immortality, but writes about social immortality: "We Confucians also have our own doctrine of immortality. Yanzi died at the age of 32, and yet still lives today" (Ching 1973, 4–5). Yan Hui (Yanzi) was the favorite disciple of Confucius, and Wang means that his reputation was still alive.

Wang himself certainly gained social immortality and his ideas are studied in Korea, Japan, Taiwan, Singapore, and with a resurgence of interest in Confucianism even in the People's Republic of China. During the Ming and later Qīng 清 dynasty (1644–1911/1912), shrines were built to Wang Yangming and rituals at these shrines encouraged social immortality, with even some overtly religious overtones.

Shrines (*cí* 祠) were an omnipresent feature of the Chinese landscape in the Ming-Qing period. They were of different types and included shrines to worthies in the Confucian tradition. Shrines to worthies existed in the Han dynasty, but gained in popularity from the time of the Song. These worthies were men, and occasionally chaste women, who were sacrificed to after their deaths as moral exemplars but not as gods. Shrines to Wang were established in his home province, as well as in provinces where he had served. An example is the "Shrine of the Five Worthies" (*wǔxiān cí* 五仙祠) built by a local man on Mount Qingyuan, Jiangxi Province during the late Ming and restored in the early Qing in order to sacrifice to Wang Yangming and four of his most prominent disciples from Jiangxi. Another late Ming shrine to the fellowship around Wang was established in Wang's home province of Zhejiang, to worship him and twelve of his disciples who were mainly from Zhejiang or studied there with Wang.

In a show of powerful antagonism to Wang's teachings, however, the holdings of this shrine were seized by the government and held from the years 1579 to 1584 so that sacrifices could not be carried out. This happened in spite of the fact that the court had agreed to enshrine Wang in the Confucian temple in 1573. The shrine's property was likely returned to it in 1584 because this was when Wang was actually installed in the temple.

Wang's legacy has followed the highs and lows of his own life. Particularly from the 1600s on, Wang's late-Ming followers were blamed (or praised in the People's Republic of China) for acting on their questioning of the traditional social order and moral codes. Some scholars thought these ideas so subversive as to bring about the collapse of the Ming dynasty. Although the Qing returned to an earlier interpretation of Confucianism as state orthodoxy, and the majority of thinkers turned away from Wang's ideas, Wang's teachings remained compelling to many Koreans, Japanese, and twentieth-century Chinese political reformers.

Kandice HAUF
Babson College

Further Reading

Chan, Wing-tsit. (1977). Biography of Wang Yangming (as Wang Shou-jen). In L. C. Goodrich and Chaoying Fang (Eds.), *Dictionary of Ming biography, 1368–1644*. New York: Columbia University Press.

Chang, Carsun. (1962). *Wang Yang-Ming: Idealist philosopher of sixteenth-century China*. New York: St. John's University Press.

Ching, Julia. (1976). *To acquire wisdom—The way of Wang Yang-ming*. New York and London: Columbia University Press.

Ching, Julia. (1973). *The philosophical letters of Wang Yang-ming*. Columbia: University of South Carolina Press.

Cua, Antonio S. (1982). *The unity of knowledge and action: A study in Wang Yang-ming's moral psychology*. Honolulu: University of Hawaii Press.

de Bary, W. T. (1970). Individualism and humanitarianism in Late Ming thought. In W. T. de Bary (Ed.), *Self and society in Ming thought* (pp. 145–247). New York: Columbia University Press.

Gu Yanwu. (1695). *Rizhi Lu* 日知录 [Records of daily learning]. Changsha, China: Pan Lei Sui chu tang.

Ivanhoe, Phillip J. (2002). *Ethics in the Confucian tradition* (2nd ed.). Indianapolis: Hackett.

Tu Wei-ming. (1976). Neo-Confucian thought in action: Wang Yang-ming's youth (1472–1509). Berkeley: University of California Press.

Sibu Beiyao (Ed.). (1985). *Wang Yangming nianpu* [Chronological biography]. In *Yangming quanshu* 陽明全書 [Complete works] (Reprint). Taipei, Taiwan: Zhonghua shuju. (Original work published 1572)

Wang, Yangming. (1963). *Instructions for practical living, and other Neo-Confucian writing by Wang Yang-ming*. (Chan Wing-tsit, Trans). New York: Columbia University Press. (Original work published fifteenth century)

Wanli, Emperor (of Ming)

Wànlì 万历

1563–1620—Emperor of the late Ming dynasty; reigned 1572–1620

Alternate names: birth name: Zhū Yìjūn 朱翊钧; temple name: Shénzōng 神宗

Summary

Emperor Wanli reigned for forty-eight years during the late Ming dynasty. After a successional dispute with his ministers, he retreated from effectual rule for nearly thirty years, leading to his reputation as a weak, profligate ruler who contributed to the downfall of the dynasty. During this period, however, China saw a flourishing of culture and technology, and its influence began to spread to the West. Wanli supported the arrival of the Jesuits in Beijing, but his rejection of influence from other countries set the tone for Chinese foreign relations for the next three centuries.

Born Zhū Yìjūn 朱翊钧, Emperor Wanli reigned from 1572–1620, toward the end of the Míng 明 dynasty (1368–1644). At forty-eight years, his was the longest reign of the sixteen Ming emperors. While most historians have considered him a failure, some have evaluated him as intelligent but weak-willed and caught in a bloated and inefficient imperial establishment. He was only nine years old when he ascended the throne, and he was a conscientious ruler while under the tutelage of Grand Secretary Zhāng Jūzhèng 张居正 (1525–1582), who initiated tax reform and anti-corruption measures. But when the emperor wanted to establish his third son as heir apparent, rather than the first as accorded with dynastic precedent, he became embroiled in a fifteen-year succession struggle with his ministers. The emperor relented in 1601 and named his eldest son heir, but from the 1580s onward he withdrew into the inner palace and refused to attend audiences, perform his ritual duties, or read and act on memorials. Since an emperor was to rule as well as reign, the emperor's strike meant that offices were not filled, officials were not promoted, and policies were not carried out.

Although politically the Wanli emperor is considered weak, the late Ming dynasty period during which he reigned was a time in which culture, technology, and the economy flourished. Throughout the dynasty, the military responded to northern incursions by Mongols, Chinese rebellions, and Japanese pirate raids along the southeast coast, as well as the Japanese invasion of Korea and the ensuing five-year war in which China supported its tributary country. The military declined in effectiveness, however, just as the Manchus grew in strength in the late sixteenth century, until they finally overthrew the Ming to establish the Qīng 清 dynasty (1644–1911/1912) just twenty-four years after Wanli's death.

Because of his position near the end of the dynasty, traditional Confucian-educated historians evaluated the Wanli emperor as a classic "bad last ruler" who helped to lose the Ming's Mandate of Heaven, or the right to rule granted by Heaven as long as an emperor was a just ruler. The late Ming state was clearly weakened by weak or inattentive emperors, but also by population pressure, a global economic depression, the onset of a "little ice age," disease, factional strife among officials, and interference by palace eunuchs.

Life Behind the Palace Walls

Zhu Yijun was born into the ruling family of the Ming dynasty founder Zhū Yuánzhāng 朱元璋, also known as *Emperor Hóngwǔ 洪武 (1328–1398; r. 1368–1398). Hongwu came from a poor peasant background and had led a successful rebellion to overthrow the Mongol Yuán 元 dynasty (1279–1368). Upon the death of his father, Emperor Longqing, Zhu Yijun succeeded to the throne with the reign name of Wanli. As was the case with all emperors, he was thought to have received the Mandate of Heaven and was referred to as the Son of Heaven, one who mediated between Heaven and Earth. In audiences, only he faced south while his officials faced north. When those officials referred to him in writing, his name was elevated above their vertical lines of writing, and his reign name was used to tell time, for example 1577 was Wanli 5. As emperor, Wanli lived in luxury behind the walls of the Forbidden City, the palace and office complex built in Beijing in the fifteenth century. His was a feminine universe of palace women and eunuchs. He was married to his empress at age fourteen. Chinese marriage among the elite was polygamous, with one legal wife and the possibility of numerous concubines. The emperor had more of everything, of course, including a harem of women. These consorts and concubines were served by maids and eunuchs in order to insure the purity of the imperial patrilineage. In spite of

*People marked with an asterisk have entries in this dictionary.

View of a large square in Beijing's Forbidden City, built in the fifteenth century. As emperor, Wanli lived in luxury behind the walls of the Forbidden City. Photo by Joan Lebold Cohen.

his wealth and privilege, only seven of the emperor's children reached adulthood. Of his eight sons, three died in infancy, and of ten daughters, eight died young.

Thinking of his own mortality, the emperor started building his enormous tomb at the age of twenty, and upon his death at age fifty-seven, he, and later his empress, and Lady Wang as mother of the next emperor, were buried there. The emperor was honored under the temple name of Shénzōng 神宗 ("spiritual ancestor"). (Centuries later, in 1969, Red Guards dragged the skeletons of the emperor, empress, and consort into the open, and denounced and burned them.)

Over time, Wanli had become an obese recluse who spent lavishly on luxuries, new palaces, and the construction of his tomb. Much of the funding came from the people's taxes as he confused the public and privy purses. In an exhibit in 2012 in Beijing's Capital Museum, the size and splendor of the underground mansion in the tomb were displayed. Carts pulled by 1,600 mules transported the large pieces of granite used in construction. The tomb was filled with precious objects and contained wooden eunuchs to serve the emperor and his ladies in the afterlife. This was a telling contrast to the famous terracotta warriors guarding the tomb of the First Emperor, the more military-minded *Qín Shǐhuáng 秦始皇 (259–210 BCE). Although Wanli was personally extravagant, it must be remembered that he also had to support a very large establishment. Historians estimate that in the late Ming there were 3,000 palace women and almost 20,000 eunuchs in the palace. One Japanese scholar puts the figures at 9,000 women and 100,000 eunuchs. In addition to supporting the imperial palace, there was the huge expense of supporting the extended imperial family. The Ming founder began the practice of sending his sons to the provinces, where they had huge estates, salaries, and personal guards. By the late Ming, several thousand of these imperial relatives were being supported by the state.

Context of Wanli's Rule

The political stalemate of the late Ming and of Wanli's rule originated as early as 1380, when the Ming founder abolished the prime ministership to emphasize the power of the emperor over the bureaucracy in a highly autocratic system that continued such Mongol practices as whipping officials at court. This left the emperor as the only strong coordinator of governmental affairs in the inner court, made up of the emperor, the Hanlin Academy (Hànlín Yuàn 翰林院) and the palace eunuchs. The Hanlin Academy consisted of the highest-ranked civil service examination graduates. Secretaries were chosen from this group to aid the emperor, and by the sixteenth century the most important of these secretaries were referred to as grand secretaries.

Until he died in 1582, Grand Secretary Zhang advised Wanli and was the main point of connection between the inner court and the bureaucracy. The emperor had chafed under Zhang's strictures against drinking and extravagance, so when he discovered after his death that Zhang had not practiced what he preached, he confiscated Zhang's extensive holdings and rescinded his titles. This episode embittered the emperor and encouraged him, along with the demands of officials in the succession affair, to rely more on the palace eunuchs and then to quit ruling altogether. This created a vacuum in communication between the inner court and the bureaucracy, which was sometimes filled by eunuchs.

In the Ming dynasty, the civil service bureaucracy was largely made up of a nonhereditary elite recruited through competitive examinations based on a Confucian curriculum. During the late Ming in particular, members of this elite were attempting to emphasize a more equal role in government against the absolute authority of the emperor. There was factional strife among officials on how to proceed on many issues. Some moralistic officials were willing to face beatings or even death in opposition to the inner court. These brutal consequences exemplified these officials' fervent desire for change, which, in some cases, seems to have reached the level of an unhealthy search for social immortality through martyrdom.

Legacy of an Emperor and a Dynasty

How have the Ming dynasty and the Wanli period been remembered? Twentieth-century Communist leader *Máo Zédōng 毛泽东 (1893–1976) praised Zhu Yuanzhang for rising from a peasant background, and Mao and other contemporary Chinese lauded the Ming dynasty for reestablishing Chinese rule over China, and reasserting China's international power and prestige. The Forbidden City, built during the Ming dynasty and used as the imperial palace, with its material treasures is for many Chinese and foreigners the symbol of the glory of imperial China.

The Wanli period is honored by Korea for successfully joining in its five-year war against Japanese invaders. This was also the time when the Jesuits arrived in China. Though he refused to meet or correspond with them, in 1601 the emperor gave *Matteo Ricci (1552–1610) and his fellow Jesuits permission to live in Beijing, some land, and a stipend. Ricci sent back accounts to Europe of the fabulous wealth of China and of its "enlightened" government. Europeans, especially in the eighteenth century, borrowed from China in many regards, from the import and imitation of the famous Ming blue-and-white porcelain to advocating the recruitment of officials through a civil service examination system as a way to reform their own governments. In contrast, the Wanli emperor's policy that a self-sufficient China did not need the goods or knowledge of the West set the tone of China's foreign relations for the next three centuries.

Kandice HAUF
Babson College

Further Reading

Goodrich, Carrington L. & Fang, Chaoying (Eds.). (1976). *Dictionary of Ming biography*. New York: Columbia University Press.

Huang, Ray (1981). *1587, a year of no significance: The Ming dynasty in decline*. New Haven, CT: Yale University Press.

Melvin, Sheila (7 September 2011). China's reluctant emperor. *New York Times* review of "Retrospect of the Ming Dynasty: Experiencing the Period of Wan Li." Capital Museum. Retrieved November 25, 2013, from http://www.nytimes.com/2011/09/08/arts/ 08iht-wanli08.html

Mote, Frederick W., & Twitchett, Denis (Eds.). (1988) *The Cambridge history of China. Vol. 7. The Ming dynasty, 1368–1644*. Cambridge, UK: Cambridge University Press.

Spence, Jonathan D. (1988). *Emperor of China: Self-portrait of Kang-hsi*. New York: Vintage.

Wèi Zhōngxián
魏忠贤

1568–1627—Powerful eunuch official

Alternate name: Lǐ Jìnzhōng 李进忠

Eunuchs carrying sedan chair of Empress Dowager Cixi in the late nineteenth century.

Summary

Wei Zhongxian has become notorious in Chinese history as a powerful eunuch who dominated a weak emperor and controlled the court in the early seventeenth century. While the young Emperor Tianqi concerned himself with carpentry and other interests, Wei Zhongxian exploited the people by levying huge taxes; he filled government posts with his own sympathizers and ruthlessly brought down his enemies. He was stopped only when the emperor died prematurely and Wei hanged himself rather than face reprisals by Tianqi's successor.

Wei Zhongxian was the most notorious in a series of eunuchs in the Míng 明 dynasty (1368–1644) who exercised power under weak or ineffective emperors. He served in the inner court of the Tiānqǐ emperor 天启 (r. 1621–1627), considered the worst among the Ming's several poor rulers. This emperor was only fourteen years old when the previous emperor died after two months in office, and was dead himself at age twenty-one. The Tianqi emperor was young, poorly educated, inexperienced, and weak both physically and mentally. His real passion was carpentry, not ruling, which provided the power vacuum into which Wei Zhongxian inserted himself.

By 1624, the emperor had given significant power to Wei, even though Wei was reportedly illiterate. Wei initially ingratiated himself into the emperor's confidence through his relationships with palace women. He had been a butler in the service of the future emperor's mother where, through a friendship with the young prince's nurse, Wei was introduced into his inner circle. Life in the inner court could be very lonely and bound by ritual. Eunuchs were often the playmates and confidants of young princes, so it is understandable that a young emperor would turn to one for comfort and advice. Wei dominated the government from 1624 to 1627. He collected irregular taxes and was head of the secret police, which had powers to imprison, torture, and execute outside the regular judiciary.

Historical Context

The late Ming was a time of factional strife among officials, and resulted in political purges, struggles, and violence. The major factions during the Tianqi reign consisted of the literati who clustered around the Donglin Academy (Dōnglín Shūyuàn 东林书院), a private center for philosophical learning established during the Sòng 宋 dynasty (960–1279 CE) and rebuilt in 1604, and opposed the forces who rallied around Wei Zhongxian. Retired officials and literati gathered at the academy to criticize government corruption and advocate strict moralistic teachings and the practice of Confucian values. Like-minded officials advocated for the same reforms, and against the same policies, officials, and eunuchs. This loose Donglin coalition was labeled a faction or party by its enemies. A faction was thought to put private, selfish interests over public, state welfare, so this was a dangerous label. The Donglin leaders at court weren't necessarily anti-eunuch, and did work with a eunuch sympathetic to their cause. This eunuch, however, was murdered in 1621 in a purge orchestrated by Wei Zhongxian.

Supporters of Wei reported auspicious omens linked to him, and built shrines to honor him. Wei terrorized, purged, and executed hundreds of officials who opposed him. In a translation by the scholar Charles Hucker of a 1624 memorial, one brave official accused Wei of twenty-four crimes including "usurping imperial authority, intriguing against upright ministers, manipulating civil service appointment procedures, murdering opponents within the palace, and, by forced abortion, preventing the empress from giving [the Tianqi emperor] an heir" (1957, 132). After the Tianqi emperor died, Wei hanged himself rather than face punishment by the next emperor. In an expression of anger and contempt, his corpse was mutilated and the head was displayed on a pike.

Eunuchs had existed in China since the ancient dynasties. Their main role had been to serve the emperor and his women in the inner palace. As castrated males, they were not considered a threat to the purity of the patrilineal line of the emperor. Males who were made eunuchs were often enemies captured in battle. Confucians looked down on eunuchs as being less than men, since they could not take part in the accepted family structure. According to Confucian teachings, the ancestors gave a person his body and it was his filial duty to return this body intact at death. So, for Confucians,

Eunuchs in Dynastic History

The primary sources on eunuchs are the biographies of mostly notorious eunuchs included in the standard histories of each dynasty, which contain the Confucian historians' vitriolic commentaries on eunuchs as scoundrels who overstepped their original role as menial servants. Nearly all indigenous Chinese dynasties had eunuchs serving in the palaces as servants and intermediaries between the emperor and the officialdom. Eunuchs in the Hàn 汉 (206 BCE–220 CE), Táng 唐 (618–907 CE), and Míng 明 (1368–1644) dynasties were blamed for the fall of these dynasties. Even when large numbers of eunuchs were evicted from the palaces and massacred by the thousands in 189 CE and 890 CE, the survivors were soon recalled and new recruits brought into the palaces. In the Han and Tang dynasties many eunuchs acquired offices, became estate owners, and terrorized the populace, interfering in court and military affairs to the point of usurping the operative powers of the bureaucracy and dethroning and enthroning emperors. The number of eunuchs varied from several dozen in short-lived dynasties to 100,000 in the Ming dynasty, during which the emperors, who distrusted the Confucian officialdom, entrusted eunuchs (such as Wei Zhongxian) to lead major military and diplomatic campaigns.

Foreign peoples who founded dynasties on Chinese territory did not have eunuchs during their nomadic stages, but they adopted this Chinese institution as part of the state-forming and sinicization process when they set up these dynasties—including, among others, the Tabgach Northern Wèi 魏 (386–534 CE), Khitan Liáo 辽 (907–1125), Jurchen Jīn 女真金 (1115–1234), Mongol Yuán 元 (1279–1368), and Manchu Qīng 清 (1644–1911/1912). The Northern Wei eunuchs gained as much power as their counterparts in the indigenous dynasties, but eunuchs in the Liao, Jin, and Yuan periods were relatively insignificant. In the Qing dynasty some eunuchs were manipulative, but they did not have the institutionalized political and military powers associated with the eunuchs of the earlier periods.

—Jennifer W. JAY, *University of Alberta*

castration was seen as an offense against one's ancestors. The Confucian thinker *Mencius 孟子 (c. 372–c. 289 BCE) taught that the most unfilial act was to not produce a son and heir, which a eunuch could not do.

Castration was sometimes meted out as a punishment. One of the most famous cases was that of China's first historian, *Sīmǎ Qiān 司马迁 (c. 145–86 BCE). Because he offended the emperor by speaking up in support of a general who had surrendered to the "barbarians," Sima was given the option of death or castration. Wanting to finish the work begun by his father, he chose the humiliation of castration. Castration could result in death through excessive blood loss or infection, but Sima survived to complete his masterful history of China. In the Ming dynasty, poor families might castrate a son and present him to the court (or a young man might volunteer himself for castration, as Wei Zhongxian seems to have done) in hopes he would be accepted for service. The family would receive remuneration, and might continue to receive aid from a successful son.

Likely the most famous eunuch of the Ming dynasty was the Muslim admiral *Zhèng Hé 郑和 (1371–c. 1433). He is an example of eunuchs serving as personal servants to the emperor who were given a wide assortment of jobs outside of the palace. From 1405 to 1433, Zheng He led seven expeditions to Ceylon (Sri Lanka), Arabia, and East Africa. The purposes of these voyages was to broadcast the might of China, to encourage countries to submit to the Chinese tributary system, and to acknowledge the emperor as the most powerful ruler in the known world. These voyages were set in motion by Zhu Di (1360–1424), who usurped the throne in 1402 to become the *Emperor Yǒnglè 永乐, and so was anxious to appear powerful and legitimate and quell any criticism of his actions by the educated elite. Zhu Di

A Ming dynasty portrait of Emperor Tianqi.

*People marked with an asterisk have entries in this dictionary.

greatly increased the use of eunuchs to control the literati. Ming eunuchs worked in the palace guard and secret police, supervised mines and the salt monopoly, and supervised government storehouses and tax bureaus. Whereas Zhu Di used eunuchs to assert his control over the bureaucracy, the weak or inattentive late Ming emperors such as Tianqi ceded much of their power to their increasingly powerful palace eunuchs. This was what happened in the case of Wei Zhongxian.

In recent scholarship, historians have presented a more balanced view of eunuchs as palace servants and intermediaries between an emperor and his bureaucracy. Some of them seem to have had good ideas and made positive contributions. This re-evaluation, however, has not changed the prevailing view of Wei Zhongxian as a power-hungry and essentially corrupt person.

Kandice HAUF
Babson College

Further Reading

Atwell, William. (1988). The T'ai-ch'ang, T'ien-ch'I, and Ch'ung-chen reigns, 1620–1644. In F. W. Mote & D. Twitchett (Eds.), *The Cambridge history of China,* vol. 7, *The Ming dynasty 1368–1644.* Cambridge, UK: Cambridge University Press.

Chan, Albert. (1982). *The glory and fall of the Ming dynasty*. Oklahoma City: University of Oklahoma.

Elman, Benjamin A. (1989). Imperial politics and Confucian societies in late imperial China: The Hanlin and Donglin academies. *Modern China, 15*(4), 379–418.

Huang, Ray. (1982). *1587, A year of no significance: The Ming dynasty in decline*. New Haven, CT: Yale University Press.

Hucker, Charles. (1981). *The Ming dynasty : Its origins and evolving institutions. (Michigan papers in Chinese studies)*. Ann Arbor: Center For Chinese Studies, The University of Michigan.

Hucker, Charles. (1957). The Tung-lin movement of the late Ming period. In John K. Fairbank (Ed.), *Chinese thought and institutions* (pp. 132–162). Chicago: University of Chicago Press.

Mammitzsch, Ulrich Hans-Richard. (1968). *Wei Chung-hsien (1568–1628): A reappraisal of the eunuch and the factional strife at the late Ming court*. (Ph.D. dissertation [No. 176], University of Hawaii.)

Tsai, Shih-Shan Henry. (1995). *The eunuchs in the Ming dynasty*. Albany: State University of New York Press.

Wú Chéng'ēn
吴承恩

c. 1505–1580—Supposed author of *Journey to the West*

Alternate names: courtesy name: Rǔzhōng 汝忠; style name: Shèyáng Shānrén 射阳山人 ("Mountain dweller of Sheyang")

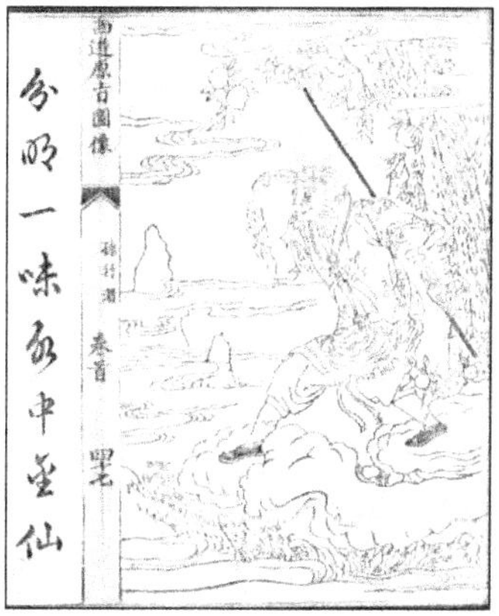

Monkey, the main character from Wu's novel *Journey to the West*.

Summary

Wu Cheng'en is generally believed to be the author of *Journey to the West*. While Wu's authorship is questionable, his life and works provide an important reference point for the modern reader seeking to understand the knowledge structure that likely prepared a literary mind during the time of the Ming dynasty. Readers of *Journey to the West* have interpreted it differently at different times in history; during the Qing dynasty, readers embraced the novel mainly as an allegorical work that expounded on the Daoist principle of supreme perfection. Modern critics have also hailed *Journey to the West* as the most fascinating romance in Chinese literary history, and a masterpiece of vernacular fiction.

Wu Cheng'en is considered an important literary figure in Chinese history largely due to his putative authorship of *Journey to the West* (*Xīyóu jì* 西遊记), a sixteenth-century novel of one hundred chapters in vernacular Chinese that is loosely based on the historical pilgrimage of Xuánzàng 玄奘 (c. 596–664 CE), also known as Tripitaka 三藏, and his fellow travelers to India. The eighty-one ordeals that the fictional Tripitaka goes through in this novel are so captivating that the members of the pilgrimage have long become household names in China and elsewhere in eastern Asia: the master whose highly desirable flesh is supposed to extend one's life; Sūn Wùkōng 孙悟空, the recalcitrant monkey king; Zhū Bājiè 猪八戒, the pig who is a somewhat comic figure prone to sensual indulgences; the Sand Monk (Shāsēng 沙僧), who is a banished immortal just like the pig; and the horse that was originally a white dragon. Among the three disciples of Tripitaka, it is Sun Wukong who wields the utmost magical power—his seventy-two modes of transformations and

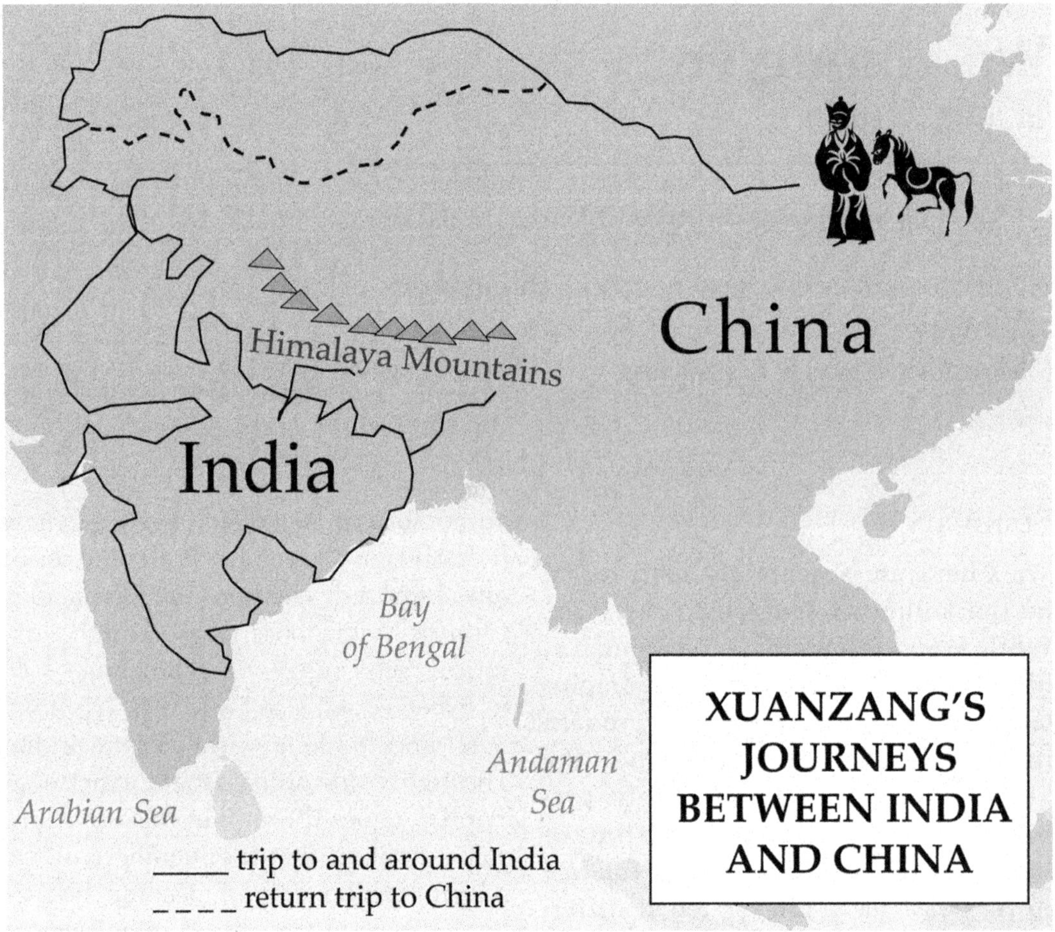

XUANZANG'S JOURNEYS BETWEEN INDIA AND CHINA

trademark somersault, which allows him to travel ten-thousand-and-eight-thousand *li*, make him the most fascinating character of the entire group.

The earliest edition of *Journey to the West* in its existing, fully developed form was published in 1592. It does not identify the author but lists one Master of Huayang Grotto 华阳洞天主人 as the collator. Most of the later editions from the Qīng 清 dynasty (1644–1911/1912) claim that the novel is a Daoist (Taoist) manual on cultivating the primordial Oneness created by Qiū Chǔjī 丘处机 (1148–1227), master of the *Quánzhēn* 全真 ("complete perfection") teachings. But as early as the eighteenth century the Qing scholar Jì Yún 纪昀 (1724–1805) challenged such an attribution by pointing out that all the institutional titles in

Journey to the West came from the bureaucratic system of the Míng 明 dynasty (1368–1644), after Qiu's time. Authorship attributed to Wu Cheng'en, however, is also open to questions. The local gazetteer of Huái'ān 淮安, Wu's home area, from the Tiānqǐ 天启 reign (1621–1627) lists *Journey to the West* under Wu's name along with his other writings, *Collection of (Master) Sheyang* (*Shèyáng jí* 射阳集) and "Preface to *The Spring and Autumn Annals*" ("*Chūnqiū lièzhuàn* xù" 春秋列传序). Since traditional bibliography typically does not include anything other than belle-lettres, it remains a question whether the *Journey to the West* listed here is identical to the full-length novel (Zhang 1983).

Challenges notwithstanding, Wu Cheng'en remains the most likely candidate to claim authorship of the novel. Master of Huayang Grotto is the literary name of Lǐ Chūnfāng 李春芳 (1510–1584), an eminent official of the Ming court who was Wu's close friend. In addition, critics since the Qing dynasty have considered the novel's sociological setting to be most likely in the Huai'an region. Wu's collected poems and essays also display a sense of familiarity with the same repertoire of knowledge that the novel draws upon. Furthermore, Wu was a contemporary and friend of such illustrious figures as the painter and calligrapher Wén Zhēngmíng 文征明 (1470–1559), the writer Hé Liángjùn 何良俊 (1506–1573), and essayist Guī Yǒuguāng 归有光 (1507–1571), which reinforces the impression that Wu belonged to the exclusive circle of cultural elite that contributed much of what modern literary history holds as canonical literature. Therefore, despite the lack of definitive evidence that Wu Cheng'en is the author of *Journey to the West*, a study of Wu's life and work will shed light on the kind of social milieu, experiences, and knowledge structure that likely prepared a literary mind of the time to produce the likes of the one-hundred-chapter novel.

Life and Social Network

Both Wu Cheng'en's great grandfather and grandfather had served as instructors of a Confucian school, and his father was a book-loving merchant. Wu grew up as an aspiring student, like most of his contemporaries from well-to-do families. In 1529, when Wu was in his mid-twenties, he entered the local Lóngxī 龙溪 Academy established by Gě Shí 葛石 (*jinshi* 1517, d. 1535), who was then prefect of Huai'an. In 1531 Wu took his first provincial exam along with two of his childhood friends, Zhū Yuēfān 朱曰藩 (1501–1561) and Shěn Kūn 沈坤 (1507–1560). While both Zhu and Shen passed the exam and proceeded to become metropolitan graduates (obtaining a *jìnshì* 进士, or presented scholar, degree after passing examinations in the capital), Wu repeatedly failed to pass the provincial exam. In 1544, he finally became a tribute student (*gòngshēng* 贡生, the degree bequeathed to talented licentiates to

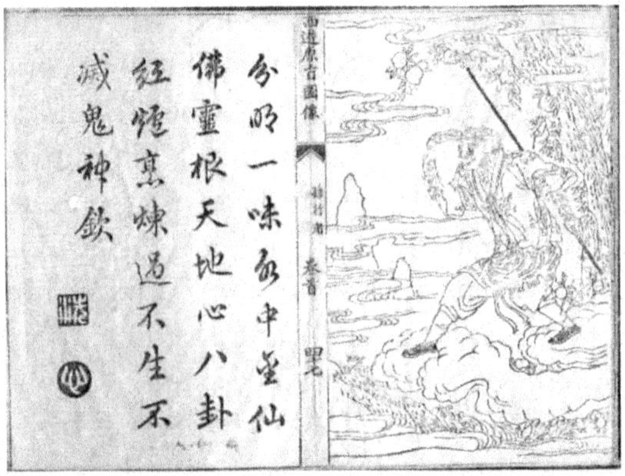

Page from Wu Cheng'en's novel *Journey to the West*. On the right is an image of the novel's main character, Sun Wukong.

allow them admission to the Imperial Academy in the capital, and then to receive official positions at the beginning level of the bureaucracy) and spent the early to mid-1550s at the Imperial Academy in Nanjing.

In 1562 or 1564, Li Chunfang, who was soon to become grand secretariat, summoned Wu Cheng'en to Beijing to seek office. It was not until 1566 that Wu became vice district magistrate in Chángxīng 长兴 County (modern-day Zhejiang Province), a post of little rewards or prestige that he took only reluctantly, because he had to leave his aged mother back at home. Within about two years he was discharged as a result of an embezzlement scandal, and in 1569 he was appointed moral mentor at the palace of Prince Jīngxiàn 荆宪 in Qízhōu 蕲州 of Hubei Province. Scholars do not agree on whether Wu assumed this post, but it is generally accepted that he spent the last decade of his life in retirement in his hometown until he died in 1582.

Wu Cheng'en had a frustrated life as a scholar, and he never was able to hold any office of significance. But this did not keep him from being an active member in a network of prestigious and affluent acquaintances. Apart from maintaining close friendships with Zhu Yuefan, Shen Kun, and Li Chunfang, all of whom held important offices, Wu was also on good terms with local officials such as the prefects of Huai'an, the directors-in-general of grain transport, and the surveillance vice commissioner of Shandong. When he was student at the Imperial Academy in Nanjing, Wu also acquainted himself with such prominent officials as the chancellor of the Imperial Academy, the minister of rites, the minister of justice, and the minister of military. Most of Wu's correspondences with high officials were carried out through panegyric writings on serendipitous occasions such as birthdays and promotions. Since many of these officials were learned Confucian scholars, quite a few—such as Hú Zōngxiàn 胡宗宪 (1512–1565) and Máo Kǎi 毛恺 (1506–1570)—were closely affiliated with *Wáng Yángmíng's 王阳明 (1472–1529) School of Mind (*xīnxué* 心学), which championed an interpretation of *Mencius's 孟子 (c. 372–c. 289 BCE) concept

---

*People marked with an asterisk have entries in this dictionary.

of the human nature (*xìng* 性) as inner knowledge (*liángzhī* 良知) that unified knowledge with action, Wu himself may also have been quite familiar with the teachings of the School of Mind (Xue 2008).

Wu also had a circle of friends with whom he wrote poems and drank in literary gatherings. One such event at the house of the director of studies of the Imperial Academy in Nanjing was recorded in He Liangjun's collected writings, in which he recalls having Wu as a guest for a literary game presided over by the director of studies. Zhāng Yǔ 张羽 (fl. 1557), in his preface for a printed edition of Dǒng Jièyuán's 董解元 *Story of the Western Chamber* (*Xīxiāng jì* 西厢记) in all keys and modes (*zhūgōngdiào* 诸宫调), mentions Wu Cheng'en and Zhu Yucfan as members of a close-knit community for "refined activities" (*yǎyóu* 雅游) among "gentlemen who cherished the past and were well versed in music" 好古知音之士. When he was serving office in Changxing, Wu also befriended poet Xú Zhōngxíng 徐中行 (1517–1578), one of the Seven Late Masters in the revivalist movement of the Ming. In addition, there were poetry exchanges between Wu and mountain hermits (*shānrén* 山人)—men who rejected public service for self-acclaimed moral principles, such as Guō Dì 郭第 (style name Cìfù 次父; fl. 1550s) and Wú Kuò 吴扩 (style name Zǐchōng 子充; fl. 1550s). Among recipients of Wu's poems on birthday events were men from different social echelons: merchants, doctors, painters, and master chess players. We can therefore see from Wu's life acquaintances that, despite his failure to pass the civil service exam, he was a cultural figure of certain stature in his time.

Praise from Peers

Although not many writings directly under the name of Wu Cheng'en survived, save for the collection of poetry and prose essays printed posthumously in 1590 by his grandson Wú Qiūdù 吴丘度 (1536–1615) under the title *Posthumous Writings by Master Sheyang* (*Shèyáng xiānsheng yígǎo* 射阳先生遗稿), Wu Cheng'en was clearly quite a sensation in his own time. The Huai'an gazetteer from the Tianqi period, for example, had the following to say about him:

> Wu Cheng'en was quick-witted by nature and equipped with many talents. He exhaustively studied books of all kinds, and when writing poetry or essays, he would finish within moments. He had a style akin to that of Qin Shaoyou [Qín Guān 秦观, a master writer of song lyrics from the Northern Song dynasty (960–1127)]—pure and elegant, fluent and polished. He was also good with jests, having composed several writings on miscellaneous matters that won him instant fame. (Zhu 2002, 164)

If Wu indeed turned the popular story of Tripitaka's journey into the current one-hundred-chapter form, then it must have been one of the sensational "writings on miscellaneous matters" noted by the gazetteer. Wu's quick wit and humor also match the image of the implied author of *Journey to the West.* The only instance in which we can get a glimpse of how Wu viewed his own miscellaneous compositions is his preface to *Records on Yu's Nine Cauldrons* (*Yǔdǐng zhì* 禹鼎志):

> I was fond of marvelous tales since my tender years. When I was studying at school as a child, every time I managed to get hold of hearsays and unofficial histories from the market, I was wary that my father and teacher would chide me and take them away. So I would find a hiding place to read them. As I grew up, I was even more drawn to them, and my stories were increasingly novel. By the time I was fully grown, I had gone out of my way in pursuit of these tales, to the extent that they almost filled my chest.
>
> I loved Tang writers such as Niu Qizhang [Niú Sēngrú 牛僧儒, 780–848 CE] and Duan Kegu [Chéngshì 段成式, 803–863 CE], because they were adept at simulating matters of various things. I always wanted to write a book to match their writings, but I was sluggish and found no time for this. . . Every single day I fought my laziness, and to my luck I was able to win. This is how my book had taken shape. (Zhu 2002, 159)

Both Niu Sengru and Duan Chengshi are well-known for their collections of tales of the strange (*zhìguài* 志怪). Therefore even though *Records on Yu's Nine Cauldrons* did not survive, this is most likely a collection of classical Chinese tales. By collecting these stories and actively creating them, Wu Cheng'en was certainly familiar with the same repertoire of knowledge that *Journey to the West* had heavily drawn upon. For example, in his poem titled "Song on the Picture of Erlang Searching the Mountains, with Preface" 二郎搜山图歌并序, Wu alludes to a whole set of details related to Erlang's saga that *Journey to the West* has also invoked, including his imperially bequeathed title, his impressive armor, and his triumphant feats that make his enemies cringe. We can also find a degree of verisimilitude—what Wu finds most inspiring about Niu's and Duan's collections—in Wu Cheng'en's inscription on his father's gravestone that is comparable to *Journey to the West*, in which he describes his father's love of books and his idiosyncratic nature as a merchant that won him the nickname as one who was "foolish" (*chī* 痴). At the very least, Wu's writings open yet another window for us to conceptualize the kind of literary

A scene from a modern Suzhou Opera performance: "Monkey creates havoc in Heaven." Photo by Joan Lebold Cohen.

qualities the author of *Journey to the West* must have aimed to achieve.

Wu Cheng'en was also an acclaimed stylist who was sympathetic with the Revivalist School but not subject to their weakness (in their attempt to emulate literary precedents from the past, Revivalists's writings are sometimes found lacking in creativity). The historian Lǐ Wéizhēn 李维桢 (1547–1626), in his preface to Wu's posthumous collection, lauds Wu's literary achievements in the following words:

> Among the Seven Masters, Renzhong [Wu Cheng'en] was closest to Xu Ziyu [Xu Zhongxing], and they maintained intimate

> correspondences. But his collected writings present a style distinct from the Seven Masters. All his writings came directly from his interior feelings not tainted by excessive embellishments, and the lines flowed at insouciant ease without the writer being flustered at having to hurry the string. He would also capture emotions of people and matters of things the way they were seen and heard without being compelled to exhaust their vagaries.

Wu's poetry rivaled that of Táng 唐 dynasty (618–907 CE) masters such as Qián Qǐ 钱起, Liú Yǔxī 刘禹锡, *Yuán Zhěn 元稹, and *Bái Jūyì 白居易. His prose was on par with writings by Sòng 宋 dynasty (960–1279) masters such as *Ōuyáng Xiū 欧阳修 and Nanfeng (Zēng Gǒng 曾巩). When it comes to concocting parallel prose the way *Sū Shì 苏轼 did, or crafting short tunes and new sounds like those from *Among the Flowers* (a *ci* anthology from the Five Dynasties) and *Grass Hut* (an anonymous twelfth-century anthology), Wu had modulated keys in songs, and sorted out weft and warp in prose essays, so that they could admonish while being intoned. These were extra skills that Wu had honed to perfection:

> In all regards, Ruzhong [Wu Cheng'en] harbored a master's mind and a craftsman's design, and he refused to take after others to fish for short-lived fame. This is why he could amount to such achievements. (Zhu 2002, 161)

Li Weizhen was not heaping praises just out of courtesy, as Zhū Yízūn 朱彝尊 (1629–1709), an eminent poet from the early Qing period, also acknowledged Wu's achievements in poetry by including him in his *Compendium of Ming Poetry* (*Míng shīzōng* 明诗综). Chén Wénzhú 陈文烛 (1525–1607), who was a close friend of Wu's during Chen's term as prefect of Huai'an, had written a preface for Wu Cheng'en's compilation of a song lyric (*ci*) anthology titled *New Compilations to Complement* Among the Flowers *and* Songs from the Grass Hut (*Huācǎo xīnbiān* 花草新编). Although Wu's compilation did not survive, he was clearly modeling his volume after Chen Wenzhu's massive collection titled *Compilation of Highlights from and Beyond* Among the Flowers *and* Songs from the Grass Hut (*Huācǎo cuìbiān* 花草粹编). Such an endeavor attests to Li Weizhen's account of Wu's "extra skills." In the same preface for *New Compilations to Complement* Among the Flowers *and* Songs from the Grass Hut, Chen Wenzhu further informs us of Wu's talent and reputation as a painter and art collector:

> Among masters within the sea who engage in the business of painting, there was none who did not know that there was Ruzhong

> [Wu Cheng'en] in Huai'an, who was born with exceptional talents. When he just reached the age of one, not yet able to walk, he was already painting on the wall with powered dust, and there were no drawings that did not fully resemble their life counterparts. One elder from the neighborhood asked him to draw a goose, and Ruzhong drew one that was flying. When the old man asked: "How could a goose fly," Ruzhong raised his head and laughed into the air. He had in fact drawn a swan. The old man stuck out his tongue in amazement, and all he could say was that this precocious child was so capable even without a teacher. (Su 1980, 65–66)

While this account verges on a miraculous tale blown out of proportion, it instantiates the kind of admiration that Wu had earned from his peers. Indeed, Wu Cheng'en did not need *Journey to the West* alone to enhance his literary name during his own time. But for the modern reader, learning about Wu's life and works can certainly help flesh out the kind of author projected by the novel.

Enduring Classic

Readers of *Journey to the West* have interpreted it differently at different times in history. Readers from the Qing dynasty embraced the novel mainly as an allegorical work that expounds on the Daoist principle of supreme perfection. Modern critics have also hailed *Journey to the West* as the most fascinating romance in Chinese literary history and a masterpiece of vernacular fiction rooted in the intellectual discourse of the School of Mind and the syncretism of the three teachings (Confucianism, Buddhism, and Daoism). One thing has remained constant: *Journey to the West* is considered a classic in Chinese literature.

Xiaoqiao LING
Arizona State University

Further Reading

Cai Teying 蔡铁鹰. (1989). Wu Cheng'en Jingfu jishan zhiren yu *Xiyou ji* 吴承恩"荆府纪善"之任与《西游记》, *Jianghan Luntan*, 75–79.

Cai Teying 蔡铁鹰. (2006). Guanyu *Xiyou ji* dingxing de xiangguan tuiding: Wu Cheng'en shiren Jingfu jishan xiangkao 关于《西游记》定型的相关推定—吴承恩实任"荆府纪善"详考, *Ming Qing xiaoshuo yanjiu*, *82*(4), 147–160.

Cai Teying 蔡铁鹰. (2012). Wu Cheng'en ci chuangzuo yu cixue gongxian chutan 吴承恩词创作与词学贡献初探. *Jinyang Xuekan*, *5*, 122–127.

Chang Kang-i Sun. (2010). Literature of the early Ming to mid-Ming. In Kang-i Sun Chang & Stephen Owen (Eds.), *The Cambridge history of Chinese literature* (pp. 1–62). Cambridge, UK, and New York: Cambridge University Press.

Li Yunfei 李云飞. (1984). Wu Cheng'en shi Changxing kao 吴承恩仕长兴考. *Jiaxing Shizhuan Xuebao*, *15*(1), 115–117.

Liu Huaiyu 刘怀玉. (1987). Wu Cheng'en shengping ershi kao 吴承恩生平二事考. *Ming Qing Xiaoshuo Yanjiu*.

Su Xing 苏兴. (1980). *Wu Cheng'en nianpu* 吳承恩年譜. Beijing: Renmin wenxue chubanshe.

Su Xing 苏兴. (1985). Yetan baihui ben *Xiyou ji* shifou Wu Cheng'en suozuo 也谈百回本《西游记》是否吴承恩所作. *Shehui Kexue Zhanxian*, *1*, 245–253.

Xue Mei 薛梅. 2008. Wu Cheng'en yu xinxue renwu jiaoyou kaozheng 吴承恩与心学人物交游考证. *Hubei daxue xuebao 35*(2), 81–84.

Yu, Anthony. (1985). *Hsi-yu chi*. In W. H. Nienhauser (Ed.), *The Indiana companion to traditional Chinese literature* (pp. 413–418). Bloomington: Indiana University Press.

Zhang Peiheng 章培恒. (1983). Baihui ben *Xiyou ji* shifou Wu Cheng'en suozuo 百回本《西游记》是否吴承恩所作. *Shehui Kexue Zhanxian*, *4*, 295–305.

Zhu Yixuan 朱一玄. (Ed.). (2002). Xiyou ji *ziliao huibian* 西游记资料汇编 [Collected reference materials for *Journey to the West*]. Tianjin, China: Nankai daxue chubanshe.

Xú Guāngqǐ

徐光启

1562–1633—Scholar-official and scientist; early convert to Christianity

Alternate names: courtesy name: Zǐxiān 子先; style name: Xuánhù 玄扈

Summary

Xu Guangqi, a colleague of the Jesuit Matteo Ricci, was a scholar-official, agricultural scientist, astronomer, and mathematician who made Western mathematics available to the Chinese through his translations. He was the most renowned Chinese convert to Christianity until the twentieth century. Xu authored one of the first treatises on agriculture; led the reform of the Chinese calendar, in perhaps the first collaboration between European and Chinese scientists; and translated many Western texts, including parts of Euclid's *Elements*.

Xu Guangqi was born in Shanghai, Songjiang Prefecture, in 1562 (the forty-first year of the reign of Emperor Jiājìng 嘉靖) and died in 1633 (the sixth year of the reign of Emperor Chóngzhēn 崇祯) at the age of seventy-two years. His family was not well-off, and his ancestors were farmers and traders. The invasion of the Jiāngnán 江南 area (the area directly south of the lower Yangzi River, including parts of Jiangsu, Anhui, Jiangxi, and Zhejiang provinces) by Japanese pirates aggravated their hardship. During Xu Guangqi's time, his family was barely able to subsist or to send Xu Guangqi to school. Due to his hard work, Xu earned the *xiùcai* 秀才 title, the equivalent of a bachelor's degree, in 1581 when he was twenty years old. In 1597, Xu surpassed his peers and was awarded the *jǔrén* 举人 (selected scholar) title. In 1604, at the age of forty-one years, he passed the metropolitan examination at the capital and was awarded the *jìnshì* 进士 (presented scholar) title. His essays had impressed the chief examiner Jiāo Hóng 焦竑 (1540–1620), who later became his mentor and introduced him to the philosopher and historian *Lǐ Zhì 李贽 (1527–1602).

*People marked with an asterisk have entries in this dictionary.

Xu started his career as a trainee at the Hanlin Academy 翰林院—a prestigious cultural and secretarial apparatus set up under the Táng 唐 dynasty (618–907 CE) *Emperor Xuánzōng 玄宗 (r. 712–756)—and subsequently served as Compiler, Assistant Director of the Household Administration of the Heir Apparent, and Deputy Minister of the Ministry of Rites. He was Grand Secretary of the Cabinet and concurrently Minister of Rites when he died in 1633.

Introduction to Christianity

Exposure and conversion to Catholicism was the turning point of his life. In 1596 Xu met the Italian Jesuit father Lazzaro Cattaneo in Shaozhou, and in 1600 was introduced to *Matteo Ricci 利玛窦 (Lì Mǎdòu) (1552–1610) in Nanjing. Xu was impressed with Ricci's Christian doctrines and scientific knowledge and was baptized by Jesuit missionary Joao de Rocha in 1603 with the Christian name "Paul." In 1604, Xu met Ricci again in Beijing and studied with him. He became an advocate of Christianity, believing that the teachings of God would be able to supplement Confucianism, and was the first Chinese scholar to translate European books into the Chinese language. Together with Ricci, Xu translated Western books on mathematics, hydraulics, astronomy, and geography. Among their most famous translation was Euclid's *Elements* (*Jǐhé yuánběn* 几何原本), which introduced new concepts in mathematics and Western logic to China and has had a great impact on Chinese mathematics (Needham 1986a, 3:52; Hashimoto and Jami 2001).

Scientific Knowledge and Political Strife

In 1607, Xu moved back to Shanghai to mourn his father's death. It was during this time that he put his agriculture knowledge into practice and tested Western-style irrigation methods. He also experimented with the cultivation of sweet potatoes and cotton. By the time he returned to Beijing in 1610, Ricci had passed away. Xu moved to Tianjin and continued to learn European science from Sabatino de Ursis as well as other Jesuit missionaries.

Xu's knowledge of astronomy contributed to his being promoted to full Minister of Rites in 1630. On 21 June 1629, when the Imperial Astronomical Bureau failed to predict the exact date of an eclipse, Emperor Chongzhen appointed Xu Guangqi to revise the imperial calendar. With the assistance of three missionaries (German Jesuits Johann Terrenz—also known as Johann Schreck—and Johann Adam Schall von Bell, and Italian Jesuit Giacomo Rho), Xu correctly predicted the eclipse and subsequently helped lead the calendar reform of the late Ming era.

The Chinese Calendar

China has a long tradition of astronomical observation. Unlike other calendars, it does not count years in an infinite sequence. The main calendars used in East Asia were Chinese in origin until the nineteenth century; today such long-established calendars are still used to mark religious and traditional holidays and festivals; the Gregorian calendar regulates only civic affairs.

The origin of the Chinese calendar is steeped in myth; the legendary Yellow Emperor Huáng Dì 黄帝 (discussed in the article "Mythological Figures," in Volume 1) is supposed to have created the calendar in 2637 BCE. Historical evidence, however, dates the invention of the calendar much later: well into the fourteenth century BCE. An ordinary year in the Chinese calendar, as in the Jewish calendar, has twelve months, whereas a leap year has thirteen months. As a result, an ordinary year has 353, 354, or 355 days, and a leap year has 383, 384, or 385 days.

To determine the Chinese year, first the dates of the new moons are established. A new moon is interpreted as a completely "black" moon (when the moon is in conjunction with the sun), not the first visible crescent, as stipulated in Islamic and Jewish calendars. The date of a new moon is the first day of a new month. Calculated next are the dates when the sun's longitude is a multiple of 30 degrees. These dates, called the "principal terms," are used to calculate the number of each month. Each month therefore carries the number of the principal term that occurs in that month.

All astronomical observations are made for the meridian 120 degrees east of Greenwich, England, which approximately aligns with the east coast of China. The Chinese calendar, unlike other calendars, does not count years in an infinite sequence. Instead, years have names that are repeated every sixty years. Within a sixty-year cycle each year is assigned a name composed of two parts: the celestial stem, the terms of which cannot easily be translated into English, and the terrestrial branch, the terms of which correspond to the familiar animals of the Chinese zodiac. This method of using a sixty-year cycle is ancient: the cycles are numbered from 2637 BCE.

—Nirmal DASS, *Wilfrid Laurier University*

During Xu Guangqi's tenure as a government official, Ming-era China suffered from a series of crises, in particular the invasion of the Manchus from the north in Liaodong Province and factional struggles at the imperial court, such as the persecution of members of the Dōnglín 东林 Academy by the powerful eunuch *Wèi Zhōngxián 魏忠贤 (1568–1627), that cost the lives of many Donglin scholars. (This was an academy dating from the Song dynasty that had been revived by scholars in the Jiangnan area.) From the outset Xu Guangqi remained neutral and refrained from supporting any of the factions. To save the country from catastrophe Xu put forward the idea of "Enrich the country, strengthen the military" (*Fùguó qiángbīng* 富国强兵).

To enrich the country, he proposed agricultural reform and wrote an outstanding agricultural treatise *Encyclopaedia of Agriculture* (*Nōngzhèng quánshū* 农政全书), which was published by the famous Jiangnan scholar Chén Zǐlóng 陈子龙 in 1639. The book covered important topics such as land distribution, field management, methods of irrigation, irrigation equipment, horticulture, silk production, cotton and hemp plantation, forestry preservation, animal husbandry, and famine control. In his preface to the *Encyclopaedia*, Chen Zilong said that throughout Xu's life he had examined the relationship between "heaven and man," based on the principle of practical usage. In many ways, his ideas are comparable to those set forth by the Yuan-dynasty scholar *Wáng Zhēn 王祯 (1290–1333) in his work, *Agricultural Treatise* (*Nóngshū* 农书). Thus, Xu said: "to enrich the country, it has to be from the foundation"; and "to strengthen the country, we have to rectify the army."

Xu's concept of "strengthen the military" was fully elaborated in his book on military techniques and strategies entitled *Master Xu's Kitchen Talk* (*Xúshì Páoyán* 徐氏庖言). The book also included measures he recommended in the numerous memorials he submitted to emperors Shenzong and Chongzhen on military reforms and frontier defense. But due to the fact that his time spent at the cabinet was relatively short and political struggles at the court intense during his time, Xu's recommendations were not implemented.

Nevertheless, his interest in Western science and technology should not be regarded only in the context of his Christian faith. Xu Guangqi was essentially a pragmatic scholar-official who wished to employ his knowledge of science and technology to transform his country.

LEE Cheuk Yin 李焯然
National University of Singapore

Further Reading

Chen Weiping, & Li Chunyong. (2006). *Xu Guangqi pingchuan* 徐光启评传 [A critical biography of Xu Guangqi]. Nanjing, China: Nanjing University Press.

Han Qi. (2001). Astronomy, Chinese and Western; The influence of Xu Guangqi's views in the early and mid-Qing. In Catherine Jami, Peter Engelfriet, & Gregory Blue (Eds.), *Statecraft and intellectual renewal in late Ming China: The cross cultural synthesis of Xu Guangqi (1562–1633).* Leiden, The Netherlands: E. J. Brill.

Jami, Catherine; Engelfriet, Peter; & Blue, Gregory. (Eds.). (2001). *Statecraft and intellectual renewal in late Ming China: The cross cultural synthesis of Xu Guangqi (1562–1633).* Leiden, The Netherlands: E. J. Brill.

Keizo, Hashimoto, & Catherine, Jami. (Eds.). (2001). From *The Elements* to calendar reform: Xu Guangqi's shaping of scientific knowledge. In Catherine Jami, Peter Engelfriet, & Gregory Blue (Eds.), *Statecraft and intellectual renewal in late Ming China: The cross cultural synthesis of Xu Guangqi (1562–1633).* Leiden, The Netherlands: E. J. Brill.

Liang Jiamian 梁家冕. (1981). *Xu Guangqi nianpu* 徐光启年谱 [Chronology of Xu Guangqi]. Shanghai：Shanghai Guji Press.

Luo Guang. (1982). *Xu Guangqi chuan* 徐光启传. [Biography of Xu Guangqi]. Taipei, Taiwan: Chuanji wenxue.

Needham, Joseph (1986a). *Science and civilisation in China: Volume 3, mathematics and the sciences of the Heavens and the Earth.* Taipei, Taiwan: Caves Books.

Needham, Joseph (1986b). *Science and civilisation in China: Volume 6, biology and biological technology, part 2: agriculture.* Taipei, Taiwan: Caves Books.

Wang Chongmin 王重民. (1981). *Xu Guangqi* 徐光启. Shanghai: Shanghai renmin Press.

Xi Zezong 席泽宗, & Wu Deduo 吴德铎 (Eds.). (1986). *Xu Guangqi yanjiu lunwenji* 徐光启研究论文集. Shanghai: Xuelin.

Xu Guangqi 徐光启 (1984). *Xu Guangqi ji* 徐光启集 [Collected works of Xu Guangqi]. Shanghai: Shanghai Guji Press.

Xu Guangqi 徐光启. (1956). *Nongzheng quanshu* 农政全书 [Encyclopaedia of agriculture]. Beijing: Zhonghua. (Originally published in 1639 by Chěn Zílǒng)

Xú Xiákè

徐霞客

1587–1641—Explorer and travel writer; discoverer of source of the Yangzi River

Alternate name: given name: Hóngzǔ 弘祖

Summary

Xu Xiake was the most famous travel writer and explorer of pre-modern China. During the late Ming dynasty, he traveled to the Five Sacred Mountains and as far afield as Yunnan Province. In the face of enormous difficulty and personal danger, he succeeded in reaching western Yunnan in order to ascertain the source of the Yangzi (Chang) River. He is admired to this day not only for his inquisitive mind and the pioneering spirit of his journeys to remote parts of the Chinese empire, but also for the literary quality of his travel diaries.

Xu Xiake, the foremost travel writer of imperial China, covered large areas of the country in his wanderings during the final years of the Míng 明 dynasty (1368–1644). Famous for his single-mindedness, fortitude, and stoic endurance of difficult traveling conditions, he is also held up as a model of Confucian rectitude: he did not undertake long journeys while his mother Wáng Rúrén 王孺人 (1545–1625) was still alive, he famously commissioned poems in her honor from his literati friends, and, following her death, he completed the requisite three-year period of mourning before embarking on his greatest expedition to southwest China.

Over thirty years of traveling, he visited nineteen provinces, writing lengthy accounts of his journeys that run over 400,000 Chinese characters. He visited and wrote in exhaustive detail about mountains and rivers, volcanoes and caves, as well as man-made constructions that he saw on his travels. In his exploration of the karst landscape of southwest China, for example, he explored some three hundred caves in the provinces of Guangxi, Guizhou, and

Yunnan. As he wrote in a preface to a series of poems about a mountain close to his home town, "In my boundless roaming there is nothing I wish to omit" (Xu 1993, 1149). In the face of enormous difficulty and personal danger, Xu Xiake carried out his goal of reaching western Yunnan in order to ascertain the source of the Yangzi (Chang) River. The literary quality of his diary, often written in wholly adverse conditions, is remarkable, his approach always painstaking.

Much of the academic debate about Xu has centered on the extent to which he was the archetypal solitary traveler, a recorder of information who merely stacked up details of the places he visited. As he wrote in Yunnan in 1639 towards the end of his last journey, "When I travel I require neither a horse nor a companion: rather than traveling together, it would be better if you could simply point out the way to me. When I am about to travel, what I am apprehensive about is precisely the idea of having companions while those with whom I do not wish to travel are just worried about getting a horse" (Xu 1993, 1044). This image of the reclusive, impulsive traveler was heightened by the foreword penned for the diaries by the scholar Pān Lěi 潘耒 (1646–1708), "He did not plan the dates of his journeys and did not seek traveling companions. For Xiake, traveling was both his innate sensibility and his whole life. He went without a reason and that was his reason" (Xu 1993, 1268).

In fact, it was not the case that he always operated in isolation. He was well known to many leading intellectual figures of the first half of the seventeenth century and his biography can be pieced together not just from his own diaries, but from his contacts with these notables. In addition, he sought out local intellectuals in the course of his travels, using the letters of introduction from his friends in eastern China partly to find financial assistance but also to find people who could provide him with information about the landscape of the particular locale through which he was passing.

Early Travels

Xu Xiake was born on 5 January 1587 near the city of Jiāngyīn 江阴 in present-day Jiangsu Province (and would die there on 8 March 1641). His birth name was Hóngzǔ 弘祖, which means "to honor ancestors." His literary name Xiake, which means "guest of the sunset clouds," was chosen for him by his friend Chén Jìrú 陈继儒 (1558–1639), a renowned late Ming literatus, who described Xu this way:

> He has a dark complexion and snowy white teeth. At a height of six feet, he looks as spare as a Taoist priest. His outward deportment is that of a mountain recluse, but there resides in him a rich spirit and the essence of courage. When I spoke with him, his words were

> upright and lofty, full of the stuff of strange journeys and extreme danger. (Xu 1993, 1235)

Xu Xiake's travels can be divided into two discrete periods, the first between 1609 and 1628 when he visited many of the famous sites of northern and eastern China, and the second when he set out, in 1636, on an epic three-year journey to remote parts of southwest China. To a certain extent, Xu's early diaries fit the conventional mode of Chinese travel diaries of the time: short accounts of visits to well-known picturesque spots, though even here he showed an innovative approach.

The early tradition of travel writing can be traced back to the Táng 唐 dynasty (618–907 CE) and the short accounts written by Liǔ Zōngyuán 柳宗元 (773–819 CE), who had been sent on internal exile from the imperial capital Chang'an, about his new home in the town of Yǒngzhōu 永州 in Hunan Province. By the Sòng 宋 dynasty (960–1279), the travel diary was evolving and longer accounts were beginning to emerge, the most prominent examples being *Diary of a Boat Trip to Wu* by Fàn Chéngdà 范成大 (1126–1193) and Lù Yóu's 陆游 (1125–1210) *Journey to Shu*, both written by officials traveling large distances in order to take up new positions.

Where the earlier accounts concentrated on place and involved small groups of literati admiring the scenery while citing apposite literary texts, the longer versions brought in the process of travel itself. In his pioneering study of Fan Chengda's diary, James Hargett, professor of Chinese studies, examined how these writers drew upon a vast lexicon to describe the process of movement (Hargett 1989). This model was further developed in the sixteenth century by Wáng Shìxìng 王士性 (1547–1598), a geographer who took advantage of official postings to provinces such as Sichuan and Yunnan to write comprehensive geographical works. His *Drafts of Travels to the Five Sacred Mountains* (*Wǔ Yuè Yóucǎo* 五岳游草), printed in 1593, covered such topics as the varying climactic conditions of northern and southern China and the customs of the minority peoples of the southwest.

Wang's writings were a major source of inspiration for Xu Xiake, as can be seen most clearly in the latter's lengthy diary of his trip to southwest China, which represents more than three quarters of the diaries as they exist today, and which constitutes his greatest achievement. Like Wang, Xu was not interested solely in visiting well-known places and repeating the words of earlier visitors and information found in geographical texts. Rather, he investigated his destinations in exhaustive detail, questioning received wisdom as he went. Again like Wang, Xu was obsessed with visiting each of the Five Sacred Mountains, a configuration which can be traced back to the Qín 秦 dynasty (221–206 BCE), at which time there were just four:

Mount Tài 泰山 in Shandong Province (eastern), Mount Héng 恒山 in Shanxi Province (northern), Mount Huà 华山 in Shaanxi Province (western), and Mount Héng 衡山 in Hunan Province (southern). A fifth, central, mountain, Mount Sōng 嵩山 in Henan Province, was added during the Han dynasty.

During his early years of travel, when the Confucian code of filial piety prevented him straying far from his ageing mother, Xu was able only to visit sites relatively close at hand, such as Mount Tai and the birthplaces of the philosophers *Confucius 孔子 (551–479 BCE) and *Mencius 孟子 (c. 372–c. 289 BCE). In 1613, he went to the Buddhist island of Mount Pǔtuó 普陀山 and to two mountains in present-day Zhejiang Province, Tiāntái 天台山 and Yàndàng 雁荡山. In 1616, he visited Mount Báiyuè 白岳山, and Mount Huáng 黄山, and Mount Wǔyí 武夷山. Over the next few years he traveled to many of the most famous sites of eastern China, including Mount Huang, Mount Song, Mount Hua, and Mount Wǔdāng 武当山. Following the death of his mother in 1625, he spent three years mourning her, after which he went south to Mount Luófú 罗浮山 and north to Mount Pán 盘山 and Mount Heng. So far, his travels had been extremely conventional. In 1636, however, he embarked on the journey for which he is best known, filling his diaries from this period with what would be the most dramatic moments of his life.

*People marked with an asterisk have entries in this dictionary.

Pushing the Boundaries of Travel

It was an epic expedition that was to last more than three years, passing through the present-day provinces of Zhejiang, Jiangxi, Hunan, Guangxi, Guizhou, and on to Yunnan. As a filial son, Xu had felt he could not wander far from home while his mother was still alive. In a letter to Chen Jiru written prior to his departure, he described his desire to move beyond the constraints of the central China plains in order to explore the southwest of China (Xu 1993, 1147–1148). Although he did not refer directly to the Yangzi River in this letter, it is clear from comments he made elsewhere that he wished to ascertain the true source of the river. At the time of his departure in 1637, Xu was accompanied by two servants (Wáng Èr 王二, who fled after a few days, and Gù Xíng 顾行, who was to stay with Xu until almost the last diary entry) and a Buddhist monk, Jìngwén 静闻, who was carrying a copy of the *Fǎhuá Jīng* 法华经 (Lotus Sutra) written in his own blood, to offer to Mount Chickenfoot 鸡足山, a prominent Buddhist retreat in northwestern Yunnan. Early in his journey, Xu visited Mount Heng, located in present-day Hunan Province and the only one of the Five Sacred Mountains that he had not seen.

Shortly after their departure from the nearby town of Héngzhōu 衡州, the travelers were robbed while on a boat on the Xiang River 湘江. Jingwen, who suffered serious injury in the course of the robbery, died of dysentery eight months later. Xu Xiake carried the monk's remains in a casket for more than a year, until his arrival at Mount Chickenfoot, where they were buried in an auspicious location. Xu was unusually forthcoming about his feelings for Jingwen, writing a series of six poems in his honor. The preface and opening poem read:

> Jingwen, a Buddhist monk, and I, having sworn allegiance to the great mountains, came ten thousand *li* on pilgrimage here to Mount Chickenfoot. Unable to recover from an illness, he took lodging at the Songshan Temple in Nanning. Not long after, a parting became *adieu*. The pain of life and

The tomb of Xu Guangqi's travelling companion, a Buddhist monk named Jingwen, at Mount Chickenfoot, a prominent Buddhist retreat in northwestern Yunnan Province. Photo by Julian Ward.

death will be seen in these lines.
Looking westwards we had a life and death pledge to go to the mountains.
Now gazing eastwards alone, to carry on brings pain.
At home we said that few could climb on high,
Now at the end of the world, my soul broken, I can only look alone.
(Xu 1993, 1153)

In the latter stages of his diary, the increasingly weary Xu Xiake was suffering from a succession of ailments, stating, "After forty years exploring our great mountain ranges, I have now reached the end of the line" (Xu 1993, 1119). The diaries came to a sudden and unexplained end while he was still on Mount Chickenfoot, and just four days after Gu Xing had absconded. The diaries thus do not record his journey back to Jiangyin, where he was to die just over a year later.

According to a contemporary account, by Chén Hánhuī 陈函辉 (1589–1646), Xu spent three months compiling the first gazetteer of Mount Chickenfoot, a task which he had undertaken at the request of the local chieftain Mù Zēng 木增 (1587–1646), the leader of the ethnic Móxiē 麽些 people based in the nearby town of Lìjiāng 丽江. He then set off on the long journey home, initially on a sedan chair provided by Mu, before taking a boat along the Yangzi River back to Jiangyin, arriving home in the summer of 1640, where his health faded rapidly (Xu 1993, 1190–1198). According to Xu's friend, Jì Mèngliáng 季梦良, "From now on, the only traveling he could do was in his mind. On many occasions I sat at the end of his bed till midnight, and he never once tired of recounting his travels" (Xu 1993, 1).

Travel Diaries

The diaries went through a convoluted history over the next century, narrowly avoiding destruction in the midst of the chaos that accompanied the collapse of the Ming dynasty, before finally being published in 1776. Xu Zhen's foreword to this edition reads:

> My ancestor Xiake was born with a great *wanderlust*. Unfortunately, he died before his work was completed. . . . Not long afterwards, it was destroyed in a fire caused by rampaging soldiers. It was only as a result of Xu's son Jieli compiling the edition he picked up from visiting the Shi and Cao families of Yixing that the diaries were again formed into a book. . . . Now one hundred and forty years on, I have made my own edition, with the aim of verifying for the present and transmitting for the future. (Xu 1993, 1)

It was, however, to be many years before Xu Xiake's critical reputation was firmly established. In the nineteenth century, the Qing dynasty official and literary scholar Lī Címíng 李慈铭 (1830–1894), wrote:

> In his desire to experience in person the unfathomable, [Xu] Xiake scaled the precipitous and clambered up into the void, merely in order to satiate his taste for the strange and certainly not out of a desire to convey either a profound aesthetic appreciation or the true love of the ancients for clouds and mists. Moreover, his intentions are muddled, his narrative a mess, to the extent that the mystique of marvelous sites is lost, and the allure of beautiful regions obscured, and compilers of travelers' guides are unable to find the true path within his writing, and those interested in famous sites are left dissatisfied. Furthermore, his interests lie in the orientations of ridges, theories akin to those of the geomancer, which are quite without foundation. He has certainly not carried out his investigations on the basis of either ancient or modern geography, totally ignoring the names and places of past glories. Accordingly since the end of the Ming dynasty, scholars have not read his work. I cannot imagine why it should be studied. (Li 1963, 472–473)

The upsurge in Xu's reputation did not start until the early years of the twentieth century, when his contribution was acknowledged first by the late Qing reformer *Liáng Qīchāo 梁启超 (1873–1929), and later by the Western-trained geographer Dīng Wénjiāng 丁文江 (1887–1936), who produced an edition of the diaries in the 1920s. After a relatively fallow period in the first thirty years of Communist rule, the study of Xu and his diaries has, since the start of the reform era in the late 1970s, entered a golden age. This can be attributed partly to the opening up of China and the growth of a huge tourist industry, which has adopted Xu as a quasi-patron saint of travel. His popularity increased even more when an edition of the diaries that covered a section of his trip to southwest China in greater detail was discovered in the National Library in Beijing. From this additional information and its literary flourish, a more rounded and soulful figure emerged. In place of terse entries, we find detailed descriptions of the scenery and of his emotions. Following the Xiang River robbery, he and his companions returned to Hengzhou, where they spent three weeks waiting for Jingwen's health to recover, all the while seeking funding for the onward journey. One evening Xu wrote, "This was my second visit here, each time as the sun was setting; the scenery had not changed, but my affairs were in turmoil, how could I not feel overcome with emotion" (Xu 1993, 206).

The diaries contain numerous passages of lyrical description alongside the factual accounts of geographical features.

Like Fan Chengda and Lu You, Xu wrote of the physical movement through landscape as matched by a metaphysical appreciation of the sublime, the goal being to arrive at a fusion of the physical scene with one's human feelings. While it is overly reductive to say that Chinese travel writers are drawn by the desire to harmonize with Nature while Westerners think in terms of conquest, it is undeniably the case that the diaries resound with a love of, and immersion in, the landscape. He writes of plunging into the hills, feeling "shaken" and "chilled," and of feeling overwhelmed by the sights and smells that he experienced. While at Mount Chickenfoot, he wrote:

> Pushing through the waterfall to enter the inlayed cliff, I looked beyond at Lanzong 兰宗 and the other monks, stretched out like silk threads separated by mist. To the front, the shadows of the trees and the blossom on the branches were like flying souls and cleansed spirits, marvels of concealed beauty. On the western path of the bank a screen of green moss like an array of elegantly colored floss, almost dripping in greenness like a painting of nature that was neither rock nor mist, created another illusory scene. By the side of the bank, mountain and trees piled up together, jasper branches and jade roots forming a dark forest curtain, in an array of colors. (Xu 1993, 839)

As James Hargett stressed when discussing Fan Chengda's account of a visit to Mount Éméi 峨眉山 in 1177, the travel writer is concerned with more than just a physical ascent; there is an important spiritual element to the journey (Hargett 2006). This is evident in Xu Xiake's description of traveling through Guangxi;

> When I enquire about the names of the crags and the division of the villages in this region, I receive many mistaken answers. When I pace them out, working side by side with the mountain spirits, the outline of the landscape becomes ever clearer. In this way, none of the landscape's charms remain concealed. (Xu 1993, 432)

Geographic Discoveries

There was much that was new about China in the seventeenth century, and much for Xu to investigate and correct. The terrain of southwest China was notoriously difficult to traverse, with the steep mountains and unnavigable rivers of Guizhou and Yunnan in particular resulting in the emergence of many different ethnic groups, often with scant knowledge of the ways of central China. Unsurprisingly, mistakes in the extant geographical texts were numerous and Xu undertook the mission of rectifying them. In the words of Andrea Riemenschnitter, professor of modern Chinese studies: "the designated aim of Xu's explorations was to correct traditional imaginary geographies by empirical means" (Riemenschnitter 2003, 299).

In western Yunnan, he corrected the entry in the official Ming gazetteer that stated that the Red River joined up with the Mekong at Yuánjiāngfǔ 元江府 to form the Yuán River 元江, noting that the Láncāng 澜沧江 (Mekong), Lù 潞江 (Salween) and Lǐshè 礼社江 (Red) rivers were in fact three separate rivers. This is not say that his methods were always successful. In tracing the course of the Northern 北盘 and Southern Pan 南盘 rivers in Guizhou and eastern Yunnan, he was unable to cover the whole area and instead relied on information passed on to him. The short essay he wrote on the subject therefore contained a number of mistakes.

One of Xu's most celebrated writings discussed the source of the Yangzi River, which had long been assumed, on the basis of *The Tribute of Yu* (*YǔGòng* 禹贡), a proto-geographical text written during the Warring States 战国 period (475–221 BCE), to be in the Min mountains of northern Sichuan. In his revisionist essay, Xu referred to the Golden Sands River 金沙江 which passes though Yunnan and is in reality the upper reaches of the Yangzi:

> The source of the Yangtse, has never been properly investigated, with the result that it is merely the tributaries which are close at hand which have come to be considered. In fact the Min river entering the Yangtse is, like the Wei [River] entering the Yellow River, one of the tributaries of the central plains: the Min River is passable for river traffic, while the Golden Sands River twists and turns through the mountainous barbarian regions, and is passable neither by land nor water . . . all (existing Yunnan records) merely return to the sentence in the "Yu Gong" which states that "from Mount Min he surveyed the Yangtse" as disclosing the source of the Yangtse . . . The Min River flows into the Yangtse but it is not its source, in the same way that the Wei River flows into the Yellow River but is not its source. (Xu 1993, 1128)

Such comments on the views acquired from a revered canonical text and entrenched in China's *weltanschauung* for many centuries did not pass unnoticed. Hú Wèi 胡渭, (1633–1714) wrote: "The 'Yu Gong' clearly states that the Min mountains guide the Yangzi, those such as Xiake who claim the Li water (Golden Sands River) to be the true source are not worthy of mention" (*Siku Quanshu* 67.739).

A Man of His Times

It is important to remember that Xu Xiake was not operating in a vacuum; his life and work must be considered in the context of the customs of his age. Like Wang Shixing, for example, he commented adversely on the customs of the minority peoples of the southwest. Wang Shixing described the Yáo 傜 people as "the most evil and hard to cultivate" and the Luóluó 罗罗 as being "constantly grubby from not washing and the men and women went round in bare feet" (Wang 1993, 214–219). In a similar vein, Xu Xiake, while in Téngyuè 腾越 in western Yunnan, referred to the wild people living in the outlying regions, which had formerly been part of China but were now untouched by imperial culture (Xu 1993, 981). In his fondness for strangeness (*qí* 奇), his devotion to the notion of obsession (*pǐ* 癖) and, not least, his analysis of the landscape through the application of *fēngshuǐ* 风水 terminology, Xu was very much of his time. In fact, what is perhaps most interesting about the belittling comments of Li Ciming, quoted above, is that he was criticizing Xu for precisely those aspects of his writing that chimed closely with the interests of the late Ming period.

Xu wrote the following when looking for a suitable spot to bury the monk Jingwen's remains:

> When I first arrived at Mount Chickenfoot, on reaching Dajue 大觉 [Temple], I examined the mountain's setting from every angle: each of its circling peaks was dotted with Buddhist shrines and retreats, all perfectly placed. The only imperfection was the lack of a pagoda here at the heart of the mountain. On arriving at Xitan 悉檀 Temple and looking into the distance, the summit appears even more remarkable, I think I understand why it was that King Ayu 阿育王 (Asoka) manifested his numinous power here. (Xu 1993, 844)

This passage illustrates how Xu's aims were by no means solely utilitarian, but imbued with a deep appreciation of the landscape. The spiritual dimension of his visits to mountains, which was closely connected to the notion of obsession, was no less important for him than for earlier travelers such as Fan Chengda. Because of his familiarity with the Chinese canon and his obsession with travel, Xu Xiake, like other Chinese travel writers, was able to draw on a wealth of literary and cultural allusions.

Xu Xiake's life and work also reflected the changing patterns of travel in China. Travelers were no longer only officials on the way to a new posting, or religious pilgrims visiting sacred mountains. Since the end of the Yuan dynasty, the outlying regions of China had become increasingly stable, and the transportation systems had developed into a much more extensive network, all of which contributed to a huge growth of information about geography and places in China. Apart from the national gazetteer *Comprehensive Gazetteer of the Great Ming Dynasty* (*Dà Míng yītǒng zhì* 大明一统志) published in 1461, and introduced with a preface written by Emperor

Yīngzōng 英宗 (r. 1457–1464), around three thousand gazetteers were compiled during the Ming dynasty, not just about the familiar urban centers but also places in the more remote provinces. In addition, the sixteenth century saw the emergence of route books, which provided basic information such as the availability of inns, ferry schedules and the distances between towns and villages on a wide variety of routes. All of this led, as the academic Flora Li-tsui Fu and other researchers have pointed out, to a steady expansion in travel to increasingly remote parts of China (Fu 2009).

For Xu Xiake, visiting southwest China allowed him to see the unfamiliar, to rectify mistakes in existing geographical texts, and, above all, to indulge his love of mountains: nowhere is this more evident than in his writings about Mount Chickenfoot. Although only fragments of the gazetteer he compiled for Mu Zeng have survived, the diaries contain lengthy passages outlining the time he spent there and his passion is evident. Furthermore, the act of recording information about the mountain's history, the temples, and the people, can be seen as a part of the process whereby Yunnan, which for many years in its recent past had not been part of China, was fully assimilated into the imperial fold. As Xu wrote in the introduction to the Mount Chickenfoot gazetteer:

> The outward manifestations of a mountain's scenes are its peaks and caves. A scene is created when a passer-by chances upon it: only once it has been transmitted through his emotions does the scene become unique. (Xu 1993, 1141)

The contribution of the travel writer was to record these sites for future generations. Xu Xiake's writings about Mount Chickenfoot provided authenticity both for the location and for the peoples of the region.

Xu Xiake Today

It is worth noting that some international scholars remain equivocal about Xu Xiake's contributions. The expert on modern Chinese literature, Leo Ou-fan Lee, for example, described Xu's aim as being "merely to traverse the geographical landscape of China and to surpass his predecessors in the detail and accuracy of his findings" (Lee 1985, 283), while Chou Chih-Ping, professor of East Asian studies, described Xu's work as "utilitarian" (Chou 1988, 112). Others have painted a rather more nuanced picture of Xu as not simply an explorer who happened to write, but as a writer of great acuity.

At the same time, interest has spread to Xu's contemporaries. The diary of a visit to Mount Huang written by Qián Qiānyì 钱谦益 (1582–1664), who also wrote a biography of Xu, inspired a well-received book by the historian Stephen McDowall called *Qian Qianyi's Reflections on Yellow Mountain*. McDowall calls for more attention to be paid to the specific cultural contexts in which the descriptive passages of the Ming travel diary were formed, and not just to their tendency towards accurate historical and physical records (McDowall 2009).

Within China, Xu Xiake's reputation today is higher than ever. There have been many complete and edited editions of his writings, along with books of maps of his travels, and a version in modern Chinese. *Xu Xiake Research* 徐霞客研究, a journal devoted to the study of his life and works, contains academic papers and records the numerous events held in his honor. Jiangyin and also some towns and cities through which Xu passed, now boast statues in his image. In 2011, 19 May was designated National Tourism Day, marking the start of Xu's earliest extant travel diary, a visit to Mount Tiantai in 1613, and in the following year a Xu Xiake study center was formally opened in Jiangyin (Chen 2012, 7). Although only extracts of the diaries have appeared in translated form in any of the European languages as of yet, a Korean version of the entire text was published in 2012.

Xu Xiake was a man driven by the need to explore the outer realms of China and to describe what he saw in meticulous detail. Before Xu's expeditions, travel writing had been for the most part a leisurely pursuit. His great contribution was to build on the longer form of the diary pioneered by Fan Chengda, Lu You, and Wang Shixing, and then use this form to accommodate his exploratory zeal, all the while retaining the literary flourishes that so distinguished the genre. The words of Qian Qianyi, his biographer, provide an eloquent final assessment:

> He would travel with a servant, or sometimes with a monk and just a staff and a cloth bundle, not worrying about carrying a traveling bag or supplies of food. He could endure hunger for several days, eating his fill when he found some food. He could keep walking for several hundred *li*, ascending sheer cliffs, braving bamboo thickets, scrambling up and down, hanging over precipices on a rope, as nimble as an ape and as sturdy as an ox. He used towering crags for his bed, streams and gullies for refreshment and found companionship amongst fairies, trolls, apes and baboons, with the result that he became indistinct, retiring and unable to speak. However when it was a matter of discussing mountain paths, distinguishing water sources or seeking out superior geographical terrain, his warm heart would suddenly open out. (Xu 1993, 1199)

Julian WARD
University of Edinburgh

Further Reading

Brook, Timothy. (1988). *Geographical sources of Ming-Qing history*. Ann Arbor: University of Michigan, Center of Chinese Studies.

Chen Zhongmei 陈仲梅. (19 May 2012). Xu Xiake yu luyouri 徐霞客与旅游日 [Xu Xiake and National Tourism Day]. Renmin Ribao *People's Daily*, p. 7.

Chou, Chih-ping. (1988). *Yuan Hung-tao and the Kung-an School*. Cambridge, UK: Cambridge University Press.

Clunas, Craig. (1991). *Superfluous things: Material culture and social status in early modern China*. Urbana: University of Illinois Press.

Fu, Flora Li-tsui. (2009). *Framing famous mountains: Grand tour and Mingshan paintings in sixteenth-century China*. Hong Kong: Chinese University Press.

Hargett, James, M. (1989). *On the road in twelfth-century China: The travel diaries of Fan Chengda (1126-1193)*. Stuttgart, Germany: Franz Steiner Verlag Wiesbaden.

Hargett, James, M. (2006). *Stairway to heaven: A journey to the summit of Mount Emei*. Albany: State University of New York.

Hu Wei 胡渭. *Yugong zhuizhi* 禹贡锥指 [Basic guide to the "Yu Gong"]. In *Siku Quanshu* (vol. 67, pp. 211–850).

Lee, Leo Ou-fan. (1985).The solitary traveller: Images of self in modern Chinese literature. In Robert Hegel (Ed.), *Expressions of Self in Chinese Literature* (pp. 282–307). New York: Columbia University Press.

Leed, Eric J. (1991). *The mind of the traveler: From Gilgamesh to global tourism*. New York: Basic Books.

Li Chi. (1974). *The travel diaries of Hsu Hsia-k'o*. Hong Kong: The Chinese University.

Li Ciming 李慈铭. (1963). *Yuemantang du shu ji* 越缦堂读书记 [Reading notes in Yueman Hal. Beijing: Zhonghua shuju.

McDowall, Stephen. (2009). *Qian Qianyi's reflections on Yellow Mountain: Traces of a late-Ming hatchet and chisel*. Hong Kong: Hong Kong University Press.

Munakata, Kiyohiko. (1991). *Sacred mountains in Chinese art*. Urbana: University of Illinois Press.

Naquin, Susan, & Chün-fang Yü, (Eds.). (1992). *Pilgrims and sacred sites in China*. Oxford, UK: University of California Press.

Riemenschnitter, Andrea. (2003). "Traveler's vocation: Xu Xiake and his excursion to the southwest frontier." In Nicola di Cosmo & Don J. Wyatt, (Eds.). *Political frontiers, ethnic boundaries, and human geographies in Chinese history* (pp. 286–323). London: RoutledgeCurzon.

Strassberg, Richard E. (1994). *Inscribed landscapes: Travel writing from Imperial China*. Berkeley: University of California Press.

Wang Shixing 王士性. (1993). *Wang Shixing dilishu sanzhongç* 王士性地理三种书 [Three geographical works by Wang Shixing]. Shanghai: Shanghai Guji.

Ward, Julian. (2000). *Xu Xiake (1587–1641): The art of travel writing*. London: Curzon.

Xu Xiake 徐霞客. (1993). *Xu Xiake Youji* 徐霞客游记 [The travel diaries of Xu Xiake] (Chu Shaotang & Wu Yingshou, Eds.). Shanghai: Shanghai guji.

Yongle, Emperor (of Ming)

Yǒnglè 永乐

1360–1424—Third emperor of the Ming dynasty

Alternate names: birth name: Zhū Dì 朱棣; temple name: Tàizōng 太宗, Chéngzǔ 成祖

Summary

Emperor Yongle, son of the founder of the Ming dynasty, came to the throne after raising an army and overthrowing his nephew. During his reign, he led military campaigns north to the Mongol steppe, moved the capital from Nanjing to Beijing, commissioned the wide-ranging sea voyages of Zheng He, and made his court the center of intellectual life in China by commissioning vast encyclopedias of knowledge, most notably the 11,095-volume *Grand Compendium of the Yongle Era*. The Ming dynasty saw an apex of power under his forceful reign, though it was at such great cost that his predecessors had to scale back immediately upon his death.

Emperor Yongle, born Zhū Dì 朱棣, was the fourth of the twenty-six sons of Emperor Hóngwǔ 洪武 (Zhū Yuánzhāng 朱元璋, 1328–1398), founder of the Míng 明 dynasty. Information about Zhu Di's early years is unreliable, as he ordered the family records altered to frame his usurpation of the throne from his nephew in a positive light. His official historians declared him to be a son by Empress Ma, his father's primary wife, but it is widely believed that his mother was a consort of Korean or Mongol descent. Zhu Di was born only a few years after his father established his base (and later his capital) at Nanjing, and the dynasty (in power 1368–1644) was consolidated and established over the course of his childhood.

The founder of the dynasty had arranged for all of his sons to have a comprehensive education in classical texts, ritual etiquette, history, literature, and other subjects. In 1373, he compiled a collection of clan regulations, the *Ancestral Admonitions* (*Zǔxùnlù* 祖训录), to which his progeny were bound to adhere. Zhu Di and his brothers were taught by the most famous scholars in the realm, and throughout his life, Zhu Di demonstrated a facility with classical texts and with the history of previous dynasties. Despite this academic training, however, Zhu Di's disposition and talents were more focused on the military arts, much like his father. From an early age, he distinguished himself with his physical strength and his skills in archery and horsemanship. By the age of fourteen, he was already accompanying military campaigns led by his father or by prominent generals. His father encouraged these talents in his sons, for he viewed them as important to the defense of the empire. Reviving an ancient precedent from antiquity, the emperor enfeoffed his sons with domains across the empire, intending that they would provide a strategic defense of the capital at Nanjing. (The term "enfeoff" refers to the feudal practice of giving a vassal property in exchange for pledges of service.)

In 1370, when Zhu Di was ten, he was given the title of Prince of Yan at Beijing (then called Beiping), a crucial point of defense against the peoples of the steppe, though he did not take up this post until he was twenty. As he travelled to his post accompanied by 5,700 troops in 1380, the prince was well aware of the challenges that lay before him. The Mongol court and its forces had been driven from the city only twelve years earlier and the regions around it had been ravaged by warfare and natural disasters over the past several decades.

Zhu Di received extensive tutelage in military affairs from the leading generals of the realm, particularly Xú Dá 徐达 (1332–1385). A military leader of great talent and achievement in defeating Mongol forces and securing the new dynasty, Xu was very close to Emperor Hongwu. The emperor rewarded Xu handsomely with noble titles and numerous honors and even arranged for the general's daughter to marry Zhu Di in 1376, such marriage arrangements being common among the children of the Hongwu emperor.

Usurping the Throne

In 1392, the court was rocked by the sudden death of the heir apparent, Zhū Biāo 朱标 (1355–1392). After extensive discussion, Hongwu named Zhu Biao's son, the fifteen-year-old Zhū Yǔnwén 朱允炆 (1377–1402) as the new heir-apparent. This decision caused tension among the princes, some of whom had imperial ambitions of their own. By this time, Zhu Di's entourage included advisors like the Buddhist monk Dàoyǎn 道衍 (1335–1418) who believed that the Prince of Yan's fortitude, experience, and wisdom made him the much more suitable choice for succession to the throne.

Soon after the emperor died in 1398 and Zhu Yunwen ascended the throne as Emperor Jiànwén 建文 (r. 1399–1402), tensions between the Nanjing court and the princes of the realm became apparent. Concerned with stabilizing his own position, Jianwen enforced his grandfather's ban on princes attending the funeral services for the deceased emperor, arousing the ire of Zhu Di and his brothers. Under the advice of the scholar officials of the court, Jianwen began to further curtail the power of the imperial princes, with the goal of eliminating their domains. Five princes were charged with crimes and removed, one of them dying in a fire in his palace.

By 1399, Zhu Di was the oldest and most powerful of the princes and a clear target of the court. At this time, he invoked a clause in his father's *Ancestral Admonitions* which allowed for members of the imperial family to intervene when the ruler was endangered by malicious advisors. Zhu Di declared that the court of his nephew was beset by "treacherous officials," naming the officials most closely associated with the policies aimed at the imperial princes. As the oldest member of the clan, it was incumbent that he, as Prince of Yan, undertake punitive measures. Zhu Di was careful to insist that he had no aspirations to the throne and that his actions were in keeping with the wishes of his father.

As his rebellion began, Zhu Di's forces were significantly disadvantaged, his troops and resources dwarfed by those of the imperial court. But his well-trained and experienced soldiers were superior to those of Nanjing. His military included an imposing Mongol cavalry force. Zhu Di himself was a gifted strategist and he had accumulated considerable experience as a military leader. There were claims that the court at Nanjing was ill-prepared in military matters and more focused on civil affairs. Some scholars have argued that the purges of the military in the 1390s had weakened the imperial forces, particularly in terms of the leadership in the upper echelons.

In late 1399, open hostilities began as Emperor Jianwen deployed his armies to the north to subdue the Prince of Yan, but these attempts were unsuccessful as Zhu Di's forces rebuffed and outmaneuvered them. There were several prominent defections to the north and the prince had numerous informers at the imperial court. By the beginning of 1402, Zhu Di's forces were pressing southward, with the imperial army desperately defending the region around Nanjing. In early July, as the northern forces approached the capital, emissaries from the court failed in negotiating a peace settlement with the prince. Forces within the fortified city of Nanjing capitulated and opened the gates for Zhu Di's armies, which entered without a fight. In the ensuing chaos, the palace was burned and the emperor probably perished inside. Stories circulated that the young ruler escaped disguised as a monk and wandered in hiding through the southern and western regions of the empire, rumors that persisted for centuries afterwards.

On 15 July, four days after the fall of Nanjing, Zhu Di ascended the throne, after rituals of modest refusal. He declared a reign title of Yǒnglè 永乐, meaning Eternal Joy, and moved quickly to consolidate his new court and to restore the administrative apparatus of the empire. Yongle sought to obliterate the legacy of his nephew's rule, ordering that the official records of the four reign years of Jianwen be subsumed under those of the dynasty's founder. He instructed his officials to cull the records of Jianwen's reign, destroying all documents except those pertaining to economic or military affairs. Early on, he ordered the compilation of an official account that vindicated his usurpation of the throne, the *Record of Quelling Troubles in Obedience to Heaven* (*Fèngtiān jìngnàn jì* 奉天靖难记), portraying his nephew as immoral and inept, and presenting himself as the rightful heir to the throne in keeping with the wishes of the founder.

Establishing Rulership

Yongle purged the court of many loyalists to the old regime, but he was also eager to recruit those willing to serve him. From among the leading Nanjing officials who surrendered, he selected a core advisory staff of capable officials, most of whom were veterans of both the Hongwu and Jianwen reigns. Close advisors to the emperor had become necessary at the Ming court after Hongwu abolished the position of prime minister in 1380, leaving a void at the top of the bureaucracy. Under Yongle, this body regularly advised the ruler on governmental matters and gradually became formalized as the Grand Secretariat (*nèigé* 内阁), one of the most important institutions at the top of the civil bureaucracy during the Ming.

Although the grand secretaries and top ministers played important roles in shaping the new court, they were kept tightly under Yongle's control and frequently suffered his wrath and imprisonment. Convinced that his nephew had been overpowered by willful advisors, he was determined to ensure that his ministers understood their subordinate place. In his advice to his sons and grandsons, he repeatedly emphasized that proper relations between ruler and minister was the key to order within the empire. The leading grand secretary, Xiè Jìn 解缙 (1369–1415), angered Yongle with his forthright remonstrance and died in prison after being charged with a violation of protocol. The minister of revenue, Xià Yuánjí 夏原吉 (1367–1430), was imprisoned for three years for opposing one of the emperor's costly northern military campaigns. The grand secretary, Huáng Huái 黄淮 (1367–1449), tutor to the heir-apparent, was imprisoned for ten years along with several colleagues when the emperor was dissatisfied with his heir's behavior.

Several of the leading officials of Yongle's court outlasted their ruler, however, and continued to dominate court politics into the 1440s. Prominent among these were the grand secretaries known as the "Three Yangs," Yáng Pǔ 杨溥 (1372–1446), Yáng Róng 杨荣 (1371–1440), and Yáng Shìqí 杨士奇 (1365–1444), who tutored and guided Yongle's son, grandson, and great-grandson. Their policies, which focused on stability and order within the realm, were credited with consolidating the dynasty. These men presided during the apex of a civil bureaucracy that gradually became more ordered, after the chaotic years of the late Yuán 元 dynasty (1279–1368) and the purges of Hongwu's reign. From Yongle's reign onward, the civil service examination system became a more regularized form of recruitment, after more than a century of fluctuating policies.

Like his father, however, Yongle was more comfortable with military men than with scholars. He generously rewarded those who had supported his usurpation, granting noble titles to his leading generals from that war and from later campaigns to the north and in Vietnam. Yongle also relied upon his eunuch staff to a greater degree than his father, assigning them to serve in special administrative tasks, important diplomatic positions, and in surveillance. The Eastern Depot (*Dōngchǎng* 东厂) was established in 1420 as an investigating agency, staffed by eunuchs and independent from civil bureaucratic control.

As he consolidated his authority over the realm, Yongle sought to recruit more scholars to his court by commissioning several ambitious academic projects. These projects served to assert his legitimate authority as a truly Confucian ruler. They also drew in hundreds of scholars from across the realm to work in his court. One of the first of these was a vast encyclopedia endeavor, the *Grand Compendium of the Yongle Era* (*Yǒnglè dàdiǎn* 永乐大典). This project was inaugurated shortly after Yongle's reign began and was completed rapidly in 1408, with 22,877 chapters in 11,095 volumes. Both Hongwu and Jianwen had initiated projects of this kind, but none on the scale of the *Yongle dadian*. Over time, the project drew on the skills of over 2,000 scholars. The emperor remained closely attentive to the progress of the encyclopedia, intervening to expand its scope. He clearly saw the project as part of his imperial legacy, and boasted upon its completion that it would be a boon to scholars everywhere.

Next was the consolidation and organization of the Confucian curriculum, with a particular focus on the Neo-Confucian doctrines that had predominated since the twelfth century. This project included the production of authoritative versions of the classics: the *Great Comprehensive Compilation on the Four Books* (*Sìshū dàquán* 四书大全) and the *Great Comprehensive Compilation on the Five Classics* (*Wǔjīng dàquán* 五经大全). These were completed in 1415 and presented to the court. The series also included a broad topical anthology of Neo-Confucian concepts and themes: the *Great Comprehensive Compilation on*

Two volumes from the 11,095-volume encyclopedia *Yongle Dadian*: volume (*juan* 卷) 489–490 (left) and 8,908 (right).

Human Nature and Heavenly Principle (*Xìnglǐ dàquán* 性理大全), completed in 1417. These works were intended as reference material for students preparing for the civil service examinations and the compendia were published and circulated to schools and government offices throughout the realm.

In these projects and in other ways, Yongle made his court the center of the intellectual and cultural life of the realm. Although he was a skilled and experienced warrior, he frequently asserted his own scholarly credentials. Like his father, he took the dictates of Neo-Confucianism seriously and personally. In 1409, for example, he compiled his own work of Neo-Confucian teachings, the *Method of the Mind in the Learning of the Sages* (*Shèngxué xīnfǎ* 圣学心法), an anthology of Neo-Confucian writings on the moral cultivation of the ruler.

While Yongle was trained and conversant in Neo-Confucian doctrines, he also gave significant attention and patronage to Buddhist and Daoist (Taoist) teachings and institutions, and demonstrating a pious reverence to each. His closest advisor and confidant was the Buddhist monk Daoyan, the abbot of the august Qingshou Monastery (Qìngshòu sì 庆寿寺) in Beijing. Yongle wrote extensively on Buddhist topics himself; he was particularly taken with Tibetan Buddhism and invited prominent spiritual leaders from Tibet to lecture and perform ceremonies at court, after which they were presented with titles and gifts. In 1410, he arranged for a printing of the Tibetan Tripitaka (Buddhist Canon). In 1420 in Beijing, he commissioned a reprinting of the Chinese Tripitaka in 6,361 chapters, revising the edition sponsored by his father nearly fifty years earlier.

Yongle was also keenly engaged in Daoist teachings, practices and institutions. In 1406, he commissioned a new printing of the Daoist canon, a project that took until the 1440s to complete (like the Buddhist canon). The emperor venerated several prominent Daoist deities. In particular, he believed his military successes had been supported by the Dark Warrior deity (Xuánwǔ 玄武), and so he refurbished temples to him.

Yongle's primary wife, the Empress Xu (1362–1407), was similarly concerned with the promulgation of moral virtue. Under her auspices, the court produced a collection of exemplary female biographies, the *Lives of Virtuous Women, Ancient and Modern* (*Gǔjīn liènǚ zhuàn* 古今列女传). Two other works were also attributed to her, the *Women's Admonitions* (*Nǚ xùn* 女训) and the *Book of Encouraging Goodness* (*Quànshàn shū* 劝善书), a collection of moralistic passages and historical anecdotes.

Moving the Capital

Yongle brought about a dramatic shift in the geography of the empire by moving the capital from Nanjing north to his old fiefdom at Yan. From the beginning of his reign, it was clear that the emperor was not satisfied with Nanjing. Despite the fact that the demolished imperial palace buildings had been quickly rebuilt, Nanjing retained the air of a conquered city. Having lived for 20 years at his fief in Yan, Yongle was more comfortable in the north. In his mind, the northern city was a better strategic location from which to project the power and authority of the Ming northward onto the steppe. Nanjing had an important cultural legacy as an ancient capital, and it was well-situated amidst the flourishing trade networks of the wealthy Yangzi (Chang) region. But for Yongle, the northern city and its location represented the kind of political and military engagement with inner Asia that he envisioned for the empire. The city had been named Běipíng 北平 or "Northern Peace," but in the first year of his reign, Yongle changed the name to Běijīng 北京, meaning "Northern Capital." To further reaffirm the legitimacy of his capital, he renamed the prefecture Shùntiān 顺天, "Compliant with Heaven," matching his father's naming of the Nanjing prefecture as Yingtian, "Responding to Heaven." For a time, Beijing and Nanjing acted as dual capitals, and Yongle ordered imperial altars built in the north to match those in

Nanjing, allowing him to fulfill his ritual responsibilities in either city.

Yongle was deeply involved in the reconstruction of Beijing as the new capital, although his time was mostly divided between Nanjing, where he spent many of the early years of his reign, and the steppe on the Mongol campaigns. His eldest son, the heir-apparent, (Zhū Gāochì 朱高炽, [1378–1425]) was installed in Beijing to represent him in his absence. After 1409, Yongle himself spent more time in the north, while his heir managed affairs in Nanjing. Over time, auxiliary branches of all the imperial ministries and agencies in Nanjing were set up in the north. When Beijing became the official capital in a transition between late 1420 and early 1421, these branches became the main offices of the imperial government and those in Nanjing were relegated to a secondary status.

The logistics and costs of building the new capital and moving the administration from Nanjing were a major preoccupation of the Yongle reign. In Beijing, parts of the old Yuan Dynasty structure of the city had decayed and required extensive refurbishment, and the city itself had to be redesigned to suit Yongle's ideas for the new imperial capital. Hundreds of thousands of workmen were recruited, and construction materials were ordered from across the empire and as far south as Annam (in present-day Vietnam). To expand the population of his new capital, Yongle ordered that 10,000 households be moved to the city from Shanxi Province to the west, following a precedent set by his father in the building of Nanjing. To provide provisions for the expanding capital, Yongle ordered the extensive refurbishment of the Grand Canal. The canal system had been extended up to Beijing under the previous Yuan dynasty, but chronic silting made transport inefficient and coastal routes were generally preferred. By 1415, both the lower and the upper sections of the canal had been dredged and redesigned, drawing on corvée laborers in the hundreds of thousands. ("Corvée" labor is another term related to feudalism; it refers to unpaid labor provided by a feudal vassal to his lord.)

Throughout his reign, Yongle claimed a deep concern for the welfare of the peasantry, seeking to echo his father's vision of a peaceful agrarian order. In numerous edicts, he called upon his officials to relieve the conditions of the peasants and to be lenient in the collection of taxes. The Yongle reign placed heavy burdens on the tax base of the empire, however, with the expansive scope of military and civil projects such as the moving of the capital.

International Relations

Yongle's vision of the scope and prestige of the Ming empire was more expansive than that of his predecessors. Using both diplomacy and military force, he sought to extend his power, authority, and influence over the territories and peoples beyond the Ming borders in every direction. Under his reign the reach of the empire was more vast than at any other time in the dynasty.

The emperor had long been focused on asserting an offensive posture towards the Mongols and other neighboring peoples to the north. Defense of this border had been his official charge since he was first assigned to the fief of Yan, and his preoccupation with conditions to the north was one of the reasons that he moved the imperial capital to Beijing. Relations with northern peoples were not entirely hostile, and early in his career, Yongle had built alliances with Mongol groups, including some who had provided military support during the war to usurp the throne. Some groups had chosen to settle in north China, accepting Ming authority and engaging in military service.

Through diplomatic efforts, Yongle sought to build a network of alliances along the northern border, reaching as far to the west as Turfan, Samarkand, and Herat. Although some leaders in these regions agreed to friendly relations and accepted Chinese titles, others did not, warring with the Ming empire and raiding across its borders. The largest foreign threat to the empire was the Timurid Empire to the far west, whose ruler Tamerlane (1336–1405) sought to restore the glorious realm of his ancestor *Chinggis (Genghis) Khan (c. 1162–1227). Tamerlane intended to crush the Ming, launching a powerful expedition in 1404. He died a year later, however, before his forces reached the Chinese borders, sparing the Ming a costly invasion.

Over the course of Yongle's reign, various Mongol groups continued to be a significant threat to the empire. The emperor chose not to maintain costly fortifications established by his father in the far north, except for those in Manchuria. Instead he was determined to strengthen the region around his new capital at Beijing. After a Ming envoy was executed by a khan in eastern Mongolia, however, Yongle launched the first of a series of five major military campaigns that he led personally between 1410 and 1424 to reassert Ming authority over much of the steppe. The campaigns included as many as 300,000 troops and lasted for months, keeping the emperor away from his capital, and leaving his heir-apparent in charge. His ministers raised frequent objections to the cost of these expeditions, which placed a heavy burden on the finances of the realm. Although there were several military victories, the campaigns failed to bring the diverse Mongol forces fully under Ming authority, and in spite of his efforts, Yongle left a legacy of instability and defiance along the northern border of the empire.

Although the Mongols were the primary security concern for the empire, the Yongle court also became embroiled in matters on the southern border.

*People marked with an asterisk have entries in this dictionary.

Emperor Yongle (also known under his title Ming Chengzu) sitting on the Dragon chair. National Palace Museum, Taipei, Taiwan.

During the last decade of the fourteenth century, there was turmoil in the kingdom of Annam, a tributary state to China since the tenth century. In 1400, the throne of the reigning Trãn (Chén 陈) dynasty was usurped by a powerful member of the court, Lê Quí-ly (c. 1335–1407, Hồ Quý Ly 胡季牦 or Lê Quý Ly 黎季牦) just as the Ming dynasty was preoccupied with its own civil war. The Ming court subsequently became involved, siding with a Trãn claimant to the throne. After Lê's forces launched a surprise attack on a delegation of Ming officials and troops escorting the Trãn clansman back to assume the throne, Yongle ordered a full-scale invasion punitive force of over 200,000 men into Annam. The Ming military routed the forces of the Annam court and captured Lê and his son in 1407.

That year, Yongle announced the annexation of Annam as a Ming province, giving it the old Chinese name Jiāozhǐ 交阯, a decision that had disastrous results. The establishment of Chinese rule and administration throughout Annam was deeply unpopular, inspiring widespread resistance, led by members of the Trãn clan and others. Open rebellion required the Ming court to commit large numbers of troops to pacify the region. Despite a number of significant military victories, Chinese forces were unable to overcome persistent guerrilla-style resistance throughout Annam. Over the course of the Yongle reign, this resistance was fueled by the demands for resources from the region to support the construction of the new capital at Beijing. By Yongle's death, Annam had still not been pacified and the court was compelled to abandon the project in 1427.

Yongle also actively courted cordial relations with other peoples on the Ming periphery. He invited leading religious leaders from Tibet, gave them official titles, and welcomed them to perform ritual ceremonies at his court. In Manchuria, his eunuch emissary cultivated warm relations with the Jurchen tribal chieftains far to the north and established a regional military commission and a Jurchen guard. Twenty battalions were stationed throughout Manchuria to maintain peaceful relations with the Jurchen and to protect the rich trade in horses, furs, and other commodities from the region. From Korea, the Yongle court secured a bountiful tribute in gold, silver, horses, furs, and women for the imperial harem. Diplomatic and trade relations were also established with Japan, a reversal of the ban imposed by the Ming founder on exchanges with Japan.

Perhaps the most logistically ambitious of Yongle's foreign relations efforts was the launching of a series of six maritime expeditions into the Indian Ocean between 1405 and 1421. This enterprise was closely linked to the emperor himself, overseen by Yongle's eunuchs and drawing heavily on the imperial household treasury. The voyages were led by *Zhèng Hé 郑和 (1371–c. 1433), a Muslim eunuch from Yunnan who had served

Yongle faithfully since 1380. The expeditions were made up of large armadas manned by up to 27,000 men, made up of over 200 vessels that varied in size, but including some over 120 meters (400 feet) long. These were probably some of the largest wooden ships and the largest armada the world had ever seen. The purpose of the voyages appears to have been primarily diplomatic and exploratory, projecting Ming power and authority throughout the Indian Ocean. The voyages reached as far as the Maldives, Hormuz in the Persian Gulf, Aden in the Gulf of Suez, and Malindi on the African coast.

The ships were well-armed and manned with soldiers, even though these were not primarily military expeditions. The first voyage included a battle in which Zheng He's men routed a force of several thousand pirates near Palembang in Indonesia. On the third voyage, the king of Ceylon (modern-day Sri Lanka) attacked the armada and was defeated. Zheng He's voyages were broadly successful in asserting Ming authority in the Indian Ocean and affirming tribute relations with the various states of the region. The court sent a bounty of treasures to present to local rulers—mostly paper money, silk, and Chinese calendars (which regional rulers were expected to use in their correspondence with the Ming)—and received a wealth of tribute in return. Included among the gifts to the Ming court were exotic animals such as giraffes and lions that were presented at the capital.

Yongle's Death and Legacy

Yongle died in the summer of 1424 as he was concluding his last northern campaign in Mongolia. At sixty-four, he had already suffered several strokes and possibly some paralysis. His body was placed in a coffin and brought back to Beijing. He was buried in a large and elaborate mausoleum and given the posthumous title of "Grand Ancestor" or Tàizōng 太宗, the traditional designation for the second ruler of a dynasty. His eldest son, Zhu Gaochi, ascended the throne as Emperor Hóngxī 洪熙 (r. 1425). He was not as martial as his father, usually remaining at the capital while his father went out on campaigns. Upon his ascent to the throne, he reversed several of his father's policies, granting amnesty to imprisoned officials, reducing military campaigns, discontinuing the Indian Ocean voyages and, most notably, making arrangements to move the capital back to Nanjing. Concerned about the burdens that his father's projects had placed upon the populace, he sought to reduce tax obligations and to alleviate economic hardship across the realm. Hongxi did not live long enough to carry out these plans, however, and died nine months after ascending the throne.

Soon after, Yongle's grandson Zhū Zhānjī 朱瞻基 (r. 1426–35), was enthroned as Emperor Xuāndé 宣德. Yongle's irascible second son, Zhū Gāoxù 朱高煦 (1380–1429), attempted to repeat his father's seizure of the throne from his nephew. This time, however, the bureaucracy and the military establishment stood firm in support of the young emperor and the rebellion was quickly suppressed. While sharing his grandfather's military prowess, Xuande's reign also saw the curbing of the expansive projects of the Yongle reign and policies that focused upon economic, political, and social stability.

Over the course of his reign, Yongle had had a dramatic impact, consolidating and reshaping the dynasty. His legacy, however, was a mixed one. On the one hand, the remarkable achievements of his reign—the move of the capital, the voyages throughout the Indian Ocean, the colossal compendia of knowledge, the campaigns against the Mongols—were each a testament to the grand ambitions and determination of the emperor. On the other hand, the endeavors of Yongle also took their toll. At the time of his death, the budget of the empire had been severely overstrained from Yongle's relentless expenditures, leaving his son and grandson with little choice but to curtail his projects and restore the treasury and the economy of the realm. While his military exploits successfully dampened the ambitions of his adversaries to the north, the relocation to Beijing and his military arrangements left the capital vulnerable to raids and attacks from the steppe. Vacillation over the risks and logistical challenges of the northern capital continued for more than two decades after Yongle's death. The emperor's usurpation of the throne from his nephew also left a dangerous precedent for his successors, beginning with his own son. Despite these problems in his legacy, however, Yongle was revered throughout the Ming and beyond as a sage and capable ruler. In 1538, Emperor Jiājìng 嘉靖 (r. 1522–1566) revised Yongle's posthumous name from Taizong to Chéngzǔ 成祖, "Accomplished Progenitor," acknowledging his profound impact upon the realm.

Peter DITMANSON
University of Oxford

Further Reading

Farmer, Edward L. (1976). *Early Ming government: The evolution of dual capitals.* Cambridge, MA: Harvard University Press.

Li Zhuoran 李焯然, & Mao Peiqi 毛佩琦. (1994). *Ming Chengzu shilun* 明成祖史论 [Essays on the history of Ming Chengzu] Taipei, Taiwan: Wenjin.

Shang Chuan 商傳. (1989). *Yongle huangdi* 永樂皇帝 [The Yongle Emperor]. Beijing: Beijing Publishing.

Shih-shan Henry Tsai. (2001). *Perpetual happiness: The Ming Emperor Yongle.* Seattle: University of Washington Press.

Zhu Hong 朱鴻. (1988). *Ming Chengzu yu Yongle zhengzhi* 明成祖與永樂政治 [Ming Chengzu and the governance of the Yongle reign]. Taipei: Taiwan National Normal University.

Yuán Chónghuàn

袁崇焕

1584–1630—Magistrate and military commander

•袁崇焕•

Summary

Famous for the defeat of Nurhaci at the Battle of Ningyuan, Yuan Chonghuan was a powerful military leader who defeated the Jin outside the borders of the Great Wall and kept them at bay during his lifetime. The surprising news of the Ming victory at Ningyuan was greeted with joy in Beijing, as it was the most serious defeat Nurhaci had ever suffered as a military commander; as the Ming minister of war proclaimed, "This proves that China still has men after all!" It was only upon Yuan's execution for supposed treason (and, before that, Yuan's execution of the warlord Mao Wenlong), that the Ming were made vulnerable to further attacks that would bring about the downfall of their empire.

A Míng 明 dynasty (1368–1644) civil official and military commander, Yuan Chonghuan is best known as the defender of Ningyuan (modern-day Xingcheng, in Liaoning Province) and executioner of the semi-independent warlord Máo Wénlóng 毛文龙. Yuan's own subsequent execution by mercurial Emperor Chongzhen (r. 1628–1644) is considered by many (including early Qing historians) to have been one of the key blows that aided the eventual Qing conquest of the Ming by removing one of the greatest obstacles to their success in the northeast. Though his life and actions were somewhat controversial in his own day, he was later remembered as one of traditional China's greatest patriots, especially in the late Qing and the early twentieth century as a wave of Han Chinese nationalism swept the country. No less a luminary than the intellectual and reformist *Liáng Qǐchāo 梁启超 (1873–1929), considered Yuan to have been China's greatest (Han) soldier.

*People marked with an asterisk have entries in this dictionary.

Shrines and memorials to his memory and exploits can still be found in several places, including an impressive complex in his hometown of Dongguan, Teng County, Guangdong Province; another in Shaowu, Fujian Province, where he held his first official post; and a small shrine in Longtan Park, in the southern part of Beijing, not far from the Temple of Heaven. Yuan also continues to be the subject of popular historical works and television dramas.

Yuan's Rise to Power

As is the case for many officials in traditional China, relatively little is known about Yuan's life prior to when he passed the imperial civil service exams and earned his *jìnshì* 进士 (presented scholar) degree in 1619 at the age of thirty-five. The following year, he received his first official appointment as Prefect of Shaowu, Fujian. From this point onwards Yuan's rise to prominence would be rapid, owing in large part to the pressing military situation in the northeast.

In 1616, the Jurchen leader *Nurhaci 努尔哈赤 (1558–1626) had declared the creation of his state of Latter Jin and subsequently articulated a series a grievances against the Ming state and its emperor, *Wànlì 万历 (r. 1573–1620). Nurhaci seized the strategically important city of Fushun in 1618, prompting the Ming to take military action. In 1619, the veteran official Yáng Hào 杨镐 assembled a Ming army of around 90,000 to crush Nurhaci. Though Yang urged caution, others at court wanted to press the attack, so Yang's forces advanced in four columns towards the Jin capital of Hetu Ala in the early spring of 1619. The decision to divide his forces proved a grave mistake, and bad weather and poor coordination resulted in the destruction of three of the Ming armies. This led to Yang Hao's dismissal and imprisonment and his replacement by Xióng Tíngbì 熊廷弼, another official with long experience in the northeast. The Ming state also implemented the so-called "Liao surtax," the first of the tax increases that would plague the late Ming people, in an effort to raise funds for military supplies and operations in the northeast. Taxes would be increased again in 1620 and Xiong Tingbi would be dismissed because of differences over strategy with other powerful figures at the Ming court. Xiong favored a gradual, more defensive approach to the Jurchen threat until the Ming had trained their armies and marshaled their resources.

Meanwhile, Yuan Chonghuan exercised his duties capably in his post in Shaowu, rescuing the locals from natural disaster, suppressing banditry, and contributing to the reconstruction of a local pagoda. In short, he was a model official. Then matters in the northeast got even worse, and the Jurchens captured a number of key Ming forts and cities, including Liaoyang, in Liaoning Province, which would become their new capital. Xiong Tingbi's replacement was cashiered and Xiong was reinstated. About the only positive development that occurred for the Ming was a series of minor triumphs against the Jin along the Korean border engineered by a maverick military commander named Mao Wenlong. The court was delighted, and the new emperor, Tiānqǐ 天启 (r. 1621–1627), soon promoted Mao to the post of regional vice-commander. It was against this backdrop that Yuan Chonghuan went to Beijing to examine the situation more closely, though the exact reasons for Yuan's visit are not revealed in the extant sources.

While in Beijing, Yuan took advantage of the opportunity to go to the frontier alone and personally examine the state of affairs. Upon his return to the capital he told the court that he personally could oversee the defense of the passes if properly supplied. Even at an early stage in his official career, Yuan demonstrated the cockiness that would become his trademark. Such was the desperation of the Ming court that within the month he was appointed as a scrutinizing secretary in the Ministry of War, given official credentials, and dispatched to the front. While still in Beijing Yuan conferred closely with Xiong Tingbi, but Xiong was soon dismissed again, along with the military administrator Wang Huazhen, after the latter's plan to take a more aggressive stance and make use of Mongol allies to fight the Jurchens ended in more humiliating defeats for the Ming. Xiong's initial replacement this time was Sūn Chéngzōng 孙承宗, with whom Yuan would work fairly well in the coming years. But other appointments were also made and jurisdictional authority in Liaodong was fragmented, undermining Ming efforts there. Xiong was subsequently imprisoned and sentenced to death, and Yuan was made a supervising censor in Shandong in charge of military supplies.

Success Against the Jin

Over the next couple of years, the various high Ming officials would debate different strategies for holding Liaodong and recovering lost territory. Though particulars varied, there were essentially three major strategies. The first involved pulling back all the way to the Great Wall and could be considered primarily a defensive strategy. The second was a gradual recovery strategy that emphasized defense in the short run and more aggressive activity as Ming power and readiness improved. This was essentially the strategy advocated by Xiong Tingbi. The third strategy was a more aggressive forward strategy. In this plan, the Ming would not abandon any cities beyond the Great Wall but would look to keep their advance bases and expand their control by using a variety of means, including locally raised troops, Mongol allies, and naval forces such as those commanded by Mao Wenlong. After going on a personal inspection tour of the frontier in the sixth month of 1622, Minister of War Sun Chengzong decided to adopt the forward strategy and appointed Yuan Chonghuan to defend the city of Ningyuan, located northeast of Shanhaiguan, not far from the coast. This decision was strongly opposed by the newly appointed military commissioner of Liaodong, Wang Zaijin. After Sun pled his case to the emperor, Wang was removed and transferred to a position in Nanjing.

With the backing of Sun Chengzong, Yuan Chonghuan went about reinforcing the defenses of Ningyuan and even extending the Ming defense corridor further to the east, to the cities of Jinzhou and Songshan. In addition to rebuilding the defenses of these towns, the Ming court stepped up the manufacture and deployment of firearms for the frontier, spurred by Christian converts at court such as Xu Guangqi and Sun Yuanhua, who had access to Western firepower and technology. They also continued to send supplies and bestow honors upon Mao Wenlong, still stationed far to the east. It appeared that the initial Jin tide had been stemmed and the recovery of lost lands was a possibility. Yuan stepped up his construction activities at Ningyuan and the Ming sent a pair of accomplished generals, Zu Dashou and Man Gui, to train the troops and oversee combat operations. Simultaneously, Sun Chengzong pushed for the use of the Liao people to defend Liaodong and argued that the Ming should facilitate more productivity in the region so that the people and armies could shoulder the burden of feeding themselves.

In 1624, Mao Wenlong suffered a defeat at the hands of the Jin and pulled back to the islands in the Bohai Gulf, requesting the dispatch of more supplies. Still in Ningyuan, Yuan learned of the death of his father and requested permission to return home for the mourning observations, which typically lasted twenty-seven months. But repeated requests to resign his post were refused due to the importance of his position. At the same time, the court was embroiled in factional strife as a censor named Yang Lian publicly attacked the powerful eunuch official *Wèi Zhōngxián 魏忠贤 (1568–1627) for abuses of authority. Though Yuan continued to receive promotions, his patron Sun Chengzong was eventually replaced because of his opposition to Wei Zhongxian. In the next year, the Jin pressure increased and they moved their capital to Shenyang. In response, Gao Di, who was Sun Chengzong's replacement, ordered a withdrawal of all Ming forces beyond the Great Wall. Yuan Chonghuan refused to comply with the directive, as he and Sun had already devised their forward base strategy and they believed that it had progressed too far already to merely abandon. Xiong Tingbi was executed and dismembered in the marketplace in Beijing as the partisan strife intensified. And despite his refusal to comply with Gao Di's directive, Yuan Chonghuan would be promoted to censor-in-chief at the end of the year.

Yuan's decision to remain at Ningyuan would be justified early in 1626 when the Jin khan surrounded the city with 60,000 of his best troops. The other isolated forts of Songshan, Jinzhou, had fallen to the enemy and their forces had pulled back to Ningyuan, where Yuan amassed barely 20,000 troops. But he had done a good job of reinforcing the city's defenses over the previous years and in addition to reinforcing the walls he had arrayed a large number of cannons around the walls, most notably the large "Western Ocean Cannon," purchased from the Portuguese or modeled after their designs. As the Jin cavalry approached the city walls, Yuan opened fire and the defenders reaped a grim harvest. Hundreds allegedly fell before some of the blasts and repeated assaults were turned back, as Yuan personally oversaw the defense of the city from atop the walls. The ground shook and the air was filled with smoke. Whereas earlier Ming defense plans had called for placing cannon outside the city walls, this time they were atop and inside the fortress and the enemy could not get close enough to overrun them. Efforts to breach the walls with scaling ladders were repulsed by incendiaries and arrows. Night attacks also failed, though the Jin were able to capture the offshore weapons storage base on Juehua Island in part because cold temperatures over the previous several decades resulted in the freezing of the sea all the way out to the island. But Ningyuan did not fall and Yuan was vindicated. Nurhaci himself was wounded in the battle and he would die several months later.

The surprising news of the Ming victory at Ningyuan was greeted with joy back in Beijing and the very men who had ordered Yuan to withdraw were now claiming credit for it. It was certainly the greatest triumph the Ming had gained over the Jin in the war thus far and it made Yuan the toast of the town. Indeed, it was the most serious defeat Nurhaci had ever suffered as a military commander. As the Ming minister of war gushed, "This proves that China still has men after all!" Gao Di was predictably cashiered and replaced by Wang Zhichen, and Yuan Chonghuan was promoted again and given oversight of all military operations outside the Great Wall. The court also initiated plans to manufacture and deploy more heavy artillery, recognizing their importance in the Ming victory. The Jurchens recognized this as well and Nurhaci's successor, Hóng Tàijí 洪太极, would later embark upon a program of cannon manufacture and training for his own troops, buoyed by Chinese collaborators and weapons acquired in the Siege of Dalinghe in 1631.

Slaying of a Rival

His success apparently stoking an already considerable ego, Yuan's relationship with Man Gui and Mao Wenlong started to deteriorate. Yuan had Man transferred back to Beijing and replaced by Zhao Shuaijiao. He complained that Mao was trumping up his victories and in fact doing little to help the Ming cause while siphoning valuable supplies from the court. And on top of this, there were reports that Mao's men were looting and causing problems in Korea. There were also rumors that Mao was opening his own negotiations with the Jin. Then, in the ninth month of 1626 when Hong Taiji (1592–1643) assumed the throne, Yuan opened his own talks with the Jin, hoping to buy time for consolidating Ming control over their advance bases. Though the talks and exchange of envoys lasted for months, nothing much came of them. In fact, many historians suggest that Hong Taiji used them to distract the Ming from his own preparations for the invasion of Korea, which would take place the following year.

As the Jin ran roughshod over Korea's defenses and again dislodged Mao Wenlong from the mainland, Yuan scrambled to find supplies and equipment for his forces. He also moved to reinforce the defenses of Songshan and Jinzhou. Fresh from their successful operations in Korea, the Jin attacked these cities and Ningyuan in the early summer of 1627, but were again defeated by Ming forces led by Man Gui and Zu Dashou. These defeats reinforced upon the Jin khan the need for more firepower to take Ming cities. But the factional battles were continuing at the Ming court and Yuan submitted a request for resignation due to illness and a desire to take care of his aged mother. This request was granted, but Yuan would be recalled soon thereafter, as the sickly Emperor Tianqi died and was succeeded by his younger brother, who reigned as Emperor Chóngzhēn 崇祯 (1611–1644) until the end of the Ming dynasty.

Among the new emperor's first acts was the purge of many of the eunuch elements from court, along with the members of various factions. He reinstated Yuan with sweeping authority and promised him full imperial support. In a personal meeting with the emperor in the Forbidden City in the summer of 1628, Yuan bragged that with proper support and funding he could recover all of Liaodong in just five years. This was music to Chongzhen's ears, for the emperor loved concrete timetables and swift action. In fact, Yuan's overall plans were not that different from those of Sun Chengzong or even Xiong Tingbi. He was just more confident and outspoken in his promises of success. And the potential problems he faced were in turn highlighted by a troop mutiny over lack of rations in Ningyuan itself, followed by one in Jinzhou a couple months later. Still, by the time he reached the front again in late 1628, Yuan was receiving supplies and more rewards from the throne.

Upon his return to the front, Yuan continued to bump heads with Mao Wenlong. Yuan resented Mao's freedom of action and independent status. He was also concerned by the continuing rumors of Mao's dealings with the Jin. Mao aggravated matters by paying a surprise visit to a Ming city on the Shandong peninsula that was clearly designed as a show of force. Yuan tried to get Mao to relocate closer to the main Ming forces near Ningyuan, but Mao refused, arguing that his advance position was needed to keep the Jin attentions divided. This argument actually made sense, though other records indicate that Mao was indeed attempting to set himself up as an independent maritime power broker in the Bohai Gulf. Yuan in turn moved to confiscate some of the supplies earmarked for Mao.

Matters finally came to a head when Yuan personally visited Mao's base on Shuangdao. The ostensible reason for the visit was to inspect defenses and discuss strategy, but in fact Yuan had decided to liquidate Mao. After the two exchanged pleasantries for a couple days and Yuan watched archery displays, Yuan started questioning Mao's men about various aspects of their lives and orders. He also distributed cash among the troops, telling them that funds sent from the capital had been repeatedly embezzled by Mao for his own ends. In a dramatic episode, Yuan then arrested Mao in front of his troops and summarily decapitated him based on a dozen allegations of malfeasance, the most serious of which involved embezzling, insubordination, and treating with the enemy. Mao's troops were reorganized into four divisions under subordinate commanders in a move that would have dire consequences later.

The court was rocked upon hearing the news of Mao's execution. Though Yuan indeed had the authority to do it (contrary to what some opponents at court claimed later), the execution was not carried out upon the command of the emperor, as Yuan told Mao at the time. And whatever his dealings with the Jurchens, Mao was a charismatic leader and he had distracted their attentions from the fighting in western Liaodong. None of Mao's subordinates could compel the loyalty of as many men and they soon fell to fighting one another. Many at court supported Mao's activities as well, including the emperor, and they were not pleased that Yuan had acted so drastically. On top of this, Yuan continued his own negotiations with Hong Taiji.

Yuan's Downfall and its Aftermath

In late autumn of 1629, in coordination with Mongol allies, the Jin launched a raid upon Beijing and its environs. They swept to the north through the Great Wall, circumventing the strongest Ming defenses around Shanhaiguan. The raid proceeded rapidly and the Ming defenders were caught unawares. Zhao Shuaijiao rushed back from Manchuria and was killed in an ambush. Man Gui arrived in time to help mount a defense of Beijing, followed shortly thereafter by Yuan Chonghuan and Zu Dashou. These men eventually managed to rally the Ming forces and repulse the attackers, but Man Gui was wounded in a friendly fire incident that was blamed on Yuan Chonghuan, even though most sources indicate that the two were fighting on opposite sides of the city. But this incident, coupled with a planted Jin report that Yuan had secretly reached an agreement with them and aided their invasion, cast a cloud of suspicion over Yuan. Though Chongzhen initially rewarded Yuan for his valor, charges of treason started rolling in, circulated by the many enemies he had made over the years. The fact that Yuan had in fact been talking with the Jin ruler gave these allegations further credence. The emperor had Yuan arrested in a court audience on 13 January 1630.

At the time of Yuan's arrest, it is said that many of his soldiers were greatly upset and called for his reinstatement. Some high officials also requested exoneration for Yuan, but the emperor would not listen. He had a pathological fear of factions and was very sensitive to any allegations that he might seek some kind of accord with the Jin. But somebody needed to be blamed for the recent humiliating attack upon the capital and Yuan was a very visible scapegoat. In his absence, the Jin would capture several more Ming cities and fortresses in the northeast, though they would all be abandoned by late spring of 1630 as the Ming forces finally rallied under the leadership of generals Zu Dashou and Ma Shilong.

Unlike many other disgraced officials (such as Yang Hao, who spent ten years in prison) Yuan did not languish long in jail. He was sentenced to death by dismemberment, with his remains to be scattered along the frontier. The sentence was carried out in the western marketplace in Beijing on 22 September 1630. It is related that the indignant commoners of the capital fought over scraps of his flesh. It is also said that one of his loyal followers managed to recover Yuan's head so that it, at least, could be given a proper burial. In a pattern that would become sadly familiar in the ensuing years, the emperor's rash temper and desire for quick solutions and visible results would lead to disaster.

After the deaths of Mao and Yuan, the Ming never really took the offensive again in Liaodong, as they were forced to alternate their attentions between the northeast theater and the northwest, where massive peasant uprisings emerged in the late 1620s. Many argue that had Mao and Yuan (or even just one of them) remained alive, the Ming might have mounted a more consistent plan of defense in Liaodong.

Perhaps the most immediate aftereffects were seen in the subsequent Jin siege of Dalinghe and the so-called Wuqiao Mutiny (1631–1633). With Yuan out of the way, the Jin attacked the Ming base of Dalinghe, which was still under construction, in the summer of 1631. It fell after several months and the Jin captured large numbers of cannon as a result. These became the basis for the weaponry in the artillery corps that Hong Taiji created with the help of Chinese defectors in the following years. Meanwhile, a Ming relief force led by Kong Youde, one of Mao Wenlong's former lieutenants, mutinied while traveling through Shandong en route to Dalinghe. This mutiny lasted over a year and a half and even though it was eventually put down, its ringleaders and many of their followers escaped and joined the Jin, bringing their weapons and skills in naval and artillery warfare with them. Many Chinese scholars suggest that their expertise was crucial for later Qing success in siege warfare. They argue that had Mao Wenlong not been assassinated on flimsy evidence, perhaps this course of events would never have transpired.

Thus the saga of Mao Wenlong and Yuan Chonghuan has been recounted by proponents of both men over the ensuing centuries. Supporters of Mao argue that he was merely buying himself breathing space and that he had achieved considerable success against the Jin when everyone else was retreating or backbiting each other. Had he only been properly supplied, he could have opened a second front that would have crippled the Jin. Yuan's champions, on the other hand, note that many of Mao's so-called victories were only minor skirmishes. He had also raided Korea continuously and took steps to ensure the loyalty of the troops to him alone, withholding supplies and getting all of his men to change their surnames to Mao, signifying their personal bond. Mao also repeatedly ignored directives from Yuan to cooperate with the Ming units on land. In any case, the tragic nature of both of their deaths has provided fodder for discussion ever since. While one is not inclined to completely agree with it, the final line from Yuan Chonghuan's biography in the *History of the Ming* (*Míngshǐ* 明史) is telling: "First Chonghuan ignorantly killed Wenlong, then the emperor foolishly killed Chonghuan. From the time of Chonghuan's death there was no one who could deal with border affairs and the fate of the Ming was decided."

Kenneth M. SWOPE
University of Southern Mississippi

Further Reading

Jung Byol-chul. (2006). Late Ming island bases, military posts, and sea routes in the offshore area of Liaodong. In Angela Schottenhammer & Roderich Ptak (Eds.), *The perception of maritime space in traditional Chinese sources* (pp. 41–50). Wiesbaden, Germany: Harrassowitz Verlag.

Li Guangtao 李光濤. (1986). Mao Wenlong niangluan Dongjiang shimo 毛文龍釀亂東江本末 [Complete story of the chaos caused by Mao Wenlong in the northeast] In *Ming-Qing Dang'an lunwenji* (pp. 163–250). Taipei, Taiwan: Lianjing chubanshiye gongsi.

Swope, Kenneth M. (2013). *The military collapse of China's Ming dynasty, 1618–1644*. London: Routledge.

Swope, Kenneth M. (2014). Competing strategies for the defense of Liaodong in the late Ming. In Kai Filipiak (Ed.), *Civil-military relations in Chinese history*. London: Routledge.

Yan Chongnian. (2006). *Yuan Chonghuan zhuan* 袁崇焕传 [Biography of Yuan Chonghuan]. Beijing: Zhonghua shuju.

Yan Chongnian, & Yu Sanle. (Comps.). (1984). *Yuan Chonghuan ziliao* 袁崇焕资料 [Materials on Yuan Chonghuan] (2 vols.). Nanjing, China: Guangxi minzu chubanshe.

Yuán Hóngdào

袁宏道

1568–1610 CE—Poet, essayist, literary theorist; one of the "Three Yuans"

Poet and playwright Xu Wei, whose work Yuan Hongdao knew and advocated.

Summary

Yuan Hongdao was a major poet, essayist, and literary theorist of the late-Ming period who advocated natural self-expression in literature and championed vernacular fiction. Yuan and his brothers, leading figures in a movement that came to be known as the Gong'an School, rejected the imitation of ancient styles, stressing instead that poetry should reflect a writer's unaffected individuality; appropriating the lines of ancient poets was, for Yuan, like "wearing summer clothes in the middle of winter." His literary collections later found favor with like-minded scholars of the Republican era. His lively short essays represent some of the finest examples from the late-Ming period.

Yuan Hongdao was born in Gōng'ān 公安, in modern-day Hubei Province, and rose to prominence during the reign of *Emperor Wànlì 万历 (r. 1573–1620) of the Míng 明 dynasty (1368–1644), a period of great political uncertainty. Yuan and his brothers Yuán Zōngdà o 袁宗道 (1560–1600) and Yuán Zhōngdào 袁中道 (1570–1624), who together were known as the "Three Yuans," championed spontaneity and self-expression in literature at a time when the prevailing orthodoxy demanded a stricter adherence to ancient styles. Although the initial reception of these theories was mixed, Yuan's rediscovery by Republican scholars in the early twentieth century helped to cement his place as a major figure in the history of Chinese literary thought. From a twenty-first century standpoint, his lively short essays represent some of the finest examples from the late-Ming period.

Life and Career

Yuan was by all accounts a talented and precocious youth, heading a literary

*People marked with an asterisk have entries in this dictionary.

society as a teenager, and eventually passing his *jìnshì* 进士 (presented scholar) civil service examination in 1592, at the age of twenty-four. Yuan was appointed to his first official post, that of magistrate of Wú 吴 County (modern-day Suzhou) in 1595, but he found neither the administrative duties of his new career, nor the hustle and bustle of Suzhou itself to be to his taste. A series of personal letters, written during this time in Suzhou, documents Yuan's extreme and increasingly obsessive distaste for his official life, which, he claimed, rendered him "no longer human." "Whenever I encounter my superiors I am forced to grovel like a slave," he lamented on one occasion. "How very poisonous is my existence!" (translated in Campbell 2002, 175–176).

Desperate to quit his post, Yuan composed the first of a series of seven petitions (Qian 1981, 313–323) requesting release from (*qǐ gūi* 乞归) or transfer of (*qǐ gǎi* 乞改) office in the third month of 1596, less than a year after his arrival. (See sidebar.) His final, ultimately successful petition refers repeatedly to illness, but when at last given permission to return home in the spring of 1597, Yuan chose instead to spend several months travelling, or devoting himself "to my hiker's stick" as he recorded in the poem that celebrated his dismissal (translated in Chaves 1978, 31). This decision may have been influenced in part by his father's reportedly unfavorable reaction to the news that his son had resigned after such a short period in office.

"Only Quitting Office Will Cure Me"

In 1597, Yuan Hongdao was finally granted (after several attempts) his most fervent wish: permission to quit his official post in Suzhou.

I am not blessed with a strong constitution and was not intended for public office. As soon as I felt the fetters of office close around me, an overwhelming sense of oppression came over me, an oppression that persisted until I fell prey to consumption. My illness stems from melancholy and this melancholy is caused by my holding of office. It becomes worse each day that I remain at my post. Ordinary medicines merely treat the symptoms of my disease. Only quitting office will cure me.

Source: Translated by Duncan M. Campbell. Letters by Yuan Hongdao, *China Heritage Quarterly 30/31*. Retrieved December 22, 2013, from http://www.chinaheritagequarterly.org/scholarship.php?searchterm=030_yuan.inc&issue=030

The poetry and essays written during the period immediately following his release from office, and collected under the revealing title *Deliverance Collection* (*Jiětuō jí* 解脱集), perhaps best exemplify Yuan's natural prose and verse style. In the opening essay, he claimed to share an "obsession" (*pǐ* 癖, an important concept in late-Ming culture) with the famous Song-dynasty scholars *Sū Shì 苏轼 (1037–1101) and *Wáng Ānshí 王安石 (1021–1086), so that whatever he found himself doing, "there is never a moment in which my mind is not touring the hills and lakes" (Qian 1981, 419). His essays describing several months' travel on and around West Lake (Xīhú 西湖) in Zhejiang Province are some of the best examples of his work, and display a number of the characteristics he advocated in his literary theory.

Yuan resumed his official career in Beijing in 1598, but illness again got the better of him and, following the death of his elder brother Zongdao in 1600, he retired to and spent the next six years on a secluded estate near Gong'an. Here Yuan devoted himself to the study of Buddhist thought, and his poems from this period reflect this preoccupation far more than those of earlier collections. His official life continued, sporadically, from 1606 until his death in 1610 at just forty-two years of age. The sometimes graphic details of Yuan's illness and eventual death are recorded in his younger brother Zhongdao's diary *Notes Made Travelling and at Rest* (*Yóujūfèilù* 游居柿录).

Reception and Significance

Yuan Hongdao was a leading member, and the most important literary theorist, of the movement that came to be known as the Gōng'ān School. This group, of which Yuan's two brothers and the poet and essayist Jiāng Yíngkē 江盈科 (1553–1605) were prominent members, argued against the blind imitation of ancient models, advocating instead the expression of one's own *xìnglíng* 性灵 (natural sensibility) in poetic composition. Appropriating the lines of ancient poets, who had themselves been writing about a very different world, was for Yuan, like "wearing summer clothes in the middle of winter" (Qian 1981, 709). It followed that traditionally marginalized genres such as vernacular fiction, drama, and even folk songs held genuine literary value—for these, Yuan argued, were the works of "real people" (*zhēn rén* 真人), unencumbered by the suffocating constraints of learning (Qian 1981, 188). Yuan himself claimed to have been responsible for the popularity of the poet and playwright Xú Wèi 徐渭, (1521–1593) (Qian 1981, 715–719), and he was an early admirer of the novel *The Plum in the Golden Vase* (*Jīn Píng Méi* 金瓶梅), which he seems to have examined in manuscript form before its publication.

Although not universally admired, Gong'an literary values were certainly influential to a generation of thinkers in the early seventeenth century, even if some eventually rejected the emphasis

Page from a Ming dynasty edition of the novel *Jin Ping Mei* (*The Plum in the Golden Vase*), one of Yuan Hongdao's favorite works.

on unstudied spontaneity on the grounds of vulgarity. Gong'an ideals were clearly important in the development of late-Ming poet Zhōng Xīng's 钟惺 (1574–1624) early thought, although he and his Jìnglíng 竟陵 School colleagues later moved in a different direction and were themselves heavily criticized by early-Qing scholars such as Qián Qiānyì 钱谦益 (1582–1664). The poet *Yuán Méi 袁枚 (1716–1797) was a rare champion of Gong'an literary values during the eighteenth century, by which time they had generally fallen out of favor.

Yuan's contribution to the development of the informal essay (*xiǎopǐn* 小品) during the late-Ming was considerable, and an annotated selection of his essays was published as early as 1632 by Lù Yúnlóng 陆云龙 (republished as Lu 1997). Writing at a time when the travel essay (*yóujì* 游记) had assumed an important self-fashioning role for educated literati, Yuan's work clearly informed that of later exponents, such as Xú Hóngzǔ 徐宏祖 (1586–1641), also known as *Xú Xiákè 徐霞客, Qián Qiānyì, and Zhāng Dài 张岱 (1597–c. 1684), although all three of these men went on to stretch the genre in new and arguably more exciting directions (McDowall 2009). The "History of the Vase" (*Píng shǐ* 瓶史), a work on flower arrangement that Yuan completed in 1599, became extremely influential in Japan.

Yuan's collected works were officially banned during the long reign of Emperor *Qiánlóng 乾隆 (r. 1736–1795) as part of the monumental *Complete Library of the Four Treasuries* (*Sìkù quánshū* 四库全书) compilation project, although the extent and efficacy of Qing censorship is a point of contention (Qian 1981, Li 1994). It is clear, however, that copies of Yuan's works continued to circulate privately until they were republished in the Republican era in several different editions. This was a period of renewed interest in Yuan and his writings, with many populist May Fourth Movement (Wǔsì yùndòng 五四运动, 1919–1923) thinkers regarding him as a precursor of the twentieth-century vernacular movement. Zhōu Zùorén 周作人 (1885–1967), an influential writer of that generation, admired the freshness and natural charm of Gong'an writing, while admitting that it lacked depth (Pollard 1973, 158–166). In recent decades, Yuan's short essays have continued to command more critical attention than his poetry, and these have frequently been anthologized (Ni 1985) or published as separate collections (Xiong 1996). The original divisions under which Yuan's various writings were published during his own lifetime are retained in the editor Qián Bóchéng's 钱伯城 excellent edition (Shanghai, 1981).

Stephen McDOWALL
University of Edinburgh

Further Reading

Campbell, Duncan M. (2002). The epistolary world of a reluctant 17th century Chinese magistrate: Yuan Hongdao in Suzhou. *New Zealand Journal of Asian Studies*, 4(1), 159–193.

Chaves, Jonathan (Trans.). (1978). *Pilgrim of the clouds: Poems and essays from Ming China*. New York: Weatherhill.

Chaves, Jonathan. (1983). The panoply of images: A reconsideration of the literary theories of the Kung-an School. In Susan Bush & Christian Murck (Eds.), *Theories of the arts in China* (pp. 341–364). Princeton, NJ: Princeton University Press.

Chou, Chih-p'ing. (1988). *Yüan Hung-tao and the Kung-an School*. Cambridge, UK: Cambridge University Press.

Li Jianzhang 李建章. (1994). *Yuan Hongdao ji jianjiao zhiyi* 《袁宏道集笺校》志疑 [Uncertainties in the *collated and annotated works of Yuan Hongdao*]. Wuhan, China: Hubei renmin chubanshe.

Lu Yunlong 陆云龙. (Ed.). (1997). *Huang Ming shiliu mingjia xiaopin* 皇明十六名家小品 [Informal essays from sixteen famous masters of the Great Ming]. Ji'nan, China: Qilu shushe.

McDowall, Stephen. (2009). *Qian Qianyi's reflections on Yellow Mountain: Traces of a Late-Ming hatchet and chisel*. Hong Kong: Hong Kong University Press.

Ni Qixin 倪其心. (Ed.). (1985). *Zhongguo gudai youji xuan* 中国古代游记选 [A selection of ancient Chinese travel records]. Beijing: Zhongguo youji chubanshe.

Pollard, David E. (1973). *A Chinese look at literature: The literary values of Chou Tso-jen in relation to the tradition*. London: C. Hurst & Company.

Qian Bocheng 钱伯城. (Ed.). (1981). *Yuan Hongdao ji jianjiao* 袁宏道集笺校 [The collated and annotated works of Yuan Hongdao]. Shanghai: Shanghai guji chubanshe.

Ren Fangqiu 任访秋. (1983). *Yuan Zhonglang yanjiu* 袁中郎研究 [Research on Yuan Hongdao]. Shanghai: Shanghai guji chubanshe.

Vallete-Hémery, Martine. (1982). *Yuan Hongdao (1568-1610): théorie et pratique littéraires*. Paris: Collège de France.

Xiong Lihui 熊礼汇. (Ed.). (1996). *Yuan Zhonglang xiaopin* 袁中郎小品 [The informal essays of Yuan Hongdao]. Beijing: Wenhua yishu chubanshe.

Zhèng Hé

郑和

1371–c.1433—Muslim eunuch; land and sea military commander

Summary

Zheng He, originally named Ma He, was born in south China to a Muslim family. After being selected to become a eunuch at the Ming court when he was ten years old, he went on to become a successful military commander in the Ming army. For his loyal service he was awarded the title of Grand Eunuch, also receiving the Chinese surname Zheng. After the accession of Emperor Yongle, Zheng became the commander of several successful maritime expeditions, unmatched in Chinese history, reaching as far as India and the east coast of Africa. These expeditions, along with his many military successes, have assured his heroic legacy.

Born in 1371 at Kūnyáng 昆阳 (in present-day Yunnan Province) to a Muslim family, probably of Mongolian-Arab descent, Zheng He was originally surnamed Mǎ 马, the first syllable in Mǎhāmá 马哈麻 or Mǎhāmò 马哈末. These are two of the many common Chinese transliterations of the name Muhammad, and Ma was therefore a common surname for Muslims in China. Ma He's birth came only three years after the founding of the Míng 明 dynasty (1368–1644) by the peasant rebel leader Zhū Yuánzhāng 朱元璋 (1328–1398), who reigned as *Emperor Hóngwǔ 洪武 from 1368 to 1398. The Hongwu emperor's establishment of the Ming in 1368 was a monumental event. It was the culmination of the effort to expel the Mongols, who had subjugated China since the time of *Khubilai (Qubilai) Khan 忽必烈汗 (1215–1294; r. 1260–1294), and the ensuing power struggle among Chinese contenders to fill the power gap they left behind. China was now finally restored to Chinese rule, and Emperor Hongwu sent out emissaries to all

*People marked with an asterisk have entries in this dictionary.

foreign countries with which it had relations to proclaim this news to the world. The founding of the Ming also had a profound effect on the life of Ma He.

Selected as a Eunuch

Ma He's home in Yunnan was one of several areas in the empire initially outside the Ming government's firm control. Once power in the political center—which was then in the Jiangnan area, near the capital at Nanjing—had been consolidated, the new rulers turned their attention to "pacifying" such outlying areas as Yunnan (i.e., expelling any Mongol power bases) and incorporating them into the newly founded regime. A campaign to this effect was launched in Yunnan in 1381–1382. Some of the generals were also charged with scouting out young boys who could be made eunuchs to serve the imperial family. In 1381, during the Yunnan campaign, when he was only ten years old, Ma He was selected to become a eunuch. He was then taken into the service of Prince Zhū Dì 朱棣 (1360–1424), the fourth son of Emperor Hongwu, at his principality in Yān 燕 in the region of present-day Beijing, thousands of kilometers from his homeland.

Military Commander

While in Zhu Di's service, Ma He distinguished himself as a military commander, first in campaigns against Mongol forces in the north between 1393 and 1397, and then in the Civil War launched by Zhu Di in 1399 against his nephew Zhū Yǔnwén 朱允炆 (1377–c. 1402), who reigned as Emperor Jiànwén 建文 (r. 1399–1402). Yunwen's father, Zhū Biāo 朱标, had been Hongwu's eldest son and heir apparent, but when Zhu Biao died prematurely, Hongwu appointed the latter's son Yunwen as heir apparent. In doing so, he was bypassing his other sons and choosing his grandson to inherit the throne. This angered Hongwu's other sons and put the young grandson in the precarious position of being threatened by a number of disgruntled uncles. Zhu Di, who was the most powerful of these uncles, raised an army against Jianwen in 1399. Ultimately, after three years of civil war, Zhu Di was victorious. He stormed the capital and usurped the throne in 1402, proclaiming himself *Emperor Yǒnglè 永乐 (r. 1403–1424). For his loyal military service in the campaign, Yongle rewarded Ma He with the title of Grand Eunuch (*tàijiàn* 太监) and conferred on him the Chinese surname Zhèng 郑. This occurred on New Year's Day in 1404, and he was known as Zheng He from this day forward.

Almost immediately after ascending the throne, Yongle began planning the maritime expeditions that would make Zheng He famous. In some respects these expeditions were continuations of the regular practice of foreign relations that had gone on for centuries—the sending and receiving of envoys (often eunuchs) to and from neighboring polities, and the exchange of gifts to formalize relations. Even under Hongwu, who was not known for his interest in diplomatic affairs, envoys and gifts were exchanged with other countries, especially with nearby polities in East and Southeast Asia. As early as the ninth month of 1402, only three months after taking power, Yongle stepped into his new imperial role and, following in his father's footsteps, sent ambassadors to the various foreign countries to proclaim his accession to the throne.

Overseas Expeditions

An indication that Yongle had increased overseas activity in mind can be seen in the reopening, in 1403, of the three maritime supervisorates (*shìbósī* 市舶司) that had operated under Hongwu, in Zhejiang, Fujian, and Guangdong. These supervisorates would facilitate the arrival of foreign embassies into China and control their trading and other activities. It was not until Yongle ordered the construction of substantial quantities of ocean-going ships, as well as the conversion of ocean-going grain transports, however, that the scale of his ambition was revealed. The *Veritable Records of the Ming Dynasty* (*Míng Shílù* 明实录), a daily chronicle of the court's activities, records imperial orders for the construction or conversion of 525 ships in 1403 (in three separate orders: 137, 200, and 188), and another 55 ships at the beginning of the following year. The emperor then issued the order for the first expedition to the "Western Oceans" (*xīyáng* 西洋) on 11 July 1405 and appointed Zheng He commander of the fleet. The fact that he had more than one of these expeditions in mind at this time is evident; seven days later he ordered another 1,180 ships to be constructed, presumably in preparation for the second voyage.

In all there were seven major expeditions and several minor ones. The various reports of Zheng He's activities in certain parts of the world, scattered in a number of sources, including stone inscriptions, have allowed scholars to piece together a chronology of the voyages, which is also a chronology of Zheng He's life. This effort was greatly aided by the discovery in the 1930s of stone steles in Liujiagang, at Taicang near Shanghai, and at Changle in Fujian. From these sources, scholars have been able to determine the following dates of the major expeditions:

- First expedition 1405–1407
- Second expedition 1407–1409
- Third expedition 1409–1411
- Fourth expedition 1413–1415
- Fifth expedition 1417–1419
- Sixth expedition 1421–1422
- Seventh expedition 1431–1433

Each one of these major voyages took approximately two years from departure to return, and followed a regular seasonal pattern and trajectory due to the monsoons. The ships left Nanjing in the early autumn and congregated in the

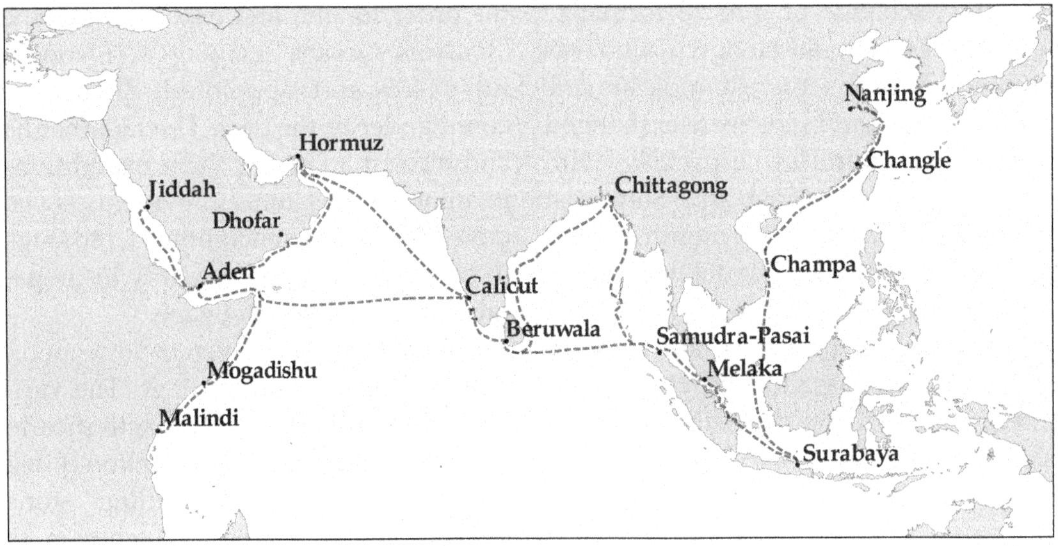

Map of Zheng He's voyages. Map provided and created by Sally K. Church.

port of Tàicāng 太仓 (near present-day Shanghai). When the whole fleet had assembled there, it sailed down the coast to the port of Changle, where it stayed until December or January to wait for the monsoon. It then sailed on to Champa (present-day Qui Nhon in Vietnam), and to Java, Palembang, Melaka (Malacca), and various places on the island of Sumatra, including Samudra-Pasai. After crossing the Bay of Bengal, the ships (perhaps now only part of the fleet) reached Ceylon (present-day Sri Lanka), and then proceeded to Quilon, Cochin, and finally Calicut, then a major emporium in the Indian Ocean trading network. The first three expeditions proceeded in quick succession; no sooner had one returned than the next one departed in a matter of months. These three all traveled as far as Calicut. After the third voyage the expeditions traveled further and left a two-year gap between each expedition. The fourth voyage ventured as far as Hormuz and Aden, the fifth sailed to Arabia, and the sixth traveled to Arabia and the east coast of Africa.

Between the sixth and seventh expeditions there was a hiatus of nine years. This was due to Emperor Yongle's death in 1424 and the subsequent policy swing under his successor, Emperor Hóngxī 洪熙 (r. 1424–1425). Supported by a number of like-minded officials, Hongxi saw the expeditions as unnecessary extravagances and ordered them to be stopped immediately. His reign lasted less than one year, but his successor Emperor Xuāndé 宣德 (r. 1425–1435) did not launch the final expedition until six years into his reign.

During the nine-year hiatus from 1422 to 1431, Zheng He served as defender (*shǒubèi* 守备) of Nanjing. At this time Nanjing was the secondary capital of China, as the main capital had been moved to Beijing in 1421. There is not much information available about Zheng He in general, but this is particularly true for this period of his life. One source says that he consulted with other eunuchs who had served on the expeditions in Nanjing, and that he was engaged in repairing palace buildings. He was called up again to command the final expedition in 1431 under Emperor Xuande. This voyage traveled as far as Arabia and Africa, and is also said to have visited Makkah (Mecca). It was a glorious finale to a significant chapter of China's history.

Final Days

The precise time and place of Zheng He's death is not known for certain. Some scholars say he died abroad on the last voyage in 1433, too far away to be brought back to China for burial. Others say he passed away after he returned to Nanjing in 1435. A tomb on Niúshǒu 牛首 (Cow's Head) Hill in Nanjing is now venerated as his.

Other than the brief records of the expeditions telling about their departure and return, and giving a few details of some key episodes, we have very little other evidence to document Zheng He's life. There is almost nothing written by him; the three travel accounts of the voyages are all by those who sailed with him—Mǎ Huān 马欢, Fèi Xìn 费信, and Gǒng Zhēn 巩珍. Even the stone inscriptions bearing his name, set up in Liújiāgǎng 刘家港 and Changle in 1431 and 1432 respectively, were probably drafted by others. There are a number of scattered references to Zheng He in disparate sources, but most concern the expeditions, and none is comprehensive. The references to him in the *Veritable Records* usually take the following form: "The Grand Eunuch Zheng He and others were sent out as envoys to (or returned from) the various foreign countries of the Western Oceans" (*Ming* [*Taizong*] *Shilu* 83.3b, 1114). Since we know very little about his sentiments or personal life, his biography primarily consists of the record of these voyages.

Unanswered Questions

Several perennial questions arise concerning the expeditions. Two of the most common are: "Why were they launched?" and "Why did they stop?" In fact, their ultimate purpose is not entirely clear, though there were probably a number of different motivations. The main reason given in the *Official History of the Ming* (*Míngshǐ* 明史)—and the official reason given by Emperor Yongle himself—is that their object was to find the dethroned Emperor Jianwen, who was believed to have escaped in 1402 when Yongle's troops took the capital at Nanjing and burned the former emperor's palace to the ground. Jianwen's remains were never found, and it was rumored that he went into hiding, pretending to be a monk, with some even speculating that he went overseas. This may have been the excuse that Yongle gave to justify the effort and expense of the voyages, but it is not an explanation to be taken seriously. It would be highly impractical to send such a large fleet, consisting of hundreds of ships and tens of thousands of men, over such vast distances to search for a single person. Nor would it explain the political, military, and diplomatic activities that took place in the regions they visited, or why so many expeditions were sent out over the course of twenty-eight years.

The *Official Ming History* offers a secondary explanation that seems closer to the truth: the desire to "spread awe of China's wealth and power" (*shì Zhōngguó fùqiáng* 示中国富强) (*Mingshi* 304.7766). The expeditions served a combined diplomatic and domestic purpose: to enhance the emperor's prestige both abroad and at home. Having experienced a century of subjugation by the Mongols, China now needed to appear strong to her neighbors, and to assert her cultural and military superiority, in order to ward off any future invaders. There was a threat in the northwest from the Timurids, and China was in fact spared from an invasion in 1405 only by the death of Timur (1336–1405) himself. (Timur is commonly known as Tamerlane.) On the domestic side, Yongle's ascendance to power was at first despised by the bureaucracy because he had usurped the throne. He needed to prove his legitimacy not only to these officials but also to the rest of the imperial family. If he could show himself to be a great world leader, to whom all other rulers on Earth kowtowed and paid respects, this would help to boost his prestige. He took other measures as well to win over the bureaucracy, such as involving them in producing that great compendium of past literature, the *Yǒnglè dàdiǎn* 永乐大典.

As for the second perennial question, "Why did they stop?," it is often asserted that China suddenly turned inward at this crucial time, just before the arrival of the Europeans in the Indian Ocean, rejecting the way of science, technology, and progress, willingly forfeiting a prominent role in international relations, and thus sealing her fate in the nineteenth and twentieth centuries. This is seen as a conscious and rather ignorant decision, and creates an image of China retreating into its entrenched traditional worldview, isolating itself and closing itself off from the rest of the world. Instead, a more likely explanation for the end of the maritime expeditions is financial. Scholars argue over whether the expeditions ultimately brought profit or loss, but most scholars see them as a drain on the Chinese economy. The expeditions were expensive and there were other demands on the imperial coffers at the time as well. These included not only military expeditions against the Mongols in the north and Nam Viet (Annam) in the south, but also palace construction in the new capital at Beijing, and the refurbishment of the canal system for the transport of grain and other supplies from China's breadbasket in Jiangnan to the new capital. This is not to mention such routine concerns as famine relief and dyke repair. By the end of Yongle's reign, the people were exhausted and the empire's finances were under considerable strain.

Another of the unanswered questions regarding the voyages concerns the size of the ships and the fleet. Despite the many investigations that have been made into the nature and size of the ships that were used on the voyages, we still do not know very much about them. It is generally thought that they were probably not as large as stated in the *Ming shi* (44 *zhang* long and 18 *zhang* wide), which would have made them 136 meters by 55 meters (447 feet by 183 feet), but there is considerable disagreement about exactly how big they were. There are also various reports concerning the size of the fleet, taken from the number of ships requisitioned at various times and other records in the sources. The numbers are not consistent, and it is very difficult to go beyond a guess. The number of people who travelled on each voyage is surprisingly consistent, however, with figures of around twenty-seven to twenty-eight thousand recorded for most of the voyages. Scholars are hopeful that wrecks discovered along Zheng He's route may yield more detailed information about the ships.

One question that does not seem to have been addressed in the sources is how Zheng He, a seasoned land-combat commander, could have achieved sufficient naval competence to command such a fleet without any previous naval training. He must have been successful at it, to have launched so many major voyages and returned safely himself, as well as transporting large numbers of foreigners back and forth to China. There are only a few references to shipwrecks occurring during the period, though this does not guarantee that they were negligible. One can only speculate that Zheng He must have relied on the maritime knowledge and experience of his underlings. He was not the only commander of the voyages—there was an entire eunuch team, and a number of others also led some of the main and side expeditions. Moreover, while the voyages were going on, at least sixty different embassies were sent out on diplomatic missions separate from Zheng He's expeditions, each requiring its own ambassadors and commanders.

Commerce and Trade

The longest lasting commercial impact of Zheng He's voyages was probably the establishment of Melaka as the key emporium for the Arab and Indian trade with China. Arab and Indian ships could obtain Chinese goods, such as porcelain and silk, in Melaka, without having to go all the way to their place of origin. The development of this emporium realigned the Indian Ocean trade, giving Melaka a monopoly for over one hundred years, and transforming it for a time into the richest city in the world. The trade was handled by Chinese merchants, who warehoused and sold the goods to be transported westward on Arab and Indian ships. This development also contributed to the Chinese diaspora in Southeast Asia. The monopoly continued under Chinese suzerainty until the arrival of the Portuguese in 1511; only when the ports of Macao and Manila were established did Melaka lose its role as the chief emporium for products from China to the rest of the world, although under the Portuguese and Dutch it still continued to play a prominent role in the Indian Ocean trade.

The voyages also resulted in changes to the value of some commodities. A good example was pepper. Before Zheng He's voyages, pepper was a very expensive luxury in China, as it was in Europe before the Portuguese discovery of the Cape of Good Hope route to India around the southern tip of Africa. As a result of the huge amounts of pepper brought in during the Ming expeditions, however, there was a glut of pepper on the Chinese market. It became so plentiful and cheap that it was used by the Ming government to pay its officials and soldiers, and this caused problems of its own.

Historical and Scientific Data

Information about the voyages was suppressed in China during the Chenghua period (1465–1487) due to internal politics. Fearing an increase in eunuch power, and citing the extravagant expense of the expeditions, the official Liú Dàxià 刘大夏, who later became president of the Ministry of War, discredited the accounts of the voyages, calling them "deceitful exaggerations of bizarre things far removed from the testimony of people's ears and eyes" (Duyvendak 1938, 395–396; translated from Gu 1987, *Kezuo zhuiyu* 1:30a). He is thought to have destroyed the documents in the official archives relating to the voyages. Despite this destruction, however, a substantial number of sources concerning the expeditions still survive. The first-hand travel accounts written by the three scribes mentioned above were kept in private collections and are now reprinted in modern editions. They contain detailed descriptions of rulers, governments, societies, products, trade, and relations with China of the major polities that were visited. Although they did not circulate widely, they had considerable impact on China's knowledge of other lands. Much of the information they contain was included in various chapters of the *Official Ming History*, which circulated in the subsequent Qīng 清 dynasty (1644–1911/1912). Among these are the first Chinese accounts of Hormuz, Aden, and Makkah, to say nothing of the East African ports that became such avid consumers of Chinese porcelain. These accounts not only contain information on the countries visited, but also provide equally important information about sea routes, sailing conditions, and navigation.

Study of the voyages also brings to light the importance of the *Veritable Records* as a source for China's relations with other states and polities in the Ming period, as well as the history of these states and polities themselves. The *Veritable Records* provides meticulous documentation of foreign visits to China, as well as China's voyages to other countries, in which names of emissaries, kings, and ruling families are mentioned, and dates are given in precise terms. For this reason, the *Veritable Records* has been used, particularly by the historian Geoff Wade, to corroborate existing records of other polities and to reconstruct aspects of their history.

The transfer of scientific knowledge was an important impact of the voyages. The so called Mao Kun map, named in modern Chinese *Zhèng Hé hánghǎitú* 郑和航海图, or "Zheng He's Navigation Chart," is thought to have derived from the charts, or rutters, used by Zheng He on his voyages. It contains clear references to a technique used by Arab seafarers to determine latitude: using finger widths to measure the height of certain stars above the horizon. Printed in 1621 and presented to the throne in 1628, the map has acquired this name because it occurs in a collection of military documents compiled by Mao Yuanyi (1597–1661), grandson of Mao Kun (1512–1601), whose knowledge about naval matters came from his involvement in the coastal defense of Fujian from pirates in the mid-sixteenth century. Technological ideas were also transmitted from east to west during the voyages. The survival of Chinese-style fishing nets on the Kerala coast of India, with their sophisticated use of counter-weights, is often cited in this regard. The British sinologist and chemist Joseph Needham argued that *material medica* (i.e., compendia of the medicinal qualities of various substances) from foreign lands were studied and collected on the voyages, and that information from these sources later found its way into pharmacopoeia like the *Běncǎo gāngmù* 本草纲目. These are just a few of the scientific aspects of the voyages that deserve further study.

Legacy

In the popular imagination, apart from inspiring both a Ming drama and a novel, Zheng He acquired supernatural status in some quarters, particularly in Southeast Asia. Temples were erected in his honor and he was (and still is in some places) worshiped as a god. This may have arisen partly because of the general tendency in China to deify historical figures, but also because of the worship of the Celestial Goddess (Tiānfēi 天妃) by Zheng He and his crew, to whom they prayed for safety on the voyages. Temples are dedicated to her in Nanjing, Taicang, and Changle. Images of Zheng He were later included in some of these temples. Sailors worshiped these images for centuries afterward to secure his protection on sea voyages. Later, particularly in Southeast Asia, temples were also dedicated to "Sanbao"—a term meaning "three treasures," perhaps referring to the *triratna* of Buddhism—which derives from the title *Sanbao taijian* (Grand Eunuch Sanbao) given to Zheng He in 1431 by Emperor Xuande.

The modern Chinese image of Zheng He, particularly since the six-hundredth anniversary celebrations of 2005, is of a hero who stands for China's friendship and generosity to the rest of the world. This image is epitomized by the four-character expression associated with him, *hòuwǎng bólái* 厚往薄来, "giving generously to foreigners overseas and bringing very little back home," emphasizing the two qualities of humility and magnanimity for which China wants to be known. Underlying this expression is the contrast between China's behavior and Western colonialism, a message China is anxious to promote: Zheng He did not colonize or proselytize; he extended the hand of friendship to foreign states, and gave to them generously of the things that were most treasured in Chinese culture (porcelain, silk, jade, seals of office, status, and so forth). The Chinese government is sometimes willing to allow history to be distorted to fit this image, emphasizing the peaceful aspects of the voyages and shoving the military ones to one side.

In fact, the military aspects should not be overlooked. Of the large numbers of passengers and crew recorded for the voyages, substantial proportions were soldiers. Zheng He had several occasions to show off his military prowess as a commander in battle, and these are documented in the records. During the first voyage, Zheng He's troops fought and captured the Chinese pirate Chén Zǔyì 陈祖义, originally from Guangdong, and his band, who were terrorizing the Melaka strait at the time. In the battle, over five thousand pirates were killed and Chen Zuyi was brought back to China, where he was decapitated in 1407. On the return of the third voyage in 1411, a violent conflict broke out in Ceylon between Zheng He's forces and those of the Sinhalese king Alagakkonara, ruler of the Rayigama kingdom near Columbo. The Chinese stone inscriptions say he "was guilty of a gross lack of respect and plotted against the fleet" (Duyvendak 1938, 347; translated from the inscription). Zheng He's forces captured the king, along with his wife, children, and functionaries, and took them to China. In the end, the emperor pardoned the king and allowed him and his family to return home. A third major incident occurred during the fourth voyage. The ruler of Samudra-Pasai, Sultan Zain Al-'Abidin, had previously requested China's assistance against Sekandar, a local usurper who was causing havoc in his country. The emperor had instructed Zheng He to lead troops against the usurper and restore the "rightful" king. The Grand Eunuch's troops pursued Sekandar to Lambri, captured him along with his wife and child, and took them to China, where he was executed in 1415.

These instances show that even though China's actions on the voyages were generally peaceful, and fell into the diplomatic rather than the military realm, China sometimes played the role of an international policeman, and this should not be forgotten. This image of China as generally peaceful but potentially threatening suits contemporary politics, and is conveyed in some of the statues of Zheng He one sees today. He stands heroically braving the wind and waves, with one hand behind his back holding a sword.

Emperor Yongle's goals for the voyages seem to have been achieved: his own prestige was enhanced and the voyages were a great boost to China's prestige overseas. Not only did they impress the governments and people of the countries they visited, but they also gave large numbers of foreign emissaries and others—including kings and royal families—the opportunity to visit China and see for themselves. This was one of the ways in which word spread about Chinese culture, products, and ways of life to the rest of the world.

Although information about the voyages was suppressed in China for many hundreds of years, it has now resurfaced, and the expeditions have become a source of pride: Zheng He's achievements are now recognized all over the world. It was truly an amazing feat for his day to have commanded seven huge fleets and to have sailed as far as India, Arabia, and East Africa nearly a century before Vasco da Gama rounded the Cape of Good Hope. It is not necessary to claim absurdities, like the discovery of the Americas or other continents, in order for Zheng He, or China, to be called great. One only has to look at what he accomplished and what is documented in both the written and archaeological records.

Sally K. CHURCH
University of Cambridge

Further Reading

Chiang Kui-sheng. (1976). Cheng Ho. In L. Carrington Goodrich, and Fang Chao-ying (Eds.), *Dictionary of Ming biography* (pp. 194–200). New York: Columbia University Press.

Church, Sally K. (2002). Changing attitudes toward foreigners from overseas: An investigation into the policy of the Ming Emperor Yongle, 1403–1424. *Nanyang xuebao [Journal of the South Seas Society]*, *56*, 45–73.

Church, Sally K. (April 2004). The giraffe of Bengal: A medieval encounter in Ming China. *Medieval History Journal*, *7*, pp. 1–36.

Church, Sally K. (2005). Zheng He: An investigation into the plausibility of 450-ft treasure ships. *Monumenta Serica, 53*, 1–42.

Dabringhaus, Sabine, & Ptak, Roderich. (1997). *China and her neighbours: Borders, visions of the other, foreign policy 10th to 19th century*. Wiesbaden, Germany: Harrassowitz.

Dreyer, Edward L. (2007). *Zheng He: China and the oceans in the early Ming Dynasty, 1405–1433*. London: Pearson Longman.

Duyvendak, J. J. L. (1938). The true dates of the Chinese maritime expeditions in the early fifteenth century. *T'oung Pao, 34*, 341–412.

Gu Qiyuan 顧起元. (1987). *Kezuo zhuiyu* 客座贅語 (Tan Dihua 譚棣華 & Chen Jiahe 陳稼禾, Eds.). Yuan-ming shiliao biji congkan series. Beijing: Zhonghua shuju. (Original work published in 1618)

Lo Jung-pang. (1958). The decline of the early Ming navy. *Oriens Extremus, 5*, 149–168.

Lunde, Paul. (2007). Arabic sources for the Ming Voyages. In J. P. Starkey & T. Wilkinson (Eds.), *Natural resources and cultural connections of the Red Sea* (pp. 229–246). Oxford, UK: Society for Arabian Studies Monographs No. 5. BAR International Series 1661.

Mills, J. V. G. (1970). *Ma Huan, Ying-yai sheng-lan: "The overall survey of the ocean's shores" [1433]*. Cambridge, UK: Hakluyt Society.

Mills, J. V. G., & Ptak, Roderich. (1996). *Hsing-ch'a sheng-lan: The overall survey of the star raft by Fei Hsin*. Wiesbaden, Germany: Harrassowitz.

Ming Shilu 明實錄 [Veritable records of the Ming dynasty]. (1963 to 1968). Photolithographic edition. Taipei, Taiwan: Institute of History and Philology, Academia Sinica.

Needham, Joseph, Wang Ling, & Lu Gwei-djen. (1971). Nautical Technology (Section 29). In *Science and civilisation in China*. Vol. 4, Pt. 3: *Civil engineering and nautics* (pp. 379–699). Cambridge, UK: Cambridge University Press.

Ptak, Roderich. (1998). *China and the Asian seas: Trade, travel, and visions of the others (1400–1750)*. Aldershot, UK: Ashgate.

Ptak, Roderich. (1999). *China's seaborne trade with South and Southeast Asia, 1200–1750*. Aldershot, UK: Ashgate.

Tian Rukang (T'ienJu-kang). (1981). Cheng Ho's voyages and the distribution of pepper in China. *Journal of the Royal Asiatic Society*, 2, 186–197.

Tsai, Henry Shih-shan. (1996). *The eunuchs in the Ming dynasty*. Albany: State University of New York Press.

Wade, Geoff. (1997). Melaka in Ming dynasty texts. *Journal of the Malaysian Branch of the Royal Asiatic Society, 70*(1), 31–69.

Wade, Geoff (Trans.). *Southeast Asia in the Ming Shi-lu: An open access resource*. Singapore: Asia Research Institute and the Singapore E-Press, National University of Singapore. Retrieved October 31, 2013, from http://epress.nus.edu.sg/msl

Wade, Geoff. (2000). The *Ming Shi-lu* as a source for Thai history—Fourteenth to seventeenth centuries. *Journal of Southeast Asian Studies, 31*(2), 249–294.

Yan Congjian 嚴從簡. (1993). *Shuyu zhou zilu* 殊域周恣錄. Zhong-wai jiaotong shiji congkan series. Beijing: Zhonghua shuju. (Original work published in 1574)

Zhang Tingyu 張廷玉, et al., (Eds.). (1974). *Ming shi* 明史 [History of the Ming]. Beijing: Zhonghua shuju.

Zheng He sheng 鄭鶴聲, & ZhengYijun 鄭一鈞. (1980–1989). *Zheng He xia Xiyang ziliao huibian* 鄭和下西洋資料匯編 (3 vols.) Ji'nan, China: Qi Lu shushe.

Berkshire Dictionary of Chinese Biography Index

Bold entries and page numbers denote people with an article about them in the *DCB*. Roman numerals before page numbers indicate the volume number.

C

D

Bold entries and page numbers denote people with an article about them in the *DCB*. Roman numerals before page numbers indicate the volume number.

E

F

Bold entries and page numbers denote people with an article about them in the *DCB*. Roman numerals before page numbers indicate the volume number.

J

Bold entries and page numbers denote people with an article about them in the *DCB*. Roman numerals before page numbers indicate the volume number.

M

P

Q

Bold entries and page numbers denote people with an article about them in the *DCB*. Roman numerals before page numbers indicate the volume number.

R

S

T

U

V

Bold entries and page numbers denote people with an article about them in the *DCB*. Roman numerals before page numbers indicate the volume number.

W

X

Y

Bold entries and page numbers denote people with an article about them in the *DCB*. Roman numerals before page numbers indicate the volume number.

Z

CPSIA information can be obtained
at www.ICGtesting.com
Printed in the USA
BVOW04s0034210817
492613BV00001B/3/P

9 781614 720072